Memoirs of the Museum of Anthropology
University of Michigan
Number 31

The View from Madisonville

Protohistoric Western Fort Ancient Interaction Patterns

Penelope Ballard Drooker

Ann Arbor
1997

Printed in the United States of America
ISBN 978-0-915703-42-5 (paper)

ISBN 978-1-951519-95-7 (ebook)

Cover design by Katherine Clahassey

The University of Michigan Museum of Anthropology currently publishes three monograph series: Anthropological Papers, Memoirs, and Technical Reports. We have over seventy titles in print. For a complete catalog, write to Museum of Anthropology Publications, 4009 Museums Bldg., Ann Arbor, MI 48109-1079.

Library of Congress Cataloging-in-Publication Data

Drooker, Penelope B.
The view from Madisonville : protohistoric Western fort ancient interaction patterns / Penelope Ballard Drooker.
p. cm. -- (Memoirs of the Museum of Anthropology, University of Michigan ; no. 31)
Includes bibliographical references and index.
ISBN 0-915703-42-4 (pbk. : alk. paper)
1. Madisonville Site (Ohio) 2. Fort ancient culture--Ohio--Madisonville. 3. Excavations (Archaeology)--Ohio--Madisonville. (Ohio)--Antiquities. I. Title. II. Series
GN2.m52 no. 31
[E99.F67]
306 s
[977.1'77]--DC21 97-28211

The paper used in this publication meets the requirements of the ANSI Standard Z39.48-1984 (Permanence of Paper)

James Bennett Griffin
without whom none of this would have been possible

Contents

Tables

Figures

Acknowledgments

This project had its inception in two events: an observation by James B. Griffin during a Southeastern Archaeological Conference symposium in late 1990 that excavations at Madisonville had "provided a preliminary report...but an adequate study should still be attempted by an energetic graduate student" (Griffin 1992:55), and my participation during the spring of 1991 in a seminar on Fort Ancient archaeology organized by Gary Wright. Rashly, I decided to tackle a reanalysis of materials from the Madisonville site as the basis for a dissertation project. It never could have happened without the help of scores of people, who generously shared with me their knowledge and experience of Fort Ancient and eastern North American archaeology. Because so many individuals contributed so much, I cannot begin to describe the special help provided by each one, but I extend my sincere appreciation and thanks to all.

Jimmy Griffin's work is the foundation for all subsequent Fort Ancient research. Whenever I thought I had discovered something new, inevitably I found that he had been there before me. Even from a neophyte, though, he was willing to listen to speculations, examine fuzzy photographs of puzzling sherds, answer very basic questions, and suggest new sources of data. His encouragement (and needling) helped to keep me going, and his support opened the door to publication. My grateful appreciation goes beyond words.

The members of my dissertation committee, Gary Wright, Robert Jarvenpa, Dean Snow, and Richard Wilkinson, were helpful and encouraging throughout the project, as was Michael Smith, who honed my ability to conceive and refine a research project and to write a grant proposal. During my graduate career at Harvard and SUNY-Albany I was blessed with a fine cadre of teachers. Of them, I must single out one for special thanks: Ian Brown, my master's thesis advisor, who introduced me to the rigors of archaeological analysis and to the Contact Period as a focus for research, and who has been a generous mentor and friend ever since.

A huge number of Fort Ancient archaeologists helped to bring me up to speed when I first began this project. Pat Essenpreis worked to put me in touch with students and colleagues currently involved in Ohio Fort Ancient projects. Ken Tankersley gave me much background information when I was just starting out. Not only did Wes Cowan welcome me to the Cincinnati Museum of Natural History (now Museum of Natural History and Science) collections, share basic knowledge about southwestern Ohio artifact styles and horizon markers, and make his own ongoing research available to me, but, in addition, he and his family generously opened their home to me during one long research visit. Specialists who have analyzed recently excavated Madisonville and related Ohio and Kentucky Fort Ancient artifacts and who went out of their way to share insights and results included Sandy Dunavan, Chris Turnbow, Jack Rossen, Gail Wagner, and Robert Warren, among others. My particular thanks to Rodney Riggs, who answered questions on southwestern Ohio chronology and ceramics, and made portions of his almost-completed dissertation manuscript available. Farther east in Ohio, Jeff Carskadden and Jim Morton showed and discussed type ceramics from both early Middle and protohistoric sites, plus Contact Period metal artifacts, and Jim has continued to provide a wealth of information on Wellsburg and eastern Fort Ancient sites, ceramics, and other artifacts. Gwynn Henderson and Dave Pollack gave me an abundance of background information from "south of the border," showed me Kentucky Fort Ancient and Caborn-Welborn ceramics and Contact Period horizon marker artifacts, and are always ready to answer questions and discuss problems. Bob Maslowski, during a visit to West Virginia that he initiated and facilitated, took me to see museum collections in Huntington and Parkersburg not currently open to outside researchers, showed me the Clover and Rolf Lee sites, and provided copies of unpublished documentation. Nick Freidin displayed artifacts and shared insights from his recent work at Clover. Roland Barnett shared his large collection of artifacts and his knowledge of lower Kanawha Valley sites, and he and his wife took me on a memorable tour of Orchard and related sites in areas where he has excavated. Ron Moxley also shared his collection, plus much information gleaned from his own and other West Virginia amateurs' excavations. Other collectors in West Virginia and Ohio who showed and discussed their artifacts include Bob Ferrell, Everett Schwartz, and William Wertz. Many of these generous people have continued to correspond, answer questions, and share unpublished papers, to my great benefit. Others who have made thesis and dissertation work-in-progress available include Sarah Evans, Diana Greenlee, Brett Harper, William Holmes, and Patricia Tench.

Many archaeologists working in surrounding regions and other specialties also have been generous with data and advice. Chief among them has been Marvin Smith, whose work with interior Southeast Contact Period sites was one of my major inspirations, and who has been more than willing to discuss problems, help me out with needed information, and warn me against careless mistakes. He kindly read and commented on my entire dissertation manuscript, to the great benefit of the published version. Bill Fitzgerald shared critical details of his important work with Contact Period Neutral site chronology and European trade goods, as did Jim Bradley with his Onondaga work, Bill Johnson with his Monongahela research, and Martha Sempowski and Lorraine Saunders with their Seneca project. Duane Esarey went far out of his way to provide Oneota ceramics information, as well as share his ongoing work on spider shell gorgets. Larry Conrad stimulated me to take a closer look at early shell gorget types, generously answering questions and sharing information on a range of Illinois River valley-related concerns. Cheryl Munson has kept me updated on relevant data from Caborn-Welborn sites, while answering an endless stream of questions. J.E.B. Bowen has been an ongoing source of information on northern Ohio archaeology. Steve Williams has been helpful in many ways, including, among other things, his discovery and rescue of John Swanton's 1897 Madisonville map. Others who have helpfully answered (sometimes many) key questions about protohistoric horizon markers, unpublished sites, and methodology include Ernie Boszhardt, Jeff Brain, Jim Brown, Jim Collins, Ken Farnsworth, Bill Fox, David Hally, Jim Hatch, Jim Herbstritt, Rochelle Lurie, Jim Pendergast, Stephen Plog, Brian Redmond, Margaret Schoeninger, Kathryn Stark, Vin Steponaitis, Dave Stothers, Lynne Sullivan, and Greg Waselkov.

Several people were directly responsible for identifying or suggesting lines of inquiry about particular Madisonville European artifacts. Martha Sempowski brought my attention to chemical and physical differences in "early blue" glass beads. Jim Bradley suggested that certain iron artifacts might be lugs from iron-fitted copper kettles. He and Terry Childs viewed the Madisonville metal collection at Harvard to confirm that possibility, at which time Terry drew my attention to the spiral made from a thin metal tube. Ian Brown and Jeff Brain confirmed the identity of the Clarksdale brass bell (at least, as far as was possible from photographs). Donald LaRocca confirmed identification and provided a date range for the iron dagger guard.

Ron Hancock, of the University of Toronto SLOWPOKE Reactor Facility, went far beyond mere helpfulness in providing trace element analysis of glass beads from Madisonville and Rolf Lee and metal samples from Madisonville, part of it on a *pro bono* basis, plus initial interpretation of the results. At the NSF-Arizona AMS Facility, Timothy Jull generously instituted an additional round of testing after I raised questions about some of the corn kernel radiocarbon dates.

Geologists and archaeologists who showed me rock specimens, examined photos of artifacts, answered questions about local and exotic minerals and fossils, and put me in touch with other knowledgeable experts include Jim Murphy, who gave me a great deal of useful information and advice, Dale Gnidovec, Michael Hansen, Barbara Luedtke, Bob Converse, and Bob Kuhn. I am grateful to N'omi Greber for information and cautions on pipestone analysis and sourcing.

People at many institutions provided access to relevant collections, often generously sharing their own knowledge to add immeasurably to what I was able to discover on my own. At the Peabody Museum, Lane Beck, Viva Fisher, Scott Fulton, Bob Ganong, Gloria Greis, T. Rose Holdcraft, Martha Labell, Pat Lieberson, Roxanne Reddington-Wilde, Beth Sandager, and Scott Spurlock each contributed to my work over a long period of time, giving me access to collections and to special expertise, always with friendly interest. Lane very generously provided consultation and advice on osteological analysis. Professor. Nikolaas van der Merwe, of the committee on destructive analysis, helped with additional information and leads on metal analysis. At the Cincinnati Museum of Natural History, Bob Genheimer and Wes Cowan went far out of their way to make my work productive and efficient. Hetty Jo Brumbach, at SUNY-Albany, made it possible for me to borrow Madisonville metal artifacts from Cincinnati for analysis. Very generous with their time and help were Anibal Rodriguez at the American Museum of Natural History, Bill Mercer at the Cincinnati Art Museum, Laura Chace and Scott Gampfer at the Cincinnati Historical Society, Bill Green at the Iowa Historical Society, Dawn Scher Thomae at the Milwaukee Public Museum, Mary Jane Lenz at the National Museum of the American Indian, Martha Potter Otto and Don Bier at the Ohio Historical Society, Malinda Blustain at the Robert S. Peabody Museum, Guy Aaronson and Deborah Wood at the Smithsonian Institution, and Mary Powell at the University of Kentucky William S. Webb Museum of Anthropology. Others who helpfully answered questions about collections I did not visit include Janice Klein at the Field Museum, Sandy Dunavan at the University of Michigan Museum of Anthropology, Linda Thomas of the Pratt Museum of Natural History at Amherst, and Jane Ketcham and Rebecca DuBey at Beloit College's Logan Museum.

Master photographer Steve Burger was extremely generous with his talent and time, going far beyond what I requested in providing pictures of artifacts curated at the Harvard University Peabody Museum. Likewise, Bill Collier provided all that I asked for, and more, in his fine photographs of specimens from the Museum of Natural History and Science, Cincinnati. Barbara Alexander's drawings of artifacts curated in Cincinnati are a significant enhancement to this volume.

My first three years under the aegis of The University at Albany, SUNY, were made possible by a very generous Presidential Fellowship, and my dissertation was supported by NSF Dissertation Improvement Grant No. DBS-9213382.

Finally, my heartfelt thanks to my husband Mike, other family members, and friends, who forgave my dropout from normal everyday life while I worked on this project, and were waiting for me when I finally was able to step back and rejoin them in the real world.

CHAPTER 1

Introduction

In recent years, events and processes of the Contact Period in eastern North America have received much attention from archaeologists and ethnohistorians. Changes in Native American subsistence, settlement patterns, social organization, and interaction networks during this crucial time have been traced out in the Northeast, the Great Lakes, the coastal and interior Southeast, and many areas adjacent to the Mississippi River. However, the protohistoric Ohio River valley still is largely unknown. Although this region is far from where the earliest contacts between Europeans and natives took place, it is a major node in an ancient system of trails and waterways stretching from Florida to Canada and from the Atlantic to the Mississippi and beyond. By the mid-sixteenth century, its residents were receiving European goods, but where they obtained them, how they used them, and what influences for change came along with them have not been studied. Without knowledge of Ohio Valley people's participation in regional interaction networks, no picture of the Contact Period can be complete.

Historical sources are little help. Not until the mid-eighteenth century do reliable descriptions of the region begin to become available, and even then, they are unsatisfyingly fragmentary. Indeed, even the best Euroamerican eyewitness descriptions are not capable of providing a complete picture of early Contact Period interactions and influences, because so much of the experience involved down-the-line interaction rather than face-to-face exchanges between newcomers and natives. Given these circumstances, archaeology offers a unique and valuable source of additional information about this important period in North American history.

Many early assessments of the post-Columbian contact period characterized Native Americans as the passive or savagely resisting recipients of change forced upon them by powerful and culturally advanced outsiders. More recently, researchers have emphasized the mutual effects of contact, the positive initiatives taken by Native Americans in contact situations, and the importance of the respective European and native ideologies in shaping their responses to each other. Particularly during the past decade, ethnohistorians and archaeologists have clarified the circumstances and results of early interactions along the Eastern Seaboard. Fine-grained temporal analysis of European and indigenous trade goods from successively occupied sites, plus new advances in absolute dating techniques, are beginning to allow reconstruction of small-scale fluctuations in exchange relationships, demographics, settlement patterns, and mortuary practices, as well as changing responses by Native Americans to newly introduced European materials and tools. Contact-era disease, warfare, prosetylization, and demands for furs, skins, and slaves took their toll on indigenous peoples, but did not necessarily strike immediately nor result in instantaneous, overwhelming cultural change.

In theory, interior communities, far from the immediate impact of direct European contact, would have been more subject to gradual and controlled cultural transformation, a transformation that would be "expressed in their social, exchange, mortuary, and other ritual subsystems" (Hamell 1986-87:84), many aspects of which can be observed in the archaeological record. The central Ohio River valley, occupied from the eleventh century onward by members of what archaeologists term the "Fort Ancient tradition," is one such region.

The currently accepted portrait of protohistoric Fort Ancient society is *not* one of gradual, controlled change. In fact, historians have proposed that the previously populous Ohio Valley was largely abandoned between about 1670 and 1730 (e.g., Tanner 1987:31-33). Despite historical evidence refuting the "myth of Iroquois conquest" (Jennings 1984:16), many researchers still attribute seventeenth-century change in this region to Iroquois incursions connected with the fur trade, possibly aggravated by epidemic disease. No matter what the ascribed cause, words like "chaos," "upheaval," "disruption," and "collapse" are not uncommonly applied (e.g., Cowan 1988:8-13).

One alternative to this picture of externally imposed disastrous upheaval is that at least some changes observed in the late Fort Ancient archaeological record reflect deliberate responses to new outside influences rather than social disruption and collapse. If so, such responses should be conditioned upon existing patterns and conventions of interaction, and should reflect prevailing procedures for handling external influences. Thus, "effects" of the European presence need to be evaluated in the context of previously existing interactions. In fact, the relatively short-term interactions represented by European-derived goods at Fort Ancient sites can serve to illuminate interactions and changes in relationships among native groups, with European materials and artifacts acting as visible and time-sensitive tracers.

A key site for interpreting interaction and change in this region is the Madisonville village and cemetery, now encompassed by suburban Cincinnati. Excavated primarily over a period of three decades at the turn of the century, Madisonville is the most completely explored protohistoric Fort Ancient site, and among the most populous. It was important in James B. Griffin's original formulation of the "Fort Ancient Aspect," being the type site for one of four geographically oriented "foci" within the Fort Ancient region (Griffin 1943: Map 1; see below, Figure 4-1). It also is the type site for the recently defined "Madisonville Horizon," a temporally oriented construct that includes Late Fort Ancient settlements active between approximately 1450 and 1700. As the apparently last-occupied settlement in western Fort Ancient territory, Madisonville has much to teach us about the interactions of interior peoples with the gradually expanding European presence in eastern North America.

The site is located on the Little Miami River about eight kilometers above its confluence with the Ohio River. Between 1879 and 1911, it was excavated first by members of the Madisonville Literary and Scientific Society and then by a series of expeditions sponsored by Harvard University's Peabody Museum. It contained over 1450 burials within the same area as some 1300 corn storage/refuse pits, and yielded almost five hundred European-derived metal and glass artifacts. The 1920 site report, exemplary for its day, included illustrations and normative descriptions of important artifact and feature types, statistics on burial orientations and pottery grave goods, and biometric analyses of selected human remains (Hooton and Willoughby 1920). Griffin's analysis (1943:119-43) included much additional information on museum-curated ceramics from the site.

Besides undocumented pot-hunting, more recent work at Madisonville, almost all of it restricted to the southwest corner of the site, has included amateur excavation of sixteen burials and several dozen pits during the 1930s and 1940s, limited salvage from the 1958 construction of a swimming pool, a small-scale excavation in 1984 from which were obtained two ^{14}C dates, and a 1988-89 salvage excavation of a midden and several refuse pits by the Cincinnati Museum of Natural History (Starr 1960:78-79; Tankersley 1986b; Cowan, in press; Conover, n.d.). The stratigraphic information and additional radiocarbon dates from this last project made it possible to begin construction of a site chronology tied to important ceramic types (Glowacki et al. 1993). Madisonville clearly is multicomponent, spanning at least the eleventh through seventeenth centuries. Occupation probably was most intense toward the end of that time period. However, no spatio-temporal analysis of artifacts, remains, and features ever has been carried out for the site as a whole.

In order to evaluate the events and interactions in which Madisonville residents took part during the sixteenth and seventeenth centuries and how these might have affected their social and economic life, I undertook a reanalysis of Madisonville archaeological collections and excavation data from work carried out between 1879 and 1911, with emphasis on site chronology, spatial organization, mortuary patterns, and exotic materials and artifacts. These data were evaluated in light of similar evidence from other late prehistoric and protohistoric Fort Ancient sites, with the goal of defining local and regional socioeconomic organization, interaction, and change.

Questions addressed include the following. When and for how long was Madisonville occupied? With whom did Madisonville residents interact, locally, regionally, and interregionally? What were the nature of these relationships? Did they change over time? Were they affected by Contact Period events? If so, in what ways?

To extend current understanding of Madisonville occupation history, I utilized AMS radiocarbon dating, horizon marker artifacts, and intrasite spatial and stratigraphic relationships. Contemporaneity with other settlements was established by means of horizon marker traits and absolute dates from radiocarbon assays. To determine the context of local and intraregional interactions, I examined social organization by means of mortuary analysis, settlement pattern analysis, and information exchange theory (Binford 1971; Chang 1968; O'Shea 1984; B. Smith 1978; Willey 1956; Wobst 1977). Prehistoric and protohistoric long-distance exchange patterns were explored through distribution patterns of exotic materials and artifacts, both indigenous and European.

The model of social interaction that I found most applicable was Peer Polity Interaction (Renfrew and Cherry 1986). Peer polities are autonomous sociopolitical units, usually of similar size and situated within the same geographical region. Relationships among such entities, and their political development, are conceived as driven by both competition and cooperation. Initial, tentative identification in the archaeological record is primarily by settlement pattern analysis, with other potential markers including technological similarities, stylistic similarities and oppositions, and supralocal symbols with nonhierarchical distribution patterns. An important consideration was to demonstrate how Madisonville fit into such a model, and if so, whether it functioned alone or in conjunction with other southwestern Ohio Fort Ancient communities as a polity, which other Fort Ancient polities could be considered as peers to Madisonville, whether at any time these Fort Ancient polities came together into a larger polity, and what were the external, non-Fort Ancient interactions of these smaller or larger polities. In considering these external interaction patterns, my working hypotheses for protohistoric Fort Ancient peoples were (1) that interaction networks already in place would not be abandoned, (2) that new connections might be forged deliberately, and (3) that new positive and/or negative interactions, perhaps requiring new patterns of socioeconomic organization, might be forced by external events.

This volume first lays out theoretical and methodological considerations, then gives geographical, historical, archaeological, and ethnographical background information and summarizes Contact Period studies for interior eastern North America, the Fort Ancient culture area, and the southwestern Ohio subregion. Next, it focuses on the Madisonville site: its occupation history, mortuary patterns, and exchange relationships. The data from Madisonville are employed with data from other sites to analyze larger interaction patterns and address the research questions posed above.

Chapter 2, *Social Organization, Interaction, and Change*, describes the theoretical and methodological frameworks used to interpret Madisonville and contemporaneous Fort Ancient interaction patterns over time. Models of social organization and interaction, including Peer Polity Interaction, are summarized and discussed, as are preferred approaches to analysis of settlement patterns and site structure, mortuary patterns, interaction, and acculturative and non-acculturative change.

Chapter 3, *Contact and Change in Eastern North America after 1492*, presents a condensed overview of fifteenth- to seventeenth-century eastern North America, drawing upon evidence from history, ethnohistory, and archaeology. Maps and event tables summarize indigenous culture areas, population centers, and communications systems, as well as European expeditions and settlements. Documented direct and indirect effects of European contact are summarized and generalized, and important horizon marker artifacts are identified for eventual comparison with central Ohio Valley evidence.

Chapter 4, *The Central Ohio River Valley*, briefly describes the Fort Ancient archaeological culture area, its residents' characteristic subsistence strategies, settlement patterns, and technology, and what is known or has been inferred to date about their social organization, interaction networks, and involvement in Contact era events. Significant changes over time in site and settlement organization, mortuary treatments, and exchange patterns are noted. Locations, short descriptions, and relative chronologies are included for southwestern Ohio sites and for protohistoric Fort Ancient sites that probably were contemporaneous with Madisonville.

Chapter 5, *The Madisonville Village and Cemetery*, describes the Madisonville site and its local surroundings. The excavation history of the site is briefly reviewed, in order to evaluate the influence of pre-modern excavation and curation procedures on the interpretation potential of the archaeological collections. Problems with the published site map are presented, and the bases for construction of a revised version are summarized. The revised master map, entered into the computer in a GIS format, makes it possible to relate site features to site topography, and conveys a very different picture of settlement spatial organization from the published version. Rather than having a disorganized, unstructured plan, this village, like the majority of thoroughly excavated Fort Ancient sites, is shown to have been organized around a communal open area or plaza.

Chapter 6, *Madisonville Occupation History*, addresses the question of intrasite temporal components. Radiocarbon dates, horizon marker artifacts, and crosscutting features tentatively identify late prehistoric (fifteenth–early sixteenth century and earlier) and protohistoric (late sixteenth–early seventeenth century) components at the site. Continuities and changes in settlement size, spatial organization, and lifeway characteristics over time are explored. To form a basis for discussion of local settlement patterns and culture change over time, lower Little Miami Valley sites contemporaneous with temporal components at Madisonville are identified. Using the data developed in this chapter, the chronological position of Madisonville relative to other protohistoric Fort Ancient sites is discussed.

Rather than having been a very large settlement, the Late Fort Ancient component at Madisonville appears to have been comparable in size with Early–Middle Fort Ancient southwestern Ohio villages, but was occupied for a significantly longer time. Changes in site use patterns between late prehistoric and protohistoric components probably were related to changes in subsistence patterns, specifically, the addition of bison hunting to an earlier focus on maize horticulture. From currently available data, there appears to have been no hierarchical settlement pattern in the area around Madisonville. For most of its existence, this village apparently functioned as an independent polity rather than as a member of an interdependent group of settlements. European horizon marker artifacts present, all of which would have been available by the end of the sixteenth century, imply a relatively early chronological position (and/or a different exchange sphere) compared with protohistoric Fort Ancient sites farther east.

Chapter 7, *Madisonville Internal Relationships*, uses site layout and mortuary data to analyze intrasite socioeconomic organization. It includes a short methodological summary, discussion of high- and low-value artifacts at the site, delineation of large-scale spatial patterns and significant burial types, and implications for village and local-area social organization and internal interaction. Particular attention is paid to the occurrence and significance of exotic materials and artifacts as status indicators in the mortuary context.

Significant continuity over time can be seen in mortuary treatment, with no evidence for ascribed elite status during any period. However, social organization does appear to have become more complex over time. At least two types of leadership roles were filled by men throughout the periods of interest, one apparently related to ritual/healing, and the other to more secular concerns, probably including hunting/warfare and external relations. The first, marked in many cases by possession of the equivalent of a medicine bundle, probably involved a vision quest and training/experience that commenced in early adolescence. The second, marked most strongly by possession of an important pipe, seems to have been limited to adult males. By the end of the Madisonville occupation, it is very likely that an additional leadership function, marked by sheet-copper symbol badges, had developed. Since similarly shaped copper pendants have been excavated with burials at three other contemporaneous western and central Fort Ancient settlements, it is hypothesized that they were related to peer polity confederacy-level interaction and alliance. However, a close consideration of all extra-community interactions by Madisonville residents shows that this was by no means the only external relationship maintained.

Chapter 8, *Madisonville External Relationships*, explores the patterns of interregional interaction implied by various nonlocal materials and artifacts present at Madisonville, both European and indigenous. Directions of interaction are investigated largely by means of artifact distribution maps. Intensity of interaction is inferred through quantities of exotic items from particular external sources, through local imitations of nonlocal artifact types, and through similarities and differences in use patterns compared with source areas. Madisonville's intraregional interactions with other Fort Ancient settlements as well as its extraregional interactions with non-Fort Ancient peoples are summarized, as are the most important external interactions maintained by other contemporaneous Fort Ancient settlements. European artifacts are used to trace changes and continuities in protohistoric versus prehistoric interaction patterns.

During the Late Fort Ancient Madisonville Horizon, eastern and western Fort Ancient peoples apparently were in regular and intimate contact, as evidenced by similarities in ceramic styles, pipes, functional artifacts, settlement locations and organization, and supralocal symbols such as marine shell maskettes. However, regional differences were maintained in lifeways and in non-Fort Ancient interaction networks, as evidenced by differences in mortuary treatment, personal adornment, and types and quantities of exotic materials and artifacts between roughly contemporaneous western and eastern Fort Ancient settlements.

Contacts external to Fort Ancient territory conform in many ways to a risk-pooling model involving heterarchical interactions. Ceramics and other functional artifacts from mortuary and nonmortuary contexts provide evidence of positive relationships between Fort Ancient and northern Ohio peoples throughout the Fort Ancient period. At Madisonville, a significant northwesterly (Oneota) connection, evident in western Ohio Early-Middle Fort Ancient contexts (ca. 1100-1450), appears to have been continued and intensified by Late Fort Ancient Madisonville residents. Evidence comes from bison products, stone clubs, bone rasps, pipe styles, medicine bags, and a striking group of tubular metal serpent-shaped pendants. Less common at Madisonville, but forming a significant assemblage, are items such as ceramics and particular types of shell ornaments associated with central Mississippi Valley peoples. From this direction, too, might have come the European brass bell of a type connected with the de Soto entrada. Evidence for an apparently new direction of interaction, toward the northeast, comes from the presence of European metal and glass items traded in the St. Lawrence estuary by late sixteenth century Basque fishermen, and fragments of Iroquoian ceramic pipes from several different sources including Neutralia. This connection apparently flourished only briefly, during the late sixteenth and early seventeenth centuries. While it lasted, it brought a fair amount of copper and brass to Madisonville, which local residents apparently fashioned into symbolically significant ornaments, some of which probably were exchanged with allies to the west, perhaps in connection with obtaining bison products. Madisonville people also made fine pipes of nonlocal styles, probably for ceremonial gifts. It seems likely that during this time the settlement served some of the functions of a gateway city between Fort Ancient territories and people farther west.

Protohistoric eastern Fort Ancient communities appear to have had different external relationships than did Madisonville/western Fort Ancient. Evidence for interaction to the south includes relatively large numbers of engraved marine shell gorgets originating in eastern Tennessee. Evidence for interaction with Riker/Wellsburg and Monongahela peoples to the north comes from ceramics and from bone and cannel coal ornaments. European-related artifacts appear to have been obtained through both of these networks, as well as through Susquehannock peoples more directly east.

It seems that Fort Ancient peoples and polities were not monolithic, but forged a variety of internal and external ties, ties that they maintained and extended during the increasingly turbulent Contact era. Almost all of the European artifacts excavated from protohistoric Fort Ancient settlements could have been obtained prior to the mid-seventeenth century. If this signals the departure of at least some groups from the central Ohio Valley after that time, it is very likely that different Fort Ancient groups migrated in different directions, toward the locations of their protohistoric interaction partners.

CHAPTER 2

Social Organization, Interaction and Change

The central question addressed in this volume is what effects (if any) the early presence of Europeans in North America had on the interior peoples of the central Ohio River valley, with a particular focus on their interaction networks. Any attempt to answer it requires attention to both general diachronic processes and particular historical contexts. For effects to occur, interaction, whether direct or indirect, must have taken place. For effects to be assessed, there must be some indication of change. Thus, it is necessary to understand the general nature of "interaction" among the natives of eastern North America and between them and the sixteenth-century newcomers to their shores. It also is necessary to delineate what changes might be instituted through interaction, and how these might be recognized in the archaeological record. And because interaction takes place between particular people, filling particular roles in their own societies, through whom the results of interaction are transmitted to others, it is necessary to have a grasp of intrasocietal interaction patterns—in synchronic terms, "social organization." Additional important background for this project includes known prehistoric interregional relationships, known historical events attendant to the European presence, and the specific archaeologically recoverable evidence of this presence.

These last matters are addressed in Chapter 3, which examines the historical context for interaction in eastern North America during the late prehistoric and early historic periods. The current chapter looks at more general issues related to the theoretical and methodological bases for examining and evaluating social organization, interaction, and change. It is not an exhaustive review, but an introduction to the major concepts that have guided my analysis of protohistoric Fort Ancient continuity and change. The first three sections discuss manifestations of change, of social organization, and of interaction in the archaeological record. A fourth section describes selected models that incorporate aspects of these phenomena.

Archaeological Manifestations of Change

The irreductable dimensions of archaeology have been defined as temporal locus, spatial locus, and form (Spaulding 1960). Thus, a minimalist definition of archaeologically visible change would be differences in locations and/or forms of features, artifacts, and/or ecofacts in successive time periods. In order to recognize and assess change, it is essential to establish a chronological framework and to define relative chronological relationships among clearly identified components. In order to effectively interpret Contact Period archaeological patterns, prehistoric baselines must be established for comparison.

Temporal Scales

Drawing from the work of historian Fernand Braudel, Michael Smith reminds us that "different historical processes operate at different temporal rhythms or levels" (Smith 1992:26). These differences must be taken into account in all aspects of archaeological research, including project design, data collection, analysis, and interpretation, in order to make legitimate comparisons and conclusions.

Braudel's hierarchical temporal levels include (1) *events*, which pertain to individuals and relatively short-term actions like battles, coronations, or childbirth, (2) *conjonctures,* which pertain to group-level, longer-duration actions and interactions, and which can be divided into (a) *intermediate-term conjonctures*, including processes such as wars or economic cycles and (b) *long-term conjonctures*, including processes such as long-term demographic changes or the rise and fall of empires, and (3) the *longue durée,* which pertains to "man in his environment, a history in which all change is slow, and history of constant repetition, ever-recurring cycles" (Smith 1992:27, quoting Braudel). Bradley calls these levels individual time, social time, and geographical time (Bradley 1991:210). Smith adds a fourth level, corresponding to the third of Karl Butzer's adaptive systems modes: (4) a time scale at which very long-term "adaptive transformations," such as the inception and adoption of agriculture, can take place.

Very little prehistoric archaeological data can be comprehended on the level of the event. One exception is primary inhumations. For this reason, gravelots are considered particularly valuable for seriation (Rowe 1962). However, the seriation process cannot pinpoint the time of the event, only place it within a relative scale of decades to a half-century or more. Because of the nature of both dating technology and formation processes (such as the accumulation of debris in and around a dwelling, sometimes over the course of several generations), most archaeological information is retrieved only at the level of the *conjoncture*. Very often the remains of events with potential ethnographic analogs are superimposed upon each other, rendering direct analogy and detailed interpretation difficult if not impossible.

Due to inherent statistical uncertainties, modern methods of absolute dating such as radiocarbon dating and thermoluminescence can provide information no finer than the *conjoncture* level. At a similar temporal scale, assemblages of "horizon marker" artifacts and styles can be used to build relative chronologies. Such chronologies can be refined further when artifacts of known absolute date or with very short-term cycles of style or availability are included, such as in New World assemblages containing European artifacts (Fitzgerald 1990; Kidd 1954; Kidd and Kidd 1983; Quimby 1939; Smith 1987:23-53). However, interpretations must always take into account archaeological formation processes, which can affect precision significantly (Schiffer 1987:305-21).

Contact Period Change (1): Non-Acculturative

Marvin Smith, who studied the Contact Period interior Southeast, argues strongly for a distinction between culture change (including "deculturation," or loss of culture) instigated indirectly by Contact Period conditions and events, and "acculturation," or increased similarity of one culture to another, which generally occurs due to prolonged contact (Smith 1987:113-14, 127-28). Smith identified much culture change, but little acculturation, in his region of interest during the sixteenth and seventeenth centuries (1987:54-128; see summary in Chapter 3 below).

Formal models of acculturation and its manifestations in the archaeological record have been developed. They will be described and discussed in the next section. Here, I will briefly list significant non-acculturative changes identified by Smith and others as important during the Contact Period, together with the types of archaeological evidence used to identify their presence and magnitude.

Epidemic disease has been proposed by Dobyns and others as a major and immediate factor in post-Columbian culture change (e.g., Crosby 1972; Dobyns 1983; Ramenofsky 1987), although its timing and effects now are known to have varied considerably from region to region (e.g., Snow 1995a; Baker and Kealhofer 1996). Archaeological evidence that might be present includes both direct evidence of nontraumatic mass death and indirect evidence of drastic population decline (e.g., Milanich 1996:65; Smith 1987:54-85). Because epidemic deaths are, by definition, relatively swift, the bones of the deceased rarely offer positive evidence, although diseases such as smallpox sometimes produce skeletal lesions. Data that might (considering all factors) be interpreted as direct evidence of epidemic deaths include rapid increase in nonindividual burials (Milner 1980:48-49), demographic curves with over-representation of very young, very old, adolescent, and young adult individuals (Milner 1980:49), and multiple delayed burials evidenced by disarticulated remains and/or evidence of gnawing (Smith 1987:60-61). An increase in items interpreted as charms against sickness or shamanistic curing devices might also accompany high death rates (e.g., Fitzgerald 1992; Mandzy 1994:142). Indirect evidence would include fewer or smaller-sized villages or houses, and population movement that could be attributed to people fleeing from disease areas (Snow and Starna 1989; Smith 1987:67-84). Smith has proposed that the latter would manifest itself initially as scattered, small settlements, then as a single consolidated site, smaller in total population than the aggregate of pre-epidemic sites; he also discusses "slower movements brought about as tribal balances of power shift with changing demography" (1987:75). Individually, of course, almost all of these manifestations can be explained by alternative scenarios. It is multiple lines of evidence, and elimination of alternative possibilities, that would prove a case.

Ann Ramenofsky has proposed a general model of differential persistence of communities in the wake of European-introduced disease, based on settlement location, duration, and form (Ramenofsky 1990). She suggests that sedentary settlements located on navigable drainages, that is, directly accessible to a frequent axis of communication, would have a high impact from newly introduced diseases, while mobile groups living in dispersed settlement patterns would have a low impact from disease, no matter what their location. She makes no predictions for mobile, nucleated groups or for sedentary groups on secondary drainages or even farther removed from major communication routes.

Warfare is known to have been an important factor in people's lives during the early historical period (e.g., Dye 1990; Hunt 1960; Jennings 1984:145-219; Trigger 1971). If endemic, it would be attended by high proportions of violent deaths, evidenced by "arrow wounds, parry fractures, scalping, decapitation, and other mutiliation," particularly among adult males, plus completely or partially disarticulated remains, some perhaps showing indications of exposure prior to burial, nonstandard burial positions and locations, and mass burials (Milner 1995; Milner et al. 1991; Santure 1990:158). Sometimes a case can be made for the presence of captives or refugees based on multiple lines of evidence such as osteological evidence for differential genetic ties, abrupt introduction of nonlocal pottery traits, an excess of physically abused females in a population, differential burial treatment, or a contemporaneous destroyed settlement that could have been the source of displaced people (e.g., Wilkinson and Van Wagenen 1993; Wray et al. 1987:242-48). Cannibalism of enemies is known to have been practiced historically among Iroquoian and other groups (e.g., Heidenreich 1978:386; Trowbridge 1938:88-90, 1939:21, 53-54). Skeletal evidence for cannibalism, including fragmentary remains with cutmarks, intentional fracture, and signs of burning, is outlined by T. White (1991:393-406). Evidence for warfare at the settlement and regional level would include palisades, moats, embankments, and buffer zones (Anderson 1994:263-71; DeBoer 1981; Dye 1990:214; Larson 1972; Peregrine 1993). If warfare were culturally paramount, depictions of it would be expected in media such as rock art, effigy pipes, and engraved shell, bone, and stone, as is true for the Missisippian "falcon warrior" and associated motifs (e.g., see Brown 1985, 1991; Strong 1989).

Social organization, as evidenced by settlement patterns and mortuary practices, will be discussed below (Archaeological Manifestations of Social Organization). Contact Period changes in some cases were toward lesser organizational complexity (e.g., the devolution of Southeastern complex chiefdoms) and in others were toward greater organizational complexity (e.g., the expansion of the Iroquois Confederacy).

Changes in subsistence patterns are known to have been associated with the European presence during historical times, particularly for (1) groups involved in the fur or skin trade, (2) Plains groups who obtained horses, and (3) groups coming under the influence of missionaries who attempted to mold them into European-style farmers. It is mainly the first instance that is potentially relevant to interior sixteenth-seventeenth century eastern North America. Direct evidence for increased acquisition and processing of hides might include numerical increases in hunting camps, hunting and hideworking tools, and appropriate animal remains (e.g., beaver). Warren DeBoer argues, from ethnohistorical analogy, that large underground storage pits are indicative of seasonally abandoned settlements, such as for extended hunting expeditions, rather than a hallmark of sedentism (DeBoer 1988). In addition, he argues that they also can "be viewed as a stress marker, one that is as much keyed to socioeconomic turmoil as it is to climatic vagaries" (DeBoer 1988:14). Other evidence for seasonal abandonment of settlements might come from paleoethnobotanical and faunal analyses to establish the seasonal nature of remains. In some cases, buffer zones might be connected with hunting as well as with warfare (Hickerson 1965). New hunting strategies aiming for increased yields, such as large-scale deer drives, would be reflected by the presence of faunal remains of all ages rather than selected very old or immature specimens (Waselkov 1978). New plant species, such as peaches and melons, were introduced by Europeans (but arguably had far less effect on subsistence patterns than the adoption by Europeans of plants such as maize, potatoes, and tobacco). Their presence would be indicated by pits and seeds.

Interaction networks and exchange patterns certainly were influenced by the advent of new trading partners along the Eastern Seaboard (Chapter 3). Archaeological manifestations of exchange are discussed below, under Archaeological Manifestations of Interaction and Exchange, and models of interaction are discussed at the end of the chapter, under Models of Interaction and Change.

Contact Period Change (2): Acculturative

Under what circumstances and by what means groups of Native Americans have become "acculturated" to European ways has been one of the significant concerns of Contact Period anthropologists and archaeologists. In actuality, this is only one part of a larger picture, encompassing interaction in general and acceptance or rejection of styles, technology, and ideology of one group by another. Much of the North American work is couched in terms of indigenous groups gradually accepting aspects of a more powerful "donor" culture, in spite of the fact that "acculturation" actually flowed in both directions (e.g., Deagan 1983; McWilliams 1953; Waselkov and Paul 1981). Acculturation studies did, however, result in the development of formal models for archaeologists that can be applied not only to indigenous-to-European acculturation, but also to European-to-indigenous, indigenous-to-indigenous, and even European-to-European.

The archaeological models are direct descendants of work by mid-twentieth century "diffusionist" anthropologists studying interaction between industrialized and nonindustrialized peoples around the world, whose models of culture change were tied to the initiation and spread of innovations (e.g., Broom et al. 1954; Keesing 1953; Linton 1940; Malinowski 1945; Redfield et al. 1936; Spicer 1961, 1972; Walker 1972). The Society for American Archaeology went on to develop a classification of culture contact situations for use by archaeologists (Wauchope 1956). Its two main aspects were "trait unit intrusion," in which a new trait was introduced to a region, and "site unit intrusion," in which a completely new culture was introduced to a region, via the immigration of a group of its proponents. A spectrum of possible outcomes was specified for each type of intrusion, representing lesser to greater acceptance of the intruded trait or culture, along with other possibilities.

Object-oriented models are of particular affinity to archaeologists. One such widely used model was developed by John White from a classification of European influence on indigenous ethnographic artifacts set up by George Quimby and Alexander Spoehr (Quimby and Spoehr 1951; White 1975). White's model (Table 2-1) classifies newly introduced artifacts, and indigenous artifacts influenced by newly introduced technology and materials, in terms of increasing levels of acculturation. He organized each of these two divisions from "least externally influenced" to "most externally influenced," with the expectation

TABLE 2-1
Classification of Archaeological Remains from Contact Period Sites

Category	Examples
A. Artifacts NEW to the adopting culture	
1. New types of artifacts for which there is a native counterpart	Glass beads, some European clothing, iron knives
2. New types of artifacts for which there is no native counterpart	Firearms
3. New types of artifacts made from native materials but copying introduced models	
a. Where the techniques are introduced along with the new artifact	Pottery-making, where none existed before
b. Where the techniques come from within the recipient group	Stone bullet molds
4. New types of artifacts where the introduced model is decorated after the native manner	Carved knife handles, modified European clothing
5. New types of artifacts where the manufacture is local but the maker employs imported material and techniques	Clothing made from imported cloth, using metal needles and scissors
B. Artifacts TRADITIONAL in the adopting culture	
1. Old types of artifacts where there is a substitution of an imported material for a local one	Glass projectile points, porcelain scrapers
2. Old types of artifacts where there is a substitution of material and technique	Metal projectile points, metal awls
3. Old types of artifacts modified by the introduction of a new element of subject matter	Non-local designs on traditional pottery or baskets

(White 1975:161). A.5 represents the highest degree of change. B.3 and A.4 are essentially similar in degree of change.

that differing proportions of artifacts in each category could be "used to show the degree of acculturation in a particular sphere of activity" (1975:156). Adrian Mandzy developed a more unified scheme of six categories that indicate successively more-acculturated material culture (Table 2-2) (Mandzy 1992:33-34, 1994:137-38). A formal method for scoring artifact "innovation" was devised by Jeffrey Brain (Table 2-3), to be utilized along with "configuration" values, assigned at the level of artifact assemblage, to determine degree of acculturation. A more detailed quantitative system was developed by Paul Farnsworth for application to the direct, extended contact situation at Spanish missions in California. It made use of Stanley South's functional artifact groups (kitchen group, arms group, personal group, etc.) (South 1977), scoring assemblages from different proveniences as to percentages of native and European types present, and analyzing the differences in terms of greater or lesser acculturation (Farnsworth 1989).

Ian Brown has cautioned that acceptance of foreign material items does not necessarily indicate cultural change (Brown 1979a, 1979b). For example, the same artifact can serve a different function among different groups (e.g., European brass spoons utilized as pendants). Brown advocated the perusal of ethnohistorical documentation for clues as to the functions of European items in aboriginal cultures. For archaeologists with little relevant historical documentation, context becomes essential in interpreting an artifact's function.

Because Brain's system is somewhat difficult to use, Marvin Smith's solution was to take White's scoring system (similar to Brain's calculated innovation value), then informally consider context (Smith 1987:119). In so doing, he not only considered the general nature of the assemblage as advocated by Brain (Table 2-3B), but also clearly defined what sorts of items (technomic, sociotechnic) the newly introduced artifacts substituted for, and differentiated between different sorts of disposal contexts (e.g., elite burials, commoner burials, midden). Although his method is informal, its interpretive value is high.

Behind all of these models are ethnohistorical observations making it clear that many Native Americans in early contact situations were most interested in acquiring European items that fit into their sociotechnic rather than technomic categories (see Table 2-4 for definitions) (cf. Hamell 1983; Miller and Hamell 1986, but see also White 1994). These items commonly have been found as grave goods, but also are known to have been curated within temple buildings in the Southeast. Later, as trade goods became more common, they were increasingly deposited in village middens or refuse pits, as well as with burials. At this point, technomic items began to be utilized as such—first in native ways (often modified to conform to known tools, as with ax blades cut into celt forms), and much later, after longer term contact, in European ways. Region-specific examples of these generalizations are included in Chapter 3.

Long-term changes in lifestyle will be signaled by deeper changes than the adoption of foreign artifacts and technology. Brad Bartel has suggested additional, nonartifactual bellwether attributes for analysis of acculturative effects. These include alterations in food preparation, consumption, and disposal, in mortuary practices, and in material symbols of self-identification (Bartel 1989:176-77). House configurations appear to be particularly resistant to acculturative change (Scarry and McEwan 1995).

TABLE 2-2
Artifact Categories Used to Assess Seventeenth Century Cayuga Change Due to European Interaction

Category	Examples
1. Traditional artifact types made from local materials	Local pottery vessels, bone awls, flint points, stone celts
2. Traditional artifact types made from non-local native and European materials	Marine shell ornaments, iron awls made from nails, brass points cut from kettles
3. European artifacts that are functionally equivalent to traditional artifact types	Iron knives, metal kettles, white ball clay pipes
4. New artifacts (either European or indigenous) that are functionally equivalent to no known traditional artifact type	Firearms, panes of window glass
5. Artifacts that are functionally equivalent to European artifact types but are made from local materials	Native gunflints
6. Artifacts that service new European artifact types in use. No corresponding traditional tools are observed	Bullet molds

(Mandzy 1994:138)

Archaeological Manifestations of Social Organization

In current practice, two bodies of theory and method commonly are employed to define social (or socioeconomic) organization through the archaeological record. The first describes spatial organization of the living community: relative locations and sizes of settlements and special-activity sites, and of households, activity areas, and public or communal sectors within settlements. The second describes treatments of the dead, and how their physical manifestations might reflect social relationships among the living.

Settlement Patterns and Site Organization

Spatial patterning and relative sizes of activity areas within buildings—of buildings and activity areas within settlements, of settlements, special purpose areas, and resource areas within regions, and of regions with respect to each other—reflect the socioeconomic relations of their residents (cf. Chang 1968; Douglas 1972; Parsons 1972; Smith 1978; Trigger 1968; Willey 1956). As Wendy Ashmore defines it: "Settlement archaeology is the study of past human behavior through the evidence of settlement patterns" (Ashmore 1981:38). The data of settlement patterns—sites and features—can be used to evaluate human behavior associated with both social organization and environmental exploitation. The framework for the following discussion is taken from Sharer and Ashmore (1979:421-34), with additions from other sources as indicated.

In evaluating architectural-social relationships, Amos Rapoport emphasizes that "built environments are created... to support desired behavior," as well as "to communicate and assert status, power, roles, etc." (Rapoport 1990). If so, they can be decoded to gain understanding of those behaviors and social dimensions. At the level of the dwelling, size, configuration, and associated activity areas can be used to infer the size and nature of household units, from nuclear families to lineages or clans. Their positions and orientations relative to other dwellings tell us about interactions between households. Within settlements, sizes and general configurations of structures and spaces give clues to the interactions among residents. Size, construction materials, elaborateness, location, accessibility, and diversity of public structures can be used to help identify the presence of elite segments of society or ritual specialists, and of the social control or cohesion required for the labor necessary to erect them. Activity areas, segregated or grouped, can echo economic specialization and role differentiation. Number, size, accessibility, and location of public spaces relative to public and private buildings can be taken as indicators of community interaction and coherence. Regular versus irregular layouts reveal the presence or absence of imposed planning. K.C. Chang has suggested that segmented settlement plans might reflect predominance of a social system based on segmented lineages (1958); numerous others have suggested that hierarchical settlement layouts reflect social stratification.

Similar principles are applied to the distribution of settlements within a region. For example, villages of equal size, approximately equivalent in function and distributed evenly within a region (considering physiographical and ecological constraints), would be taken to represent egalitarian social relationships, while hierarchical distributions, with a large central settlement surrounded by smaller satellite communities, would be indicative of a more complex, multilevel society. Usually within a region there are not only different-sized settlements but settlements that differ in function (e.g., farming communities, hunting camps, quarries, religious centers), which together make up a settlement system. For archaeologists to analyze such systems, they must determine contemporaneity, relative sizes, functions, and lines of communication among the constituent communities.

Given a complete roster of contemporaneous sites within a region, location theory, developed by economic geographers, can be used to investigate relationships among them. One often-invoked model is the central place theory, which predicts that, given a featureless landscape, settlements will tend to be spaced equidistantly, following an hexagonal lattice, and that central places (larger centers, in a hierarchy of sizes from high-level to low-level) will tend to develop among them at regular intervals to provide goods and services. Different lines of communication/transport among settlements indicate different net-

TABLE 2-3
Method for Assessing Degree of Acculturation Based on Archaeological Artifact Modifications and Total Assemblage

A. Determining Artifact "Innovation Value"
(sum of all assigned values)

Artifact Attributes	Old	New
Material	0	1
Form	0	1
Manufacturing technique	0	1
Use technique	0	1
Function	0	1

B. Determining Artifact Assemblage "Configuration" Value
(indicative of context and associations)

Assemblage Context	Configuration Value
Occasional European trinkets in otherwise native assemblage and configurations	0
Predominantly native assemblage, with European trinkets and hardware, in native configurations	1
Considerable array of European artifacts and traits, but still a strong native representation All in native configurations	2
All Euro-American artifacts and traits, but predominantly in native configurations	3
All Euro-American artifacts and traits in Euro-American configurations (difficult to distinguish from nonnative remains)	4

(Brain 1979:271-273)

works of relationships among same-level and different-level centers (Smith 1974:173-75). The restrictive conditions and purely economic orientation of this model make it inappropriate for direct application to most prehistoric situations, but various researchers have developed modified models based on hypothesized socioeconomic characteristics of the particular regions under study, such as redistribution rather than market-driven economic forces (e.g., Steponaitis 1978; Welch 1991). Alternative patterns to central place organization include solar systems, with small settlements hierarchically organized around a higher-order center but poorly articulated with other such systems; dendritic systems, in which "all lower-level centers are tied to a single higher-level center in a chain that is entirely vertical without horizontal links" (Smith 1974: 177); and linear systems, which might be constrained by the landscape, such as along river valleys.

Another model from economic geography that has been applied successfully, with some modification, within prehistoric and protohistoric North America is the concept of gateway cities (Hirth 1978; Kelly 1991; Riley 1978). These typically are high-level communities located near the edges of regions, through which long-distance exchange is carried out with other regions. They tend to be located along natural corridors of communication, such as rivers, at "critical passages between areas of high mineral, agricultural, or craft productivity...and at the interface of different technologies or levels of sociopolitical complexity" (Hirth 1978:37). Usually they are connected in dendritic or linear patterns to lower-level communities in their hinterlands.

It is important to note that not only permanent settlements but also periodic meeting places can serve as "central places" or "gateway communities," as with historically documented ren-

TABLE 2-4
Selected Definitions Relevant to Analysis of Socioeconomic Relationships

HETERARCHY: "the relation of elements to one another when they are unranked or when they possess the potential for being ranked in a number of different ways" (Crumley 1995:3).

IDEOTECHNIC ARTIFACTS: "signify and symbolize the ideological rationalizations for the social system and further provide the symbolic milieu in which individuals are enculturated" (e.g., clan symbols, idols) (Binford 1962).

RANK: "positions in a structure" (Rothschild 1975:32, after Fried 1967:35). A rank society has a fewer positions of valued status than individuals to fill them.

ROLE: "behavior appropriate for a specific status" (Rothschild 1975:32, after Linton 1936:113-114).

SOCIAL IDENTITY: "a category of persons, or what has been called a social position or status" (Saxe 1970:4, after Goodenough 1969). Goodenough's original definition is more general: "an aspect of self that makes a difference in how one's rights and duties distribute to specific others" (1969 :313).

SOCIAL PERSONA: a "composite of several social identities selected as appropriate to a given interaction" (Goodenough 1969:316). In simple societies, the number of age-grades through which a person has passed is expected to be important in establishing his/her social persona at death; in complex societies, social rank and other factors also will come into play (Saxe 1970:8).

SOCIOTECHNIC ARTIFACTS: "the material elements having their primary functional context in the social sub-systems of the total cultural system/ ...the... means of articulating individuals one with another into cohesive groups capable of efficiently maintaining themselves and of manipulating the technology" (e.g., king's crown, warrior's coup stick) (Binford 1962:219).

STATUS: collection of rights and duties that define an individual's place in society (Linton 1936:113-114) Status can be ascribed at birth, or achieved during life. Any individual holds more than one status. All statuses are relative to other statuses (Rothschild 1975:32).

STRATIFIED SOCIETY: "one in which members of the same sex and equivalent age status do not have equal access to the basic resources that sustain life" (Fried 1967:186).

TECHNOMIC ARTIFACTS: "those artifacts having their primary functional context in coping directly with the physical environment"; their variability is explained in terms of ecological differences (Binford 1962:219).

WEALTH GOODS: "primitive valuables used in display, ritual, and exchange and special, rare and highly desired subsistence products" (Brumfiel and Earle 1987:4). Often used as equivalent to PRESTIGE GOODS, which "symbolically embody wealth and function in social exchanges and ritual" (McGuire and Downum 1982:118), but there are conceptual differences (see discussion in text). Also called HIGH VALUE GOODS and STATUS GOODS. Although the latter two terms are not used as widely as the former ones, they have the advantage of being more neutral with respect to the imputed social system in which they circulate.

dezvous points in the exchange networks of western North America (Ewers 1954; Swagerty 1988, 1991; Wood 1972, 1980).

Needless to say, locations and sizes of settlements alone are not sufficient to derive regional social organization. Site functions, determined from analysis of intrasite features, artifacts, and ecofacts, are essential in interpreting the regional spatial relationships. Other data, such as exchange patterns, subsistence patterns, and mortuary patterns, also must be brought to bear.

Mortuary Patterns

Based on the seminal work of Arthur Saxe and Lewis Binford, the fundamental tenet of mortuary studies holds that "the form and structure which characterize the mortuary practices of any society are conditioned by the form and complexity of the organizational characteristics of the society itself" (Binford 1971:23; Saxe 1970). Although ordinarily only a fraction of the total mortuary treatment is preserved in the archaeological record (e.g., Bartel 1973, 1982; O'Shea 1984:27-31; Schiffer 1987:80-89), and although this record must be interpreted with caution (e.g., Kristiansen 1984; Pader 1982; Ucko 1969; Whittlesey 1978), it now is generally accepted that archaeological evidence of mortuary treatment can be used to study larger social dimensions within a society (e.g., Levy 1989; O'Shea 1984; Tainter 1978).

Most archaeological mortuary studies involve statistical correlations between the age and sex of individuals interred and attributes of body treatment, interment facility, and associated grave goods, reflecting the theoretical concept that an individual's social persona (composite of social identities: see Table 2-4) can be correlated with her/his burial treatment, and that the social personae evidenced in a burial population will

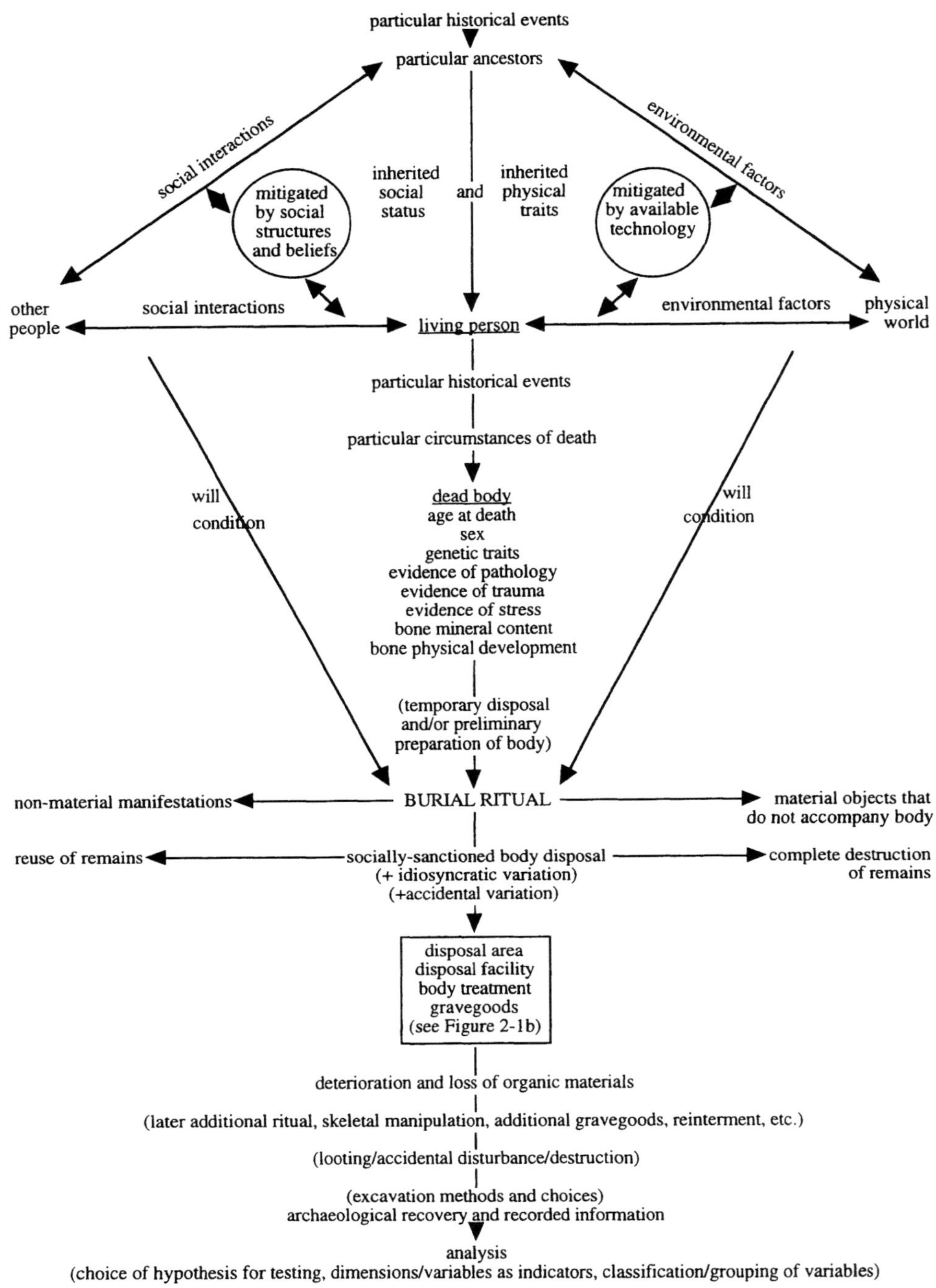

Figure 2-1a. Diachronic relationships among categories of archaeological data drawn upon in mortuary studies.

mirror at least some aspects of social relationships adhering among living members of that community (Goodenough 1969:316; Saxe 1970:8). In addition, spatial patterning of burials within cemeteries and of cemeteries within larger settlement patterns often mirror subgroup memberships among the living (e.g., Chapman and Randsborg 1981:14-19; Goldstein 1980, 1981, 1995; Howell and Kintigh 1996; O'Shea 1988). Each of these archaeologically recoverable aspects of mortuary ritual is discussed in somewhat greater detail below, followed by a summary of analytical principles.

<u>Disposal location</u>

- Nature of disposal area
  - Form (e.g., cemetery, mound, house-floor)
  - Location (vis-à-vis settlement/territory)
    - Access
    - Spatial pattern (e.g., center/periphery, within/outside settlements)
  - Visibility
    - To social group members
    - To outsiders
  - Boundedness
  - Size
  - Shape
  - Geographical orientation
  - Geographical/geological constraints
- Location within disposal area
  - Location vis-à-vis other disposals
  - Visibility
    - To social group
    - To outsiders
  - Patterning (e.g., random, sub-group clusters, overall comprehensive organization such as circles or rows)
  - Characteristics of nearest neighbors
  - (Special mortuary processing facility)
- Location within disposal facility
  - Single vs. multiple disposal
  - Grouping of contemporaneous vs. non-contemporaneous deaths
  - Patterning of multiple disposals

<u>Disposal facility</u>

- Type of facility (e.g., tomb, grave)
  - Above/below ground
  - Sealed/accessible
  - Material
    - Perishable/non-perishable
    - Common/rare
    - Heavy/light
  - Size
  - Shape
- Visibility (to social group members and/or outsiders)
  - Facility itself (e.g., tomb, mound)
  - Markers
- Orientation of facility
- Body containment within facility
  - Type (e.g., special wrapping, receptacle)
  - Material
    - Perishable/non-perishable
    - Common/rare
    - Heavy/light

<u>Disposition of remains</u>

- Evidence of prior preparation
  - Articulated/disarticulated
  - Complete/missing parts
  - Defleshed/not defleshed
  - Inhumation/cremation
- Posture
  - If articulated
    - Extended/flexed
    - Prone/supine/right side/etc.
    - Details of limb, face positioning
  - If not articulated
    - Bones formally arranged/not
- Orientation
  - (compass orientation of head-trunk)

<u>Grave furnishings</u>

- Types
- Materials
- Quantity
- Quality
- Variety
  - Within single burial
  - Within cemetery
- Sources
  - Exotic/local
  - Foreign/native
- Location vis-à-vis body
  - Directly connected with body (clothing, ornaments, etc.)
  - Separate from body
  - Precise location vis-à-vis body parts

Figure 2-1b. Detail: archaeologically visible aspects of socially sanctioned body disposal.

Anticipating this discussion, Figure 2-1 summarizes the relationships between mortuary data generally available in the archaeological record and "real-world" mortuary events. The vertical axis in Figure 2-1a represents time. At top is a simplified diagram of environmental, social, and historical factors impinging upon the living individual to shape his/her physical body and social persona. Below it are arrayed factors with the potential to affect the nature of the original depositional record. These are followed by postdepositional factors, excavation factors, and analytical factors that also could alter the original depositional pattern. In spite of its inherent simplifications, this diagram is intended as a reminder of real-world complexity that the archaeologist must attempt to unravel.

As should be obvious from Figure 2-1, many aspects of mortuary ritual, and thus of the social identities revealed by it, will not survive in the archaeological record. Those with the potential to survive include grave goods (especially non-perishable items such as ceramics or lithics), some aspects of grave construction, placement and orientation of cemeteries and burials, and skeletal material itself. Although each has been used alone in at least a few mortuary studies to interpret social relationships among the living, far more information can be obtained by considering as many different types of data as possible. Below, I first discuss these four aspects of mortuary data separately, then describe how their various types of information can be incorporated fruitfully into multidimensional studies of social organization.

Biophysical Attributes and Body Treatment. Over the past few decades, great strides have been made in gaining socioeconomic information about mortuary populations directly from their skeletal remains. Although sophisticated biophysical analysis was not the focus of this investigation, certain basic attributes, such as the age and sex of as many individuals as possible within the population (e.g., T. White 1991:305-56), are essential for almost any mortuary analysis. Such information can provide the basis for reconstruction of the demography of the living population from which the burials were derived, including population estimates and life expectancies (e.g., Weiss 1972, 1976). Expectations in regard to roughly equal divisions between sexes and to proportions of various age groups can be compared with actual distributions in the burial sample, both as a whole and within subgroups. If a mortuary population subgroup does not match the profile of the total group, or if the group as a whole does not match a regional profile, differences might relate to nonequivalent treatment on the basis of social status (e.g., Blakely 1971, 1977; Buikstra 1979, 1981).

Correlation of mortuary treatment of individuals with their age and sex is basic to understanding the social roles played by men, women, and children in a given society (see below, Modeling Status Differentiation). Beyond that, particular physical attributes of subgroup members such as differences in diet, health, and stature can be ascertained and compared with other mortuary traits such as grave good assemblages to see whether they co-vary in accordance with postulated social relationships, and genetic traits can be used directly to test hypotheses on intermarriage and kinship (e.g., Buikstra 1972; Cook 1981; Hatch and Willey 1974; Haviland 1967; Howell and Kintigh 1996; Lane and Sublett 1972). Deliberate mutilation/mutation such as cranial deformation, foot binding, or tooth shaping, decorating, or extracting can signal group or subgroup membership (e.g., Dragoo 1963:Figs. 20B, 20C, 20D, 52; Garrett 1988). Events such as warfare, famine, or epidemics that might be connected with sociocultural change can be deduced from evidence of trauma or pathology or sudden unexpected mass death (e.g., Blakely and Mathews 1990; Boyd and Boyd 1991; Goodman et al. 1984; Milanich 1996:65; Milner and Smith 1990; Ramenofsky 1987; Smith 1987:54-85; Wilkinson and Van Wagenen 1993). Premortem episodes of stress due to starvation or disease might be marked by growth arrest (dental hypoplasia, Harris lines in long bones) (T. White 1991:334-35, 354).

Besides the biophysical indicators of pre-death conditions discussed above, postmortem, preburial treatments such as defleshing, disarticulation, rearticulation, mummification, cremation, exposure to animal gnawing, or transformation into ornaments or functional items can be indicators of social status, social affiliation, or circumstances of death (e.g., Binford 1971:Table 4; Brown 1971; Dragoo 1963: Figs. 20E, 20G; Kenyon 1982; Mathews 1988:103-8; O'Shea 1988:77; Raemsch 1991, 1993).

Obtaining, analyzing, and interpreting evidence for these types of relationships requires specialized training, experience, and sometimes sophisticated technology that archaeologists rarely attain. The ideal, but rarely achievable, situation is to have archaeologists and physical anthropologists working in concert to obtain as much interrelated information as possible from features, artifacts, and human remains (e.g., Santure et al. 1990; Wray et al. 1987; Wray et al. 1991).

No specialized knowledge is required to ascertain body position within the grave, usually an important culturally determined factor. Within a given group, there most often is a single normative posture for the dead, such as flexed, or extended and supine, or (after preparatory treatment) as a disarticulated bundle. Differences can be significant indicators of age, sex, or class (e.g., Goldstein 1976:153-54; Pader 1982:141). Minor differences in limb positions in some instances can be significant, either by specific attributes, such as a tradition of clasped hands on chests among certain Christian groups, or by a more rigid treatment afforded members of some groups compared with others (e.g., Goldstein 1976:154; Pader 1982:95-97).

Single versus multiple burials can be objectifications of belief systems, such as young children needing help to reach the Land of the Dead, warriors being desirable escorts on that journey, family members requiring proximity in death as in life, paramount leaders warranting retainer sacrifice, or ceremonial staging of mythological events (e.g., Beck 1990:67-68; O'Shea 1988:77; Peebles and Kus 1977:439, 444; Sugiyama 1992). Dual or small-group burials can be due to simple expedience in cases of nearly simultaneous deaths, such as a mother and infant in childbirth, in cases such as house-floor burial where space is at a premium so that old graves must be shared, or in cases of old burials accidentally encountered when digging a new grave. They also can be indicators of special situations such as epidemics or massacres (see above). Interpretations by archaeologists often are ad hoc, but special attention to percentages of individuals found in mass graves, indicators of simultaneity or nonsimultaneity of death and interment of bodies found together, consistency within an entire cemetery of body treatments and of relative body positions and orientations, and the presence of possible war-related trauma can help indicate whether a given situation is normal or special within a particular society.

Grave Goods. The use of grave goods as prime indicators of social identities and social personae has been common in mortuary studies (e.g., Hodson 1977; Pader 1982; Randsborg 1974; Rothschild 1975, 1979; Shennan 1975; Van de Velde 1979). Some of this research has involved hypothesis testing or model building, but much seems merely to consist of virtuoso exercises in statistical analysis (for critiques of selected examples of the latter, see Orton and Hodson 1981 and the reviews associated with Van de Velde 1979). Where mortuary inclusions are present, they can be very useful as data, but they are by no means always present nor is their symbolic function necessarily related to the social persona of the deceased. For example, Rothschild's comparative study of 7700 burials at 66 different archaeological sites in eastern North America found that "more individuals do not receive grave goods than do, and more artifact categories are randomly distributed (in relation to age and sex classes) than nonrandomly" (1975:148). One cross-cultural survey found that grave goods symbolized status (rank) distinctions in less than 5% of 93 ethnographically reported groups (Tainter 1978:121; see also Ucko 1969). Grave goods can relate to the formerly-living person (e.g., personal possessions or ceremonial badges of the deceased, gifts from mourners commemorating various social identities of the deceased), or to the mourners (e.g., gifts intended to display the social status of the giver or of family members of the deceased), or to the new status of the deceased as a non-living being (e.g., food for a journey to the Land of the Dead, amulets to ward off predation on the living by the spirit of the dead). As previously noted, perishable grave goods often do not survive in the archaeological record, resulting in biased data sets.

Pointing out shortcomings of studies relying heavily or entirely on the analysis of grave goods should not be taken as dismissing out of hand the utility of this line of evidence. Artifactual evidence can be extremely valuable when used in conjuction with other dimensions of mortuary treatment.

The choice of which grave goods to include in an analysis and how to categorize them is extremely important—and difficult. Unless an archaeologist is working with historically documented materials, it is almost impossible to pre-judge the emic social significance of a given artifact or burial practice: "A priori, the archaeologist has no idea which of the observable attributes may be significant, nor can it be assumed that any single attribute will be both a necessary and a significant indicator of any social distinction" (O'Shea 1985:91-92). Because there is "nothing intrinsic in the form of a symbol to limit it to any particular referent" (Binford 1971:16), the same trait can symbolize different things in different cultural or temporal settings. Conversely, a particular meaning can be symbolized by different traits, not only within different cultures but also within a single culture (e.g., Bloch 1981; Ucko 1969; Zentai 1979). As O'Shea has demonstrated empirically, poor choices of traits to analyze can significantly obscure the results of objective analytic techniques (O'Shea 1985). Sometimes the statistical model itself dictates inclusion or exclusion. For instance, particular grave goods may be discarded from consideration in a cluster analysis if they occur in fewer than a certain number of burials (e.g., O'Shea 1984:66). In this case, the researcher must be careful not to completely ignore rare items of potential symbolic value.

Categorization of artifacts creates larger classes for quantitative analysis and allows more general comparison among sites. A variety of approaches are employed. Sometimes artifact types, particularly pottery, are categorized stylistically (e.g., Peebles 1974; Van de Velde 1979), but this may or may not be done consistently, or toward a specific purpose. Too often, artifact types assigned by the excavator, which may include haphazard application of stylistic, functional, and material-based criteria, are utilized expediently in a mortuary analysis, with a real potential for obscuring mortuary relationships. Larger-scale classification usually is tied to the particular problem being addressed, but is not always unambiguous.

In investigating vertical social distinctions (see below, Modeling Status Differentiation), the most common artifact categories used in mortuary analysis include the following.

(1) Binford's distinction between technomic and sociotechnic/ideotechnic artifacts (Table 2-4) (Binford 1962:219) often is seen as useful in distinguishing achieved versus ascribed social identities (e.g., Peebles 1974:54-57). Sociotechnic artifacts are expected to accompany persons in positions of leadership. In practice, the identification of nontechnomic artifacts is not always clear-cut when working from the archaeological record alone.

(2) The distinction between local and exotic materials (Winters 1968) has been taken as a prime marker of special status and wealth. Justification for this common-sense categorization comes from exchange theory and numerous specific exchange-based studies (e.g., Brose 1990; Brown et al. 1990). Braun (1977, 1979) attempted to capture emic notions of value by categorizing mortuary artifacts not only as to local or nonlocal material but also as to whether they occurred in midden as well as non-midden (burial) contexts. Those rarely deposited in nonmortuary contexts were considered to have been highly valued.

(3) Supralocal versus local symbols have been pinpointed by Peebles (Peebles 1974; Peebles and Kus 1977) as important in identifying the highest-ranking members of a panregional polity. Where they exist and can be recognized, such markers can be useful, but they are not always clearly indicated.

(4) Wealth, variously distinguished, is often used as the basis for identifying individuals of high rank (e.g., weight of bronze grave goods [Randsborg 1974], value of raw materials plus estimated time of production of artifacts [Shennan 1975], value of Contact Period trade goods in monetary cost [Orser 1980] or made beaver [Mainfort 1985]). Cautions to this approach include the fact that wealth and authority do not always coincide, and the fact that European notions of wealth are not always realistic bases for application to non-European peoples. For example, George Hamell has convincingly argued that the glass beads disdained by European traders as "trinkets" were highly valued by Native Americans because they embodied powerful symbolic and ritual meanings within a long cultural tradition (Hamell 1983, 1986-87, 1995; Miller and Hamell 1986).

(5) Prentice distinguishes between status items ("restricted in use to a specific social segment") and wealth items ("attainable by many people" and "valued by everyone because they give the owner prestige" due to their scarcity and/or convertibility). "Wealth items are... quantifiable in that more, larger, or better made items represent greater wealth." Status items might or might not be wealth items. In distinguishing wealth items from status items, quantity is "critical since the importance of status items depends not on how many one has but on whether or not an individual is allowed to possess them" (Prentice 1987:198-99).

(6) Among the living, the items most intimately associated with personal identity are those related to costume. Only permanent or temporary body modification such as cranial deformation, tooth shaping, tattooing, scarification, painting, or hair arrangement are "closer" to the individual (Wallace 1993). According to information theory tested by European ethnographic case studies, stylistic messages targeted at larger, more socially distant audiences will be conveyed by large-scale, highly visible decorative motifs and items of costume (such as headdresses); such highly visible items commonly are used to convey group affiliation, while items visible only at close range convey "an individual's position along a ranked scale, such as wealth, status, or age" to a socially less-distant audience (Wobst 1977:335). More intricate items, requiring high skill and significant energy input, often are associated with higher-status individuals (Kuttruff 1988, 1993). Although perishable clothing (and hair and skin treatments) rarely survive burial, headdresses and ornaments of non-perishable materials often do. Their size, form, color, and placement can provide clues to the social identities with which they might be associated.

In a research project with somewhat different objectives than most of those mentioned above, Rogers developed a function-based typology for analysis of early Contact Period change in Arikara culture (Rogers 1990). The 25 categories included containing, scraping, cutting, piercing, abrading, pounding, painting, knapping, perforating, smoothing, chopping, digging, grinding, drilling, decorating, incising, straightening, fastening, wedging, scooping, joining, personal appearance, gaming, smoking, and worshipping. Such a classification allows straightforward consideration of changes over time in style, material, or exchange source within artifact categories, as well as changes in the categories that are deemed appropriate for mortuary inclusion.

Interment Facilities. Like grave goods, burial facilities (Figure 2-1b) can be distinguished on the basis of size, shape, materials, construction techniques, decoration, and style. In turn, these attributes can be used in interpreting the status and social relationships of the person(s) interred within them. However, graves and tombs have additional properties that can serve as objectifications of social values and/or relationships. These include location, orientation, visibility (e.g., above or below ground), identification markers (e.g., headstones, clan markers), amount of energy expended (e.g., stone-lined versus bark-lined graves), number of people involved in construction (e.g., burial mounds, log-lined tombs, pyramids), individual versus collective facility (e.g., group ossuaries), and temporary versus permanent facility (e.g., facilities for burial programs where bodies are defleshed or mummified before final interment). Again as with grave goods, comparison is essential: it is the differences and similarities among attributes of interment facilties afforded to individuals and subgroups within the larger group that can provide information pertinent to social relationships among living members of a society. Many of these attributes will be discussed below, under Spatial Relationships. Here, I will touch briefly upon energy expenditure and communal involvement.

Unlike grave goods, interment facilities rarely have been the primary focus of mortuary analyses. One exception is a series of studies by Tainter, who undertook an ambitious program to develop a general, objective measure of social complexity for use on archaeological mortuary data (1973, 1975a, 1975b, 1976, 1977a, 1977b, 1978, 1980, 1981). This measure was based on labor expenditure, stemming from Binford's hypothesis (1971) that dead people of higher rank will be "entitled to a larger amount of corporate involvement in the act of interment" (Tainter and Cordy 1977). Attributes of body preparation, grave goods, and type and location of burial facility originally were factored into Tainter's model, but his later applications relied almost totally on burial facility data. Although his model (constructed by means of information theory and systems theory), methodology, and data have been criticized for a broad range of problems (Beck 1990:28-35; Braun 1981; Drooker 1992b:16-17; Goldstein 1976:22-24; O'Shea 1984:17-20), the theoretical basis remains valid: individual or group burial facilities that require large amounts of labor, time, or construction skill often mark interments of important social personae. For example, in Mississippian large-scale complex chiefdoms, burial in mounds seems to have been the prerogative of members of an elite subgroup (e.g., Milner 1984; Peebles 1974; Peebles and Kus 1977), and the communal effort expended to this end is seen as a significant aspect of Mississippian society. In some Mississippian groups where almost everyone was buried within a mound (e.g., Lewis 1934; Lewis and Kneberg 1946:136-43), communal effort was directed more broadly, toward a larger segment of the population, and thus is interpreted in different social terms. Likewise, the communal effort expended in historically documented group rituals such as the Huron "Feast of the Dead" has led many archaeologists to interpret large communal ossuaries (e.g., Kenyon 1982; Kidd 1953) and similar ceremonially processed multiple burials as marking the renewal rites of well-organized but essentially egalitarian societies.

Spatial Patterning. Spatial relationships—among cemeteries, their associated settlements, and neighboring territories, among groups and subgroups of burials within cemeteries, and among human remains, grave goods, and other features within graves—can be crucial in interpreting social relationships from mortuary data (Chapman and Randsborg 1981:14-19; O'Shea 1984:40). Spatial analysis provides a context lacking in mortuary studies that consider only material goods, and can provide a crosscheck on and reinforcement of analyses based on other types of data: "Coincidence of spatial organisation and grave associations must imply coincidence of cultural elements" (Goldstein 1981:57). According to Lynne Goldstein, the spatial component provides "a way to organise the various components so that co-variations and interrelationships become clear" (1981:57). Because many aspects of funerary behavior are not represented in the archaeological record, only by considering co-variation can reliable inferences be generated. In her own study of Mississippian mortuary sites, Goldstein employed cluster analysis of grave goods plus burial position and orientation to define group memberships not revealed by analysis of grave good assemblages alone (Goldstein 1976, 1980). Particularly powerful for kinship analysis are cases in which hereditary traits can be considered in terms of spatial relationships (e.g., Howell and Kintigh 1996; Lane and Sublett 1972).

Regional studies of spatial relationships among cemeteries, settlements, and resource procurement areas have provided insights not possible from analysis of single cemeteries alone. People of different class or status may be interred at separate locations as well as being given very different postmortem treatment (e.g., Bradley 1995; Brown 1971; Buikstra 1981; Goldstein 1976, 1980; Peebles 1971). Ethnic boundaries may be demonstrated by fine-grained analysis of otherwise similar burial programs in adjacent regions (Beck 1990, 1995). Resource areas may be mapped or territories marked by large-scale, visible burial structures (e.g., Chapman 1981, 1995; Charles 1995; Goldstein 1995; Larson 1995:250-52; Mallam 1976; O'Shea 1988:88; Renfrew 1976; Syms 1979). In general terms, inward-directed versus outward-directed focus of a mortuary program can be inferred by high or low visibility to nongroup members. Physical boundary-marking between groups (by large-scale constructions or by smaller-scale stylistic differences) denotes perceived social difference ("us" versus "them"), and can be intensified by economic stress (e.g., Beck 1990:76-77; Hodder 1979).

Locations of burials within (and outside of) a cemetery often pertain to corporate group membership or to special status. It is almost axiomatic that members of kin groups frequently are buried close to each other. Although this cannot be taken for granted, groups consisting of a man, woman, and child(ren) usually are assumed to represent family members. Such a conclusion is more tenable when supported by other evidence, such as a burial location in or around a dwelling in which the dead presumably resided while still alive.

Historically, some peoples are known to have buried "special status" individuals such as young infants, lepers, suicides, warriors, or prominent leaders separately from other group members. Binford, using Human Relations Area Files ethnographical data from 40 non-state societies, found that people with different subgroup affiliations (e.g., clans) were separated by burial location within 37.5% of the societies, people of different social position were buried separately in 20% of them, and people of certain age groups were buried separately in 17.5% of them (Binford 1971: Table 4).

People belonging to groups with ascribed membership, such as moieties, clans, and hereditary classes, are frequently buried close to each other and separate from members of opposing groups (e.g., Zentai 1979:131). For example, in many Mississippian communities, members of apparently elite classes were buried in mounds, while commoners were consigned to nonmound cemeteries (e.g., Peebles 1974; Peebles and Kus 1977). This hierarchical treatment of human remains echoes the hierarchical settlement patterns typical of many Mississippian complex chiefdoms (Smith 1978; Steponaitis 1978; see below, Chiefdoms and Complex Chiefdoms). Vernon J. Knight has proposed that paired burial and elite residence mounds arrayed around the plaza at the large ceremonial site of Moundville, Alabama, were loci for hierarchically ordered corporate kin groups, analogous to the organization of ranked dual-division (moiety) and clan members' dwellings in historically described Chickasaw encampment circles (Knight 1993).

One very important principle for interpreting burial location has come to be called the Saxe-Goldstein Hypothesis. It is based upon the idea that "the emergence of formal cemeteries was caused by increasing competition for access to vital resources, and the formation of agnatic descent groups which tried to monopolize those resources, justifying their claims through lineal descent from the dead" (Morris 1991:147, after Saxe 1970:119, 233-24). As reformulated by Lynn Goldstein, and corroborated by ethnographic data, it states that "if there is a formal bounded disposal area, used exclusively for the dead, then the culture is probably one which has a corporate group structure in the form of a lineal descent system. The more organized and formal the disposal area is, the more conclusive this interpretation" (Goldstein 1976:35-69, quotation from 72, 1980:7-8; Brown 1995:13-15; Morris 1991; Saxe and Gall 1977).

Besides location, orientation of burials can be a significant attribute. For example, some cemeteries show a consistent correlation between head orientation and a given compass direction, often either toward the rising or the setting sun (e.g., Gruber 1971; Robinson et al. 1985). In some cases, as with the historical Narragansett cemeteries documented by Robinson and colleagues, this can be linked definitively to religious beliefs such as the direction to the Land of the Dead. Although attempts have been made to use this trait to tie an unknown prehistoric group to a known historical group (e.g., Voegelin 1944), this is risky because within-group practices can change within a few generations (Sempowski 1991). Burial orientation can, however, be useful (together with other attributes) in hypothesizing social relationships between contemporaneous settlements, where similar treatments might indicate similar belief systems, or in pinpointing individuals within a cemetery who are accorded treatment that contrasts strongly to that of their peers. Putative solar alignment also sometimes can be linked to seasonal use of a site (Gruber 1971). Also widely noted are alignment to a topographical feature, such as a bluff edge or the contours of a hill (e.g., Santure et al. 1990:69), or to a socially demarcated feature, such as a distant ceremonial center (e.g., Milner 1984:470), around a central charnal house (e.g., Milner 1984:Fig. 4), toward the center of a group burial mound or ossuary (e.g., Kenyon 1982:Fig. 124; Oehler 1973:47; Starr 1960:57), around the edges of a plaza (e.g., Nass 1987:110), or along house structure walls (e.g., Hally 1994).

The above-listed spatial organizing principles for cemetery areas, plus others such as discrete rows (e.g., Goldstein 1976, 1980) or the grids of boxed individuals in modern American cemeteries, all can be interpreted in social terms, most broadly in terms of whole-community integration, subgroup integration, or individualization (cf. O'Shea 1988). Per Goldstein's suggestion quoted at the beginning of this section, the discovery of covariation of spatial organizing principles with other dimensions of mortuary treatment can allow the development of robust models of social organization.

Spatial relationships of grave goods to people or (in multiple burials) of people to each other within graves can be socially significant. For grave goods, one of at least two organizing principles might be important. The location of grave goods relative to a body can mark differences in social identity. For example, a pot on the left versus the right side of the head might correlate statistically with male versus female gender. However, different grave goods in the same locations in some cases can be substitutes for each other, marking the same identity, as with rings and brooches at the same location on the body for female burials in certain Anglo-Saxon cemeteries (Pader 1982:114, 119-23). For multiple burials, placement of people relative to each other can provide information about social relationships, as with the consistent placement of the bones of older

TABLE 2-5
Typical Patterns of Mortuary Variation Indicative of Vertical, Horizontal, and Special Status Social Distinctions

	Vertical Differentiation	Horizontal Differentiation	Special Status
Size of Subgroups	HIERARCHICAL PYRAMID, with higher-ranked groups smaller in size	EQUAL-SIZED comparable groups	SMALL / INDIVIDUAL
Age/Sex Distribution within Subgroups	NORMAL = hereditary classes ADULT MALES (usually) = apical leadership status ADULT = achieved leadership statuses	NORMAL = lineage groups SINGLE-SEX and/or -AGE = age/sex classes ADULT = membership societies	Variable
Spatial Separation within Cemetery	Likely for hereditary classes	Likely for lineage groups	Likely
Symbolic Designation of Subgroups	Differential energy expenditure in burial treatments and grave goods Symbolically-significant and/or exotic grave goods for members of highest-level groups	Equal levels of energy expenditure in burial treatments and gravegoods Use of non-exotic items as marker symbols	Low levels of energy expenditure, non-normative treatments (but see Table 2-6)

(after O'Shea 1984:64, 1981:42)

males at centers and female and subadult remains at peripheries of small-group ossuaries in Late Woodland Michigan (O'Shea 1988:77, 80).

Modeling Status Differentiation. To date, much attention in archaeological mortuary studies has been focused on the identification and delineation of individual rank (ascribed or achieved) and hierarchical organization of complex societies (e.g., J. Brown 1971, 1981; Hatch 1976; Peebles 1974; Peebles and Kus 1977). For a complete social analysis, however, it is necessary to investigate not only vertical distinctions (e.g., rank, wealth), but also horizontal distinctions (e.g., clan, descent group, secret society) and special status differentiation (e.g., suicides, traitors, sourcerers) (Beck 1990; Mainfort 1979; O'Shea 1981, 1984, 1988; Shennan 1982). See Table 2-4 for definitions of some of the important terms used in the following discussion.

John O'Shea has produced the most comprehensive general model of relationships between archaeologically visible mortuary attributes and within-group social status, incorporating vertical, horizontal, and special-status differences (1984). Tables 2-5 and 2-6 summarize the primary indicators and configurations of O'Shea's model, the broad outlines of which are described briefly below.

Vertical differentiation within a society is, in essence, its "structure of rank grading" (Tainter and Cordy 1977:96). The complexity of a society is related (among other things) to the number of vertical levels present. It is expected that each higher rank will consist of fewer members, and that people of higher rank will be "entitled to a larger amount of corporate involvement in the act of interment," that is, a greater amount of energy expenditure (Tainter and Cordy 1977:97). O'Shea based his model on work by Peebles and Kus (Peebles 1974; Peebles and Kus 1977). Their markers for superordinate and subordinate social classes or divisions are summarized in Table 2-7.

Rank can be ascribed or achieved—or, from ethnographic analogy, a combination of the two, as with chiefs selected (based on achievement) from one specified clan (with ascribed membership). Achieved rank levels will be held by adults, most frequently males. Ascribed rank levels will include both sexes and all ages. Vertically differentiated ascribed-status groups can be recognized by shared sociotechnic/ideotechnic markers found with subadults as well as adults (Brown 1981:29-30). That is, markers of high rank will crosscut markers of most other identities.

Information theory predicts that the highest leadership levels will be marked by symbolic redundance (Braun 1979:67; Neitzel 1995:397, 409). Because of this redundance, such roles will have the highest archaeological visibility, particularly if their markers are both redundant and exclusive (O'Shea 1985). Such a situation is associated most strongly with ascribed rank.

For any given individual, particularly an older person, markers of more than one social identity (Table 2-4) are expected to be present in death. In societies where leadership is primarily achieved rather than ascribed, mortuary assemblages even for the highest leaders are likely to reflect an additive accumulation of social identities peculiar to a particular individual. This is reflected in William Rathje's model of mobile and non-mobile social systems (Rathje 1973). He postulated that "social identities in non-mobile societies tend to occur in mutually exclusive, consistently replicated sets," whereas in a mobile system, with

TABLE 2-6
Social Categories and Their Archaeological Attributes

	Sex	Age	Frequency	Symbolic Designators	Possible spatial element
Rank Differentiation					
Apical leader	Male (usually)	Adult	Lowest	Supralocal sociotechnic symbols. Most energy intensive mortuary treatment.	Yes
Ranked males	Male	Adult	Low	Local sociotechnic symbols. Wealth.	Yes
Ranked females	Female	Adult	Low	Local sociotechnic symbols. Wealth.	Yes
Ranked subadults		Subadult	Low	Local sociotechnic symbols. Adult-ascribed artifacts. Wealth.	Yes
Priest/doctor[a]	Male (usually)	Adult	Low	Local sociotechnic symbols. Artifact quantity and variety, esp. exotic items.	No
Wealth	Male/female	Adult (usually)	Varies	Wealth.	No
Horizontal Differentiation					
Moiety	Male/female	Normal distrib.	50%	Possible formal differentiation (location, orientation). Ideotechnic symbols. Cross-section of vertical dimensions.	Yes
Clan	Male/female	Normal distrib.	Depends on no. of clans	As above; specific ideotechnic symbols	Yes
Societies (non-kin-based)	Male/female or male	Adult	Low	Local sociotechnic symbols	No (us.)
Age-grade categories	Male/female	Similar	Varies	Local sociotechnic symbols	No (us.)
Gender categories	Male or female[b]	Normal distr.	50%	Local sociotechnic &/or technomic symbols	No
Special Status Distinctions					
Circumstantial	Male/female	Adult/subadult	Low	Interment away from usual area. Alternative mortuary treatment. Normal inclusions.	Yes
Deviants[a]	Male/female	Adult	Low	Alternative mortuary treatment. Interment away from usual area. Atypical inclusions or absence of grave inclusions.	Yes

(after O'Shea 1981:42). Designators are additive for individuals. Note that gender and age-grade differentiation can be considered vertical rather than horizontal.
Berdache-type categories will have physical males with female (or special) symbols, or vice versa.
Shamans may be considered deviants, and treated accordingly.

potential for achieved rank, the "general status level of identities in individual social persona[e] is not always consistent": identities are changeable and may be incongruous, and symbols for them will not necessarily co-vary directly (1973:743). This is consistent with the recently introduced concept of "heterarchy" (Table 2-4), which relates to collective organization of elements that have the potential to be ranked in more than one way (Crumley and Marquardt 1987; Ehrenreich et al. 1995).

In theory, horizontal differentiation of a society "encompasses structural components equal at each hierarchical level. Examples... include sodalities, individual descent units of segmentary descent systems, task groups, territorial bands" (Tainter and Cordy 1977:96). O'Shea's model specifies that horizontally differentiated groups will be approximately equal in size (Table 2-5). Subgroup membership can crosscut society (as with moieties or clans), in which case the age-sex distribution should be comparable to that of the group as a whole. Alternatively, it can be based on age or sex, or require adult status (Tables 2-5, 2-6). Spatial differentiation in mortuary treatment is most likely in the case of ascribed horizontal group membership (e.g., moieties). According to O'Shea, "since the number of social subdivisions that can be expressed through the spatial segregation of interments is limited, social units so expressed should represent a (if not the) significant horizontal social subdivisions distinguished within the society" (1988:70). Symbolic designators of horizontal group membership are expected to be made of local rather than exotic materials. In North America, they are known from ethnohistorical records often to have consisted of markers such as hairstyles that rarely survive under archaeological conditions (e.g., O'Shea 1984:70-86; Fletcher and La Flesche 1992 [1911]: Figs. 4-8), so that fine-grained horizontal distinctions often are difficult to pinpoint in the archaeological record (O'Shea 1984:302).

Other factors further complicate this record. For example, it is not unusual for "horizontal" components, particularly segmentary descent units, to be ranked with regard to each other, as has been found by ethnographers for many eastern North American groups (Knight 1990). In fact, truly horizontal social dis-

TABLE 2-7
Expectations for Superordinate and Subordinate Dimensions of Mortuary Differentiation in a Ranked Society

Superordinate Dimension	Subordinate Dimension
1. Some infants, some children, and some adults will be found in every scale category except the paramount category.	1. As the chronological age of the individual buried increases, so will the energy expended in that individual's burial.
2. The apical class will contain only adults, and probably only adult males.	2. Children and infants will have some items as grave goods that will not be shared by adults; women will have some items as grave goods not shared by men.
3. Some infants and children will have greater amounts of energy expended in their mortuary ritual than some adults, some women more energy expended in their treatment than some men.	3. Energy expended in the lowest level of the superordinate dimension will be greater than that expended in the highest level of the subordinate dimension.
4. The numbers of burials in each scale category will markedly decrease as one goes higher on the scale, thereby reflecting the rank pyramid.	4. The number of individuals in each scale category of the subordinate dimension should reflect the age and sex pyramid of the population through time.

(O'Shea 1984:Table 3.4, after Peebles and Kus 1977)

tinctions between members of different socially distinguished groups or identities probably are relatively rare (Table 2-8). For these reasons, among others, more-nuanced mortuary analyses are beginning to allow for the possibility that socioeconomic relationships among members of a group might not adhere to a strictly dichotomous model in which organization is either hierarchical or egalitarian, but might partake of both (e.g., McGuire and Saitta 1996).

Special-status distinctions arise, and are reflected in the mortuary record, usually either when circumstances of death are unusual or when an individual's social persona is considered so deviant as to warrant mortuary treatment distinct from the norm. They are recognizable in the archaeological record mainly because they differ in odd ways from the norm and usually affect only a small proportion of the population (Tables 2-5, 2-6).

People dying away from home, as with warriors in battle, might be buried (or otherwise disposed) close to their place of death, and/or borne home, perhaps to be buried as disarticulated remains, but otherwise accorded their expected treatment. Victims of epidemics or mass violence might be consigned to multiple burials and might lack expected inclusions if not enough living people survive to provide them.

Social deviants might include physically disabled people, people considered antisocial such as murderers or witches, or non-persons such as small infants, slaves, or war captives. Such individuals often are interred separately, but might receive special treatment within a cemetery such as a non-normative orientation or body position. Premortem and/or postmortem body mutiliation might be expected on enemy remains. Grave goods, if present at all, very likely would have unusual characteristics.

If certain people are interred away from the group, only discovery of a separate burial area or expert, fine-grained demographic analysis might discover that they are missing (cf. Buikstra 1981).

Based on O'Shea's model, analyzing status distinctions is a matter of establishing a data base that defines the significant, archaeologically visible mortuary attributes of each individual under consideration (Figure 2-1), utilizing statistical analysis to aid in the recognition of groups of individuals having similar attributes, and comparing the characteristics of these groups with characteristics predicted for groups differentiated by status (Table 2-5). As O'Shea states, "The advantage of working with a predicted structural arrangement of variability is that it is unnecessary to determine in advance which particular attribute or set of attributes will function symbolically in a given mortuary occurrence" (1984:48). It is the pattern that is important, rather than any particular attribute. When working with historically known groups, as in O'Shea's case study of Pawnee, Omaha, and Arikara cemeteries (1984:71-301), it is possible to search for attributes known to have functioned as symbols of rank or of group membership, and for horizontal divisions, such as specific numbers of clans, known to have been present. This is a part of O'Shea's procedure, but it is not possible when working with prehistoric groups of unknown affiliation.

All societies have at least some categorical identities based on age and sex. Thus, the first step in analysis is to establish normative group and age-sex subgroup characteristics before attempting to discern differences related to other aspects of social status (Beck 1990; O'Shea 1984). Analysis consists of descriptive statistics to establish mean, mode, and range of variation for mortuary attributes (Figure 2-1) of group and subgroups, plus simple measures of correlation to establish the statistical significance of particular attributes (such as particular grave goods) associated with each subgroup. O'Shea not only utilizes a measure of association (Kendall's *tau*) to evaluate statistical significance of the association of a particular practice or grave good with a particular age-sex group, but also follows the rule that: "Any type that occurred in two or more grave units and

Table 2-8
Social Statuses Generally Conceived as "Vertical" or "Horizontal"

Vertical Distinction (usually)	Either Vertical or Horizontal Distinction	Horizontal Distinction (usually)
supernatural being/human	male/female/berdache	sister/brother
ancestor/descendent	husband/wife	
grandparent/parent/child*	family/family	
different age grades*	clan/clan	
hereditary classes or castes	moiety/moiety	
leader or organizer	special membership society/other such societies	
paramount chief	non-subsistence craft specialist	
peace chief	shaman	
war chief	alive/dead	
priest		
task leader		
ceremonial specialist		
sub-leaders or organizers		
special talent or skill		
master/slave		
rich/poor		
healthy/unhealthy		

Statuses in central category can be distinguished vertically (e.g., ranked lineages, strongly patriarchial family structures) or horizontally, depending on the society. Within group categories, such as hereditary classes, clans, or age grades, statuses can be vertical or horizontal.
*Youngest always at bottom, but oldest not necessarily at top

that had a constant age and/or sex association was considered to be constrained" (1984:65).

In distinguishing other aspects of social differentiation, O'Shea employs a two-step procedure (1984:66-69; cf. Brown 1987; Goldstein 1980:53-96; Mainfort 1979:298-302; O'Shea 1985; Peebles 1972; Shennan 1988). Factor analysis is used to determine sets of artifacts that tend to occur together, and cluster analysis is used to identify similarities among groups of burials. Groups thus established are compared for relative size, age-sex composition, spatial relationships, and symbolic designators (Table 2-5) to determine what social dimensions they might represent (Table 2-6).

Group or subgroup solidarity or differences in social control can be indicated by communally centered, small-group-centered, or individually centered mortuary programs. For example, O'Shea has contrasted the social-unit focus of communal ossuaries with few grave goods utilized at the thirteenth-century Younge site in Michigan against the individualistic focus at the fur trade era Fletcher site, with its separate, individual inhumations and marking of individual and family (competitive) wealth and prestige by means of grave goods (Mainfort 1979, 1985; O'Shea 1988).

Archaeological Manifestations of Interaction and Exchange

Interaction between individuals or groups can take many forms, which might or might not include material aspects. Trading myths, songs, or gossip, pricking fingers for rituals of blood-brotherhood, or ceremonially counting coup on an enemy are important social acts that ordinarily leave no trace in the archaeological record. Archaeologists studying interaction must work exclusively with physical evidence, attempting to discover meaningful patterns in an often-ambiguous record. Selected models for interpretation of interaction and change will be discussed in the final section of this chapter. First, I will describe data and methods used to define the nature of interaction between groups, including its occurrence, its direction, its extent, and its intensity.

Defining Interaction

My dictionary has but one definition for the concept of interaction: "To act on each other" (Morris 1969:683). For the anthropologist, however, interaction has many faces. It can be fortuitous or planned, direct or indirect, positive, negative, or neutral, and consciously or unconsciously directed toward obtaining material rewards (subsistence or prestige goods), services, information, political alliances, or productive or reproductive rights, or enhancing status, power (secular or sacred), health, social ties, or productive or reproductive success (e.g., Bohannan 1955; Ford 1983; Helms 1988; Mauss 1957; Sahlins 1972:188-95; Spielmann 1989; Wilmsen 1972; Wobst 1974).

Strictly speaking, interaction is always between individuals, but depending on the circumstances, individuals might interact either at a person-to-person level or, in unison with others, as members of groups. At the person-to-person level, an individual might consciously represent only him/herself, or a larger group. Interaction can be one-time or short-term, or longer-term, comprising many individual acts that serve to bind people or groups of people into enduring relationships.

In considering different types of interaction, Marshall Sahlins's concept of reciprocity is a useful starting point (Sahlins 1972:188-95; cf. Mauss 1957). It is defined as a symmetrical, "*between* relation, the action and reaction of two parties." The pure gift anticipates no return. Generalized reciprocity involves "transactions that are putatively altruistic," but that rely on a diffuse obligation. Balanced reciprocity is equivalent to "direct exchange... the reciprocation is the customary equivalent of the thing received and is without delay." Often, as in friendship pacts and peace agreements, it is exactly equal. Negative reciprocity is "the attempt to get something for nothing with impunity," as in chicanery and theft. Depending on its circumstances, warfare might be seen as negative or as balanced reciprocity. Sahlins correlates his continuum of interaction forms with increasing social distance: pure gifts (if such indeed exist) and generalized reciprocity take place between people who know each other well and interact regularly, while negative reciprocity is more likely to take place between relative strangers or people who consider themselves "other."

Large-scale interactions in one region can have ripple effects elsewhere, as with refugees fleeing warfare in their homeland. In general, down-the-line interaction takes place through third parties, such as traders, who might or might not leave evidence of their involvement (e.g., Ray 1974, 1978; Rogers 1990).

All interactions, by definition, have an element of exchange. Many, but by no means all, exchanges do leave traces in the archaeological record. Table 2-9 illustrates the complexity of ethnohistorically observed exchange relationships, including those that would leave little archaeological evidence (cf. Ford 1972, 1983). Because of the nature of the available data, archaeologists most often deal with large-scale, longer-term (*conjoncture* level) exchange relationships, between groups rather than individuals, and involving nonperishable rather than perishable items. Figure 2-2 and Table 2-10 summarize two archaeological models of exchange, specifically oriented to the movement of material goods. The processually oriented model (Figure 2-2) emphasizes economic use and disposition of exchanged materials (Torrence 1986). The geographically oriented model (Table 2-10) emphasizes the "shape" of exchange networks in time and space (Plog 1977). Aspects of them will be discussed further below.

Evidence of Interaction

For archaeologists, the "smoking gun" that indicates interaction is usually the presence of nonlocal materials, artifacts, styles, or motifs. Sometimes special tests are necessary to establish a nonlocal origin (see below). In order to interpret interaction relationships, it is desirable to obtain as much information as possible on how exotic items were obtained and used. Acquisition can be through positive, negative, or neutral interaction, or, in some cases, without any person-to-person interaction at all. Use can range from the display of a prestigious sociotechnic symbol to the gradual wear on a utilitarian technomic tool to the distainful breakage and discard of a captured enemy's possessions. Nonartifactual indicators of interaction patterns include large-scale spatial data such as locations and configurations of settlements, and biophysical data related to intermarriage or conflict.

Rituals of Greeting and Incorporation. Most North American groups had formal rituals for greeting strangers and incorporating them into the group so that interaction could take place. Sometimes these paralleled or incorporated formal adoption ceremonies (Hall 1987). Much of this ritual involved nonmaterial or perishable components, such as singing, speechmaking, feasting, or the presentation of clothing, but nonperishable items such as beads often were included (Clayton et al. 1993:1:278; Lankford 1984, 1988; Smith and Hally 1992:100-102). Greeting rituals for known outsiders, such as regular trading partners, invariably included the exchange of gifts (e.g., McClellan 1975:501-7; Spielmann 1983); in fact, trade itself often was "phrased in terms of gift-giving" (Wright 1967:190).

Throughout the Great Lakes region, smoking was an integral part of greeting ceremonies. In Iroquoia, interaction with visitors involved group smoking but not usually pipe presentation (Fenton 1953). In the western Great Lakes and upper Mississippi Valley, however, greeting ceremonies often included the presentation or exchange of pipe bowls (Blakeslee 1981; Brown 1989; Hall 1987), so communities with regular outside contacts should show evidence of this in their pipes.

In temporal terms, greeting ceremonies are at the event level, so it is rarely possible to recognize them as such in the archaeological record. However, people strongly associated with them, such as leaders who habitually enacted such rituals, often were buried with associated paraphernalia such as important pipes. Likewise, other ritual gifts—prestige goods—received during formal greeting ceremonies elsewhere, such as beads or clothing, might well be considered appropriate as grave goods for an individual whose social persona included an identification with interregional interaction.

For more detailed descriptions of greeting rituals and their material correlates utilized in different regions of eastern North America, see Chapter 3 (Early Historical Period Protocols for Inter-Polity Interaction).

Exchange. Exchange per se usually can be recognized in the archaeological record by the presence of nonlocal materials or finished items. The first step in considering such items is to establish that they are exotic. It must be kept in mind, of course, that exotic materials and items often can be obtained through channels other than face-to-face interaction, including direct acquisition of a material by traveling to the source, transport of a material by natural forces such as rivers or glaciers, accidental loss by visitors, stealing, or capture in warfare (Table 2-9, Fig-

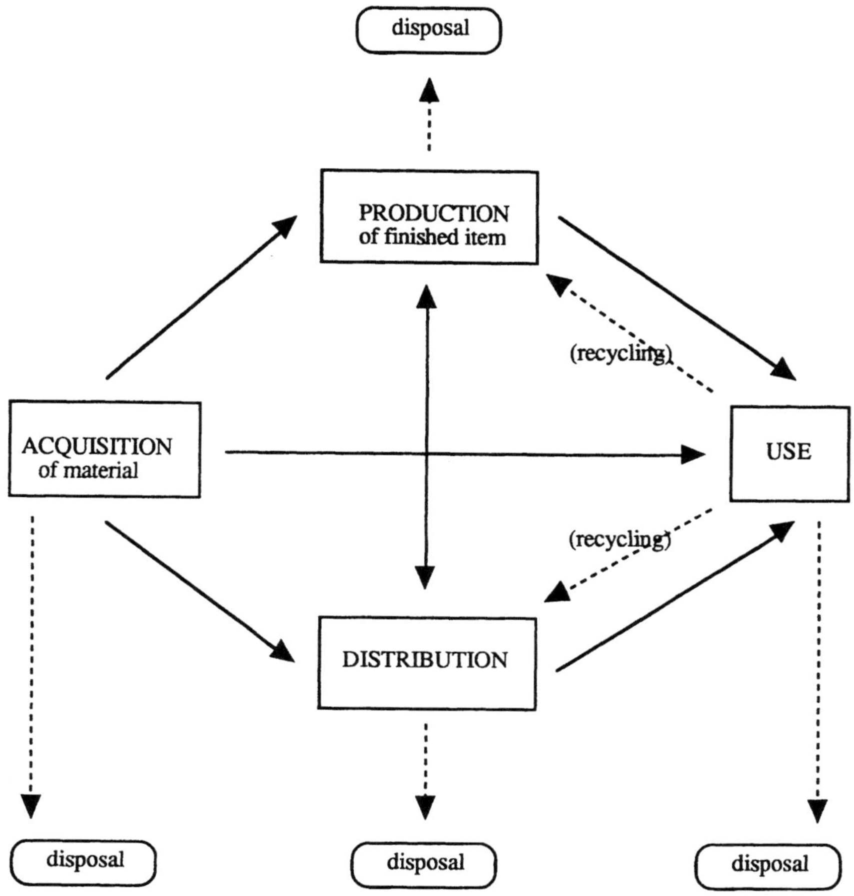

Figure 2-2. Dimensions of an exchange system: processually oriented model (after Torrence 1986:5).

ure 2-2) (Drooker 1993e:26-27; Hodder 1980; Latta 1991; Torrence 1986:171-217).

Sometimes visual inspection will suffice to establish the exotic nature of a material (e.g., glass beads in early Native American contexts), but more often, physical or chemical tests or microscropic examination by an expert will be required (cf. Drooker 1993e:10-16). Nonlocal manufacture of an object made from an exotic material usually is established by the absence of evidence for local crafting, including tools, raw materials, and manufacturing debris (Drooker 1993e:26-27). Nonlocal artifact styles often can be recognized by eye, but local craftspeople—either natives or non-natives such as in-marrying spouses, adoptees, captives, or slaves—can choose to utilize techniques, styles, and motifs originating elsewhere. Since local materials often are employed for this purpose (e.g., local clays or tempering materials in ceramics), detection might involve chemically or physically analyzing the material, and comparing the results with both nonlocal finished products and locally available materials (e.g., Plog 1980, 1986; Trigger et al. 1980). When nonlocal styles or motifs are borrowed, they often are mixed with local stylistic attributes. Widespread occurrence of this in a community, or the rapid development of a clearly hybrid style, usually is interpreted as indicating a mixture of people from different backgrounds living together on a long-term basis.

European artifacts present at Native American settlements represent unequivocal examples of exotic goods. Most European materials, such as glass or glazed pottery, are readily recognizable, but copper (and to some small extent silver and iron) is a different story, because it was available from a number of indigenous sources (Goad and Noakes 1978; Rapp 1985; Rapp et al. 1990). Trace element analyses or metallurgical analyses are necessary to determine whether copper is North American or European, and whether artifacts fashioned from such metals were made by native or European techniques (e.g., Childs 1994; Fitzgerald and Ramsden 1988; Hancock et al. 1991; M. Wedel 1959:63-71).

An overwhelmingly important nonmaterial exotic resource is information. In and of itself, knowledge of and from distant regions often is viewed as a source of power (Helms 1988), and individual pilgrimages often are associated (for instance) with shamanistic training and functions, or with coming-of-age rituals (e.g., Helms 1988:69-72, 76, citing examples from Australia, South America, and the Northwest Coast of North America).

TABLE 2-9
Dimensions of an Exchange System: Ethnohistorically-Oriented Model.

- DID EXCHANGE TAKE PLACE?
  - Could potential participants have interacted in time and place?
  - Can types of interaction other than exchange be eliminated?
    - Direct acquisiton of materials by user
    - Transport by natural forces (water, wind)
    - Local application of manufacturing techniques or styles learned non-locally
      - By natives, visitors, in-marrying or adopted individuals, captives, slaves, etc.
    - Accidental deposition (loss, breakage) of items belonging to visitors
    - Stealing, raiding, looting
    - Capture in war
- WHAT was exchanged?
  - Types of resources
    - Materials (perishable/non-perishable)
    - Manufactured items (production by specialists/non-specialists)
    - Animals, birds
    - People (slaves, hostages, adoptees, marriage partners)
    - Services (labor, spiritual, medical, sexual, entertainment, "protection")
    - Information, ideas, methods, styles, motifs
    - Land/land use privileges
  - Pertinent qualities of resources
    - Effective life
    - Transportability (size, weight, breakability, etc.)
    - Rarity/perceived value
  - What was exchanged in return? similar items? different items?
- WHERE did exchanged resources come from?
  - Location of source
  - Effective distance from source to user
    - Travel distance
    - Topography
    - Intervening social groups
- HOW MUCH was exchanged?
  - Were particular items rare/high-value or abundant/low-value?
  - Were exchanged resources similar or different in amount and/or value?
- WHO did the exchanging?
  - What groups?
    - How closely related to each other?
      - Socially
      - Geographically
    - With what socioeconomic characteristics?
      - Mobile/sedentary
      - Hunter-gatherer/agricultural
      - Vertically ranked/horizontally segmented
  - What individuals or types of individuals within each group?
    - Elite members of society
    - Individuals with special knowledge/talent/training
      - Shamans
      - Witches
      - Ceremonial specialists
      - Organizers of ceremonies
      - Owners of particular ceremonial songs, dances, rituals
      - Midwives
      - Prostitutes
      - Craftspeople
      - Bards, entertainers
    - Dedicated middlemen/"professional" traders
    - Specified trading partners
    - Men/women/children
  - Did particular types of individuals or groups deal only with particular types of items/materials?
- WHEN did exchange occur?
  - Over time
    - Great continuity and time depth?
    - Only during some time periods?
  - For a given time period
    - On a regular or irregular basis?
    - On demand/as needed?
    - At a particular time of year?

TABLE 2-9 (cont.)
Dimensions of an Exchange System: Ethnohistorically-Oriented Model.

- WHEN did exchange occur? (cont.)
    - (cont.)
        - Harvest/hunt related
        - Weather/season related
        - Annual ceremonial cycle
    - Associated with life-crisis events?
        - Births/naming ceremonies
        - Initiation ceremonies
        - Weddings
        - Funerals
- WHERE did exchange take place?
    - At a settlement? Whose settlement?
        - Type of settlement
            - Gateway settlement (at regional boundary)
            - Central place/regional distribution center
            - Smaller-scale settlements
        - Location vis-a-vis settlement
            - Near but outside settlement boundary
            - Within settlement
                - Dedicated market area
                - Inside public building
                - In or near dwelling of a participant
    - At a "trading post" (location exclusively dedicated to trade)
    - At a neutral location, not "owned" by either party
        - Resource acquisition area (e.g., fish spawning area, salt lick)
        - Agreed-upon rendezvous
- HOW did the system function?
    - How (and by whom) were materials/items/services acquired?
    - How (and by whom) were materials/items transported?
        - Method (boat, back, horse, etc.)
        - Route
    - How (and by whom) were materials/items altered?
        - Production workshops/centers
        - Associated tools
    - How (and by whom) were materials/items stored?
    - How were materials/items/services exchanged?
        - Ceremonial protocol
        - Within particular "spheres of exchange"
        - Simultaneous or delayed presentation
            - Gift
            - Barter
            - Use of "money"
        - Gambling
        - Stealing/pillage
    - How were materials/items used, once acquired?
        - Were they reexchanged? to whom? interagroup or intragroup?
        - Were they consumed/otherwise removed from the system?
            - Subsistence/survival
            - Adornment/other "non-essential" uses
            - "Sacrificial" offering to supernatural powers
            - Ceremonial costumes, badges of office, ritual bundles
            - Grave goods
        - Were they used only by particular individuals/types of people?
- WHY did exchange take place?
    - To acquire immediatedly-required items or services
        - Why were they needed/desired?
        - Could they, if necessary, be acquired/produced locally rather than by exchange?
    - To forge alliances/social links for future needs
        - Why were they needed/desired?
            - To buffer subsistence fluctuations (temporal and/or geographical)
            - To maintain mating networks
            - To wage war or defense
        - How strong and necessary were the links thus forged?
    - To establish prestige, status
        - Via acquisition, display (social separation and/or competition)
        - Via generosity (social leveling)
    - To resolve conflicts

TABLE 2-10
Dimensions of an Exchange System: Geographically-Oriented Model

TEMPORAL DURATION of network
CONTENT of network (range of materials exchanged)
MAGNITUDE of network (quantity of goods exchanged)
DIVERSITY of exchanged materials (number of types of items involved)
SIZE/TERRITORIAL EXTENT of network
DIRECTIONALITY of exchange (direction[s] of flow of goods)
SYMMETRY of exchange (amount of goods flowing in given direction)
CENTRALIZATION of network ("collection" of resources at a few selected loci)
COMPLEXITY of network (variation in diversity, directionality, symmetry, and/or centralization over network territory/between loci of exchange)

(after Plog 1977:129)

Archaeological indicators of this type of long-distance interaction, when they do exist, often take the form of individualistic assemblages of exotic grave goods including what might seem to be very low-value items, such as small pebbles of quartz or other nonlocal minerals.

Intermarriage, Visiting, and Migration. Intermarriage between groups is a very important form of exchange, with great potential for cultural change if the partners come from very different backgrounds (e.g., Deagan 1983). The most reliable methods for establishing in-marriage are through analysis of human remains, for instance by comparison of DNA or of nonmetric osteological characteristics (e.g., Lane and Sublett 1972; Riggs 1977).

For many years, archaeologists attempted to equate pots with people, frequently explaining the presence of nonlocal pottery or stylistic elements by the presence of so-called captive brides or other foreign women (Latta 1991:376-78; cf., Trigger et al. 1980:131). Of course, life is not that simple. Exchange of pottery, either as such or as containers for foodstuffs, is one of many alternative explanations. For example, Martha Latta has proposed, from archaeological and ethnohistorical evidence, that the infrequent, diverse nonlocal sherds usually present at early Contact Period Iroquoian sites are the results of accidentally broken vessels used by males for cooking or carrying cooked food in canoes during long-distance travel (1991). She notes that pottery styles during that period—relatively small, squat jars with protruding castellations and handles through which a cord could be passed—are ideal for such a purpose.

This does not mean that pottery cannot be used for recognition of intermarriage, only that quantity, specific attribute variations, and context of disposition must be taken into consideration, and a broad range of evidence must be evaluated to rule out other possibilities. For example, at the large ceremonial center of Moundville, most of the nonlocal whole vessels were found with burials—women or adults of unknown sex. Since pottery was never found in identifiably male burials, the unknown sex burials are assumed to be women. The women were interpreted as having married in from the regions represented by their mortuary vessels (Welch 1991:172).

Foreigners can live among a group on a temporary or permanent basis without intermarriage being a major factor, as with the regular wintering-over of Plains hunter-gatherer bands at particular Southwestern pueblos (Ford 1983:712; Spielmann 1983:269). Recognition of such situations in the archaeological record usually focuses on definition of a spatially coherent area of a settlement with significant differences in dwelling style or layout and/or in domestic implements such as pottery. Spatially segregated cemeteries with significantly different burial practices and foreign grave goods also might constitute evidence, if contemporaneity could be shown (cf. Reyman 1978). However, in the absence of other evidence, these could be interpreted as manifestations of intragroup differences, such as by class. As mentioned above, common and consistent stylistic hybridization (such as of ceramics) within a settlement usually is taken as an indication of long-term co-residence of originally separate groups, gradually merging together.

Having reviewed and critiqued previous approaches to migration in prehistory, David Anthony recently proposed an archaeological migration model based on anthropological, geographical, and demographic models developed from modern data (Anthony 1990; Sutton 1995). Conditions most favorable to migration would include "negative (push) stresses in the home region," "positive (pull) attractions in the destination region" based on an adequate flow of information, and acceptable transportation costs (Anthony 1990:899). Information about new regions usually comes from relatives or friends there, and from short-term visits; migration is unlikely to take place without it. Motivation is usually economic, with "great differences in economic opportunities between two regions" being a good predictor of movement (Anthony 1990:900). Factors such as lower population densities or higher energy uptake per person in the destination region would "pull" migrants, while factors such as drought or military invasion would "push" them. Groups engaged in a "focal" subsistence strategy (dependent on relatively few highly productive, localized resources) are seen as more likely to engage in long-distance migration than groups engaged in a "diffuse" subsistence strategy, such as broad-spectrum hunter-gatherers. Long-distance migration patterns include: (1) leapfrogging based on information relayed by advance scouts, (2) migration streams along a defined pathway from circumscribed home regions, and (3) return migration. Their archaeological correlates include: (1) evidence of pre-migration penetration by members of the migrating group (usually young adult males), "islands" of population surrounded by less desirable areas, a founding population skewed toward young adult males; (2) "trails" between old and new homelands (recognizable by, for instance, distinctive artifacts or linear distributions of small transient sites), initial narrow ranges of artifact traits perhaps followed by an explosion of stylistic change; (3) exotic artifacts that might be interpreted as "long distance trade."

Boundary Markers. Boundary markers, setting off a settlement or a region from its nearest neighbors, can be physical, as with moats, palisades, and buffer zones, or stylistic, as with significant differences in costume or other highly visible material culture (Wobst 1977). Ethnohistorical studies have found that style differences between groups can be crisp or permeable, but are "accentuated by socioeconomic stress," accentuation taking the form of both differentiation and redundancy (DeBoer 1990; Hodder 1979; Wiessner 1983: quotation from 271, 1985, 1990). Proximity or frequent contact do not breed similarity in material culture if intergroup socioeconomic competition is present, as with African groups studied by Ian Hodder (Hodder 1979; Byers 1995; Logan and Schmittou 1995). Boundary-marking differences also often persist between groups that engage in complementary, interdependent economic practices (Barth 1969; Bloom 1969:83-84).

Polly Wiessner makes a useful distinction between "emblemic" and "assertive" styles, the former transmitting "a clear message to a defined target population... about conscious affiliation or identity," and the latter transmitting information about personal identity (Wiessner 1983:257). Indicators of "emblemic" style, which is closely related to group boundary-building, are expected to "undergo strong selection for uniformity and clarity," and should be recognizable in the archaeological record by their discrete distribution, an "all or nothing" phenomenon (Wiessner 1983:257, 259). The distribution of assertive stylistic indicators would range "from random to clinal," depending on particular conditions of interaction (Wiessner 1983:259).

Warfare and Other Negative Interaction. Evidence for warfare includes biophysical evidence for relatively high frequencies of weapon-induced injury, mutilation, and traumatic death, and for delays in burial; mass burials; protective structures such as palisades or moats around settlements; buffer zones; and depictions of warfare in various artistic media, most evocatively on status emblems such as marine shell gorgets. In an archaeological context, it would be difficult to identify exotic items acquired by practices such as stealing or raiding unless other indicators of intergroup conflict were present.

Direction and Extent of Interaction

The primary evidence identifying interaction partners comes from exotic materials and artifacts at a site, and from distributions of artifacts known to originate from the home site or region. A broader range of data, of course, is utilized when it is available, but here I will concentrate on artifactual evidence.

Source Characterization. Simple visual inspection rarely suffices to pinpoint the origin of raw materials and finished products. Depending on the resource being studied, physical, chemical, or stylistic analysis can be used for sourcing.

Typically, procedures for source characterization include: a geological survey to take samples from as many potential sources as possible; analysis of selected attributes in the samples; graphical or statistical analysis to define the characteristics of a given source or source region; collection and chemical/physical analysis of archaeological samples; and statistical analysis to assign them, as possible, to particular sources (for overviews, see Drooker 1993e:10-16; Harbottle 1982; Leute 1987:99-155; Rice 1987:309-446; Shotton and Hendry 1979). Distinguishing among varieties of a particular mineral often calls for trace element analysis, with neutron activation analysis being one of the most widely used techniques (Harbottle 1976), but many other methods are used, depending on the material to be analyzed and the information sought (Drooker 1993e: Table 4). Materials such as shell, bone, or feathers that come from living creatures generally are sourced on the basis of species ranges.

Stylistic studies of artifacts require either a typology or an attribute analysis to assign artifacts to groups (e.g., Hill and Evans 1972; Rice 1987:244-88; Shennan 1988:190-95; Spaulding 1977; Whallon and Brown 1982). As has become evident through a variety of ceramic studies, style alone often is not adequate to define the source of an artifact (Deutchman 1980; Hantman and Plog 1982; Kuhn 1985:19-42; Plog 1983:133). However, the use of stylistic types or attributes in conjunction with physicochemical analysis can be extremely fruitful.

Sourcing European materials and artifacts can involve not only stylistic and physicochemical analysis (e.g., Chafe et al. 1986; Kidd and Kidd 1983), but also evidence from historical documents and paintings (Brain 1979; Dimmick 1987; Kidd 1954, 1983). Two different objectives may be pursued: determination of the identity of the exporter or manufacturer in Europe, or determination of the supplier or point of entry into North America. The former has included both searching of manufacturers' and trading companies' records and archaeological excavation of important European manufacturing sites (e.g. Baart 1988; Fitzgerald et al. 1993; Karklins 1985; Ray 1974; Sleen 1963). Because some manufacturing centers, such as Venetian bead makers, supplied goods to a variety of European trading companies, defining the place of manufacture usually is not sufficient to trace dissemination of artifacts in the New World. Point-of-entry determination is more useful (e.g., Turgeon 1990:84-86). Archaeological association of particular types or styles of artifacts with particular exploring expeditions (e.g., Brain 1975; DePratter and Smith 1980), with colonial sites or regions occupied by a single European power (e.g., Noel-Hume 1982; South et al. 1988; Waselkov 1989), or with native sites occupied by people primarily in contact with a single European nationality (e.g., Brain 1979) are rosetta stones for such determinations. Abrupt changes of trade-good types in the archaeological record sometimes can be tied to newly awarded trade monopolies or to newly established trading settlements documented in the historical record (e.g., Ceci 1977, 1982, 1988; Fitzgerald 1982:43-44; Kenyon and Fitzgerald 1986; Pena 1990). Artifacts associated with particular European powers or entrepôts in eastern North America are discussed in Chapter 3.

Source identification studies can be oriented toward determining the distribution of a given resource from its source, in which case spatial analysis methods such as map distributions are employed (see below), or toward determining the sources of exotic resources found at a given archaeological site, in which case the results are expressed as absolute or relative abundances at the site of material from a given source. In either case, satisfactory results depend on recovery and analysis of samples from as many potential sources as possible.

Few such studies already have been done for types of resources present at Madisonville and other protohistoric Fort Ancient sites. They include source identifications for native copper (Goad 1978; Rapp 1985; Rapp et al. 1990), catlinite and related red pipestones (Gundersen 1993; Sigstad 1973; the latter study should be approached with caution), cherts used in southwestern Ohio projectile points (Litfin et al. 1993:24, 27-41), some marine shell species and gorget styles (Esarey 1990; Hally et al. 1990:133-34; Pendergast 1989), some pipe styles (Brown 1989; Salter 1977; West 1934), and a number of European artifact types (Bradley and Childs 1991a; Brain 1975; Drooker 1993b, 1996b; Fitzgerald 1990; Fitzgerald et al. 1993; Hayes 1983; Mitchem and McEwan 1988; M. Smith 1992; Waselkov 1989). Data, results, and supplementary analyses are discussed in Chapter 8.

Resource Distribution. Establishing distribution patterns of important raw materials and artifacts is an integral part of defining sources and nature of exchange. Methods and tools include fall-off curves and regression analysis, map distribution studies, trend surface mapping, and network analysis. Of these, map distribution studies are the most suitable for the goals and available data of the current study.

Fall-off curves and regression analysis are two-dimensional methods of representing distribution data, which plot or mathematically represent resource frequency versus distance from source (Drooker 1993e:18-19; Hodder 1974, 1978; Hodder and Orton 1976; Renfrew 1969, 1975:156-58, 1977). Ultimately, these methods, which were most popular during the late 1970s, were conceded to be unable to cope adequately with the complexities of reality, due to their unidimensionality and oversimplification. However, some general concepts first expressed in connection with these types of analysis are worth stating.

In general, the abundance of a commodity was expected to decrease at a regular rate with distance from its source. Deviations from that pattern would reflect different exchange circumstances. The most common deviation was an almost horizontal portion of the fall-off curve close to the source, then a negatively-sloping portion farther away. The former was equated to a "supply zone," in which goods were distributed from the source by a single transaction, while the latter, called the "contact zone," was thought to represent a series of down-the-line exchanges, or alternatively, dedicated long-distance traders (Renfrew 1969:157, 1977:84-85). The steepness of the contact zone slope was seen as reflecting the types of resources involved. High-value goods would manifest a gentler slope (and a broader supply zone) than low-value or more-readily-substitutable goods (Renfrew 1977:76-77), reflecting their association with "prestige chain" rather than down-the-line exchange (Renfrew 1975:45-46, 1977:77; cf. Bohannan 1955). As an idea of distances that might be involved with movement of low- versus high-value goods, a sourcing study of exotic materials and artifacts at Spiro, Oklahoma, found that low-value goods such as pottery and projectile points were limited to a 450-kilometer import range, but high-value goods such as marine shell were imported from much farther away (Brown 1983:143-49).

Map distribution studies add the second spatial dimension that graphical methods lack. They are a good way to quickly visualize spatial relationships for given raw materials and artifact types, but do contain some pitfalls (Drooker 1993e:17-18). In the literature, distribution maps most often have been a purely descriptive tactic. However, they also can be a useful analytical tool, following principles such as those stated above.

Types of distribution maps include: single-resource maps, depicting either presence alone or relative number of artifacts per site; maps with several different items superimposed in order to indicate a trade corridor or to contrast differential distributions of two or more items; and series of maps, indicating changes in resource distribution over time. The problem with the more complex maps is to present as much information as possible in an unconfusing way. If this can be accomplished, results can be as useful as trend surface mapping (see below).

In studies of individual trade centers, maps can be used to show source areas from which occupants obtained exotic materials and artifacts (e.g., Bell 1947; Brown 1983; Di Peso 1974; Ford and Webb 1956; Kelly 1991; Welch 1991). This can be useful, for instance in attempting to reconstruct travel routes and methods of transport, but only if source locations are not simply guesses on the part of the mapper. For example, there are many sources of native copper in eastern North America other than the obvious Lake Superior region (cf. Goad 1978; Goad and Noakes 1978). Few such studies have included maps of identifiable exports as well as imports, but contrasts and congruencies between the two can be very useful in interpreting interaction spheres (e.g., Di Peso 1974; Welch 1991:188-89).

While ethnohistorians have the wherewithal to map actual routes of exchange, this is usually difficult for researchers working exclusively with archaeologically recovered artifacts and materials. In that case, the simplest method for visualizing distribution systems is to map the occurrence of types of artifacts or materials. The use of this method is mainly descriptive rather than interpretive, but suites of maps or maps with several superimposed bodies of data can be used to infer either common or disparate exchange systems. Once distributions have been mapped, it is possible to correlate them with natural corridors of travel, such as river systems or mountain passes, and to consider the implications of spatial clustering associated with regional settlement patterns.

Artifacts and raw materials involved in exchange are expected to be most abundant at their sources and at centers of distribution and intensive use including ports of trade, gateway cities, and central places (Burghardt 1971; Chapman 1957; Hirth 1978; Smith 1974; see above, Settlement Patterns and Site Organization, and below, Network Analysis). However, archaeological studies of North American aboriginal sites known historically to have been distribution centers or home bases for intermediary traders have demonstrated that sometimes they actually are deficient in the highly visible exotic goods that their residents were gathering and passing on to others. Examples include the northern fur trade, the Plains fur trade, and the Southwestern turquoise trade (Kidder 1932:103; Ray 1974; Rogers 1990). Even in the absence of finished goods, production centers often can be recognized in the archaeological record by the presence of spatially discrete workshop areas, specialized tools or toolkits for craft production, caches of raw materials, manufacturing debris, and/or storage facilities for completed craft items (e.g., Creel 1991; Torrence 1986; Yerkes 1983, 1989). Proximity to a source of raw materials is another potential indicator (e.g., Cobb 1989:83).

Trend surface or synagraphic mapping is essentially a contour map of the frequency of occurrence of a resource, extrapolated from data collected at individual sites. Given adequate archaeological data, the primary value of this technique lies in its ability to graphically represent both the magnitude and the direction of resource movement. Irregularities in resource frequency contours, combined with consideration of topography and source locations, can be used to indicate trail systems, social boundaries, and the relative importance of alternative resources, and a time series of maps can be used for diachronic studies of resource movements (Earle and Ericson 1977:7-8; Ericson 1977, 1981; Erickson and Baugh 1994:10-13; Findlow and Bolognese 1982; Hodder and Orton 1976:155-74). Both a relatively abundant resource and a very well surveyed archaeological region are necessary to use this method effectively, as is stringent chronological control.

In contrast to models focusing on either export or import of resources from/to a given site, network analysis (Drooker 1993e:20-22) is designed to identify and analyze interaction among sites, in terms of "patterns produced by repeated exchange events" (Irwin-Williams 1977:143). The basic building blocks of networks are "nodes" (sites) and "linkages" (relations between pairs of sites). The first step in an analysis is to establish contemporaneity among nodes. Linkages then can be measured in several different ways, including: presence/absence of items from one node within assemblages from another; within a given class of items, the proportion from one node that is present in the total from another node; the proportion of items of the same class that originates at given nodes; the directional flow of items, as measured by the import-export ratio between nodes; the variety of items exchanged between nodes, as measured by the number of classes of items; and the kinds of classes of items exchanged between nodes. In considering linkages and nodes, distinctions are made between bidirectional and (apparently) unidirectional linkages, linkages involving only one class of items versus those involving multiple classes, and nodes at which imported items make up a large proportion of a given class versus nodes where import percentages are small. "Connectivity" between nodes can be expressed in matrix form (presence/absence or numerical) or graphical form (points connected by lines or arrows). Connectivity for a given node is expressed as a sum of rows and/or columns from the matrix; relative values of connectivity for different nodes can be used to define a hierarchy of sites. "Density" of connections within a zone is the ratio of actual zonal links to total possible links, while "multiplexity" involves the ranking of linkages and nodes in terms of uni- or bidirectional exchange and number of classes of items involved. Using these two concepts, "it is possible to differentiate zones with maximum internal linkage bounded by zones of relative low density and few multiplex relations"; such boundaries may differentiate separate social systems or spheres of influence (Irwin-Williams 1977:146).

Theoretically, such an analysis can be a powerful tool. In practice, however, it is difficult to carry out. Without a complete site data base, results will be distorted (Plog 1977:127-28). Even with a nearly complete site data base, evidence for certain classes of trade goods will be lacking because of the differential preservation of some materials over others in the archaeological record. The perishable resources that have been demonstrated to play such a large role in historically documented exchange networks (e.g., Ford 1972; Wright 1967; Drooker 1991a:94, 1992e:234-37) generally can only be postulated or inferred from indirect evidence. As an alternative, the less formal model of an exchange network summarized in Table 2-10 (Plog 1977) can be used as a template even when input data are incomplete. Most of its attributes can be assessed by means of map distributions.

Related to network analysis of exchange systems are the concepts of central place and gateway community, introduced from economic geography (see Settlement Patterns and Site Organization above). Central place systems involve two dimensions of exchange: distribution of goods from a regional center to a hierarchy of smaller local centers (and vice versa), and horizontally organized exchange among lower-level centers of equivalent rank. The central place also is the locus of interregional exchange, exporting items and raw materials produced within the entire region, and importing items and raw materials from other regions (Smith 1974:168-73). Gateway cities are the distribution centers for asymmetrical, dendritic hierarchical exchange systems; in theory, little or no exchange interaction takes place among lower-level communities (Burghardt 1971; Hirth 1978). Gateway communities tend to be located near regional boundaries (which often are equivalent to physiographic boundaries) and at key points along natural communication corridors, and to fulfill intermediary roles in long-distance trade systems.

Both central places and gateway cities are recognized archaeologically by various measures of site size rank, concentration of exotic goods, and patterns of intraregional linkage. As mentioned above, however, cautions have been raised about the possibility of adequately assessing sites that served intermediary functions, since all materials and finished items handled there would not necessarily be preserved in the archaeological record.

Nature and Intensity of Interaction

Establishing the fact of interaction is only the first step in identifying the nature of the relationships embedded in it. Some of the discussion above has touched upon interpretation of interaction relationships through evidence in the archaeological record. In this section, I will round out that discussion, with strongest emphasis on exotic artifacts and exchange-related analyses. Quantities, types, and disposal contexts of exotic goods all are important in interpreting the socioeconomic relationships they objectify.

The strength of an economic relationship between two settlements or two regions can be assessed, in part, on the basis of the attributes of their mutual exchange system, as modeled in Table 2-10. A strong relationship would be apparent if the temporal duration of the exchange network was long-term, if a large quantity of goods was exchanged, and if many different types of items were involved. The nature of that relationship would be interpreted differently depending on what types of goods were provided from and to each of the two parties, whether similar amounts (or value) of goods flowed in both directions, and whether the relationship was exclusive—i.e., whether one or both of them had additional exchange partners (see discussion of central place and gateway city linkage configurations above).

The strength and nature of social relationships between two settlements or two regions can be assessed, in part, by how people on each side of their mutual exchange system use the items or ideas obtained through it. Models of acculturation developed to describe culture changes in North America during the Contact Period have been based mainly on acceptance of newly introduced materials, objects, styles, and techniques (see above, Contact Period Change (2): Acculturative). For example, from Mandzy's model (Table 2-2), a group of people would be said to be increasingly acculturated to a foreign group if their artifact assemblage included (1) some local traditional items made from foreign materials, (2) foreign items functionally equivalent to local types, (3) foreign items with no known local traditional antecedent, and/or (4) local imitations of foreign items. Examples from prehistoric archaeological contexts can be put forth for each category: (1) locally made obsidian knives at eastern North American sites, (2) Oneota catlinite disk pipes at Fort Ancient sites, (3) a Mississippian engraved marine shell gorget at an Ontario Iroquoian site, and/or (4) a Fort Ancient jar (local paste and form) with a modeled face, like Middle Mississippi human portrait vessels. Note that items in categories 1-3 all could be obtained by down-the-line exchange, with no face-to-face interaction between originating and receiving group members. Direct interaction is more likely for category 4 items (see below).

Even more telling, however, than the presence of foreign or foreign-influenced items are the ways in which they are used. Based on a combination of ethnohistorical and archaeological data (e.g., Brown 1979a), it is clear that the more similar the use of a "foreign" item in the receiving group to its mode of use in the originating group, the closer in contact and more attuned the two populations are likely to be. Similarity of use includes both how and by whom an item is used.

Besides obvious function-related attributes such as form and size, how an item was used can be inferred from use wear and disposal context. Depending on the item, use wear encompasses blunt or chipped cutting edges, frayed or broken yarns, worn suspension holes on shell ornaments, broken and mended pipes, sooty ceramic vessels, etc. Pristine, unused items formally disposed (for instance, as grave goods or in a cache) obviously differ in use history—and value—from broken items thrown into a midden. Residues such as blood, plant fibers, or carbonized food can be analyzed for additional information. Repair, especially careful and painstaking repair (as with riveted embossed copper symbol badges found at some Southeastern ceremonial centers), would indicate high value or difficulty of replacement. Disposal context includes type of feature (e.g., storage pit, midden, house floor, ceremonial structure interior, burial), location within feature (e.g., close to central hearth versus close to wall in a domestic structure, or on the shoulder, held in the hand, or between the thighs of a skeleton in a grave), and associated artifacts.

Users of particular exotic items sometimes can be determined by artifact disposition in nonmortuary contexts, as with artifacts found only in portions of a site independently determined to have been used primarily by particular subgroups, such as elite residences on Mississippian mounds. Items serving as grave goods might well have been used by the deceased, but this would not neccessarily be true in all circumstances. Mortuary associations, however, can be considered as themselves constituting a sort of use pattern, in that certain items would be considered appropriate and others inappropriate for association with a person of a given age, sex, and social identity. If disposition of a given type of exotic artifact (or better yet, multiple types of artifacts) is the same in the receiving as in the originating region (e.g., engraved marine shell masks found only in burials, with subadults or adult males, placed over faces, with unworn eye holes; smoking pipes of a particular style ubiquitous on a site but never found in mortuary contexts), there is a strong implication that the receiving group was in relatively close and positive contact with the originating group. When foreign objects are present but disposed of differently than in the originating region (e.g., engraved shell masks hung on thongs around necks of adult female remains; smoking pipes of a particular style never found in middens, but always in burials of adult males, held in the right hand), such differing local customs imply social distance: either minimal direct contact or deliberate differentiation between groups.

The nature and strength of intersettlement or interregion relationships also are related to who, from each group, actually interacts. When high-value goods (see Grave Goods, above) are exchanged and they remain with people who, based on other evidence (such as from the mortuary record), probably were members of an elite class and/or served as leaders, then participation in "prestige chain" interaction is likely. Such interaction consists of, or incorporates, exchange of wealth goods or prestige goods (Table 2-4) among a limited number of people, often members of a social elite or otherwise specially designated segment of society. Prestige chain interaction can lead to, or signify, strong relationships between certain segments of two settlements or regions, not necessarily between the populations as a whole (Earle 1994:430-35; Schortman and Urban 1992a:237-40). When exotic goods are dispersed more broadly among the population of a site or region, there is a higher possiblity that exchange took place among greater numbers of the population, as in trading partner relationships, ceremonies like potlatches, seasonal gatherings, or situations where relatively large groups of people visit each other frequently or for extended periods of time (Table 2-9).

As discussed above (see Evidence of Interaction), one indicator of social boundaries can be stylistic differences between the material cultures of the people involved. Among other alternatives, this can signal interaction and economic competition. Broadly-similar material culture styles can signal interaction on less competitive terms. For example, among African hunter-gatherer groups studied by Polly Wiessner, who combined foraging with risk-pooling by means of widespread reciprocity, style was homogeneous for a variety of attributes within the risk-pooling population, and no attributes were used as emblems of identity for subgroups within that population (Wiessner 1983). In their archaeological model of tribal social networks, David Braun and Stephен Plog predict that intergroup connectedness will be accompanied by comparable "stylistic similarity between localities and...decorative homogeneity or standardization within each locality" (Braun and Plog 1982:512). Large-scale, consistent contrasts or similarities in items of clothing and adornment would be particularly evocative of boundary-building versus inclusiveness between groups (Wobst 1977).

For objects that are local imitations of, or hybrids with, foreign styles, two things must be considered. First, there must have been an opportunity for the craftsperson to see the nonlocal object on which the local imitation was modeled (although a verbal description is an outside possibility). This could be accomplished in a number of ways, including origin of the craftsperson from the foreign group, a visit by the craftsperson to the foreign group, or transport of a foreign object to the local group, where it could be seen by the craftsperson. Second, the desire to emulate must have been present. This implies the opposite of competitive boundary-building (cf. DeBoer 1990). In spite of the "captive brides" theory of what is sometimes called ceramic miscegenation, local imitations in most cases would seem to be indicators of positive interaction. (Of course, nostalgia for familiar attributes by a person forcibly removed from home and expected to produce items in a local style is an alternative possibility.)

Models of Interaction and Change

In their most general sense, interaction studies are concerned with "understanding the effects of interactions among spatially distinct population units on processes of local social change" (Schortman 1989:52; cf. Schortman and Urban 1992b). Interaction, of course, also occurs at smaller scales, and interaction patterns at local levels can affect those carried out over greater distances.

Interaction Studies

Currently, there is no general, over-arching model for studying interaction. According to Edward Schortman and Patricia Urban, interaction studies have developed along several different trajectories, each influenced by the prevailing archaeological paradigm of its day (Schortman and Urban 1987, 1992a, 1992b). Briefly, these include (1) models and concepts such as interaction spheres (e.g., Caldwell 1964) and acculturation (e.g., Linton 1940) that developed out of, and beyond, the diffusion perspective of the 1930s and 1940s, "in which culture change was equated with the fortuitous interregional borrowing of traits and trait complexes" (Schortman 1989:53); (2) the broad field of trade studies (e.g., Adams 1974; Earle and Ericson 1977; Renfrew 1975, 1977; Renfrew et al. 1966), which attempted to quantify variables and generalize "laws" of exchange and interaction, in parallel with the "cultural ecology" and processualism of the 1950s through 1980s; (3) development and application of modified versions of Wallerstein's (1974, 1980) capitalism/colonialism-based core-periphery world systems model (e.g., Blanton and Feinman 1984; Champion 1989a; Schneider 1977); (4) development and application of cluster-interaction (Price 1977), peer-polity (Renfrew and Cherry 1986), and heterarchical (Ehrenreich et al. 1995) models, which propose codevelopment among roughly equivalent autonomous sociopolitical units, based on interaction and competition; and (5) an increasing focus on "the interactions themselves," including the contexts in which they occur and the social identities, social affiliations, and world views of the participants (e.g., Hamell 1993; Miller and Hamell 1986; Schortman 1989: quotation from 53), in parallel with the postprocessualist concern with historical context and symbolic significance (e.g., Hodder 1982).

Not all of these categories are really full-fledged models, useful in studying the complete range of interaction and change. For example, "models" based simply on fortuitous interregional borrowing of attributes and technology are not really models at all, merely reactive explanations. Thus, while I have highlighted some useful aspects of acculturation theory above (see Contact Period Change [2]: Acculturative), I cannot utilize it as an over-arching concept.

The second category, trade studies, is not broad enough to encompass all aspects of interaction (Schortman and Urban

TABLE 2-11
Factors Promoting Organizational Change in Chiefdom Societies

	Increases in Complexity (decision making levels stable or increasing)	Decreases in Complexity (decision making levels unstable or decreasing)
Regional physiography:	homogeneous	irregular
Climate:	favorable	unfavorable
Resource structure:	predictable/even	unpredictable/irregular
Subsistence production:	surplus	shortfall
Storage technology:	present/extensive capability	absent/minor capability
Tribute mobilization:	bearable	excessive
Prestige goods exchange:	constant/increasing flow	decreasing/interrupted flow
Alliance network:	strong	weak
Information flow:	regular	erratic
Territorial boundary maintenance:	aggressive	passive
Population levels:	increasing	decreasing
Population movement:	sanctioned	unsanctioned
Ritual institutions:	strongly supported	weakly supported
Authority structures:	strong	weak
Factional competition:	minor/channeled	major/uncontrolled
Nature of sucession:	regular/institutionalized	uncertain/weakly institutionalized
	Complex Chiefdom Formation	Complex Chiefdom Collapse

(after Anderson 1994: Fig. 3)

1987:53). Strictly speaking, trade only pertains to interactions involving "(1) personnel; (2) goods; (3) carrying; and (4) two-sidedness" (Polanyi 1975:136), while interaction encompasses much more. Furthermore, it is important to note that in pre-capitalistic nonstate societies, trade per se rarely is the direct cause of culture change. Far more often, it is the interpersonal interaction accompanying trade that fuels change. As previously discussed, if the interaction is close or frequent, it can generate either cultural/stylistic similarities (connected with cooperation) or deliberate differences (connected with competition).

Thus, Schortman and Urban's fifth category, focusing on the actual contexts and participants of intergroup interaction, is of key importance (see Evidence of Interaction, and Nature and Intensity of Interaction). In support of it, Schortman has developed the concepts of "salient identities," which are those social identities (Table 2-4) used most commonly by an individual, and "salient affiliations," which "focus on those points of interest among a group of interacting people which are perceived to be of particular importance to those involved and bring a number of individuals into consistent, repeated contact" (Schortman 1989:54-55). Such affiliations can exist at a local or supralocal level, and can bridge long geographical distances. They replace the archaeological concept of a "culture" by a focus on interaction networks (often overlapping) maintained by members of significant social categories. However, by itself, this concept does not "explain the distribution of material patterns nor [does it] account for the importance of intersocietal contacts. In order to do this, salient social categories must be integrated into a larger theoretical system of related assumptions" (Schortman 1989:59). One example of such a system is the peer-polity interaction model, which will be discussed further below.

Three other interaction models are summarized. They include: social networks related to "risk-pooling," including heterarchical social systems with permeable and shifting boundaries; a review of the chiefdom/complex chiefdom concept and recent theoretical work on the evolution and devolution of chiefdoms; and certain aspects of world systems interaction. World systems and complex chiefdom models emphasize asymmetrical socioeconomic relationships, while peer-polity and risk-pooling models emphasize symmetrical relationships (competitive and cooperative, respectively). Some of these models incorporate not only social interaction but also environmental factors as impetus to change. Each framework appears to have some potential utility for assessing late prehistoric-protohistoric Fort Ancient interaction patterns and change.

It must be noted that the commonly used typological distinctions between tribe, chiefdom, and various subtypes of them has not been upheld in detailed comparative studies of real-world socioeconomic attributes. A cross-cultural survey of New World sedentary prestate societies by Gary Feinman and Jill Neitzel reveals a wide range of variation in organizational attributes and leadership duties (Feinman and Neitzel 1984). Among their sample of over 100 historically described groups, there was continuous rather than discrete variation in leadership functions, status differentiation, levels of political decision-making, and settlement patterns. In fact, they found it impossible to separate out chiefdoms from less complex types of socioeconomic organization, due to the fact that within a given group, "increasing complexity along one societal dimension may or may not imply similar variation along other dimensions" (1985:77). Rather than using sets of archaeological correlates chosen to fit a theoretical organizational type, they recommend studying "change and variation along a set of societal dimensions concurrently" (1985:77, 44-45). This is, in fact, the strategy that I follow in my study. However, since several important archaeological models are based on just such typological distinctions, I present separate discussions of chiefdom and tribal models.

Chiefdoms and Complex Chiefdoms

Models developed to recognize chiefdom-level socioeconomic organization in the archaeological record also can be used to determine that this organizational type was not present in a region, or to track evolution or devolution between less complex and more complex socioeconomic organization over time. As such, they are important to the analysis of Fort Ancient interaction patterns and change, whether or not the Fort Ancient region can be equated with chiefdom-type attributes and organization.

What Is a Chiefdom? Many classificatory systems have been devised for prestate sedentary societies (cf. Feinman and Neitzel 1984: Table 2-1), with chiefdoms, if included as such, generally conceived as the most complex types in the system. Archaeologically oriented definitions of chiefdoms have evolved from models originally put forth by anthropologists Elman Service (1962) and Morton Fried (1967). Based on current usage, chiefdoms can be defined as "multicommunity political units under the control of a hereditary decision-making group or elite," with simple chiefdoms containing one decision-making level (i.e., two hierarchical levels), complex chiefdoms containing two decision-making levels with direct control of all subordinate groups, and paramount chiefdoms containing two decision-making levels with both direct and indirect control of yet larger numbers of lower-level communities/regions (Anderson 1994:4-9, quotation from 7).

Archaeological Manifestations of Complex Chiefdoms. The most complete archaeological model of a complex chiefdom (ranked society) was developed, tested, and refined in conjunction with analyses of data from the large Mississippian ceremonial center of Moundville, Alabama, and its surrounding region (Peebles and Kus 1977; Knight 1993; Peebles 1971, 1974, 1978, 1987; Powell 1988, 1992; Steponaitis 1978, 1983; Welch 1991; Welch and Scarry 1995). Contrary to the chiefdom constructs of Service and Fried, redistribution has not been found to be a constant correlate of chiefdoms (Earle 1977; Feinman and Neitzel 1985:44; Peebles and Kus 1977:424-27; Welch 1991:8-22). In their cybernetics-based model, Christopher Peebles and Susan Kus singled out "mortuary differentiation, ritual-regulatory networks, subsistence autonomy, and part-time craft specialization" as indicators of the hierarchical social organization and other factors associated with chiefdoms (1977:421). Specifically, their model predicts (and Moundville data confirm): (1) ascribed ranking, visible in the mortuary record (Tables 2-5, 2-7) and perhaps in separate residential areas, (2) a hierarchy of settlement sizes and types, (3) settlement locations consistent with a high degree of local self-sufficiency in subsistence, (4) organized productive activities transcending the basic household group, including construction of monuments and at least part-time craft specialization, and (5) "evidence of society-wide organizational activity to buffer" environmental uncertainty, including (a) mixed strategies for food production, (b) evidence for food storage, (c) defensive organization for warfare, and (d) management of intersocietal trade, with actual attributes present dependent upon which environmental variables were most uncertain (1977:431-33, quotation from 433). Peebles also notes a hierarchy of symbolism in sociotechnic grave goods, distinguishing between items acting as supralocal symbols (found only with the highest-ranking individuals at higher-order sites) and those functioning as local symbols (Peebles 1971:69). Long-distance prestige-goods exchange also is mentioned in connection with (4), but not emphasized.

Mary Lucas Powell brought together biophysical data from Moundville and four other large Mississippian sites to test expectations with regard to ranked status. Model predictions in connection with diet were that elite class members (1) would have greater adult body size than non-elites, due to better diet and selection for leaders of imposing stature, (2) would evidence less growth disruption (hypoplasia) and better dental health (specifically fewer caries, and less tooth wear), (3) would have higher bone strontium levels indicating a diet richer in meat, and (4) would evidence stronger immune response to infections. Elite males were expected to show more warfare-related trauma than non-elites, due to the importance of warrior prowess in achieved status. Elite females were expected to show less trauma related to daily work than non-elites. Some, but not all, sites showed the expected differences in stature, trauma, and meat ingestion, but skeletal and dental pathology generally did not differ between classes. Analysis of floral and faunal remains and pottery assemblages at Moundville versus lower-order sites within its purview showed differences in foodways between elite and non-elite contexts, suggesting that the former received meat as tribute and that they, and the central Moundville settlement, were associated with greater elaboration in foodways and large-group feasting (Welch and Scarry 1995).

Lower-order chiefdoms would be congruent with the complex chiefdom model, but exhibit fewer hierarchical levels and encompass a smaller region with fewer settlements. Settlement patterns, mortuary evidence for or against an ascribed elite class, and employment or nonemployment of supralocal symbols are probably the most accessible classes of data for determining the level of complexity in a multisettlement polity.

TABLE 2-12
Factors Associated with Different Forms of Intertribal Relationships

	Symbiosis	Merger/Coalition	Warfare
Economic Systems	Functionally differentiated - in production and/or - in distribution Surplus production - of foodstuffs and/or - of durable goods	Functionally parallel	Functionally parallel
Relative Location	Adjacent (Short-term use of common territory) (Short-term co-residency)	Use of common territory Permanent co-residency	Competition for territory
Population Size	Self-sustaining	Reduced (e.g., by epidemic)	
Type(s) of Exchange	Generalized reciprocity (delayed return) Balanced reciprocity - Ceremonial - Individual Negative reciprocity (raiding, to adjust temporary imbalances)	Generalized reciprocity (sharing, pooling)	Balanced reciprocity (trade, often through go-betweens) Negative reciprocity (raiding, to permanently acquire resources, labor)
Proprietary Rights of Respective Groups	Held separately	Held jointly	Contested
Alliance Making	Marriage (usually between leading families of different bands) Fictive adoption ("father-son")	Marriage (widespread) Fictive adoption ("sibling") Cross-cutting sodalities	Kinship through captives

(from Albers 1993)

Cycling and Devolution. From archaeological and historical evidence, polities that can be typed as chiefdoms are not stable over time, but tend to fluctuate from simple to complex, with centers of power shifting as one or another community gains prominence (Anderson 1994:1-52). Under some conditions, fissioning and out-migration may take place (Anderson 1994:45-48). According to David Anderson (1994:9),

> Cycling encompasses the transformations that occur when administrative or decision-making levels within the chiefdom societies occupying a given region fluctuate between one and two levels above the local community...the recurrent process of the emergence, expansion, and fragmentation of complex chiefdoms amid a regional backdrop of simple chiefdoms.

Table 2-11 lists the factors important in promoting cycling, to either a higher or a lower level of administrative complexity. Anderson postulates that the most important factor is "competition for prestige and power between rival elites" (1994:50). Among the late prehistoric Savannah River chiefdoms that he studied, he also found external factors, including climatic change, to have been significantly important in promoting cycling (1994:274-89, 327). A broad regional perspective and close chronological control were required for complete analysis; for instance, to demonstrate that the rise of two large polities in adjacent river basins led to the depopulation of a significant portion of the Savannah River valley, which then served as a buffer zone between them (1995:326-29).

Although Anderson's model is specific to ranked societies, many of the factors that he found important for fostering organizational change also may be important for fostering change in societies of lesser complexity. At the very minimum, the multidimensional approach and regional perspective can be applied to organizational change at any level.

Not only cycling among hierarchical chiefdoms, but also devolution from a hierarchical to a more-or-less nonhierarchical system, is known to have taken place, for example, in the sixteenth- and seventeenth-century Southeast. No general model has been developed, but it is presumed that major and abrupt external/environmental stresses would be involved in such a change, such as widespread so-called virgin soil epidemics with accompanying population decimation (Smith 1987:54-112).

Tribes

As discussed above, tribes probably should be treated in a continuum with chiefdoms, rather than separately, but the discussion here is organized around previously developed models based on typological distinctions. Models developed for tribal-level interaction and change may well be applicable to the Fort Ancient region, whether or not the socioeconomic organizational complexity of its residents can be designated as completely tribal.

What Is a Tribe? In contrast to centralized, hierarchical chiefdoms, tribes have been conceived as decentralized and nonhierarchical, although at least one classification system assigns them one administrative tier, thus equating them with the simple chiefdom model described above (Feinman and Neitzel 1985:47). They have been described as "bounded groups of culturally similar people...generally consisting of individual communities or extended kin units...largely independent of one another economically, but politically and ceremonially interdependent" (Creamer and Haas 1985:739; see also discussions in Helm 1968, e.g., Dole 1968 and Fried 1968). There is limited surplus production or specialization. Individual social ranking and leadership positions are generally based on achievement, although kin groups may be ranked in status, and certain leadership positions may be filled primarily by individuals from designated kin groups (i.e., some ascribed status differentiation may be present; cf. Knight 1990). Decision-making is carried out at the group level, not by individual leaders. As with chiefdoms, there is considerable variation within historically known groups designated as "tribes."

Archaeological Manifestations of Tribes. Winifred Creamer and Jonathan Haas have proposed the following archaeolgical correlates for tribes, which they tested with data from Panama and Costa Rica (1985:742-43): (1) a nonhierarchical settlement pattern, with "sites composed of similar constituent units dispersed over a definable region," (2) nondifferentiated residential architecture, (3) no supralocal storage facilities, (4) limited evidence of vertical ranking in mortuary treatment and grave goods, (5) possible religious specialization (shamans), (6) low frequency of "valuables" in either caches or rich burials, (7) possible intraregional exchange of subsistence goods, (8) some interregional trade, with exotic goods "distributed among the populace, not concentrated in any place." They also predict that there will be environmental stress indicators (evidence of warfare or restricted subsistence) contemporaneous with the time of formation of the tribal unit (see next section).

Implicit in this construction is territorial boundedness. An alternative model has been proposed by Rhea Rogers for application to late prehistoric-protohistoric communities in the northwestern Carolina Piedmont, based on the concept of heterarchical organization (Table 2-4) developed by Carole Crumley (1987, 1995). She concluded that, "Far from being a series of small, autonomous sociopolitical units, the[se] tribes... are better understood as protean and interactive networks that were unbounded in terms of both personnel and space.... Traditional archaeological constructs that emphasize or reify the spatial boundedness of social groups may obscure patterning indicative of an egalitarian heterarchy" (1995:7). Egalitarian heterarchy is characterized by high levels of individual (rather than centralized) interaction, including alliance-forging, intermarriage, and high mobility, manifested archaeologically as different spatial patterning for material remains associated with different socioeconomic networks.

Tribal Social Networks and Risk Aversion. David Braun and Stephen Plog's model of tribal social networks and risk aversion (Braun and Plog 1982; Saitta 1983) was formulated and tested in conjunction with analysis of evolution in nonhierarchical social systems. Its formulators view the development of social integration at the tribal "level" as a response to environmental unpredictability.

Braun and Plog view tribal social networks as integrating factors within nonhierarchical societies, describing them as:

> lines for the transmission of material and information through reciprocity and reciprocal roles, that is, as lines of cooperation, communication, and control among individuals and groups. The diversity and relative strength of such links define the social distances among the connected parties. Such networks have the effects of (1) distributing environmental risks and benefits among the participants; (2) providing channels of communication about environmental conditions of different spatial scales; (3) defining lines of fusion and fission for any cycles of spatial aggregation and dispersion; and (4) delegating decision making responsibilities. [1977:507]

"Environment" is defined as encompassing both the social and the natural landscape, each of which can be the source of risk and uncertainty (Braun and Plog 1977:507). Braun and Plog predict that region-wide social interconnectedness will intensify in response to increases in environmental risk and uncertainty, leading to greater regional integration. However, complete social disruption is possible if environmental changes are so large and abrupt that social adaptation cannot keep pace. Alternatively, no socioeconomic change will take place if increases in environmental uncertainty are minor.

Increasing social connectedness should be detectable in the archaeological record by (1) "increasing stylistic similarity between localities, and increasing decorative homogeneity or standardization within each locality," (2) "an increase in the quantity of goods exchanged," and (3) "a shift towards the exchange of goods indicative of a decreasing social distance between the interacting parties, for example, towards the exchange of goods that are less costly, less standardized, or made of less scarce materials" (Braun and Plog 1977:512-13).

If applicable to the Fort Ancient region, the Braun-Plog model has potential usefulness for assessing effects of increasing uncertainty due to either natural factors, such as the so-called Little Ice Age initiated during the fifteenth century, or social factors, such as the increasing presence of Europeans along the eastern seaboard during the sixteenth and seventeenth centuries. However, it does not consider the potential role of negative reciprocity in risk aversion.

It might be useful here to consider a model of intertribal relationships developed by Patricia Albers from nineteenth-century Plains data, which views the range of intertribal socioeconomic relationships, including merger or coalition, symbiosis, and warfare, as a frequently-shifting continuum (Albers 1993; but see Foster 1994:x-xii). Building upon the work of Joseph Jablow, who first highlighted the important role of exchange among Plains groups (Jablow 1994 [1951]), Albers highlights the interdependence of all three of these relationships and the roles played within them by exchange and alliance making (Table 2-12). Interdependent relationships, alliances, and exchange were by no means constrained by differences in ethnicity, nor were conflicts absent within tribal groups, many of which are known to have fissioned and separated.

In nineteenth-century Plains history, warfare often erupted when long-standing exchange relationships were disrupted by European traders, cutting out one group or another from valued goods. However, non-hostile interaction often continued between members of warring groups, and kinship ties continued to function, leaving the door open for future reconciliation (Albers 1993:122-28). Although intergroup relationships were particularly dynamic in the nineteenth-century Plains due to specific economic and environmental factors, archaeologists should view this historically based model as a caution against reliance on simplistic theories of interaction and change.

Confederations

Among prestate sedentary groups in Feinman and Neitzel's sample, administrative flexibility was apparent in a large proportion. Twenty-six out of 72 groups were recorded as participating in "occasional confederations" or "larger concentrations" of groups (1985:62-63). Eleven of these otherwise were administered by a village chief and the remainder by village chiefs and a district chief; that is, confederations were recorded among groups with both one and two decision-making levels. Participation was temporary and contingent upon circumstances, for instance, during times of warfare. It can be considered as a sort of "risk sharing."

I have found no generalized models or formal sets of archaeological correlates for confederations, although there is an accessible literature on historically known long-term and short-term indigenous confederations in eastern North America. Some examples, to illustrate the range of variation in scale and complexity, include the League of the Iroquois, the Huron and Neutral Confederacies, the Creek Confederacy (Muskogee, Hitchiti, Uchee, Natchez, Alabama, some Shawnee and others), Three Fires (Potawatomi, Ottawa, Chippewa), the Illinois Confederacy and (on a smaller scale) the Confederated Peoria, and the five functionally differentiated "divisions" of the Shawnees (Bauxar 1978:599; Callender 1962, 1978c:673, 1978f; Crane 1929; Howard 1981; Hudson 1976; Jennings 1984; Smith 1987:129-42; Tooker 1978; Trigger 1976; Wright 1986). Large-scale amalgamations of groups for warfare, such as Pontiac's and Tecumseh's late seventeenth- and early nineteenth-century intertribal movements (Edmunds 1984), rarely seem to have included whole polities, so cannot really be considered confederations. As with chiefdoms, confederations evolved and devolved within years, decades, generations, or centuries, based on historical circumstance and the needs of their participants.

Many (but by no means all) of the longer-term confederations united groups at the same level of administrative complexity, residing in separate settlements (e.g., Iroquois Five Nations, Shawnee Divisions). Ceramics have been proposed as archaeological correlates to at least two such confederations. Pottery styles among members of the League of the Iroquois are said to have become increasingly similar from the fifteenth century onwards, perhaps correlating with the formation of the League (Tuck 1978:331-32), and the rapid development and spread of a particular ceramic horizon style (brushed pottery, typed as Chattahoochee Brushed or Walnut Roughened) has been proposed as a correlate to the development of the eighteenth-century Creek Confederacy (Smith 1987:141). In eastern North America, alliance rituals usually involved reciprocal gift-giving (Dye 1995:299). At least sometimes there were supralocal badges of office or group membership, such as Iroquois wampum belts, that objectified the highest levels of participation. Such items might or might not reach the archaeological record; for instance, they might be passed on between successive office holders. However, if extant, they would be expected to form not a triangle of ascending levels of higher office (as with paramount chiefdoms), but a trapezoid, with several equivalent contemporaneous "highest" indicators.

Center-Periphery Models

"Center-periphery" or "world systems" models are concerned with economic systems that bind together separate polities of differing scale and complexity. They facilitate analysis of asymmetrical relationships operating across vast geographical regions. Their potential relevance to the current study lies in their intimate connection with colonial economic systems.

A world system is defined as a spatially extensive economic system containing more than one cultural-political unit, but only a single division of labor. It consists of "core states," which control and benefit from the system, "peripheral areas," which in the modern world produce low-value goods or raw materials, "semi-peripheral areas," which lie between them, and "external areas," only weakly (if at all) tied to the system (Schortman and Urban 1987:55-56). The original model, developed by Immanuel Wallerstein (1974, 1980), is tied to modern capitalism and thus not directly applicable to prehistory, but it has been both reinterpreted and used as a modeling device, that it might be more so (e.g., Blanton and Feinman 1984; Champion 1989b; Pailes and Whitecotton 1979; Schneider 1977; Upham 1986). According to Schortman and Urban, "the general aspects of world systems theory which have the greatest relevance to such a [pre-capitalist] conceptual system are the specification that at least one unit of analysis should be a set of closely interacting societies, and the notion that the interactions among the elements of the system, and the interdependence of the elements, are crucial to an understanding of the system as a whole" (1987:61). Unlike peer polity models, world systems models emphasize dominance and subordination rather than interaction among roughly equivalent polities.

A particularly influential critique of Wallerstein's model is that of Jane Schneider (1977). She argued that he had not adequately considered large-scale pre-capitalist exchange (such as along the Silk Road between China and the West), particularly the crucial importance of luxury goods, or "preciosities." Wallerstein had dismissed the exchange of such items as unimportant to the functioning of the system, but in fact both luxury and utilitarian goods (labels that can be applied to the same item, depending on the circumstances) have both economic and social importance. To establish the relative importance of particular items one must know how they function in the originating and receiving groups: "meaning is given to them by the rôle they play in the social relations of a specific society at a specific time" (Champion 1989b:8).

According to Champion, current archaeological applications of core-periphery relationships have "moved away from Wallerstein's concern with trade, and [have] concentrated more on the growth and nature of long-distance interactions and their capacity for producing social transformations, on the interrelationship of cycles of economic activity in spatially distant areas, and on diachronic patterns in the location of power centres" (1989:11). Two analytical concepts of importance are "prestige goods economies" and "modes of production." Prestige goods "symbolically embody wealth and function in social exchanges and ritual" (McGuire and Downum 1982:118). Even more than wealth, they convey and symbolize status: their exchange is confined to a limited number of people, usually a social elite or an otherwise specially designated segment of society. Prestige-goods exchange is a common "means of articulating societies with very different structures of economic and social organization" (Champion 1989b:12). "Mode of production" is a concept that many have found useful in defining peripheral economies and tracking changes to them as they interact with core states; "kin-ordered" and "tributary" modes are considered particularly appropriate to these circumstances (Wolf 1982:79-100, 400-404).

Recognition of centers and peripheries in the archaeological record requires the identification of an economic relationship involving dominance and inequality. One approach is the analysis of trade volume between polities, but complete definition and quantification are difficult, if not impossible, for reasons discussed above (Archaeological Manifestations of Interaction and Exchange). Analysis of exchange linkages between regions can be useful, because peripheries may develop dependence on a particular core area due to the fact that they have the opportunity to interact with it and it alone. Another approach is to examine patterns of consumption and discard within core, periphery, and semi-periphery (Champion 1989b:14, 16).

Variations of the center-periphery model have been applied successfully to economic relationships between Mesoamerica and the Southwest (e.g., Ericson and Baugh 1993; McGuire 1989; Wilcox 1986), but have been tried and roundly rejected in prehistoric eastern North America (Dincauze and Hasenstab 1989; Griffin 1993). The model is well-suited to examining relationships between colonial powers and local indigenous groups, as long as it is demonstrated, rather than assumed, to have been in effect. For example, it can be used to analyze European-native economic relationships in North America during the later fur trade era, when a few peripheral Native American groups, such as the Woodland Assiniboine, Cree, and Ojibway in central Canada, eventually became dependent for survival upon the goods they received in exchange for furs from monopolistic trading companies such as the English Hudson Bay Company (Ray 1974:137-65). However, as Ray's book makes clear, core-periphery relationships in most cases were complex and shifting, not simplistic and monolithic patterns of dominance and subordination.

The center-periphery model is much less pertinent to relations during the early Contact Period, when numerous European powers were vying for a foothold in the New World, would-be traders needed the knowledge and contacts of their indigenous allies to survive, and interior peoples could pick and choose which of them (if any) with whom to interact. In my analysis of Fort Ancient socioeconomic relationships I kept this model in mind for its potential utility, but in the end did not find it applicable to my region and period of interest.

Peer Polity Interaction

Colin Renfrew has offered peer polity interaction (similar to Barbara Price's concept of "cluster interaction") as a process through which sociopolitical change can be analyzed and understood (Price 1977; Renfrew and Cherry 1986). It is defined as:

> the full range of interchanges taking place (including imitation and emulation, competition, warfare, and the exchange of material goods and of information) between autonomous (i.e., self-governing and in that sense politically independent) socio-political units which are situated beside or close to each other within a single geographical region, or in some cases more widely. [Renfrew 1986:1]

This approach emphasizes the nonisolation of autonomous political entities, and de-emphasizes "relations of dominance and subordination" (Renfrew 1986:1). It also emphasizes the importance of style as an essential component of communication systems, and symbolic systems as links among political peers (Renfrew and Cherry 1986:vii-viii). Material, technological, and symbolic systems are seen as interacting and changing together, within a particular social matrix.

A polity is the "highest order sociopolitical unit" within a given region, an independent entity under no higher jurisdiction (Renfrew 1986:2; cf. Price 1977:210). Polities can exist at different scales, including the early states studied by Renfrew and his colleagues, chiefdoms, tribal units, and villages. More complex polities often are formed from previously-independent smaller polities, either by one polity gaining ascendance over its former peers, or by an amalgamation of more-or-less equal units into a confederacy.

Peer polities share structural homologies. Settlement patterns, site plans, architecture, writing and numerical systems, languages, political institutions, and religious beliefs are recognizably closely related. Such similarities are more specific than would result from a simple response to similar environmental conditions. Renfrew gives the example of Mayan ceremonial centers organized around a central complex that incorporates square-based pyramids, plazas, and courtyards in a particular pattern, as well as carved stone stelae using the same system of glyphs (1986:4-5). These material homologies are seen as manifestations of nonmaterial homologies, and as developments closely related to long-term interaction.

Renfrew distinguishes cultural change related to peer polity interaction from "exogamous" and "endogamous" change (1986:5-7). According to him, the former often is used as an explanation in "models of dominance," where change is considered to be due to contact with more "advanced" polities. External influences are seen as essential in diffusionist, center-periphery, and systems analysis approaches. For example, James Hill states that systems will remain in equilibrium unless outside sources act upon them: "no system can change itself" (Hill 1977:76). "Endogamous" change is brought into play by analysts examining a political entity in isolation from external socioeconomic interaction. Prime mover explanations, such as population increase or irrigation plus intensification of agriculture, coupled with postitive feedback, often are tied to this sort of change. Change due to peer polity interaction is intermediate between endogamous and exogamous change. It is not instigated from outside the system as a whole, but also is not situated entirely within a given polity. It operates regionally, from "the assemblage of the interacting polities" (Renfrew 1986:6). Although external interactions are not ignored, they are seen as less significant than intraregional interactions.

An analysis of peer polity interaction runs the risk of circularity if it centers exclusively on trait distributions. To avoid this, it must first establish the prior existence of contact among roughly equivalent polities, then establish the occurrence of contemporaneous mutual change (usually related to an increase in organizational complexity), and finally propose a mechanism through which the observed contact could have facilitated the observed change. Change may be manifest as new architectural features, new conceptual systems, "assemblages of specific and special artifacts which may be associated with high status," or new customs, such as burial practices, "reflecting and perhaps reinforcing the social organisation" (Renfrew 1986:8). Among participating polities, there ordinarily are webs of relationships, not single monolithic contact points (cf. McKivergan 1995). Of importance to a complete analysis are the exact nature of the interactions, and the particular individuals or groups of individuals between whom they take place. Interaction may take the form of, or result in: (1) competition, including warfare (cf. Carniero 1977) or competitive emulation (including gift exchange and the erection of large monuments); (2) "symbolic entrainment," defined as "the tendency for a developed symbolic system [e.g., of writing, of social organization] to be adopted when it comes into contact with a less-developed one with which it does not strikingly conflict"; (3) transfer/acceptance of innovations, both technomic and ideotechnic; or (4) increased exchange in material resources, eventually resulting in increased production, craft specialization, or the development of new institutions for receiving and distributing goods (Renfrew 1986:8-10, quotation from 8).

One difficulty in applying this model to nonliterate societies is determining that archaeologically recognizable units are indeed politically equivalent and autonomous; another is determining system boundaries (Cherry and Renfrew 1986:150, 152). In nonhierarchical societies, in particular, it is difficult to recognize the "highest order political unit," because "it is characteristic of many such societies to be organised on a segmentary basis, so that what represents an operationally relevant unit is defined relativistically, with reference to a particular situation" (Cherry and Renfrew 1986:151; Shennan 1986:148). In response to this problem, peer polity principles have been used to carry out analyses between "whole 'core' regions or culture areas" that might well include a number of autonomous groups. Examples include Stephen Shennan's study of third millennium B.C. European regions and David Braun's exploration of relations between Illinois and Ohio Hopewellian regions (Braun 1986; Shennan 1986). Joseph Caldwell's concept of "interaction spheres" was a forerunner to analysis on this scale (Caldwell 1964; Renfrew 1986:6). As Shennan puts it, "as far as peer polity interaction is concerned, the key question is whether the parallel developments in a number of adjacent regions have any connection between them, and whether they would have been different if the connection had not been present" (1986:147).

The peer polity model appears to have possible relevance to several aspects of indigenous interaction and change in eastern North America. Thus, I looked at possible peer polity interactions among late prehistoric Fort Ancient autonomous units (settlements or settlement systems), and also between the Fort Ancient culture area (in whole or in part) and adjacent culture areas with which they seem to have close, long-term relations and structurally homologous material culture. Considering protohistoric times, I looked, in addition, for a possible coupling of exogamous change, ultimately from European sources, with changes promoted by peer polity interaction.

CHAPTER 3

Contact and Change in Eastern North America after 1492

During the sixteenth and seventeenth centuries, the European presence in eastern North America increased sporadically, gradually impinging upon Native American territories. Disease, warfare, prosetylization, and the demand for furs, skins, and slaves engendered a ripple effect of demographic changes from coastal contact locations to hundreds of miles inland. However, demographic change was nothing new to this region. Large-scale political dynamics and population shifts, some of them within less than a century of European contact, had been going on long before the voyages of Columbus and his competitors. To assess post-Contact changes, an overview of pre-Contact conditions is necessary. For ongoing consultation, Figure 3-1 provides important physiographic and hydrographic information that is not included in other maps.

Late Prehistoric Eastern North America

The 500 years prior to the advent of Europeans to eastern North America saw some large-scale trends in subsistence, settlement patterns, and sociopolitical organization, some significant regional differences in adaption and interaction, and much intraregion smaller-scale variation and change over time. Figure 3-2 shows the general locations of selected late prehistoric and protohistoric archaeological phases and culture areas—prehistorically occupied regions defined by archaeologists on the basis of perceived similarities in material culture—that are discussed in this volume. Archaeologists have become increasingly aware that these were not uniformly populated territories with long-term, well-defined borders, but regions in which settlements or settlement groups, often clustered along waterways, were surrounded by unpopulated areas used for hunting or buffer zones (Anderson 1991; Dye 1990:214; Gramly 1977, 1988; Hickerson 1965; Milner et al. 1991; Snow 1994, 1996). Neither were they static: over time, particular localities waxed and waned in regional and interregional influence, and subregions were settled or emptied of population in response to both climatic and sociopolitical cycles (e.g., Anderson 1991, 1994; Milner et al. 1992; Scarry 1996; Snow 1996). The series of summary maps for eastern North America ca. A.D. 900–1100, A.D. 1250–1300, A.D. 1400–1450, and A.D. 1540 published by David Anderson (1991: Figs. 2-5), plus an unpublished map for ca. A.D. 1600–1650 (Milner et al. 1992), effectively illustrate these tendencies and trends.

Almost everywhere from the Great Lakes south, maize agriculture, sedentism, and shell-tempered pottery increased in prominence during this half-millennium period, but details of lifeways varied considerably. Four over-arching archaeological traditions recognized for the interior eastern United States of this period are Mississippian, Oneota, Iroquoian, and Fort Ancient.

Mississippian Peoples

Hallmarks of Mississippian groups included cleared-field maize agriculture, hierarchical settlement patterns, settlements centered on large plazas bordered by burial and substructure platform mounds, complex iconography, and mortuary practices interpreted as indicative of multilevel ranked societies or complex chiefdoms with ascriptive status differentiation (Anderson 1990; J. Brown 1971, 1985, 1991, 1996; Emerson and Lewis 1991; Galloway 1989; Hatch 1976; Jones 1982; Knight 1989; Larson and Kelly 1957; Milner 1984; Moore 1996; Pauketat 1994; Peebles 1974; Scarry 1994b, 1996; B. Smith 1978:479-88, 1986:53-63, 1990; Steponaitis 1978; Stoltman 1991; Welch 1991). However, cultural expression was by no means uniform across the entire Southeast (e.g. Blitz 1993; Brown 1981; Drooker 1994d; Green and Munson 1978; Lewis and Kneberg 1946; O'Brien 1994; Polhemus 1985; Pollack et al. 1996; Rogers and Smith 1995; Scarry 1994a, 1996; K. Smith 1992; Steponaitis 1991; Sullivan 1986). Interaction networks resulted in far-ranging transport of materials and artifacts, some of them probably made by specialist craftspeople, which apparently were utilized most commonly by high-ranking elites. The most important items, of embossed copper, engraved marine shell, and finely

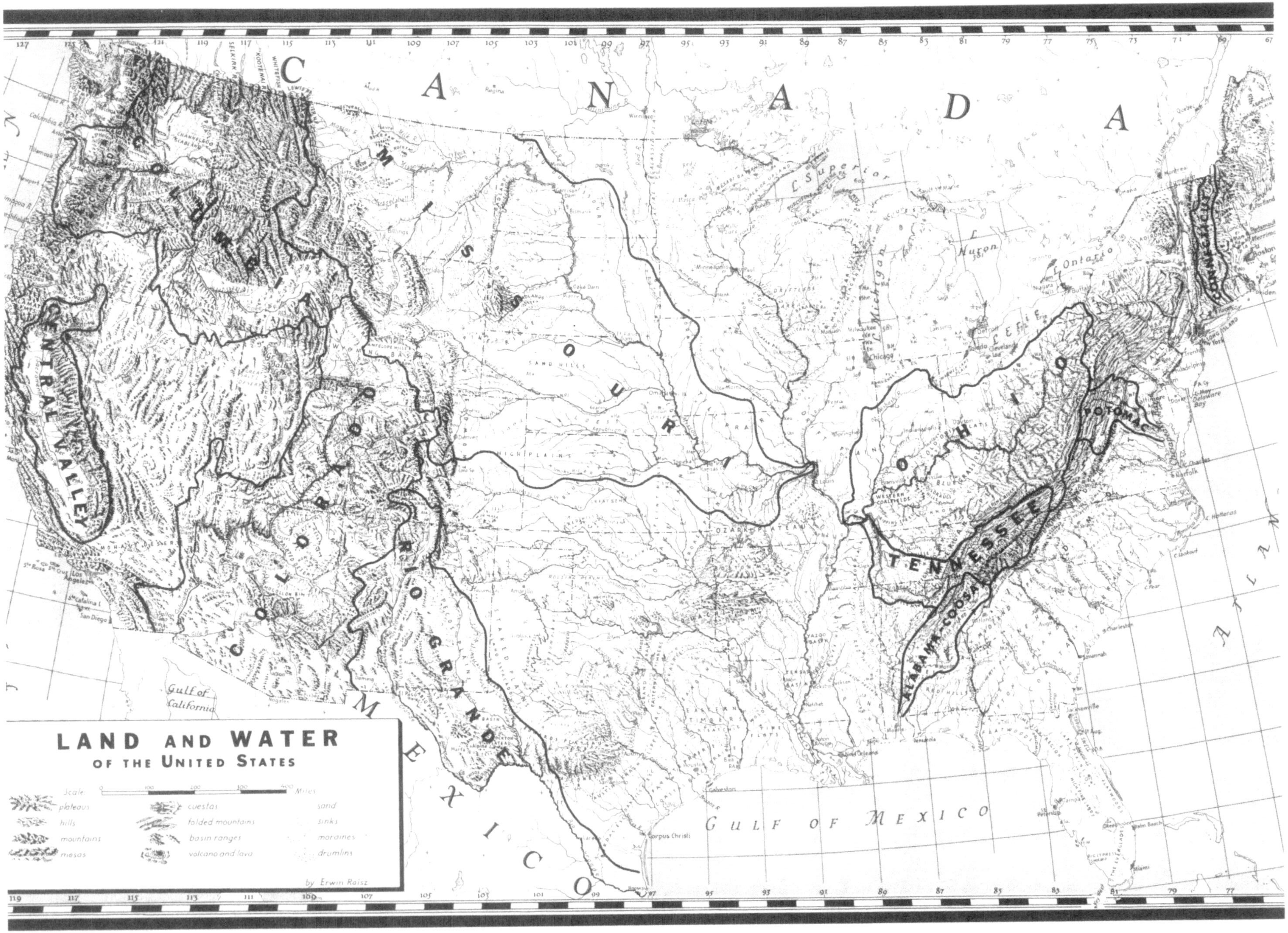
LAND AND WATER
OF THE UNITED STATES
Scale
Miles
plateaus
hills
mountains
mesas
cuestas
folded mountains
basin ranges
volcano and lava
sand
sinks
moraines
drumlins
by Erwin Raisz
CANADA
MEXICO
GULF OF MEXICO
Gulf of California
COLUMBIA
MISSOURI
COLORADO
RIO GRANDE
CENTRAL VALLEY
OHIO
TENNESSEE
ALABAMA-COOSA
POTOMAC
CONNECTICUT
L. Superior
L. Michigan
L. Huron
L. Erie
L. Ontario
SAND HILLS
HIGH PLAINS
STAKED PLAINS
Chicago
Galveston
Corpus Christi
San Diego
Miami

crafted exotic lithic materials, constituted supralocal symbols that signaled the relative ranks of leaders within multilevel complex chiefdoms (J. Brown 1975, 1983, 1996; Brown, Kerber, and Winter 1990; Drooker 1991a; Galloway 1989; Goad and Noakes 1978; Kelly 1991; Larson 1993; Peebles and Kus 1977; Phillips and Brown 1978).

Kinship structure, postulated as necessarily conducive to observed evolution and devolution cycles of social complexity, probably consisted of exogamous matrilineal ranked clans/lineages separated into ranked dual divisions/moieties and possibly crosscut by internal individual ranking associated with birth order (Knight 1990; Widmer 1994). In the Dallas sites of eastern Tennessee, marine shell gorgets with zoomorphic, anthropomorphic, and geometric motifs, usually found with women and children, have been proposed as clan symbols (Lewis and Lewis 1995:20); the same function has been proposed for zoomorphic ceramic vessels at Moundville (Peebles 1971:83), with various aspects of site bilateral symmetry there perhaps related to dual-division distinctions (Knight 1993; Peebles 1971:83-84). For complex chiefdoms, production and curation of stone, ceramic, and wood male or paired male and female statues, together with the curation and special treatment of bones of selected individuals, are seen as objectifying hereditary class distinctions through the veneration of ancestor figures (Brown 1985; Knight 1986). In general, members of elite classes were interred separately and with a greater expenditure of energy (e.g., in mounds versus cemeteries) and were given more, more "valuable," and more symbolically significant grave goods than others (e.g., J. Brown 1975; Hatch 1976; Larson 1971; Peebles and Kus 1977). Decorated ceramics were important as mortuary and ritual vessels (Emerson 1989; Sears 1973; Steponaitis 1983), and their great stylistic and iconographic variation has inspired much archaeological research. The large number of different vessel forms (see, for example, Hally 1983; Hathcock 1976; Steponaitis 1983) serves to differentiate Mississippian ceramic assemblages from those of neighboring culture areas (Hall 1986).

The pre-eminence of particular large polities with major ceremonial centers shifted in location over time, from Cahokia, in Illinois across from the Mississippi-Missouri River confluence (most active in the eleventh and twelfth centuries), to polities farther south, including Spiro in eastern Oklahoma (thirteenth and fourteenth centuries), Lake Jackson in northwestern Florida (thirteenth through fifteenth centuries), Moundville in central Alabama (fourteenth and fifteenth centuries) and Etowah and Little Egypt in northwestern Georgia (fourteenth and early sixteenth centuries) (Figure 3-2). After about 1350, major depopulation occurred in the lower Ohio Valley and the central Mississippi Valley south of the Missouri River, with new large population centers aggregating south of northern Arkansas and northern Tennessee (Anderson 1991:Fig. 4). By the beginning of the sixteenth century, there is so little evidence for active settlements in the Middle Cumberland River valley and formerly populous areas in eastern Missouri, west-central and southern Illinois, western Kentucky, and southern Indiana that they have been designated a "Vacant Quarter" (Anderson 1991: Fig. 5; Williams 1980, 1990). The only exception may be the small cluster of Caborn-Welborn villages at the confluence of the Ohio and Wabash rivers (Figure 3-2), a few of which have produced early European-derived trade goods (Green and Munson 1978; Moorehead 1906; Pollack and Munson 1995; Pollack et al. 1996). However, most radiocarbon dates center on the late fourteenth-fifteenth centuries (Pollack et al. 1996:3, Table 1). Caborn-Welborn sites differ from their Angel phase predecessors in lacking platform mounds and a single large ceremonial center. Farther south, other major population shifts took place by the late fifteenth century, including, among others, the devolution and disappearance of the Moundville polity and the abandonment of all but the extreme upper Savannah River basin (Anderson 1994; Peebles 1987). The pan-southeastern exchange in preciosities declined after about 1350, while polity nucleation and warfare increased (Anderson 1994:137; Dye 1995; Steinen 1992). Through all these changes, Mississippian peoples' chosen environment was the highest-quality horticultural land of major river floodplains, with preference for locations adjacent to differing physiographic zones that would allow a variety of subsistence activities as additions to their mainstay crop of maize. Within subregions, the locations of preeminent sites shifted from century to century (e.g., King 1995; Sullivan 1995). One important factor probably was loss of soil fertility (Baden 1995).

A number of researchers have considered and rejected climatic change, such as the onset of the so-called Little Ice Age perhaps by the early fifteenth century (cf. Keigwin 1996: Fig. 4B, n.9), as the primary cause of major demographic shifts (see, e.g., Anderson 1991:16-17; Morse and Morse 1983:301; Pauketat 1992:43; Williams 1990:175-76). Nevertheless, environmental factors probably did contribute to some extent. David Anderson's very detailed study of rainfall fluctuations and food production potential in the Savannah River basin has demonstrated significant connections between localized growing season fluctuations and the rise and fall of regional chiefdoms. Apparently equally important, however, were political pressures from the development of strong chiefdoms in neighboring river basins (Anderson 1994:274-89, 324-29; cf. Hally 1996).

Oneota Peoples

The Oneota archaeological tradition appears to have developed in the upper Mississippi Valley, in southern Wisconsin and adjacent Minnesota, Iowa, and Illinois, concurrently and in interaction with the Mississippian tradition to its south (Brown 1965; Brown and O'Brien 1990; Gibbon 1986, 1972, 1982; Hall 1962, 1986, 1991:23-27; McKern 1945; Overstreet 1978, 1995;

Figure 3-1 (*facing page*). Physiographic map of the eastern United States. (From map entitled "Land and Water of the United States," copyright by Erwin Raisz, reprinted with permission of GEOPLUS, Danvers, Mass.)

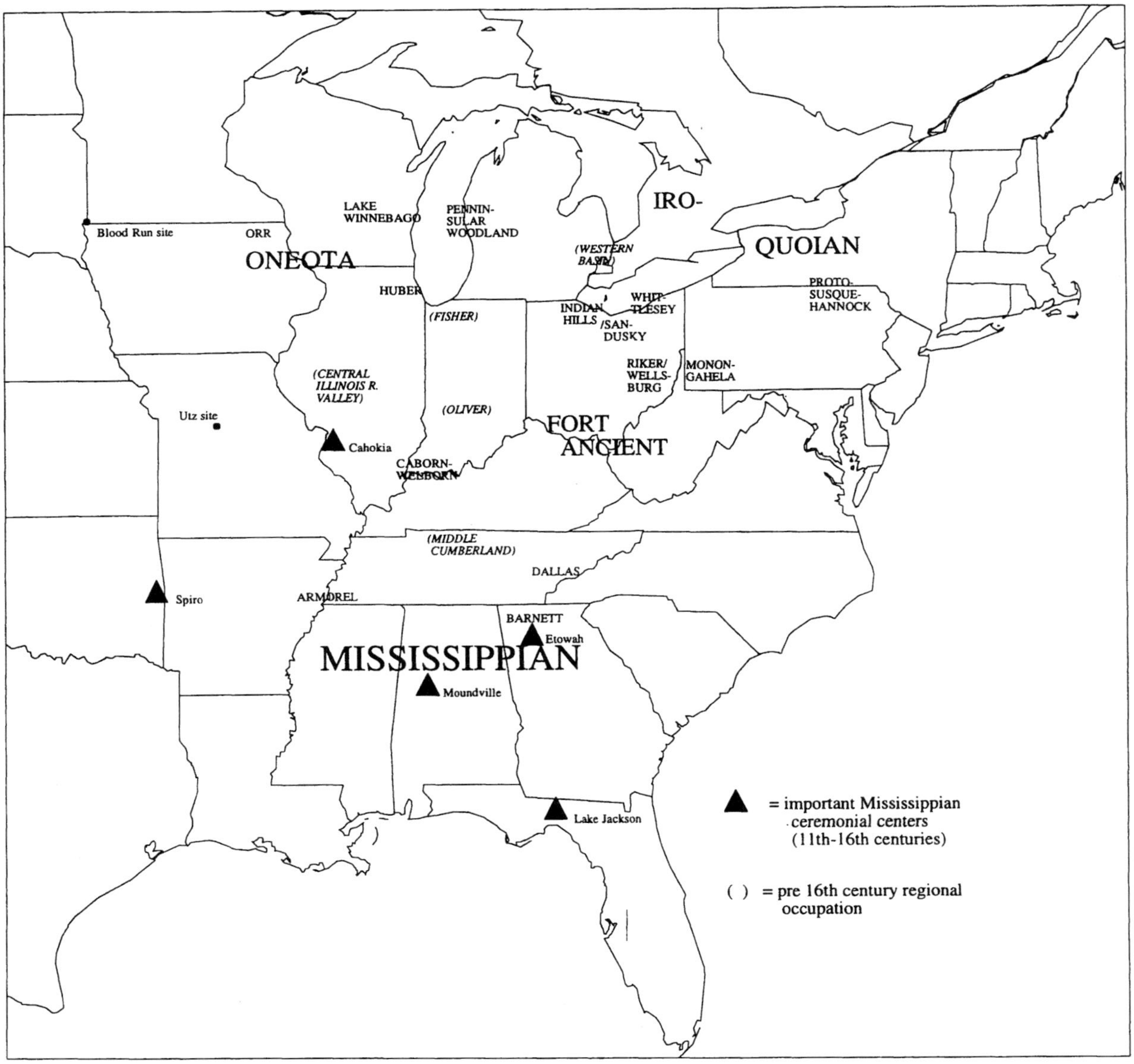

Figure 3-2. North American archaeological culture areas and selected sites mentioned in text.

Wedel 1959; cf. Griffin 1943:286-302). In Illinois after the decline of Cahokia, Oneota settlements could be found in the west-central part of the state, the Illinois River valley, and the area around Cahokia itself, but after about A.D. 1450 they seem to have persisted mainly close to the southern end of Lake Michigan, into northwestern Indiana (Anderson 1991: Fig. 5; Bettarel and Smith 1973; Brown and O'Brien 1990; Faulkner 1972; Milner et al. 1984; Nolan and Conrad 1993; Santure et al. 1990). At the same time, after about 1300 (Anderson 1991: Fig. 4), Oneota occupation in Wisconsin contracted to the area around Lake Winnebago in the east, and the Mississippi Valley around LaCrosse and adjacent Iowa and Minnesota (Orr phase) in the west (Gibbon 1986). By the protohistoric period, the Oneota center of gravity was much farther west than earlier, with settlement areas scattered across Iowa and northern Missouri, to the Missouri River valley in Kansas, Nebraska, and South Dakota (Bray 1991; Collins 1988-89; Gibbon 1994; Harvey 1979; Henning 1970, 1994; Sasso 1993; M. Wedel 1959; W. Wedel 1959:131-72); Wisconsin appears to have been virtually depopulated between about 1520 and 1620 (Green 1993). The lure seems to have been bison, which became increasingly important over time, supplementing, and in some part displacing, the maize horticulture, gathering, fishing, and smaller game hunting (all of which emphasized wetlands resources) that sustained earlier populations.

Interaction with Mississippian populations during the Cahokian heyday was significant, as indicated by the distribution of artifacts such as ritually important Ramey Incised ceramics, marine shell long-nosed god masks, and early styles of circular marine shell gorgets (Brown et al. 1990; Emerson 1989; Hall 1986, 1991; Kelly 1991). During the fourteenth century, Oneota and Mississippian peoples appear to have lived in extremely close proximity in the central Illinois River valley (Esarey and Santure 1990). Annular marine shell gorgets provide a link to Fort Ancient sites (Conrad 1991b:154, 1996). The distribution of Oneota redstone/catlinite disk pipes is one of the strongest indicators of continuing interaction after the fourteenth century with Mississippian peoples in the central Mississippi Valley, Caborn-Welborn region, and the interior Southeast, as well as with contemporaneous Fort Ancient peoples (Brown 1989; Drooker 1992a; Green 1993:300; Pollack and Munson 1994:14; Pollack et al. 1996:24; Salter 1977; Sigstad 1973). At late Oneota sites, there is a small but significant proportion of materials, artifacts, traits, and symbols associated with peoples of the Plains and Southwest (Boszhardt 1993; Green 1993:301).

Settlement patterns, burial practices, and iconography bespeak a less stratified social organization than is associated with Mississippian groups (Harn and Klobuchar 1991; Herold et al. 1990:95-97; Hollinger 1993, 1995; Kreisa 1993; Lurie 1994; Overstreet 1978; Santure et al. 1990; Wedel 1959:42-46). Villages and campsites are reported, but no clusters of hierarchically-sized ceremonial centers and satellite settlements. Platform mounds were very rare in Oneota settlements (cf. Brown 1982:108). Average house size was greatest during the Classic Horizon, ca. 1300-1650, than earlier or later, by a 1:6:2 ratio; settlement size and duration might also have been at their height then (Overstreet 1978:39-45; Hollinger 1993, 1995; Lurie 1994; cf. Green 1993). Large corn storage pits were common.

Mortuary offerings and methods of interment varied over time and space, but never seem to reflect the extreme social stratification objectified by differential grave goods and burial practices in large Mississippian polities. Burial mounds, some with adjacent cemeteries, appear to be earliest in time, their use probably ending by ca. 1300; at the same time, flexed burials gave way to extended ones, always with some proportion of secondary interments (Brown 1993; Hall 1962:134-46; Kreisa 1993). Separate cemeteries continued in use after 1300 (e.g., Henning 1995; Kreisa 1993:44; Santure et al. 1990). By 1400 in western Wisconsin, burials inside houses were very common (O'Gorman and Halverson 1993). Both cemetery and village interments are typical of later Oneota practices (Bray 1991; Henning 1970; Herold et al. 1990; Lurie 1994; M. Wedel 1959).

Grave goods included ceramic vessels, medicine bundles, pipes, flat and tubular copper emblems, and a variety of tools and ornaments (Bray 1961a; Hall 1962:134-46; Harvey 1979:135-41; Herold et al. 1990:88-92; Kreisa 1993; O'Gorman and Halverson 1993; Santure et al. 1990:75-110; M. Wedel 1959). In general, it is older adult males who seem to have had greater numbers of grave goods as well as more "special" items than other people, but children often were buried with exotic ornaments. Women, on average, had the smallest and least diverse surviving assemblages, but important exceptions include possible female ritual specialists at late northeastern Illinois sites (Herold et al. 1990:13, 18, 91; Lurie 1994).

Although Oneota peoples employed a number of symbols that were elaborated within the Mississippian "Southeastern Ceremonial Complex," they often utilized them in different ways. For example, the "hawk" and "forked eye" motifs so common on Mississippian embossed copper and engraved shell ornaments and cups (e.g., Phillips and Brown 1978, 1984; Strong 1989) are engraved onto stone "tablets" and pipes in central Missouri (Bray 1963). The nested chevron motif that is such a common decorative element on typical Oneota jars has been hypothesized to represent the tail of the hawk or thunderbird (Benn 1989; Hall 1991:24, 28-29; cf. Brown 1965:112-48). In turn, this bird motif is thought to represent the upper level of a "hierarchy of descent through [ranked] clans" (Benn 1989:252), in which an upper, sky, moiety and associated bird- and warrior-related clans would outrank an earth/water moiety containing clans with land and water creatures as totems. Benn hypothesized that both within-group and between-group relationships would be formalized by means of such ranked dualities (1989:253). This is consistent with historically documented forms of kinship among both Chiwere Siouan and Central Algonquian groups in the region, which all incorporated patrilineal lineages organized into clans. In turn, clans usually were grouped into divisions that most often took the form of hereditary earth- and sky-related moieties (e.g., Brown 1965:82-92; Callender 1962).

The Oneota archaeological tradition has been described on occasion as "ethnically mixed," because several of its recent components have been identified with historically known Algonquian and Chiwere Siouan groups, by means of the direct historical approach (W. Wedel 1937). These include the (Siouan) Ioway with Orr phase sites in northeastern Iowa, the (Siouan) Missouri with the Utz site in the Chariton River region of central Missouri, and the (Algonquian) Illini with the historical Zimmerman/Starved Rock/Hotel Plaza site area (around Fort St. Louis) and earlier and later sites in western Illinois (Figure 3-2; see also Figures 3-6, 3-7) (Bray 1978, 1991; M. Brown 1979; Emerson and Brown 1992; Grantham 1993; Schnell 1974; M. Wedel 1981, 1986). Other Siouan groups suggested as descendents from Oneota predecessors include the Oto, Kansa, Osage, Omaha, and perhaps Dakota (Hollinger 1995:142). The connection of the (Siouan) Winnebago with Lake Winnebago phase sites in eastern Wisconsin is still debated (C. Mason 1976; R. Mason 1993; Overstreet 1994:14-18). A currently ascendant hypothesis is that Winnebago-related groups occupied much of eastern Wisconsin and northeastern Illinois (including the Huber archaeological culture area at the tip of Lake Michigan) until a disastrous military defeat by the Illini and their allies ca. 1640 (Hall 1993, 1995; cf. J. Brown 1990:159). The identity of Huber phase people previously had been proposed, variously, as Illini, (Algonquian) Miami, Winnebago, or Chiwere Siouan (summarized by R. Mason 1986:216). Illini peoples presently

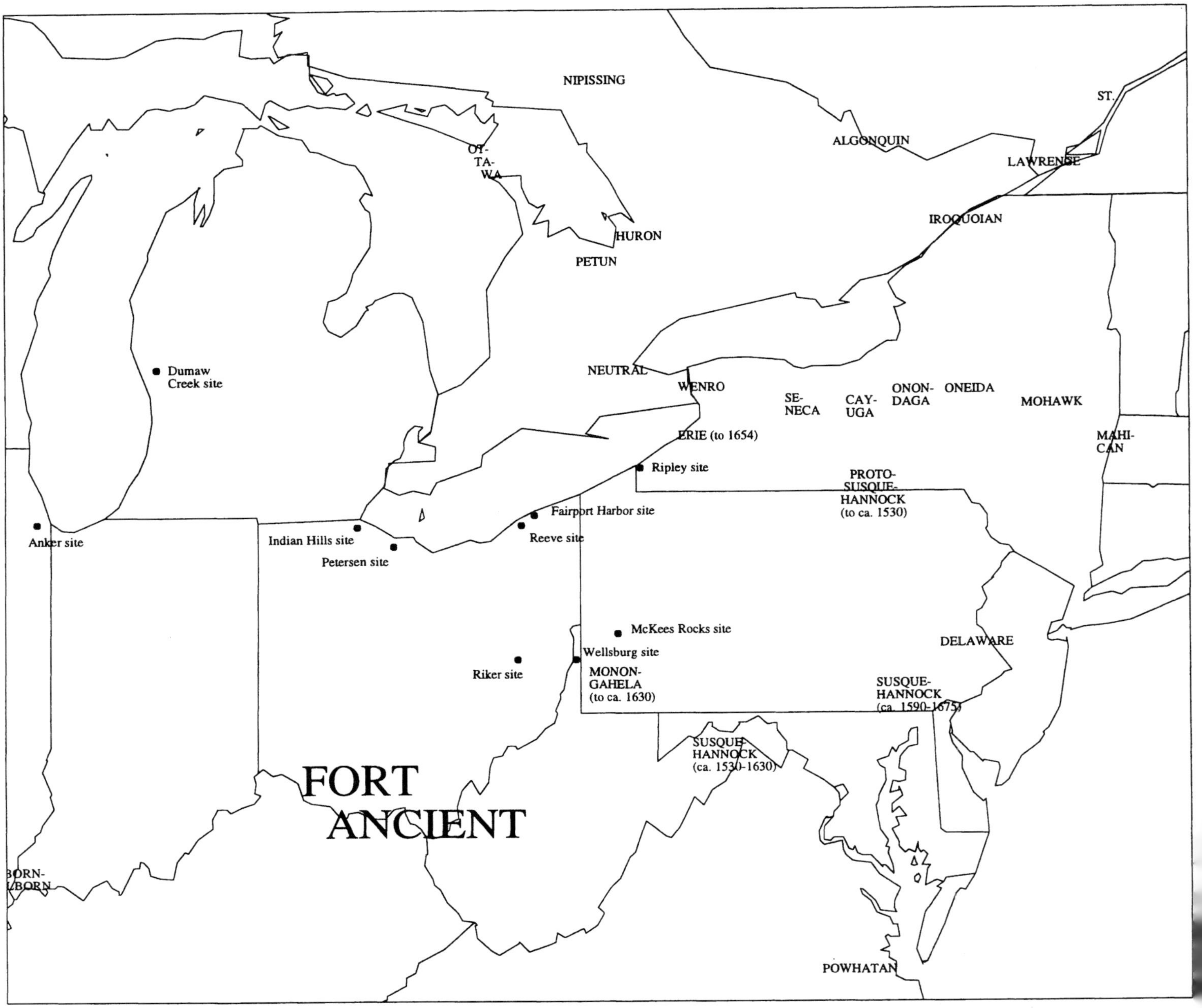

Figure 3-3. Sixteenth-century locations of Iroquoian and nearby groups, including selected archaeological sites mentioned in text.

are being described as non-Oneota, with links to Danner and Keating pottery types rather than to Huber types (Emerson and Brown 1992; Grantham 1993).

Iroquoian Peoples

Iroquoian territory encompassed southern Ontario, southern Quebec, New York, and portions of Pennsylvania (Bamann et al. 1992; Ellis and Ferris 1990; Hayes 1991; Tuck 1978). The late prehistoric Iroquoian settlement pattern, in place by the end of the fifteenth century, of very widely spaced village clusters surrounded by uninhabited areas that served as buffer zones and deer-hunting areas (Gramly 1977; Lennox and Fitzgerald 1990:437-38) was preceded, up to about the fourteenth century, by three broader areas of occupation across central New York and north of Lakes Erie and Ontario (Snow 1995b:64, 1996). Across the region, many historically known groups have been traced backward several centuries in time with enough confidence that their names have been assigned to particular clusters of prehistoric sites, although most researchers would not push this connection farther than about the late fifteenth century (Snow 1995b:62).

The Erie, Seneca, Cayuga, Oneida, Onondaga, and Mohawk, whose settlement areas stretched across New York from west to east, are reasonably well anchored, as are late prehistoric Huron-Petun and Neutral-Wenro areas at the southeastern tip of Lake Huron and the western end of Lake Ontario (Figures 3-2, 3-3) (Bradley 1987a; Engelbrecht 1991; Lennox and Fitzgerald 1990; Niemczycki 1984; Ramsden 1990a; Snow 1995c; Tuck 1971; White 1976; Wray and Schoff 1953; Wray et al. 1987; Wray et al. 1991). Other late prehistoric Iroquoian groups lived at the eastern end of Lake Ontario (Jefferson County, New York) and along the Saint Lawrence (Engelbrecht 1995; Jamieson 1990; Pendergast 1991b; Pratt 1991). Western Basin peoples living north of the western end of Lake Erie prior to the fifteenth century have been conjectured to be Iroquoian (e.g., Stothers 1978, 1991); however, many researchers see them rather as a Central Algonquian group, known historically as the Fire Nation, long-term enemies of the Neutral (e.g., Lennox and Fitzgerald 1990:438; Murphy and Ferris 1990). The historically known Susquehannocks of the lower Susquehanna River are believed to have migrated during the protohistoric period from an area near the river's headwaters, at the New York-Pennsylvania line (Funk 1993; Kent 1984). Brashler has hypothesized that the migration was not direct, but involved sequential occupation of at least two sites on the South Branch of the Potomac in West Virginia (Brashler 1987:27-28; Manson and MacCord 1941, 1944) prior to occupation of the Susquehanna River Schultz site starting in the late 1590s (cf. Sempowski 1994:61). A recently excavated proto-Susquehannock village in Moorefield, West Virginia, extends the South Branch Potomac occupation to 1600-1630 (Patrick Trader, pers. comm.) This is consistent with the presence of polychrome glass beads at yet another site in the area (Brashler 1987:2; M. Smith, pers. comm.). The Monongahela archaeological culture area at the southwestern corner of Pennsylvania might or might not be part of the Iroquoian sphere. Johnson has proposed that its protohistoric occupants were an elusive Iroquoian group known as the Black Minqua (Johnson 1992, 1994).

Although corn was being utilized as early as A.D. 700 in southern Ontario (Warrick 1990:332), both heavy reliance on maize horticulture and stable villages of at least one hectare in size appear to have developed only gradually, up to two centuries earlier in the west than the east (Bamann et al. 1992:442). For example, in Cayuga territory, this occurred ca. 1300-1350 (Niemczycki 1984), whereas in Ontario, corn was a diet staple by about 1200 (Williamson 1990:312; Williamson and Robertson 1994:36). Seasonal fishing, hunting, and nut-gathering camps also were utilized both prior to and concurrent with the larger, horticulturally centered settlements (Bamann et al. 1992:441). Iroquoians practiced swidden agriculture. Periodic village movement was by no means completely contingent upon soil depletion, but also was conditioned by factors such as depletion of firewood and game, insect infestation of cornfields, accumulation of refuse, and chronic warfare (Bamann et al. 1992:445; Starna et al. 1984). Large-scale climatic fluctuations, such as the Little Ice Age, are also thought to have been important, particularly for groups expanding into marginal areas (Bamann et al. 1992:446); this factor might help to account for the risk-buffering exchange of maize for meat and fish between Hurons and Northern Algonquian hunters and gatherers who lived still farther north (Fox 1990; Warrick 1990:372, 374; cf. Wright 1967, 1968).

During late prehistoric times, virtually all Iroquoian groups resided in rectangular longhouses within compact palisaded villages. (The Monongahela, however, built circular structures that were organized around plazas [Johnson 1992:1-2; Mayer-Oakes 1955:98-103]). In New York, most Iroquois villages—located on defensible uplands away from waterways—apparently were moved approximately every generation, a change from pre-fifteenth century practices when occupation periods were longer (Snow 1995b:66). In southern Ontario, at least some villages were occupied for 50 years or more, with repeated episodes of rebuilding due to enlargement (Ramsden 1990a:374-75). In both areas, longhouses accommodated kin groups of multiple families; an increase in average house size over time is interpreted as a response to increasingly larger matrilineages. For the proto-Huron-Petun, this seems to coincide with explosive population growth during the fourteenth century (Warrick 1990:353). In Ontario, the maximum house length, over 100 meters, was achieved during the fifteenth century, after which house size declined; in New York, houses up to 120 meters date to the same period (Fitzgerald 1992:4; Lennox and Fitzgerald 1990:444-45; Tuck 1978:328; Warrick 1990:374). In Huronia, village spatial organization changed over time, probably reflecting increasing complexity in social organization: from haphazard placement of houses, to clusters that are postulated to be associated with particular clans or other subgroups (Ramsden 1990a:374-75; Warrick 1990). Most researchers see no reason not to project early historical kinship organization—strongly matrilineal and matrilocal (Fenton 1968:309-12)—backward in time for at least half a millennium (Snow 1995b:71; but see also Williamson 1990:317-19).

Mortuary treatments differ among regions and over time, objectifying different levels of group identity and solidarity. Group interment of secondary burials, in ossuaries or multiple bundle burials, can be traced back several centuries at Ontario Iroquoian sites. Such practices culminate in the historically recorded Huron Feast of the Dead ceremonies, during which bones of many individuals from different settlements were mixed together (Dodd et al. 1990:354-56; Kenyon 1982; Lennox and Fitzgerald 1990:452-56; Ramsden 1990a:380-81; Spence 1994). Other burial forms include longhouse interment, particularly for small children (e.g., Lennox and Fitzgerald 1990:455; Williamson 1978). Prehistoric central and western New York Iroquois and Susquehannock most often were interred as primary, flexed burials in cemeteries separate from villages (Kent 1984:295-406; Tuck 1978:332-33). Historically recorded clan or lineage cemeteries may well have developed early, in the form of two or more cemeteries associated with a particular site (Tuck 1978:332; but cf. Wray et al. 1987:247-48). Monongahela burials, most often primary and flexed, were within villages, with children often inside houses (Davis 1984; Johnson 1992:3-4).

Few formal mortuary analyses directed at elucidating prehistoric Iroquoian social structure have been carried out. At Ripley, New York, a fourteenth–early seventeenth century ceremonial site on the Lake Erie shore, two tiers of social ranking were evident, based on number and variety of grave goods (Sullivan and Coffin 1995; Sullivan et al. 1995). Mortuary goods included pots (with many people of all ages and sexes), ornaments, projectile points, tools, pipes, and ceremonial items such as red ochre. Adults, mostly males, had greater numbers and more types of items, suggesting a "wider range of social roles" (Sullivan and Coffin 1995:179); more males than females had ceremonial objects, and seven males (of 238 individuals) were associated with cut bear maxilla positioned as for a headdress, probably a status marker. No horizontal differeration could be discerned, in spite of the known importance of clans, and clan matrons, in Iroquoian society (cf. Sempowski 1986). In another study, changes in mortuary treatment at a series of Seneca cemeteries from about 1540 to 1690, including reversal in burial orientation from east to west and marked increases in grave goods, have been hypothesized to reflect new beliefs associated with the late prehistoric formation of the League of the Iroquois (Sempowski 1991).

This confederacy resulted in cessation of (archaeologically apparent) hostilities among the Five Nations, but perhaps in increased warfare directed toward outside groups, and probably was consolidated by the end of the fifteenth century (Bradley 1987a:34-47; Richter 1992:30-38, 300). A later date of 1538 also has been proposed (Warrick 1990:378, citing Snow 1987). James Bradley sees League formation as directly associated with a renaissance of long-distance exchange, apparently initiated by the late fifteenth century when very small amounts of marine shell begin to appear at a few Iroquoian sites, probably transported from the Chesapeake via the Susquehanna River. This trickle grew into a significant trade axis by early historical times (Bradley 1987a:90-93). Evidence for external interaction prior to that time is extremely sparse, particularly when contrasted with significant evidence for interregional interaction during much earlier Adena/Hopewell times (Bradley 1987a:93; Fitzgerald 1992:6-7; Spence et al. 1990; Williamson and Robertson 1994; Wright 1994:53-55). Although interaction between Hurons and Northern Algonquians was probably in progress from at least the fourteenth century, when proto-Hurons expanded northward (Dodd et al. 1990:322-23), evidence for outside contacts in other directions is difficult to come by. Very little exotic raw material and virtually no exotic artifacts have been found at pre-sixteenth-century Iroquoian sites in Ontario, New York, and Pennsylvania (Bradley 1987a:90-93; Ceci 1989b:68; Lennox and Fitzgerald 1990; Pendergast 1989:97-99; Williamson 1990:300). The only example I have found of an Oneota-style redstone disk pipe in Iroquoian territory, at the late prehistoric (mid-sixteenth century) Cayuga or Seneca Reed Fort/Richmond Mills site, had been ritually "killed" (Hamilton 1967:24; Witthoft et al. 1953:92, 102). The distinctive New York and Ontario Iroquoian ceramic pipes and grit-tempered, high-collared ceramics generally are not found prehistorically outside Iroquoian-occupied territories (although selected stylistic elements do turn up in ceramic vessels of immediately neighboring groups). For example, trace element analysis of ceramic pipes has shown much interaction among contemporaneous late prehistoric Mohawk communities, but little between them and their Algonquian neighbors to the east (Kuhn 1986, 1987b).

Outside influences on Iroquoian development have been postulated in the form of core-periphery interaction emanating from Cahokia and of diffuse "Mississippification" from the broader Southeast (Dincauze and Hasenstab 1989; Jamieson 1992). However, a more likely model seems to be one of largely intraregional development, such as proposed by Ronald Williamson and David Robertson (1994), who see the increasing stylistic similarity among southern Ontario and New York ceramics after about 1300 as evidence of internal Iroquoian peer-polity interaction and gradual evolution of more complex sociopolitical systems (1994:38). All was not peace and brotherhood among Iroquoian groups just before the advent of Europeans, however. Warfare, evidenced by population movements, palisades, skeletal trauma, and cannibalism, appears to have been common during the fifteenth–early sixteenth centuries—for instance, between the Neutral and Western Basin peoples, between eastern New York Iroquois (and/or the Huron) and Saint Lawrence Iroquoians, and among western New York groups (Heidenreich 1990:483; Jamieson 1990:403; Lennox and Fitzgerald 1990:486; Trigger 1986:106-8; Warrick 1990:364, 372; Wray et al. 1987:247-48).

Northern Ohio and Central Indiana Groups

Some of the closest neighbors to Fort Ancient territory resided along the southern shore of Lake Erie (Figures 3-2, 3-3). Unlike Mississippian, Oneota, and Iroquoian archaeological cultures, the late prehistoric populations generally are not presented as monolithic, but as culturally differentiated Upper Mississippian groups occupying relatively small areas. A recent summary of northern Ohio late prehistoric traditions names the Riker/Neale's Landing Complex (which others have separated into Neale's Landing Fort Ancient and Riker/Wellsburg) on the Ohio River drainage just west of Pennsylvania, the Whittlesey Tradition on the Lake Erie shore west of Pennsylvania, the Sandusky Tradition to its west, the Fort Meigs/Indian Hills Complex at the western end of Lake Erie, and the (earlier) Younge Tradition just north of that, between Lakes Erie and Huron (Brose 1994:3; cf. Brose 1978).

In general, as of the thirteenth century, groups immediately south of Lake Erie existed as hunters, gatherers, and maize horticulturalists living in small villages (Bowen 1994; Brose 1976, 1994:161-77). Over time, settlement size and house size increased, and maize/squash/beans became more important. By late prehistoric/protohistoric times, villages as large as four hectares are known, such as the Indian Hills site, which had a central plaza surrounded by circular structures (Stothers 1981). Throughout the region, late prehistoric villages were fortified, and located on blufftop sites along rivers; inland hunting stations and lakeshore fishing/fowling stations had short-term usage. (In the Sandusky River area, ditch fortification commenced as early as the fourteenth century.) Few burials are associated with Whittlesey village sites; separate cemeteries are postulated, and at least one early (pre-1250) burial mound is known. In the Sandusky River area, extended, supine burials gave way after ca. 1425 to flexed interment and secondary reburial in ossuaries. Four ossuaries were associated with the Indian Hills site. Nonlocal ceramics and other artifacts in all three areas give evidence of interaction with Fort Ancient groups to the south. The late prehistoric Reeve site on the Chagrin River west of Cleveland produced an extraordinary number and variety of pipes, including clay Iroquoian styles and stone styles typical of late Late Fort Ancient groups, some visually identified as made from Ohio pipestone, perhaps from the Portsmouth area (Ahlstrom 1979; Greenman 1935).

A group of very late prehistoric–protohistoric sites in the upper Ohio Valley often are discussed together as Riker phase or Wellsburg phase settlements (Baker 1988; Buker 1968; Carskadden, 1992a, 1992b, Vietzen 1974; Whitman 1975; James Morton, pers. comm. 1992, 1995; Morton and DaRe 1996). Local pottery types typically are found with notable additions of neighboring types, including Indian Hills, Monongahela, and Fort Ancient. The northernmost such site, McKees Rocks, a stockaded village on a bluff across the Ohio River from Pittsburg, was described, with the Riker site in eastern Ohio, as having more similarities to Fort Ancient than to Monongahela sites (Buker 1968:49). For example, stone vasiform pipes (in a variety of forms) were far more common than ceramic pipes, and extended rather than flexed burials were common. Riker and Bosman in eastern Ohio (see Figure 4-2 below) were fifteenth-sixteenth century villages from which were excavated copper ornaments but no definitely European materials; the latter was protected by palisade and ditch, while the former was surrounded by an earthworks (Carskadden 1992a, 1992b, 1994; Vietzen 1974). The non-stockaded Cullison site has produced at least one European artifact, an iron buckle (James Morton, pers. comm.). Large storage pits have been excavated at several of these sites; small, circular structures defined by postholes were present at Bosman, while both circular and small rectangular structures are reported from Riker (Carskadden 1992a, 1992b; Vietzen 1974).

One more small group of Upper Mississippian late prehistoric settlements should be mentioned. They were located immediately west of Fort Ancient territory, along the White River in the vicinity of Indianapolis and southward. Now known as the Oliver phase, the tradition represented by these sites dates to ca. 900-1400 (Redmond 1993:39). Several Oliver phase sites were described by Griffin (1943:261-67), who drew attention to their ceramics, which show strong ties both to Middle Fort Ancient (e.g., grit and shell tempered jars with rim bands and incised guilloche motifs on necks) and to Fisher tradition Oneota sites at the southern tip of Lake Michigan. Projectile point forms also fall within the Fort Ancient range (Bailey 1993), and a number of tool types are common to both cultures (Dorwin 1971:374-75). Maize and beans were cultivated, and stored in deep cylindrical pit features (Redmond 1993:40-41). At least some of the circular to oval villages, constructed around central open areas, were palisaded, exhibiting "cultural similarities with components of the Anderson phase of southwestern Ohio" (Redmond 1993:41, 1994:15-17; Redmond and McCullough 1996:24-41; Dorwin 1971:301). Only one complete dwelling has been excavated to date, a subrectangular 3-4 × 6 m wall-trench structure (Redmond and McCullough 1996:26-31). The 40 burials at the Bowen site, almost all of them flexed, were disposed in four clusters around the perimeter of the settlement (Dorwin 1971:296-99, Fig. 14).

According to Dorwin, "Fort Ancient pottery is found all across the midsection of Indiana from the southeast to the northwest but it is not found in the southwest or in the northeast" (1971:372). In his overview of northwestern Indiana late prehistoric sites, Charles Faulkner stated that "although its most important relationships are within the Oneota tradition, the Fisher culture...also displays a strong interaction with the Fort Ancient Aspect....There is evidence that the Fisher and Fort Ancient cultures may have been in constant interaction throughout their development," but most intensely so during very late prehistoric and protohistoric times (Faulkner 1972:163). In interpreting these interactions, Dorwin characterized Oliver phase peoples as inhabiting a "frontier transfer zone" between Mississippian in the south and west and Woodland cultures in the north and east (1971:389). According to him, Oliver peoples consisted of mixed populations who interacted with and drew elements of culture from widely separated regions along that zone, which reached from the Mill Creek phase of northwestern Iowa to the Fort Ancient region of the central Ohio River valley (Dorwin 1971:382-90).

Fort Ancient Peoples

Cultural characteristics of Fort Ancient peoples will be presented in more detail below, but a brief summary is included here for comparison with the summary descriptions of prehistoric Mississippian, Oneota, Iroquoian, and other neighboring archaeological traditions.

The Fort Ancient archaeological tradition is found in the Central Ohio River valley from southeastern Indiana and adjacent Kentucky through southern Ohio and northern Kentucky to eastern West Virginia (Figure 3-2), encompassing the period from A.D. 1000/1100 to 1650/1750. Villages of these floodplain horticulturalists are found along the Ohio and its major tributaries almost to the hydrological divides with Lake Erie and the Cumberland/Tennessee river system (Figure 3-1). Hunting camps and other special-purpose sites tend to be found toward the upper reaches of the tributaries. After about 1400, the majority of settlements were located within 20 kilometers of the Ohio River.

Many villages, from all subregions and all time periods, were organized around central plazas (Church 1987:218-20; Drooker 1996a; Graybill 1981:136-39, 165-67; Henderson 1992:265, 269). At least one, the Baum site, included a substructure mound (Mills 1906). However, poor mapping by early archaeologists and little large-scale excavation by modern ones leaves the complete range and developmental sequence of site plans and sizes poorly known. Early single-family-size wall-trench houses (most evident in the west) probably were supplanted by post construction, which occurs during all time periods; semisubterranean structures also are known at earlier sites (Cowan et al. 1990; Drooker 1996a; Graybill 1981:145; Mills 1906:6). Many early dwellings were as small as 10 square meters (Church 1987:220; Drooker 1996a), but larger structures, up to 180 square meters and more, are known from both early and late sites (e.g., Hanson 1975:16; Wheelersburg 1992). At some settlements, a notably large structure adjacent to the plaza may have acted as a public building (Carskadden 1994; Church 1987:214; Hawkins 1994; Lileas 1988:45-46; Nass 1987:178-80, 255; Nass and Yerkes 1995; Robertson 1984:253-54). Large corn storage pits were ubiquitous from at least the thirteenth century onward. Sixteenth century settlements, if not necessarily larger in area than earlier ones, probably were more densely occupied.

Burial mounds were in use up to about A.D. 1300 (Church 1987:220, 223; Drooker 1996a; Henderson 1992:261, 265; Mills 1904, 1906, 1917; Oehler 1973; Smith 1910). Thereafter, and probably concurrently, burial was in villages: around plazas and in and around houses. Individual primary inhumation was the most common, extended in western Fort Ancient territory, and flexed gradually changing over time to extended in the east; multiple and secondary burials also were present (Essenpreis 1982; Evans 1994; Graybill 1981; Hanson 1966, 1975; Mills 1906; Oehler 1973). Ossuary burial is known from at least one thirteenth-century northeastern site (Carskadden 1994). Ornaments and tools, and, at some later sites, pots and pipes, were the most common grave goods. Mortuary analyses of individual sites have indicated no more than one level of authority, and no evidence for ascribed ranking (Essenpreis 1982:54-135, 213-14, 237-39; Evans 1994; Griffin 1992; Holmes 1994). At many sites, child burials frequently included ornaments and exotic materials such as marine shell.

The location of the Fort Ancient territory, at a nexus of important trails and water transportation routes (Henderson et al. 1986; Rountree 1993b; Tanner 1989), makes interaction with people from other culture areas highly likely. Interaction toward the northwest, southwest and southeast was continuous throughout Fort Ancient occupations, as evidenced by moderate amounts of marine shell, including Mississippian engraved gorgets of all style periods, small amounts of native copper, foreign pipes, and a variety of exotic ceramic sherds (Cowan 1987; Drooker 1992a, 1993c, 1993d, 1994c, 1994d; Griffin 1943; Mills 1917; Smith 1910). This is proposed to have been on the rise after about 1400 (Henderson et al. 1992:270; Jack Rossen, pers. comm.), but no diachronic quantitative studies have been done. At least some interaction with northern Ohio and southwestern Pennsylvania also is evident, mainly from ceramics (e.g., Baker 1988; Bowen 1994:2, 62; Brose 1994:163; Whitman 1975). By the late prehistoric period, a significant area apparently lacking permanent settlements surrounded Fort Ancient territory to the west; the closest known villages are in Caborn-Welborn and Huber territory (Figure 3-2; cf. Anderson 1991: Fig. 5).

The post-1400/1450 period, recently designated the Madisonville Horizon, is characterized not only by less widespread settlement locations and a possible increase in external exchange, but also by increased intraregional similarity in ceramic styles (Cowan 1988:8-9; Essenpreis 1988; Griffin 1992:54; Henderson and Turnbow 1987:220-21; Sharp 1990:469-71). Middle Fort Ancient jars, often decorated by guilloche motifs but in distinct subregional styles and a variety of tempers, gave way to shell-tempered smooth and cord-marked jars with undecorated necks and strap handles across the entire region (for many examples, see Griffin 1943).

European Expeditions and Settlements, 1500-1700

For over a century and a half after Columbus's initial voyage, there was little penetration into the interior of eastern North America by Europeans. During the sixteenth century, most activity centered around the fisheries in the north and Spanish exploration and prosetylization in the south (Figure 3-4). Exploratory voyages along the coast were carried out under many European flags, followed by a series of short-term colonization attempts (Table 3-1). Not until 1565, at St. Augustine, was any permanent settlement established.

In the north, Cartier's explorations of the Saint Lawrence and interactions with its residents during the first half of the century (Table 3-1, Figure 3-4) provided a glimpse of the interior that was not enlarged for over sixty years, until the colonization of Quebec in 1608 (Trigger 1986). Fishing and whaling off Newfoundland and in the Gulf of Saint Lawrence included incidental exchange of goods with natives, particularly in the vicinity of semipermanent processing stations (Figure 3-4). By the 1580s, large-scale commercial trade for beaver pelts was underway in the region (Borque 1994:35-42; Borque and Whitehead 1985; Fitzgerald et al. 1993; Turgeon 1990).

A series of Spanish expeditions into the Southeastern interior, of which de Soto's was the most extensive, recorded much information of interest to today's historians, anthropologists, and archaeologists, but after Pardo's expeditions from Santa Elena to eastern Tennessee in the 1560s there was very limited interior travel north of present-day Florida until the arrival of the English in South Carolina a century later (Table 3-1, Figures 3-4, 3-6) (e.g., Clayton et al. 1993; Hudson 1990; Hudson and Tesser 1994:36-122—see particularly Worth 1994; Milanich and Milbrath 1989; Thomas 1990).

Permanent colonies gradually were established along the coast and up the Saint Lawrence during the first half of the seventeenth century, with the four major powers—Spain, France, England, and the Netherlands—each jockeying to establish its own presence (Table 3-1, Figure 3-5). Each had its own priorities, with emphasis on trade, resource exploitation, colonization, and prosetylization varying among them. Rivalries and conflicts in the New World—often carried out with the help of Native American allies or wholly by means of native proxies—mirrored those in the Old. Although Lake Michigan was visited as early as 1634 by Jean Nicolet, only after about 1670 did English colonists and traders begin to travel very far beyond their coastal settlements, at about the same time that French exploration, missionization, and establishment of forts and outposts intensified and expanded westward across the Great Lakes and southward to the mouth of the Mississippi (Figure 3-6) (Braund 1993; Crane 1929; Fausz 1985; Gehring and Starna 1988; Hall 1993; Heidenreich 1990; Jennings 1975, 1984; Merrell 1989; Ray 1974; Rountree 1993a; Tanner 1987; Thwaites 1896-1901; Trigger 1971; Usner 1992; White 1991; Wood et al. 1989).

Patterns of Native American Interaction and Realignment, 1500-1700

Working with the corpus of primary historical data, from chronicles of exploratory expeditions to extensive French and Spanish missionization records to demographic data and financial records of trading companies and nascent colonies, historians are offering increasingly sophisticated analyses of events and interactions during the sixteenth and seventeenth centuries. Their accounts no longer are limited to Eurocentric records of Great Men and Historic Events, but include background and motivation for national, group, and individual action and interaction on both sides of the encounter—both "native" and "newcomer." Combinations of history, ethnohistory, and archaeology are proving particularly fruitful (e.g., Deagan 1983; Galloway 1995; Kent 1984; Walthall 1991; Walthall and Emerson 1992).

How did early Contact Period European incursions affect nearby and distant Native American groups? Among indigenous peoples, the establishment of each new European colony led to complex realignments of alliances and interactions. Shorter or longer "honeymoons" often were followed by local conflict and eventual withdrawal or decimation as a result of warfare or disease (e.g., see Table 3-1). Interior groups were affected differently depending on the history of exploration in their area, their proximity to European settlements and to major travel routes, the priorities of the particular European groups near them, their own priorities and those of their leaders, and their locations and relationships with regard to refugee groups and intermediary groups closer to European settlements.

It is far beyond the scope of this project to explain the complex web of events connected with the first two centuries of European incursion into the New World. However, for at least two reasons, the nature and timing of these events are very important to interpretation of trends and events in the central Ohio Valley. First, actions and reactions of groups close to the European presence eventually impinged on Native Americans farther inland, even if only indirectly. Fort Ancient peoples did not live in a vacuum, and their archaeological traces cannot be understood without understanding the outside influences and interactions that affected them. Second, generalizations from historically recorded or archaeologically interpreted events and processes associated with the native peoples who first encountered Europeans can be useful for interpreting the archaeological record in other regions. Therefore, the following pages briefly summarize some important trends, focusing upon well-researched case histories of interior groups who probably interacted, directly or indirectly, with Fort Ancient people during the early Contact Period. The discussion covers population movements, demographic and sociopolitical change, intergroup interaction protocol, and descriptions of important exchange goods that were typical of different time periods and thus are useful as chronological horizon markers.

Changes in Population Distribution and Organizational Complexity

Timing and effects of early Contact Period events were different in different regions. In some areas such as the interior Southeast, disease, depopulation, and "devolution" in social organization occurred rather early; in others, such as the Northeast, economic competition and conflict actually stimulated social complexity and new external relationships.

Many of the powerful, populous, socially stratified, and spatially extensive complex chiefdoms visited by the de Soto entrada between 1539 and 1542 (Figure 3-4) were disrupted by epidemic disease during the following decades. Thus, the central and lower Mississippi Valley, with its numerous polities comprising large, closely situated horticultural settlements, was greatly depopulated by the last quarter of the seventeenth century, when Marquette, Joliet, and LaSalle traveled down the Misssissippi to claim the region for the French (Table 3-1) (Dye and Brister 1986; Hoffman 1993; Morse and Morse 1983:304-20). Only the Natchez survived as a socially stratified polity (Le Page du Pratz 1763). Other groups, such as the Tunica—known as intermediary traders during the early French occupation of Louisiana—adjusted their settlement locations and lifeways to new circumstances and opportunities (Brain 1979, 1988). In east-central Mississippi during this period, the Choctaw came together as a multiethnic confederacy, drawing refugees from the lower Mississippi epidemics as well as from

TABLE 3-1
Sixteenth and Seventeenth Century European Exploration, Settlement, and Conflict in Eastern North America

	Date	Event
	1497-1498	Voyage to Newfoundland, John Cabot (E)
	1501	Voyage to Labrador, Newfoundland, Maine, Gaspar Corte-Real (P)
	1513	Voyage around southern coast of Florida, Juan Ponce de León (S)
*	1521	Colonization attempt, Charlotte Harbor, Florida, Ponce de León (S)
*	1521-?	Colonization attempt, Cape Breton Island, Joao Fagundes (P)
	1521-1525	Exploratory voyages, eastern seaboard north to South Carolina, Lucas Vásquez de Ayllón (S)
	1524	Exploratory voyage, eastern seaboard north of Georgia, Giovanni da Verrazzano (F)
	1525	Exploratory voyage, eastern seaboard esp. north from New England, Estevao Gomes (S)
*	1526	Colonization attempt, Georgia, de Ayllón (S)
	1527	Exploratory voyage, eastern seaboard, Laborador-West Indies, John Rut (E)
*	1528	Expedition through Florida, Pánfilo de Narváez (S)
	1534-1541	Exploratory voyages, St. Lawrence estuary and river, Jacques Cartier (F)
*	1539-1543	Expedition across the greater Southeast (Florida, Georgia, South Carolina, North Carolina, Tennessee, Alabama, Mississippi, Arkansas, Texas), Hernando de Soto (S)
*	1541-1543	Colonization attempt, Cap Rouge, Quebec, Cartier (F)
*	1542-1599	Basque fishing and trading expeditions, St. Lawrence area, with establishment of semi-permanent stations at Red Bay (Newfoundland) and Tadoussac (Quebec) (F)
*	1559-1561	Colonization attempt, Pensacola, Florida, and expedition to northwest Georgia Tristán de Luna (S)
*	1562	Colonization attempt, Fort Caroline, Florida, René de Laudonnière (F)
**	1565	Establishment of St. Augustine, Florida (S)
*	1566-1568	2 expeditions through Georgia, South Carolina, and eastern Tennessee, Juan Pardo (S)
*	1566-1587	Colonization at Santa Elena, South Carolina (S)
*	1570-1571	Colonization attempt, Ajacán, Chesapeake Bay (S)
	1576-1578	Search for Northwest Passage, Martin Frobisher (E)
*	1585-1587	Colonization attempt, Roanoake Island, North Carolina, Walter Raleigh (E)
**	1587-1704	Franciscan missions, coastal Georgia and northern Florida (S)
	1597	Guale rebellion against Spanish missionaries, Georgia coast
	1597-1628	5 small-scale military expeditions, interior Georgia (S)
	1604-1605	Exploratory voyage, Nova Scotia, Samuel de Champlain (F)
**	1607	Establishment of Jamestown, Virginia (E)
**	1608	Establishment of Quebec City, Samuel de Champlain (F)
	1609	Exploration of Hudson River, Henry Hudson (D)
	1610	Search for Northwest Passage (into Hudson's Bay), Henry Hudson (E)
*	1614	Establishment of Fort Nassau (New York) (D)
	1615	Expedition to Lake Huron, Samuel de Champlain (F)
**	1620	Establishment of Plymouth Colony (E)
	1622-1646	Continuing conflicts between Powhatans and Virginia colonists
**	1624	Establishment of New Netherland (D) (conquered by England 1664)
	1624-1628	Mohawk-Mahican conflict, resulting in retreat of Mahicans from direct trading with Dutch
	1628-32	English control of Quebec, with trade operated by the Anglo-Scotch Company
**	1630s	Establishment of Massachusetts, Rhode Island, Connecticut (E)
**	1633	Establishment of Maryland (E)
	1634	Expedition to Green Bay and points south, Jean Nicollet (F)
*	1636-1645	Initiation of 6 Jesuit missions among the Huron in southern Ontario (F)
**	1638	Establishment of New Sweden (Delaware) (Sw) (taken over by Dutch 1655)
	1641-1700	Continuing conflicts between Five Nations Iroquois and other, mostly French-allied, native groups and French posts in the upper St. Lawrence and Great Lakes region
**	1642	Establishment of Montreal (F)
	1640s	Dispersion of "Fire Nation" peoples by the Neutral
	1649-1653	Dispersion of Huron and Neutral from southwestern Ontario by Five Nations Iroquois
*	1654-1656	Initiation of 5 missions among the New York Iroquois (F)
	1656	Dispersion of the Erie from western New York by Five Nations Iroquois
	1655-1662	Defeats of Five Nations Iroquois war parties by refugee groups in Wisconsin and Michigan
	1664	Takeover of Dutch colonies by the English
*	1665-1672	Initiation of 6 Jesuit missions in Wisconsin and Michigan (F)
	1650s-1660s	Continuing conflicts between Five Nations Iroquois and Susquehannocks (Delaware-Maryland)
**	1670	Establishment of Charles Towne, South Carolina (E)
**	1672	Establishment of Fort Michilimackinac, between Lakes Michigan and Huron (F)
	1673-1674	Exploration of Mississippi River Valley to Arkansas River, Louis Jolliet and Pére Jacques Marquette (F)
	1674	Travel in western West Virginia, Gabriel Arthur (E)
	1674	Travel to Westo territory, interior South Carolina, Arthur Woodward (E)
*	1675	Initiation of Jesuit mission to the Kaskaskia Illinois, Illinois River Valley (F)
	1675-1676	King Philip's War, New England
	1675	Defeat/dispersal of Susquehannock by Seneca Iroquois, Maryland and Virginia colonists
	1675	Bacon's Rebellion, Virginia
	1680	Defeats of Illinois groups by Five Nations Iroquois, Illinois River Valley
*	1682-1691	Establishment of Fort St. Louis (Zimmerman Site), Illinois River Valley (F)
**	1682	Establishment of Pennsylvania (E)
	1682	Exploration of Mississippi River to mouth, Robert Cavelier, Sieur de La Salle (F)
	1680-1683	Conflict with and dispersion of the Westo by Carolina settlers
	1685	Trade expedition to Upper Chattahoochee River, Henry Woodward (E)
	1685-1687	Additional French exploration in Mississippi River Valley, including travel southwest into Texas, La Salle and Henri de Tonti (F)
*	1686	Establishment of Arkansas Post on Arkansas River, Henri de Tonti (F)
**	1699	Initial French settlement in Louisiana Territory, at Biloxi (F)

D = Dutch, E = English, F = French, P = Portuguese, S = Spanish, Sw = Swedish, * = temporary settlement/presence, ** = permanent/long term settlement

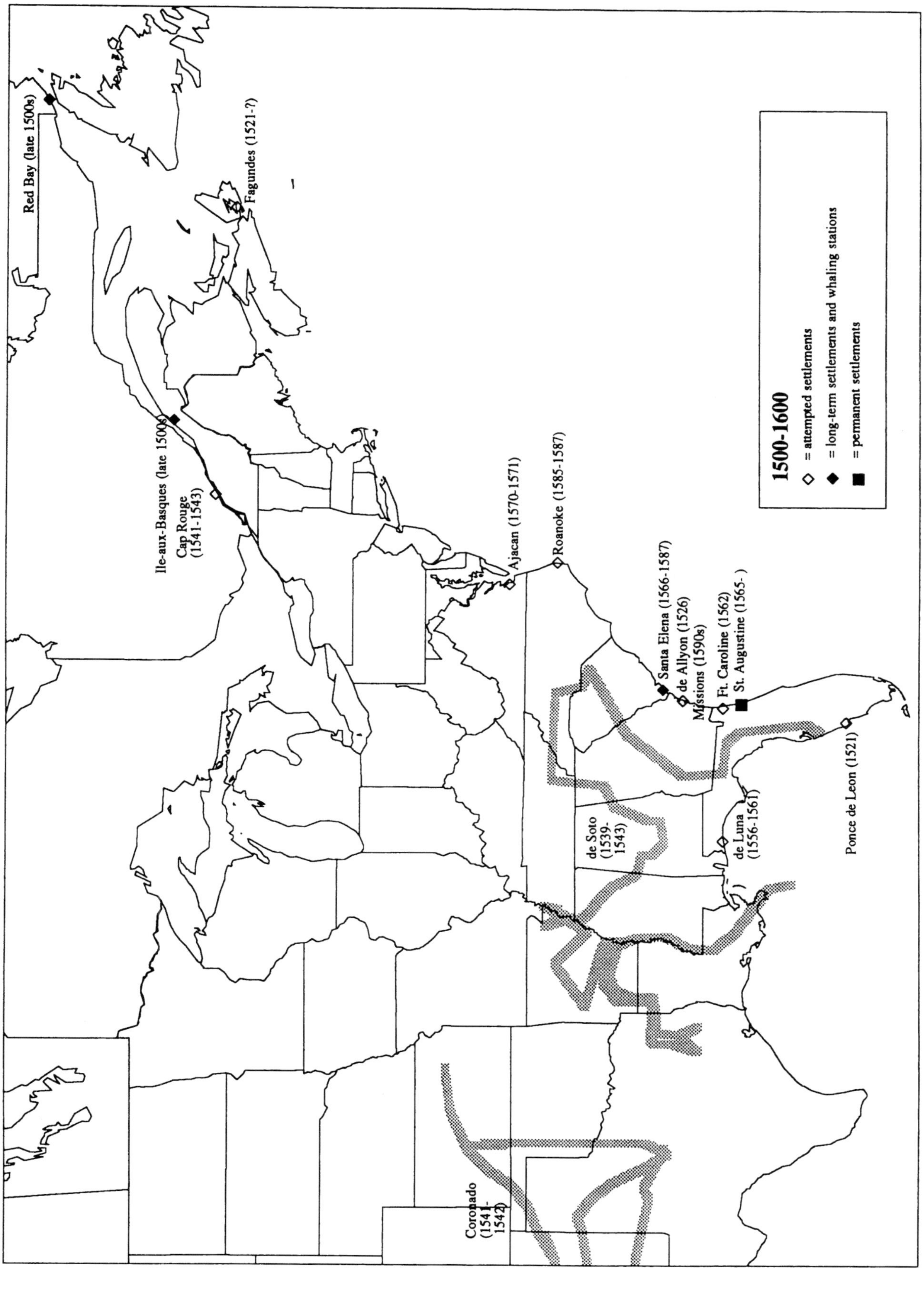

Figure 3-4. Sixteenth-century European expeditions, settlements, and areas of activity.

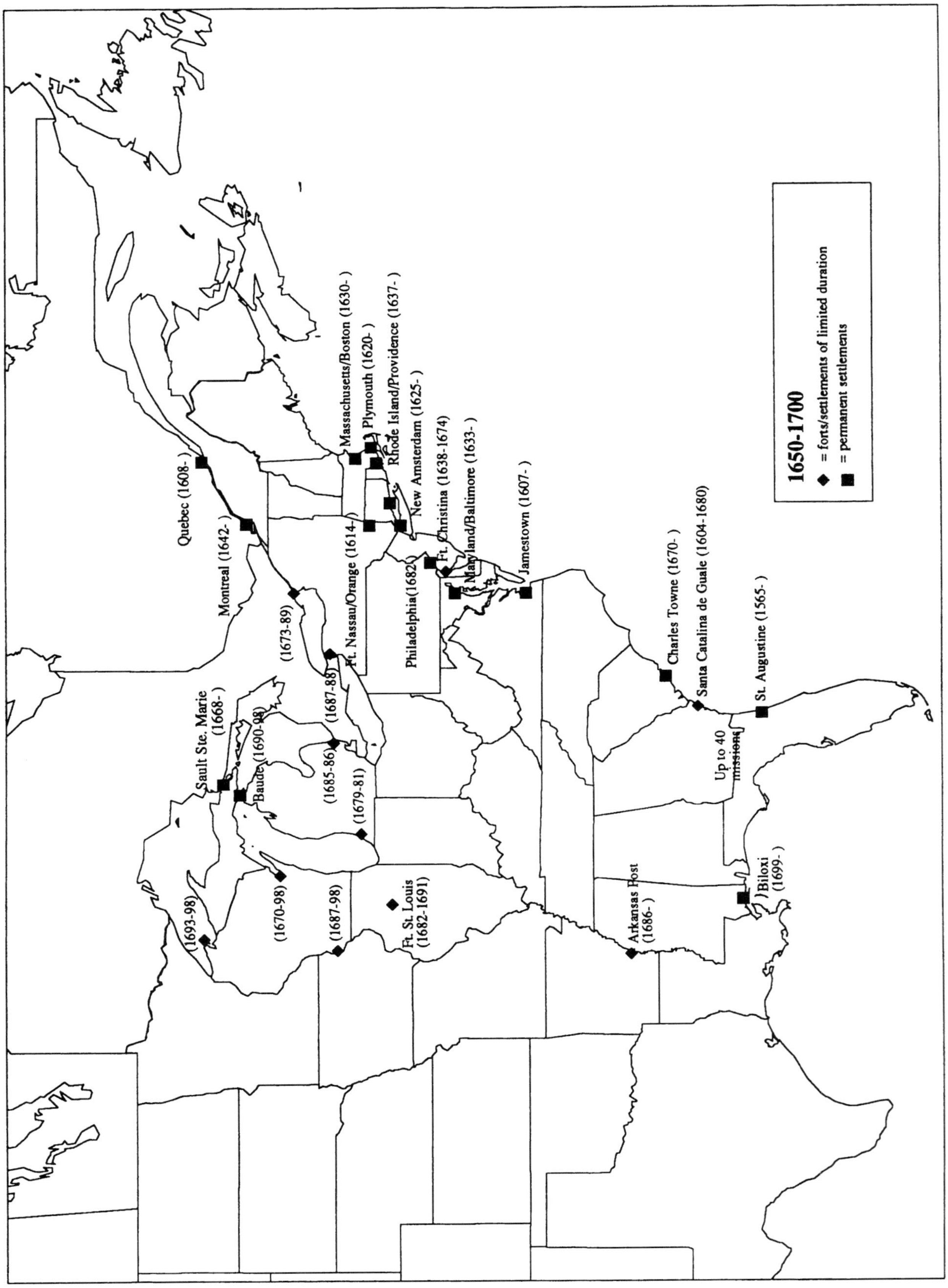

Figure 3-5. European expeditions, settlements, and areas of activity, 1600-1650.

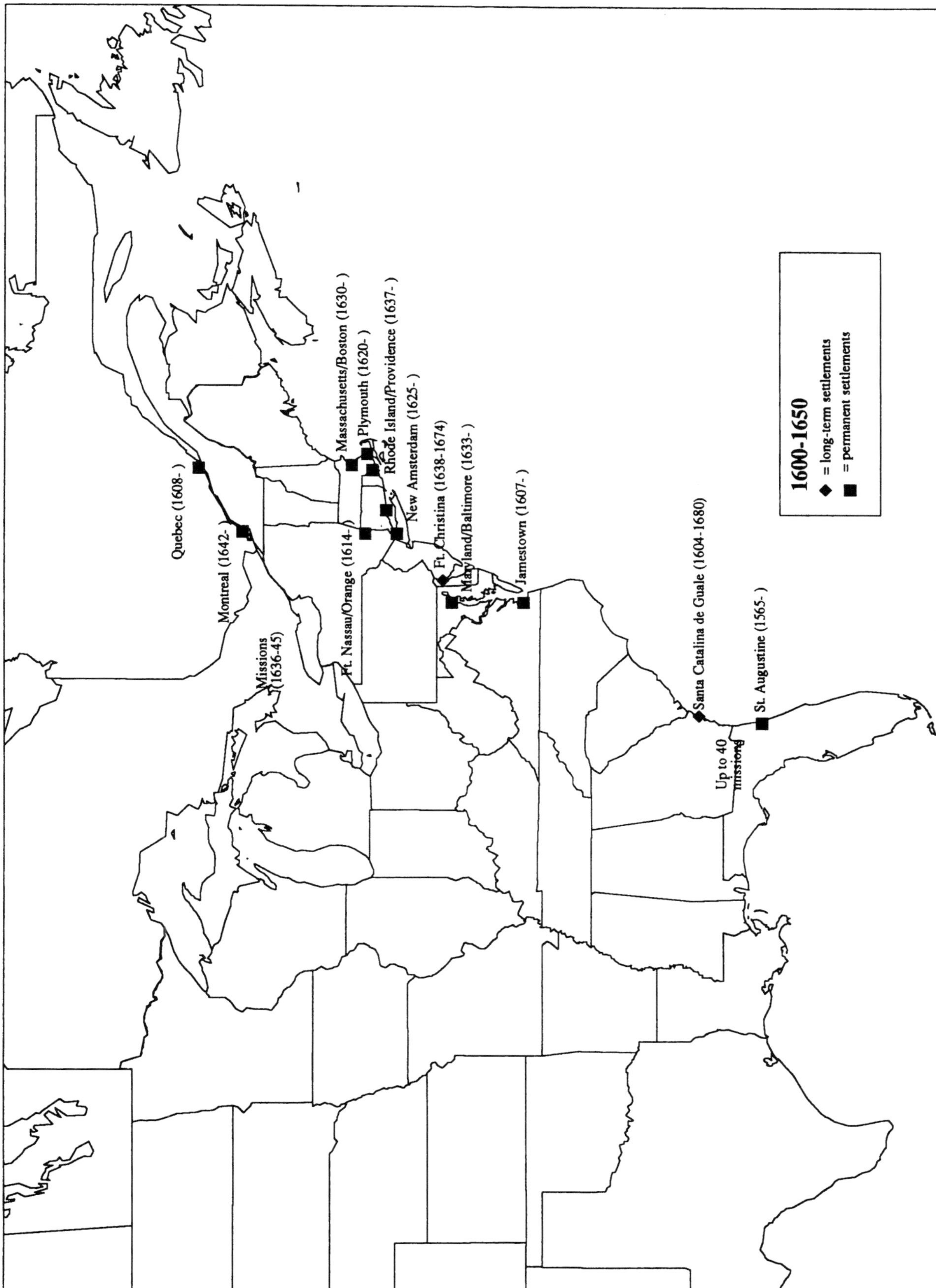

Figure 3-6. European expeditions, settlements, and areas of activity, 1650-1700.

the pre-de Soto devolution of the powerful Moundville polity that formerly controlled the Tombigbee Valley in central Alabama; the culturally diverse nature of this group is particularly well evidenced by its broad range of historically recorded burial customs (Galloway 1994, 1995).

Likewise, the powerful chiefdoms of the trans-Appalachian interior might have been devastated by disease in the decades after 1540. When later Spanish expeditions visited the formerly-vigorous polity of Coosa in the 1560s, they described it as a shadow of what had been reported by the de Soto chroniclers (Hudson 1990; Hudson et al. 1989:132-33). Most researchers have taken this as evidence of population decline due to epidemic disease, but Paul Hoffman has questioned these reports, interpreting them as a reflection of their writers' discouragement with their own attempts at colonization (1995).

Marvin Smith (1987) has used the archaeological record to trace the movements over time of settlements probably connected with Coosa. Archaeologically, this paramount chiefdom is associated with seven site clusters along the drainages of the upper Tennessee and Coosa rivers, among them sites of the Dallas and Barnett phases (Figure 3-2) (Anderson 1991: Fig. 5; Hally 1994a; Hally et al. 1990). One archaeological marker of the polity was Citico-style marine shell gorgets engraved with rattlesnakes, which were buried with high-status women and children (Hally et al. 1990:133-34). After the mid-sixteenth century, these population centers gradually moved some 150 miles southwest along the Coosa River into Alabama, settlements became smaller and fewer, and multiple and mass graves perhaps increased, among other changes (Smith, 1987:54-112, Fig. 7.1, 1993, 1994). The area east of the Tennessee River in Tennessee was abandoned until the Overhill Cherokee moved into the area.

Historical information about these inland people and members of other contemporaneous polities such as Ocute and Ichisi was not available again until well after 1670, when Charles Towne was established and English traders sought direct contact (Braund 1993; Waselkov 1994). By that time, they had devolved from a stratified society headed by hereditary chiefs and members of ascribed elite lineages, to the historically known Creek Confederation of villages organized into ranked moieties and clans and managed by peace and war chiefs and associated councils (Adair 1930; Dye 1995; Hudson 1976:184-260; Knight 1985, 1990). During their century of seclusion, they continued to receive European trade goods through intermediaries from communities connected with Spanish missions in and around northern Florida, in exchange for peltries (Table 3-1, Figure 3-5) (Waselkov 1989, 1994). By the time they were again in direct contact with Europeans, they had become a "synthetic [culture] incorporating both European trade goods and traditional artifacts, values, and activities in a new, distinctive, stable cultural format" (Waselkov 1993:125; cf. Dimmick 1987). For the next century, they were well situated to play off French and English interests, struggling for control of the interior Southeast, to their own advantage (Waselkov 1993:125-29).

Ethnohistorians argue that one important factor in eroding the influence of the hereditary elite was "the artificial dilution of symbols of exclusivity and politico-religious legitimacy produced by the opening up of common channels of access to foreign knowledge and luxury goods," particularly metal (Knight 1985:178-79)—elaborate copper regalia having been of supreme symbolic importance in Mississippian paramount chiefdoms centering on Spiro, Moundville, Etowah, and Lake Jackson. Elaborating on this point, Waselkov (1993:124) states:

> Ownership of copper during the late prehistoric period had been limited to the elite; because of its rarity, possession was limited to those with control over other scarce commodities, thereby conferring prestige on the owners and serving to validate and sanctify their chiefly rank in stratified societies. The sudden widespread availability of this formerly scarce commodity, now in the form of sheet brass, must have created a crisis in the social hierarchy. Combined with other processes..., devaluation of the metal's sacred content probably contributed to the decline in chiefly authority that evidently occurred during the protohistoric period. The sustained demand for brass artifacts throughout the seventeenth century implies that native perceptions of its sacred value still functioned. But ownership was no longer limited to particular lineages; instead, achieved status was expressed by the material that had previously symbolized certain individuals' permanent exclusion from positions of ascribed authority.

Large, shaped metal pieces, however, such as the famed Tukabatchee Plates, continued to function as group sacra well into the nineteenth century (Knight 1985:179-80; Swanton 1928).

Somewhat farther north, the Chesapeake Bay region was an important contact locus even before the permanent advent of English settlers to Jamestown in 1607 and their consequent interactions—positive and negative—with the powerful Powhatan Confederacy (Table 3-1, Figures 3-3, 3-4, 3-5) (Fausz 1985; Potter 1993; Rountree 1993a; Turner 1985). By the end of the sixteenth century (ca. 1575 according to Kent 1984:18 or ca. 1595 according to Sempowski 1994:61), Susquehannock people, who had been acting as intermediaries in exchange of marine shell and European goods to Onondaga and other New York Iroquois groups, had relocated from the upper to the lower Susquehanna River (Figure 3-3) (Bradley 1987a:89-103, 1987b; Kuhn and Funk 1994; Pendergast 1989:102-3; Witthoft 1952). During this time, some of their settlements were located as far west as eastern West Virginia (Figure 3-3) (Brashler 1987; MacCord 1952; Mason and MacCord 1941, 1944; Patrick Trader, pers.comm.).

Another group, the Massawomeck, may have been performing the same intermediary function to western New York and southern Ontario via the Potomac, Monongahela, and Allegheny rivers (Figure 3-1) (Lennox and Fitzgerald 1990:429-31; Pendergast 1991a; Sempowski 1994); at least a portion of this group might perhaps be identified with the archaeologically defined Monongahela culture (Johnson 1992:32-36). The recent excavation of a very large early seventeenth-century Monongahela village interpreted as a trading center adds evidence to this hypothesis (Anonymous 1994; Davis 1993).

Disruptions to the Susquehannock–New York Iroquois exchange connection by the beginning of the seventeenth century (Kuhn and Funk 1994; Lapham 1995; Sempowski 1989, 1994) were followed by the establishment of the Dutch–Mohawk–League Iroquois trade axis by the 1620s (Figure 3-5; see below) (Trigger 1971). The Monongahela disappeared from archaeology and the Massawomeck from history by the late 1630s, perhaps due to the efforts of the Seneca, the westernmost member of the League (Johnson 1992:35-37), although exchange relations apparently continued between Seneca and Monongahela settlements for one or two decades into the seventeenth century (Lapham 1995:28). Warfare between League Iroquois and Susquehannocks continued until the latter were dispersed by European settlers in 1675 (Jennings 1984:139-59). Over the century before that, Susquehannock settlements and cemeteries are notable for their increasing amounts of European trade goods, as well as for the use of European tools to manufacture ornaments and weapons from shell, antler, stone, and metal (Kent 1984:145-294; Figs. 28, 39, 42, 50).

The founding of Pennsylvania in 1682 (Figure 3-6) established a new focus for Native American–European interaction, and a counterbalance to the English–Iroquois Confederacy alliance in New York, with the Delaware in the front lines. Other groups, including Shawnee and Conoy, moved into southeastern Pennsylvania during this time (Jennings 1984:223-74).

In New York and southern Ontario the sixteenth and seventeenth centuries saw the continuation and amplification of hostilities and population movements initiated prehistorically (see above), with the period between about 1580 and 1655 witnessing particularly intense interactions and striking demographic changes. Unlike residents of the interior Southeast, Iroquoians outside the Saint Lawrence Valley did not experience their first round of devastating epidemics until after the first quarter of the seventeenth century (Heidenreich 1990:487; Snow 1995a; Snow and Lamphear 1988; Snow and Starna 1989). But before then, escalating warfare already had affected demographic patterns and intergroup alliances, with European-initated interactions and European rivalries constituting one part of a complex, multifaceted process (cf. Heidenreich 1990:487).

The Saint Lawrence Iroquoian settlements visited by Cartier in 1535 were gone by the time of Champlain (Table 3-1, Figure 3-3), many of their former residents (from archaeological evidence) apparently settling among the Huron and others among the Mohawk (e.g., Engelbrecht 1995; Jamieson 1990:403; Pendergast 1985; Ramsden 1990b; Warrick 1990:378). European-introduced disease, hostilities on-going from prehistoric times, and deteriorating climate all probably were contributing factors; conflict over European trade probably was not (Jamieson 1990:386, 402-4). Although some sporadic exchange was carried on with Basque whalers and European fishermen in the vicinity of the lower Saint Lawrence estuary from at least the 1530s onward, European goods did not reach interior peoples from the Saint Lawrence in any great numbers until around 1580, when large-scale trade directed toward the acquisition of furs became an important European aim (Borque 1994; Borque and Whitehead 1985; Fitzgerald 1990; Fitzgerald et al. 1993; Harper 1956; Lennox and Fitzgerald 1990; Trigger 1986:111-63; Turgeon 1990). Initial down-the-line exchange routes appear to be from Tadoussac, at the Saint Lawrence–Saguenay River juncture (across from Ile-aux-Basques, Figure 3-4), where European traders visited on a regular basis, via Montagnais and Algonquin intermediaries along an overland route west of the Saint Lawrence Valley to the Huron (Figure 3-3). Prehistoric interaction networks continued to be utilized as the fur trade increased in volume and new trading centers such as Quebec were established during the early seventeenth century, with Ottawa and Nipissing, traditional trade partners of the Huron, traveling as far west as Wisconsin and as far north as Hudson's Bay to acquire furs (Trigger 1978a; Waisberg 1977). Ottawa interaction networks also can be traced by the ornaments fashioned from upper Great Lakes red siltstone and perhaps Minnesota catlinite that appear on Petun, Huron, Neutral, and Seneca sites after 1620 (Fox 1980, 1990:464; Lennox and Fitzgerald 1990:433, 435-36; Wray and Schoff 1953:62). From relatively large amounts of marine shell at Huron and Neutral sites occupied between approximately 1580 and 1650, a persisting southern exchange route to Chesapeake Bay has been postulated (Lennox and Fitzgerald 1990:429, 431, 433). In the decades around 1600, New York Iroquois were obtaining European goods and marine shell from the south via Susquehannock and perhaps Massawomeck intermediaries (see above) and probably also, to some extent, from the north, by raiding the Saint Lawrence (Bradley 1987a:99-103, 1987b; Kuhn and Funk 1994; Trigger 1978a:345). After the elimination of the Mahicans as trade rivals, the Mohawk (the easternmost members of the Iroquois Confederacy) became the primary intermediaries in the Dutch fur trade as of the 1620s (Trigger 1971). Concurrently, by the second quarter of the seventeenth century, "true" wampum, manufactured of white and purple shell with European tools, began to appear in quantity and be utilized as both a standardized medium of exchange and—fashioned into "belts"—as a powerful symbol of alliance and condolence (Bradley 1987a:178-80; Ceci 1982, 1989a, 1989b; Kuhn 1987a; Sempowski 1989). Diachronic differences in marine shell quantities and assemblages of European goods at Mohawk, Seneca, Onondaga, and Ontario Iroquoian sites reflect differences in both primary European suppliers (e.g., Huron–Basque/French, Mohawk–Dutch/English, Susquehannock–English/Swedish/Dutch) and in intermediary exchange routes. As chronologies are refined (e.g., Kenyon and Fitzgerald 1986; Sempowski 1994), our detailed knowledge of intergroup relationships gradually increases.

By the late sixteenth century, settlement patterns among the Huron and Neutral are believed to reflect the formation of confederacies analogous to the League of the Iroquois (Fitzgerald

1990:257-59; Lennox and Fitzgerald 1990:410-11; Trigger 1986:157-59; Warrick 1990:374, 380). Neutral raiding against traditional Algonquian ("Fire Nation") enemies during the 1630s and 1640s culminated in the virtual abandonment of southwestern Ontario, adjacent Michigan, and northern Ohio (Murphy and Ferris 1990:260; Stothers 1994). In that entire area, only a small group of Indian Hills sites, at the southwestern end of Lake Erie (Figure 3-3), had access to European goods in any quantity, including small ornaments of copper and brass and a few glass beads (Brose 1994; Quimby 1966a; Stothers 1994; Stothers and Abel 1991). A Sandusky River site has produced two rolled beads and a conical tinkler made from European copper (Bowen 1994:12). With the possible exception of an iron hook found at the Reeve site and rolled copper beads or tinklers at the Fairport Harbor and Tuttle Hill sites, the Whittlesey region in northeastern Ohio provides no evidence for involvement in trade networks through which European goods circulated (Brose 1994:161-77; Greenman 1935:63, 1937:342; Murphy 1971:27, Fig. 7b). The extraordinary assemblage of late-style local and nonlocal pipes at Reeve Village (Ahlstrom 1979), including both Iroquoian and Fort Ancient types, is an intriguing body of evidence that has not yet been investigated in full. Just to the south, at least a few European artifacts were reaching Wellsburg sites, such as the iron buckle at Cullison (see above). Despite the admitted lack of archaeological evidence, David Stothers has argued from historical sources that Indian Hills people received European goods via a lower Great Lakes Algonquian trade axis (Stothers 1994).

Guns became available to League Iroquois in significant numbers by the mid-1640s, due to loosening of Dutch control of this commodity (Heidenreich 1990:488, 491; Wray 1985). During that time, only a few Christian converts among French-allied Ontario groups were allowed guns by their European trading partners. At least partially due to this weapons imbalance, by the mid-1650s League Iroquois had dispersed the Ottawa River Algonquins, the Huron, the Petun, the Neutral, the Wenro, and the Erie from their traditional homelands (Figure 3-3). Northern Ohio settlements also were abandoned by that time. For more than a half century afterwards, southwestern Ontario, Michigan, the southern shore of Lake Erie, and western Pennsylvania appear to have been virtually deserted except for hunting parties (e.g., Brose 1994:178-82; Heidenreich 1990:490). Although historians often have interpreted the bellicose actions of League Iroquois as an attempt to gain control of the beaver trade and assure access to European commodities on which they had become dependent (e.g., Hunt 1960; Trigger 1986:260-62), more recently, emphasis has been placed on Iroquois Mourning War traditions and the need to replenish population after the epidemics of the 1630s and 1640s (e.g., Heidenreich 1990:486-92; Richter 1992:30-74). Indeed, large numbers of Iroquoian peoples dispersed by the League Iroquois were resettled in New York among their former enemies.

In the upper Mississippi Valley, population movements both presaged and accompanied the growing French presence after 1650 (Table 3-1, Figure 3-6). In 1634, when Jean Nicolet traveled in Lake Michigan and its surrounding waterways, the Winnebago very likely controlled much of southeastern Wisconsin, south to the Chicago area (Hall 1993, 1995). After his visit, they were defeated by the Illini and allied peoples, eventually regrouping near Green Bay as a much smaller population. This opened areas of southern Wisconsin to immigrant Algonquian groups. Refugees from Iroquoian hostilities moved to Wisconsin and northern Illinois, adjusting to new environments and forming new alliances and multi-ethnic communities, often with syncretic or vastly altered subsistence, social structure, and ceremonial life (e.g., Brose 1983; Hickerson 1962, 1963, 1970; Lurie 1960; C. Mason 1986; R. Mason 1981:373-420, 1986:15-20, 1993; White 1991:1-49; see also various summaries in Trigger 1978b); these included groups that came to be known as Potawatomi, Sauk, Fox, Kickapoo, and Mascouten from Michigan, and Ottawa and Chippewa from north of the Great Lakes, which joined already-present Winnebago, Menomini, Miami, and Illini (Figure 3-7). On the Illinois River, the establishment of Fort St. Louis in 1682 (Figure 3-6) attracted a very large population that included Illini, Miami, Shawnee, Mahican, and Missouri peoples (J. Brown 1961; M. Brown 1975, 1979). The burgeoning fur trade, with accompanying rivalries between French and English for control of land, peoples, and resources (e.g., Ray 1974; White 1991:94-141), was a big factor, but not the only one, in the vast changes in the social landscape of the Great Lakes region during this time.

Early Historical Period Protocols for Inter-Polity Interaction

Early historical accounts document several differing protocols for intergroup interaction in eastern North America. Their material correlates frequently are deposited in the archaeological record. Knowing these ritual accompaniments to interaction, as well as who actually carried out contact with "foreign" groups, allows better interpretation of archaeological material assemblages in terms of both internal social organization and the nature of relationships with external groups.

In eastern North America, the duties of chiefs or leaders varied considerably, but among two-thirds of eighteen groups surveyed by Gary Feinman and Jill Neitzel they included duties such as ambassadorial functions, control of trade, and hosting visitors (Feinman and Neitzel 1984:50). Thus, as European members of the earliest expeditions to the Southeast discovered, it often was the chief or his or her representative who made initial contact with incoming strangers and conducted greeting ceremonies. Some sort of ceremony, usually accompanied by gift exchange, was almost universal on such occasions; in many cases it has been shown to serve the purpose of creating a fictive relationship incorporating the stranger into the group (cf. Hall 1987). Customary actions and accoutrements varied among groups. Ceremonies with similar material correlates also accompanied the arbitration of inter-polity disputes and the cementing of alliances (Dye 1995:296).

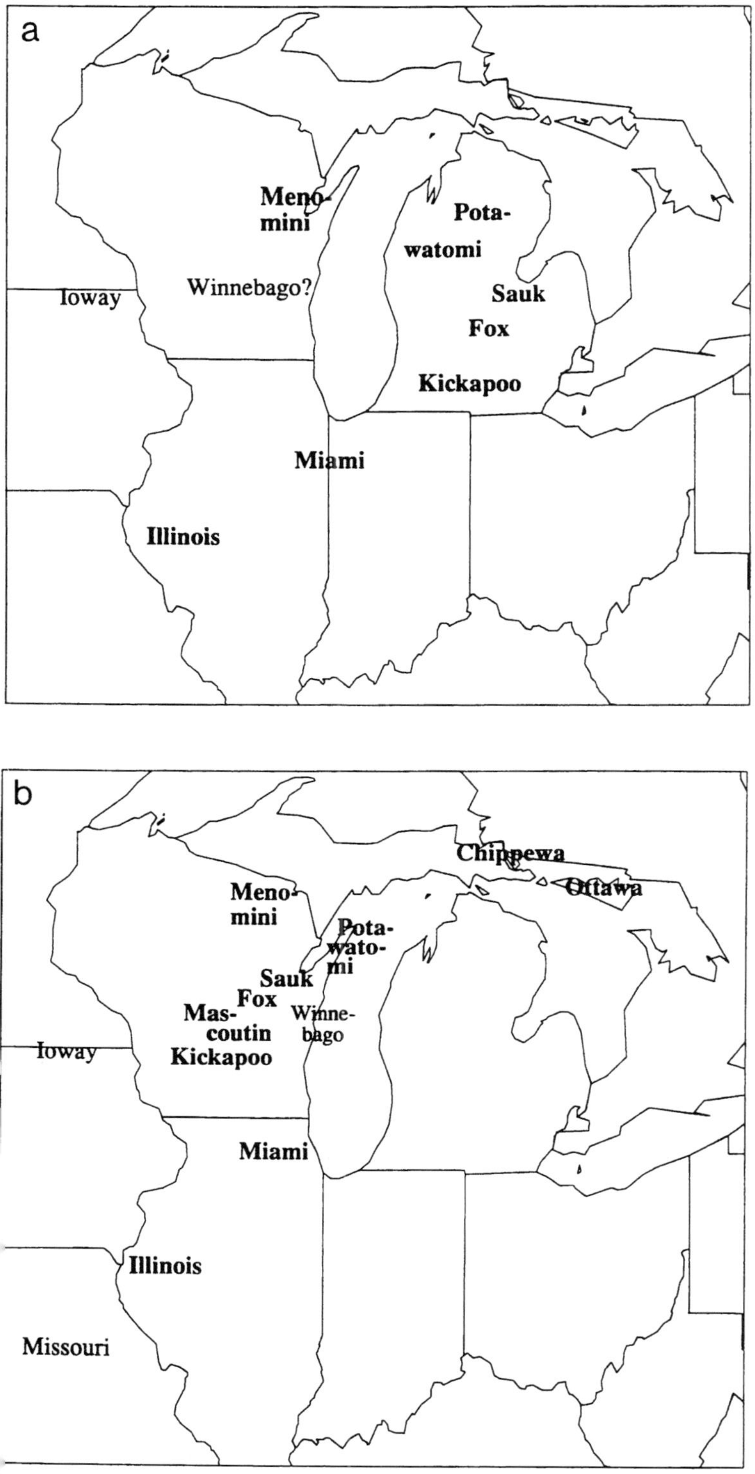

Figure 3-7. Seventeenth-century locations of selected Upper Mississippi–Great Lakes groups. *a*. Suggested distribution of Central Algonquian and Siouan groups ca. 1600 (after Callender 1962: Fig. 1; see text for additional discussion). *b*. Distribution of Central Algonquian, Northern Algonquian, and Siouan groups ca. 1670 (after Callender 1978b: Fig. 1; Bray 1961; Wedel 1981, 1986). Callender places the Shawnee in the Ohio Valley during both periods.

High-level greeting ceremonies in the sixteenth-century interior Southeast involved, among other things: preliminary encounters at town outskirts with ceremonially dressed, litter-borne chiefs or their representatives and singing, flute-playing attendants; formal speech making; and presentation of gifts, including food, clothing, and pearl or shell beads (Brown 1989:315; Clayton et al. 1993:1:278-79; Smith and Hally 1992). Intra- and inter-polity political negotiations were accompanied by "feasting, ceremonial smoking, and gift exchange" (Dye 1995:296).

Among Powhatans, Powhatan Confederacy members, and groups with whom they interacted, ceremonies included entry to the town through two lines of residents, stroking, oratory, feasting, dancing, and smoking (Rountree 1993b:39-41). Sexual hospitality was offered by local women, and long-term or regular visitors were invited to take local wives, practices common from eastern Virginia to southern Ontario (Rountree 1993b:41-42). All trade and prestige goods were controlled by the werowance (chief) (Potter 1989).

When they penetrated the western Great Lakes, Upper Mississippi Valley, and Plains in the late seventeenth century, the French learned that calumet ceremonialism was an important validation of intertribal alliance and exchange. The calumet (wand or pipe stem) was "very sacred and could be used as a safe-conduct pass when travelling through potentially hostile territory," but it also figured importantly in greeting rituals that served as adoption ceremonies "used to establish fictions of kinship between prominent Indians in different villages or different tribes and...between welcome Europeans and the bands or villages they visited" (Hall 1987:30, 31). Among the Pawnee, a child of the person involved was the putative honoree and actual recipient of the sacred objects utilized in the ceremony (Fletcher and Murie 1904; Hall 1991:30-31). The entire ritual as experienced by Europeans (with details differing in different areas) incorporated ceremonial smoking, ritualized weeping, stroking, presentation of clothing, dancing, speechmaking, and feasting (Blakeslee 1981; Brown 1989; Hall 1987:32). It often included presentation or exchange of pipe bowls. There were calumets for both peace and war, each decorated with different bird skins and other symbolic items (Brown 1989:313). Large-disk catlinite pipes appear to have been late prehistoric precursors to the more familiar elbow-shaped pipe bowls used historically in the calumet ceremony (Brown 1989). However, a number of examples of these "archaic" forms are known to have been retained through the nineteenth century in sacred bundles for ritual use by groups such as the Ioway, Osage, and Omaha (Paper 1988:87; West 1934:212-16).

In Iroquoia, interaction with visitors involved group smoking but not usually pipe presentation (Fenton 1953; Paper 1992:163-65). By the seventeenth century, wampum belts, emblems of the new Iroquois League cultural identity, were exchanged and preserved as material symbols of intergroup commitments (Ceci 1989b:72; Williams 1989:199). In both Iroquoia and the Mississippian Southeast, the symbolic associations of white shell made it particularly resonant as a metaphor of "physical, spiritual, and social well-being" and important as a high-status ceremonial material representing peace (Hamell 1988:205; Miller and Hamell 1986:324; cf. Yerkes 1989:114-15). In wampum belts, black/dark blue backgrounds denoted matters of "grave importance," including death, and red overpainting was associated with war (Hamell 1995:47-48).

Important Pan-Regional Horizon Markers

Across eastern North America, some distinctive and widespread artifact types are particularly useful as temporal markers. From late prehistoric contexts, some pipe styles and shell ornament designs, plus ceramics, serve well in this function (e.g., Williams 1980). Because of currently available dating techniques, however, temporal boundaries tend to be fuzzy. For protohistoric and historical contexts, European materials and manufactured goods offer opportunities for relatively fine-grained temporal assignments (Kidd 1954; Quimby 1939; Woodward 1932). Much work has been done in recent decades to build chronologies for different types of European goods, particularly glass beads (e.g., Hayes 1983; Kent 1984:211-23; Kidd and Kidd 1983; Rumrill 1991; Smith 1977, 1992; Smith and Good 1982). A few researchers have gone further, to build chronologies of artifact assemblages (beads plus other significant items) that are typical of particular time periods. Figure 3-8 diagrams the time ranges for horizon marker artifacts that will be important in interpreting Fort Ancient diachronic relationships, based largely on the work of Marvin Smith for the interior Southeast and William Fitzgerald for the region centering on Neutral territory in southern Ontario. These and related artifacts are discussed briefly below.

One of the earliest and most comprehensive efforts in tracking artifact assemblages and cultural practices over time was by Charles Wray and Harry Schoff, who devised a relative chronological sequence for thirteen Seneca sites occupied from the late 1500s until 1687 (Wray and Schoff 1953). They diagrammed the relative frequency of some 87 indigenous artifact types, European artifact types, and burial traits for seven sequential periods. Although the end of their sequence was dated on the basis of historical record, the earliest dates were somewhat arbitrary. Barry Kent used the Seneca artifact assemblages to date the earliest sites occupied by Susquehannock people in the lower Susquehanna Valley; again, the most recent sites could be dated historically (Kent 1984). Of particular importance is his site-by-site presentation of glass bead assemblages, based on his own formal typology but cross-referenced to the more general typology developed by Kenneth and Martha Kidd (Kent 1983; Kidd and Kidd 1983, originally published in 1970).

Ian Kenyon, Thomas Kenyon, and William Fitzgerald were able not only to trace the sequence of glass bead types over time in southern Ontario, but also to distinguish French- from Dutch-introduced types and tie changes in bead attributes to particular historical events such as the 1628-1632 English occupation of New France and the 1624 advent of the Dutch West India Company (Fitzgerald 1982, 1990:141-251; Kenyon and Fitzgerald 1986; Kenyon and Kenyon 1983). The most recent formulation (Fitzgerald 1990) defines three French-related bead horizons, Glass Bead Period 1 (ca. 1580-1600), Glass Bead Period 2 (ca. 1600-1630), and Glass Bead Period 3 (ca. 1630-1650) and two Netherlands-related horizons, Dutch 1 (1609/14-1624) and Dutch 2 (1624-1664). As Smith (1983) has noted, red beads are much more common in the Northeast than the Southeast. Some are present by the late sixteenth century (GBP1), but monochrome red seems more common from Dutch 1 onward (Kenyon and Fitzgerald 1986). The typical Dutch polychrome bead assemblages are found primarily at New York and Pennsylvania, not Ontario, sites (Kenyon and Fitzgerald 1986), and offer a direct means of tracing and relating peoples who acted within the exchange networks supplied by the Dutch, out of both New Netherlands and New Sweden (Table 3-1, Figure 3-5). Besides comprehensive summaries of bead types present over time, Fitzgerald (1990) provides detailed information on chronological changes in attributes of axes, knives, various other metal tools, Jesuit rings and medallions, and native-made brass ornaments and projectile points within southern Ontario, all tied to the three glass bead periods. His quantitative data on iron axes, for example, show a steady decline in size, from an average of 1655 g in GBP1 to 1199 g in GBP2 to 1062 g in GBP3 (1990:443). At lower Susquehanna River Susquehannock sites, which were supplied by non-French sources, the average ax weight ranges from 940 g at Schultz (now dated from 1590 to 1620; Sempowski 1994) down to 543 g at a post-1690 site (Kent 1984:235).

Trace element analysis has aided in defining one common early glass bead type in this region, known as "early blue" or "sky blue disappearing" beads for their medium turquoise blue color, their chronological placement at about 1600, and their tendency to crumble (Rumrill 1991:8; Witthoft 1966:206-7). Anne Chafe found that friable turquoise blue beads from GBP1 New York and Ontario sites were high in copper and low in manganese and calcium compared with GBP3 blue beads (Chafe et al. 1986). Medium-blue beads were not common at GBP2 sites.

Also of note as fine-grained time markers in the Northeast are the large iron-fitted copper kettles that were traded in the lower Saint Lawrence during the final decades of the sixteenth century (Fitzgerald et al. 1993; Turgeon 1990). They were quickly supplanted in the fur trade by smaller, lighter-weight, cheaper brass kettles.

Spiral pendants made from thin copper tubes have a relatively short time horizon, from about 1550 to 1625, on Iroquioan sites in New York, Pennsylvania, and Ontario, particularly those associated with Susquehannock occupations. Metallurgical analysis has shown that they were fashioned by native craftspeople from European metal (Bradley and Childs 1991a, 1991b; Childs 1994; contra Witthoft 1966:204-5). They appear to be related technologically and temporally to coil-shaped

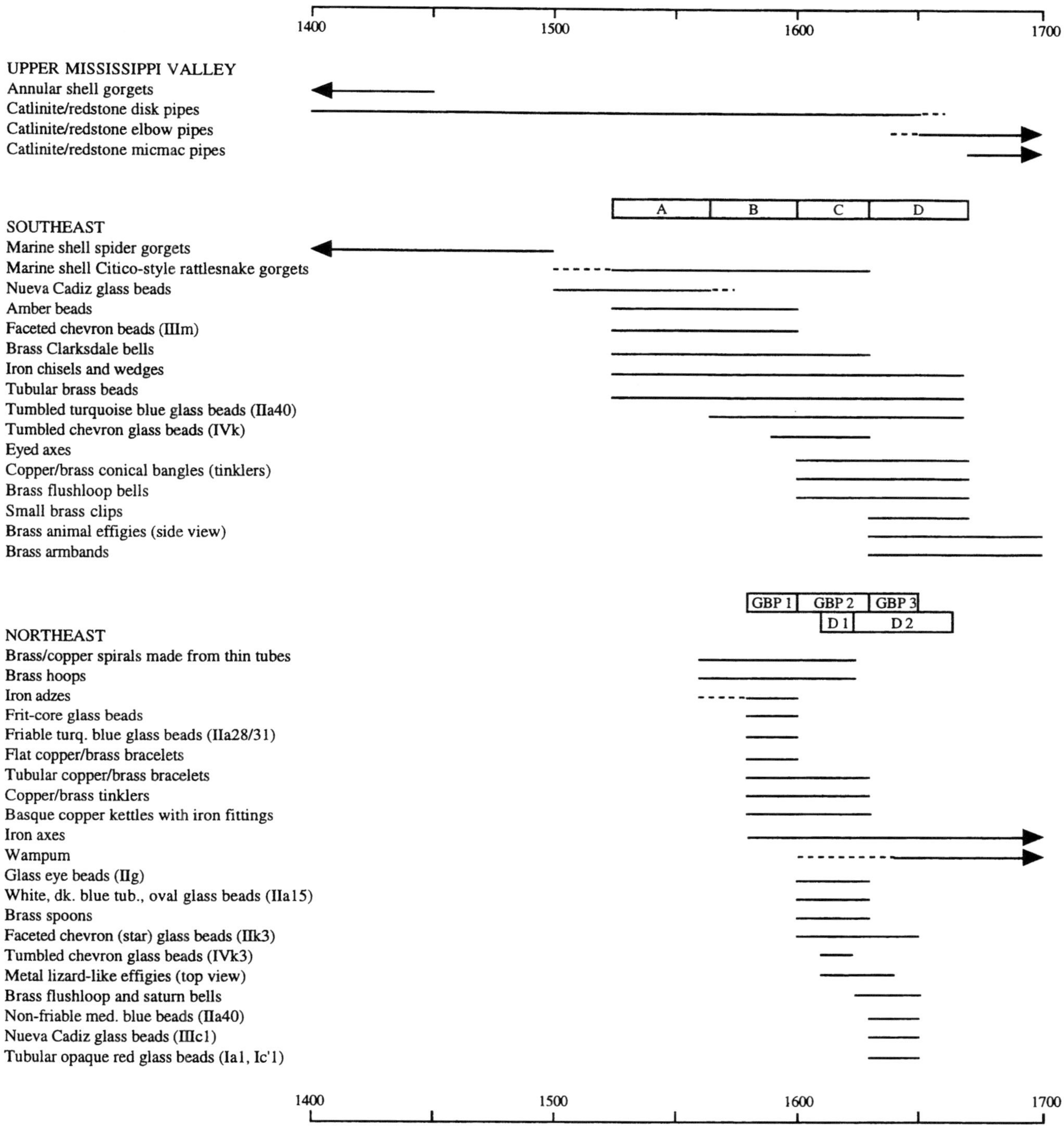

Figure 3-8. Important late prehistoric-protohistoric horizon marker artifacts. Artifacts from Southeastern sites are related in time to Assemblages A-D (Smith 1987). Artifacts from Northeastern sites are related in time to Glass Bead periods 1-3 and Dutch periods 1 and 2 (Fitzgerald 1990).

and serpent-shaped ornaments formed from thin copper or brass tubes, which enjoy different distributions than the spirals (see below, Chapter 8) (Drooker 1992a, 1993c, 1996b; Herold et al. 1990:88-91; M. Wedel 1959:63-75), and which also appear to have continued in use for a somewhat longer time. Coils and rings fashioned of thin copper and brass tubes were present at several Ontario sites during GBP1 and GBP2 (ca. 1580-1630); one has come from a GBP3 site (ca. 1630-1650) (Fitzgerald 1990:506-9). Coils were present at at least one Alabama site dated approximately 1630-1670 (as well as two others with no temporally diagnostic European artifacts) (Jolly 1969; Smith 1987:51; Webb 1939:28; Webb and Wilde 1951:123). Ornaments fashioned from thin tubes disappeared before the last decades of the seventeenth century. Between about 1670 and

TABLE 3-2
Selected European Horizon Marker Artifacts
with Different Time Frames in Southeastern and Northeastern Chronologies

	Southeast	Northeast
Nueva Cadiz beads, untwisted (IIIc1)	1500-1575 (...1600)	(1580...) 1630-1650
Seed beads	1525-->	1600-->
Turquoise/sky blue glass beads		
Undifferentiated (IIa31/40)	1575-->	
Friable, colored by copper (IIa31)		1580-1600
Solid, colored by cobalt (IIa40)		1630-1650 ...
Turquoise glass beads with white stripes (IIb56/57)	1585-->	1630-1650 (few)
Tumbled chevron beads (IVk)	1590-1650	1609/14-1624
Tubular brass beads	1550-->	...1580-->
Brass clips	1630-1670	1615-->
Conical brass/copper tinklers	...1600-1670	...1580-->
Copper/brass spirals made of thin tubes	--	1550-1625
Copper/brass rings/coils made of thin tubes	1550-1670	1580-1630...
Copper/brass lizard/beaver effigy pendants (top view)	--	1610-1640
Brass animal effigy pendants (side view)	1630-1700	--
Iron celts/wedges/adzes	1525-1675-->	1550-->
Iron axes (eyed)	1600-->	1580-->

Sources include: Fitzgerald 1990:141-241, 405-541; Kenyon and Kenyon 1983; Smith 1983, 1987, 1992; Cadzow 1936:126. Bead types from Kidd and Kidd 1983.

1720, similar shapes were constructed from European-made B-shaped (as opposed to O-shaped) brass wire (Drooker 1992a, 1996b).

Martha Sempowski and Lorraine Saunders have used Fitzgerald and Kenyon's glass bead periods to revise absolute dating for the early portion of the Seneca site sequence (Saunders and Sempowski 1991). This has implications for the Susquehannock site sequence (and probably for a number of other Iroquois sequences as well), placing the earliest-occupied lower Susquehanna Valley Susquehannock site somewhat later in time than Kent had it (Sempowski 1994).

Only a very broad "chronology" of successive European artifact assemblages has been proposed for the western Great Lakes. Carol Mason, building on earlier work by George Quimby, lists iron knives, brass bracelets, glass bottles, religious medals, brass kettles, and glass beads including "star chevrons" (very large, faceted chevron beads) as typical of the early historic period, between 1610 and 1670; however, only the beads are exclusively associated with pre-1670 contexts (1986:373-74; Quimby 1960, 1966b; cf. Kidd 1949). After 1670, European goods are present in much greater numbers and variety (e.g., Bray 1978; Brose 1970; J. Brown 1961; M. Brown 1975; Cleland 1971; Wittry 1963). It is unclear how refined the 1670 date is, since no site-by-site assemblage series has yet been published, to my knowledge.

For the interior Southeast, Marvin Smith, bowing to what he called the "Iroquois methodology" for utilizing assemblages of European goods to produce relative site sequences, built on the work of Wray, Schoff, Fitzgerald, Bradley, Pratt, and others to produce a chronology for sixteenth and seventeenth century sites in eastern Tennessee, northwestern Georgia, and eastern Alabama. His research revolved around bead types and other artifacts introduced by early Spanish explorers and later missionaries (DePratter and Smith 1980; Smith 1983, 1987:23-53, 1992; Smith and Good 1982). The end result was a series of four diagnostic assemblages for 1525-1565 (Assemblage A), 1565-1600 (B), 1600-1630 (C) and 1630-1670 (D), ending at the time of the establishment of Charles Towne (Table 3-1, Figure 3-8) and the associated English trade in slaves and skins (Braund 1993). Gregory Waselkov carried out additional research on metal artifacts that probably entered the interior Southeast via Spanish Florida, including brass animal effigies and armbands, the use of which he documented up to 1700 (Waselkov 1989). Sheet brass Clarksdale bells have been singled out as a marker of the de Soto expedition (Brain 1975; Mitchem and McEwan 1988). Smith notes that they also occur at later sites, within assemblages not typical of the de Soto time period (1987:46-47). He is of the opinion that they still were being supplied at that later time. However, the possibility of curation always is present.

The side-view brass effigies documented by Smith and Waselkov seem to have different source regions than the top-view brass "lizard"/"salamander"/"beaver" effigies known in the Northeast. William Johnson and James Herbstritt have documented the top view effigies at Monongahela, Seneca, and Fort Ancient sites (Johnson 1992:22, 1994; Herbstritt 1996), but they have not been reported farther south. The two Seneca sites at which they have been found date to 1610-1640, so these items seem to slightly precede the side-view effigies associated with the Spanish trade.

Metal "clips"—rectangular pieces with ends turned under to attach them to leather or textiles—probably can be used as temporal markers only if close attention is paid to scale and form. Based on matched sets of small clips from two 1630-1670 Alabama sites, Smith lists brass clips as a diagnostic artifact for his Assemblage D (Smith 1987:47, 49, 51). Walthall et al. describe "small brass mail rings[,]...small copper beads, which were clamped to a leather thong or to clothing to serve as decoration[,]...an excellent temporal marker for the last quarter of the seventeenth century," citing their recovery from a 1650-1715 Alabama site, a site in western Illinois, and four in the Straits of Mackinac (1992:141, 142); the form of most of these examples is cylindrical. Waselkov, who has added a variety of examples to those listed above, categorizing them as "mail (clips)," considers such artifacts to be associated primarily with late seventeenth-century French contact assemblages (1996, pers. comm.). However, in the Northeast their occurrence is earlier: a set of brass clips (noncylindrical) attached to leather thongs made into a "belt or girdle" is known from the Susquehannock Washington Boro site (Cadzow 1936:126), now believed to have been established sometime between 1615 and 1620 (Sempowski 1994:61). The larger size of these clips, along with their noncylindrical form, may be diagnostic of the earlier period.

Not included as diagnostic artifacts in Smith's Southeastern chronology, but occurring at at least four Alabama sites in context with typical Period D artifacts, are iron bracelets (Lindsey 1964; Webb and Wilde 1951:30, 116, 141). One also is reported from a Tennessee site containing items from Assemblages A and C (Smith 1987:50); it is not clear whether its context allows assignment of it to one or the other of the two time periods. In the Northeast, they are reported from two GBP2-3 Huron sites (ca. 1600-1650), and from Seneca sites currently dated 1655-1687 (Fitzgerald 1990:499; Saunders and Sempowski 1991; Wray and Schoff 1953:59-59).

As can be seen in Figure 3-8, some key "horizon markers" have different peak periods in Northeastern and Southeastern contexts. Table 3-2 lists a number of them that will factor importantly in constructing relative chronologies for protohistoric Fort Ancient sites.

Indigenous artifacts useful as pan-regional horizon markers include items with rather short-term, distinctive styles that, for one reason or another, were exchanged or copied widely. For the central Mississippi Valley, Stephen Williams has proposed the "Markala Horizon," ca. 1500-1700, with markers including flat copper bird-shaped symbol badges, rectangular engraved shell "buttons," disk pipes, and particular pottery styles and lithic tools (Williams 1980). Marine shell mushroom-shaped ear plugs also date to this period (Morse and Morse 1983:277); in eastern Tennessee, they generally have been excavated at late sixteenth–early seventeenth century sites (Richard Polhemus, pers. comm.). Robert Mainfort has fine-tuned chronological markers for western Tennessee into two pre–de Soto and two post–de Soto periods (1996). Campbell Appliqué ceramics mark the period after 1500, while unifacial snub-nosed endscrapers are present from about 1541 onward, a time-frame that is not universal across their very widespread area of use (cf. Railey 1992). Robert Hall, while not proposing any horizon marker function, documented the variety of shapes, including birds, claws, "maces"/ "keyholes," and "serpents," associated with flat copper symbol badges from Oneota contexts (Hall 1962:141-46, Pl. 79-81).

Marine shell was a highly-valued material in interior eastern North America from very early times (e.g., Goad 1978, 1980; Goad and Noakes 1978). For the late prehistoric period, marine shell gorget styles and motifs (Brain and Phillips 1996; Conrad 1996; Kneberg 1959; Muller 1966, 1989) can be useful as temporal markers, although their periods of use tend to be longer than European horizon marker artifacts. Simple annular gorgets, round with a central hole, date to ca. 1200-1450 at central Illinois River valley sites in Illinois, perhaps even as early as the twelfth century (Conrad 1991b:148, 149, 154, 1996). Spider motifs, which are concentrated on gorgets from the upper Tennessee Valley and the Illinois-Mississippi-Ohio-lower Tennessee River area, date to ca. 1200-1500 (Esarey 1990:17). Significant numbers of these gorgets were buried with females and subadults, and Esarey proposes that, at least within the Illinois River valley region, they might be related to group identity. The scalloped triskele, associated with females and infants, comes from Cumberland Valley sites dating to the fifteenth century (Kneberg 1959:15; Muller 1989:17). The Citico-style rattlesnake gorget, which Smith dates from some time before 1525 to between 1600 and 1630, has been proposed as a marker of the Coosa paramount chiefdom; it, too, generally is associated with females and subadults (Hally et al. 1990:133-34; Smith 1987:108-12). In contrast, mask gorgets are associated with males and subadults. They appear at about the same time as Citico rattlesnake gorgets, but perhaps continued in use longer: one is reported from a late nineteenth-century Kansa war bundle (Smith and Smith 1989). Smaller masks, or "maskettes," have been proposed as a later, purely protohistoric, development (Brashler and Moxley 1990:6); however, their context at the Hiwassee Island site is with prehistoric subadult burials, not with any of the burials assigned to the historic period (Lewis and Kneberg 1946:130, 134, 147, 149-52). Brain and Phillips (1996) do not treat small masks as a separate style. They suggest that unengraved masks with eye holes might be the most recent type; however, it, too, occurs in prehistoric contexts at Hiwassee Island.

For the northeast, Lynn Ceci documented the development of wampum, pinpointing successive styles that can be used as temporal markers (1982, 1989b). "Early wampum" (slightly larger and more variable in size than later types, but probably drilled by iron awls) was present at interior New York sites of the late sixteenth century. "Wampum" was present in great quantities by the mid-seventeenth century, but still coexisted with a variety of other bead shapes, while highly standardized, thinly-drilled "late wampum" was the only type of shell bead present by the beginning of the eighteenth century. The wampum belt developed mainly after 1640. Ceci's 1989 summary, with its contrasting discussion of shell-bead-producing coastal sites versus shell-bead-"consuming" interior sites, well illustrates the nonsimultaneity of "horizon marker" deposition—the fact that a given artifact might be used in one region at a somewhat different time than in another—and the fact that a given material or artifact might be treated or "valued" differently at different distances from its source, as well as at sites used by producers or intermediaries versus "end users" (cf. Cobb 1989; Ray 1978).

Bone musical rasps are a relatively late phenomenon in eastern North America, which Robert Boszhardt has tracked from their first appearance in the southern plains and pueblos around 1250-1450 (e.g., Panhandle Aspect, Grasshopper and Pecos pueblos) to late prehistoric/early historic central Plains sites (Great Bend Aspect) and protohistoric Oneota sites in the vicinity of LaCrosse, Wisconsin. He believes their spread may have occurred mainly during the 1500s (Boszhardt 1993, pers. comm.).

Smoking pipes are very common during the late prehistoric and early historic periods, and tend to have distinctive diachronic stylistic variations in all regions of eastern North America. Although particular materials, stylistic attributes, and motifs are peculiar to different geographic regions, pipes often were transported far from their places of origin. Thus, they have great potential as pan-regional chronological markers. Unfortunately, few exhaustive studies have been undertaken. There seem to be more chronologically oriented studies of Iroquoian pipes (e.g., Lenig 1965:54-56; Noble 1992) than for pipes of other regions, but even these studies are few and often equivocal (cf. Pendergast 1992:59-61). Since Iroquoian pipes are relatively rare outside their home territories, they are more useful as local than pan-regional horizon markers.

Large Mississippian figure pipes (over about four inches maximum measurement), including human, human-animal, and fantastic and naturalistic animal depictions, are a prehistoric phenomenon, most common in the eleventh through fourteenth centuries (e.g., C. Brown 1926:247-67; J. Brown 1976:245-70; Drooker 1994d; Emerson 1982, 1983; Farnsworth and Emerson 1989; Fundabark and Foreman 1957: Pls. 99-103).

Catlinite disk pipes, and the use of catlinite in general, occur after 1400 at Oneota sites in southern Wisconsin, the region where they are most common (Gibbon 1986:328). They have been found at at least a few sites with European goods (e.g., Hamilton 1967; O'Brien 1994:239). Although some have survived in historically utilized war bundles, Ian Brown places their production mainly within prehistoric-protohistoric times; they do not appear to have been fashioned with metal tools (Brown 1989:317-22; West 1934:207). According to William Green (1993:300), most "prototypical" late Oneota catlinite disk pipes date to around 1450-1650.

Unfortunately, little research has been done on changes of disk pipe styles over time. They may have become smaller. For example, more-compact shapes (short handle, relatively small disk), often rendered in limestone rather than catlinite or other red pipestone, are known to be associated with very late prehistoric or protohistoric Orr phase (Ioway) sites (M. Wedel 1959: Fig. 11; West 1934: Pl. 259); however, their total time frame is unknown. Slightly less compact limestone disk pipes with cylindrical or ovoid handles ending in points or pointed edges have come from protohistoric Caborn-Welborn sites like Murphy (Moorehead 1906: Fig. 23). Production of large-disk, long-handled catlinite disk pipes may perhaps have been confined almost entirely to prehistoric times (Brown 1989:322).

Catlinite elbow pipes, strongly associated with calumet ceremonialism, are a later form that probably dates from the mid-seventeenth century onward (Brown 1989:311, 322-26). Likewise, catlinite Micmac-style pipes apparently date to the late seventeenth or early eighteenth centuries and after (Brown 1989:317; Witthoft et al. 1953). Vase-shaped pipe bowls, occasionally in redstone/catlinite, but generally in a variety of other lithic materials, are assigned to the late prehistoric or early protohistoric (Witthoft et al. 1953:94).

These valued materials and artifacts, both indigenous and European, are useful both for establishing site occupation time frames and for tracing interaction among settlements and regions. The latter topic is explored in Chapter 8. In Chapter 4, horizon marker artifacts, together with absolute dating methods, are used to develop relative chronologies for Fort Ancient sites. The place of the Madisonville site in this chronological sequence is considered in Chapter 6.

Chapter 4

The Central Ohio River Valley

In contrast to the Eastern Seaboard and Great Lakes area, there are almost no eyewitness historical accounts for the Ohio River valley until the middle of the eighteenth century, nearly 250 years after Europeans and indigenous peoples of eastern North America began to interact. Furthermore, unlike regions such as New York, there is no clear sequence of prehistoric-protohistoric-historic archaeological sites that make it possible to use the "direct historical approach" to work backward from known to unknown lifeways, worldviews, and interaction patterns.

In later chapters, the Madisonville site is considered as a case study of protohistoric Fort Ancient interaction patterns, continuity, and change. This chapter sets the stage with a summary of relevant available intraregional information. First, it briefly reviews the meager historical record and the archaeologically defined Fort Ancient tradition, including overviews of chronology, environment, and subsistence, and models of settlement patterns, social organization, and exchange. Then it describes two groups of sites that provide contexts for analyzing Madisonville as the westernmost well-excavated protohistoric Fort Ancient settlement: (1) southwestern Ohio Fort Ancient sites that preceded or overlapped in time with Madisonville, and (2) other known protohistoric Fort Ancient settlements. In these descriptions, particular attention is paid to horizon marker artifacts and attributes that make possible the identification of contemporaneous sites. The final section is a very short summary of attempts that have been made to link the Fort Ancient archeological culture with a known historical group or groups.

The Early Historical Record

There are only a small handful of pre-1750 written records with reliable information about the Ohio Valley. The earliest eyewitness account dates to 1674, when an illiterate English trader was captured by Indians, with whom he probably visited the Kanawha-Ohio River confluence area. French maps of the late seventeenth century do place named groups in the central Ohio Valley (e.g., Griffin 1943: Maps 2-10; Steckley 1990). However, all locations appear to be based on hearsay evidence (e.g., see discussion of sources in Griffin 1943:12-31).

It was the French who first sought to explore this interior region, under René-Robert Cavelier de La Salle in 1669, and who later asserted that these explorations gave them first claim to it. However, it is extremely doubtful that La Salle ever reached the Ohio (Hunter 1978:588; Witthoft and Hunter 1955:46). The information available from Native American informants to the French in Montreal before they organized this expedition has been summarized by Witthoft and Hunter:

> They knew that there was a great river to the southwest, called Ohio by the Iroquois; it flowed westward, and at a distance of six or seven months' march, emptied into the sea....On this river lived a great number of tribes, people who came to French Canada. There were such great numbers of these people that each tribe might consist of fifteen or twenty villages. [Witthoft and Hunter 1955:45-46]

> In 1668...La Salle...understood from some visiting Iroquois that "this river [the Ohio] took its rise three days' journey from Seneca, that after a month's travel one came upon the Honniasontkeronons and the Chiouanons, and that, after passing the latter, and a great cataract or waterfall [Falls of the Ohio, near Louisville]...." [Hunter 1978:588, translating from Margry 1876-86:1:116].

In another account from around this time, Galinée reported that a Frenchman, residing with Nipissing Indians (see Figure 3-3) in 1668-1669, obtained from them a captive taken from the Ohio Valley, who described the "great number of tribes" that resided there (Witthoft and Hunter 1955:45-46, after Margry 1876-86:1:141-43). Similar descriptions were given to Louis Joliet and Father Jacques Marquette, who passed the mouth of the Ohio River on their way down the Mississippi in 1673:

> This river flows from the lands of the East, where dwell the people called Chaouanons in so great numbers that in one district there are as many as 23 villages, and 15 in another, quite

> near one another. They are not at all warlike, and are the nations whom the Iroquois go so far to seek, and war against without any reason. [Griffin 1943:31, quoting from Edna Kenton's translation of Marquette's journal]

In 1671, a group of traders from Virginia under Col. Abraham Wood traveled as far inland as (probably) the headwaters of the New River, a tributary of the Kanawha that in turn runs into the Ohio, near the present-day Virginia–West Virginia border (see Figure 3-1) (Olafson 1960). Three years later, a servant of Wood, Gabriel Arthur, returned to the same area and was captured by "Tomahittan" Indians, with whom he traveled to a large "Moneton" village farther down that same river. He traveled with the Tomahittans to attack members of another Indian group who lived on a larger, westward-flowing river a day's journey downstream. Arthur was wounded and captured by these people, who apparently never had seen a paleface before. Arthur, who gave their "king" a hatchet and knife, reported that he did not see any other iron tools while he was with this group, nor did they know how to use guns. They were described as members of a populous "nation" dispersed along the Ohio, 20 days' travel from end to end. Arthur eventually made his way home, and his adventures later were recorded by his employer, Abraham Wood (Alvord and Bidgood 1912:210-26). Over the years, there has been much speculation as to exactly where Arthur traveled, although it generally is acknowledged that he did reach the Ohio (e.g., Griffin 1943:32-33; Lewis and Lewis 1995:258-60; Myer 1928:736, 780; Swanton 1943:57-58; Williams 1928:23-27). Olafson suggests that the village he visited was the Buffalo site, about 24 miles up the Kanawha from its junction with the Ohio (Olafson 1960). Others have suggested that Arthur eventually traveled as far as the confluence of the Scioto River with the Ohio (summary by Henderson et al. 1986:23).

Received wisdom from traditional historians has been that the Ohio Valley was virtually devoid of population by the last few decades of the seventeenth century, its residents having been "almost completely disrupted and evicted...in the so-called Beaver Wars" with the Iroquois (Hunter 1978:588; cf. Callender 1978f; Hanna 1911:158; Tanner 1987:32-33; White 1991:11-13) or devastated by epidemic disease. For example, Griffin, who believed there was a strong but not ironclad case that the Fort Ancient people could be equated with the historical Shawnee (1943:34-35), quotes the Frenchman Perrot as saying that after about 1671 the Iroquois made war upon "the Andastes [Susquehannock] and Chaouanons [Shawnee], whom they routed in several encounters" (Griffin 1943:30, from Blair 1911-1912:1:226; see also the quotation above from Marquette). Certainly, Shawnee and other captives probably from this general area are known to have been brought back to Iroquoian territory in Ontario and western New York during the 1670s (e.g., Griffin 1943:30, 31; cf. Richter 1983:539-41). However, the wholesale devastation and forcible expulsion later claimed by the English as having been accomplished by their Iroquois League proteges never was backed up by eyewitness accounts. Over the past decade, evidence refuting the "myth of Iroquois conquest" has been vigorously and effectively marshaled (e.g., Jennings 1984:16; McConnell 1987:93-94), but positive historical evidence related to Ohio Valley demographics during this time remains nil.

The earliest firsthand information and reliable maps of the Ohio were provided through a 1739 expedition by Charles Le Moyne de Longueuil from Lake Chautauqua, New York, to the Mississippi River, and a 1749 expedition by Pierre Joseph Céloron de Blainville along the same route down the Ohio as far as the mouth of the Great Miami River (Hunter 1978:588; Henderson et al. 1986:33-35; White 1991:206-8). In 1750-51, Christopher Gist surreptitiously explored along the river for the Ohio Company of Virginia (Darlington 1893). By that time, a thriving European–native trade center existed at Lower Shawneetown (the Bentley site), opposite the mouth of the Scioto River (Hanna 1911:145-46; Henderson et al. 1986:21-40).

Whether or not the region was "empty" at the end of the seventeenth century, the first eighteenth-century historical records of its residents dealt with at least some groups of Native Americans who had resided elsewhere until the early part of that century. Delawares and Shawnees from Pennsylvania and Senecas from New York are known to have migrated to the Upper Ohio Valley and westward starting around 1725 (Hanna 1911:145-47; Hunter 1978:589, 591-92; Kent et al. 1981). At least some of the Shawnees probably were returning to places where they or their families previously had lived (e.g., Witthoft and Hunter 1955). Information about French and English traders on or near the Ohio River has been compiled from about 1728 onward (Hunter 1952), but there are tantalizing hints in the Pennsylvania records that commercial trade was in swing by the 1710s (Hagadorn 1991). Given the half-century hiatus in eyewitness descriptions of this region after Gabriel Arthur's 1674 account of a thriving, populous region, what can archaeological evidence add to our knowledge of this important period in the central Ohio Valley?

The Fort Ancient Archaeological Tradition

Because the historical record tells us so little about the Ohio Valley for the first two and a half centuries of the Contact Period, the archaeological record is particularly important. Ohio Valley excavations have been reported for well over 150 years. Some of them were well planned and methodically conducted to obtain particular archaeological data, but many others were fortuitous and haphazard, with much information lost in consequence.

Early interest centered on the many mounds and earthworks that dotted the landscape (Atwater 1820; Metz 1878, 1881; Squier and Davis 1848; Thomas 1894). The most arresting of them now are known to have been constructed by Hopewell and Adena peoples during the centuries just before and after the beginning of the Christian era. However, until fairly recently many people believed that these sites, with their caches of exotic materials and sophisticated artifacts, must postdate (or at

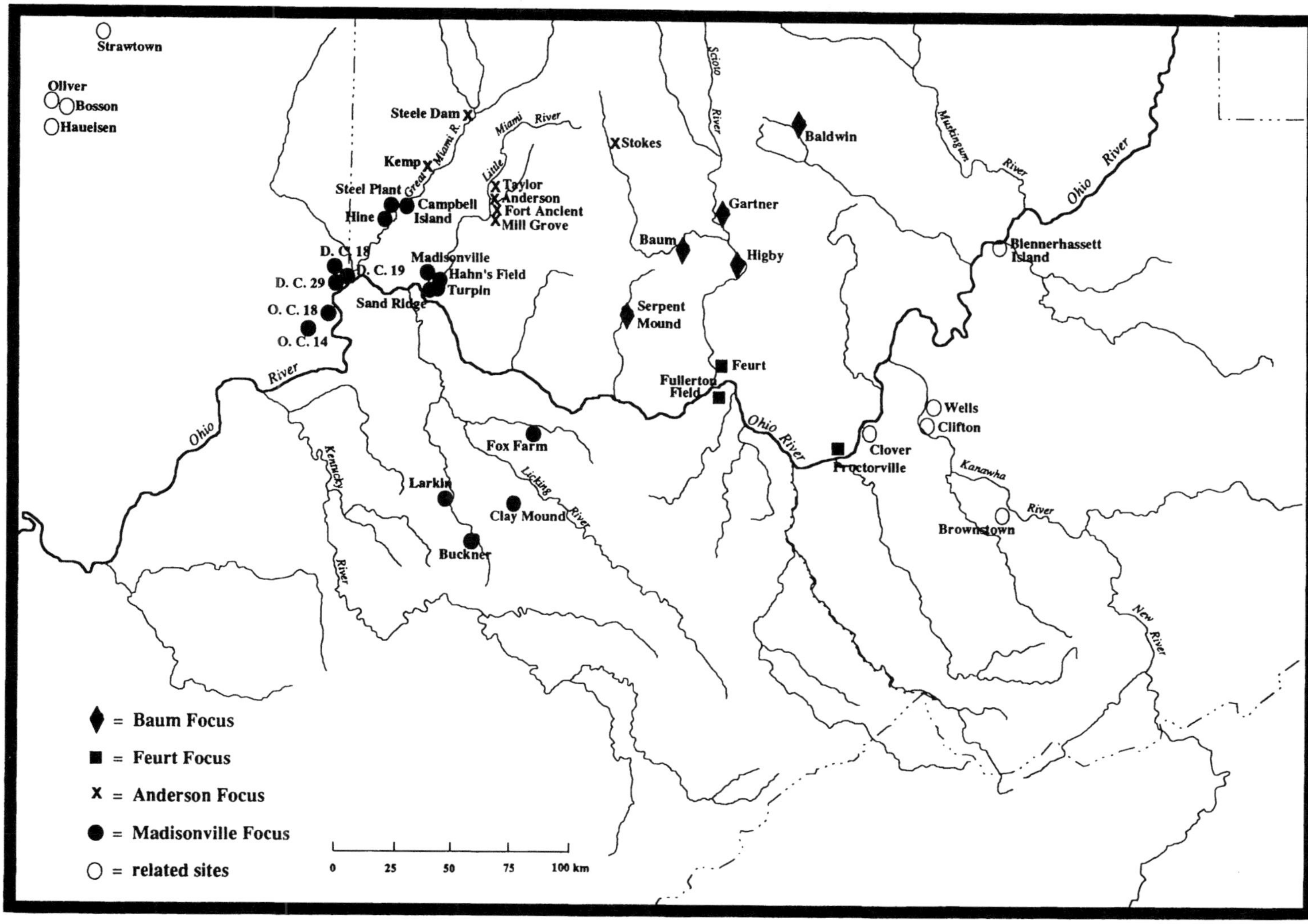

Figure 4-1. Sites and foci included in *The Fort Ancient Aspect* (after Griffin 1943: Map 1).

least must have been concurrent with) the more mundane village sites that now are assigned to the Fort Ancient archaeological tradition.

Recognition and Development of the Fort Ancient Concept

It was Frederic Putnam of the Peabody Museum at Harvard who first recognized in print the entity that we now call "Fort Ancient" (Putnam 1886:500). However, it was William Mills of the Ohio Historical Society who formally assigned a name to it (Mills 1906:135-36; Griffin 1943:210). Unfortunately, the site after which the tradition was named is multicomponent, and has yielded more evidence for Hopewellian than Fort Ancient occupations. However, the name had precedence and was retained by James Griffin, the primary definer of the Fort Ancient culture area (1943:222). His own opinion, though, was that "it might have been better to have called the culture 'Madisonville' " (1943:119), as originally advocated by Charles Willoughby (Hooton and Willoughby 1920:135; Willoughby 1923a, 1923b).

After painstaking analysis of archaeological collections obtained by many different excavators from the late nineteenth century through WPA days, Griffin assigned thirty-one sites in southeastern Indiana, southern Ohio, and northern Kentucky to what was called the "Fort Ancient Aspect." Of these, Madisonville was the most populous and had produced by far the greatest number of ceramic vessels. Based on differences and similarities in ceramics and other material culture traits, Griffin divided the sites into four geographically oriented "foci," also recognizing a fifth closely related region centering on the Kanawha Valley area of West Virginia and a sixth in central Indiana now designated the Oliver phase (Figure 4-1). Concepts and terminology were based on the Midwestern Taxonomic System that recently had been developed by William McKern (Griffin 1943:327-41; McKern 1939). Temporal relationships within the Fort Ancient tradition were not a significant part of Griffin's analysis, but European artifacts from a single site, Madisonville, demonstrated the persistence of the tradition into post-Contact times. Griffin also demonstrated, through stratigraphic relationships, the temporal precedence of Hopewell-Adena over Fort Ancient occupation in this region (1943:210-15).

Griffin, with McKern, placed Fort Ancient within an "Upper Mississippi phase" that included the Oneota peoples of the upper Mississippi River valley, the belief being that they both "derived their Mississippian complexion from Middle Mississippi" (Griffin 1943:301). In his comparisons of traits among culture areas, Griffin found greatest similarities between Oneota (with its easterly offshoots in the northeastern Illinois/northwestern Indiana Fisher Focus) and western Fort Ancient (Madisonville Focus); southern Fort Ancient sites also exhibited many traits typical of Mississippian sites of both the upper Tennessee Valley and the central Mississippi Valley. In addition, Griffin recognized "a significant number of traits—pottery, nonpottery, and burial" that were common to Fort Ancient and Woodland cultural divisions, particularly at northern Fort Ancient sites (1943:207). This latter correspondence is now understood to be a result of the *in situ* development of Fort Ancient from Woodland culture and lifeways (e.g., Church 1987; Riggs 1986).

Griffin's extensive trait lists, descriptions and illustrations of artifacts (particularly ceramics), measurements and attribute lists for selected ceramic vessels, reviews of excavation history for each site, examination of historical documentation, and comparisons between traits of Fort Ancient and other recognized culture areas and archaeological aspects are extraordinarily thorough, reliable, and insightful. They represent a benchmark and a data base from which modern researchers are still benefiting. However, they lack quantitative information about site artifact assemblages that can be analyzed by statistical methods. Because they were not intended to address time-related questions within the Fort Ancient tradition, and because of limitations in early excavation techniques, they also lack much information on stratigraphic relationships and do not emphasize (even though often recognizing) the multicomponent nature of many Fort Ancient sites.

Since the original formulation of the Fort Ancient culture area, many additional sites have been excavated in the region. Figure 4-2 shows the locations of the most thoroughly investigated Fort Ancient sites that are currently recognized—almost triple the number included in Griffin's original study. Considerably more have been located, but many are of limited extent or have been described only from small-scale surface surveys. For example, five major sites are shown in Figure 4-2 within 25 km of the Hardin site, but a recent study lists a total of sixteen sites with Fort Ancient components within this area, on the Kentucky side of the Ohio River alone (Holmes 1994:41-46); Graybill (1981:30-31) maps forty-five sites along the Kanawha and the Ohio north to the West Virginia line where Figure 4-2 shows thirteen; see also Figure 4-6 below for southwestern Ohio. Many additional sites have been lost to the picks and shovels of early highway crews, the backhoes and bulldozers of later industrialists and developers, and the uncontrolled scavenging of avaricious collectors (for example, see descriptions in Metz 1878, 1881; Starr 1960). Extant museum collections, some well documented, some not, remain, as they were for Griffin, a prime source for new research.

Fort Ancient Chronology

With the advent of new excavations and radiocarbon dating after World War II (Corskadder and Morton 1977; Oehler 1950, 1973; Pruter 1970; Rattery 1974), a Fort Ancient chronological sequence began to emerge. Instead of the essentially synchronic system of foci that Griffin had put forth, a diachronic system of phases (local developmental stages) was gradually developed, following the model of Willey and Phillips (1958). A number of projects were initiated specifically to develop subregional chronological sequences based on small-scale stratigraphically controlled excavations, radiocarbon dating, and seriation of horizon marker artifacts and feature attributes (e.g., Church 1987; Cowan 1986; Graybill 1981; Riggs 1986, 1994). By the beginning of the 1980s, as many as seven diverse subregional traditions were proposed to have developed *in situ* during the Early-Middle Fort Ancient periods, ca. A.D. 1000-1450 (e.g., Graybill 1981: Fig. 1; Griffin 1978: Fig. 1), which eventually merged into a more coherent Late Fort Ancient regional tradition that has been designated the "Madisonville Horizon" (Cowan 1988:8-9; Essenpreis 1988:9; Henderson and Turnbow 1987:220-21; Sharp 1990:469-71). Ceramics have been instrumental in developing distinctions among phases: relatively diverse styles and a variety of tempering materials differentiate Early-Middle Fort Ancient subregions, whereas Madisonville Cordmarked and Madisonville Plain jars with strap handles, undecorated necks, and unthickened, everted rims (see below, Figure 4-9) seem to be common at Madisonville Horizon sites in all subregions.

Figure 4-3 shows time frames proposed for some of these phases. Boundary dates assigned to phases do vary among subregions, as indicated by the broad boundary lines at the left of the diagram. This reflects (1) variation in archaeological conditions among subregions, (2) decisions on whether to mark boundaries primarily by transitions in important horizon marker attributes or primarily by absolute dates (radiocarbon or thermoluminescence), and (3) inconsistent calibration procedures for radiocarbon dates. The latter factor has not been explicitly addressed for most currently recognized Fort Ancient phases, but can make a significant difference in absolute timing. For example, when radiocarbon dates from sites assigned to the Early Fort Ancient Turpin phase (Cowan 1986:135) are calibrated, they fall between A.D. 1100 and 1300, rather than 1000 and 1250 as diagrammed in Figure 4-3 (Drooker 1996a). A primary horizon marker for these sites is burial mounds. However, in northern Kentucky, where radiocarbon dates consistently are calibrated using the standard University of Washington calibration

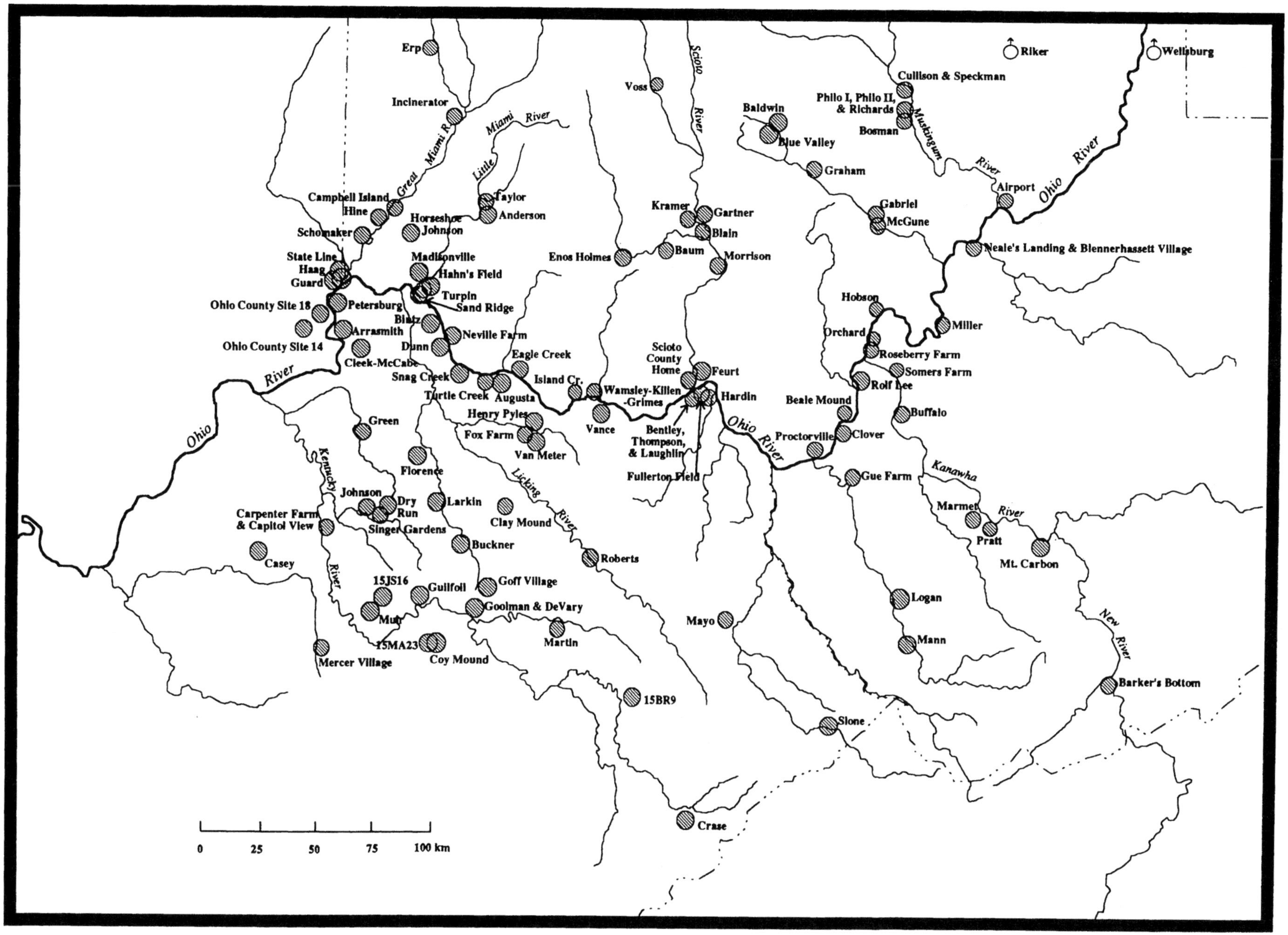

Figure 4-2. Important currently recognized Fort Ancient and related sites (base map after Henderson 1992: Fig. I-1).

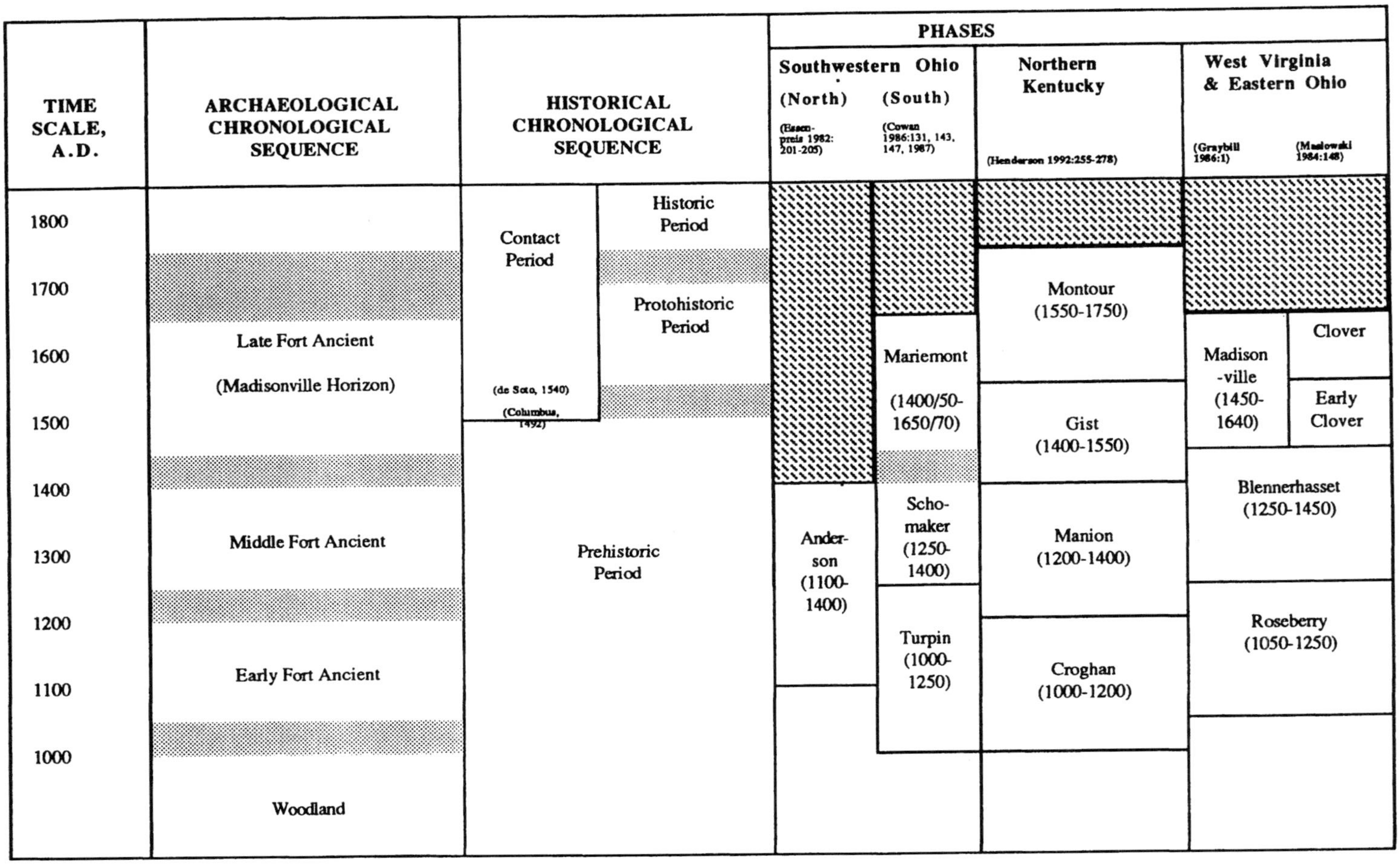

Figure 4-3. Fort Ancient temporal relationships for selected subregions (source: Henderson 1992:3).

curve (Stuiver and Reimer 1986, now superseded by Stuiver and Reimer 1993) and phases are bounded by absolute dates approximately two centuries apart, all sites with burial mounds have been assigned to the Middle Fort Ancient Manion phase, A.D. 1200-1400 (Henderson 1992:262-66). Mounds thus are not considered an Early trait in this subregion. In fact, it seems very probable that an early burial mound horizon occurs across both subregions at approximately the same time, centered on the thirteenth century.

When comparing phases primarily distinguished by absolute cutoff dates versus phases primarily distinguished by the rise and fall of assemblages of horizon marker attributes, another factor must be kept in mind. Because different horizon markers often change at different rates, there is bound to be overlap (in terms of absolute time) between Early, Middle, and Late periods, even within a given subregion.

Differences in phase boundary definitions also reflect the fact that some subregions, such as those assigned by Griffin to the Anderson Focus and the Baum Focus, seem to have contained few if any settlements during the Late Fort Ancient period. On the other end of the time scale, one subregion, in northern Kentucky, includes the Lower Shawneetown site, known to have been occupied historically; the temporal limit of the late Late Fort Ancient Montour phase has been adjusted accordingly.

Indeed, the upper temporal limit of Late Fort Ancient phases seems frequently to waver as new theories and evidence are brought to bear (e.g., in Cowan 1986 and 1987)—which of course is not at all a bad thing. Various dates also have been proposed for the boundary between the two Late Fort Ancient phases. Most researchers, if they do subdivide Late Fort Ancient, do it on the basis of presence or absence of European goods—in other words, early Late Fort Ancient would be considered prehistoric and late Late Fort Ancient would be considered protohistoric. However, Graybill and Cowan recently have employed a dividing line of A.D. 1640 (Cowan 1992:15-16; Graybill 1987). After that date, Graybill argued, the "pristine" Fort Ancient cultural system became disrupted by population movements and other pressures induced by Iroquois aggression. He assigned Madisonville to the post-1640 phase. The data for this model, unfortunately, are marred by inconsistent consideration of horizon marker artifacts and radiocarbon dates for sites assigned to each phase. The model is described in more detail below in Recent Research on Fort Ancient Settlement Patterns, Social Organization, and Exchange.

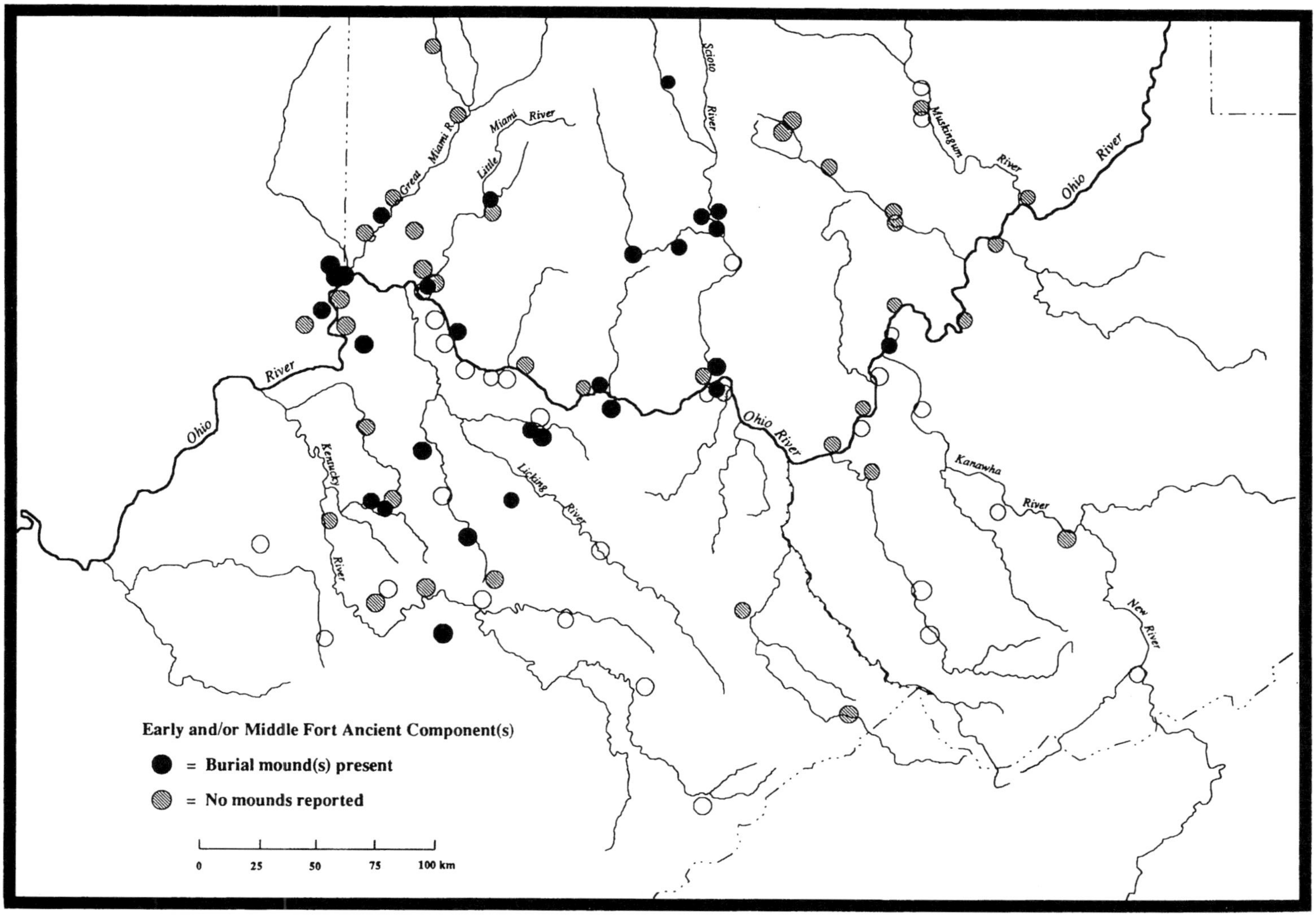

Figure 4-4. Early-Middle Fort Ancient components (Carskadden 1994; Church 1987; Drooker 1996a; Graybill 1981; Henderson et al. 1992; Prufer 1970; Prufer and McKenzie 1967; Sharp 1990).

In this manuscript, I do not attempt to resolve differences among phase boundaries assigned within subregions, but, in discussions of relative temporal placement, refer to time periods in very general terms as Early Fort Ancient (1000/1050-1200/1250), Middle Fort Ancient (1200/1250-1400/1450), and Late or Madisonville Horizon Fort Ancient (1400/1450-1650/1750), the last subdivided into prehistoric Early Madisonville Horizon or early Late Fort Ancient (1400/1450-1550) and protohistoric Late Madisonville Horizon or late Late Fort Ancient (ca. 1550-1650/1750). Whenever possible, I tie these periods to concrete variation in horizon marker attributes.

Gwynn Henderson (1992:3; cf. Cowan 1986:148) has drawn attention to the problem of multicomponent sites, which confounded early attempts to develop consistent pan-Fort Ancient chronologies, and which until very recently often were shoehorned into a single phase. Matters were complicated, and still are, by the continued uncritical use of Griffin's synchronic pottery types as phase markers. Stratigraphically controlled excavations at multicomponent sites and radiocarbon dates from samples in direct association with particular pottery types are starting to allow fine tuning of this system to make it useful for diachronic analysis (Drooker 1996a; Glowacki et al. 1993; Riggs 1986, 1994; Turnbow 1992; Turnbow and Henderson 1992), but a revised definitive, encompassing ceramic chronology has yet to be published.

Radiocarbon dates and horizon marker artifacts for the western Fort Ancient developmental sequence and for late prehistoric-protohistoric sites contemporaneous with Madisonville are presented and discussed below. Figures 4-4 and 4-5 are included here as a preview, to give a general idea of Fort Ancient settlement locations over time. Figure 4-4 indicates sites that contain components assigned to pre-Madisonville Horizon time peri-

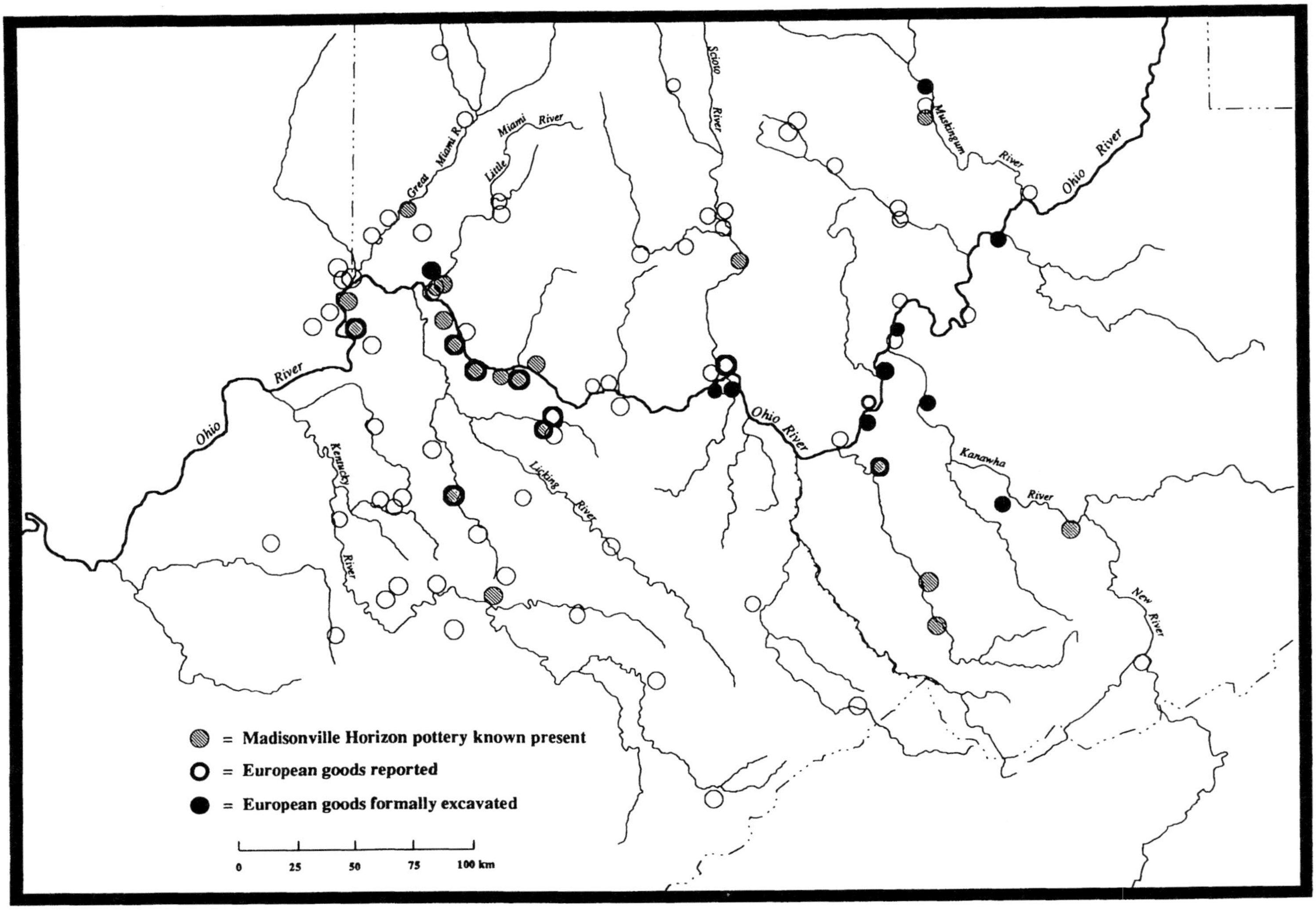

Figure 4-5. Late Fort Ancient and related components, defined on the basis of ceramics and European goods present (for references, see Table 4-9).

ods, A.D. 1000/1050-1400/1450. It highlights sites known to have burial mounds, which appear to be an early attribute. Although almost no radiocarbon dates have come from mound contexts, it seems likely that most mound building ceased by 1300 (Drooker 1996a).

Figure 4-5 shows Late Fort Ancient sites, so designated by the presence of late Madisonville series ceramics (which might not be clearly delineated in site reports, due to the definitional problems mentioned above). The most recent Fort Ancient sites are those that have produced European materials and artifacts. These have been obtained by controlled excavation from only a few (definitely protohistoric) sites. Additional sites from which European artifacts have been reported were not necessarily occupied primarily after 1492 (see Protohistoric Fort Ancient Sites below for descriptions of recovery contexts at different sites).

Keeping these caveats in mind, the maps do reveal at least two significant time trends for Fort Ancient settlement locations: (1) over time, the center of gravity for Fort Ancient sites apparently shifted from west to east, and (2) later sites appear to be less dispersed, the majority (but by no means all) of them situated near the Ohio River.

Fort Ancient Territory and Subsistence

Fort Ancient communities all were located within the drainage system of the central Ohio River valley (Figures 3-1, 4-2). North of the Ohio, sites have been found from the Muskingum River in eastern Ohio to the lower reaches of Laughery Creek in southwestern Indiana, and north almost to the Ohio River–Lake Erie divide. South of the Ohio, they are located from the mouth of the Little Kanawha in the east to the upper Salt River drainage in the west, and south to the upper reaches of all major tributaries. As illustrated in Figures 4-4 and 4-5, the range of preferred settlement locations changed over time, and much of this territory may well have been utilized primarily for hunting after about 1450.

The main southeastern portal through the Appalachians was via the New/Kanawha River valley, which gave access to the headwaters of a number of major rivers south of Chesapeake Bay, such as the James, Roanoke, and Peedee (Rountree 1993b: Fig. 1.3; see Figure 3-1). The Ohio River provided a major northeast-southwest communication axis. Northwestern Ohio could be reached readily via the Great Miami and the northeast-draining Maumee, and the upper reaches of the Wabash provided a route toward the west. Historically and probably prehistorically, an important system of trails led south cross-country from the Ohio River near Cincinnati to the Cumberland Gap and southwesterly along the northern flank of the Appalachians (Henderson et al. 1986:18-21; Myer 1928; Tanner 1989).

The central Ohio Valley has a temperate continental climate (Church 1987:41-45; Graybill 1981:50-52; Wagner 1987:12), characterized by significant differences between summer and winter temperatures, from minima of about -10°F to maxima of about 105°F, and also significant day-to-day fluctuations. Frost-free days average 150 to 180. Precipitation, which ranges from about 90 cm per year in the north to about 115 in the south, is heaviest during the late spring and summer. However, most flooding occurs between December and April. Based on pollen studies and analysis of Lake Erie western basin paleoclimates by Lawrence Graves, the climate probably was warmer and drier until ca. A.D. 640, becoming cooler and wetter through the end of the late prehistoric (Church 1987:44). Less localized climatic analysis has postulated fluctuations within this period, with a warm/dry period between A.D. 1300 and 1450 followed by a return to cooler and moister conditions around 1450-1700 (Graybill 1981:57).

The Fort Ancient territory encompassed much geomorphological and biological diversity, including portions of three physiographic provinces (Church 1987:40-60; Graybill 1981:40-58; Henderson 1992:23-27; Nass 1987:15-27; Wagner 1987:11-32; cf. Figure 3-1). In the east, the Allegheny Plateau province comprises an unglaciated, maturely dissected landscape of rugged topography, with greatest elevations and relief southeast of the Ohio River. Its locally varied bedrock, soils, exposure, and elevation supported a mosaic of deciduous forest covers falling broadly within the mixed mesophytic (moderate-moisture) type. The Interior Low Plateau province, mainly west of the Licking River in Kentucky, is characterized by gently rolling topography underlain primarily by limestones. Its western mesophytic forest type is transitional from the mixed mesophytic to its east to an oak-dominated mixture farther west. The Central Lowlands province, covering western Ohio, coincides with glacial incursion into the region, and with the beech-maple forest region. Its generally flat topography is due to burial of much surface relief by glacial drift. In all provinces, floodplains of the Ohio River and its major tributaries provide fertile agricultural soil, while upland soils vary in their suitability for horticulture.

The varied hydrology, topography, and plant cover supported a broad range of wildlife, including fish, shellfish, and turtles in and near the rivers, pigeons, wild turkey, and waterfowl, small mammals such as squirrels, raccoons, and woodchucks, and large mammals such as deer, elk, bear, bobcat, and, some time after A.D. 1450, bison (Graybill 1981:55-56; Henderson 1992:25-26; Miller and Duerksen 1995; Tankersley 1986a, 1992; Tankersley and Adams 1991). Salt licks, attractive to large game animals, are common in northeastern Kentucky and southeastern Ohio (Henderson 1992:26).

Fort Ancient people utilized a wide range of plant resources, including wild fruits and nuts, but with fairly heavy emphasis on corn. They also cultivated beans, squash, sunflowers, chenopod, and tobacco (Rossen 1992; Wagner 1983, 1984, 1986, 1987). According to Rossen and Edging, nut collecting may have decreased from the Woodland period, and may have been less important for Fort Ancient than for Mississippian peoples (Rossen and Edging 1987). Maize, too, may have been less important: from $\delta^{13}C$ measurements on human remains, Schurr and Schoeninger conclude that occupants of four Early-Middle Fort Ancient sites ate significantly less maize than people at two lower Ohio Valley/Mississippi Valley Mississippian sites (1995:328). Although there are local differences, the Fort Ancient subsistence system probably remained relatively stable over time (Dunavan 1993; Rossen 1992:208; Wagner 1987:229). Nass's catchment analysis of six southwestern Ohio sites supported Graybill's assertion that Fort Ancient settlements were self-sufficient in horticulture (Graybill 1981; Nass 1988). Shell hoes were the common agricultural implement throughout the region. Elk antler mattocks also were used, but appear, along with bone agricultural implements, to have been most common in the west. At least by Middle Fort Ancient times, the use of deep storage pits for corn was widespread (e.g., Cowan 1987:20-21; Nass 1987:150-72). Large jars, probably for food storage, have come from many sites, while smaller jars suitable for cooking and serving were very common. Bowls, of individual serving size, and some large, flat "saltpan" vessels make up the remainder of vessel types. (See Griffin 1943 for photographs of typical vessel forms.)

Emanuel Breitburg recently summarized animal resource utilization data for fifteen Fort Ancient sites (Breitburg 1992), concluding that four faunal resources formed the subsistence backbone: deer, elk, bear, and turkey. At most sites, deer did not dominate the assemblage, but there was considerable variation among sites and subregions. Bison came into the region late, and are known with certainty to have been utilized only by residents of the Madisonville site (Baker 1994; Tankersley 1986a, 1992; Tankersley and Adams 1991). In Kentucky, upland hunting sites were frequented, and salt licks probably figured in large-animal hunting strategies. Since the area is not on a major flyway for migratory birds, they were not an important part of the diet. Aquatic resources were utilized, but also did not form a large part of the diet (cf. Warren, in press). This is in contrast to major Mississippian sites, whose occupants relied more heavily on floodplain faunal resources (cf. Smith 1978:480-

88). (Essenpreis reports slightly different conclusions based on a smaller sample of sites examined by Orrin Shane and Gail Wagner [1982:246].) Bone fishhooks, triangular arrowheads, bone "beamers" (hide scrapers) and flint endscrapers, reflecting fishing, hunting, and hide-processing activities, were almost universally present at Fort Ancient sites.

Evidently, in many communities the diverse subsistence base of hunted and gathered foodstuffs did not adequately supplement corn, the Fort Ancient dietary mainstay. High reliance on corn, deduced at many sites from the high frequency of kernels in flotation analyses, was confirmed for the Turpin site through bone carbon isotope studies (van der Merwe and Vogel 1978). Two studies that compared demographics and bone and dental health indicators between people from Fort Ancient sites (Hardin, Turpin, State Line) and Archaic and Woodland sites both concluded that the Fort Ancient population had worse health than earlier people, probably due both to diet and to higher population densities in nucleated villages (Cassidy 1984; Perzigian et al. 1984).

Previous Research on Fort Ancient Settlement Patterns, Social Organization, and Exchange

For many years, Griffin's original magnum opus, along with followup summaries at intervals of one or two decades (Griffin 1943, 1952, 1978), were the major sources for a complete overview of Fort Ancient material culture and lifeways. Although the emphasis was on artifacts, particularly ceramics, no important trait was left unmentioned. A good summary of house types and site layouts by focus (Baum, Anderson, Feurt, and Madisonville/Clover), plus information on mortuary treatments, was included in Griffin's *Handbook of North American Indians* overview, but the author attempted no diachronic analysis, concluding that "the pitifully few dates from Fort Ancient sites and the almost complete lack of stratigraphic data or carefully compared site or site segment complexes make significant temporal subdivisions of Fort Ancient an interesting game, but the results cannot be definitive" (1978:557).

Reconstruction of Fort Ancient social organization and its development over time requires a sizable body of data on settlement patterns (including location, size, layout, and function of contemporaneous settlements during successive periods), mortuary treatments (including burial locations, types of interment including likely group involvement and energy expenditure, and types and distribution of grave goods), and outside interaction (objectified by the presence of exotic materials such as marine shell and valued finished items of identifiable source such as catlinite pipes).

The first attempt at a comprehensive summary of Fort Ancient settlement patterns (Essenpreis 1978) was hampered by the meager published record. This tentative identification of a Madisonville phase hierarchical settlement pattern—later refuted—was based on the erroneous identification of a Fort Ancient component at Marietta, a mound site in southeastern Ohio (Essenpreis 1988; Graybill 1980, 1981; Griffin 1992; Yerkes 1991). In actuality, the only Fort Ancient site with a documented substructure mound (perhaps analogous to those at Mississippian ceremonial centers) is Baum, active during Early Fort Ancient time to around 1200 (Church 1987:123-35, 213-25; Griffin 1992:54; Mills 1906), but it never has been proposed as an upper-level site in a settlement hierarchy.

Only by the 1980s had enough data from stratigraphic excavations, radiocarbon dating, and detailed, comprehensive mapping of site features accumulated to allow diachronic treatment of all aspects of material culture, including artifact attributes and types, building construction, settlement layout, mortuary treatment, and external interaction objectified by exotic materials and artifacts. Since then, several studies have focused on defining subregional developmental patterns, from Early through Late Fort Ancient. These have focused on the central Scioto Valley of south-central Ohio (Church 1987), the Muskingum River valley of southeastern Ohio (Carskadden 1992, 1994; Carskadden et al. 1992; Carskadden and Morton 1977; Morton 1984, 1992a, 1992b), West Virginia from the lower Kanawha Valley north along the Ohio to the Muskingum confluence (Graybill 1981), northern Kentucky including the North Fork of the Licking River and the Ohio Valley between the Little Miami and Scioto rivers (Henderson et al. 1992; Pollack and Henderson 1992), and the Great and Little Miami valleys of southwestern Ohio (Cowan 1986, 1987; Drooker 1996a). Although no comprehensive synthesis of Fort Ancient development, covering all currently available subregional data, has been published, several of the subregional studies have presented models of Fort Ancient social development through protohistoric times. Significant data and conclusions are summarized below.

Because available published data and comprehensive models developed for south-central and southeastern Ohio mainly cover the period prior to Late Fort Ancient, I will mention them only briefly here. Flora Church's work centered on elucidating the Late Woodland–Early Fort Ancient transition in the central Scioto Valley. The six Early Fort Ancient villages she reports had plazas, storage pits, burial mounds (at least five sites) plus village burials, and no palisades (1987:218-25). The substructure mound, with burials, in the center of Baum Village has been interpreted by some, but not by Griffin or Church, as pre-Fort Ancient (Griffin 1992:54; Mills 1906:5-11; Schurr and Schoeninger 1995:319). To the northeast, in the central Muskingum Valley, four late thirteenth–early fourteenth century Philo phase settlements, containing relatively small domestic structures generally organized around plazas, are the last known occupations in this subregion until a Wellsburg phase occupation in the sixteenth century, discussed below (Carskadden 1994; Carskadden and Morton 1977).

In West Virginia, Jeffrey Graybill (1981) examined changing settlement patterns over time, using a data base of 22 sites. Maize agriculture and shell-tempered pottery were in place by the mid-eleventh century. Settlements consistently were organized around a central plaza. Average site size increased over time (0.62 ha for Early Fort Ancient, 1.24 ha for Middle, and 1.89 for Late), while numbers of sites decreased (4 to 7.6 per 100 years for the Early-Middle periods, versus 3 for Late). Site locations shifted from high terraces alone to mainly floodplain settings (67% of Late sites), with Late sites concentrated in the southern part of the study area. Based on excavations at two sites, Roseberry Farm and Buffalo, a significant enlargement of house size took place between Early and Late periods, from an average of 28 m^2 at Roseberry Farm to one of 98 m^2 at Buffalo. Based on information from two Middle and two Late sites, only Late sites were found to have palisades. Burial mounds were present at 25-33% of Early sites. The Roseberry Farm mound bordered the plaza and contained adult and adolescent interments; infant burials were found in the domestic zone. At Middle and Late sites, all burials were within the domestic zone, with the majority of them inside houses at Buffalo.

From these data, Graybill drew attention to population amalgamation and geographic constriction over time, paralleling similar trends in Oneota, Whittlesey, Monongahela, and New York Iroquois culture areas. He postulated increasing warfare as the cause for the "appearance of fortifications at about A.D. 1450" (1981:169), tying the warfare to climatic deterioration that affected more northerly peoples' ability to sustain agriculture, leading to competition over hunting/gathering places located between culture areas. In a later paper, he elaborated this conclusion, based on the recent recognition of a "Madisonville horizon" representing similarities in material culture across the entire Fort Ancient area (Graybill 1986). Increased village size during this period was attributed at least partially to population influx, and material culture similarities to increased interaction within Fort Ancient region as a whole. In turn, these changes might signal the development of a society formerly consisting of autonomous villages into a larger tribal entity. After 1550, an influx of non–Fort Ancient people is postulated, following the abandonment of the Whittlesey culture area in northeastern Ohio.

A still later paper (Graybill 1987) offered a revised interpretation of the Madisonville Horizon, drawing upon data from protohistoric sites reported by Maslowski (1984) and Henderson et al. (1986), plus historical accounts of Shawnee locations and movements during the seventeenth century. Based on James Herbstritt's comparison of some 1000 glass beads from Rolf Lee (the Fort Ancient site that has produced by far the largest number of European artifacts) with glass beads from Susquehannock sites, the terminal date for Rolf Lee was put at 1630. (It should be noted that this work does not take into account Sempowski's revised chronology—1994, discussed in Chapter 3—which would result in a somewhat later date.) Because historical accounts, summarized above, describe the presence of a considerable population in the centra! Ohio valley as late as the 1670s, and at least one Fort Ancient site, Orchard, was reported to have produced a few post-1630 glass beads, Graybill postulated a severe restriction on access to European goods around 1630, due to the collapse of a north-south trade network linking Fort Ancient people to Dallas people in eastern Tennessee and to Neutral people in Ontario. However, he emphasized that this did not necessarily mean that the region was depopulated after this time. Thus, he proposed two Late Fort Ancient phases: "Clover" (A.D. 1450-1640), including the Marmet, Buffalo, Rolf Lee, Clover, Hardin, Fox Farm, Buckner, and Augusta sites, and "Orchard" (A.D. 1640-1690), including the Marmet, Neale's Landing, Orchard, Bentley/Thompson, Morrison, Larkin, Madisonville, and Campbell Island sites (Figures 4-2 and 4-5). For the latter time period, he postulated a westward population shift (linked to Iroquois incursions from the northeast) and cultural discontinuity including a change from nucleated to dispersed settlement patterns and alterations in mortuary practices including increased proportions of grave goods, mortuary vessels, and extended interments.

Robert Maslowski's 1984 paper presented radiocarbon dates and quantitative data on diagnostic artifact attributes, settlement location and organization, mortuary practices, and exotic goods for seven protohistoric sites in West Virginia (late Clover phase, per Figure 4-3), comparing them with three "early Clover" sites that lacked European goods. He saw continuity between the early sites (Gue Farm, Goldcamp, and Mann) and five of the late sites, Clover, Buffalo, Logan, Marmet, and Rolf Lee. Orchard's location away from the river's edge and its high proportion of burials with mortuary vessels were seen as more similar to the Madisonville site than to other Clover phase sites. Neale's Landing's preponderance of mortuary vessels and the distinctive pottery type, with similarities to Whittlesey types, also placed it apart from other Clover sites. Marine shell artifacts and some "southern" pottery attributes were seen as linking Clover settlements with settlements in eastern Tennessee, and Maslowski proposed that Clover peoples migrated south "prior to European settlement of the Ohio Valley," perhaps ultimately joining the Creek Confederacy (1984:161).

Stanley Baker presented a somewhat differing protohistoric scenario for eastern Fort Ancient. In a discussion of glass beads from Rolf Lee, he linked them specifically to a Susquehannock source, postulating that the Herriot Farm site in eastern West Virginia—one of the most westerly known Susquehannock settlements (Figure 3-3) (MacCord 1952)—might have been a locus for down-the-line trade (Baker 1986). He suggested that there might have been some curation and delay in passing on "current" bead types from the coast (consistent with Ray's 1978 model), so that the assemblage at Rolf Lee might not have reached there before the middle of the seventeenth century. The drop in availability of trade goods then would have coincided with a known drop in lower Susquehanna River Susquehannock population between 1647 and 1670 due to disease and warfare (Baker 1988:49). (This scenario is complicated by the fact that West Virginia Susquehannock sites contain no post-1630 horizon markers; Brashler 1987; MacCord 1952; Mason and MacCord 1941, 1944; Trader 1996.) In his analysis of ceramics from the small Neale's Landing site, Baker found approximately 30% Madisonville, 33% Wellsburg, and 24% Neale's Landing types, which he interpreted as representative of an amalgamated population from three different cultural backgrounds, the first from farther southwest, the second from farther north (but not as far north as the Whittlesey culture area), and the third locally developed, which came together due to both Iroquois pressure and depletion of population attributed to trader-transported disease (Baker 1988). All three ceramic types, plus a McKees Rock style jar, were found as mortuary vessels.

The Neale's Landing ceramic assemblage and Baker's interpretation of it have interesting correspondences with assemblages from four late prehistoric-protohistoric Wellsburg phase sites in the central and upper Muskingum River valley (Figures 3-3, 4-2). Based on ceramics present at the late prehistoric Riker site, which has produced 44 copper ornaments but no definitely European-derived artifacts (Vietzen 1974), and on its location at a crossroads of historical trail systems, Janice Whitman proposed that this village-cemetery site served as a center of north-south and east-west trade (1975:79). The predominant ceramic types were relatively large Wellsburg vessels (70%), used for storage, and local "Riker" ware (23%), used for cooking, but Madisonville, northeastern Ohio Tuttle Hill Notched, northwestern Ohio Parker Festooned, and Monongahela types also were present. Each of four excavated mortuary vessels was of a different type: Wellsburg, Riker, Madisonville, and Monongahela (Whitman 1979:29, 31, 73-78). Some 80 km downstream from Riker, the circular, palisaded Bosman settlement (with a few copper ornaments and later radiocarbon dates than Riker; see Table 4-8 below) produced about equal proportions of Madisonville and Wellsburg ceramics (each over 45%), with minor proportions of Tuttle Hill Notched, Indian Hills Stamped, and Neale's Landing Grooved-Paddled; none of the types were segregated from each other on the site (Carskadden 1992, 1994; Carskadden et al. 1992:60). Two nearby later sites, Cullison, with European artifacts and sixteenth-seventeenth century radiocarbon dates, and Speckman, with seventeenth century dates, contained no Madisonville ceramics. Wellsburg types predominated; Indian Hills types and a type related to ceramics at the McKees Rock site were present, but little pottery that could be tied to northeastern Ohio types such as Tuttle Hill Notched (James Morton, pers. comm.). From these assemblages, particularly the sparse representation of northeastern Ohio ceramics, Morton, with Baker, discounts any strong presence of Whittlesey-related peoples, but not the possible presence of Indian Hills-related peoples (cf. Figure 3-3).

Overall Fort Ancient development in the west seems to exhibit many similarities to that in the east. Based on small-scale excavations at three Great Miami River sites (Campbell Island, Hine, and Schomaker) and compilation of data from other southwestern Ohio sites discussed by Griffin, Wesley Cowan has presented the following portrait for the lower Miami drainages (Cowan 1986:130-56, 1987). Early Fort Ancient Turpin phase settlements were larger than preceding Late Woodland villages, and at least some had plazas or palisades. They were characterized by burial mounds (considered a horizon marker for this phase), although village burial, sometimes in stone-box graves, also took place. Shell-tempered pottery, a spatulate-shaped stone ax, stone discoidals, and wall-trench architecture were seen as evidence of interaction with Mississippians farther west. After about A.D. 1250, numbers of settlements sharply decreased. Middle Fort Ancient Schomaker phase settlements (based largely on data from the Schomaker site) had plazas, and at least two sites (Sand Ridge and Hine) were located on blufftops rather than the floodplain locations more typical of Fort Ancient villages. Artifacts and site layouts showed many similarities to more northerly Anderson phase sites like Incinerator, which had both plaza and palisade. Based on analogy with that site and Anderson, burials were characterized as occurring in a belt ringing the plaza. Late Fort Ancient Mariemont phase sites listed by Cowan are relatively few, with Steel Plant, Campbell Island, and Hahn's Field probably prehistoric and Madisonville protohistoric; the Augusta site in Kentucky was seen as related to Madisonville. No house patterns had been published from these sites, and no evidence of plazas was known to Cowan. Mortuary vessels frequently accompanied burials. Ceramics were characterized as strikingly different than those from Schomaker, and a suite of new objects, including many different worked bone tools and ornaments, was in evidence (see Horizon Markers). A number of traits were noted as similar to protohistoric assemblages from the upper and central Mississippi Valley, including bi-pointed knives, thumbnail scrapers, and bison bone tools. The European goods recovered from Madisonville were thought to have been obtained by down-the-line exchange, probably from French or Spanish sources. From Turpin and Schomaker phase structures, research from Incinerator (see below), and evidence for much larger, probably multifamily, houses at the Late Fort Ancient Hardin site in Kentucky, Cowan postulated development over time from self-sustaining nuclear families in small villages to a later more complex clan-based social structure.

In a more recent paper, Cowan (1988) emphasized the differences between western and eastern Early-Middle Fort Ancient house structures (wall trench versus posthole), exchange connections (Mississippi Valley versus eastern Tennessee), and mortuary programs (extended versus flexed burials). In this and other later presentations, Cowan has offered a model of late protohistoric cultural upheaval congruent with that of Graybill (Cowan 1988, 1992). He has painted a picture of Middle Fort Ancient subregional diversity followed by the Madisonville Horizon (ca. 1540-1640) as a "single, monolithic unit" (1988:8-9), replaced in turn by Late Madisonville (ca. 1640-1690) diversity. He cited increased frequencies of multiple burials, bundle burials, and mass graves, suggesting "a far different pattern of mortality than...earlier counterparts" for Late Madisonville, specifically the Madisonville and Orchard sites (1988:10, 1992:15). The late Madisonville Horizon appearance of a number of artifact types such as musical rasps, animal-shaped flat amulets and three-dimensional effigies, engraved pebbles, possible "sucking tubes," and appliqué "salamanders" on ceramic vessels was interpreted as an upsurge in ritual behavior, previously evidenced only by effigy tobacco pipes (1992:16). Cowan suggested that: (1) "it is unlikely that the Ohio Valley populations would have escaped" the epidemics that struck Huron, Iroquois, and Susquehannock peoples during the mid-seventeenth century; (2) the "Iroquois and Susquehannock demand for furs" led to increased hunting by Madisonville Horizon folk, evidenced by greater projectile point density in storage pits at Madisonville versus earlier sites (Cowan 1988:13, 1992:19-20) and by a Madisonville Horizon winter hunting camp in Kentucky (Turnbow and Jobe 1984; Turnbow et al. 1983); and (3) Iroquois raiding after 1650 eventually led to abandonment of Fort Ancient territory (1988:12). Cowan cautioned that "no burned villages, no prostrate, arrow-filled corpses, and no ransacked dwellings have been recorded through archaeological research," but specified the Late Madisonville "change in community plan from structured to unstructured, and probably population composition, increased frequency of redeposited burials, often lacking body parts, [and] the increased occurrence of...ritual paraphernalia" as easily detectable indirect evidence for Iroquois raids (1992:21).

Kenneth Tankersley (1992) has presented a hypothesis of protohistoric subsistence and interaction that is specific to Madisonville, rather than covering a larger portion of Fort Ancient territory. Based on the presence of bison bone and large corn storage pits at Madisonville and of a known bison kill site at Big Bone Lick, Kentucky (Figure 4-2), he postulated seasonal abandonment of Madisonville for the purpose of group bison hunting at Big Bone Lick, analogous to historically known practices of the Mandan and Illini. This new subsistence system was estimated as dating to around 1650, even though calibrated radiocarbon assays for Big Bone Lick appear to be limited to the fifteenth century (see Table 4-1 below). It would differ considerably from subsistence at other known protohistoric Fort Ancient sites, none of which have produced any bison bone—although most of them, like Madisonville, have produced significant numbers of skin processing tools such as bone beamers and flint endscrapers. Based on perceived similarities between examples of ceramic, lithic, bone, and metal artifacts from Madisonville and from the Starved Rock and Zimmerman sites in the vicinity of the French Fort St. Louis (Figure 3-6) where known bison licks also were located, and on historical records of where different ethnic groups settled around the fort compared with where Madisonville-like artifacts have been excavated, Tankersley argued that Madisonville residents moved to Illinois around 1673-1677, and that they were members of an Illini group (1992:126-27):

> The protohistoric Madisonville site population likely exploited bison for two reasons; their close proximity to Big Bone Lick, an area that attracted and concentrated bison; and their ethnic ties to the Illinois, a Central Algonkian group whose subsistence strategy was largely dependent upon bison hunting....A migration to the upper Illinois River valley can be explained in terms of an increased dependence on bison meat....[t]he protohistoric Madisonville population moved to an area where bison were more abundant and more predictable.

The most recent and detailed overview is by Henderson and colleagues (Henderson et al. 1992; Pollack and Henderson 1992), elaborating on data from surveys, excavations, and private collections in four northeastern Kentucky counties (Henderson 1992; Henderson et al. 1986). Almost no Early Fort Ancient Croghan phase sites (A.D. 1000-1200) were found within their study area, only a component at the Thompson site that contained Baum series pottery. Also assigned to this phase were two Ohio sites, Feurt (a large site with burial mounds) and Scioto County Home (Figure 4-2). Based on evidence from sites in other regions such as Muir, Graham, and Baldwin, they suggested a settlement pattern of small communities lacking burial mounds for this phase, proposing that larger communities with burial mounds and central plazas, more typical of their Middle Fort Ancient Manion phase, developed toward the end of the Croghan phase. No nonlocal artifacts have been recovered from Croghan phase sites or from Early Fort Ancient deposits at Muir, leading them to suggest that "spheres of interaction were restricted to smaller subregions within the Fort Ancient culture area at this time, in contrast to later phases" (Henderson et al. 1992:261). (In this suggestion, they appear to be omitting from consideration the significant amounts of marine shell found at burial mound sites such as Feurt and the Baum phase settlements of Baum and Gartner; see Mills 1904, 1906, 1917; Turnbow and Sharp 1988.)

During the Middle Fort Ancient Manion phase (A.D. 1200-1400), which includes components at Feurt, Fox Farm, Fullerton Field, Hardin, Island Creek, Killen-Grimes, Van Meter, Vance, and Wamsley, houses and settlements became larger, sites were occupied longer, and burial mounds often were present (six sites). Ceramics were tempered with both shell and nonshell materials. Both circular villages with central plazas (two sites) and linear settlements (two sites) were identified, based on excavation or visible middens. Mortuary practices from these sites plus Florence and Clay Mound include flexed or extended interment within the village (around the plaza if present) plus mound burial mainly of adults, with only small amounts of grave goods (except for burials in Clay Mound). Higher social standing for mound burials, and thus "some sort of social difference," was hypothesized (Henderson et al. 1992:266). Recovery of "small quantities" of marine shell artifacts in recent excavations at Fox Farm and central Kentucky sites was taken as evidence of limited-scale extraregional exchange, probably with Southeastern groups. (Again, significant amounts of marine shell excavated at Fox Farm in the early twentieth century [Smith 1910] appear to have been omitted from consideration.)

Early Madisonville Horizon Gist phase (A.D. 1400-1550) sites, including components at Bintz, Dunn, Fox Farm, Fullerton Field, Snag Creek, Turtle Creek, and Wamsley, were large, permanent villages, some circular or oval with plaza (two sites specified) but most said to be linear (no sites specified). At least two (Bintz and Dunn) consisted of two separate or overlapping villages, occupied successively. Extended burials, some covered with stone slabs, were found in cemetery areas within villages but apart from structures. Differences in community plan and size, mortuary practices, and material culture (e.g., a more diverse ceramics assemblage) from previous phases suggest changes in social organization "in response to the larger numbers of people living together," perhaps including the "development of new rituals or ceremonies" (Henderson et al. 1992:269). The appearance of "saltpan" vessels in this phase might indicate the increased importance of salt production, possibly for exchange. Marine shell artifacts were present, and pottery attributes such as beaded rim strips, effigy rim riders, and painted vessels were taken as additional evidence for extraregional interaction toward the south.

Late Madisonville Horizon Montour phase (A.D. 1550-1750) sites, including Augusta, Bentley, Hardin, Henry Pyles, Laughlin, and Old Fort Earthworks, have all produced European goods. These were permanently occupied villages, larger than Gist phase settlements. No formally arranged community plans have been revealed by excavation, and evidence for palisades is "equivocal" (Henderson et al. 1992:273). Villages might have been unplanned or segmented with two or more clusters of houses. Structures at Hardin were large enough for 13-26 individuals, probably housing extended families or lineage groups. Historical sources and one excavation, at Goolman, indicate that small winter hunting camps also were utilized. Burials (mainly extended) were within villages, between or sometimes within structures. Grave goods were common with people of all ages. A few individuals, including children, were buried with large amounts of nonlocal items. Multiple burials excavated at Hardin and reported from Augusta are taken as possible evidence of foreign disease. "Extensive, well established, far-reaching, extraregional exchange networks" brought both European and indigenous goods to the region during this phase (Henderson et al. 1992:276). At the post-1700 historical sites, European goods were the primary exchange items; some catlinite/redstone was present, but marine shell was absent.

From this evidence, Pollack and Henderson (1992) proposed a model of Fort Ancient development from family level groups in Early times, to larger Middle Fort Ancient "acephalous local groups" consisting of settlements divided into clan/lineage segments (Johnson and Earle 1987:20), to a Big Man pattern of community-wide leadership (overarching the clan/lineage leadership) based on participation in a prestige-goods economy during the Madisonville Horizon. They saw little evidence for Graybill's scenario of increased warfare with groups to the north during this time period: except for Buffalo, no strongly palisaded community is known, and most villages are located in nondefensive positions, many directly alongside the Ohio River. Evidence for the violent death of a few individuals buried at Hardin, Buffalo, and Larkin suggested that conflict or competition was present, but only on a small scale. Evidence from ceramics, in fact, (they noted) showed interregional interaction with northern Ohio groups during this time. Evidence from marine shell gorgets showed significantly increased interaction with Mississippian groups to the south, also thought to be reflected by the rise in mortuary vessel usage. No evidence for interaction with non–Fort Ancient downstream Ohio River groups was seen. With other Fort Ancient archaeologists, Pollack and Henderson take the widespread, stylistically similar artifact assemblage of the Madisonville Horizon to indicate increased intraregional interaction, and suggest a possible alternative to Big Man social organization that might be more congruent with these circumstances: the development of a panregional tribal system, divided into separate-village formal social divisions such as those known for the historical Shawnee.

None of these models of Late Fort Ancient social development employed quantitative data from formal mortuary analysis, and most presented only impressionistic coverage of interregional exchange patterns over time. Many of the timetables were based on uncalibrated radiocarbon dates, unrefined glass bead chronologies, unrecognized of multicomponent sites, or inaccurate concepts of site occupation extent and timing, particularly for Madisonville. Published presentation of southwestern Ohio settlement patterns and site comparisons has been general rather than quantitative. To test and extend these various hypotheses utilizing data from Madisonville, I found it necessary to develop a quantitative data base of relevant comparative information.

Selected Site Descriptions and Relative Chronologies

Data from two sets of Fort Ancient sites were compiled for comparison with Madisonville: southwestern Ohio sites, for assessing prehistoric developmental changes within the subregion, and protohistoric Fort Ancient sites, for assessing characteristics and external relationships of Madisonville residents during its most intensive occupation. Although many such sites are known, large-scale or stratigraphically controlled excavations have been carried out at only a few of them. Of these, only a fraction have been comprehensively reported with accurate site maps and quantitative data on artifacts and burials. They are the ones of which I made most use. For them, I attempted to gather as much comparative data as possible on settlement characteristics, mortuary patterns, and the presence of exotic materials and artifacts. Following are very brief descriptions of sites employed as major data sources, with an emphasis on quality of data and relative chronological placement. For immediate comparison with the models presented above, I include some summary information of frequencies of occurrence of traits earmarked by previous researchers as important in interpreting Madisonville Horizon trends and events, but most comparison and discussion will be left to Chapter 8.

TABLE 4-1
Radiocarbon Dates for Southwestern Ohio and Nearby Fort Ancient Components, plus Some Related Woodland Components

	Sample No.	Date B.P.	Calibrated Date, A.D., with One-Sigma Range	2-Sigma Cal. Range, A.D.
Anderson, OH	DIC 776	730±65	1217(1284)1388	1065-1416
Arrasmith, KY	RL 801	230±100	1527(1664)1954	1444-1955
	UGA 5625	650±60	1287(1302,1373, 1381)1397	1263-1418
	RL 800	650±100	1280(1302,1373,1381)1411	1211-1442
Big Bone Lick, KY (?)	M 1352	500±100	1330(1429)1480	1289-1642
	UGA 4291	530±105	1318(1414)1447	1282-1635
Bunnell Kame, OH	DIC 1033	590±60	1302(1332,1342,1395)1416	1286-1439
Campbell Is., OH	BETA 17995	440±70	1424(1443)1610	1333-1642
	BETA 14222	540±60	1330(1412)1436	1297-1449
Carroll-Oregonia Rd., OH	DIC 1042	480±90	1406(1436)1486	1298-1642
Cleek, KY	RL 218	830±90	1070(1218)1283	1005-1383
Erp (Pleasant Hill), OH	M 831	470±150	1326(1437)1635	1264-1954
	M 1086	515±75	1332(1423)1443	1296-1616
Guard, IN	BETA 17992	860±60	1070(1210)1260	1025-1284
Haag, IN	DIC 240	680±100	1262(1294)1404	1162-1436
	DIC 239	730±120	1212(1284)1391	1030-1434
	GX 2930	950±160	902(1039,1093,1117,1141,1149)1260	694-1388
Hahn's Field, OH	AA 10223-2	285±45	1527(1646)1660	1488-1954
	AA 10223-1	345±45	1483(1522,1584,1625)1642	1442-1654
	AA 10222	375±60	1443(1491)1637	1428-1654
Hine, OH	BETA 14223	420±70	1431(1448)1623	1407-1648
	BETA 14225	680±60	1282(1294)1390	1258-1410
	BETA 14224	680±80	1278(1294)1394	1213-1423
Horseshoe Johnson, OH	BETA 17993	780±50	1216(1263,1273,1275)1285	1161-1297
Incinerator (Sunwatch), OH	I 7087	395±80	1436(1483)1637	1408-1662
	OWU 448	555±100	1300(1409)1440	1279-1620
	B 20403	560±90	1305(1408)1436	1285-1483
	M 1965	640±100	1282(1305,1316,1371,1386)1413	1214-1444
	B 20401	660±60	1285(1299)1394	1261-1414
	CWR 156	770±320	986(1265,1266,1277)1439	652-1954
	B 20402	780±60	1214(1263,1273,1275)1287	1156-1378
	CWR 141	800±190	1027(1259)1389	890-1443
	CWR 140	820±110	1066(1221,1253,1256)1289	999-1394
	CWR 150	820±115	1059(1221,1253,1256)1290	996-1398
	CWR 145	820±115	1059(1221,1253,1256)1290	996-1398
	CWR 153	830±130	1034(1218)1291	983-1407
	CWR 151	890±100	1024(1160,1173,1188)1262	983-1293
	CWR 148	900±160	994(1158)1283	780-1404
McCabe, KY	RL 217	1220±90	689(780,791,803,854,856)977	647-1017
	RL 216	1680±100	256(394)534	129-616
Petersburg, KY	BETA 46936	500±50	1409(1429)1442	1329-1485
	BETA 46937	880±60	1043(1163,1169,1192,1203,1206)1256	1021-1280
	BETA 46935	980±50	1101(1027)1153	984-1208
Sand Ridge, OH	WIS 1876	560±70	1321(1408)1434	1289-1449
	WIS 1748	1080±70	893(986)1022	780-1152
	UGA 1333	1135±60	783(898,920,944,952,957,971,976)990	775-1022
	WIS 1747	1230±70	690(779,793,800)939	657-985
Schomaker, OH	BETA 31965	390±50	1442(1486)1627	1429-1645
	BETA 17994	470±80	1410(1437)1487	1320-1638
	BETA 14226	540±60	1330(1412)1436	1297-1449
	BETA 31966	710±50	1278(1288)1376	1222-1393
	BETA 17996	720±60	1262(1286)1376	1213-1394
South Fort, OH (?)	BETA 74459	360±80	1442(1498,1512,1516,1599,1618)1648	1416-1953
	BETA 74460	730±60	1260(1284)1298	1211-1392
	BETA 74461	910±70	1026(1156)1216	996-1278
State Line, OH	UGA 2152	695±60	1279(1291)1387	1221-1407
	UGA 2154	715±55	1264(1287)1376	1217-1394
	UGA 2153	785±60	1213(1262)1286	1155-1300
Turpin-1, OH	M 907	675±150	1219(1295)1417	1028-1491
	WIS 1793	820±70	1160(1221,1253,1256)1281	1033-1296
	UGA 4483	855±65	1070(1211)1262	1024-1287
	WIS 1749	1140±40	785(897,922,943)983	779-998
	UGA 4486	1155±245	649(893,927,939)1156	418-1299
	WIS 1750	1320±20	664(688)762	655-773

Data from Brose and White 1983; Cowan 1986, 1992; Drooker 1993f, 1996b; Essenpreis 1982; Harper 1994; Henderson 1993; Nass 1987; Litfin et al. 1993; Riggs 1986; Sharp 1990; Tankersley 1986b. Calibration after Stuiver and Reimer 1993. **Boldfaced** sites have Late Fort Ancient component(s) (Sand Ridge includes the Middle-Early Late transition). See Table 6-1 for Madisonville site dates.

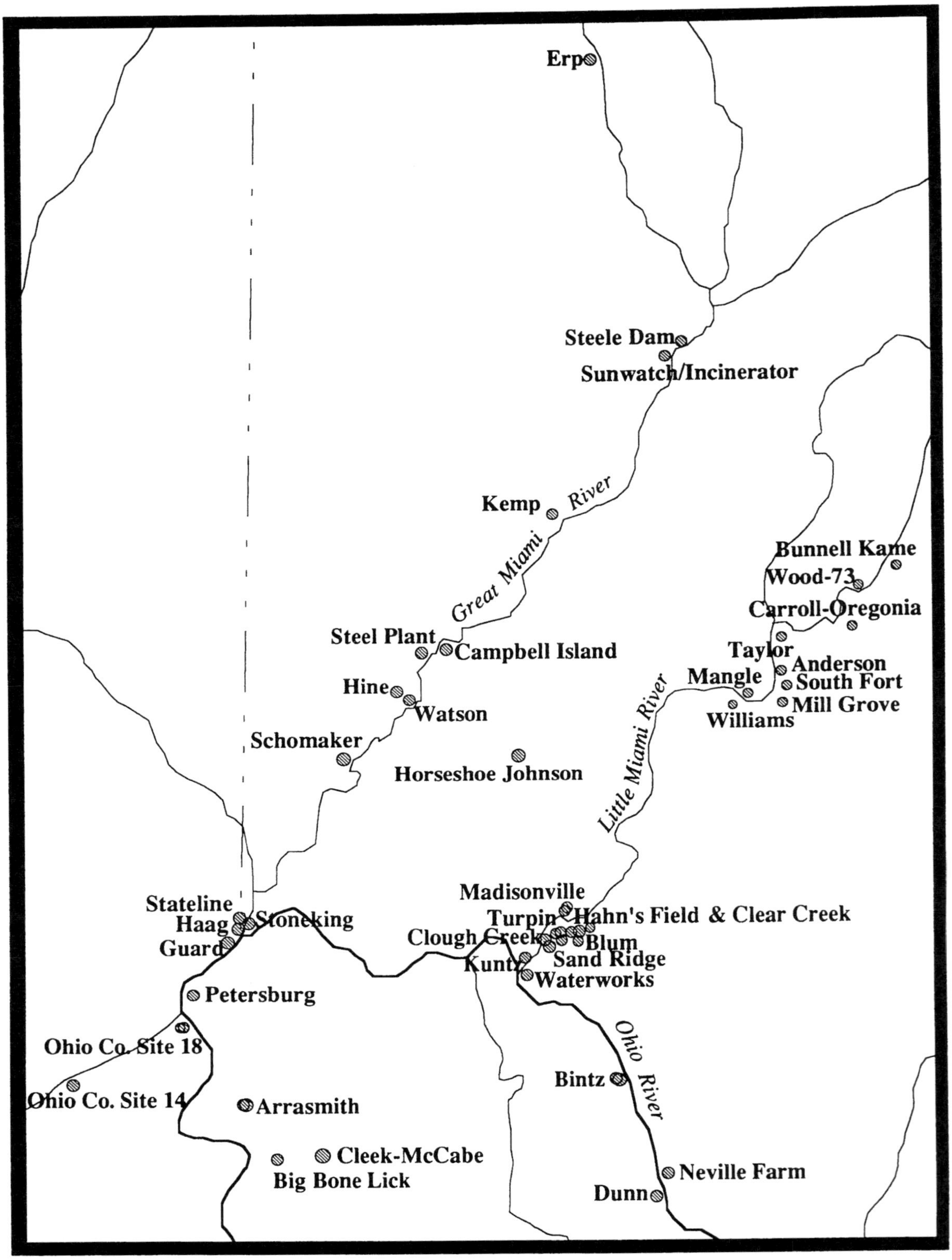

Figure 4-6. Fort Ancient sites in and near southwestern Ohio.

Southwestern Ohio Fort Ancient Sites

Southwestern Ohio was home base to both the Anderson Focus, in the upper Great Miami and Little Miami valleys, and the Madisonville Focus, in the lower Miami drainages, southeastern Indiana, and adjacent northern Kentucky (Figure 4-1). Since Griffin's original formulation, a significant number of additional sites have been recognized (Figure 4-6), and the relationship between Anderson and Madisonville Focus sites has been redefined. Essential to this work has been the use of radiocarbon dating (Table 4-1) and ceramics seriation to clarify the developmental sequence of important attributes of Fort Ancient material culture within the subregion.

Elsewhere, I have presented a detailed overview of excavation history, settlement patterns, and chronological relationships among southwestern Ohio Fort Ancient sites (Drooker 1996a). Here, I draw selectively from its data. Below are summaries of important local horizon marker artifact attributes, gross relative chronologies, a tabular summary of excavation history and important attributes of selected Early, Middle, and Late Fort Ancient sites, and a brief comparative discussion of settlement, mortuary, and exchange patterns over time in the subregion, elaborating on information presented by Cowan (described above).

Horizon Marker Artifacts and Relative Chronology. Figure 4-7 is a graphical summary of approximate time ranges associated with important local horizon marker artifacts in southwestern Ohio. Additional information is presented below.

Most Fort Ancient ceramic vessels were jars, with bowls also present during some time periods (e.g., Griffin 1943: Pls. LXVIII.1, LXVIII.3, LXXXV.2, CIII). Large, heavy, shallow "saltpan" vessels have been found at a few sites such as Fox Farm (Griffin 1943: Pls. CI, CII). One of Griffin's main distinctions between Madisonville and Anderson ceramic types was shell versus non-shell temper (Griffin 1943:117, 192, 344). However, Essenpreis and Riggs have demonstrated that, although shell temper does predominate in the more southerly sites, in both areas there was a development from grit tempering to shell tempering over time (Drooker 1996a; Essenpreis 1982:197; Riggs 1986, 1994). The type that Essenpreis named "Anderson Shell-Tempered" has been excavated at both Anderson Focus and Madisonville Focus sites. Although there was considerable stylistic diversity in ceramics during the Early-Middle Fort Ancient period, the thickened rims and decorated necks typical of Anderson jars (Figure 4-8; see also Cowan 1987: Fig. 6; Griffin 1943: Pls. XXXVI-XXXIX, XLI-XLIII) are found across the entire subregion (Henderson 1993), with shell tempering occurring earlier in the south but becoming universal by the fourteenth century (late Middle Fort Ancient). At all sites, the guilloche was the most common decorative motif, followed by triangular motifs. There was an overlapping transition to the thinner walls, unthickened rims, more everted lips, smooth, undecorated necks, and two or four convergent-sided or hourglass-shaped strap handles typical of classic shell-tempered Madisonville jars (Figure 4-9; see also Cowan 1987: Fig. 16; Griffin 1943: Pls. LX-LXVII), which includes, for example, jars with thin, everted lips and decorated necks (Figure 4-10; see also Griffin 1943: Pls. LXXX.1, XCI.3, CVI.1). Along with rims, handles became less massive.

Figure 4-11 gives a general idea of the absolute chronology associated with these ceramic types (keeping in mind, of course, that the dated refuse pits were not sealed features, so the ceramics in them could predate or postdate the materials subjected to radiocarbon dating). At Turpin, grit-tempered Anderson ceramics were excavated from two midden levels with radiocarbon dates that calibrated to the thirteenth century (Riggs 1986). Both a midden level at Madisonville and a pit at Hine from which have been excavated sandy shell-tempered Anderson pottery produced radiocarbon dates that calibrated to the late thirteenth century, the same period to which the single radiocarbon date from Anderson itself has been calibrated (Table 4-1). From associated radiocarbon dates, Anderson Shell Tempered and Madisonville ceramic types might have coexisted during the early fifteenth century (Drooker 1996a; Turnbow and Henderson 1992; Riggs 1994). For example, Anderson Shell Tempered ceramics have come from features with dates that calibrate to the fifteenth century at Hine, Schomaker, and Sand Ridge, and classic Madisonville ceramics have come from features with a similar range of dates at Campbell Island and Madisonville (Figure 4-11). The transition to classic Madisonville probably was complete by the sixteenth century. The reason that classic Madisonville jars were concentrated in the southern portion of the Anderson Focus–Madisonville Focus territory (Figure 4-1) is simply that most Late Fort Ancient settlements were located within that area (Figure 4-5), not that there is a major geographical division in contemporaneous material culture. Rodney Rigg's ceramics chronology for the lower Little Miami Valley used cluster analysis and multidimensional scaling of attributes of sherds from stratigraphic contexts to construct a detailed picture of the transition from Woodland to Late Fort Ancient ceramic attributes, and will be an extremely valuable reference when it is widely available (Riggs 1994).

Stratigraphic excavations at Fox Farm, Kentucky, found that saltpans and bowls both appeared after 1400 in conjunction with transitional (decorated neck) and classic (undecorated neck) Madisonville ceramics (Turnbow and Henderson 1992; cf. Griffin 1943: Pls. CI-CX). Bowls trimmed with beading, along with transitional Madisonville jars, were early (assigned to the Gist phase, ca. 1400-1550), and bowls and jars trimmed with lip notching were late. Early Late Fort Ancient cord-marking at Fox Farm was primarily S-twist, while late Late assemblages had mainly Z-twist impressions. Whereas plain and cord-marked jars were present throughout Late Fort Ancient assemblages, net-impressed and grooved-paddled/simple stamped surface treatments are considered typical of late Late Fort Ancient by Turnbow and colleagues (Glowacki et al. 1993; Henderson et al. 1992:271; Turnbow and Henderson 1992:135). Likewise, out of 25 West Virginia sites, Graybill found grooved-paddled ceramics only at two protohistoric locations, Orchard and Buf-

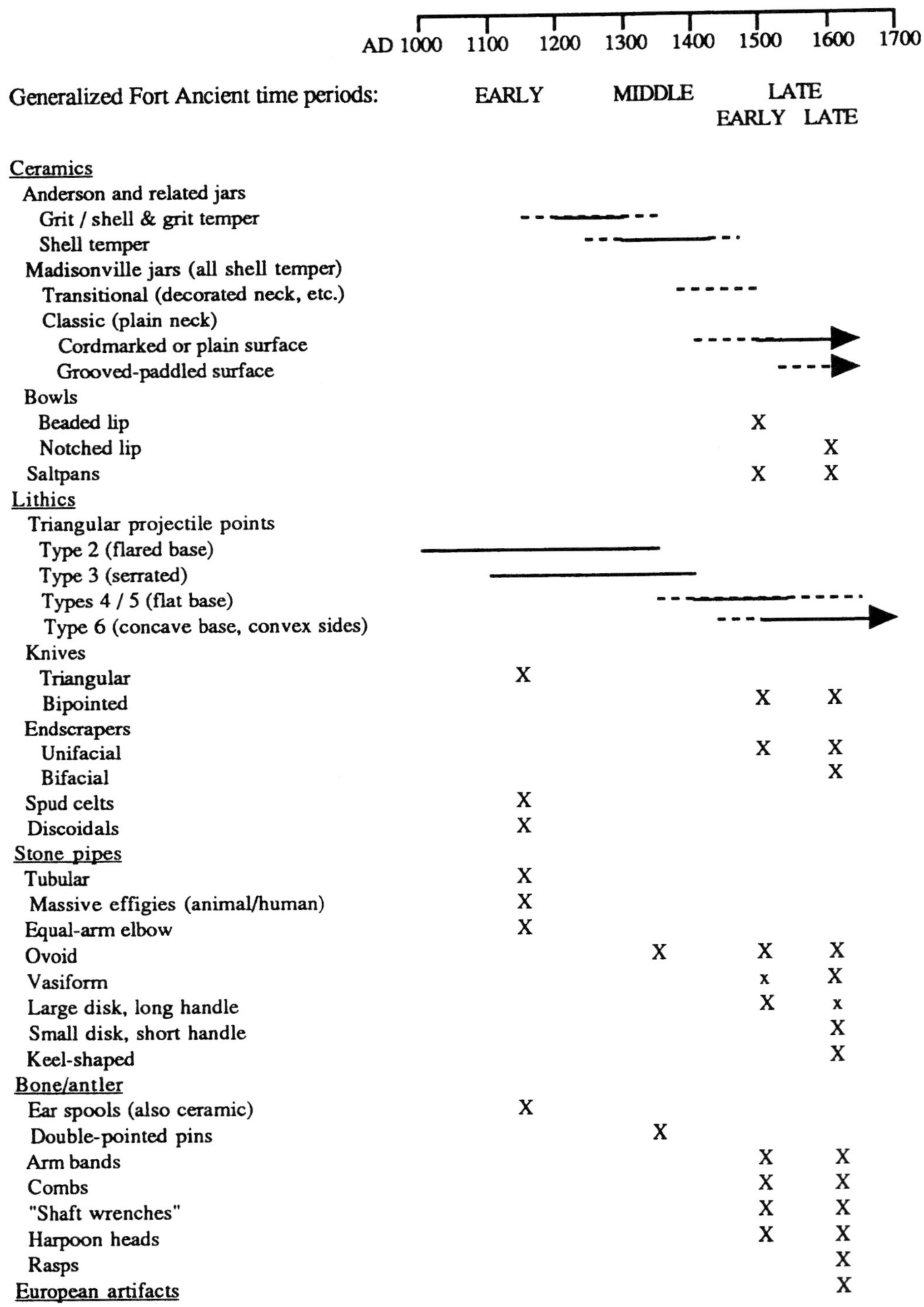

Figure 4-7. Important local southwestern Ohio Fort Ancient horizon marker artifacts.

Figure 4-8. Examples of Anderson Shell Tempered ceramics. Rims are thickened and handles are massive. Four sherds at left are from Turpin 1/2 (HUPM Cat. Nos. 84-68-10/36201, 84-68-10/36303, 84-68-10/36204, 84-68-10/36217). Two sherds at right are from Madisonville, Trench 4, Pit 30 (both HUPM Cat. No. 01-38-69471). Photograph by Hillel Burger (HUPM Photo No. N33850). Copyright 1997 by the President and Fellows of Harvard College; used by permission.

falo (1981:102). In addition, this surface treatment is common on both Madisonville and Wellsburg ceramics at Neale's Landing, and it is typical of Wellsburg ceramics at late prehistoric Wellsburg phase sites farther north (Baker 1988; Buker 1968; Moxley 1988b: Fig. 5; Whitman 1975; James Morton, pers. comm.). Along with net-impressed surfaces, grooved-paddled surfaces also occur on Whittlesey ceramics (e.g., Brose 1978: Fig. 7).

Vertically stacked compound vessels (Figure 4-12), vessels with lizard/salamander appliqué or handles (Figure 4-13), and a human face effigy pot (Figure 4-14) have been identified by Cowan with his Late Fort Ancient Mariemont phase (1986:151-152; see also Cowan 1987: Figs. 18, 19; Griffin 1943: Pls. LXIII.3, LXVI.1, LXVI.3, LXVI.4, LXIX.1-5). According to Morse and Morse, pots modeled with human faces ("head pots"), common in Late Mississippian contexts, are "almost certainly protohistoric" in the central Mississippi River Valley (1983:280). Jars and bowls with lizards or other animal effigies peering over the rim or forming handles seem to be most common at Late Madisonville Horizon sites, including Augusta, Hardin, Clover, and Orchard (Hanson 1966: Fig. 41; Moxley 1988b; Turnbow and Jobe 1992:96; personal inspection of Clover collection at the Huntington, West Virginia, Museum of Art), but also occur in small numbers at Fox Farm and Feurt, where the major site occupations are earlier, with only possible minor protohistoric components (Griffin 1943: Pl. XXIII.19; Mills 1917:365-66; Smith 1910: Pl. LIV; Turnbow 1992:67-68; cf. Table 4-1, and Table 4-4 below), and at the Early Fort Ancient Baum and Gartner sites (Griffin 1943:46, 53, Pls. VI, IX). At least one of the two appliqué animals from Feurt has ears (Ohio Historical Society specimen 161/74); these effigies are described by Mills as a mountain lion and a raccoon (1917:365). Such animals might perhaps be

Figure 4-9. Typical Madisonville Horizon jars from the Madisonville site, all with notched lips and four handles. The only other decoration at all common on "classic" Madisonville vessels such as these is a line of punctates or notches around the shoulder, aligned with the bottoms of the handles. *Left*: plain surfaced vessel from Burial 4-21 (HUPM Cat. No. 97-38-10/62963). *Middle*: grooved-paddled vessel, with Burial E-19 (HUPM Cat. No. 08-3-79682). *Right*: cord-marked vessel from Burial 4-5 (HUPM Cat. No. 97-38-10/62964). Photograph by Hillel Burger (HUPM Photo No. N33842). Copyright 1997 by the President and Fellows of Harvard College; used by permission.

an early manifestation of later lizardlike effigies. An "eared" animal effigy on a jar fragment from the Orendorf Village site in the Central Illinois River valley (ca. A.D. 1150-1250) has been identified as a "Tadpole Effigy Handle" (pop-eyes?) (Conrad 1991a: Fig. 26). Another example, with two bearlike appliqué effigies peering over the rim of a pot with a sharply everted lip (i.e., not a typical Fort Ancient form) came from a bluff-top mound east of Cahokia in Illinois, a region that was little utilized after the fourteenth century (Harvard University Peabody Museum Cat. No. 83-76-10/38879).

Stemmed pedestal pots (Griffin 1945; Murphy 1974) are a well-known and slightly controversial Madisonville ceramic type that also probably can be assigned to the Late Madisonville Horizon (Figure 4-15). Chalicelike vessels of similar concept, all consisting of local-style container forms atop a thin, pedestaled base, have been identified in protohistoric and early historical contexts from several far-flung locations. These include mid-sixteenth-century Caddoan sites in East Texas (Perttula 1992:27; Turner 1978:98-102), mid-sixteenth to early seventeenth-century Huron and Neutral sites in southern Ontario (Latta 1987, 1990; Ramsden and Fitzgerald 1990), and a late seventeenth-century Susquehannock site in southeastern Pennsylvania (Kent 1984:377).

The designation of horizon marker attributes is an iterative process. Very often, ceramics seriation, together with radiocarbon dates, are used to establish a basic temporal framework. After that, other significant artifacts are identified and used to refine the sequence. A first-pass relative ordering such as this can be accomplished for Fort Ancient sites based on radiocarbon dates, presence or absence of burial mounds, gross differences in ceramics, and presence or absence of European goods. Table 4-2 is such an ordering, based on data presented in Drooker 1996a. Many of these sites are poorly known, with pottery identified only from a few illustrations or a brief description, so this listing should not be taken as gospel. Included in the table, for discussion below, are data on plazas and palisades/enclosures. As can be seen, this information is missing or inconclusive for most of the sites.

In contrast with earlier stemmed and notched points, Fort Ancient projectile points are triangular. For West Virginia sites, Graybill used seriation to demonstrate an overlapping stylistic sequence for projectile point base shapes that runs from early convex through flat to concave (Graybill 1981:104-7). This has been corroborated by Morton in eastern Ohio and Church in central Ohio (Morton 1984; Church 1987:122-23). Using northern Kentucky data, Jimmy Railey employed additional attributes to refine this sequence (Railey 1992). He distinguished five diagnostic types (Figure 4-16). (A sixth type is probably pre-1400 but not diagnostic.) Type 2 has convex or straight sides combined with convex or straight bases to give a flared base. It occurs early (pre-A.D. 1000 through ca. 1300). Type 3, with coarsely serrated lateral edges and straight or convex base, is associated with Middle Fort Ancient components, ca. A.D. 1200-1400. Type 5, with straight base and sides, may occur before 1400, but is most common from 1400 to the early 1500s, persisting until the late 1600s. Type 4, short (<25 mm long) with convex sides and straight or convex base, also is most common ca. A.D. 1400 to the early 1500s. Type 6, with concave base and

Figure 4-10. Atypical Madisonville Plain jars with decorated necks. *a*. Madisonville site, Block 1 Burial 108 (Low 1880:Fig. 10). *b*. Madisonville site, Burial E-27 (HUPM Cat. No. 08-3-10/79684). Photograph by Hillel Burger (HUPM Photo No. N33848). Copyright 1997 President and Fellows of Harvard College; used by permission.

convex or straight sides, is "a diagnostic trait of post-1400 deposits and persist[s] as the latest stone point type in the middle Ohio Valley and some neighboring regions" (Railey 1992:63).

James Litfin and colleagues (1993) defined fifteen "types" based on most of the possible combinations of serration/non-serration, concave/convex/straight base, and concave/convex/straight sides. They assigned tentative relative ages to them, based on their occurrence at southwestern Ohio sites considered Early, Middle, or Late; unfortunately, several of these sites contain more than one Fort Ancient component, so no definitive chronological sequence can be shown for the point shapes.

Railey's study also identified bifacial endscrapers as a Late Madisonville Horizon phenomenon, with unifacial endscrapers occurring during the entire horizon (1992:143). Cowan has noted bipointed ("leaf-shaped") flint knives as another typical Madisonville Horizon tool (Cowan 1986:153, 1987:15).

Several other mostly locally produced artifacts have been specified by Cowan as chronological markers for southwestern Ohio sites. For Early Fort Ancient Turpin phase sites these include stone discoidals and spud celts, and stone and ceramic earspools (1986:137-39). Bone and copper-covered earspools occur during this period as well, as evidenced by a pair of the latter found with a skeleton interred just below the west edge of the Turpin burial mound and above the Woodland village component (Oehler 1973:45-46); the former were present at State Line (Vickery and Genheimer 1994).

For the Middle Fort Ancient Schomaker phase, ceramic scraping tools and double-pointed bone pins are singled out as "index fossils"; the latter also occur at the Anderson phase Incinerator and Anderson sites farther to the north and the Gartner and Baum sites in the Scioto drainage farther east, where they apparently often were used as hairpins (Cowan 1986:145; Cowan et al. 1990:3; Griffin 1943: Pl. XLIV; Mills 1906:60, 64; Mills 1907:48, 49). Although Incinerator conventionally has been associated with Early Fort Ancient, its radiocarbon dates (Table 4-1), decorated pottery (Heilman 1988; Robertson 1984), and layout, including lack of mounds, provide additional congruences with the Schomaker site. Both Incinerator and Anderson Village (with slightly later radiocarbon dates and more shell-tempered pottery) should be considered Early to Middle rather than Early Fort Ancient.

Late Fort Ancient Mariemont phase sites are typified by a rich assemblage of bone artifacts, including bone/antler arm bands, and antler combs, arrow shaft wrenches, and harpoon heads (Cowan 1986:153, 1987:15), but it is not known whether any of these types are concentrated in either the Early or the Late Madisonville Horizon. Bison bones, bison teeth, and bison bone artifacts, including beamers and rasps, also appear during this phase (Cowan 1986:152). Although bison were fairly common in the central Ohio River valley during the eighteenth century, they probably did not begin to reach the region until the fifteenth century at the earliest (Tankersley 1985, 1986a, 1992; Tankersley and Adams 1991). Madisonville is the only Fort Ancient village from which bison remains have been excavated. At Big Bone Lick, a salt spring location known as a hunting site (Figure 4-2), a deposit containing a bison kill and two shell-tempered cord-marked sherds was radiocarbon dated to the early fifteenth century (Table 4-1, sample UGA 4291) (Tankersley 1986a:295).

As noted in Chapter 3, pipes are excellent horizon marker artifacts. Within Fort Ancient territory a wide variety of styles is found (see West 1934 for examples of all types discussed below). Although many sites where they occur are multicom-

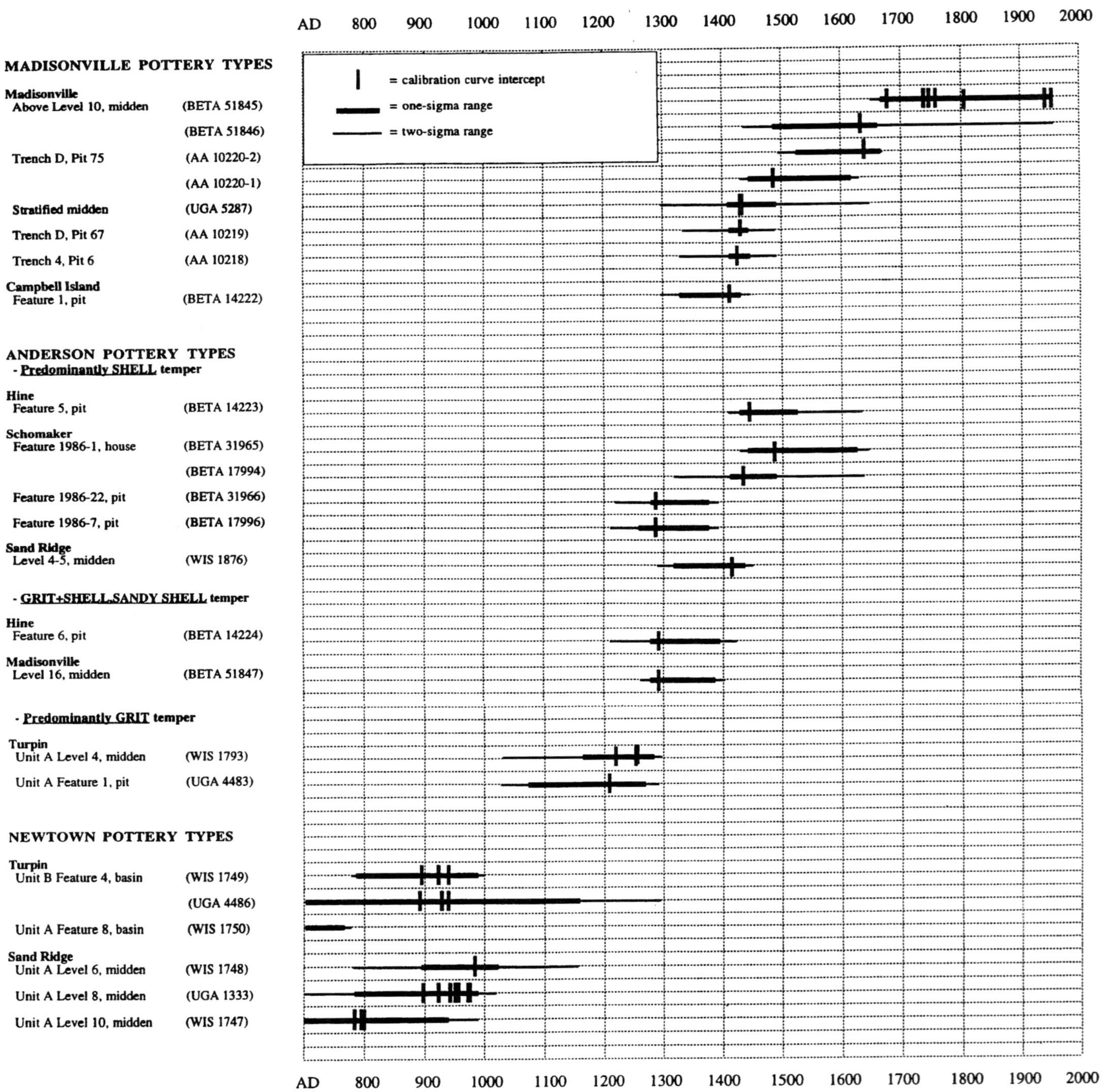

Figure 4-11. Radiocarbon dates from features with which particular pottery types were associated (Cowan 1986:37-41, 76-90; Cowan et al. 1990: Fig. 1; Drooker 1993f; Glowacki et al. 1993; Riggs 1986, 1994; Tankersley 1986:296; calibrated after Stuiver and Reimer 1993).

Figure 4-12. Grooved-paddled vertical compound vessel. Madisonville site, Burial 2-17 (HUPM Cat. No. 97-38-10/62885). Photograph by Hillel Burger (HUPM Photo No. N33845). Copyright 1997 by the President and Fellows of Harvard College; used by permission.

ponent and many site reports do not contain complete quantitative data, it is possible to do a very rough ordering based on types present across the entire Fort Ancient territory (Table 4-3). A few types do appear to be horizon markers. Full-figure human and animal effigies, which can be of massive size (e.g., Figure 4-17), appear to be early (pre-Madisonville Horizon), correlating well with their occurrence outside of Fort Ancient territory (Chapter 3; cf. Emerson 1982; Farnsworth and Emerson 1989). Many of the best-known ones, such as two crouching shamanistic figures illustrated by Squier and Davis and another by Schoolcraft (Schoolcraft 1851: Pl. 13; Squier and Davis 1848: Figs. 146, 148), were discovered in non-settlement contexts, which makes them difficult to date (Drooker 1994d). Full-figure perching bird effigies apparently came into use during the Madisonville Horizon, although it is possible that a few very large ones might have earlier affiliations. Tubular, semi-platform, and massive equal-arm pipes appear to be early: none have been excavated from components with European goods. Disk, vasiform, and keel-shaped pipes occur only at sites with Late Fort Ancient components. For disk pipes, this is consistent with their period of florescence in Oneota territory, ca. 1450-1650 (Chapter 3). Not only site-comparative data, but also stratigraphic evidence places vasiform pipes in the Madisonville Horizon. At Feurt, they were found only in the plow zone, not in the Early-Middle Fort Ancient mounds and village excavated by Mills (Mills 1917:398), and at Hardin, they increased in frequency from lower to higher excavation levels (Hanson 1966:140). Both vasiform and disk pipes are reported from the early historical Bentley (Lower Shawneetown) site (Pollack and Henderson 1984). Keel-shaped pipes appear to be a Late Madisonville Horizon phenomenon. According to Maslowski (1984:156) they are absent from all Clover phase sites except Orchard. However, outside of Fort Ancient territory they might occur earlier. For instance, many specimens have come from the Reeve Village site in northeastern Ohio, which lacks provenienced European goods (Ahlstrom 1979: Pl. xviii). At least one was excavated at the Riker site, which produced copper ornaments but no definite European goods (Vietzen 1974:111).

Settlement Patterns, Mortuary Practices, and External Interaction over Time. Table 4-2 (below) includes 26 out of three dozen published Fort Ancient sites in southwestern Ohio and two in Indiana for which I could glean any sort of chronological indicator. Information comes from early surveys by Metz, a mid-twentieth century survey by Frederick Starr, Griffin's compendium, and a few recent excavations (Drooker 1996a; Griffin 1943; Metz 1878, 1881; Starr 1960). Most of the sites are nucleated villages, directly adjacent to arable land. The special-purpose sites on Caesar's Creek above Taylor (Figure 4-6) include seasonal hunting/gathering camps utilized by Fort Ancient people into the fifteenth century (Brose and White 1983; Essenpreis 1982:249-52). Other such components are known from farther up the Little Miami River (Brose and White 1983:23; Riordan 1994).

From the many question marks on Table 4-2, it can be seen that broad-area formal excavations, or even large-scale surface surveys, have not been accomplished for many sites in this region. All village sites, of all time periods, for which layouts are known have a domestic area surrounding a central plaza. Most known palisades (or earthworks in the case of Erp) surround Early-Middle components near the periphery of occupied Fort Ancient territory. Although most villages are on floodplains or terraces, a few occupy bluff tops fifteen or more meters above the floodplain: Erp, Hine, Taylor, South Fort, and Sand Ridge.

Table 4-4 lists selected sites, in approximate chronological order, for which more detailed information is available. It includes all sites in the Great and Little Miami valleys for which quantitative burial data are available. All excavated southwestern Ohio sites with Madisonville Horizon components except Madisonville itself are included. As can be seen, the data base is not huge. Few sites were excavated under modern conditions, and many lack spatial and stratigraphic data.

Figure 4-13. Some effigy vessels from the Madisonville site. *Top*: Madisonville Cordmarked vessel with humanoid head topping handle (Low 1880: Fig. 33; CMNH 1918.3682, with Burial 1 from Block 4). *Bottom*: lizard effigy vessels, one with effigy handles (Low 1880:Fig. 39, Burial 1 from Block 7), and one with appliqué lizards (Low 1880: Fig. 38, Cincinnati Art Museum 1888.714, with Burial 34 from Block 6).

Table 4-5 summarizes spatial information and important features for these sites. Unlike Kentucky and West Virginia, there is not a steady increase in site size over time. At least some Early Fort Ancient settlements with burial mounds (e.g., State Line) were quite large—4 hectares or more—larger than any known Madisonville Horizon components in the subregion. This is consistent with other Ohio mound sites such as Baum and Gartner, both estimated as over 8 hectares in size (Church 1987:85-86, 88; but note that Schurr and Schoeninger [1995] accept only a small proportion of these areas as Fort Ancient). Southwestern Ohio Early-Middle Fort Ancient settlements without burial mounds that are not listed on Table 4-4, including Horseshoe Johnson and Schomaker (Cowan et al. 1990; Hawkins 1994), range from around 0.5 to 2 hectares. No evolution in size is apparent among them. For example, the functionally equivalent, similarly organized, and closely contemporaneous Incinerator and Anderson villages differed significantly in size (both area and mortuary population). Without considering the Madisonville site, average settlement size appears to have decreased rather than increased from Early to Late Fort Ancient.

The largest structure at State Line is larger than any excavated elsewhere in Fort Ancient territory (see Table 4-11 below). House types are poorly documented, but a variety of shapes and construction methods are known from Early-Middle Fort Ancient sites, including rectangular wall trench (State Line, Turpin 3, Schomaker), circular semi-subterranean (South Fort, Anderson), rectangular semi-subterranean (Schomaker, Horseshoe Johnson), and rectangular pole (Turpin 1, Incinerator, possibly South Fort) (Drooker 1996a: Table 4). At Horseshoe Johnson and Incinerator, one or two structures, adjacent to the plaza, were noticeably larger than the rest. They have been interpreted variously as a men's house, a council house/communal building, and a chief's house (Hawkins 1994; Lileas 1988:45-46; Nass 1987:178-80, 255; Nass and Yerkes 1995:76-78;

Figure 4-14. Human portrait vessel, Madisonville Plain, from Madisonville site, Burial D-64 (HUPM Cat. No. 08-3-10/79660). Photograph by Hillel Burger (HUPM Photo No. N33843A). Copyright 1997 by the President and Fellows of Harvard College; used by permission.

Robertson 1984:253-54). At Incinerator, a large cedar pole, astronomically aligned with one such building, had been placed in the center of the plaza, and structures interpreted as sweathouses were also within the plaza area (Goss 1988; Lileas 1988:40-41, 43).

Because of multiple components and incomplete reporting for most sites, it is difficult to discern diachronic trends for burial practices at southwestern Ohio Fort Ancient sites (Table 4-6). At all sites the majority of burials were extended but at least 10% were flexed or semi-flexed. At Turpin 1, a Late Woodland stone mound contained "flexed primary burials, partial secondary burials and pulverized bones," in contrast with mainly extended burials in the Fort Ancient component (Oehler 1950:2, 1973:47); it is possible that some flexed, semi-flexed and sitting burials reported from other multicomponent sites such as State Line may be pre-Fort Ancient. Whereas burials in the Fort Ancient mound at Turpin were almost entirely extended, 22 bundle burials and at least one semi-flexed burial were reported from the Taylor mound (Griffin 1943:103); patterns of burial placement in the latter appear much less structured than at Turpin, where an outer ring of bodies was arranged with heads toward the mound center (Oehler 1970: Photo 54; cf. Starr 1960:57). Graves with stone slabs over, under, and/or around the sides appear to be more common at earlier than later sites and, from the limited available evidence, at northern than at southern sites within this subregion. Based on the evidence from Turpin 2 versus Hahn's Field, there might be more double and multiple burials at later sites: at the former, these included only 5% of all individuals excavated, compared with 22% at the latter.

The proportion of burials with grave goods does appear to increase over time, from 5-22% at mound sites to 24-30% at

Figure 4-15. Stemmed, pedestaled Madisonville Cordmarked vessel from Madisonville site, Block 1, Burial 283 (Low 1880: Fig. 26; Cincinnati Art Museum Cat. No. 1888.715).

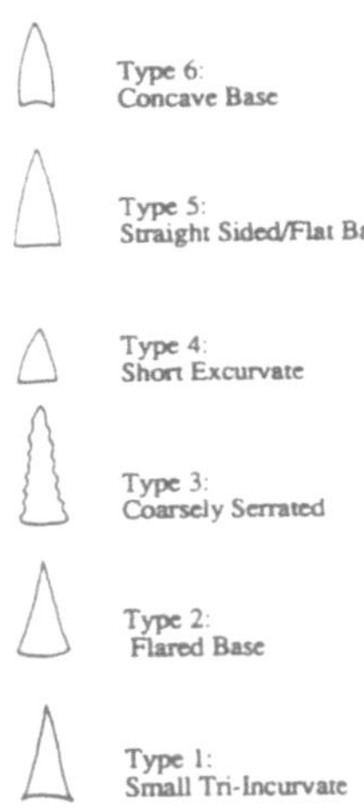

Figure 4-16. Fort Ancient time-sensitive triangular projectile point types (after Railey 1992:155-68).

non-mound Early-Middle Fort Ancient sites to 38-43% at sites with Late Fort Ancient components (Table 4-7). There were significantly more mortuary vessels at later than earlier sites. Shell ornaments were fairly common as burial accompaniments at Early-Middle Fort Ancient sites, but were not present at the Late ones in this sample. Copper was present in a few burials at most of the Early-Middle sites, most often in the form of copper-covered wood or bone ornaments. Pipes have been found with only a few individuals at non-mound Early-Middle Fort Ancient sites.

Two major approaches have been developed to determine social complexity within archaeologically known societies; one involves the study of settlement hierarchy and the other, burial patterning (e.g., O'Shea 1984; Peebles and Kus 1977; Steponaitis 1978). As noted above, no site hierarchies or large ceremonial centers have been identified within the Fort Ancient area, including southwestern Ohio, that might be interpreted to indicate a multilevel social organization. Within some individual settlements, site layout provides evidence of ceremonialism, as with the large central pole and sweathouses in the Incinerator plaza. The large council or chief's houses and other special-purpose structures at Horseshoe Johnson and Incinerator, which also occur at the early Baum and Philo II sites (Carskadden 1994; Church 1987:214), have implications for both ceremonialism and social structure.

Only a few formal mortuary analyses have been carried out for Fort Ancient sites, the majority of them from southwestern Ohio (Essenpreis 1982; Evans 1994; Hemmings 1977; Holmes 1994; Riggs 1977). They confirm anecdotal evidence from many other sites (Griffin 1992). No high-ranked elite group of ascribed status has been identified on the basis of burial location or grave good assemblage, nor has any adult been identified as filling an ascribed leadership role. A few people have been identified as possibly filling achieved leadership roles. At both the Anderson Village and Incinerator/Sunwatch sites, one individual was identified as a shaman-leader on the basis of grave goods that included pipes, awls, and bundles of objects including items historically identified with healing; at the latter site, a second individual, with a wolf-jaw headdress, was interpreted as high status (Essenpreis 1982:219). One of 335 burials at the Middle-Late Fort Ancient Hardin site (see below) also was identified as a possible shaman from the red ochre and hematite object accompanying him, and a second male, buried with two shell gorgets, was noted as a possible Big Man although he was rather young for that status (Holmes 1994:164-65, 170). All 32 burials at Neale's Landing have been described (Hemmings 1977:5.10–5.14, Appendix D; Broyles 1970). Two middle-aged males were considered to have been accorded special status. One had a large mortuary assemblage that included 28 shafted projectile points and a modified fisher skull, probably associated with a medicine bag, while the other was buried with a variety of grave goods including 13 shafted projectile points and a necklace of 43 marine shell beads. None of these studies has identified any standardized Fort Ancient high-status indicators. At many Fort Ancient sites, including all southwestern Ohio sites for which data are available, subadult burials received more exotic and ornamental grave goods than adults.

A communal focus in burial patterning seems to hold at all three of the southwestern Ohio sites for which there is significant information. At Turpin 1, a presumably communally constructed burial mound contained most of the dead. At Incinerator and Anderson, most of the dead were buried in a ring di-

TABLE 4-2
"First-Pass" Relative Chronology and Site Characteristics for Southwestern Ohio Fort Ancient Sites

	1000-1200	1100-1300	1200-1400	1300-1500	1400-1550	1500-1650	Plaza	Enclosure/ Palisade	Blufftop
Wood-73	x						?	?	--
Haag	x	x	x				?	?	--
Incinerator	x	x	x	x			x	x	--
South Fort	x	x	x	x	x	x	?	x	x
Guard		x	x				x	?	--
Turpin-1		x	x	x			?	?	--
State Line		x	x	x			?	(x)	--
Neville Farm		x	x	x			?	?	--
Horseshoe Johnson		x	x	x			x	?	--
Anderson		x	x	x			x	?	--
Taylor		x	x	x	((x))		?	?	x
Hine		x	x	x	x		x	?	x
Schomaker		x	x	x	x		x	?	--
Steele Dam			x				?	?	?
Kemp			x	x			?	?	--
Bunnell Kame			x	x			--	--	--
Mill Grove			x	x			?	?	--
Watson			x	x			?	?	--
Erp			x	x	x		?	x	x
Carroll-Oregonia Road			x	x	x		?	?	--
Sand Ridge			x	x	x		?	?	x
Waterworks			x	x	x		?	?	--
Campbell Island			x	x	x	x	?	?	--
Turpin-2			x	x	x	x	?	?	--
Hahn's Field				x	x	x	x	x	--
Steel Plant					x	x	?	?	--

Chronology based on radiocarbon dates (sites active ca. 1000-1200), radiocarbon dates and/or presence of burial mounds (ca. 1100-1300), radiocarbon dates and/or presence of Anderson-like pottery (all temper types) (ca. 1200-1400), radiocarbon dates and/or presence of Anderson Shell-Tempered pottery (ca. 1300-1500), radiocarbon dates and/or presence of Madisonville-type pottery (decorated and/or undecorated necks) (ca. 1400-1550), radiocarbon dates and/or presence of "classic" Madisonville pottery (ca. 1500-1650).
(Parentheses) indicate probable presence of attribute; ((double parentheses)) indicate possible presence of attribute.

rectly adjacent to the plaza. At all three sites, some graves were found within the domestic zone, in or among house structures, but they were in a minority.

Little research has been directed toward the identification of moieties, clans, or other horizontal social divisions at most Fort Ancient sites. However, at Incinerator/Sunwatch, pathological evidence has been used to postulate burial organization in separate family or clan burial plots, with one sector possibly containing members of a wolf clan (Essenpreis 1982:210; Lileas 1988:48). Evidence from female skeletal traits and pottery technology and decoration associated with clusters of 3-4 houses has been interpreted as a reflection of matrilocal residence (Essenpreis 1982:212-13; Heilman 1988; Robertson 1984). In her preliminary mortuary analysis of Incinerator burials, Evans examined types and amounts of grave goods with burials in each of the sectors around the plaza identified as possibly clan-related. Within each sector, she found one or a few burials with more or higher-status grave goods than others (different items in different sectors), and interpreted these as possible clan leaders (Evans 1994). The cluster of graves near the largest structure contained only males and children, supporting the idea that this was a male-dominated area, but the grave goods were not significantly different from examples found in other sectors, thus providing no evidence for a separately buried "elite" group.

Throughout the Early-Middle Fort Ancient in southwestern Ohio there does seem to have been extraregional interaction, with strongest connections (as noted by Cowan) to the west (Drooker 1992a, 1994c). Ceramics, discoidals, pipes, pipestone, and marine shell gorgets all show westerly affiliations. The following brief discussion is included to set the scene for discussion in Chapter 8 of sixteenth-seventeenth century continuities and changes in western Fort Ancient interaction patterns.

At State Line, ceramics with Middle Mississippi affiliations include painted/negative-painted sherds, a water bottle, a plate, and human head and owl rattle adornos, plus a wide variety of non-rattle adornos (Vickery and Genheimer 1994). Turpin has produced a few negative-painted sherds, pots with "Cahokia shoulders," and a vessel with a Ramey Incised-like design (Griffin 1943: Pls. LXXXI, LXXXII; Oehler 1973: Photos 8 and 10). Discoidals have come from both sites, as have large frog effigy

Figure 4-17. Human effigy pipe from Turpin, Ohio, probably of local Waverly sandstone (HUPM Cat. No. 86-46-10/A3889). Found in the crook of the right elbow of a child buried in a grave pit lined with yellow clay (Metz 1885b: Pt. 1:107). Photograph by Hillel Burger (HUPM Photo No. N33841). Copyright 1997 President and Fellows of Harvard College; used by permission.

pipes such as are well known from the Cahokia area (Conrad 1991a: Fig. 30; Emerson 1982:33-36; Oehler 1973:15, 18, 23-24; Vickery and Genheimer 1994). A frog pipe also was obtained by Moorehead in Warren County, where the Anderson, South Fort, and Taylor sites are located (Moorehead 1897:252-53). The large crouching human figure pipe from Turpin 2 (Figure 4-17) and two smaller human effigy pipes from Turpin 1 and Blum (Cowan 1987:28-29; Oehler 1973: Photo 28; Starr 1960:59, 66) had headdresses or hairdos like those on effigies from places such as the Kincaid site and the Illinois River region in southern and central Illinois (Emerson 1982: Figs. 11, 12; Conrad 1991a: Figs. 33, 34). The facial treatment of the large Turpin effigy can be compared with that of the Kingston Lake and Blind Eye pipes illustrated by Emerson (1982: Figs. 11, 16). A massive block pipe with a figure on all fours was unearthed north of Dayton, in the area between the Erp and Incinerator sites (Squier and Davis 1848: Fig. 146). Like other such pipes from Fort Ancient territory (e.g., Schoolcraft 1851: Pl. 13; Squier and Davis 1848: Fig. 148), it was similar in theme and style to shamanistic pipes from north of Cahokia (Emerson 1983, 1982: Figs. 7, 11, 16; Drooker 1994d).

Disk pipes, associated with an upper Mississippi Valley heartland (see Chapter 3), have been excavated at most Late Fort Ancient components in southwestern Ohio. Besides examples listed in Table 4-3, a redstone disk pipe almost identical to the limestone one from Campbell Island, has come from an uniden-

TABLE 4-3
Pipe Types from Fort Ancient and Related Sites

	Sample Size	TUBU-LAR	SEMI PLAT-FORM	ELBOW Equal -Arm	ELBOW Short Stem	ELBOW Long Stem	OVOID	VASI-FORM	DISK Lrg.Disk, Long Handle	DISK Sm.Disk, Long Handle	DISK Sm.Disk, Short Handle	KEEL-SHAPED	FULL-FIGURE EFFIGY [a] Human	FULL-FIGURE EFFIGY [a] Animal	FULL-FIGURE EFFIGY [a] Bird
EARLY-MIDDLE FORT ANCIENT [b]															
Turpin	15+	X(?)	X	X									X	X	
Roseberry Farm	5+		X	?-----X-----?											
Gartner	4 type exmples		X	X	X										
Incinerator	4		X	X	X										
Baum	++	X	X	X	X		X								
State Line	?	X		(elbow pipes present)		X									
Feurt (excavation)	approx. 50		X	X	X		X			X(?)			?-----X----?		
Anderson	7+				X		X								
Taylor	2				X	X									
LATE FORT ANCIENT AND RELATED [c]															
Campbell Is.	3			X			X		X						
Hahn's Field	10		X				X			X					
Feurt (plow zone)	>20	X		X	X		X	X		X	X				
Fox Farm	many		X	X	X	X	X	X	X (red)						
Riker	20+			X		X	X	X				X			X
Orchard	many				X	X	X	X		X		X			X
Buffalo	7					X		X	X(red)						X
Neale's Landing	8					X		X						X	
Hardin	22						X	X	? (frags)		? (frags)				
Rolf Lee	6+						X	X	? ("disk")		? ("disk")				

[a] Some effigy types were omitted due to space constraints. Other types present include *human heads* (State Line, Baum, Feurt [from both excavation and plow zone], Fox Farm, Buffalo, and sites related to Neale's Landing (Hemmings 1976), *animal or bird heads* (Turpin, State Line, Feurt [from both excavation and plow zone], Fox Farm, Buffalo, sites related to Neale's Landing, Hardin, and Orchard), and *other* (Gartner, Feurt [from both excavation and plow zone], Fox Farm, and sites related to Neale's Landing).

[b] References: Turpin (Metz 1885a; Oehler 1973; HUPM & CMNH collections), Roseberry (Graybill 1981), Gartner (Mills 1907; Griffin 1943), Incinerator (postcard from site museum), Baum (Mills 1906; Griffin 1943), State Line (Vickery and Genheimer 1994), Feurt (Mills 1917), Anderson (Griffin 1943), Taylor (Griffin 1943).

[c] **Boldface** indicates sites from which European goods were excaved under controlled conditions; underlining indicates sites from which European goods have been reported. See Tables 4-4 and 4-10 for references. Note that "clean" seriation was impossible because many of the sites have Early-Middle Fort Ancient components.

TABLE 4-4
Excavation Histories of Selected Southwestern Ohio Fort Ancient Sites, Including All Known To Have a Madisonville Horizon Component

	Formal excavation?	Est.% excavated	Extant Site Map?	Ft. Ancient Temporal Components	Comments	References
State Line	small	< 25% scale	no	E-M	Major Early Fort Ancient site, excavated in piecemeal fashion: 1 mound by Black in 1930s, and salvage work by CMNH and Univ. of Cincinnati.	Black 1934; Griffin 1943; Wheelersburg 1992; Vickery and Genheimer 1994
Turpin-1	yes	?	no	E-M	Village site with large burial mound, partially excavated by CCMNH during 1940s and 1960s, plus small-scale stratigraphic excavation in 1980s. First site where superimposed Fort Ancient and Woodland components were recognized.	Oehler 1950, 1973; Riggs 1977, 1986; Genheimer 1994
Turpin-2	yes	? (0.2 ha)	no	E-M, *EL*	Second component on Turpin land, east of Turpin-1. Village site with Anderson Shell-tempered and some "classic" Madisonville ceramics, and at least 1 disk pipe. Excavated by Metz and Nickerson to 19th-century standards.	Metz 1885b; Nickerson 1885; Griffin 1943
Turpin-3 ("Peach Orchard Ridge")	yes	?	no	E-M	Third component on Turpin land. Village and cemetery site, perhaps same as No. 3, Group E (Metz 1881). Excavated by Metz.	Metz 1881, 1885b; Griffin 1943; Starr 1960
Incinerator ("Sunwatch")	yes	60%	yes	E-M	Single-generation village, first in s.w. Ohio known to have circular form. Best-mapped site in the subregion. Excavated during 1970s-80s by Dayton Mus. of Nat. Hist.	Essenpreis 1982; Robertson 1984; Nass 1987, 1989; Heilman 1988; Evans 1994; Nass and Yerkes 1995
Anderson	yes	≥80%	yes	E-M	Small circular village excavated and mapped by C.C. Anderson during 1930s & 40s, after some work by Moorehead in 1880s. Analyzed by Essenpreis.	Griffin 1943; Essenpreis 1982
Taylor	no	?	no	E-M	This is a large, important multi-component "site" that includes village(s), burial mound, and burials on an adjacent knoll. Dug in 1891 by Moorehead, who provided minimal information on provenience; also collected by C.C. Anderson. Based on pottery temper, portions may be later than Anderson.	Griffin 1943; Essenpreis 1982
Sand Ridge	yes	?	no	M-EL	Village-cemetery excavated by Metz in 1883. Riggs utilized later stratigraphic excavation to define a subregional ceramics chronology.	Griffin 1943; Riggs 1986
Campbell Island	yes	≥20%	yes	E-M, L	Small settlement: concentrated area of burials plus dispersed storage pits. Shetrone excavated ca. 0.1 ha, Cowan, 13 m^2.	Griffin 1943; Shetrone 1926; Cowan 1986
Hahn's Field	yes	? (0.1 ha)	no	?, L	Village-cemetery site excavated by Metz in 1885; examined by CMNH in 1990s.	Metz 1885a; Griffin 1943; Genheimer 1994
Clear Creek	yes	?	yes	L	Midden and storage/refuse pits directly adjacent to Hahn's Field. Surface collection and salvage excavation by CMNH, 1994.	Genheimer 1994

"Temporal components" indicate phase assignments: E-M = Early-Middle Fort Ancient, L = Late Fort Ancient (Madisonville Horizon), EL = Early Late Fort Ancient (late prehistoric), LL = Late Late Fort Ancient (protohistoric) (see Figure 4-3). Minor components are *in italics*.

tified location in Butler County, which is just north of Cincinnati (West 1934: Pl. 53). Not only disks but a variety of other pipe forms from Fort Ancient settlements were fashioned from red pipestone. At least some of them very likely were made from Minnesota catlinite or related upper Mississippi Valley redstone, as apparently confirmed by an early trace element analysis project (Sigstad 1973). Unfortunately, analytical methods from this sourcing study were not adequate by today's standards. Current analyses of additional redstone material by Gundersen (1993) will be extremely useful in checking and extending the earlier work.

The most typical marine shell pendants at early sites were in geometric shapes. One common form is annular (a circle with large central hole), found at at least eleven Early-Middle Fort

TABLE 4-5
Site Characteristics of Selected Southwestern Ohio Fort Ancient Sites

	Location	Est. Total Area, ha	Number of Burials Excavated	Burial Mound(s)	Plaza	Palisade	Structure Type(s)	Maximum Structure Size, m2
State Line	Terrace, Great Miami River	4-6 ha	90	5-6	(x)	(x)	rectangular, wall trench	225
Turpin-1	Terrace, Little Miami River	?	mound: 193 village: 26	1	?	?	rectangular, poles	?
Turpin-2	Terrace, Little Miami River	?	≥230	1?	?	?	?	?
Turpin-3	Ridge top?	?	28	1?	?	?	rect., wall trench	23
Incinerator	Floodplain, Great Miami R.	2 ha	168	--	x	x	rectangular, poles	70
Anderson	Floodplain, Little Miami R.	0.5 ha	125	--	x	?	circular, semi-subterranean	64
Taylor	Blufftop, near L. Miami-Caesar Cr. confluence	24-28 ha	mound: 79 village: ±17 knoll: ±12	1	?	?	?	?
Sand Ridge	Blufftop, Little Miami River	≤1.5 ha	≥ 23	--	?	?	?	?
Campbell Island	Floodplain, Great Miami R.	0.5-1 ha	21	--	?	?	?	?
Hahn's Field	Floodplain, Little Miami R.	?	31	?	x	?	?	?
Clear Creek	Floodplain, Little Miami R.	1.3 ha	1	--	--	?	?	?

x = definitely present; (x) = probably present; ((x)) = possibly present. For references, see Table 4-4.

TABLE 4-6
Burial Characteristics of Selected Southwestern Ohio Fort Ancient Sites

	Burial Sample Size	Graves w/Stone Slabs	% Extended Burials / % Flexed Burials	Double Burials (% of People)	Multiple Burials	Disarticulated Burials	Burials with Trauma [a]	Burials with Gravegoods
State Line	90	present	68%/ <32%	----------a	few------------	--	?	present
Turpin-1	mound: 193	?	most extended	few if any	few if any	≥0.5%	?	6%
	village: 26	?	most extended	?	?	?	?	≥8%
Turpin-2	223	6%	78% / 11%	4%	1 of 3	11%	?	24%
Turpin-3	28	0	50%/32%	7%	--	18%	?	14%
Incinerator	145	>50%	both present	?	?	?	?	30%
Anderson	93	47%	84% / 15%	?	?	≥0.8% [b]	≥6%	28%
Taylor	mound: 79	19%	some / some	present	present	>22%	?	22%
	village: ±17	24%	? / ?	?	?	?	?	6%
	knoll: ±12	17%	67% / ?	?	?	?	?	17%
Sand Ridge	23	?	?	?	?	?	?	?
Campbell Island	21	5%	81% / 9.5%	0	0	5%	?	38-43%
Hahn's Field	23	0 [c]	≥61% / 13%	9%	1 of 3 [c]	13%	?	39%
Clear Creek	1	0	?	0	0	0	?	0%

For references, see Table 4-4.
[a] "Trauma" is intended to cover possible war-related injuries, including projectile points in bone, crushing blows to head, etc.
[b] 1 of 125 completely disarticulated, 15 partially disarticulated (mostly missing minor body parts)
[c] A group burial of eight individuals in a large stone-filled pit, possibly part of a multi-step mortuary program, is omitted from consideration as probably pre-Fort Ancient.

TABLE 4-7
Gravegood Characteristics of Selected Southwestern Ohio Fort Ancient Sites

		Burial Sample Size	Burials with Gravegoods	Burials with Ceramic Vessels	Burials with Copper	Burials with Shell Ornaments	Burials with Pipes
State Line		90	present	≥1%	? [a]	≥ 1%	?
Turpin-1	mound:	193	6%	2%	≤0.5% [b]	?	0?
	village:	26	≥8%		0	≥ 4%	0
Turpin-2		223	24%	3.1%	1.3%	8%	0.5%
Turpin-3		28	14%	7.1%	0	4%	3.6%
Incinerator		145	30%	0.7%	0?	≥17%	1.4%
Anderson		93	29%	4.3%	1.1%	8%	1.1%
Taylor	mound:	79	22%	2.5%	1.3%	15%	0
	village:	±17	6%	0	0	6%	0
	knoll:	±12	17%	17%	0	8%	0
Sand Ridge		23	?	?	?	?	?
Campbell Island		21	38-43%	19%	0	0 [c]	0
Hahn's Field		23	39%	35%	0	0	0
Clear Creek		1	0	0	0	0	0

For references, see Table 4-4.
[a] Copper is present at site.
[b] One individual with copper-covered ear spools buried below mound surface but above Woodland village level.
[c] One individual had a marine shell cup (*Fulgur perversum*).

Ancient sites, including Anderson, Taylor, and State Line in southwestern Ohio (Carskadden 1994; Griffin 1943: Pls. xliv, xlviiXCviii, cxx, cxxi; Mills 1904: Figs. 12, 13, 54, 1906: Figs 58, 59; Smith 1910: Pl. L; Vickery and Genheimer 1994; HUPM Cat. Nos. 86-46-10/A3679, 86-46-10/A3681 from Turpin, 08-3-10 from Madisonville; Ohio Historical Society Cat. No. 161/45, from Feurt). The other concentration of annular gorgets appears to be at a half dozen twelfth through early fifteenth century sites in the central Illinois River valley, but they also have been reported from Spiro, Etowah, and elsewhere (see Figure 8-19, below) (Brain and Phillips 1996:125; Brown 1976:104, 399, Fig. 81; Conrad 1991b:148, 149, 154, 1996; Santure et al. 1990: Fig. 10.6; Smith and Hodges 1968).

More complex gorgets, of the fenestrated cross-in-circle design with or without additional engraving or punctuation, have been found at State Line, Taylor, and Anderson, as well as Somers Farm in Kentucky (Figure 4-2) (Brashler and Moxley 1990:59; Essenpreis 1978:229; Funkhauser and Webb 1928:103-4; Griffin 1943:96-97, 106, Pl. xlvii.a; Hanson 1966:160; Vickery and Genheimer 1994). They are most closely related to Brain and Phillips's Pine Island and Russell cruciform styles, which have a wide distribution that lies mainly outside of eastern Tennessee; examples similar to those from Fort Ancient sites have come from Oklahoma (Spiro), Missouri, Illinois, and Indiana (Angel), among other places (see Figure 8-21, below) (Brain and Phillips 1996:28-33; but cf. Conrad 1996).

Another gorget style utilized during the twelfth to fourteenth centuries was the spider. Esarey has demonstrated that there are two distinct style zones, centered on Illinois and eastern Tennessee (Esarey 1990). One gorget of each style has been reported from a small area in northern Kentucky, unfortunately, neither one from formal excavations (see Figure 8-20, below). The gorget from Bracken County, between the Fox Farm and Augusta sites, is most similar to examples from the American Bottom region, around Cahokia (Esarey 1990: Fig. 6; Wagers 1993), while one from Fox Farm (Glass n.d.:7) is congruent with a specimen from Etowah, Georgia (Esarey 1990: Fig. 2a). Fox Farm also has produced a cross-in-circle gorget, in Brain and Phillips's unfenestrated Ruffner style, that is closest in style to examples from the eastern Tennessee region (Funkhauser and Webb 1928:104). It appears to be identical to one from Hixon, Tennessee (Kneberg 1959: Fig. 3).

The significant amounts of shell ornaments at Early-Middle Fort Ancient sites in southwestern Ohio (cf. Table 4-7) and at mound sites farther east such as Fox Farm (accompanying at least 11% of mound burials), Gartner (accompanying 22% of mound burials), and Baum (marine shell "found in every section of the village, especially in the burials"; Mills 1906:73), plus the presence of copper (Table 4-7), argue against a significant restriction on Fort Ancient extraregional interaction prior to Madisonville Horizon times, as has been proposed for northern Kentucky and West Virginia (see above). Whereas southwestern Ohio sites might have been interacting primarily toward the west, marine shell was probably also coming in from the southeast, perhaps through Fox Farm. The lower frequency of shell ornaments with burials at Feurt (only 3.5%; see Table 4-

TABLE 4-8
Radiocarbon Dates for Late Fort Ancient and Related Sites East of the Little Miami River Drainage

	Sample No.	Date B.P.	Calibrated Date, A.D., with One-Sigma Range	2-Sigma Cal. Range, A.D.
Augusta, KY	BETA 13365	210±60	1650(1669,1783,1797,1948,1952)1954	1527-1955
	BETA 11855	470±90	1408(1437)1490	1301-1645
	BETA 18183	470±70	1412(1437)1481	1327-1631
Bentley, KY	BETA 18182	230±50	1647(1664)1954	1527-1954
Buffalo, WV	UGA 304	270±120	1485(1650)1954	1423-1955
	UGA 303	780±70	1212(1263,1273,1275)1289	1070-1386
Bosman, OH	I 16589	340±80	1447(1523,1565,1578,1627)1653	1427-1954
	I 16593	360±80	1442(1498,1512,1516,1599,1618)1648	1416-1953
	I 16604	400±80	1435(1454,1457,1478)1635	1407-1660
Cullison, OH	I 16955	310±80	1484(1638)1664	1436-1954
	I 16954	340±80	1447(1523,1565,1578,1627)1653	1427-1954
Clover, WV	DIC 3366	370±45	1448(1492,1604,1610)1633	1437-1648
	DIC 3367	400±50	1440(1454,1457,1478)1623	1426-1642
	DIC 3087, -88, -89	750±190	1044(1281)1409	898-1610
Fox Farm, KY	BETA 11856	390±70	1439(1486)1635	1413-1656
	BETA 11857	530±70	1330(1414)1440	1295-1488
	BETA 13364	590±60	1302(1332,1342,1395)1416	1286-1439
	BETA 13363	790±70	1209(1261)1287	1065-1383
Goolman, KY	DIC 2339	130±55	1675(1695,1727,1813,1920,1954)1955	1659-1955
	DIC 2509	210±50	1653(1669,1783,1797,1948,1952)1954	1638-1954
	DIC 2338	210±100	1638(1669,1783,1797,1948,1952)1954	1450-1955
	DIC 2508	550±40	1331(1410)1427	1316-1439
Larkin, KY	BETA 19067	210±70	1647(1669,1783,1797,1948,1952)1954	1519-1955
	BETA 19068	370±80	1441(1492,1604,1610)1645	1413-1952
Morrison Village, OH	M 1761	260±100	1496(1653)1954	1438-1955
	M 1760	290±100	1485(1645)1954	1431-1955
	OWU 181	400±115	1421(1454,1457,1478)1646	1321-1954
Neale's Landing, WV	UGA 955	365±100	1438(1494,1601,1616)1651	1406-1954
	UGA 954	370±155	1415(1492,1604,1610)1952	1293-1955
	UGA 951	430±75	1426(1445)1620	1333-1648
	UGA 952	660±135	1260(1299)1417	1066-1487
Reeve Village, OH	CWRU 71 [a]	580±130	1288(1334,1338,1402)1441	1214-1635
	CWRU 71 [b]	580±65	1303(1334,1338,1402)1425	1287-1442
	CWRU 19	740±55	1259(1282)1294	1210-1389
	CWRU 13	885±65	1038(1162,1171,1190)1256	1003-1281
Riker, OH	OWU 175	390±170	1408(1486)1667	1284-1955
Rolf Lee, WV	UGA 2638	220±95	1534(1667)1954	1450-1955
Speckman, OH	I 16953	230±80	1638(1664)1954	1482-1955
	I 17358	300±80	1488(1642)1667	1438-1954
	I 16952	400±80	1435(1454)1635	1407-1660
Thompson, KY	BETA 11851	110±60	1679(1710,1718,1820,1831,1882,1914,1954)1955	1664-1955
	BETA 11853	400±70	1437(1454,1457,1478)1631	1411-1653
	BETA 13367	810±60	1164(1224,1227,1245,1257)1281	1065-1294
	BETA 13368	920±100	1003(1071,1080,1128,1136,1154)1256	900-1287

Data from: Brose 1994; Freidin 1987; Graybill 1981; Hanson 1975; James Morton, personal communication 1994, 1995; Murphy 1974; Prufer and Andors; Sharp 1990. Calibration after Stuiver and Reimer 1993. See Tables 4-1 and 6-1 for western Fort Ancient sites.
[a] As reported by Murphy 1974.
[b] As reported by Brose 1994.

13) and the apparent lack of them in West Virginia during this time argues against a route through West Virginia. However, issues of contemporaneity must be addressed as well: no definitive analysis has been accomplished to determine absolute dates of occupation periods at Feurt, Gartner, and Baum, which generally have been assigned to Early Fort Ancient.

Southwestern Ohio interaction patterns during the Madisonville Horizon, most apparent from artifacts at the Madisonville site, will be discussed in Chapter 8.

Protohistoric Fort Ancient Sites

Although Madisonville remains the primary protohistoric Fort Ancient settlement in Ohio, European artifacts also have been found in good archaeological context at a number of sites in West Virginia and Kentucky (Figure 4-5). However, only a handful of ^{14}C

TABLE 4-9
European and Other Important Exotic Artifacts at Late Prehistoric-Protohistoric Fort Ancient and Related Sites, and Associated Relative Chronological Placement

	European and Other Exotic Artifacts	Assemblage(s)	Dates	References
SITES WITH DIAGNOSTIC ASSEMBLAGES FROM GOOD ARCHAEOLOGICAL CONTEXT				
Buffalo, WV	**Amber bead**, white glass seed bead; copper and brass tubular beads, **brass clips**, flat brass "serpentine" fragment, **serpentine thin copper tube**; redstone disk pipe; marine shell mask, maskette, and Citico rattlesnake gorget, and "mushroom" earplugs	A, S	1525-1625	Hanson 1975
Hardin, KY	Copper and **brass** tubular beads, tubes, **clips**; **brass coil** made from thin tube and flat bracelet; copper pendant and tubular bracelet; marine shell Citico-style, mask, and maskette gorgets	S/GBP1-2	1550-1625	Hanson 1966
	Redstone pipes (incl. disk)			Sigstad 1973
(R)	**Glass beads: tubular**, aqua blue spherical; iron celts; copper/brass pendants and **"salamanders"**	GBP2, L	1600-1630	Henderson et al. 1986
Neale's Landing, WV [a]	**Friable blue glass beads** (IIa31/28), **iron ax** (two type 4 maker's marks, 1225 g), marine shell mask and maskette gorgets	GBP1, GBP2	1580-1630	Hemmings 1977; Baker 1984
(Henry Stahl Coll.)	Glass beads: white, blue; copper/brass "tinklers," tubular beads, pendants, tubular bracelets; iron ax			Hemmings 1977; personal inspection
Clover, WV	Glass beads: **tumbled chevron** (IVk3), dark blue seed, turquoise blue (IIa31/40); **brass/copper kettle fragments**, tubular beads, **tinklers**, thin tube in C-shape, **"lizard"** (top view), button*; **brass fish effigy** (side view); marine shell Citico rattlesnake gorget	C, D/"E," GBP2, D1, *?	1590-1700	Maslowski 1984, 1991; Freidin 1987; Mayer-Oakes 1955; personal inspection
Rolf Lee, WV	Glass beads: **white cored** (IVa11/13), turquoise blue (IIa31/40), **white & indigo tubular** (Ia5, Ia19), **indigo** (IIa52/55), **tumbled chevron** (IVk3), **blue and white striped** (IVb33), **black** (IIa7), white (IIa11), blue cored (IVa19)	C, GBP2, D1, D2	1590-1664	Graybill 1981; Baker 1986
	Copper and brass tubular beads, brass strips, flattened **thin copper tube in "spiral"/C shape**; **brass armbands**, marine shell Citico rattlesnake and mask gorgets (one with copper eyes)	S/GBP1-2, D	1550-1700	Youse 1965
	Glass beads: turquoise blue (IIa31/40), **dark blue with white** (IVb32/33); **large brass armbands**	C-D/"E"	1600-1700	Kapp 1961-68; Drooker 1994b
	Marine shell "spider"* (R), Citico rattlesnake, mask and maskette gorgets, and "mushroom" earplugs		(*pre-1500?)	Brashler and Moxley 1990
(R)	Copper/brass spoons used as pendants, 2 flat metal serpents, **brass clips**, iron celts	D		R. Maslowski, R. Moxley; E. Schwartz (pers. comm.)
Orchard, WV [b]	Glass beads: turq. blue (IIa31/40), **red tubular twisted** (Ia1, Ic'); **copper/brass** tubular beads, tinklers, **arm bands** (small); brass tubes, " 'dog head' effigy"*; marine shell mask and maskette gorgets, and "mushroom" earplugs; disk pipes	GBP3, D, *?	1630-1700	Moxley 1988a, 1988b; personal inspection
Bentley, KY	Gun parts, gunflints, lead shot; iron nails, knives, shears, kettle frags., key, etc.; brass jew's harp, pendant, tinklers, etc.; glass beads; etc.	Z	1700-1800	Henderson et al. 1986; Pollack and Henderson 1984
Old Fort Earthworks, KY	Iron axes, picks, gunbarrels, etc.; lead shot; silver crosses and buckles; brass kettles, jew's harp; glass beads; etc.	Z	1700-1800	Henderson et al. 1986
SITES WITH 16TH-17TH CENTURY RADIOCARBON DATES BUT NO DIAGNOSTIC ARTIFACTS [c]				
Morrison Village, OH				Prufer and Andors 1967
Speckman, OH				J. Morton, pers. comm. 1992
Goolman, KY				Henderson et al. 1986; Sharp 1990
Thompson, KY				Henderson et al. 1986

TABLE 4-9 (cont.)
European and Other Important Exotic Artifacts at Late Prehistoric-Protohistoric Fort Ancient and Related Sites, and Associated Relative Chronological Placement

	European and Other Exotic Artifacts	Assemblage(s)	Dates	References
SITES WITH FEW DIAGNOSTIC ARTIFACTS OR PROBLEMATICAL CONTEXT				
Pratt, WV (R)	Marine shell Citico rattlesnake gorget	Y	1500-	Brashler and Moxley 1990
Eagle Creek, OH	Marine shell maskettes, non-redstone disk pipes	Y	1500-	Snider 1991
Dunn, KY and vic. (R)	Copper/brass pendant, rolled copper tube	Y	1500-	Henderson et al. 1986
15JS16, KY	Tubular copper/brass beads, marine shell rattlesnake gorget, copper-covered earspool	Y	1500-	Henderson et al. 1986
Clear Creek, OH	Tubular copper bead	Y	1500-	Genheimer 1994
Sandstone Shelter, WV (near Barker's Bottom) (R)	**Amber bead**	A	1525-1600	Maslowski 1984
15MA23, KY (S,R)	Light blue glass seed bead	A-	1525-	Henderson et al. 1986
Gue Farm, WV (S,R)	Glass bead	A-	1525-	Maslowski 1984
(R)	Mask gorget			Brashler and Moxley 1990
Logan, WV	Glass beads	A-	1525-	Maslowski 1984
Larkin, KY (R)	Tubular copper beads, piece of **brass**, marine shell "spaghetti," rattlesnake, and mask gorgets	A-	1525-	Foley and Lipscombe 1961; Henderson et al. 1986
	Rolled copper bead, lead shot (?)			Pollack et al. 1987
Feurt, OH	Copper/brass tubular beads and conical **tinklers**; marine shell Citico rattlesnake gorget fragments	GBP1-	1580-	Mills 1917
	Redstone pipes (not disk)			Sigstad 1973
(R)	Glass beads: turquoise blue (IIa31/40), turquoise blue with **white stripes** (IIb56/57), tubular red with green core*	B/C, *?	1585-	W. Wertz, pers. comm. 1993
Marmet, WV	**Friable blue glass beads** (IIa31/28)	GBP1	1580-1600	Barnett and Paxton 1955
	Glass beads; **brass spoon** and tubular bead	GBP2	1600-1630	Youse 1988
(R)	Glass beads: **Nueva Cadiz, non-red tubular**, faceted purple*, **brass "lizard" effigy**	A, GBP2, L, *ca.1675?	1525-1640 -1675?	R. Moxley, pers. comm. 1994
(R)	Marine shell mask gorgets			Brashler and Moxley 1990
Augusta, KY (R)	Light blue glass(??) beads; **iron bracelets**, tubular copper beads, "copper face mask," **copper tubular serpent pendant**	S, C-D	1550-1670	Henderson et al. 1986
	Marine shell mask and maskette gorgets, disk pipe			Webb 1955
Beale Mound, OH? (R)	**Brass animal** (bear?) **and fish effiies, brass/copper spiral,** copper tinklers	S, D	1550-1670	W. Wertz, pers. comm. 1993
Riker, OH	Copper tubular beads & hair tubes	GBP1-2	1580-	Vietzen 1974
Bosman, OH	Copper tubular beads & tinkler	GBP1-2	1580-	Carskadden et al. 1992
Cullison, OH	Brass/copper tube, iron buckle*	GBP1-, *?	1580-	J. Morton, pers. comm. 1995
Snag Creek, KY (R)	Copper/brass conical tinkler	GBP1-2	1580-	Henderson et al. 1986
Henry Pyles, KY (R)	Copper/brass conical tinklers and tubular beads; marine shell rattlesnake gorgets; redstone items	GBP1-2	1580-	Henderson et al. 1986
Fox Farm, KY	Sheet lead pendant (S)*, rolled copper beads, marine shell mask and maskette gorgets	*?		Griffin 1943
Western edge (R)	Melted **red glass bead**; copper pendant and tubular beads; redstone disk pipes; marine shell spider, mask, and Citico rattlesnake gorgets	D1	1610-	Henderson et al. 1986; Glass n.d.
	Redstone pipes (not disk)			Sigstad 1973
Devary, KY (S)	Red glass bead	D1	1610-	Henderson et al. 1986
Laughlin, KY (S)	Spall and blade gunflints	Y,Z	1640-1800+	Henderson et al. 1986
Arrasmith, KY (S)	Hexagonal, cored blue glass bead (IIIf)	X, Z	1700-	Henderson et al. 1986

See Figure 4-18 (and/or Figure 3-8 and Table 3-2) for time ranges associated with letter designations A-D, GBP1-GBP3, D1-D2, S, and L. X = pre-1500 indigenous assemblage; Y = non-diagnostic assemblage, but probably post-1500; Z = post-1700 European assemblage. Bead type designations are from Kidd and Kidd 1983. (S) indicates sites from which European artifacts have come only from surface collection; (R) = diagnostic artifacts reportedly excavated, but location not verified. * = artifacts of uncertain time range. Dates encompass the entire period(s) represented by diagnostic European artifacts, and thus give a very broad estimate of protohistoric occupation dates. Important diagnostic artifacts are **boldfaced**.

[a] Two people have reported to me the possibility that red tubular beads were excavated at Neale's Landing and were curated at the Blennerhassett Museum (J. Morton, pers. comm. 1996; M. Smith, pers. comm. 1996), but I have been unable to confirm this. Such beads have not yet turned up in the current inventory of collections formerly housed at the Blennerhassett Museum (S. Yoho, pers. comm. 1997). The site report (Hemmings 1977) does not mention them. It is possible that the beads seen by Smith and Morton were excavated from a protohistoric pit on the grounds of the Blennerhassett mansion, not at the Neale's Landing site (R. Maslowski, pers. comm. 1996). Neale's Landing is one of several prehistoric and protohistoric sites recorded on the island.

[b] According to Ron Moxley (pers. comm. 1993), the red tubular beads reported from Orchard (Moxley 1988a, 1988b) might actually have come from Rolf Lee.

[c] See Table 4-8.

Table 4-10
Excavation Histories of Important Protohistoric Fort Ancient and Related Sites

	Formal Excavation?	Est.% Excavated	Extant Site Map?	Ft. Ancient Temporal Components	Comments	References
Riker, OH	no	<<50%	no	early LL	Excavated over many years by private individuals and 1965-66 by OAS Sugar Creek Chapter. No overall grid. Ceramics approx. 70% Wellsburg, 23% "Riker"; Madisonville, Monongahela, and northern Ohio types present. Earthen embankment reported in 1840.	Vietzen 1974; Whitman 1975
Bosman, OH	yes	30%	yes	early LL	Ceramics approx. 50-50 Madisonville and Wellsburg.	Carskadden et al. 1992; J. Morton, pers. comm. 1992
Feurt, OH	yes	20%	yes	E-M(2), *LL*	Moorehead dug in the mounds; no map. Mills finished mounds and dug part of village. Charles Wertz made a large surface collection; from pipe types present (Mills 1917:331, 398; personal inspection) this appears to represent a later component than excavated by Mills.	Moorehead 1897; Mills 1917; Griffin 1943; Henderson et al. 1992; W. Wertz, pers. comm. 1993
Fox Farm, KY	yes	? (prob. <<50%)	topo only	E-M, EL, *LL*	Smith dug 5 mounds and some proportion of the village; no map. Funkhauser and Webb dug 25 burials. Turnbow dug 4 excavation units. Smith and Turnbow found no European goods, but modern informants have, in a restricted area on the west side of the site. A local collector has developed a map.	Smith 1910; Webb 1927; Funkhauser and Webb 1928; Griffin 1943; Henderson et al. 1986; Turnbow 1992
Buffalo, WV	yes	15%	yes (WVGES)	EL-LL (2)	Site consists of two overlapping circular components. Graybill questions Hanson's designation of the Downstream Village as the earlier. Private individuals, the WVAS Kanawha Chapter, and the WV Geological and Economic Survey have excavated, the latter two approx. 0.2 and 0.6 ha respectively. Published maps of burials and structures are separate.	Griffin 1943; Mairs 1960; McMichael 1962, 1963; Broyles 1970; Guilday 1971; Metress 1971; Hanson 1975; Graybill 1981
Marmet, WV	no	?	no	?, LL	Information is from notes by private excavators, over 40 years, at 2 separate but close sites. Griffin reported on 19th-century collection from same town (then called Brownstown), which may or may not have come from same locus. Only 4 of at least 50 burials are published.	Griffin 1943; Barnett and Paxton 1955; Youse 1988; R. Barnett, pers. comm. 1993; R. Moxley, pers. comm. 1993
Hardin, KY	yes	10%	yes	*E-M*, LL	Excavated by WPA team, documented later. Map shows only approximate locations of burials. Not enough area excavated to show site layout. Digging by private individuals has been common, with significant recovery of European goods and pipes. Site much eroded by river.	Hanson 1963, 1966; Henderson et al. 1986; Henderson et al. 1992; D. Pollack, pers. comm. 1994; Holmes 1994
Neale's Landing, WV	yes	20%	yes	LL	Site on eroding blufftop. Extensively collected by individuals; a large collection by H. Stahl from the entire island is curated at the Blennerhasset Museum. Formal excavation was under the Nat. Park Service. Similar proportions of Wellsburg, Madisonville, and Neale's Landing ceramics present.	Hemmings 1976, 1977; Broyles and Hemmings 1978; Baker 1984, 1988
Augusta, KY	small scale	1%	no	E-M, LL	Large village site overbuilt by town of Augusta. Piecemeal excavations: a group of burials excavated in a cellar, CRM work at sewage plant, and 3 test units along waterfront. Hale recognized 2 components, the earlier similar to Fox Farm, with stone slab graves, and the later with burial practices and ceramics similar to Madisonville. Turnbow and Jobe found only a LL component, and disagree with Hale et al. that Fox Farm ceramics were present.	Webb 1955; Hale 1981; Henderson et al. 1986; Turnbow and Jobe 1992

Table 4-10 (cont.)
Excavation Histories of Important Protohistoric Fort Ancient and Related Sites

	Formal Exca-vation?	Est.% Exca-vated	Extant Site Map?	Ft. Ancient Temporal Components	Comments	References
Clover, WV	yes	<3%	<3%	?, LL	First reports of site based on amateur collections; Adams Collection currently curated at Huntington Mus.of Art. Griffin reported 3 mounds, no longer prominent. Excavation data are from Marshall U. field schools led by Freidin, plus 1 burial described by Griffin.	Griffin 1943; Mayer-Oakes 1955; Maslowski 1984, 1991, pers. comm. 1993; Freidin 1987
Rolf Lee, WV	yes	3%	no (WVAS)	?, LL	Village site extensively excavated by amateurs. Formal excavation (.09 ha) by WVAS Kanawha Chapter. Graybill divided the site into 2 components, both LL. No. 2, the larger, seems to include the area excavated by the WVAS and most of the burials excavated by Kapp (1961-68). All tabulated data herein refer to that component.	Kapp 1961-68; Youse 1965; Graybill 1981; Baker 1986; R. Barnett, pers. comm. 1993; R. Maslowski, pers. comm. 1993; R. Moxley 1993, pers. comm. 1993
Orchard, WV	no	ca. 60%	no	?, LL	Village site extensively excavated by amateurs over about 40 years. Field notes kept but no map available. Ceramics mainly Madisonville, but some Wellsburg present. Treated as single component in the literature, but quite possibly multi-component.	Mayer-Oakes, 1955; Graybill 1981; Moxley 1988a, 1988b, pers. comm. 1993; R . Barnett, pers. comm. 1993

Order is from European artifact assemblages (see Table 4-9). "Temporal components" indicate phase assignments: E-M = Early-Middle Fort Ancient, EL = Early Late Fort Ancient (late prehistoric), LL = Late Late Fort Ancient (protohistoric) (see Figure 4-3). Minor components are *in italics*.

dates exist for these sites (Table 4-8), and precise temporal relationships still are being worked out. For comparison with Madisonville, I have compiled as much information as possible on European goods present at Fort Ancient sites, and have used this to develop a very rough relative time frame. For selected well-excavated sites, I also have compiled quantitative information on settlement characteristics and mortuary patterns.

European Goods and Relative Chronology. Table 4-9 summarizes European and other exotic items that have been reported from late prehistoric-protohistoric Fort Ancient sites, along with the broad time frames that can be assigned to each assemblage. The table is divided into three parts: sites from which diagnostic European goods have been excavated under controlled conditions, sites from which few diagnostic items have been excavated or from which European goods have been obtained only under uncontrolled circumstances, and sites with radiocarbon dates that place them within the protohistoric period, but from which no diagnostic artifacts have been excavated.

Figure 4-18 is a more graphic summary of time spans associated with diagnostic assemblages. Because Fort Ancient communities might have acquired European items from several different directions and sources, there is some ambiguity in directly applying chronologies worked out from horizon marker artifacts for separate geographic regions, as noted in Table 3-2. Figure 4-18 indicates the regional time frame that I considered most appropriate for each horizon marker artifact in assigning relative chronological positions to well-excavated Fort Ancient sites; alternatives also are included. For sites from which Southeastern-style engraved gorgets have come, I had no hesitation in using dates developed from Southeastern assemblages (e.g., Smith 1987; Waselkov 1989), but for other sites, particularly those producing glass bead types or other artifacts that have not been found in the Southeast, I was more likely to employ time ranges associated with Northeastern assemblages (e.g., Chafe et al. 1986; Fitzgerald 1990; Fitzgerald et al. 1993; Kenyon and Fitzgerald 1986; Kenyon and Kenyon 1983; Sempowski 1994). I have personally examined and photographed portions of the assemblages from Buffalo, Neale's Landing, Clover, Orchard, Rolf Lee, and Feurt, but have not done a complete analysis for any of them. Thus, my judgments on temporal assignments have relied to a great extent on descriptions and comparisons published, and in a few cases communicated to me informally, by others (see references in Table 4-9). They should be considered as tentative, subject to future revision. The broad time ranges are due not only to problems in assigning dates to particular artifacts, but also to the fact that many if not most of the sites are multicomponent and could have been occupied, sporadically or continuously, over a relatively long time period. Some of these temporal ranges will be discussed further, and refined, in Chapter 8. For now, it is enough to note that virtually all European artifacts present at Fort Ancient sites would have been available prior to 1650.

Settlement Patterns and Mortuary Practices. Table 4-10 summarizes excavation information for nine important Fort Ancient sites from which European artifacts have been excavated or reported. Fox Farm and Feurt, with much larger Early-

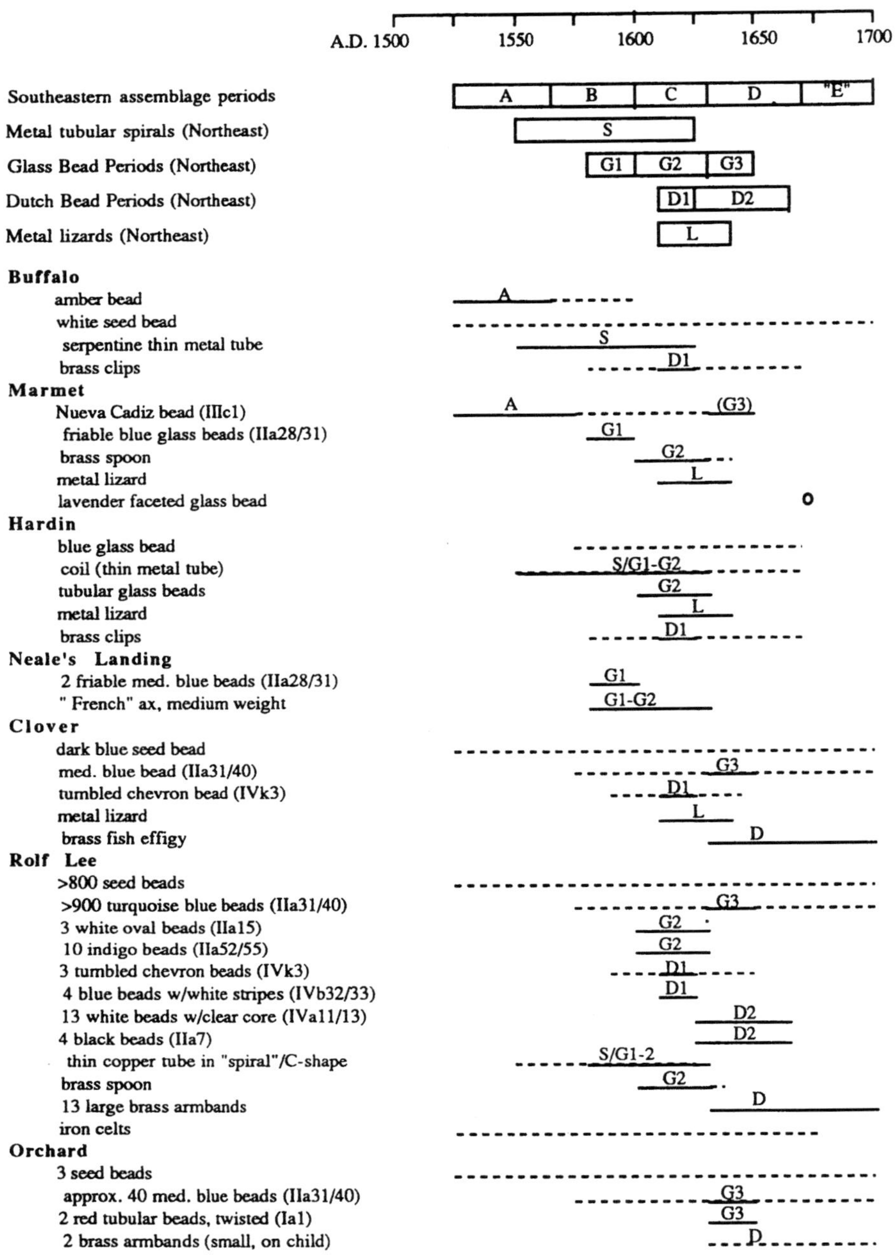

Figure 4-18. Time spans associated with diagnostic assemblages at protohistoric Fort Ancient sites.

Middle than Late components and no European artifacts excavated from good context, have been included because of their general significance in interpreting Fort Ancient development over time. From the table it should be clear that the data base for protohistoric sites rests on only limited formal, coordinated excavation (some but not all of which was well reported), plus much additional information, of greater or lesser quality, from amateur excavators and surface collectors who have operated over the course of the last century.

Table 4-11 summarizes recorded information on settlement location and spatial organization. Many of the sites are directly adjacent to, and being eroded away by, the present-day Ohio River channel, which is controlled by a series of dams. Thus, they often are described as occupying nondefensible locations. However, most of them would have been more distant from the channel in prehistoric times, except during flooding. The channel, too, would have been less continuously navigable than today, particularly during low-water periods, so it is quite possible that overland access routes were equally or even more important than water access.

A central plaza appears to have been present at the majority of these sites. Considering the generally small proportions of each site excavated, a plaza or plazas cannot be ruled out for any of them. Palisades definitely were present at Buffalo, and

TABLE 4-11
Site Characteristics of Fort Ancient and Related Sites with Protohistoric Components

	Location	Est. Total Area, ha	Number of Burials Excavated	Burial Mound(s)	Plaza	Palisade	Structure Type(s)	Maximum Structure Size, m2
Riker, OH	Bluff, 15 m above Tuscararus R.	0.8-4.0	est. 200-250	--	?	((x))	Rectangular and circular, poles	7.4
Bosman, OH	Floodplain, Muskingum R.	0.4	0	--	(x)	x	Circular, poles	26
Feurt, OH	Bluff/terrace, 12 m above Scioto R. floodplain	2	403	3	?	?	Oval?, poles	?
Fox Farm, KY	Ridgetop, 100 m from small stream; near salt licks	10-16	233	5	(x)	?	?	?
Buffalo, WV	First terrace, Kanawha R.	4.6	562+				Rectangular, poles	
(Downstream Vill.)			(561+)	--	x	x		164
(Upstream Village)			(1)	--	?	x		121
Marmet, WV	Floodplain and terrace, Kanawha R.	2-3	>50	--	?	?	?	?
Hardin, KY [a]	First terrace, Ohio R.	4.6+	335-351	--	?	((x))	Rectangular, poles	196
Neale's Landing, WV	Bluff/terrace on island, 11 m above Ohio R.	0.4	32	--	x	x	Rectangular, poles	>53
Augusta, KY [b]	First terrace, Ohio R.	24	hundreds	?	((x))	?	?	?
Clover, WV [c]	Second terrace, Ohio R.	3	7	3?	x	(x)	Rectangular?, poles	?
Rolf Lee, WV	First terrace/floodplain, Ohio R.	3	250-400	--	x	?	?, poles	?
Orchard, WV [d]	Second terrace, Ohio R.	1.6	300-800	1?	(x)	?	?	?

Order is from European artifact assemblages (see Table 4-9). For references, see Table 4-10. x = definitely present; (x) = probably present; ((x)) = possibly present.

[a] Number of individuals excavated is problematical (Holmes 1994:48-53). 335 were reported in the field notes, but at least one researcher has counted as many as 445 individuals within the extant remains. The figure of 351 is based on Hanson's 301 "burials," with 264 containing 1 individual, 28 containing 2, 4 containing 4, and 5 containing 3 or more; I used it for percentages of burial types (Table 4-12). For percentages of grave good types (Table 4-13), which were extracted from the original field notes, I used 335.

[b] Early residents report large numbers of burials. For example, one cellar, 60'x70', produced 110 individuals (Hale 1981:1). "Mass burials" might be burial mound(s), perhaps analogous to stone-box grave mounds at Middle Cumberland Mississippian sites (K. Smith 1992): an amateur excavation in 1981 yielded at least 30 individuals (2 extended, remainder jumbled), "layer-caked" with stone slabs; marine shell and a possible infant burial inside a ceramic vessel were present (Hale 1981:86-88). 10 were either excavated or closely observed by archaeologists (Webb 1955; Hale 1981).

[c] Palisade deduced from reported pattern of abrupt midden termination (Freiden 1987).

[d] Numbers of excavated burials have been reported as over 300 (Moxley 1988a, 1988b), over 600 (Maslowski 1984, based on information from Roland Barnett), and ca. 800 (Graybill 1981:61, based on information from Everett Schwartz). Although Graybill reports the presence of a plaza and domestic zone (1981:94), Orchard also has been characterized as "an unplanned, scattered village" (Moxley 1988a:4, based on Graybill 1987).

possibly or probably present at Orchard, Clover, and Hardin; again, they cannot be ruled out for any of the other sites. Houses all appear to have been posthole structures, more or less rectangular (perhaps oval at the earlier Feurt site). Structure sizes are available for only a few sites, but they tend to be relatively large. Hardin and Buffalo are multicomponent and overlap in time, so little can be said about the fact that the six completely excavated structures at the former are smaller, on average (145 m^2, calculated from data in Hanson 1975:7-13) than the twelve competely excavated structures at the latter (164 m^2, calculated by Carskadden 1994). It certainly can be said that these structures are significantly larger than any known from earlier Fort Ancient sites, with the exception of State Line. The close proximity and enlargement over time of houses at both sites, the overlapping of burials within house structures at Buffalo, and the crosscutting of burials at Hardin all bespeak intensive usage of restricted areas over significant time spans. Whether this was the rule or the exception for protohistoric Fort Ancient settlements requires additional data for clarification.

Table 4-12 summarizes burial characteristics for protohistoric sites, plus the largely Early-Middle Fort Ancient mortuary data from Feurt and Fox Farm. There are both temporal and east-west differences, the latter corroborated by data from southwestern Ohio (Table 4-6). Omitting sites where the burial sample size is ten or fewer (Marmet, Augusta, and Clover), graves with stone slabs are common only at the earlier, more westerly Fox Farm site. Except for Fox Farm and the Rolf Lee sample excavated by Kapp, the proportion of extended burials generally is not much over half, much lower than in southwestern Ohio. Judging from the very low proportion at Feurt, extended burials

TABLE 4-12
Burial Characteristics of Fort Ancient Sites with Protohistoric Components

	Burial Sample Size	Graves w/Stone Slabs	% Extended Burials / % Flexed Burials	Double Burials (% of People)	Multiple Burials	Disarticulated Burials	Burials with Trauma [a]	Burials with Gravegoods
Feurt, OH [b]	403	0.2%	0.2% / 96%	≥ 5%	1 of 4	3%	≥ 0.7%	8%
						3 of 3		
Fox Farm, KY [c] (in both mounds and village)	233	common	extended common, but many semi-flexed	common	common	common	≥ 1.7%	"nearly always"
Buffalo, WV [d]	562	0.2%	54% / 33%	present, but not noted as common		13%	≥ 2.3%	22%
Marmet, WV	4	?	75% / ?	0	1 of 3	0	75%	100%
Hardin, KY [e]	335-351	0.6%	44% / 23%	16%	5 of ≥ 3	≥ 15%	1.0%	47%
						4 of 4		
Neale's Landing, WV	32	0	44% / 22%	12.5%	1 of 3	6%	9%	53%
Augusta, KY [f]	10	30%	70% / ?	0	0	≥ 10%	10%	≥ 40%
Clover, WV [g]	6	16.7%	67% / ?	0	0	0-33%	0	33-50%
Rolf Lee, WV								
(WVAS)	19	?	47% / ≤ 47%	≥ 22%	1 of 3	≥ 11%	≥ 5.3%	≥ 32%
(K. Kapp)	82	0	72% / 26%	12%	0	0	1.2%	57%
Orchard, WV [h]	>300	?	ca. 50% / 40%	present	present 1 of almost 40	ca. 10%	"several"	>>30%

Order is from European artifact assemblages (see Table 4-9). For references, see Table 4-10.
[a] "Trauma" is intended to cover possible war-related injuries, including projectile points in bone, crushing blows to head, etc.
[b] Most disarticulated burials were in Mound 3. "Several" double burials of adults were in Mound 3, but most double and multiple burials were found in the village, and involved small children. 76% of village burials were small children.
[c] Burials often had one articulated plus one or more disarticulated individuals.
[d] Information is from the WVEGS excavations; at least 51 additional burials were excavated previously (Mairs 1960). 72% of the 561 in the Downstream Village were in house floors, the rest within the village but not in the plaza. A greater proportion of extended than flexed burials had grave goods.
[e] Extended burials most frequently had grave goods; only extended burials had European goods.
[f] See Note 2, Table 4-11. Sample in this table includes published burials only.
[g] The five burials excavated by Marshall University were all "closely associated with domestic structures" (Freidin 1987:11).
[h] Number of burials is from Moxley (1988a, 1988b); see Note 4, Table 4-11. For multiple burials, see discussion in text.

increased over time in eastern Fort Ancient territory. This pattern differs from western sites, where extended burials always considerably outnumbered flexed.

Double and multiple burials are present at all sites. They may be more common in protohistoric than prehistoric components, but trends or differences among sites during the protohistoric period are difficult to pinpoint. Will Holmes, who carried out the only large-scale mortuary analysis from this region, is of the opinion that most of the double or multiple burials at Hardin did not represent simultaneous death, but rather disturbance and redeposition of earlier burials due to later grave digging (Holmes 1994:103, 108). The reported mass burial of almost 40 people at Orchard, attributed to epidemic disease (Moxley 1988b:4), never has been described in detail. At least one different interpretation—a possible accretional burial mound—has been made of 70 burials in close proximity that were excavated by Oscar Mairs at this site (Mayer-Oakes 1955:165; contra Graybill 1981:139). Except for Kapp's sample from Rolf Lee, disarticulated burials at protohistoric sites seem to run around 10-15%, but no post-Contact trends are readily apparent. Burials with embedded arrows or other conflict-related trauma seem to run well under 10%, but no formal studies have been made, and data have been incompletely reported.

Table 4-13 summarizes grave goods. Proportions of burials with mortuary offerings do appear to be higher at protohistoric than prehistoric eastern Fort Ancient sites, and may perhaps increase over time during the protohistoric period. At any rate, Buffalo, which may be relatively early in the protohistoric sequence, has the lowest percentage of burials with grave goods, and one group of burials from Rolf Lee, which may be relatively late, has the highest. The very low proportion of European goods with burials at Buffalo, Neale's Landing, and Hardin indicates that most residents of the two larger sites, at least, probably died before such items were available—that is, prehistorically rather than protohistorically. The use of mortuary vessels may well have increased over time.

Some differences in burial practices among sites might perhaps be qualitative rather than temporal. The predominantly in-

TABLE 4-13
Gravegood Characteristics of Fort Ancient Sites with Protohistoric Components

	Burial Sample Size	Burials with Gravegoods	Burials with Indigenous Goods	Burials with European Goods	Burials w/ Indigenous & European Goods	Burials with Ceramic Vessels	Burials with with Shell Ornaments	Burials with Pipes
Feurt, OH	403	8%	8%	0	0	0	3.5%	0
(in mounds)	(340)	(9%)	(9%)				(3%)	
(in village)	(63)	(6%)	(6%)				(6%)	
Fox Farm, KY								
(published)	233	"nearly always"	most	--	?	4%	≥ 11%	≥ 2%
(reported)						a few		
Buffalo, WV	562	22%	≥ 20%	2.1%	?	1.6%	14%	0.7% [a]
Marmet, WV	4	100%	100%	50%	50%	0	50%	0
Hardin, KY [b]	335	51%	50%	3.6%	3.0%	4.5%	19%	1.2%
Neale's Landing, WV	32	53%	50%	3.1%	0	≥ 9%	≥ 6.3%	9%
Augusta, KY	10	≥ 40%	≥ 40%	0 [c]	0 [c]	20%	10%	0-10%[3]
Clover, WV	6	33-50%	33-50%	17%	17%	17%	33%	0
Rolf Lee, WV								
(WVAS)	19	32%	32%	11%	11%	0 [d]	32%	0
(K. Kapp)	82	57%	49%	19%	13%	0 [d]	37%	0
Orchard, WV	>300	>>30%	≥ 30%	present	present	ca. 30%	"common"	6-15%

Order is from European artifact assemblages (see Table 4-9). For references, see Table 4-10.

[a] According to Hemmings (1976), the bird effigy pipe was with a burial; according to Graybill, all four published pipes were "from mortuary contexts" (1981:119). At least one privately-excavated burial had a pipe (Moxley, pers. comm. 1993).

[b] Numbers of burials with grave goods are from the original fieldnotes curated at the University of Kentucky Museum of Anthropology.

[c] Local collectors report metal artifacts from burials. Disk pipe reported by Webb probably was with a burial.

[d] According to R. Moxley (pers. comm. 1993), only one excavated Rolf Lee burial had a mortuary vessel; it was a bowl.

house burial program at the Buffalo Downstream Village was not duplicated at the Upstream Village (Hanson 1975; cf. Holmes 1994), nor has it been documented at any other site, early or late (but well-documented sites admittedly are few). Even considering the difficulties with their data bases, the three sites that produced the most recent glass bead types—Orchard, Rolf Lee, and Marmet—stand in striking contrast with each other and with earlier sites like Buffalo and Hardin. No pots or pipes were included as grave goods with the Rolf Lee and Marmet burial samples, whereas almost a third of Orchard burials are reported to have had pots as mortuary vessels and over 50 to have been buried with pipes; the apparently large proportion of burials with pipes at the non-Fort Ancient Riker site is also notable. Both pots and pipes are present, but in smaller proportions than at Orchard, with burials at Buffalo, Neale's Landing, and Hardin. The proportions of extended versus flexed burials at these sites are also more congruent with Orchard than Marmet or Rolf Lee. Discrepancies like this might perhaps herald cultural or ethnic differences rather than temporal ones—consistent with Gabriel Arthur's account of (probably) Kanawha and Ohio river settlements with different alliance patterns *vis-à-vis* his Tomahittan hosts—but interpretations based on the current data base can only be pushed so far. Additional quantitative information clearly is needed.

Fort Ancient external interaction during the protohistoric period, including data from Madisonville, will be discussed in Chapter 8.

Theories of Fort Ancient Ethnic Affiliations

No evidence has been advanced that conclusively ties the Fort Ancient archeological culture area to a known historical group or groups. The currently most-cited summaries of ethnographic, historical, and linguistic evidence see the Central Algonquian Shawnee connection as the most likely (Callender 1962, 1978f; Hunter 1978; Witthoft and Hunter 1955; cf. Henderson et al. 1986:168-72). During the late seventeenth century, Shawnees were encountered traveling in the interior Southeast to trade with Spanish-allied Florida groups (Waselkov 1989:118; Swanton 1930:406-7). The first historically described large groups of Shawnees were living on the Savannah River in South Carolina by 1674, soon after the settlement of Charles Towne (Callender 1978f:630, citing Swanton 1922:307-17), in the vicinity of Fort St. Louis in Illinois soon after its establishment, from 1684 to 1688/89 (Brown 1961:8, 75-76; Margry 1876-86:1:505-7), and near Philadelphia by 1689, soon after the establishment of Pennsylvania (Jennings 1984:197-99). A group of Savannah River Shawnees formed a town in the Creek

Figure 4-19. Two Madisonville-like vessels from the Seneca Dann site, Honeoye Falls, New York, occupied ca. 1655 to 1670 (NYSM Cat. Nos. 20938 and 21134). Photograph by John Yost. Courtesy of the New York State Museum, Albany, New York.

Confederacy, moving after A.D. 1715 with other towns to central Alabama and remaining there through much of that century (Swanton 1922:277-79). All of these are peripheral locations consistent with, but certainly not proof of, an origin in the central Ohio Valley.

Among archaeologists, opinions still are mixed. Over the years, Griffin has marshalled the most evidence for an Algonquian/Shawnee connection, but never has found conclusive proof (Griffin 1937, 1942, 1943:308-13, 1972:ix, 1978:556-57). He saw, and continued to see, similarities between Madisonville Cordmarked and Grooved Paddle pottery and Danner pottery types, found in northern Illinois and at the Zimmerman and Hotel Plaza sites close to Fort St. Louis (Brown 1961:43-45, 74-76, Figs. 8, 13; Griffin, pers. comm.; Keller 1950; Orr 1949:102; Schnell 1974:23-26). However, interpretation by others of subsequent excavations at Zimmerman is that Danner ceramics are not connected with the historically mapped location of the Shawnee group, and have attributes related to ceramic types other than Madisonville, including southern Michigan-northern Ohio types (J. Brown et al. 1990:158-59; J. Brown and Willis 1995; M. Brown 1975:68-72; Mason 1986:215-17). Most recently, Larry Grantham, finding significant amounts of Danner ware at an Illini site in eastern Missouri probably visited by Marquette and Jolliet in 1673, ties this ceramic type to the Illini (1993:10). Kenneth Tankersley uses the data from Zimmerman and Hotel Plaza to argue that a group of Fort Ancient people did move from Madisonville to the vicinity of Fort St. Louis, but that they actually were Illini, unlike other Fort Ancient people, who probably were Shawnee (1992:116-26).

No analyses of ceramics or other diagnostics from historically known Shawnee village sites in South Carolina/Georgia and Pennsylvania have been published. The late seventeenth-century Susquehannock Byrd Leibhart site has produced a few examples of pots somewhat reminiscent of classic Madisonville ware, as has the 1660s Seneca Dann site (Figure 4-19) (William Johnson, pers. comm.; Kent 1984:378; Parker 1922: Pl. 30). Shawnees are known to have lived with both of these ethnic groups, both forcibly and voluntarily. The archaeological association of classic Madisonville pottery with post-1700 European goods at Lower Shawneetown (Bentley site, Kentucky) (Henderson et al. 1986:131-37; Henderson et al. 1992:270-78; Pollack and Henderson 1984) has been questioned by some archaeologists (C. Wesley Cowan, pers. comm.).

Erminie Wheeler Voegelin failed to find significant congruencies between Fort Ancient and nineteenth and twentieth century Shawnee burial customs; archaeological traits at Madisonville, such as storage pits within the village, were seen by her as most similar to Eastern Plains Siouan groups (Voegelin 1944). In her scrupulous summary of all seventeenth-century references to the Shawnee, she notes that only one of the earliest group of references (1661-72) gives any definite location for the Chiouanons (Shawnee?) (Wheeler-Voegelin 1974:34). That location happens to be the Ohio River, above what probably are the Falls of the Ohio. Nevertheless, Wheeler-Voegelin favored the Cumberland River as the Shawnee homeland, and the Madisonville Focus area along the Ohio (Figure 4-1) as the homeland of the Mosopelea. This poorly known group, the last written reference to which dates to 1682, was posited on linguistic grounds to have been a Central Algonquian group closely related to the Shawnee (Wheeler-Voegelin 1974:43-52).

John Swanton argued on historical and linguistic grounds that Fort Ancient people were most likely Eastern Siouan (specifically Ofo, which he asserted was another name for Mosopelea) (Griffin 1943:25-26, 35; Swanton 1943). No archaeological evidence has been mustered for this case. Based largely on data collected by Voegelin (1944) on historically known Plains Siouan groups, Robert Maslowski proposed that "it is most likely that [eastern Fort Ancient] Clover complex sites were occupied by Yuchi or Eastern Siouan speaking groups who migrated south prior to European settlement of the Ohio Valley" (Maslowski 1984:161). Because cordage construction varied significantly between a sample of eastern (Z-twist) and western (S- and Z-twists) Fort Ancient settlements, Maslowski and Christopher Carr argue that Fort Ancient "probably represents a culture area with several ethnic groups" (Carr and Maslowski 1995:324).

Reaching back farther into prehistory, and citing both archaeological and glottochronological data, Charles Niquette and Jonathan Kerr recently have proposed that the Late Woodland (A.D. 700-1000) Parkline phase in West Virginia represents "displaced Proto-Algonquian speaking people whose homeland formerly was Canada and the Northeast" (1993:57). Key attributes such as settlement pattern, ceramics, lithics, and cordage twist vary significantly from traits associated with Late Woodland components at (for instance) Haag, Turpin, and Sand Ridge in southwestern Ohio and southeastern Indiana (1993:56). Niquette and Kerr advance no theory as to what linguistic group or groups might be represented at western settlements.

Two biophysical studies also point to diversity among Fort Ancient peoples. Louise Robbins' study of Fort Ancient physical types, based on measurements taken by Georg Neumann, aimed to assess biological affinities between Fort Ancient and historically known peoples (Giesen 1992:16-20; Robbins 1968; Robbins and Neumann 1972). Groups of individuals from three to six sites within each of Griffin's four Fort Ancient foci (Figure 4-1) were compared with groups considered representative of five eastern North American physical types (Lenid, Ilinid, Iswanid, Muskogid, and Dakota) and of historical Seneca and Shawnee. Samples from the Feurt, Baum, and Anderson foci were identified as "Ilinid." Both "Ilinid" and "Muskogid" types were present at Madisonville Focus sites. Based on an admittedly small sample of Shawnee, Robbins concluded that this group had descended from the Fort Ancient population (1972:109).

In a recent study, Myra Giesen compared biological affinities and stress indicators between early and late Fort Ancient and early and late northern Ohio Sandusky populations, utilizing cranial metric and nonmetric and postcranial metric data to assess biological affinities, and dental pathologies and stature to assess biocultural stress (Giesen 1992). Early sites (approximately 1200-1300) included Anderson, Incinerator, and Pearson (Sandusky), late sites (placed at 1600-1650) were Madisonville and Buffalo, while two Sandusky sites, Indian Hills and Petersen, were assigned dates between about 1450 and 1550. (Indian Hills has, in fact, produced early seventeenth century European goods, and Petersen has produced two copper or brass beads (Stothers 1994; Stothers and Abel 1991:124-25), so they probably were roughly contemporaneous with Madisonville and Buffalo.) Unlike Late Archaic and Early and Middle Woodland groups studied by others, osteological evidence from these sites did not confirm closest biological relationships between groups in closest geographical proximity. Giesen concluded that "the Fort Ancient and Sandusky traditions represent diversified descendants from a common ancestral stock" (1992:201), and that biological diversity was associated with temporal rather than spatial differences. She also noted (while critiquing the typological approach championed by Neumann) that the Fort Ancient sites from which came populations designated "Ilinid" by Robbins tended to be early ones (1992:19).

The range of hypotheses and results illustrate well, I think, the difficulties of (1) working back in time from historically named "tribes" to prehistoric groups across several centuries of intergroup interaction, including intermarriage, and (2) drawing firm conclusions from only one or two categories of available data. No study so far has fully utilized historical, ethnographic, archaeological, linguistic, and biophysical evidence in attempting to trace ethnic affiliations of those who inhabited settlements within the Fort Ancient archaeological culture area. The closest thing to a comprehensive study was the encouragement (financial and otherwise) by Eli Lilly of archaeological work by James Griffin, linguistic and ethnohistorical work by Charles Voegelin and Erminie Wheeler Voegelin, and physical anthropology by Geoge Neumann and Louise Robbins, but results of the separate efforts were not completely compatible. The most promise for the future probably lies in newly developed techniques such as DNA analysis, but availability of mortuary populations for testing is problematical under current legislative mandates such as the Native American Graves and Repatriation Act. Griffin's remark of a quarter century ago still holds true today: "interpretations...will continue to be altered as additional materials appear and are combined with the reevaluation of data now available" (1972:viii).

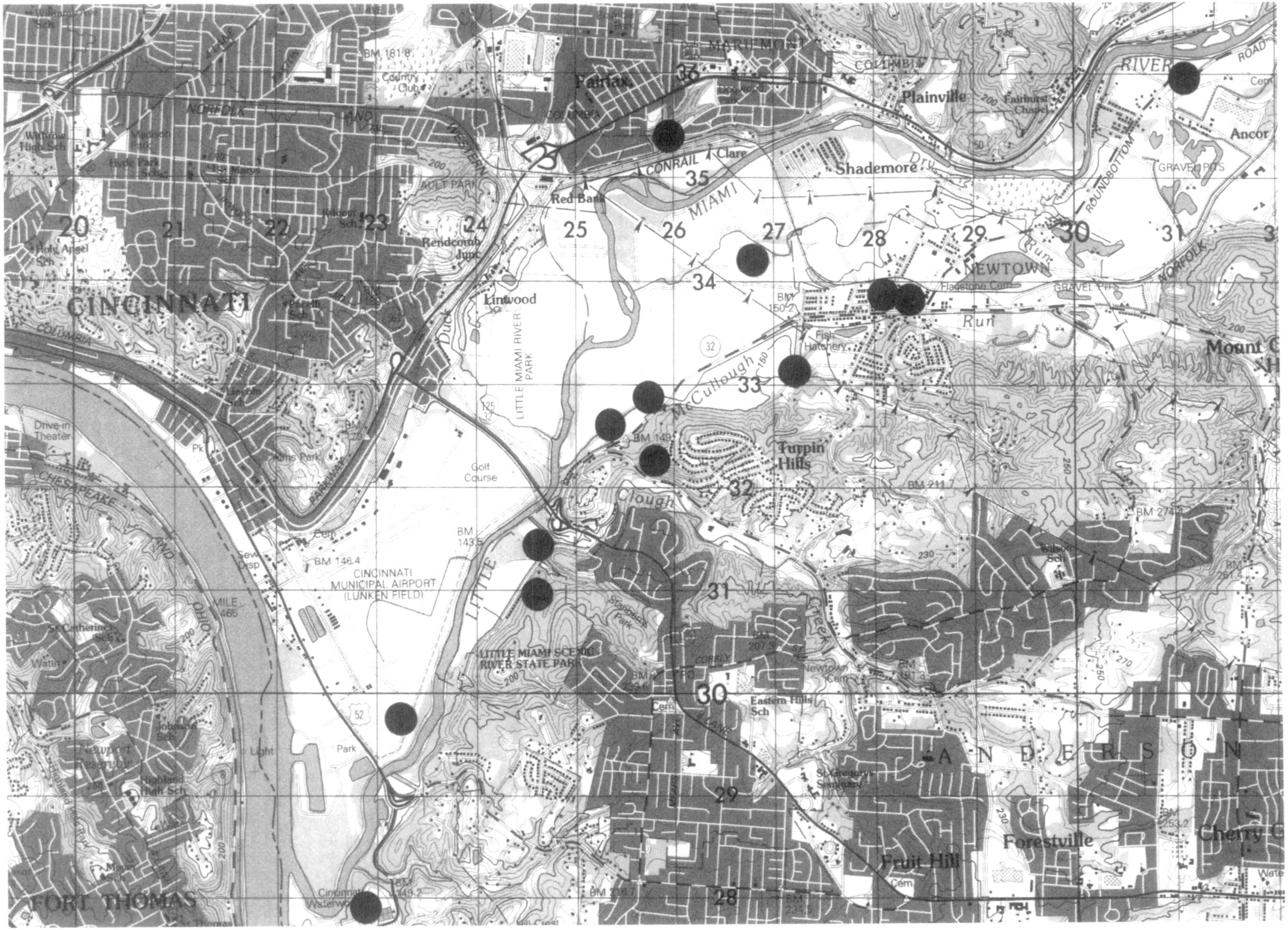
CINCINNATI
Fairfax
Mariemont
Plainville
Shademore
Ancor
Newtown
Red Bank
Clare
Linwood
Rendcomb Junc
Turpin Hills
Fish Hatchery
Fairhurst Chapel
LITTLE MIAMI RIVER PARK
CINCINNATI MUNICIPAL AIRPORT (LUNKEN FIELD)
Golf Course
LITTLE MIAMI SCENIC RIVER STATE PARK
Eastern Hills Sch
St Gregorys Seminary
ANDERSON
Forestville
Fruit Hill
FORT THOMAS
MIAMI
LITTLE
OHIO
CONRAIL
NORFOLK
COLUMBIA
ROUNDBOTTOM
Drive-in Theater
Country Club
Withrow High Sch
Hyde Park Sch
Highland High Sch
Johnson Sch
Holy Angel Sch
Kilgour Sch
St Catherines Sch
Wilson Sch
Park
Light
Water
Mount

CHAPTER 5

The Madisonville Village and Cemetery

Madisonville is the westernmost and most completely excavated protohistoric Fort Ancient site. As such, it is a lynchpin for any model of Late Fort Ancient socioeconomic development and interaction. Its relative chronological position, social organization, and interaction patterns will be explored in Chapters 6 through 8. As a prelude, this chapter briefly describes the site and its immediate physical surroundings, along with its excavation history.

Lower Little Miami River Valley Geography and Resources

The Little Miami River flows south into the Ohio, just west of present-day municipal Cincinnati (Figure 5-1). The floodplain of the Lower Little Miami Valley is much broader than that of the adjacent Ohio River, with the river meandering across it and, from the evidence of old meander scars, not infrequently changing its location. Both valleys are bounded by very steep slopes along much of their northern edges, with high land also lying to the south, rising at a somewhat lesser gradient. Both riverine and upland forest resources would have been readily available.

It is not surprising that this area was occupied throughout the Fort Ancient and preceding Late Woodland periods (Figure 4-6; cf. Drooker 1996a). At least a dozen village sites with Early, Middle, and/or Late Fort Ancient components have been documented, most of them along the southeastern edge of the floodplain (Figure 5-1). Unfortunately, a large number of them, including Clough Creek, Kuntz, Waterworks, Blum, two burial mounds in Newtown, and a village adjacent to the Hopewell Turner site across from modern-day Terrace Park, are known almost exclusively from surveys (Metz 1878, 1881; Starr 1960; cf. Drooker 1996a). Others have been partially excavated but never completely reported (Table 4-4), including Sand Ridge (just north of "Little Miami Scenic River State Park" in Figure 5-1); Hahn's Field (between "34" and "27" in the middle of the Little Miami Floodplain); Clear Creek (directly adjacent to Hahn's Field); and Turpin (a name that refers to at least three different locations on Turpin family land, clustered around "BM 149" in Figure 5-1, and one that Metz referred to as the Johnson Turpin Farm). Most Lower Little Miami settlements occupied floodplain or terrace locations, but Sand Ridge and Madisonville (just south of Fairfax and Mariemont in Figure 5-1) occupied higher ground. Madisonville is the only reported village site on the north or west side of the floodplain.

The Madisonville site occupies approximately 2 hectares on a broad bluff 40-60 feet (12-18 m) above the floodplain, about 3.7 miles (6 km) straight up the valley from the Ohio River. Bounded along its western and northern sides by Whiskey Run, an intermittent stream in a steep, narrow ravine, this is the most accessible high land along the northern side of the floodplain, and the largest area of relatively flat land outside of the floodplain itself. The upper plateau surface slopes up gradually from southwest to northeast, continuing for over a mile eastward (see also Figure 5-7).

The geology of this bluff area offers several advantageous features (Tankersley 1986b; Tankersley and Meinhart 1982; Robert Genheimer, pers. comm.). Clays and silty clays derived from underlying shales and limestones are overlain by very porous coarse sand and gravel, which is capped by sandy clay loam ("hardpan") deposits, over which black soil has formed. On top of that, the most recent layer, not yet broken down into soil, is designated "leafmold." Storage pits dug through the hardpan into the sand/gravel layer would be particularly well suited for food preservation because of their good drainage. Artesian springs flow out above the clay layer. Both good clay resources for pottery and coarse sandstone for smoothing tools outcrop along the bluff. In fact, mineralogical analyses have demonstrated that the hardpan, as well as the clay, was used for ceramic production (Tankersley 1986b:14-15). The latter could have been obtained from storage pit backdirt.

Figure 5-1 (*facing page*). Topography and Fort Ancient site locations, confluence area of Ohio and Little Miami Rivers. 1979 Cincinnati East USGS topographic map. Squares are 1 × 1 km.

TABLE 5-1
Plant Remains from the Sand Ridge and Madisonville Sites

Sand Ridge	Madisonville	
SEEDS	SEEDS	
bedstraw	amaranth	little barley
blueberry	bean, common	nightshade, black
chenopod	bean family	nightshade
grape	bedstraw	paw paw
grasses	blackberry	persimmon
honey locust	buckwheat family	plum
knotweed	chenopod (including domesticated)	pink family
maygrass	elderberry	pokeweed
paw paw	grape	purslane
plum	grass, barnyard	rush
raspberry	grass, panic	smartweed
sedges	grass family	sumac
sumac	hackberry	sunflower
sunflower	hawthorne	sunflower family
vervain	honey locust	tobacco
	knotweed, erect	unknown, possibly mint family
MAIZE	MAIZE	
		WOOD/BARK
NUTSHELL	NUTSHELL	ash
acorn	acorn	beech
hazel	hazelnut	chestnut
hickory	hickories	elm
walnut, black	walnut, black	hickory
walnut, white	walnut family	Kentucky coffeetree
		locust
RINDS	RINDS	maple
squash	gourd, bottle	mulberry
	squashes	oaks, red
WOOD		oaks, white
	MONOCOT STEMS	oaks
	grasses	sycamore
	grass, big bluestem?	walnut

Plant remains from Madisonville are based on 500 liters of flotation samples from middens and pit features excavated in 1987-88, including both early and late Fort Ancient features, ca. thirteenth-seventeenth centuries (Dunavan 1993, n.d.). Except for plum pits, screened specimens have been omitted. Floral remains from Sand Ridge were floated from levels 2, 4, 5, and 6; although these were Fort Ancient deposits, Wagner believes that they were mixed with Late Woodland plant remains from lower levels (Featherstone, 1977; Wagner, 1987:91-92).

Good agricultural land abounds. Nass calculated that there were 1350 acres (550 hectares) of Class 1 soils on the south side of the Little Miami River within a 3 km (1.9 mile) radius of the Turpin 1 site (1988: Table 9, Fig. 12), on the opposite side of the floodplain from the Madisonville site (Figure 5-1, just left of "BM 149"). For a village of 200 people, each using 9 bushels of maize per year, this would offer 79 years of occupation (Nass 1988:343). Similar figures would pertain to Madisonville, depending on the position of the river during its occupation. From total areas of Class 1 soils available, probably three to four villages of that size could be supported simultaneously for at least a century in the portion of the Little Miami valley within 5 miles (8 kilometers) of the Ohio River.

Residents of this area did indeed utilize maize as a diet staple. From stable carbon isotope ratios in 10 bone collagen samples from Turpin, Broida calculated that maize (or C-4 plants) formed 68% of the diet (Broida 1984:80). Wagner reported 8-row and 4-row corn from Turpin, 8-row from Madisonville, and 8-row and 12-row from Hahn's Field (Wagner 1984:121-23, 153-56). A few rather large caches of charred corn have been retrieved from storage pits at Madisonville (e.g., Dunavan 1993:3; Low 1880:66-67). Other domesticated plants and possible cultigens from Late Woodland through Fort Ancient contexts in this region include chenopodium, knotweed, Maygrass, squash, and sunflower (Table 5-1) (Wagner 1987:91-92).

The floodplain and surrounding uplands offered Madisonville residents a variety of nondomesticated edible and medicinal plant resources, including nuts, fruits, and seeds. Fiber plants like

TABLE 5-2
Faunal Remains from the Madisonville Site

MAMMALS	FISH
badger	bass
bear, black	carpsucker
beaver	catfish, channel
bison	catfish
bobcat	Centrarchidae
deer, white-tailed	drum, freshwater
dog	gar
coyote	*Ictiobus* spp.
elk	perch?
fox	redhorse, river
human	sucker
lynx	walleye or sauger
marten	
mole	SHELLFISH
mouse, deer & white-footed	*Marginella apicina*
muskrat	*Margitana rugosa* (Barnes)
opossum	mussels
otter	(*Unio*, at least 34 species)
porcupine	whelk, knobbed
puma	(*Busycon carica*)
rabbit	whelk, lightning
raccoon	(*Busycon perversum*)
rice rat, marsh	
skunk, striped	REPTILES
squirrel	turtle, box
vole	turtle, common musk
wolf	turtle, eastern box
woodchuck	turtle, Emydid
	turtle, leatherback
BIRDS	turtle, softshell
coot	viper, pit
duck, black/mallard	
duck, dabbling	
duck	
pigeon, passenger	
raven	
swan?	
turkey	

Fauna are as reported from burials, from "over one hundred" refuse pits excavated in 1897 (Hooton and Willoughby 1920:32-33), and from one pit (Feature 10) excavated 1987-88 (White and Styles 1993). Contents of the latter were screened with 1/4-inch mesh. The possible swan is a tentative identification of material used for large bone beads (Tonya Largy, personal communication 1994). Freshwater mussel analysis is of specimens recovered from a trench and 20 refuse pits excavated 1987-88 (Warren 1994). The remainder of the shells are as reported from pit features excavated in 1897 and from marine shell ornaments identified by Hooton and Willoughby and discussed by Warren.

rushes and bluestem grass, plus inner bark from trees, were available for production of matting, cordage, bags, and clothing, a few small samples of which have recovered from Fort Ancient sites (e.g., Hooton and Willoughby 1920: Pl. 21), and which are also evidenced by ubiquitous impressions on cord-marked, net-impressed, and fabric-impressed pottery. Dye plants such as bedstraw also have been recovered. At least a dozen tree species have been identified at Madisonville (Dunavan n.d.).

TABLE 5-3
Frequencies of Major Categories of Faunal Remains at Sand Ridge and Madisonville

	SAND RIDGE	MADISONVILLE 1	2	3
Deer	36.3%	54.3%	80.0%	75.0%
Cervidae (deer or elk)		10.5%		
Turkey	3.0%	15.5%	8.0%	(p)
Elk	37.9%	0.3%	2.5%	7.5%
Dog		(p)	2.5%	7.5%
Bear	11.9%	1.0%	2.5%	5.0%
Turtle		2.1%	2.5%	(p)
Raccoon		(p)	0.5%	(p)
Beaver		(p)	0.5%	(p)
Fish		4.3%	(p)	(p)
Water birds		1.1%	-	-
"Other mammals"	9.1%	10.9%	<1.0%	<5.0%
BY CLASS:				
Mammals	97.0%	82.2%	89.5%	>95.0%
Birds	3.0%	15.1%	8.0%	< 5.0%
Fish		2.4%	< 1.0%	< 5.0%
Reptiles		0.3%	2.5%	< 5.0%

Faunal remains are as reported from the Sand Ridge site (Breitburg 1992:232, after Theler 1978) and three refuse pits at Madisonville (Hooton and Willoughby 1920:32-33; White and Styles 1993).
1 = Feature 10, 1987-88 excavations (screened with 1/4-inch mesh)
2 = Trench 3, Pit 6, excavated 1897
3 = Trench 3, Pit 8, excavated 1897.

Available animal resources included large and small mammals, birds, reptiles, fish, and shellfish (Table 5-2), used for food, tools, leather, fiber, and ornaments. As at other Fort Ancient sites (Breitburg 1992), large mammal remains, particularly deer, seem to have predominated at Lower Little Miami settlements (e.g., Table 5-3), but proportions of different species apparently varied widely among them. For example, unlike many northern Kentucky Fort Ancient sites (Breitburg 1992:241), bear does not seem to have been an important part of the diet at Madisonville. However, the Madisonville data come from only about 0.3% of the excavated refuse pits, and may well not be representative. In addition to fish remains obtained from screened samples, many small bones were recovered from flotation samples (Sandra Dunavan, pers. comm.). Bison bone was recovered from over 40 of the 669 refuse pits excavated at Madisonville between 1897 and 1911. Much of it (or at least, most of what was saved by excavators) consisted of thoracic vertebrae modified for use as scrapers (Hooton and Willoughby 1920: Pl. 8d). Entire animals do not seem to have been butchered at the site. Bison were very late arrivals to the Ohio River valley, and Madisonville is the only Fort Ancient settlement from which bison bone has been recovered (Tankersley 1981, 1986a, 1992; Tankersley and Adams 1991). Tankersley (1992) has proposed that the animals were obtained at the Big Bone Lick saline site, about 40 kilometers southwest of Madisonville as the crow flies (Figure 4-6).

Although univalves of a wide variety of species are very common on Lower Little Miami sites (Table 5-2), shellfish, with their low levels of protein, would have been only secondary food sources. They also provided raw material for ceramic temper, tools (spoons, hoes, scrapers), and ornaments (Hooton and Willoughby 1920: Pls. 15, 16). Judging from proportions of large-river species at the Madisonville and Sand Ridge sites, Warren estimates that people traveled no more than 3 kilometers from their homes to forage for mussels (Warren, in press:21).

Chert from at least sixteen different sources in Indiana, Ohio, Kentucky, and West Virginia was used for chipped stone weapons and tools at Lower Little Miami sites including Sand Ridge, Turpin 1, Hahn's Field, and Madisonville (Litfin et al. 1993:27-34). Twelve of these chert types, used for the vast majority of recovered artifacts, could have been obtained locally from river and glacial deposits (Litfin et al. 1993:38-39). Seven of them have been found at Madisonville, including Boyle, Kentucky Flint Ridge, and Paoli cherts from Kentucky, and Delaware, Ohio Flint Ridge, Upper Mercer, and Cedarville-Guelph cherts from Ohio. Projectile points made from two additional cherts, Laurel and Harrison County, also have been found at Madisonville (as well as at Turpin and Hahn's Field). Their source areas are southeastern and south-central Indiana, so they would have had to have been carried to the site.

Madisonville Excavation and Curation History

During the late nineteenth century, the tract of land near Madisonville, Ohio, later known as the Madisonville site was owned by two adjacent farming families, the Ferrises and the Stiteses. Much of it had never been cultivated, but remained covered with old-growth trees, many of them three to five feet in diameter (Langdon, 1880:524). Ceramic sherds were ubiquitous, probably helped to the surface by hogs put to root in the woods, and the location was known locally as the "Pottery Field" (Langdon 1880:525). However, until the spring of 1879, the attention of local antiquarians was directed mainly toward mapping and excavating earthworks and mound sites in the vicinity (Metz 1878, 1881).

In late 1878 and early 1879, Charles L. Metz, a local physician with antiquarian interests, hired a workman, Matthias Britten, to excavate mounds on the property of Charles Stites, about 300 feet from the edge of the bluff top overlooking the Little Miami River floodplain to the south (Figure 5-2, upper right corner; Low 1880:41-44). In early spring, Britten "prospected" southwest across the terrace, digging pits at intervals until he reached the southwestern corner, on the property of Phoebe Ferris. It was there, on March 19 or 20, that he uncovered the first skeleton of what soon became known as the Ferris Cemetery or the Madisonville Ancient Cemetery.

For over a century after that discovery, formal and informal excavations were carried out at the site, under the aegis of five different institutions and numerous private individuals (Table 5-4). Field methods, documentation, and curation varied considerably in scope and quality. In reanalyzing data from this site, it has been necessary to develop a thorough understanding of the scope and limitations of collection practices, supporting documentary data, and surviving collections of artifacts and human remains. These are discussed briefly below. The companion CD-ROM will contain these data bases (Drooker, in press).

Excavation History, Methods, and Documentation

Between April 1879 and August 1881, excavations were supported by the gentlemen of the Madisonville Literary and Scientific Society (MLSS), who underwrote expenses, then met at intervals to divide the spoils. Although Metz became the nominal supervisor, he had other obligations. Workmen may well have proceeded on their own, with documentation mainly after the fact. There are at least four extant sets of "field notes" for the MLSS excavations, no two are exactly alike (Drooker 1996c: Table A2). None appear to be notes actually made in the field, but are lists and descriptions of features discovered, in chronological order. These features consisted of burials, deep corn storage pits later filled in with refuse, and a few hearths. Not until decades later were any postmolds recorded at the site. Sketches of interesting artifacts and of individual burials are included to a greater or lesser degree, and relative age (adult, child, infant) and sex are provided for many of the skeletons. A published account (Low 1880) describes features and artifacts encountered through June 1880.

MLSS-sponsored excavations started at the southwestern corner of the site and appear to have progressed generally northward, eventually proceeding back and forth across the southern portion of the site in 40-foot-wide trenches (Figure 5-2, O and N). Almost no spatial data were recorded for the first 350 skeletons unearthed, but after that the "field notes" included descriptions of burial locations relative to landmarks such as trees, the orientation of burials to the cardinal directions, important grave goods, and (in general terms) contents and stratigraphy of refuse pits. Unfortunately, only an extremely small proportion of extant artifacts unearthed during this time can be tied to their intrasite provenience. No contemporaneous site map survives.

After the summer of 1881, many of the original supporters decided not to continue, but some individuals, including Metz and Charles F. Low, continued to underwrite the work into the spring of 1882. Private collections by erstwhile members of the MLSS began to come on the market as early as February 1882. A number of institutions, including the Smithsonian, the National Museum of the American Indian, the Cincinnati Museum of Art, and the Cincinnati Museum of Natural History, currently

Figure 5-2 (*facing page*). Madisonville village and cemetery map from Hooton and Willoughby 1920: Pl. 30. Reprinted courtesy of the Peabody Museum, Harvard University.

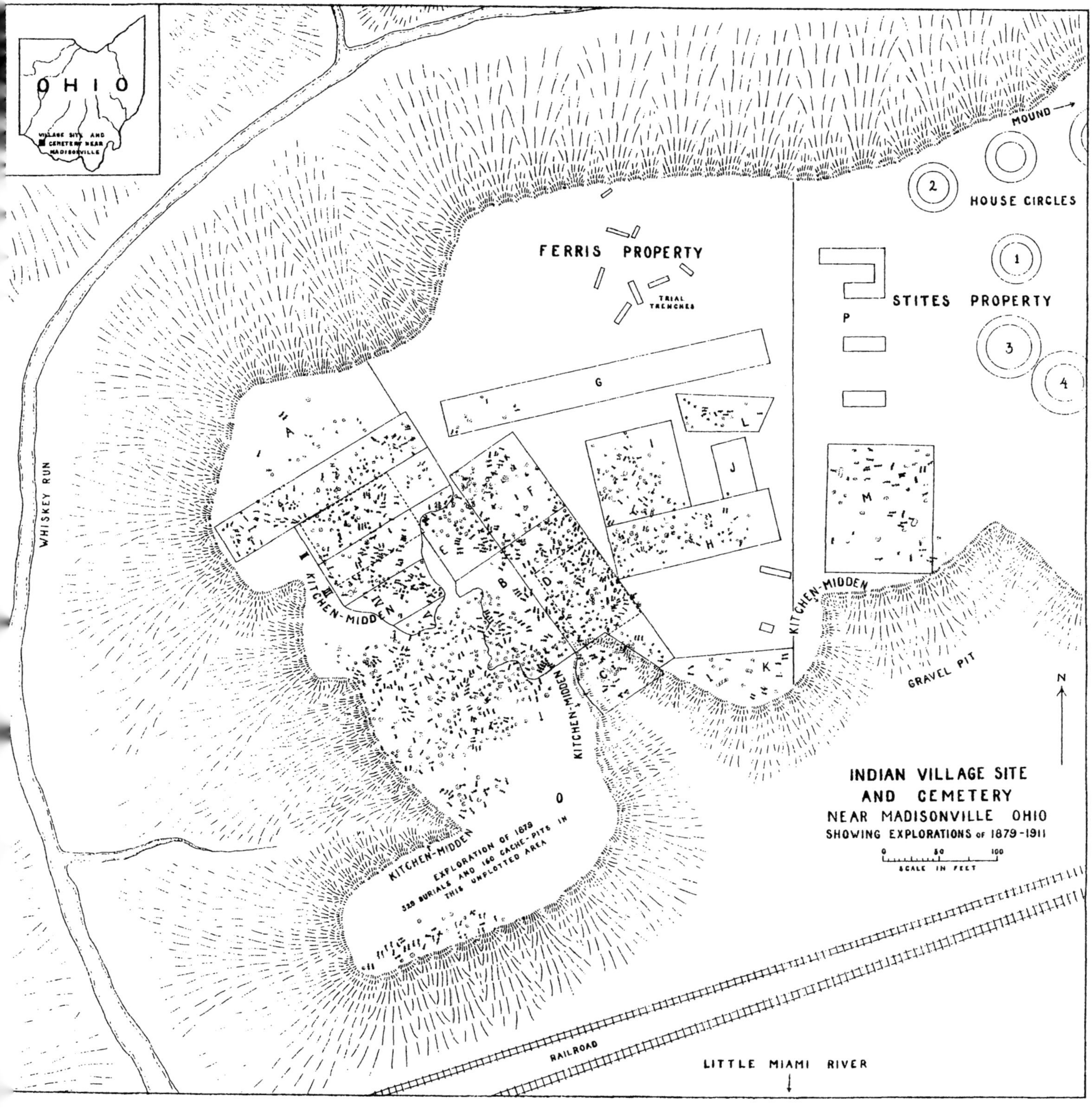

I-V	Peabody Museum Explorations, 1897, J. R. Swanton, Field Director	
A-C	" " " 1907, R. E. Merwin, " "	
D-F	" " " 1908, " " " " "	
G-K	" " " 1911, B. W. Merwin, " "	
L	" " " 1882, F. W. Putnam, " "	
M	Dept. Anthropology Exp., 1891, World's Columbian Exposition, C. L. Metz, Field Director	
N	Madisonville Literary and Historical Society, Cincinnati Hist. Soc. and Peabody Museum Explorations, 1880, C. L. Metz, Field Director	
O	Madisonville Literary and Historical Society, 1879, C. L. Metz, Field Director	

P Trial Trenches, 1882 — 1-4 House Sites

Owing to the small scale of this plan, some of the minor burials, smaller cache-pits, post-holes, etc., are omitted, to add clearness to the grouping of the more important interments and pits.

Detail plans on a larger scale are given on plates 1 and 2 of portions of Trenches II and III and the greater part of Trench D. The positions of these enlarged areas are indicated on the plan by rectangles enclosed by broken lines.

TABLE 5-4
Madisonville Excavation History

Dates	Sponsoring Institution	Field Supervisors	Locations
1878-1879	-	Charles Metz	Mounds on Stites property Test pits across Ferris property to extreme SW corner
1879-1881	Madisonville Literary and Scientific Society	Charles Metz Charles Low	Blocks 1-17 4 "house circles"
1881-1882	-	Charles Metz Charles Low	Blocks 18-22
May 1882	Peabody Museum	Frederic Putnam	Block 22 Block L 4 "house circles" 3 trial trenches on Stites property
1891	World's Columbian Exposition	Charles Metz Harlan Smith Henry Smith	Block M
1895	American Museum of Natural History	Charles Metz	?
1897	Peabody Museum	R. B. Dixon John Swanton	Trenches I-V (1-5)
1907	Peabody Museum	Raymond Merwin	Trenches A-C
1908	Peabody Museum	Raymond Merwin	Trenches D-F
1911	Peabody Museum	Bruce Merwin	Trenches G-K Mound on Stites property 21 trial trenches N & S of Tr. G-I, and N of Whiskey Run
1910s-1980s	-	Many amateur excavations	
1939-1943	-	J. D. Conover and friends	SW corner of site: various
1984	Cincinnati Museum of Natural History	Kenneth Tankersley	Deep test pit at S margin of site
1987, 1988	Cincinnati Museum of Natural History	C. Wesley Cowan	SW corner of site: pit features, midden in ravine adjacent to Block 4

See Figure 5-8 for locations of excavation blocks and trenches.

hold large collections of Madisonville artifacts from these sources (Drooker 1996c: Table A1).

The Harvard University's Peabody Museum (HUPM) gradually became involved with investigations at Madisonville through the interest of Frederic Putnam, its director. After two site visits in 1881, Putnam decided to buy into the discoveries at the Ancient Cemetery, and thus periodically receive shares of artifacts for his museum. Putnam himself directed operations for two weeks in 1882, retaining all artifacts and remains for the HUPM. In 1884, the museum acquired Metz's personal collection, unfortunately with little documentation.

As chief of the Department of Ethnology for the World's Columbian Exposition, Putnam sponsored the excavation of a large block in 1891 (Figure 5-2, Block M), as well as another in 1895, for which no field notes or maps survive, the latter in his capacity as curator of anthropology for the American Museum of Natural History (AMNH). When Miss Ferris died in 1896, she left Harvard a 25-acre tract for archaeological research. Although the will was contested, and Harvard eventually lost the land, before that happened Putnam sent students to oversee major, well-documented excavations in 1897, 1907, 1908, and 1911 (Table 5-4, Figures 5-2, 5-3). Notes were taken in the field, grids were established, features were triangulated, and most burials were documented by photographs. Unfortunately, soil screening, when it did take place, was only through very large mesh, provenience was recorded only for artifacts and remains deposited within features (others were recorded as from "general digging" within a trench), and a large proportion of bulky remains, including animal bones and pottery sherds, were discarded in the field (Figure 5-4). By the final excavation seasons, only burial goods and selected human remains and artifacts were being shipped to the HUPM (Table 5-5).

Most trenches excavated by the HUPM were mapped on a year-by-year basis. The edge of the plateau was surveyed in 1897 by a Harvard student, Ingersoll Bowditch, but no attempt was made to include topographical contours. In the decade between 1897 and 1907, topography was altered and benchmarks were disrupted: the railroad took over a strip of land south of the site, digging back into the bluff (Figure 5-5), and a major lumbering operation took place, in which most of the large trees that had served as benchmarks in earlier excavations (and had hindered total excavation of all features) were cut down. The

Figure 5-3. Raymond E. Merwin and crew at the Madisonville site, Trench E, 1908. Harvard University Peabody Museum Photo No. N3640, copyright 1997 by the President and Fellows of Harvard College; used by permission.

result was that 1907 excavations proceeded without exact knowledge of the location and orientation of previous trenches.

The final report on the Madisonville Village and Cemetery, published in 1920, was assembled from documents and materials curated at Harvard, with discussions of artifacts by Charles C. Willoughby and human remains by Earnest A. Hooton (Hooton and Willoughby 1920). Neither one excavated at Madisonville, but Willoughby did meet Metz and visit the site for a day in 1918. The report summarizes explorations undertaken at Madisonville (with the exception of those carried out from mid-August 1881 through April 1882 and in 1895, of which the authors apparently were ignorant), gives general burial statistics—age, sex, orientation, and pottery grave goods—and includes a craniometric study of 86 adults and an analysis of 112 sets of postcranial remains. Discussion of features and artifacts is normative, including drawings and descriptions of typical burials, pits, hearths, and artifacts. Burial versus pit provenience is noted for most of the illustrated artifacts, but no quantitative information is provided except for the percentage of graves containing pots. Although a master map of the site was constructed for the publication (Figure 5-2), it is incomplete and flawed (see below). Because it lacks feature numbers it cannot be used to locate particular burials or pits. For its day, this report was excellent, but it leaves much ground uncovered.

Much amateur archaeology and pot hunting took place at the Ancient Cemetery site over the years, and at least a few large collections were amassed by individuals. Some were reasonably well documented, one of which, excavated between about 1939 and 1943, was given to the Cincinnati Museum of Natural History (CMNH; now the Museum of Natural History and Science) by Donald Conover. During the 1980s, the CMNH conducted small-scale excavations in the southern portion of the site, producing samples for radiocarbon dating and some of the first controlled stratigraphic data from a deep midden left partially unexcavated by the MLSS (Cowan, in press; Genheimer 1994; Glowacki et al. 1993; Tankersley 1986b).

Figure 5-4. Refuse from Trench 1 and parts of Trenches 2 and 3, 1897. Harvard University Peabody Museum Photo No. N1643, copyright 1997 by the President and Fellows of Harvard College; used by permission.

Table 5-6 summarizes features excavated and recorded over 112 years of work at the site, compiled from all documentation available to me. These documents, including field notes, letters, manuscripts, catalog entries, photographs, and maps, currently are housed in nine different repositories at five institutions (Drooker 1996c: Table A2).

The Madisonville Village and Cemetery site now is occupied by a park containing a municipal swimming pool, with a housing development to the east. The size, shape, and topography of the plateau have been altered considerably over the past century, due to erosion, gravel excavation, and road construction, as well as to archaeological excavation itself. The only partially excavated pits discovered in 1987-88, the many features unearthed during the swimming pool excavation (Starr 1960:78-79), and the luck of twentieth-century amateurs in finding burials and grave goods underneath large trees (Robert Genheimer, pers. comm.) are all evidence that the original large-scale excavations were incomplete. Although much information has been preserved, a significant amount has been lost. All attempts at reconstruction of intrasite relationships must keep this in mind.

To recapitulate, early investigators only gradually developed a consistent and relatively complete system of field techniques and record keeping. Excavations of large portions of the site were undertaken at several different times, with no clear definition of their spatial relationships to each other. Many lack locational data, and one major excavation (1895) lacks field notes. The few maps (or field measurements to reconstruct them) that do exist from the earliest excavations, 1879-1895, are only approximate. Although field records from these early excavations describe the types of artifacts found in each grave and refuse pit, it is rarely possible to tie particular curated artifacts to specific proveniences. Maps from later excavations, and the field information and artifact collections that go with them, are far more useful. Thus, my work has concentrated most strongly on data collected between 1897 and 1911.

Figure 5-5. View of southern edge of bluff at Madisonville site (cf. Figure 5-7), probably before 1897, showing gravel removal operations. Note excavated refuse pit with shovel inside at top left, on the men's right. Photograph by M. H. Saville. Harvard University Peabody Museum Photo No. P1553, courtesy of the President and Fellows of Harvard College.

Curation Practices

Excavations at Madisonville unearthed thousands of artifacts and faunal materials, and hundreds of human skeletons. As we have seen, many were lost to archaeological analysis when they were deliberately or inadvertently discarded in the field (Table 5-5, Figure 5-4), or buried in private collections. Further losses unfortunately occurred due to standard (and some nonstandard) curation practices of the day. Just as with maps and field notes, the most complete and best documented collections come from the 1897-1911 expeditions sponsored by the HUPM, but even they suffered significant losses.

Artifacts. Collections from the Madisonville site currently are curated by at least twenty different institutions and numerous private individuals (Drooker 1996c: Table A1). Although many artifacts from the 1870-80s excavations are in museum collections, only an extremely small number of them can be tied to particular, documented features, either by means of catalog entries or by means of published or unpublished drawings or field descriptions. Because MLSS members divided artifacts among themselves by type, not by provenience, items from the same provenience, such as gravelots, rarely went all together to the same owner. As far as I can tell, none of the items from the MLSS excavations were ever labeled or catalogued as to provenience. It is only in the rare cases where a very distinctive artifact was both well-described and illustrated by a detailed sketch or drawing that provenience can be established.

The most extensive collections made during this time that were acquired directly from the field or from the original owners are curated at Harvard and at the Smithsonian Institution National Museum of Natural History (NMNH) and National Museum of the American Indian (NMAI). Another large collection is held by the CMNH. Many of the artifacts in it were acquired indirectly, through the Cincinnati Art Museum (CAM), which now retains only five artifacts—all whole vessels—from Madisonville. Quite a few of the CAM-CMNH artifacts origi-

TABLE 5-5
Examples of Numbers of Artifacts Excavated from Pit Features, versus Numbers Retained and Accessioned

Feature	Item	Number Excavated	Number Accessioned
Trench D, Pit 1	Animal bones	250+	0
	Natural rocks	100+	1
	Potsherds	25+	5
	Flints	25	0
	Shells	35	0
	Frag. bone scrapers	6	6
	Worked antler	2	5
	Antler cylinders	2	1 + frag.
	Bone awls	3	2
	Bone beads	2	2
	Notched bone	1	1
	Worked bone	2	1
	Human bones (feet)	12	16
	Perforated shells	4	3
	Sharpening stones	3	3
	Smoothing stones	1	1
	Hammer stones	1	1
	Shell discs	5	4
	Charred nut	2	1
	Worked cannel coal	1	1
	Flint scraper	3	3
	Flint drill	2	1
	Flint rejects	2	2
	Antler flaker	1	0
		490+	61
Trench H, Pit 50	Bone scraper	1	0
	Antler cylinders	3	0
	Antler points	1	0
	Worked antler	2	0
	Fragment bone scraper	1	0
	Notched rib	1	0
	Celt	1	0
	Fragment celt	1	0
	Perforated shell	1	0
	Flint point	1	0
	Flint scraper	1	0
	Worked stone	2	0
	Bone	100	0
	Stone	75	0
	Potsherds	40	0
	Shell	40	0
	Flint flakes	25	0
		296	0

Data from 1908 and 1911 field notes and from HUPM catalog entries. These features were chosen at random from the field notes, before consulting the catalog.

TABLE 5-6
Numbers of Burials and Storage/Refuse Pits within Each Excavation Area

Year(s) Excavated	Label	Number of Burials	Number of pits
1879	Block 1 ("O")	339	176±
1880	Block 2 ("O"?)	32	8
	Block 3 ("O"?)	24	12
	Block 4 ("O"?)	34	6
	Block 5 ("N")	10	6
	Block 6 ("N")	55	38
	Block 7 ("N")	10	29
	Block 8 ("N")	14	19
	Block 9 ("N")	17	12
	Block 10 ("N")	12	17
	Block 11 ("N")	31	23
	Block 12 ("N")	22	13
1881	Block 13 ("N")	3	2
	Block 14 ("N")	23	25
	Block 15 ("N")	20	29
	Block 16 ("N")	22	18
	Block 17 ("N")	23	22
1881	Blocks 18-21	20	10
1882	Blocks 18-21	19	19
1882	Block 22	≥ 8	≥13
	Putnam's Block ("L")	9-13	15
	---- ("P")	≥ 1	1
1891 (W.C.E.)	---- ("M")	36	19
1895 (A.M.N.H)	----	≥59	≥ 7
1897	Trench 1 ("I")	67	73
	Trench 2 ("II")	56	53
	Trench 3 ("III")	71	21
	Trench 4 ("IV")	41-43	31
	Trench 5 ("V")	3	4
1907	Trench A	4	15
	Trench B	61	40
	Trench C	23	33
1908	Trench D	104	143
	Trench E	40	42
	Trench F	37	58
1911	Trench G	3	7
	Trench H	43	77
	Trench I	26	60
	Trench J	0	2
	Trench K	12	14
1939-50 (Conover)	----	16	≥55
1987-88 (C.M.N.H.)	----	0	11
		1450±	1278±

"Label" indicates designation in field notes; letters in parentheses refer to designations on the published site map (Hooton and Willoughby 1920:Pl. 30), if different.

nally were owned by MLSS members, and many if not most of them probably came from the "Ferris Ancient Cemetery," but because of sketchy record-keeping most cannot be so identified with certainty (C. Wesley Cowan and Robert Genheimer, pers. comm.).

Artifacts from the fairly well documented 1891 excavations, which were supposed to have gone to the Field Museum of Natural History after the World's Columbian Exposition, are not now in that institution's collection (Janice B. Klein, pers. comm.). Conversely, the fine artifact collection made for the AMNH in 1895 has virtually no documentation except for sketchy catalog entries. Furthermore, at least some of the artifacts catalogued with the latter collection as coming from Madisonville actually were collected by Metz during a visit to the Fox Farm site near Maysville, Kentucky; thus, artifact types unique to this collection must be viewed with skepticism.

TABLE 5-7
Accessioned versus Extant Ceramics from the Madisonville Site

Accession Number(s)	Year of Excavation	Min. No. Units[a] Accessioned	No. of Units Counted 1993	Percent Still Present
		NON-MORTUARY PROVENIENCES		
97-38 and 01-38	1897	12,489	788	6.3
07-06	1907	2,098	375	17.9
08-03	1908	851	263	30.9
11-10	1911	117	97	82.9
		15,555	1523	9.8%
		MORTUARY PROVENIENCES		
97-38 and 01-38	1897	463	219	47.3
07-06	1907	34	21	61.8
08-03	1908	44	27	61.4
11-10	1911	8	9	112.5[b]
		549	276	50.3%

Numbers of ceramic vessels and sherds accessioned by the Harvard University Peabody Museum from excavations carried out at the Madisonville site between 1897 and 1911, versus numbers observed in 1993.
[a] Unit = sherd or vessel
[b] Percentage greater than 100 due to the convention of designating unknown numbers of units accessioned for a given catalog number by a minimum value of one

In general, the artifacts amassed by Harvard-sponsored expeditions between 1897 and 1911 were well provenienced, each one identified as to the burial or pit feature from which it came, or as from "general digging" (i.e., not from a feature) within a given trench. Unfortunately, problematical curation policies rendered even these collections far less useful than they might have been. As previously noted, not everything excavated under HUPM auspices was sent to the museum. This practice apparently became more pronounced over time. By 1911, only selected artifacts were being shipped to Cambridge (Drooker 1996c:578). This helps to explain the fact that relatively few artifacts were accessioned from Trenches G-K compared with areas previously dug (Table 5-7).

Once accessioned, artifacts were not necessarily retained in perpetuity. While he directed the Peabody Museum, Putnam strenuously championed the idea that all artifacts and remains excavated from a given archaeological component—site, burial, mound, shell heap—should be kept together. Even so, he sent a large number of Madisonville artifacts to the Smithsonian Institution in 1890, in an exchange. His successors at the museum continued and expanded this policy. From 1918 on, individual items and type collections of up to several hundred artifacts were removed from the Madisonville collection and exchanged to other museums and sometimes even to private individuals (Drooker 1996c: Table A1). Formal deaccessioning records remain for only a few of these exchanges. In some cases, the receiving institutions left the Harvard catalog numbers in place on artifacts, so it is possible to determine provenience for at least a proportion of them.

Many of the animal bones that did arrive in Cambridge were sent to the Harvard Museum of Comparative Zoology. Of those remaining, most were stored separately from other Madisonville artifacts, rather than being kept with other items from the same feature. They were used as a resource for zooarchaeology classes. In that connection, a fair number were sorted by type of animal, and the remainder now are jumbled together in no particular order, that is, not readily accessible by catalog number or feature lot.

Increasingly limited storage space and what might be termed "housecleaning" during the mid-twentieth century apparently led to the discard of significant proportions of bulky items like ceramic sherds and human and animal bones from the Harvard collections (Lane Beck and Gloria Greis, pers. comm.). As an example of the proportion of material that has been lost, Table 5-7 compares the number of ceramic sherds and vessels accessioned in 1897-1911 with the number still on hand in 1993. Grave goods fared better than ceramics from other proveniences, but even so, only about half remain. Among artifacts, ceramics probably represent the extreme case. For instance, most of the pipes and metal artifacts originally accessioned still are on hand. However, it is clear that any statistical analyses must be planned and assessed with extreme caution.

For this project, I examined and recorded stylistic information on all extant Madisonville artifacts curated at Harvard, taking measurements and photographs of all grave goods, exotic materials and artifacts, and other important classes of objects such as whole vessels. In examining collections at other institutions (Drooker 1996c: Table A1), I concentrated on the latter types of artifacts, particularly on objects with good intrasite provenience. Using field notes, letters, catalog entries, and other information, I made as complete a record as possible of mortuary assemblages from all excavations, compiling for each burial a descriptive list of grave goods and a photgraphic record of all extant artifacts.

Human Remains. The vast majority of human remains from Madisonville that were exhumed and retained were shipped to Harvard (Drooker 1996c: Table A1). As with ceramics and faunal remains, however, not everything was accessioned and not everything accessioned is still extant (Table 5-8). Additional problems are associated with cataloguing and post-acquisition use of these materials.

Although bone preservation was quite good on much of the cemetery site, because of the dense tree cover many skeletons were intergrown with roots, making it difficult to remove them without damage. For this reason, few burials were recovered complete. In fact, according to Hooton, "There is not one complete skeleton in good condition in all of the collections sent in by Metz, Swanton, and the Merwin brothers" (Hooton and Willoughby 1920:121). When recovery appeared too difficult, burials were left in place. Bones from MLSS excavations (1879-81) were only selectively retained, many of them were shipped

TABLE 5-8
Comparison of Madisonville Human Remains Excavated, Accessioned, and Currently in Inventory at the Harvard University Peabody Museum

Excavation year(s)	Excavated Burials [a]	Accessioned Remains (no. of lots)	REMAINS NOW IN INVENTORY No. of Lots of Remains	Identifiable Individuals [b]
1879-1882	737	113 [c]	97	8
1897	238	312	212	122 (+ 6 lots from pits)
1907	88	108	87	69 (+ 8 lots from pits)
1908	181	253	206	137 (+ 7 lots from pits)
1911	84	56	39	36
	1328	842	641	372

Number of bones still in inventory for each accession may or may not be comparable to the original number.

a Includes only recorded "burials," not individual bones discovered in ash pits or general digging.

b Individuals who can be identified with a particular burial described in field notes. Bones of extra, unidentified individuals from a particular burial are not included.

c Excludes 8 lots from Spice Bush Mound, on Stites land near "house circles."

and catalogued by type of bone rather than by individual skeleton, and almost no individual skeletons were identified as to where on the site they had come from. Thus, these remains were not part of my data base.

Material excavated by Putnam and by the later Harvard-sponsored expeditions apparently was sent from the field in burial lots, but in many cases these were not kept together after reaching the museum. Crania utilized by Hooton were catalogued separately from postcranial remains. In extreme cases, portions of a single skeleton have been catalogued in as many as four different lots. Conversely, upon examination, a number of "burial" lots were found to contain bones from two, three, or more individuals (Table 5-8). Field identification notes and laboratory notes still remain with many of the skeletons. They were used during accession and again during a recent inventory to fix identification of remains. Unfortunately, some have become jumbled and no longer are with the proper lot of bones, as I found when I compared them with field records and for internal consistency.

Over the years, many of the Madisonville bones were used as teaching aids, and retained in classroom storage. In recent years, the HUPM Osteology Laboratory sought out such "displaced" bones, identified them where possible, and returned them to storage with other Madisonville remains. However, many inevitably were lost. As the collection now stands, individuals often are represented by only a handful of bones, and only very rarely by an almost-complete skeleton. Larger parts, like crania and os coxae, are damaged more often than not. Although all remains recently were inventoried, with standard data sheets used to record bones present, number of individuals, ages, sexes, pathologies, and trauma for each catalogued lot of bones, this was done under severe time constraints and mostly by student assistants, so results must be viewed with caution (Lane Beck, pers. comm.).

Thus, assembling as complete a record as possible of "who was buried where" in Trenches 1-K was a two-step process (Drooker 1996c:518-22). First, each largely incomplete, catalogued lot of remains was scored for age and sex to the extent possible (and later cross-checked with inventory data). Following that, it was necessary to resolve inconsistencies between and within lots, and between extant remains and recorded field data, so that characteristics of a single individual could be assigned to each recorded burial.

Post-1920 Analyses of Madisonville Materials

James B. Griffin's definitive volume on the Fort Ancient cultural tradition contained summary descriptions of Madisonville features and artifacts, tables of measurements and attributes of selected whole ceramic vessels, and photographs of artifacts, with the major emphasis on pottery (1943:119-43, Tables I-V, XIV, Pls. LX-LXXIX). He used not only Harvard collections and documentation, but also materials curated at at least five other institutions. The classification system developed by Griffin for Fort Ancient ceramics leaned heavily on Madisonville data: 166 of the 224 whole vessels reported by him came from that site.

Most analyses of Madisonville materials since 1943 have been of human remains. Louise Robbins included 391 Madisonville site crania in her study of Fort Ancient physical types (Giesen 1992:16-20; Robbins 1968; Robbins and Neumann 1972; see the end of Chapter 4). Unlike populations from other Fort Ancient foci, which were primiarily "Ilinid," Madisonville Focus sites, particularly Madisonville itself, contained both "Ilinid" and "Muskogid" types.

Myra Giesen used remains from 430 Madisonville individuals as part of a study comparing biological affinities and stress indicators between early and late Fort Ancient and early and late northern Ohio Sandusky populations (Giesen 1992; see the end of Chapter 4). The majority of her Madisonville sample, which included 93 males, 110 females, 127 unknown, and 100 subadults, is said to have come from the MLSS-sponsored excavations. No individual-by-individual data base is provided. Of all sites sampled, Madisonville produced the highest within-sex variance in stature, postulated as perhaps related to class differences (1992:191). It was among the sites with the lowest measured statures; Gieson suggests that smaller statures associated with the more recent sites in her sample might reflect nutritional stress plus additional stress due to European contact (1991:122, 196). However, Madisonville people also had "what appears to be a better pattern of dental health" (1991:202), implying less nutritional stress. There was less sexual dimorphism in the Madisonville sample than any of the others, perhaps implying reduced sexual division of labor (1991:194-95).

Data from the recent inventory of Madisonville remains can be used to produce very general statistical information on traumatic injury and disease. Approximately 6% of 544 lots of remains from the 1897-1911 excavations had sustained fractures, including 1% to crania. Five had embedded lithics or piercing injuries. Approximately 18% exhibited some form of non-dental pathology, including three individuals said to evince treponemal-like symptoms and two with possible tuberculosis.

For over fifty years, Griffin's publication has stood as the final word on Madisonville site archaeology. Unpublished projects such as Rigg's Lower Little Miami Valley ceramics chronology (1994), which utilizes a sample of sherds from Madisonville, and the small-scale CMNH-sponsored excavations during the 1980s (Cowan, in press; Genheimer 1994; Glowacki et al. 1993; Tankersley 1986b) provide important temporal and stratigraphic dimensions to prior analyses of Madisonville data. Hindering further progress, however, has been the lack of intrasite provenience for previously excavated artifacts and human remains.

Madisonville Site Organization

Obviously, collection and curation practices rendered Madisonville artifacts and remains less useful than they might have been, but by no means did they erase their archaeological value. To enhance that value, one of my first tasks was to reconstruct the original locations of as many of them as possible. For that, a reliable map was required.

At first glance, the published map of the site (Figure 5-2)—constructed by Hooton from Bowditch's survey, notes and maps from the May 1882, 1891, 1897, 1907, 1908, and 1911 excavations, and one of the four extant sets of MLSS field notes—appears to be extremely detailed and useful. However, discrepancies and omissions necessitated some major revisions.

Despite the lack of spatial data for the earliest excavations (Section O), the map certainly gives a strong sense of the density of features. These consisted mainly of some 1500 burials and 1300 corn storage pits filled in with refuse, the latter generally 3 to 5 feet in diameter by 5 to 7 feet deep (e.g., Hooton and Willoughby 1920: Figs. 2-4). Several "kitchen midden" areas, where trash was deposited in deep ravines, are indicated (but not located quite accurately on this map). One wall-trench structure had been excavated, along with a number of hearths and short runs of postholes, but these features were not included on the published map.

Upon examination of this map, it is difficult to discern any pattern at all in the main area of occupation. Madisonville thus became the prototype for the unstructured village type that many consider typical of the last-occupied Fort Ancient sites (e.g., Cowan 1987:15; Graybill 1987).

On higher ground to the northeast, separated from the main part of the site, were at least eight so-called house circles—circular, probably semi-subterranean, houses with central hearths—excavated in 1879 and 1882 (Low 1880:59-60; Putnam 1882). Their locations and outlines on the map are only approximate. Near them, about 300 feet east of the eastern end of Trench G, was a low mound from which 12 burials were excavated in 1911 (Merwin 1911). According to the excavator, who found fragments of human bones in many places, the mound probably had been explored previously, so the total number of burials probably was greater. Perhaps in the same vicinity was the Spice Bush Mound excavated by Metz in 1878 and said to be one of "several small tumuli" making up No. 5 of Group A on Metz's regional map of 1878 (Low 1880:41-43, 59; Metz 1878:122). Along the bluff beyond that were five or six more mounds (Nos. 3 and 2 of Metz's Group A), and still farther, about a mile east of the "Ancient Cemetery," a circular embankment associated with two "tumuli" (Metz 1878:119-23).

Revised Site Map

I had hoped to use the published site map as the basis for a computerized Geographic Information System (GIS) map of the burials, which would link their locations to data bases listing attributes of burials and grave goods. However, when I studied the field notes from the Harvard excavations and gradually unearthed a series of field maps from the Peabody Museum Archives (Drooker 1996c: Table A3), I discovered that the published map contained some major discrepancies (Drooker 1994a, 1996c:499-509). For example, Trenches B, C, D, E, and F actually were oriented at N12°W, not at N38°W. Draft maps-in-progress, plus letters from Hooton to Willoughby, reveal considerable uncertainty as to how the excavation blocks were supposed to fit together. In the end, in order to fit everything within the surveyed boundaries of the plateau, Hooton and Willoughby overlapped Trench E with Trenches 1-5 (designated by Roman numerals in Figure 5-2), and Trench B with the MLSS excavation blocks of 1880-81 (Figure 5-6). Reconstruction of the MLSS excavations was extremely uncertain—there were no maps other

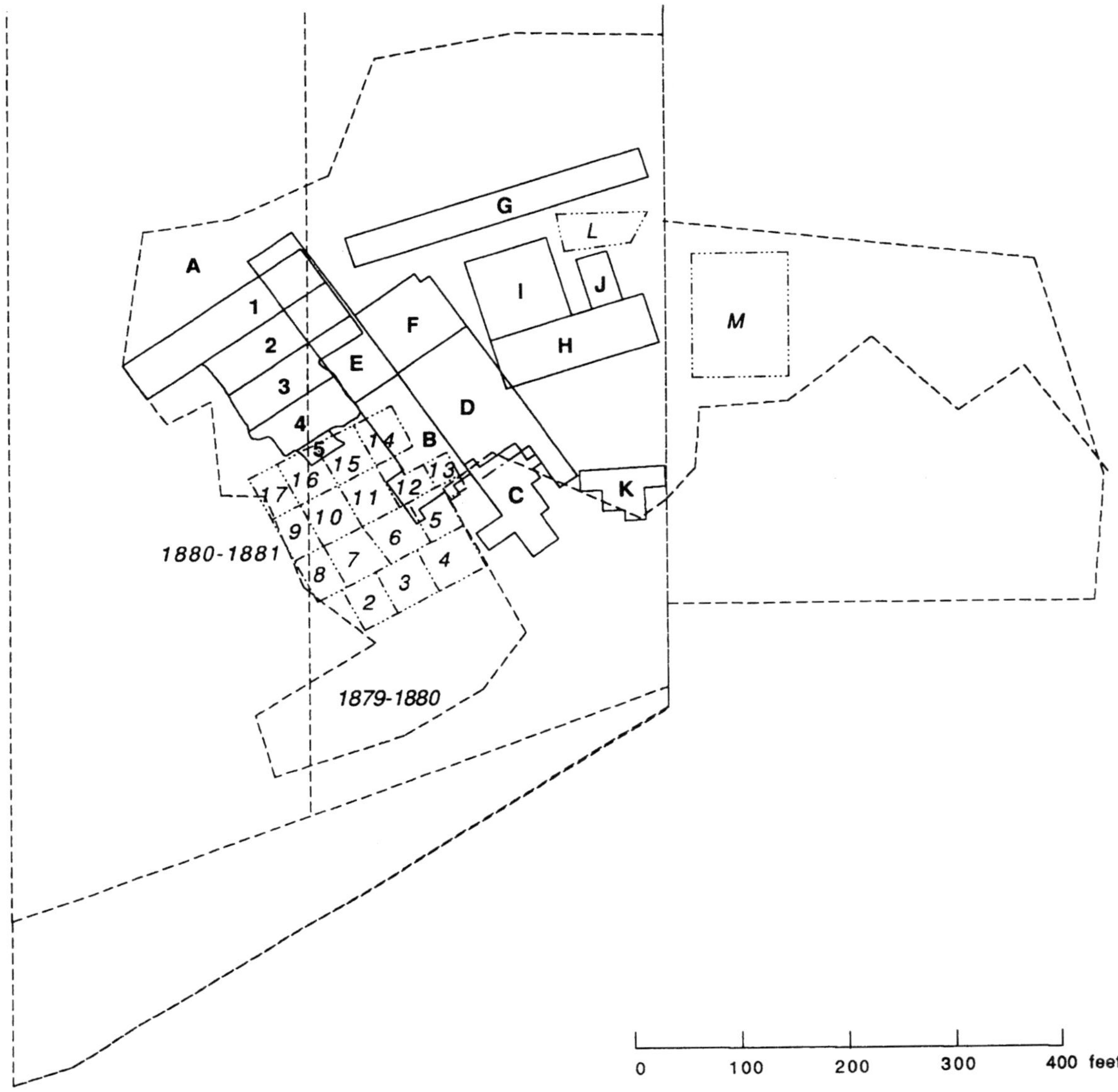

Figure 5-6. Relative positions of excavation blocks in published site map. Arrangement of Blocks 2-17 relative to each other is from a draft map in the HUPM Archives (Drooker 1996c: Table A3, Map 48).

than small-scale partial sketches, no grid was used, no compass readings were given for burial orientations, field measurements were taken from landmarks like "Large Oak No. 1," and a large proportion of the burials had no locational measurements at all. Field maps for individual trenches excavated by Harvard expeditions between 1897 and 1911 were far more accurate (although not without errors), but their relative placement on the published map is problematical in many ways.

In the end, I had to go back to square one, and reconstruct a revised site map from scratch (Drooker 1994a: Part B, 1996c:509-13, in press). I was able to superimpose survey maps of the property lines and the outline of the bluff top upon a 1952 (pre-swimming pool) large-scale topographic map, so that the approximate relationship of topography to site boundaries could be observed (Figure 5-7). Natural erosion, quarrying for sand along the edge of the bluff, and the addition of roadways had resulted in major changes to the topography, but the general trends could be seen. Using field notes, field maps, and the constraints of the property boundaries, I revised the locations of the excavation trenches to better reflect reality (Figure 5-8). The locations and orientations of most pre-1897 excavation blocks are schematic only, based on far less evidence than Trenches 1-K. Relative positions of trenches within the three groups of 1-5, B-F, and G-K are quite accurate. Orientations and locations of these groups relative to each other definitely are more accurate than on the earlier map, but still should be

Figure 5-7. Approximate relationship of Madisonville site boundaries to mid-twentieth century topography.

considered as subject to possible future revision. This tentative arrangement of excavation areas does give a concrete jumping-off place for consideration of spatial relationships among features and artifacts at the site.

The field notes document a minimum of 1450 burials and 1278 pits, unevenly distributed among over 40 excavation blocks within the Ancient Cemetery area (Table 5-6). In spot-checking Trenches 1-K with their field notes, I found that the accuracy of locations and measurements was extremely uneven, so I rechecked everything and redrew many of the individual maps to scale. Because of the vagueness of the field notes from the 1880s, I did not attempt to redraw the maps from the southern portion of the site. For this project, I dealt with the burials there on a block-by-block basis rather than individually. All of the features excavated between 1897 and 1911, in Trenches 1-5 and A-K, were diagrammed and entered into the computer as a MapGrafix GIS map (Figure 5-9) with separate layers for skeletons (Figure 5-10), graves, refuse pits (Figure 5-11), and other features (Figure 5-12). All burials and pits were identified in the GIS map by their field numbers, so that they could be linked to database information on their contents. Figure 5-13 shows the identification numbers of burials within each excavation trench.

Relative Positions of Features

The most exciting thing that emerged with the revised map was an open area that probably served as a small plaza (Figure 5-9). It approaches the same physical size as the plaza at the pre-Madisonville Horizon Anderson Village site farther up the Little Miami River (Table 5-9), but the much greater density of burials at Madisonville implies a significantly longer occupation. Many of the Madisonville burials close to the plaza appear to have been oriented parallel to the edges of the open area, as were burials at Anderson and Incinerator (Essenpreis 1982: Maps 9, 17; Robertson 1984: Fig. 1). Other burials exhibited right-angled patterns that probably mean they were associated with houses, possibly some of them interred in house floors as was the case at Fort Ancient sites like Buffalo and Turpin (Hanson 1975:23; Metz 1885b: Part 1:81). Although

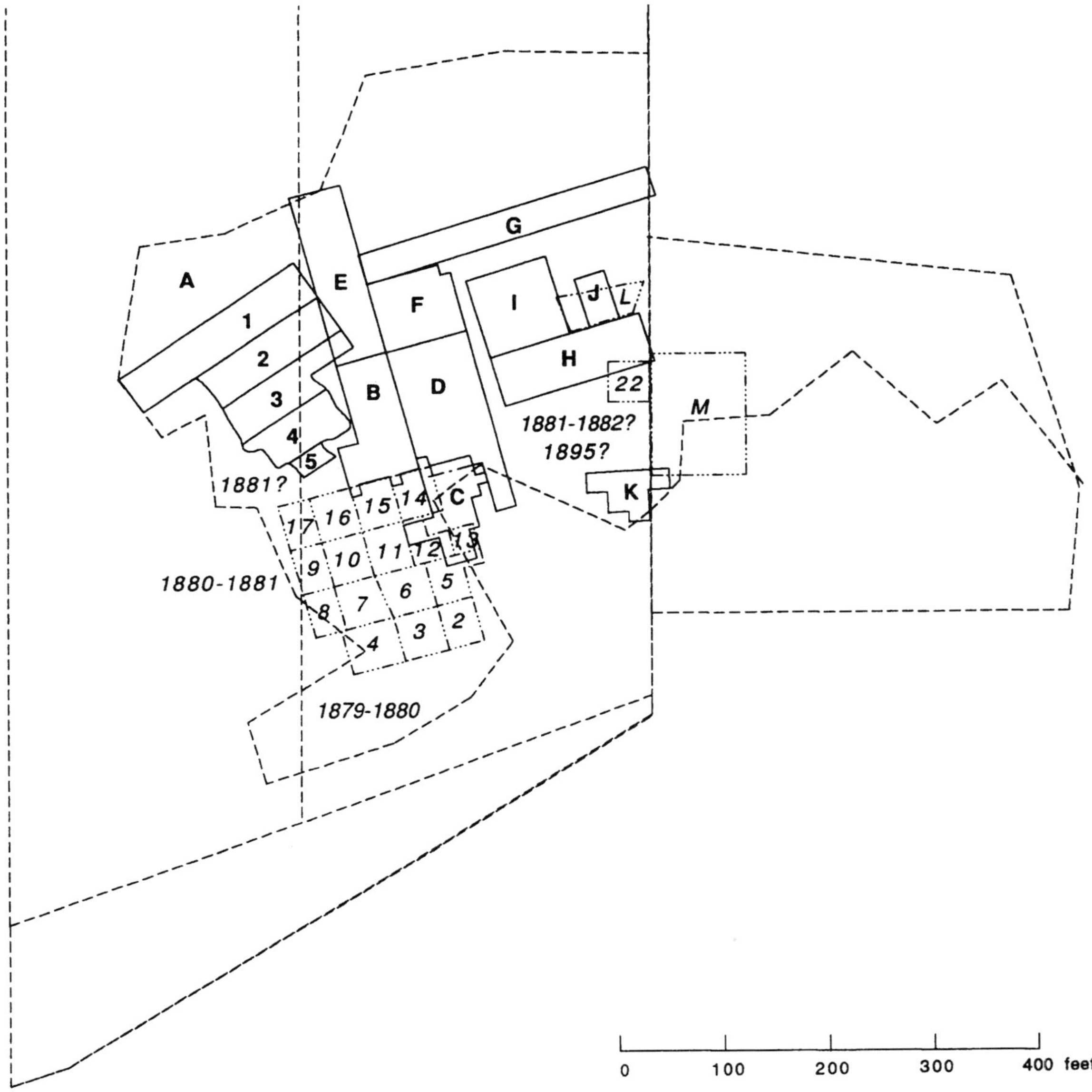

Figure 5-8. Revised excavation map, including approximate placement of excavations of 1880-91. Arrangement of Blocks 2-17 relative to each other has not been altered from Figure 5-6 except for Blocks 2 and 4, but the orientation has been changed arbitrarily for a better fit with Trenches B and C.

many burials were located close to the plaza, this zone contained relatively few pits. Farther away from the open area there were both burials and pits, sometimes mixed but often in patches where one or the other type of feature predominated.

It is of interest that a single 14-inch-diameter posthole, extending 32 inches into the hardpan layer, was excavated in the central area of the Madisonville plaza (Figures 5-9 and 5-12, upper portion of Trench B). At the Incinerator site, a four-foot deep hole near the center of the plaza held a massive cedar post over two feet in diameter, believed related to solar alignments among certain features (Goss 1988; Lileas 1988:40-41). Although the Madisonville posthole was nowhere near that size, it was among the three widest and three deepest postholes recorded from Trenches A-K (mean diameter = 8.9″, range = 5″–20″; mean depth below hardpan = 14.4″, range = 4″–36″).

Both burials and pits decreased in frequency along a line that parallels the rising ground along the northeastern side of the site (Figures 5-9, 5-7). Not only the negative evidence from Trench G but also a number of empty and almost-empty test excavations north and east of Trench G (Figure 5-2, "trial trenches" and "P") make it reasonably certain that the sloping ground between the Ancient Cemetery area and the house circles never was occupied. The small plaza and its surrounding domestic zone probably were constrained in size and shape by site topography. Besides being restricted by rising ground to the northeast, the flat area of the plateau was intruded by ravines that

Figure 5- 9. Madisonville site GIS map, Trenches 1-K, showing all features recorded in field notes.

Figure 5-10. Madisonville site GIS map, Trenches 1-K, showing locations and orientations of human remains.

Figure 5-11. Madisonville site GIS map, Trenches 1-K, showing locations of corn storage pits later used for refuse.

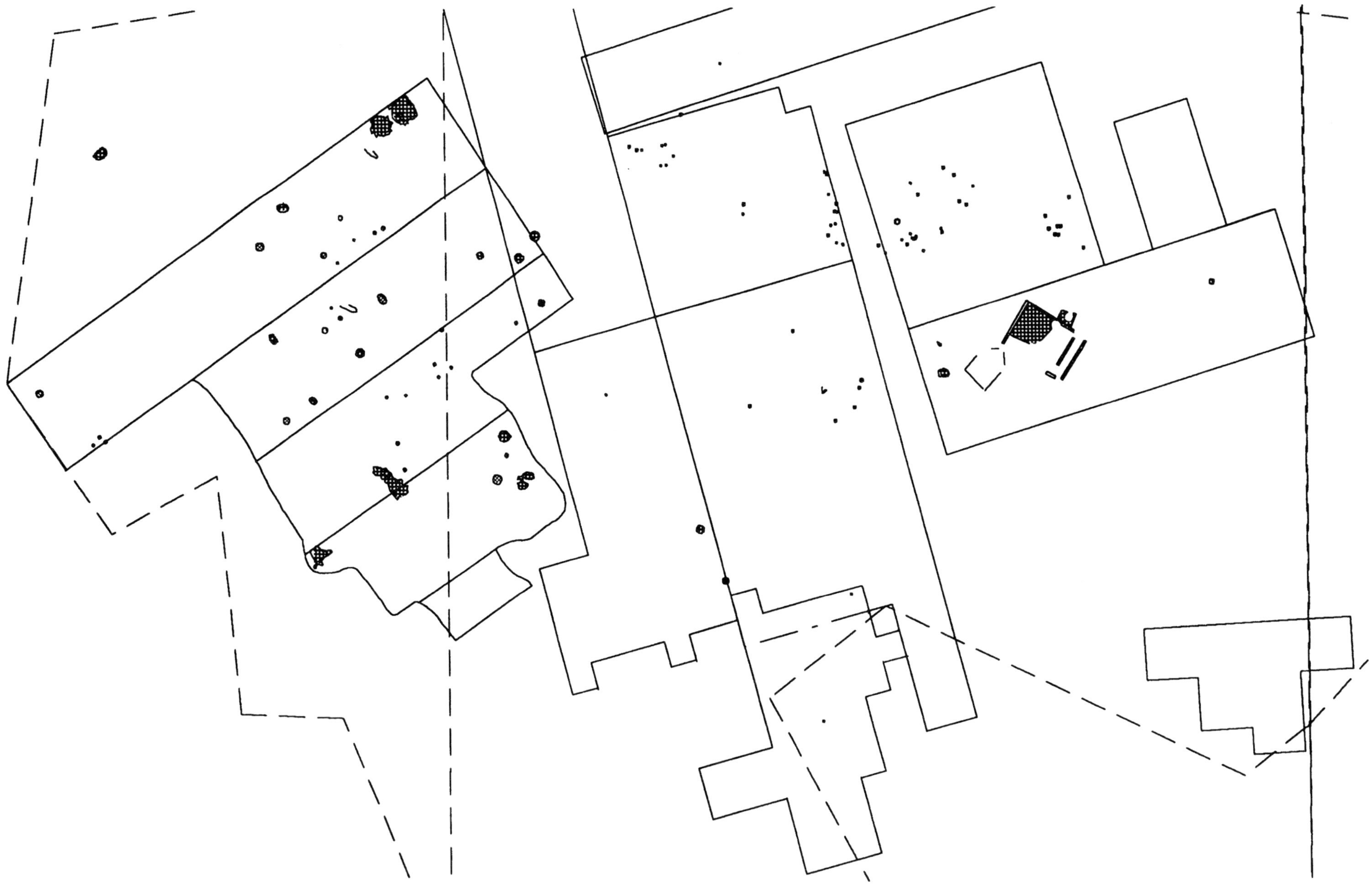

Figure 5-12. Madisonville site GIS map, Trenches 1-K, showing locations of recorded postholes, trenches, and hearths or burned areas.

Figure 5-13. Madisonville site GIS map, Trenches 1-K, showing numbered burials and their positions in relation to refuse pits.

TABLE 5-9
Comparison of Plaza and Domestic Zone Areas for Selected Fort Ancient Sites

	PLAZA		DOMESTIC ZONE
	Approximate Dimensions, m	Approx. Area, m2	Max. Diameter, m
Madisonville	21-25 x 27-36 oval	450-730	110-150
Anderson Village	25 x 40 oval	830	80
Incinerator	60 x 70 oval	3300	120
Buffalo	70 x 70	3800	180

The Buffalo site plan does not include pits and burials, so plaza dimensions are between house structures. Other sites' plaza areas were defined by presence/absence of burials and pits. Since all plazas contain some features (e.g., refuse pits, sweat lodges at Incinerator) and often are ringed by features that would not have been visible to the occupants (e.g., filled refuse pits or old, forgotten graves), dimensions are subject to variation depending on where the edge of the open area is specified. For Incinerator and Buffalo, the maximum domestic zone was defined by the palisade location; for Madisonville and Anderson, by presence/absence of features.

Table 5-10.
Density of Features in Southern versus Northern Portions of the Madisonville Site

	Southern	Northern
Area excavated (ft2)	35,450	76,900
Burial density (number/ft2)	.0168	.0077
Pit density (number/ft2)	.0130	.0082
Total feature density (number/ft2)	.0298	.0160

For the southern part of the site, data are from Blocks 1-17, excavated 1879-1881; excavation areas are approximate, particularly for Block 1. For the northern part of the site, data are from Trenches 1-K but excluding Trenches A and G, where very few features were found.

eventually were filled with midden, one running east-west across the southern corner of Trench 4 and Trench 5, another with its head at Trench C and the southeastern end of Trench D, and a third poking eastward into Block 4 (cf. Figures 5-7, 5-9, 5-14).

The open area centered on Trench B is significantly smaller than plazas at the protohistoric Buffalo site and the Early-Middle Fort Ancient Incinerator site, both of which were situated on open floodplains (Table 5-9). Additional small open spaces might have been present in the area of the Madisonville site excavated by the MLSS. Field notes report at least one section in Block 1 where few features were found, 60 × 40 feet (18 × 12 m, or 220 m²) or more in size (Low 1880:50). Unfortunately, there is not enough spatial information to fix its location more closely, or to map the surrounding features.

Although it is not possible to exactly delineate open areas *vis-à-vis* feature positions within the portions of the site excavated before 1897, it is possible to calculate and compare feature densities. Density of features was far greater in the southern than the northern portion of the site (Table 5-10), implying either longer occupation or different use of space. There were over twice as many burials per square foot and half again as many pits per square foot in the south. When densities are plotted on a block-by-block basis, it can be seen that overall density is by no means uniform. Looking at all features (Figure 5-14), densities are lowest in excavation trenches associated with the plaza area (B and E), in trenches at the outer edges of the occupied area (A, E, G, I, L, M, K), and in sectors associated with midden-filled ravines (Trenches 5 and C, Blocks 5 and 13). There are three adjacent less-dense excavation blocks (3, 7, 10) in the middle of the southern sector, indicating a relatively open area. However, they still include far more features per square foot than Trench B, which contains the major portion of the northern plaza. Densities of burials and of pits (Figures 5-15 and 5-16) do not vary together. This is consistent with the patchy concentrations of burials versus pits in Trenches 1-K, noted above (cf. Figures 5-9, 5-10, 5-11).

At least three construction methods were used for structures at and near the Ancient Cemetery site. The eight house circles northeast of the cemetery area, which may well not have been occupied concurrently with it, were formed by earthen embankments 11-12 feet wide that ranged in outside diameter from 43 to 58 feet (13-18 m). Putnam, who trenched across the centers of four of them in 1882, reported finding large fireplaces in the centers containing ashes, burnt stones, and a few fragmentary artifacts. Other artifacts, which were very few, appear to have been concentrated at the far edges of the floors (Putnam 1882).

A wall-trench structure about 17 × 18 feet (5 × 5.5 m) was excavated in Trench H (Figures 5-9, 5-17a). After occupation ceased, a portion of its floor was scraped away and used as a "fireplace" (roasting pit?), and various parts of it also were intruded by pits and burials.

I and others (C. W. Cowan, pers. comm.) have tried and failed to define the locations and sizes of other structures at the site, which certainly were present. A few recorded short runs of postholes, including several at right angles (Figure 5-12), and analogies with structures at other Late Fort Ancient sites (Table 4-11), make it likely that most structures had rectangular frameworks of poles. Since nothing identified as daub has come from the site, it seems likely that these frameworks were covered by bark, mats, skins, thatch or some such perishable material. No particular association of hearths and postholes can be discerned, nor can negative space delineated by burials and refuse pits be traced out to define house patterns with any confidence. As can be seen from the wall-trench house feature, if the trenches are taken away (Figure 5-17b), there is no recognizable pattern among the other features (some contemporaneous with the structure, others postdating it) by which the location of the building can be inferred. In fact, the closest excavated hearth was outside rather than inside the structure.

Because of these problems, I chose not to devote an excessive amount of time to attempting to locate and define dwell-

Figure 5-14. Density of features (burials and refuse pits) within selected excavation areas at Madisonville. See Table 5-6 for numbers of burials and pits excavated within each block and trench.

ings. This is worth more effort in future, and indeed, I return to it briefly in Chapter 6. Here, I propose some principles to use in such a quest. One possibility is that the primarily Late Fort Ancient site layout at Madisonville is a direct descendant of a layout similar to the well-mapped Early-Middle Fort Ancient Incinerator site (cf. Nass and Yerkes 1995: Fig. 3-3; Robertson 1984: Fig. 1). There, the houses were located at the periphery of the settlement, near a circular palisade. In front of them was a ring of storage pits, and in front of that, generally parallel with the edge of the plaza, were burials. (At least one group of burials, however, expanded out toward the plaza from the side of a structure.) Following this model, to search for house locations one would look for large empty spaces at some distance from the edge of a plaza area. At Madisonville (Figure 5-9), the south-

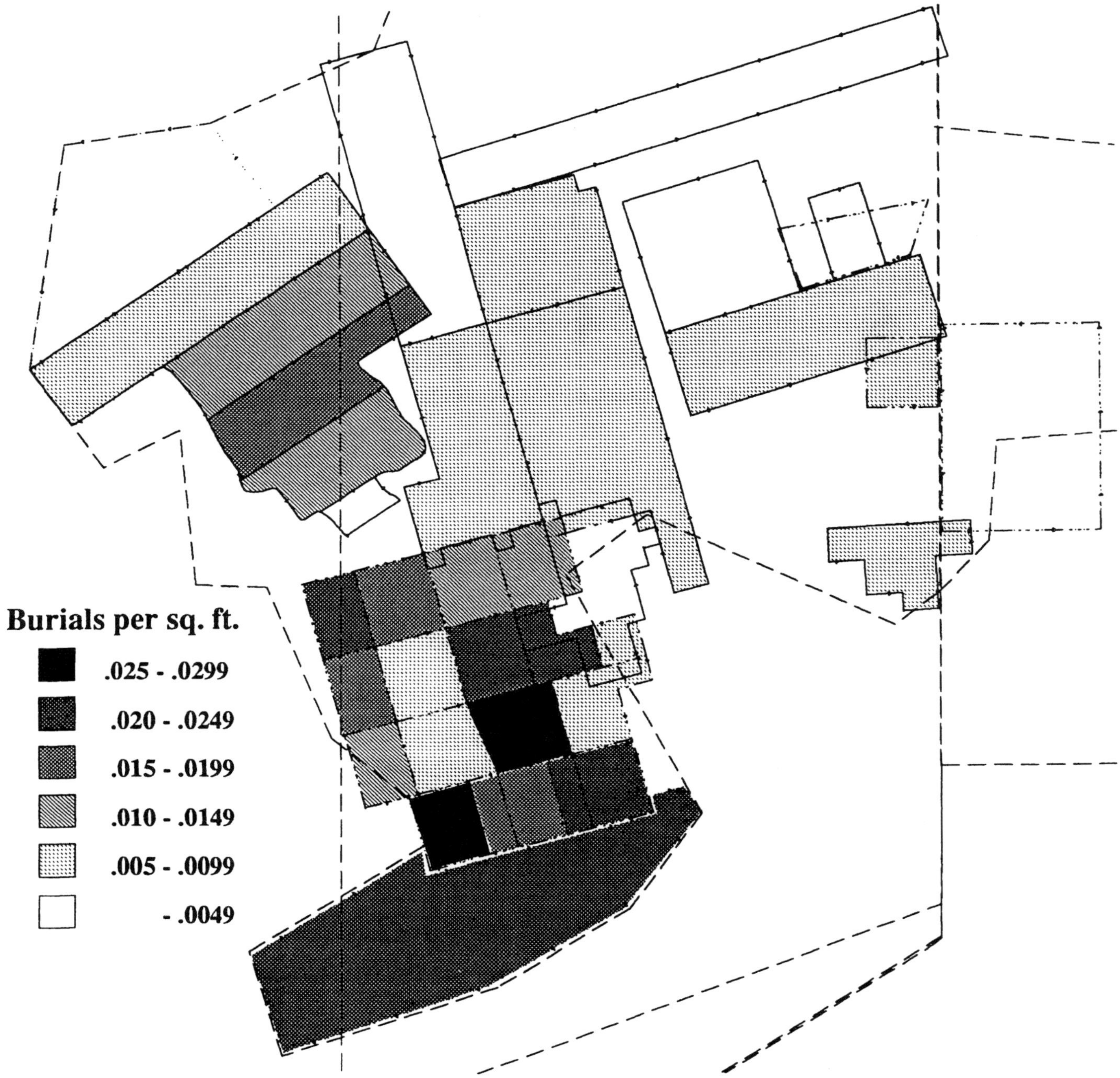

Figure 5-15. Density of burials within selected excavation areas at Madisonville. See Table 5-6 for numbers of burials and pits excavated within each block and trench.

western end of Trench 4 does not qualify, because it was a midden-filled ravine. Some areas that might fit this description are located (1) immediately south of the large group of burials at the northeastern end of Trench 1, (2) in the southwestern half of Trench 1, extending into Trench A, (3) at the extreme southwestern end of Trench 2, and (4) in the southeastern quadrant of Trench F. None of these areas contains a hearth, although there are postholes in Trench F.

A different approach ignores the precedent of Incinerator, instead looking to the Early-Middle Fort Ancient Baum site in central Ohio (Figure 4-1). There, small oval house structures had burial grounds along one side and storage pits along the

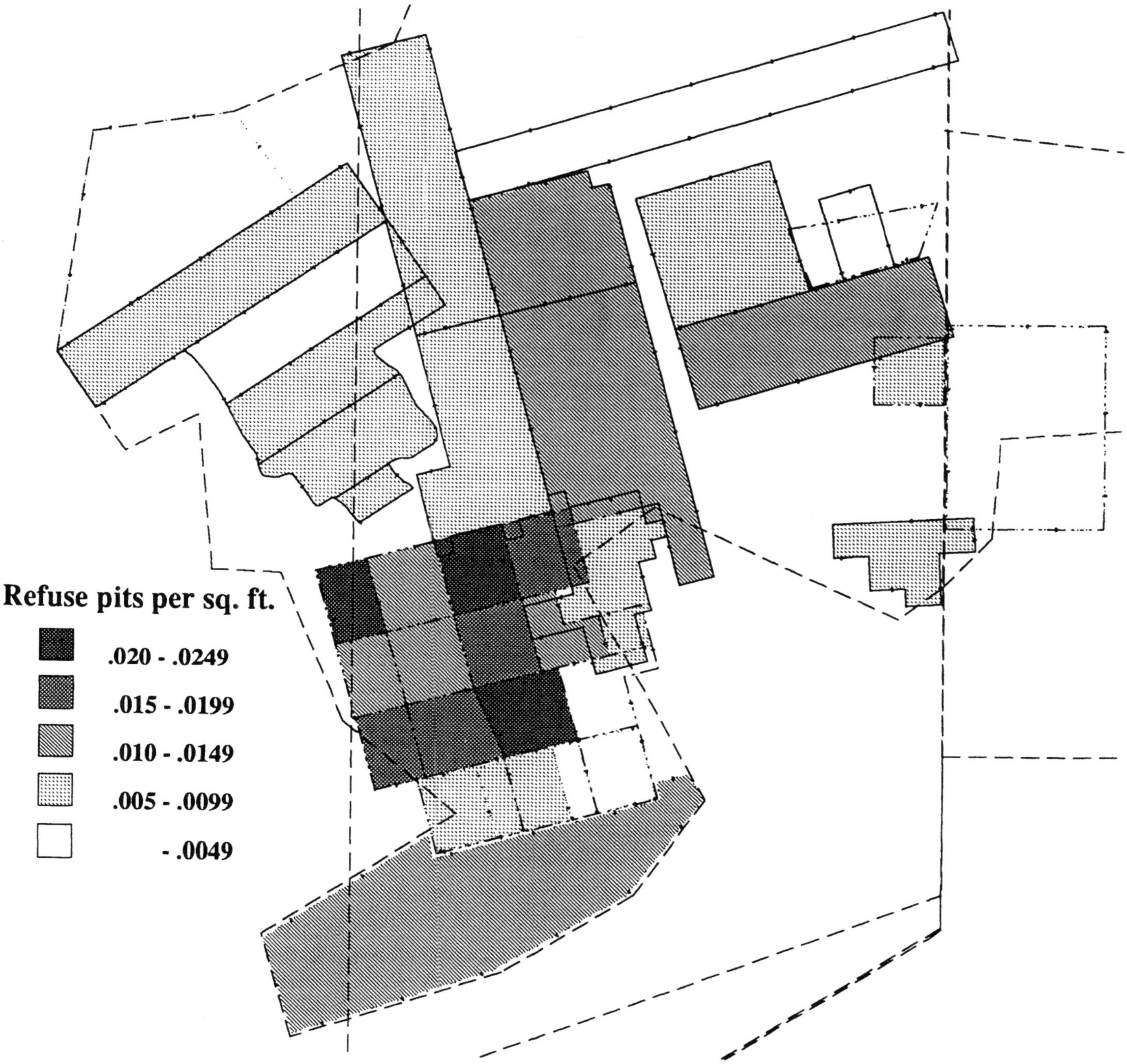

Figure 5-16. Density of refuse pits within selected excavation areas at Madisonville. See Table 5-6 for numbers of burials and pits excavated within each block and trench.

other (Mills 1906: Fig. 6). A reasonable working hypothesis is that many of the tight clusters of burials in Trenches 1-K (Figure 5-10) represent households or lineages. Quite a few of them form linear patterns that might perhaps have been constrained by an adjacent house wall. However, as with the wall trench structure (Figure 5-17), there is much visual noise in the picture due to earlier or later burials and pits obscuring the original pattern. Contemporaneous burials and pits also could muddy the visual pattern: there is much precedent for burial of family members under house floors and for storage pits utilized within dwellings. The few domestic-sized hearths recognized by the excavators at Madisonville are very difficult to tie in with other

Figure 5-17. Wall trench house feature, Trench H. *a*. All associated features, including wall trenches, burials, refuse pits, and burned areas. Dotted area indicates a depression, darker cross-hatching indicates burned areas. *b*. Burials, refuse pits, and burned areas only.

features (Figures 5-9, 5-12). Without good postmold patterns, these relationships are difficult to work out, but detailed consideration of horizon marker artifacts in graves and pits, burial depths, and other stratigraphic relationships could prove fruitful in learning more about locations and sizes of Madisonville structures (Chapter 6).

Looking at Figure 5-9 (which shows all features), Figure 5-10 (only burials) and Figure 5-13 (numbered burials and pits), there are several loci where burial patterns suggest the possibility of a nearby structure. Toward the southwestern end of Trenches 2 and 3 it is possible to discern an east-west aligned rectangular pattern, defined most strongly along its eastern and southern edges by an L-shaped concentration of burials in Trench 3; Burials 19 and 20 in Trench 2 are aligned along its northern edge. There are a hearth and some postmolds within this space, but there also are several burials and a few pits. The closely aligned burials at the north end of Trench 1 and the linear group of burials that runs into Trench E from the north end of Trench 2 might be defined by structure walls. There also appears to be a significant space between the latter cluster of burials and the large group aligned along the northern edge of the plaza. At the east end of the group along the plaza edge, in Trench D, the burials are located along a line perpendicular to the plaza edge, adjacent to an apparently empty space. At the southeastern corner of Trench D, there is an apparently empty area with a dense cluster of burials alongside. If this is not simply due to previous excavation, it could be related to a wall. Of course, there are many other areas of the site where burials are too scattered to be useful. A few additional possible dwelling locations will be discussed in Chapter 6, after temporal relationships among features have been examined in more depth.

Posthole sizes can give some clues as to structure sizes. At Madisonville, they were quite large: from 5 to 20 inches in diameter in Trenches A-K, with a mean of 8.9 inches. At the Buffalo site, houses approximately 25 × 50 feet (7.6 × 15.2 m) had three interior support posts 15 inches in diameter, but had much smaller wall posts, perhaps on the order of 2-4 inches (McMichael 1962:11; cf. Hanson 1975: Fig. 14). The best-preserved house pattern at Neale's Landing was 22 × 26+ feet (6.7 × 7.9+ m), with wall posts averaging 3.7 inches in diameter and interior roof support posts around 7.5 inches (Hemmings 1977:4-23). At Incinerator, posthole depths were taken as indicative of wall height. Ordinary dwellings, on the order of 21 × 21 feet (6.5 × 6.5 m), usually had postholes 6-8 inches deep (possibly truncated by plowing), but one large structure on the order of 23 × 30 feet (7 × 9 m) in size had many postholes 12-18 inches deep (Lambert and Heilman 1988:9-10; Robertson 1984: Fig. 1). Posthole diameters are not given for houses, but the palisade at Incinerator used poles of only 3-5 inches, set 8 inches deep (Lambert et al. 1988:4). Madisonville Trench A-K posthole depths averaged 14.4 inches below hardpan. From all these data, it seems likely that Madisonville pole-framed structures were substantial, probably approaching at least the average Buffalo structures in size.

Hearths, consisting of more-or-less circular areas of burned stones, plus larger burned areas or "fireplaces," where the hardpan surface had been discolored by fire, were found across much of the area encompassed by Trenches 1-K, but not in great numbers (Figure 5-12). A few refuse pits showed evidence on their walls of fires within, and a number of others contained quantities of burnt stones that had been heated elsewhere. The latter were reported more frequently in Blocks 1-17 than Trenches 1-K. Hooton and Willoughby interpreted the available data as showing that the "inhabitants of the village often dumped their hearth stones with their ashes into the cache-pits at the end of the season, and that they often used the depressions in the earth, caused by partially filled cache-pits, as hearths" (1920:40). I have not attempted to quantify this use of "often." The largest burned areas in Trenches 1-K, including those associated with the wall trench structure, plus many of the hearths, were located at some distance from the plaza (Figures 5-9, 5-12).

The arrangement, relative density, and types of features present at this site lead naturally to questions about its occupation history. A single, homogeneous, relatively short occupation period, such as probably occurred at the Early-Middle Fort Ancient Incinerator site, seems unlikely here. When was the site occupied? How large a population lived here at any one time? Can particular time periods be associated with particular features or particular sections of the site? Were the northern and southern portions of the site occupied concurrently or sequentially? These and related questions are considered in Chapter 6.

Chapter 6

Madisonville Occupation History

For over a century, Madisonville was treated as a single-component settlement. Until the advent of radiocarbon dating, it was unique among Fort Ancient sites in its assignability to an absolute time scale. Because European artifacts were recovered there, it was considered a protohistoric site utilized during the seventeenth century, but its length of occupation was unknown. Hooton and Willoughby reasoned that it was occupied at least 80 years—long enough for the most recent inhabitants to have forgotten locations of the earliest burials, resulting in some crosscutting of features—but not much longer, because "it seems improbable that any Indian group during this general period of tribal movements would have occupied the same site continuously for much more than one hundred years" (Hooton and Willoughby 1920:26).

During the past decade, evidence has accumulated that this site most likely was occupied, sporadically if not continuously, far longer than 100 years. Pottery analysis and radiocarbon dating point to at least two and perhaps as many as four Fort Ancient temporal components, with the major occupation apparently spanning the fifteenth to seventeenth centuries (Cowan 1986:148-49; Drooker 1993f; Glowacki et al. 1993). A few Woodland sherds indicate even earlier usage of the site (Griffin 1943:142-43). Most recent overviews (e.g., Cowan 1988, 1992; Graybill 1987; see Chapter 4) have placed the principal occupation of the Madisonville site within the Late Madisonville Horizon and during the mid-seventeenth century.

In order to consider Madisonville's external interactions, its time of occupation *vis-à-vis* contemporaneous sites must be pinpointed as closely as possible. Fine-tuned dating also allows establishment of a regional relative chronological sequence among sites, which can be used to trace socioeconomic change over time. In order to consider socioeconomic change at Madisonville itself, it is highly desirable to identify, to the extent possible, burials and other features dating to earlier and later components. In particular, my efforts were directed toward separating Madisonville Horizon materials (postdating 1400/1450) from those deposited earlier, and in attempting to identify two components within the Madisonville Horizon corresponding to protohistoric and pre-protohistoric periods.

Although I was able to pinpoint some portions of the site that were used exclusively or most intensively during one or another of these periods, there was much overlap. In the end, it did not prove possible to isolate many cemetery areas as belonging exclusively to a single temporal component. However, site occupation history is now apparent in much more detail than heretofore.

Previous Assessments of Madisonville Occupation History

Hooton, Willoughby, and Griffin all considered the question of Madisonville occupation history: What parts of the site were occupied when? Neither radiocarbon analysis nor seriation techniques were available to them, but logic, stratigraphic relationships, and horizon marker artifacts and traits all were brought to bear on the problem.

Without fully discussing his reasoning, Hooton declared the southwest portion of the site to be the earliest, postulating that the inhabited area gradually moved toward the northeast.

> [T]he strongest evidence of a long continued use of the cemetery seems to be afforded by the very large number of burials that have been disturbed in order to make room for later interments. Not only were there found frequent instances in which one body was laid in a grave over some portion of an earlier grave, but even more commonly an old grave was cleared out and its contents deposited in a heap in a corner of the new grave or nearby....Now it seems very improbable that people who buried their dead with the comparatively elaborate funeral furniture which is found in many of the earlier graves in this cemetery, would be likely to desecrate the graves of their ancestors within the time when the identity of the individuals who occupied the various graves could be remembered....Allowing twenty years to a generation it is probable that the fifth generation would have been entered upon before all the members of the first were dead and their burial places forgotten. If this argument is valid, it would then seem that the minimum period which could be considered to have elapsed between the first burials in the cem-

etery and the subsequent ones, to make room for which the former were dislodged, must have been between eighty and one hundred years. [Hooton and Willoughby 1920:26]

[T]he Madisonville cemetery must have been used for a very long time, since a considerable change in burial customs took place within the period of its utilization. Contracted burials and burials in the sitting posture were found only in the oldest portion of the cemetery—the extreme southwestern portion. There are a number of mounds in the vicinity of the cemetery and these almost certainly antedate the necropolis, although it cannot be stated with certainty that the same Indian group was responsible for both forms of burial. In the more recent portion of the cemetery the majority of skeletons were buried unaccompanied by artifacts and there are occasional finds of objects indicating European contact. [Hooton and Willoughby 1920:25-26]

The archaeological evidence as to contact with Europeans, yielded by the burials in the cemetery, seems to indicate that the inhabitants were influenced by white culture to a very slight degree, only at the close of the period during which the site was inhabited. A few glass beads and a few bits of iron and brass in the most recent portion of the cemetery are the only traces of European contact. [Hooton and Willoughby 1920:24]

The pottery finds were more numerous by far in the southwestern portion of the cemetery excavated by Dr. Metz in 1879. In the northwestern [*sic*] portion excavated by the Merwin brothers, pots and artifacts of all kinds were rare. [Hooton and Willoughby 1920:17]

Th[e] group of hut circles to the northeast would probably represent the location of the latest village on the site. The sites of the earlier houses are indicated by the hearths found from time to time by the excavators in the various portions of the cemetery. The original settlement probably was on the southwestern corner of the plateau. The dead were buried about the houses, and as rubbish and graves accumulated, the house sites gradually moved northeastward. [Hooton and Willoughby 1920:27]

In his "Conclusion" to the volume, Willoughby offered an alternative possibility.

The few artifacts found during the investigations of these [house] circles were in general of types corresponding to those of the main village. It is possible, however, that these circles antedate the occupation by the people under consideration, and that the artifacts were the result of the later occupation of the ground. The absence of such circles on the main site, where, as indicated by the cache-pits, most of the cabins stood, would seem to point to this conclusion, but the data relating to the subject are too meager to warrant definite deductions. [Hooton and Willoughby 1920:136-37]

Griffin did not wholly concur with either of them.

The description of the excavated "house circles" in the Madisonville report does not allow a statement of any degree of finality that they belonged to the peoples who left the cultural debris in the refuse pits and with the burials. The distance of the "house circles" from the refuse pits and the absence of similar structures at other Madisonville Focus sites serve to cast doubt upon the likelihood of any direct association. [1943:120]

The mounds near the site seem to belong to an entirely different cultural group than that of the Fort Ancient Aspect....Putnam reported the excavation of a near-by mound which, like that of Giauque, seems to be an Adena mound. [1943:120]

Little weight can be given to the suggestion of chronology in the slight shift from the presence of flexed burials in the southern part of the village to their reported absence in the north. In the southern part, not only were extended burials over and beside flexed burials, but they were also underneath skeletons which had been interred in a contracted position. Furthermore, the same types of artifacts and pottery were with all types of burials. Had it not been for the finding of a small number of European artifacts in the northern section of the component, the division into the earlier and later sections could not have been made....Artifacts were not found as frequently with the burials in the northern part of the burial area as in the southern. [1943:121-22]

Almost all of these conclusions are based on general impressions of quantities and locations of artifacts and burial treatments, rather than on actual mapping or statistical comparisons. For the traits mentioned above, comparative quantitative information is presented only for body position (numbers and percentages of extended, contracted, or "collective or disturbed" burials compared between 1879-1881 and 1897 excavations) and for mortuary vessels (numbers of burials with pots compared among 1879-1881, 1882, 1897, 1907-1908, and 1911 excavations) (Hooton and Willoughby 1920:11, 16). The discussion of where European artifacts were found appears to ignore significant amounts of metal, including iron, excavated from burials and pits in the southern part of the site.

Additional information can be derived from recently developed techniques and more fine-grained comparisons of temporally sensitive traits within different parts of the site. Radiocarbon analysis now offers the opportunity to obtain absolute dates. For the post-Contact period, recently refined absolute and relative chronologies for European artifacts (Figure 3-9) can provide even more finely tuned information than ^{14}C assays. Likewise, we now have available relative chronologies for certain indigenous artifact types (Figure 4-7), burial practices, and building techniques. Although collection and curation problems make it unwise to apply sophisticated statistical analysis to most categories of artifacts and impossible to use ceramic seriation for relative dating of features, it is possible to use Exploratory Data Analysis (EDA) techniques (Tukey 1977), gross spatial patterning (Allen et al. 1990), and certain stratigraphic relationships to better delineate site and intrasite occupation history at Madisonville.

TABLE 6-1
Madisonville Radiocarbon Dates

Provenience	Date No.	Date B.P.	Calibrated Date, A.D., with One-Sigma Range	Two-Sigma Calibrated Range, A.D.	Metal Present in Pit
*Pit (Fea. 10), excv. 1987-88	BETA 45674	290±45	1525 (1645) 1658	1486-1953	
*Pit (Fea. 11), excv. 1987-88	BETA 45675	710±50	1278 (1288) 1376	1222-1393	
*Pit (Fea. 19), excv. 1987-88	BETA 45676	300±60	1495 (1642) 1660	1446-1954	
*Midden, upper level, excv. 1987-88	BETA 51845	170±50	1667 (1680,1742,1750,1759, 1806,1937,1954) 1954	1650-1955	
*Midden, upper level, excv. 1987-88	BETA 51846	310±70	1488 (1638) 1660	1440-1954	
*Midden, low level, exc. 1987-88	BETA 51847	690±50	1282 (1292) 1386	1259-1401	
*Midden, upper level, excv. 1984	UGA 5287	475±95	1406 (1436) 1490	1297-1646	
*Midden, lowest level, excv. 1984	UGA 5285	985±90	987 (1025) 1187	887-1259	
*Pit, excv. 1879	AA-10215	370±45	1448 (1492, 1604, 1610) 1633	1437-1648	
*"Corn pit," excv. 1879	AA-10216-1	965±110	987 (1033, 1143, 1147) 1212	784-1282	
	AA-11774	514±66	1333 (1423) 1442	1302-1490	
Trench 2, Pit 23	AA-10217	315±40	1502 (1534,1539,1637) 1649	1454-1662	X
Trench 4, Pit 6	AA-10218	490±55	1410 (1433) 1444	1329-1491	
Trench B, Pit 27	AA-10221-1	400±55	1439 (1454, 1457, 1478) 1625	1421-1645	X
	AA-10221-2	295±50	1521 (1643) 1658	1454-1953	X
Trench D, Pit 67	AA-10219	485±45	1413 (1434) 1444	1334-1487	
Trench D, Pit 75	AA-10220-1A	400±45	1441 (1454, 1457, 1478) 1620	1429-1639	
	AA-10220-1B	385±40	1445 (1487) 1625	1436-1640	
	AA-10220-1 (weighted avg.)	*392±30*	*1445 (1485) 1619*	*1437-1633*	
	AA-10220-2A	325±50	1490 (1530,1555,1633) 1649	1444-1666	
	AA-10220-2B	265±45	1638 (1651) 1667	1498-1954	
	AA-10220-2 (weighted avg.)	*292±33*	*1529 (1644) 1653*	*1493-1666*	

UGA dates and BETA dates were on charcoal (Tankersley 1981, 1986b; Cowan 1994). AA dates were on corn kernels, using AMS. Dates labelled "-1" and "-2" are on different kernels from the same pit feature; those labelled 1B and 2B are repeat dates from the same kernels that produced dates 1A and 2A. Except for dates AA-10220-1B and AA-10220-2B, which use measured $\delta^{13}C$ values, base age calculations for AA dates assume a value of -10‰ for the $\delta^{13}C$ (Drooker 1993f). Calibration after Stuiver and Reimer (1993), with one-sigma range indicated with each date, and two-sigma range displayed separately.
* From southwestern portion of site.

Radiocarbon Dating

No radiocarbon dates were available for the Madisonville site until the past decade. In association with small-scale excavations carried out in the southwestern corner of the Madisonville site during the 1980s, eight assays were obtained on charcoal samples (Cowan 1995; Tankersley 1986b; Tankersley and Adams 1991). The results, when calibrated (Stuiver and Reimer 1993), had intercepts ranging from the early eleventh century to the mid-seventeenth century and beyond—the entire Fort Ancient chronological span (Table 6-1, BETA and UGA dates).

Some of these dates were on samples from the stratigraphically controlled excavation of a midden, probably part of a refuse-filled ravine partially excavated by the MLSS in 1879 (see Figure 5-2, southernmost "kitchen midden"). The dates, in conjunction with associated pottery, demonstrated the presence of at least two temporally distinct components (Glowacki et al. 1993). Lower layers of the midden contained "sandy" shell-tempered sherds with applied rimstrips and decorated necks typical of Early-Middle Fort Ancient Anderson Shell Tempered jars (cf. Figure 4-8), while upper layers, above a discontinuity, held typical shell-tempered Madisonville Horizon pottery (Figure 4-9). The latter included plain-necked smoothed, cord-marked, grooved-paddled, and net-impressed jars with thin strap handles and often lip notching, plain and cord-marked bowls, and a few sherds from Todd Plain saltpanlike vessels. A late thirteenth-century radiocarbon date from deep in the midden (BETA 51847, Table 6-1) is consistent with Early-Middle Fort Ancient temporal placement. Upper-level dates (BETA 51845, 51846) were sixteenth century and later.

To refine the chronology and extend it into the northern portion of the site, accelerated mass spectrometry (AMS) was used to date carbonized corn kernels excavated from refuse pits in 1879, 1897, 1907, and 1908 (Drooker 1993f). Twelve dates were obtained on ten corn kernels from seven different pits (Table 6-1, AA dates). Table 6-2 describes the pits, their fill, and mate-

TABLE 6-2
Provenience Information for Radiocarbon-Dated Corn Samples

Catalog Number of Corn Sample(s)	Intrasite Provenience	Associated Materials
79-74-10/19957 (2)	**Deep pit within Block 1.**	?
84-68-10/35900	**"Corn pit" within Block 1.** [a] Approx. 4-5' deep within 6' pit. Layers of remains and artifacts capped by 3'3" sterile soil.	Layers, from bottom: 10" ear corn; several bushels carbonized shelled corn; 4" bark, twigs, and matting; 1" animal remains, sherds, shells.
01-38-10/68811	**Trench 2, Pit 23.** In 2" layer of corn 4' from top of 4'8" pit, surrounded by ashes.	Animal bones(100+), corn, charcoal, flint flakes/rejects (40+), bone tools, sherds (50+), perf. tooth, small pc. copper. Most artifacts within or below corn layer. **Extant artifacts**: parts of 2 bear mandibles, sherd (horizontally-compound bowl, smooth surf., notched rim), perf. dog? canine, rasp frag, awl, fishhook in proc., copper/copper alloy scrap (.6 x. 65 cm).
01-38-10/69268	**Trench 4, Pit 6.** Within bottom third of 6'8" deep pit. Above layer of limestone blocks & below mixture of black soil and hard pan.	Animal bones (4), bone awl, perf. bone, sherds, flint flakes (25+). Corn and charcoal scattered within 3' layer of black soil. **Extant artifacts**: 2 flint endscrapers in proc., sherd (cordmarked jar, smooth neck, notched rim, convergent strap handle).
07-6-10/78093 (2)	**Trench B, Pit 27.** 6' deep pit.	Animal bones (350+), shells (100+), corn kernels (500+) & cobs, pawpaw seeds, sherds (16), flint flakes (75+), stone & bone tools, 3 pcs copper. [b] Mixed earth, ashes, and charcoal throughout pit. **Extant artifacts**: 3 frags bone beamers, matting needle frag, 1 flint sidescraper, 3 flint rejects, 1 reworked stemmed point.
08-3-10/71733	**Trench D, Pit 67.** In bottom of 3'8" pit, from two 1" layers separated by "mixed units."	Sherd, antler frgs, burnt animal bone, pitted stone. The 1" layers consisted of charred corn, nuts, wood, leaves, bones. **Extant artifacts**: sherd (smooth jar, notched rim, convergent strap handle), antler scraper frg, worked antler frag.
08-3-10/71802 (2)	**Trench D, Pit 75.** From 1 or more of 3 mixed layers alternating with ash in a 5'6" deep pit.	Charred corn, cobs, bean frgs, 8 sherds, bone "bead," worked pc. cannel coal, 2 sharpening stones, dog? skull. **Extant artifacts**: Sherd (cordmarked jar, smooth neck, conv. strap handle, notched rim), polished, fire-marked antler tube (7 cm. L), pc. coal.

Information on associated materials is from field notes and catalog, plus personal observation of the few extant artifacts. All extant sherds are shell tempered.

[a] See Low (1880:66-67) for description and generalized cross section of pit.

[b] Copper not mentioned in field notes, but included in Peabody Museum accession list for this pit. It is no longer in inventory at the Museum.

rials and artifacts recorded from each. Unfortunately, there were no kernels available from the northernmost and easternmost portions of the site, but proveniences were chosen to secure the greatest possible spatial spread. Figure 6-1 indicates the locations of the five pits that can be mapped, plus the general area from which the charcoal samples and the other corn samples came.

Figure 6-2 displays the calibrated dates in graphical form. Looking at calibration intercepts and one-sigma ranges (which have a 68% probability of containing the actual date of demise of the assayed sample), several distinct clusters can be observed. They are centered on the eleventh century, the late thirteenth century, and the fifteenth to mid-seventeenth centuries.

The two oldest dates hardly overlap at all with other dates from the site. They could represent a separate, very early occupation, or could be interpreted as anomalously early, and discarded. The presence at the site of at least some Late Woodland pottery (Griffin 1943:142-43) plus notched, stemmed, and flared-base triangular (type 2) points (Hooton and Willoughby 1920: Pl. 7; Litfin et al. 1993; cf. Railey 1992 and Figure 4-15) corroborate the possibility of a Late Woodland–Early Fort Ancient component.

The most recent date, which spans three centuries up to modern times, is another good candidate for discard as an outlier. The remainder of the dates are redundant enough that they probably can be accepted as "real." The two from the late thirteenth century have calibration intercepts separated by 130 years from the next-younger dates, and overlap with only one younger date at the one-sigma level. They probably represent a separate, pre-Madisonville Horizon temporal component.

Seven dates have calibration intercepts within the fifteenth century. Four of them have one-sigma ranges contained within the fourteenth-fifteenth centuries. They might constitute a separate cluster from the nine dates with one-sigma ranges that extend across the sixteenth century. Omitting the outlier BETA 17845, seven dates have seventeenth-century intercepts, from 1604 to 1645; all have one-sigma ranges extending far back into the sixteenth century. It seems likely that the primary occupation of the Madisonville site extended from the early-middle

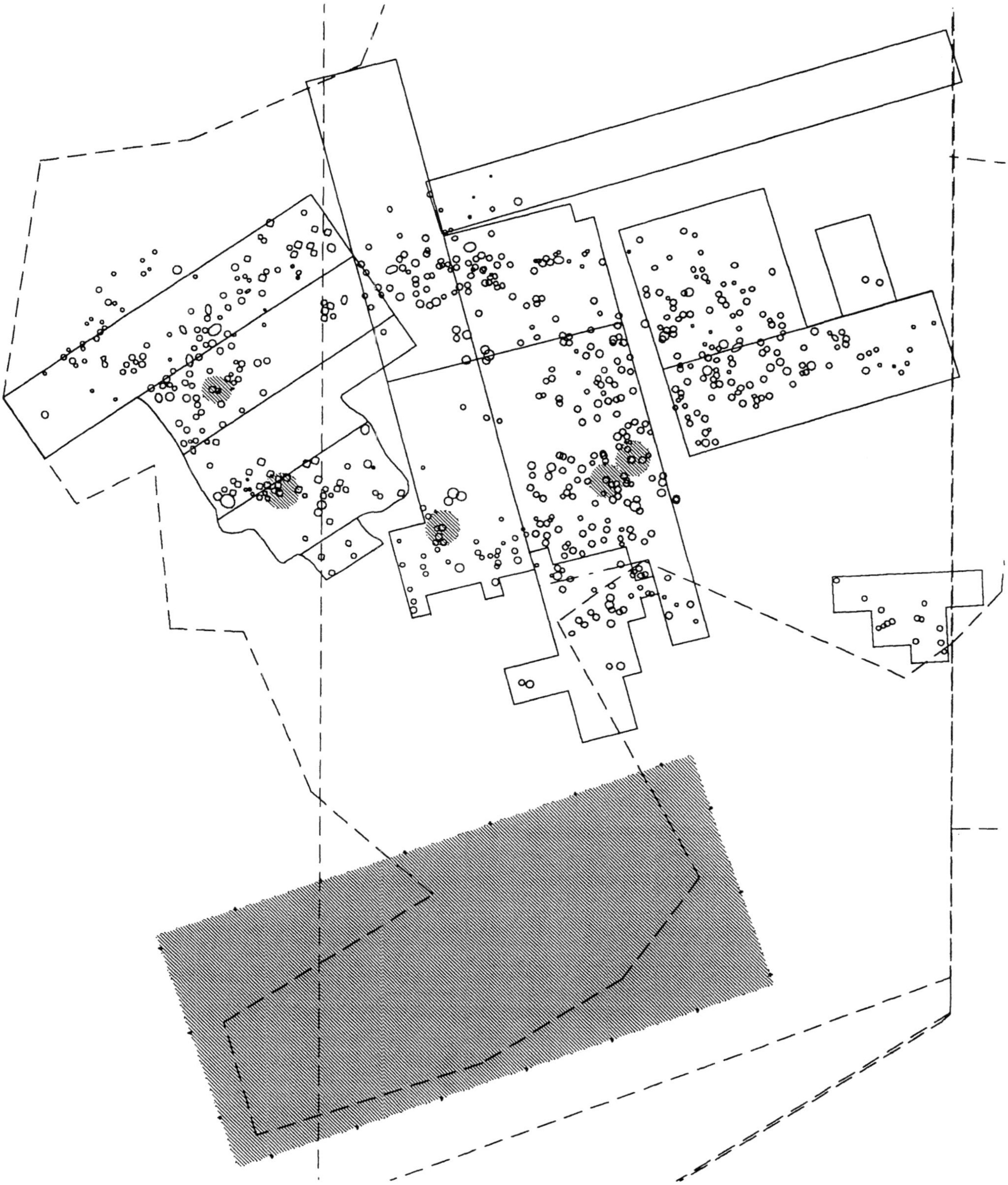

Figure 6-1. Locations of radiocarbon dated features at the Madisonville site. Pits (left to right) are 2-23, 4-6, B-27, D-67, and D-75. All other dated features were within the large shaded area. See Table 6-1 for dates.

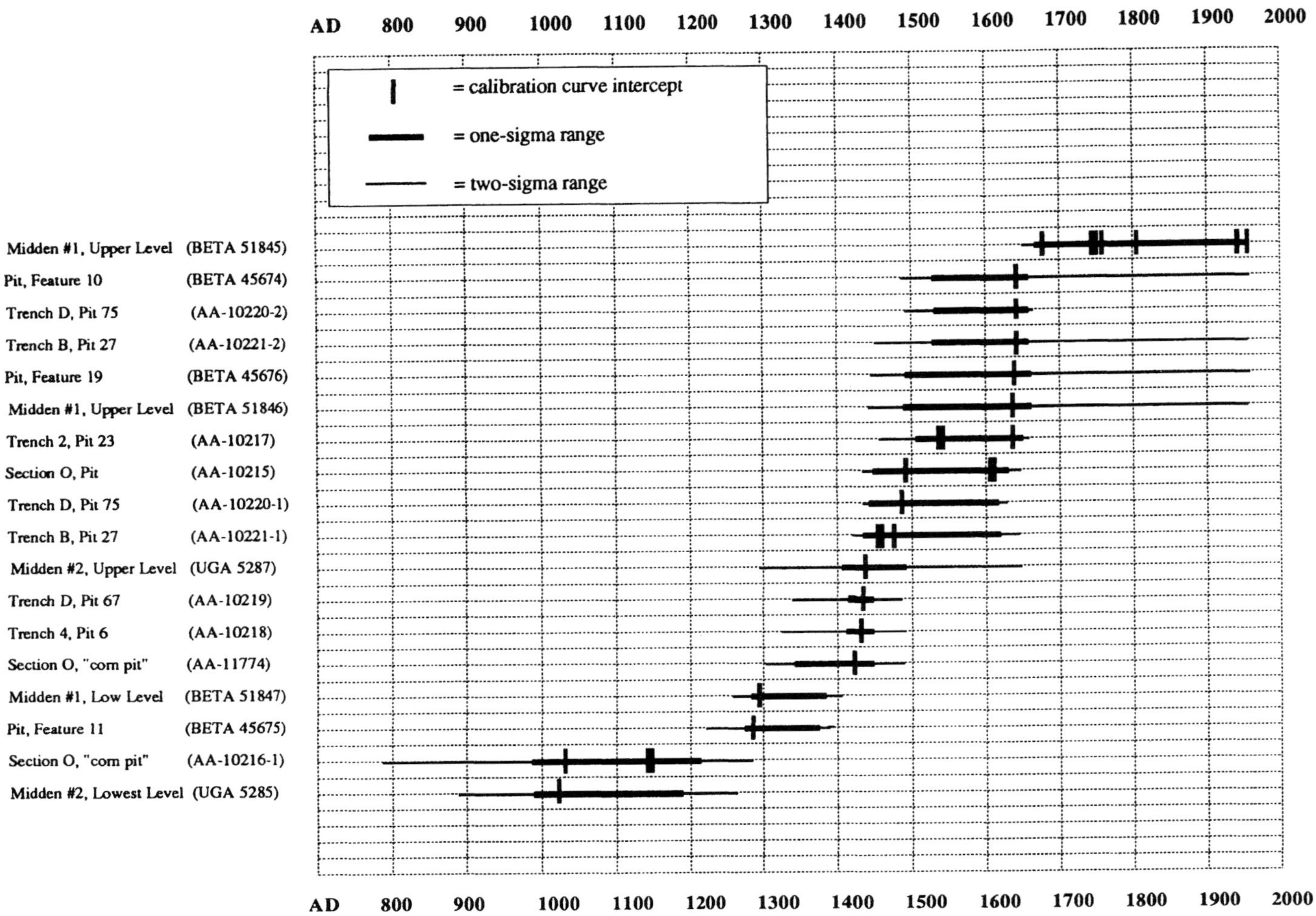

Figure 6-2. Graphical representation of Madisonville radiocarbon dates, earliest to latest.

fifteenth century to the early-middle seventeenth. The dearth of sixteenth-century calibration intercepts does not correspond to any wholesale abandonment of the site, since there is no dearth of sixteenth-century artifacts, including a variety of European-derived items (Table 6-7, below). However, it is possible that there were periods of less intense site usage during this time.

It is important to note that the dates presented in this publication were calibrated using the most recent calibration curve published by the Quaternary Research Center, University of Washington (Stuiver and Reimer 1993). The previous curve (Stuiver and Reimer 1986, 1987), which I had used for all presentations and publications prior to my dissertation (Drooker 1996c), gave somewhat different results, including four dates with sixteenth-century intercepts and a late fifteenth century "light spot" containing only one intercept. Almost all published Late Fort Ancient dates (e.g., Sharp 1990), if calibrated at all, utilized the earlier curve.

Dates from different time periods do not cluster neatly in different parts of the site—far from it. In fact, for the three cases in which two corn kernels from a particular pit, rather than just one, were analyzed, calibration intercepts for the pairs of kernels were one to four centuries apart (Figure 6-3). To double-check these results, both of the kernels from Pit D-75 were analyzed a second time, confirming that a real difference did exist between them (Table 6-1). It must be remembered that although pits generally were quickly filled with refuse after their usefulness as food storage receptacles was over, they were not sealed environments. Corn kernels can be in a pit due to primary deposition as a stored food substance, secondary deposition from an earlier midden stratum through which the pit was dug, or secondary deposition from refuse swept into a pit after it had ceased to serve its storage function.

The five earliest dates all come from the southwestern portion of the site, three from pits and two from middens (Figure 6-3). However, the two most recent dates come from this part of the site as well, as do other dates spanning much of the time period between. One of several possible scenarios is that the southwestern portion of the site was occupied first, then contin-

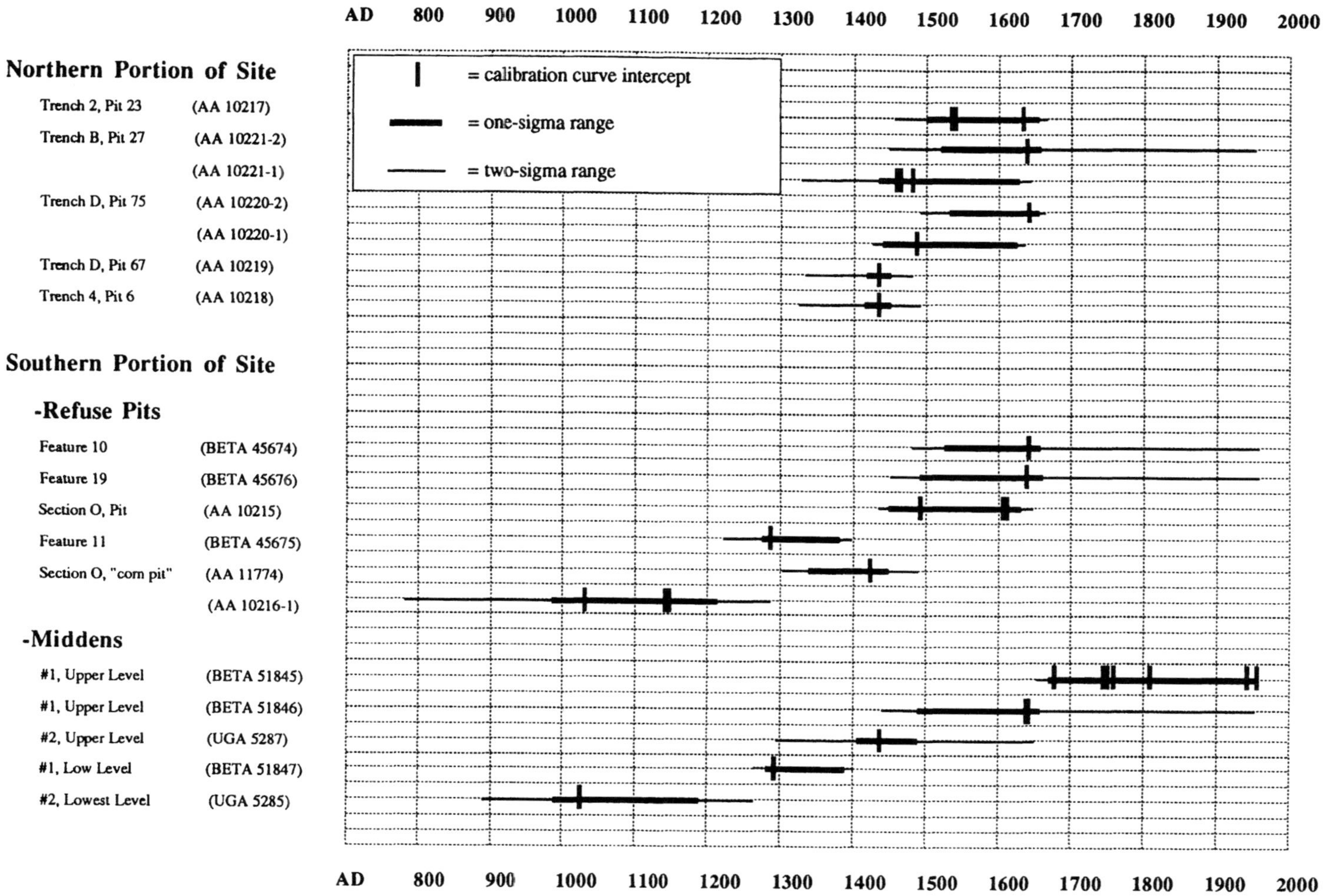

Figure 6-3. Graphical representation of Madisonville radiocarbon dates, by provenience.

ued to be used while the settlement expanded northward over time. Different occupation densities in the northern versus the southern portion of the site (Figures 5-14, 5-15) are consistent with this picture, although, as discussed below, Woodland, Early-Middle Fort Ancient, and Late Fort Ancient artifacts have come from the northern as well as the southern sectors.

Dated refuse pits in the northern portion of the site form a semicircle around the southern half of the plaza area (Figure 6-1). They span the fifteenth to seventeenth centuries, with no obvious spatial clustering of earlier versus later dates. The two dated pits from which scraps of metal were recovered, 2-23 and B-27, both have sixteenth-seventeenth century radiocarbon dates; the latter, in addition, has yielded a fifteenth-century date. The dates and relative positions of the five pits in Trenches 2, 4, B, and D are consistent with a continuous or discontinuous occupation of this part of the site from the early 1400s to the mid-1600s. The few extant horizon marker artifacts from these pits (Table 6-2) are typical of the late Madisonville Horizon (pieces of copper or copper alloy, Madisonville series pottery, rasp fragment), but they represent only a small proportion of artifacts originally present. Radiocarbon dates and extant artifacts from these pits provide no strong evidence for a pre-1400 occupation of this part of the site, but neither do they rule one out.

Structures

As discussed in Chapter 5, three types of house features have been recorded at the Madisonville site: a rectangular wall trench structure in Trench H (Figures 5-9, 5-12, 5-17), eight to twelve circular semi-subterranean structures on high ground to the northeast (Figure 5-2), and probably-rectangular pole-framed structures of undefined size at several locations in the northern portion of the site (Figure 5-12). Each probably dates to a different time period. Pre-1897 excavators recorded no postholes or trenches, so nothing can be said about house features in the southwestern portion of the site.

Rectangular wall-trench structures have been identified at the southwestern Ohio State Line and Turpin 3 sites (Table 4-5),

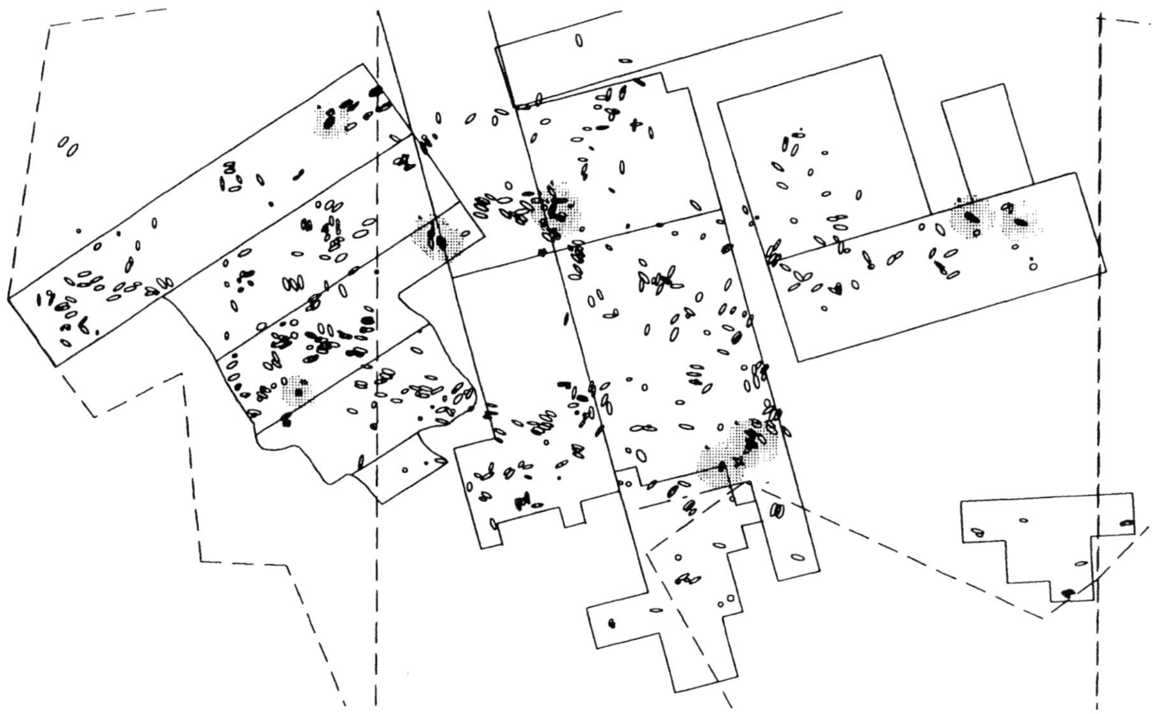

Figure 6-4. Burials associated with limestone slabs, Trenches 1-K.

and are considered diagnostic of the Early Fort Ancient Turpin phase (Cowan 1986:138; Vickery and Genheimer 1994; Wheelersburg 1992:54-55), before 1300 (Drooker 1996a). One wall-trench structure also has been excavated at the Middle Fort Ancient Schomaker site, but in this case it was semi-subterranean, lying within a 6 × 7.5 meter basin (Cowan et al. 1990:14).

The Madisonville wall trench structure, at about 5 × 5.5 meters (27.5 m²), is in the same size range as the Turpin example (cf. Table 4-5). Unfortunately, none of the burials associated with it (Figure 5-17) had grave goods, and artifacts from most of the surrounding pits were not retained by the excavator (Tables 5-5, 5-7), so not much can be learned from it that can be extrapolated to other parts of the site.

Semi-subterranean structures have not been reported from Late Fort Ancient contexts, only earlier ones. Rectangular semi-subterranean structures have been excavated not only at Schomaker but also at the thirteenth-century Horseshoe Johnson site (Figure 4-2, Table 4-1) and the Early and Middle Fort Ancient Roseberry Farm and Blennerhasset Village sites in West Virginia (Graybill 1981). Graybill argues for their widespread occurrence in the Fort Ancient region prior to around 1450 (1981:143-54). Circular semi-subterranean structures are less widely known within Fort Ancient territory. They have been reported only from very early and poorly described excavations at the upper Little Miami Valley Anderson Village and South Fort sites (Figure 4-2), both of which have thirteenth-century components (Table 4-1) (Essenpreis 1982:73-76; Harper 1994). Essenpreis interpreted those from South Fort as contemporaneous with or postdating Anderson phase materials, because they were said to have overlain deposits containing what was probably Anderson phase pottery. She believed that they could have been the house type associated with Anderson Village, but from the sketchy reports of previous investigators there she could not establish their spatial relationship relative to the other features (burials and refuse pits) actually mapped at the site.

At Madisonville, the dozen or so extant sherds of pottery from the house circles also point to an Early-Middle Fort Ancient occupation. There are decorated necks, including guilloche motifs, and a decorated rimstrip. Most, but not all, are shell tempered. Some of the shell-tempered sherds, like those from the lower levels of the midden in the southwestern portion of the site, have a sandy texture.

Rectangular structures defined by postholes alone constitute the only house type reported from Late Fort Ancient sites (Table 4-11). In the southwestern Fort Ancient region, such structures also have been excavated at Early-Middle Fort Ancient sites, including Turpin 1 and Incinerator (Lambert et al. 1988; Oehler 1973: Photo 5), but none are as large as the largest Late Fort Ancient examples (Tables 4-5, 4-11).

As discussed in Chapter 5, the diameters and depths of recorded postholes at Madisonville imply relatively large structures, some of them perhaps approaching the average at Buffalo. However, evidence is far too sparse to specify any size range with certainty. It does seem likely that this was the house type used during the Late Fort Ancient occupation of the site, but the possibility that it also was used earlier cannot be eliminated.

Burial Practices

At least three minority burial practices are probably from different time periods than are most of the interments at the site. The majority of the burials, approximately 70%, were placed in graves unlined or lined with perishable material such as bark or mats, extended on their backs. The few reported mound burials and stone-lined graves, and many of the flexed burials, probably predated most of the extended burials.

As Griffin observed (see above), it is likely that most of the mounds strung out along the bluff east of the Ancient Cemetery were built before Fort Ancient times. However, Fahrenkamps Mound, excavated in 1911 (Merwin 1911), might date to Early Fort Ancient. None of the twelve burials are known to have been subadults (three were fragmentery, with age not reported). Three of the burials were accompanied by large flint points; one of them also had worked cannel coal placed along his/her right side. One of these points survives (see below, Figure 6-17a). It is a triangular knife, considered typical of Early Fort Ancient.

Burials associated with stone slabs occur with high frequency at Early-Middle Fort Ancient sites in southwestern Ohio and nearby northern Kentucky, including Incinerator, Anderson, and Fox Farm (Tables 4-6, 4-12), but are far less common at Late Fort Ancient sites (e.g., Buffalo and Hardin, Table 4-12). At Madisonville, only 17 burials were reported to have been associated with stone slabs, 2% of those included in the burial sample. Twelve came from the Harvard-excavated portion of the site (Figure 6-4), and one each from Blocks 3, 11, 12, and 14 in the southwestern portion of the site. Just one burial, in Block M, was within a completely lined oblong "box." The others generally had been laid on stones or were partially or completely covered by them. A few graves had partial side linings of stone. One burial, not included in the above total, was found below a layer of stones in a refuse pit. The strongest cluster of clearly associated individuals that had stone slabs were the three at the northeastern end of Trench 3, an infant laid on slabs and two adults buried side by side with slabs both over and under them. The fact that they intrude upon the open plaza area might mean that they predate it, as might the fourth burial clustered with them, which lacked grave goods.

At some early Fort Ancient sites, such as Feurt, and in some neighboring territories that were occupied during periods equivalent to Early-Middle Fort Ancient, such as the Oliver phase in Indiana, there are very high proportions of flexed burials (Table 4-12; Dorwin 1971). As can be seen in Table 4-6, although flexed burials do decrease over time in southwestern Ohio, there does not seem to be a clear dichotomy between early and late sites with respect to this burial practice. Many sites of all time periods have 10-15% flexed or semi-flexed burials. Within this region, flexed burials might be most strongly associated with Late Woodland. For example, Oehler contrasted the primarily extended postures of burials he excavated from Early Fort Ancient mound and village locations at Turpin 1 with the primarily flexed postures he found in a Late Woodland stone mound at the same site (1973:52). At State Line, an Early Fort Ancient village overlying a small Late Woodland component, flexed, semi-flexed, and sitting burials are reported in addition to the extended postures of the majority of burials from both mound and non-mound contexts (Vickery and Genheimer 1994; Wheelersburg 1992).

About 7% of Madisonville burials were described as "contracted," "doubled up," or "sitting" (Drooker 1996c: Appendix B; see also Drooker, in press). The vast majority of these were located in Block 1 (Table 6-3), concentrated, in fact, within the first 150 burials excavated. Fourteen percent of the entire excavation block and 26% of the first 125 burials excavated were described with words equivalent to "flexed." Another concentration occurred in Block 16 (6 of 22).

Almost one half of the semi-flexed and flexed burials (mostly semi-flexed) scattered across the northern part of the site can be accounted for by the fact that they were disposed in or immediately above refuse pits (Figure 6-5), but this is not evident for the non-extended burials in Block 1. Both percentages and densities of flexed/semi-flexed burials are much lower in Trenches 1-K than Blocks 1-17 (4.1% versus 8.9% and .03 versus .18 per 100 ft^2), with the largest number (and highest frequency and density) in Trench F. None had grave goods, but one was associated with a Madisonville-style pot handle. The best candidates for early flexed burials in Trenches 1-K include those not associated with pits, at relatively deep levels, well into the hardpan layer, in deteriorated condition, and/or cut by other features. Only nine burials fit these specifications: Burials 2-26, 3-6, B-5, D-76, D-101, F-13, F-28, F-29, and H-14 (for their locations, see Figure 5-13). In addition to burials classified as flexed, two extended, prone individuals with slightly flexed legs (Burials H-15 and H-40) were close to or associated with the wall trench house feature (Figures 5-17, 5-13). Burial H-40 crosscut one of the house trenches, so postdates it.

It seems likely that the concentration of burials described as "contracted" or "sitting" in Block 1, only one of which had any grave goods, dates to Late Woodland or very early Fort Ancient times. Unfortunately, excavation notes for this part of the Ancient Cemetery are sparse and confusing (see Low 1880). Often all burials excavated in a day or even a whole week were simply listed and briefly described, without any information as to order of excavation, relative positions, or depths. Thus, the stratigraphic relationships between flexed and extended burials here are unknown. In other excavation blocks, more information is available. For example, five of the "doubled up" burials in Block 16 were associated with two extended burials in a pattern typical of Late Fort Ancient multiple burials elsewhere on the site (see Chapter 7).

Fort Ancient burials with grave goods generally increase in

TABLE 6-3
Frequencies of Selected Time-Sensitive Characteristics of Burials at Madisonville

		Total Number of Burials	Number of Flexed	Number with Grave Goods	Number with Pots	Number with Metal or Glass	Minimum Number with European Goods
Block	1	339	47	145	131	3	1
	2	32	3	7	7	0	0
	3	24	1	8	8	0	0
	4	34	0	12	11	0	0
	5	10	0	3	3	0	0
	6	55	1	31	26	1	0
	7	10	0	3	3	1	1
	8	14	0	6	5	0	0
	9	17	3	9	8	2	0
	10	12	1	1	0	0	0
	11	31	1	9	6	1	0
	12	22	3	8	7	1	1
	13	3	0	1	1	0	0
	14	13	1	6	5	0	0
	15	20	0	8	5	1	0
	16	22	6	3	2	0	0
	17	23	0	14	14	0	0
	22	8	1	1	1	0	0
	L	9	1	1	1	0	0
	M	36	2	7	3	0	0
Conover (SW sector)		16	0	10	8	0	0
Trench	1	67	1	28	15	4	3
	2	56	2	22	17	1	0
	3	71	2	29	19	2	0
	4	42	1	24	21	2	1
	5	3	0	0	0	0	0
	A	4	0	0	0	0	0
	B	61	4	37	27	2	0
	C	23	0	10	5	1	0
	D	104	3	42	30	4	0
	E	40	2	10	7	0	0
	F	37	4	9	6	2	0
	G	3	0	0	0	0	0
	H	43	4	4	3	1	0
	I	26	1	10	3	4	1
	J	0	0	0	0	0	0
	K	12	0	4	2	0	0
Blocks 1-17		681	64	274	242	10	3
Trenches 1-K		591	24	229	155	23	5
All non Trench 1-K		800	72	319	269	15	7

The 56 or more burials excavated in 1895 are not included, because of incomplete data. "European goods" include European-made items, materials definitely identified as iron, brass, copper alloy, or glass, and artifacts fashioned from thin metal tubes that may or may not be of European metal but that date to ca. 1550 and later. "Metal" excludes evidence from green-stained bone.

frequency over time, although not so sharply in southwestern Ohio as in eastern Fort Ancient territory (Tables 4-7, 4-13). Although it is impossible to assign a time period to a particular burial based on lack of grave goods alone, it is possible that a spatially coherent group of burials with no grave goods might date to an earlier period than a similar group with a high frequency of grave goods. Comparison of Figures 6-6 and 6-7 with Figures 6-8 and 6-9 gives some idea of the possibilities. Burials with and without grave goods occur together over much of the site, but the latter do predominate (for instance) in the north-central and northeastern portion of Trenches 1-K. Of course, numbers and types of grave goods also vary in connection with social status (see Chapter 7), so this trait cannot be used by itself as a temporal indicator.

The percentage of burials with grave goods over the entire site (39.7% for all excavations except 1895) is on a par with

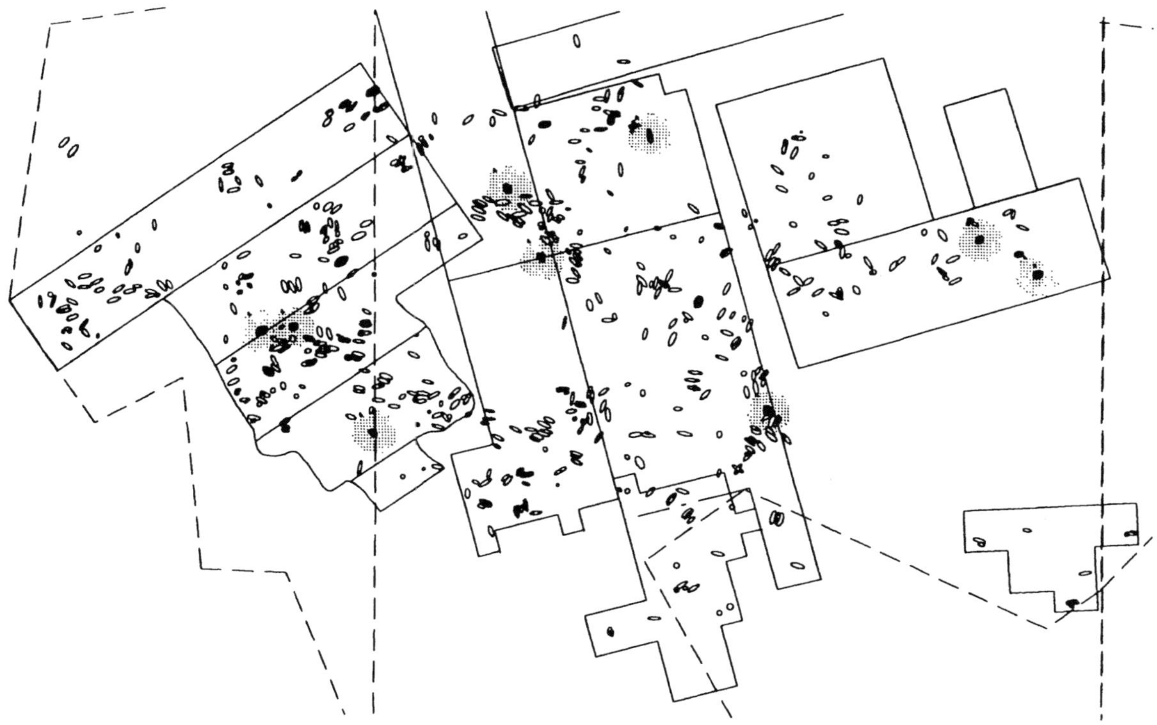

Figure 6-5. Distribution of flexed and semi-flexed burials, Trenches 1-K. Those in or over pits are highlighted.

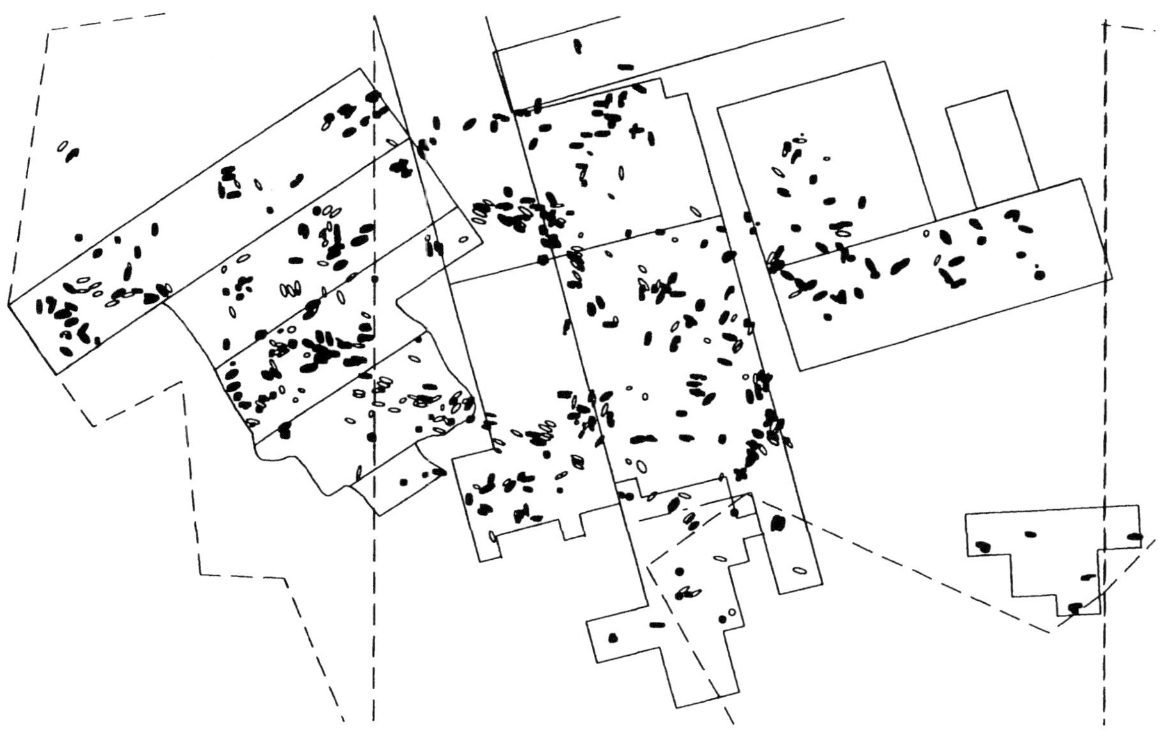

Figure 6-6. Distribution of burials with no grave goods, Trenches 1-K.

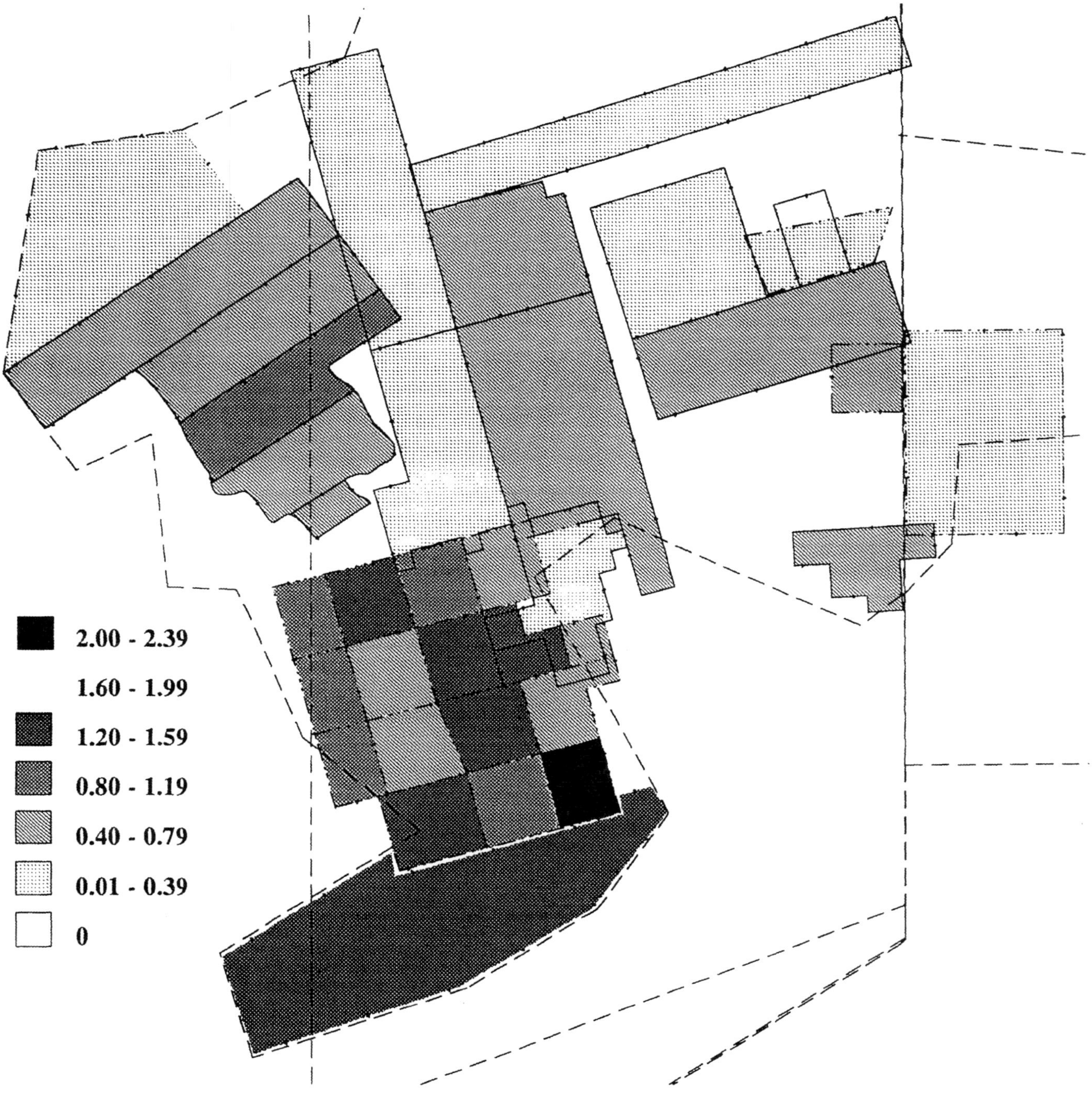

Figure 6-7. Densities of burials with no grave goods (per 100 ft^2), by excavation trench or block. Keep in mind that in larger trenches, burials were not necessarily located in all portions of the trench, and this undoubtedly holds true for Blocks 1-17 as well.

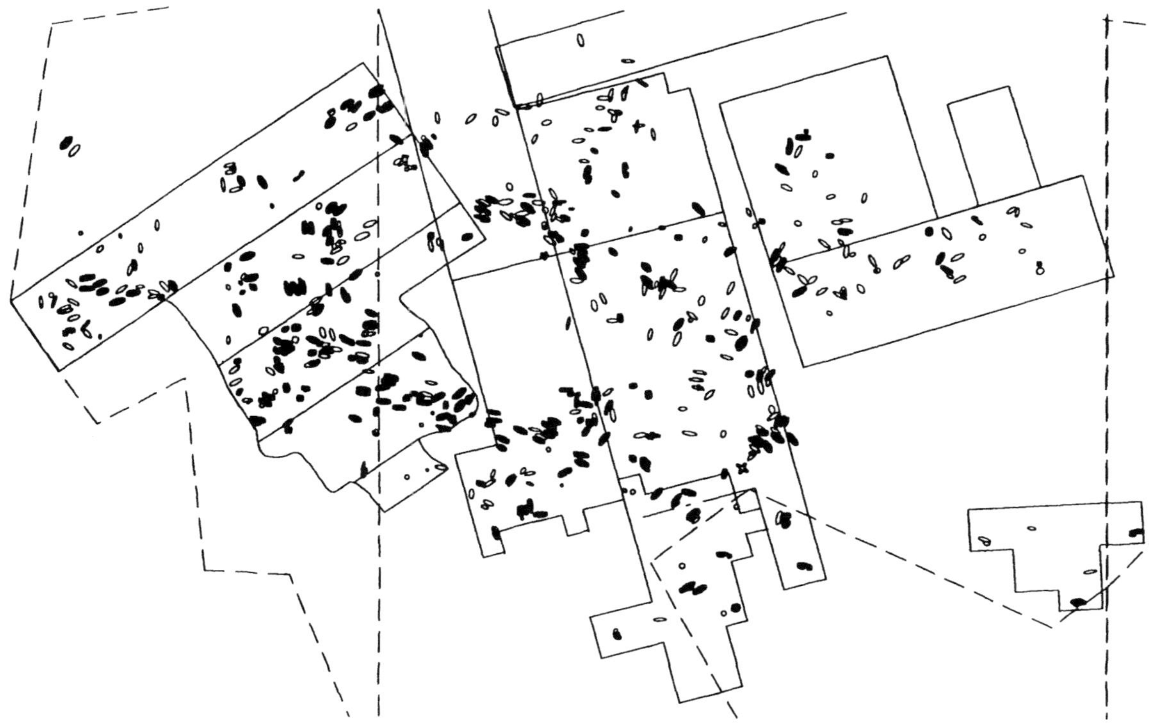

Figure 6-8. Distribution of burials with grave goods, Trenches 1-K.

other western Late Fort Ancient settlements including Campbell Island and Hahn's Field (Table 4-7). Percentages of burials with grave goods are very similar in southern versus northern portions of the site (Table 6-4). In Trenches 1-K, burials with grave goods cluster around the plaza and at the extreme ends of Trench 1 (Figure 6-8). In the southwestern portion of the site, there are particularly high concentrations of burials with grave goods in Blocks 1, 6, 9, and 17 (Figure 6-9).

The use of mortuary vessels by western Fort Ancient people apparently increased over time (Table 4-7). Certainly, the vast majority of mortuary vessels at Madisonville were classic Madisonville Horizon types (Figure 4-9), although earlier pottery types were represented in pits and midden (Table 6-5, Figure 6-34). The total frequency of burials with ceramic vessels at Madisonville (33.7% for all excavations except 1895) is exceeded at Fort Ancient sites only by that of the small sample from Hahn's Field (Tables 4-7, 4-13). Very few burials in Trenches G, H, and I and the northern portions of E and F were accompanied by pots or bowls (Figure 6-10). The very low frequency (7%) of burials with mortuary vessels in Trench H, where the wall-trench structure was located, is particularly notable. There was a statistically significant difference in frequency of burials with mortuary vessels between Blocks 1-17, where 34% of burials had them, and Trenches 1-K, where 26% did (chi square test, 1 df, $p = 0.01$). Densities of burials containing vessels also were higher in Blocks 1-17 than in Trenches 1-K (Figure 6-11), but so were densities of burials without vessels (Figure 6-12). The highest densities of both burials with grave goods and burials with mortuary vessels were in Blocks 1, 6, 9, and 17. To give perspective, the highest density of Trench 1-K burials accompanied by grave goods within a 40-foot square (similar in size to Blocks 2-17) occurred in the middle of Trench 3 (Figure 6-8). The density was .875, in the same range as Block 9 and the very large Block 1, but lower than Blocks 6 and 17. However, the density of burials with mortuary vessels in that area of Trench 3, 0.69 per 100 square feet (Figure 6-10), was exceeded by all four of the southerly blocks.

Since nonpottery grave goods were fairly frequent with western Fort Ancient interments even in Early-Middle Fort Ancient times, yet mortuary vessels were primarily a Late Fort Ancient phenomenon (Table 4-7), contrasting the locations of burials with nonpottery grave goods (some with pots as well) (Figures 6-13, 6-14) with burials containing only ceramic vessels (Figures 6-15, 6-16) gives a more focused view of where ordinary Late Fort Ancient burials were concentrated. In Trenches 1-K, this was clearly around the plaza, with a second, more distant arc running along Trench 1 then (sparsely) across Trenches F, I, and H. In Blocks 1-17, the highest concentrations appear to have been generally near the periphery of the bluff, plus Block 6. Burials with nonpottery grave goods were broadly dispersed in Trenches 1-K (Figure 6-13), but notably sparse along the northern periphery of the plaza, in spite of the fact that mortuary vessels were relatively common there (Figures 6-10 and 6-15).

Frequencies of burials with metal and identifiable European

Figure 6-9. Densities of burials with grave goods (per 100 ft^2), by excavation trench or block. Keep in mind that in larger trenches, burials were not necessarily located in all portions of the trench, and this undoubtedly holds true for Blocks 1-17 as well.

TABLE 6-4
Comparisons of Selected Time-Sensitive Characteristics
between Southern (Blocks 1-17) and Northern (Trenches 1-K) Portions of Site

	NUMBER		PERCENTAGE [a]		DENSITY [b]	
	South	North	South	North	South	North
BURIAL DATA						
Flexed burials	**64**	**24**	9.4%	4.1%	0.18	0.03
Burials with grave goods	274	229	40.2%	39.2%	0.77	0.30
Burials with pots/bowls	**242**	**155**	35.5%	26.5%	0.68	0.21
Burials with metal/glass	**10**	**23**	1.5%	3.9%	0.03	0.03
Burials with European items/materials (min.) [c]	3 [d]	5	0.4% [d]	0.9%	0.008 [d]	0.007
Number of metal/glass items in burials (min.)	107	103			0.30	0.14
PIT DATA						
Pits with metal/glass	**50**	**48**	11.0%	7.4%	0.14	0.06
Pits with European items/materials (min.) [c]	0 [d]	22	0.0% [d]	3.8%	0.00 [d]	0.03
Number of metal/glass items in pits (min.)	74	99			0.21	0.13
DATA FOR ALL FEATURES						
Features with metal/glass	60	71	5.3%	5.8%	0.17	0.09
Features with European items/materials (min.) [c]	3 [d]	27	0.3% [d]	2.2%	0.008 [d]	0.04
Number of metal/glass items in features (min.)	181	201			0.51	0.27
BASIC DATA						
Area excavated (100 ft^2)	358 (approx.)	754				
Total number of burials	681	584				
Total number of pits	455	649				
Total number of features	1136	1233				

Trenches A, G, and J, which had few features, are omitted. **Boldface** indicates statistically-significant differences at the 0.05 level or better.

[a] Percentage of all such features in sector.

[b] Number per 100ft^2.

[c] European items/materials include items and materials definitely identified as brass, iron, glass, copper alloy, or European copper, plus artifacts made from thin metal tubes, which may or may not use European metal but date after ca. 1550.

[d] Most of the metal artifacts from Blocks 1-17 could not be evaluated.

goods also are time-related, the former increasing over time at Fort Ancient sites (Tables 4-7, 4-13), and the latter, of course, being a significant marker for protohistoric sites. The distributions of these items at Madisonville will be discussed below.

Horizon Marker Artifacts

Horizon marker artifacts at Madisonville include both locally made and exotic items. They can be used both for relative and absolute dating of the site as a whole, and to aid in identifying intrasite temporal components.

Hampering any attempt to use sophisticated statistical techniques in this effort are significant problems in excavation and curation practices, discussed in Chapter 5. Field note reports of certain important types of grave goods—pots, pipes, and metal—seem to be reasonably complete for much of the site (in terms of numbers but not usually in terms of attributes or styles). Pipes and metal in pits also were closely noted after about the middle of Block 1. Excavated artifacts from pre-1897 work at the site were only haphazardly retained in museum collections. Few curated items from this time period definitely can be tied to specific burials, and even fewer to specific pits. From 1897 onward, most existing artifacts can be tied to numbered burials, numbered pits, or what was called "general digging" within a particular excavation trench. However, many bulky items (particularly ceramic sherds and animal remains) and common artifacts (including sherds and bone and stone tools) were either left in the field or later deaccessioned (discarded or exchanged for artifacts from other sites). There is no consistent record of numbers excavated versus numbers now extant for artifact types, let alone for temporally sensitive artifact styles. Absence from records or collections does not necessarily mean that a particu-

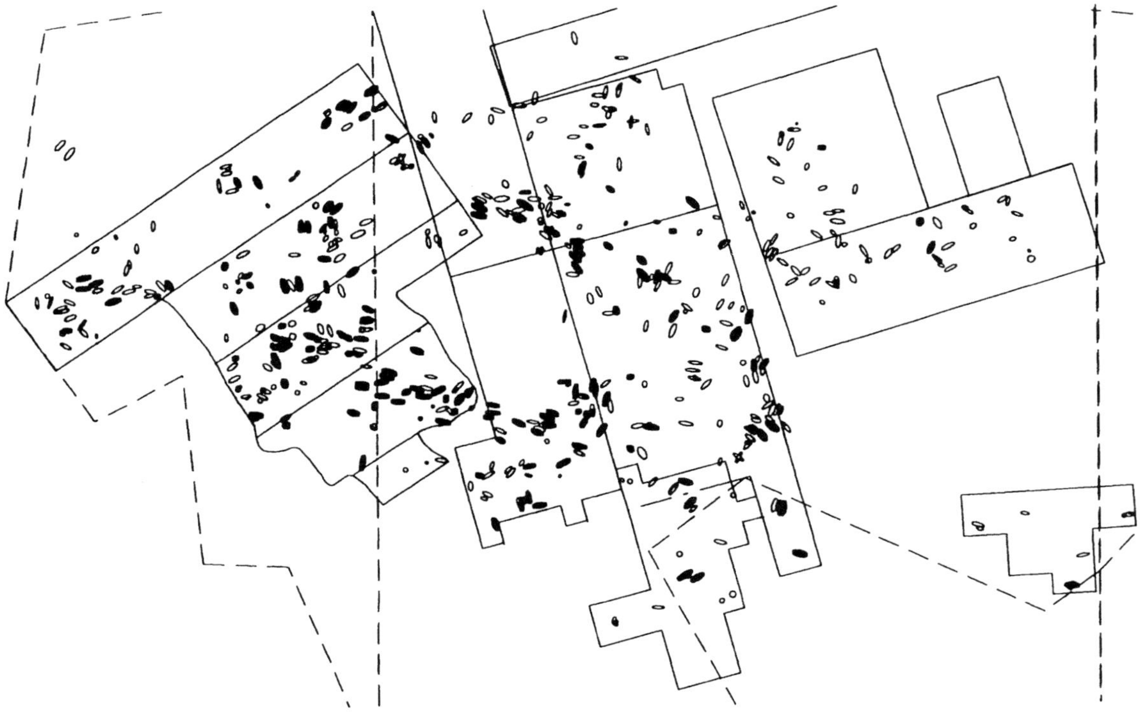

Figure 6-10. Burials accompanied by mortuary vessels, Trenches 1-K. Information from field notes.

lar item never was present. Considering all of these problems, analyses utilizing Madisonville horizon marker artifacts lean heavily on simple EDA techniques (including graphics, basic statistics, and simple measures of correlation) combined with GIS-assisted spatial patterning analysis.

Indigenous Artifact Assemblages

Only a few of the indigenous horizon marker artifacts highlighted in Figure 4-7 are not present at Madisonville, corroborating the fact that it is a multicomponent site. For very rough comparisons, Table 6-5 lists numbers of time-sensitive artifact types and attributes that I counted in extant HUPM collections from Trenches 1-K. Most of the numbers probably reflect the general proportions of artifact types and styles excavated. However, the ceramic sherds, which were heavily culled (Tables 5-5, 5-7), probably are unduly weighted toward examples with decorated necks (in addition to Figure 4-8, see Griffin 1943: Pls. LXXI, LXXV, and drawings of vessels reconstructed from sherds in Hooton and Willoughby 1920: Pl. 24c-f, i). Sherds with incised and punctated neck decoration certainly were present at the site in great numbers—there are collections from pre-1897 excavations in all the museums that I visited—but their numbers probably originally were far outweighed by less visually exciting Madisonville Horizon styles. The majority of the whole vessels, which were retained in much higher proportions than sherds, are classic Madisonville Plain and Cordmarked jars (Figure 4-9), most of them from mortuary contexts. There are no whole Anderson-style jars in any collection that I viewed, although many Anderson-type sherds were found in pits and midden (Table 6-5). All whole vessels and most of the sherds that I examined are shell tempered. Glowacki et al. (1993) found 89.9% shell-tempered sherds in the lower levels and 97.3% in the upper levels of the stratigraphically excavated midden in the southwestern portion of the site.

The Woodland period is represented in Trenches 1-K by a few prismatic blades and notched and stemmed projectile points, some reworked into scrapers, and one fabric-marked sherd. There were small numbers of typical Early Fort Ancient artifacts, including triangular knives (Figure 6-17a), type 2 (flared base) projectile points, discoidals (Figure 6-17b), and ceramics. Some percentage of shell ornaments probably spans Early-Middle Fort Ancient.

The Middle Fort Ancient presence at Madisonville is is not represented by all artifacts identified as local horizon markers for the period. Although some Anderson Shell Tempered sherds with incised and punctated neck decoration, similar to those excavated at the Schomaker site (Cowan et al. 1990), were present in Trenches 1-K (Figure 4-8; see also Griffin 1943: Pl. LXXI), no type 3 (serrated) projectile points or double-pointed bone pins were retained from that part of the site. In fact, to my knowledge, there are few if any of those two diagnostic nonceramic Middle Fort Ancient horizon markers in any Madisonville collection. The only double-pointed bone pins assigned to this site

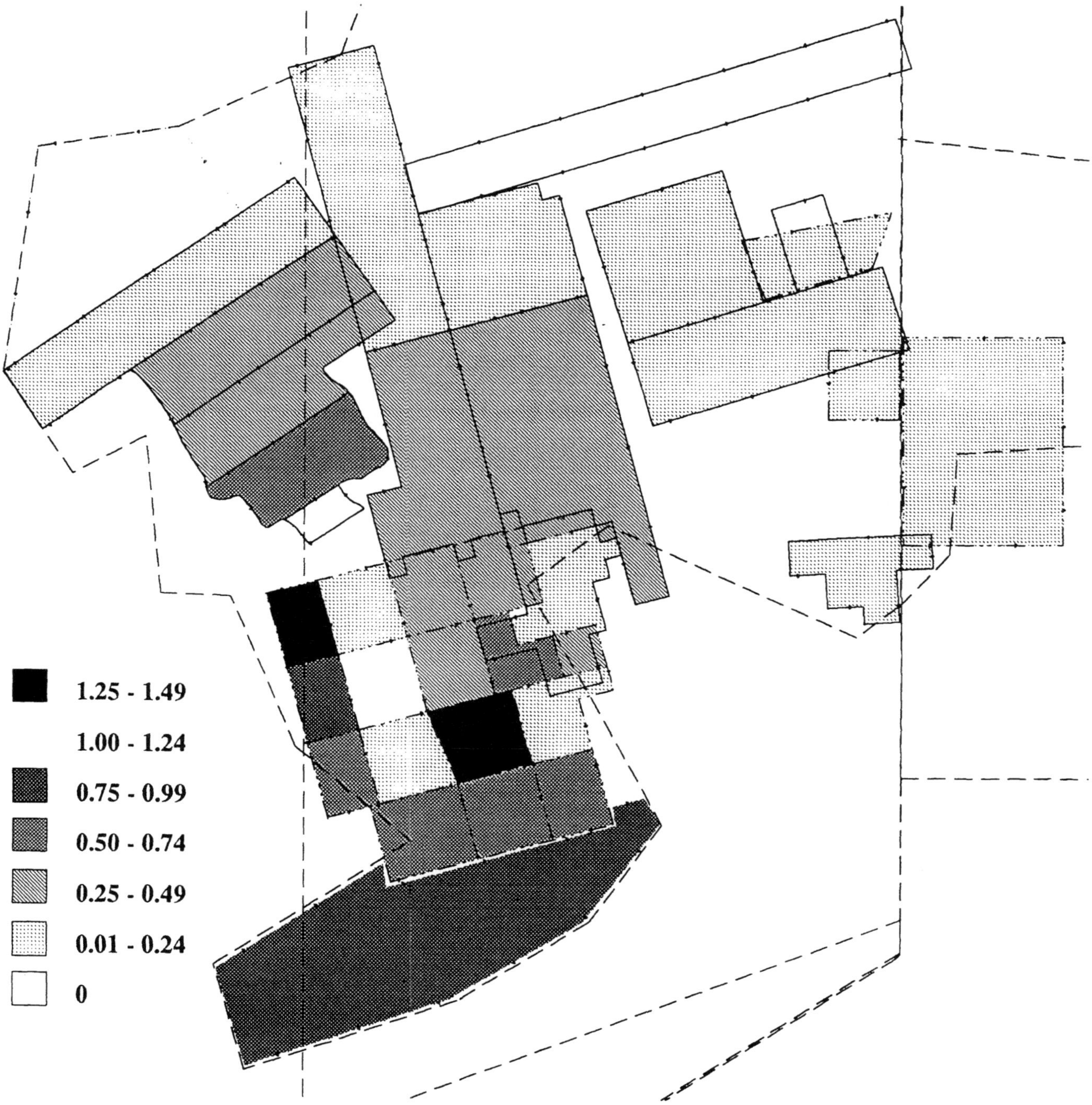

Figure 6-11. Densities of burials with mortuary vessels (per 100 ft²), by excavation block or trench. Keep in mind that in larger trenches burials were not necessarily located in all portions of the trench, and this undoubtedly holds true for Blocks 1-17 as well.

that I have seen are in the cryptic AMNH collection excavated in 1895 (Cat. No. 20/3571), and I have not seen type 3 points in any Madisonville collection. An annular marine shell gorget (Figure 6-19a, below) from the northeast quadrant of Trench F (Pit 40, near Burial 32), could date as early as the thirteenth century or as late as the mid-fifteenth: examples in central Illinois are most common in phases spanning A.D. 1300-1450 but also have come from sites with components assigned to ca. 1100-1300 (Conrad 1991b:148, 149, 154, 1996). The size and style are very similar to annular gorgets from later Illinois sites (e.g., Santure et al. 1992: Fig. 10.6).

Middle Fort Ancient includes the fourteenth century, a period for which Madisonville lacks radiocarbon date calibration intercepts (Figure 6-2). This might have been a time when the

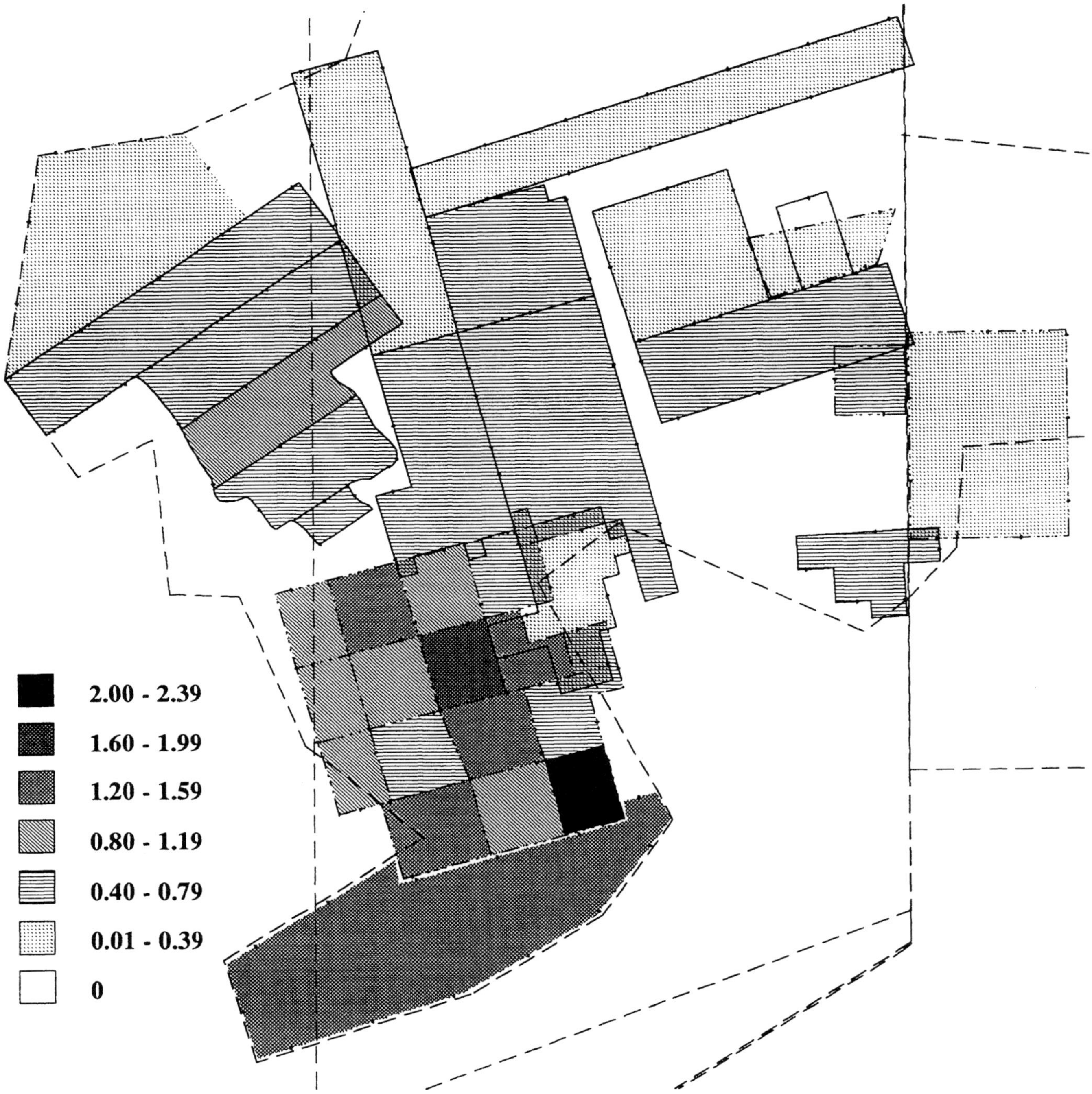

Figure 6-12. Densities of burials lacking mortuary vessels (per 100 ft²), by excavation block or trench. Keep in mind that in larger trenches burials were not necessarily located in all portions of the trench, and this undoubtedly holds true for Blocks 1-17 as well.

site was less heavily used. An apparently low frequency of transitional Madisonville decorated-neck jars and Todd Plain "saltpan" vessels and a lack of beaded bowls, assigned by Turnbow and Henderson to early Late Fort Ancient, 1400-1550 (1992:128-31), imply that this period of lesser use might have extended into the fifteenth century.

All Late Fort Ancient horizon marker artifacts are present in Trench 1-K collections, many of them in significant numbers. Late Late Fort Ancient styles, such as notched-lip jars and bowls and bifacial endscrapers (Figures 4-9, 6-17a), appear to predominate (but, as noted above, numbers present should be taken with a grain of salt). As discussed in Chapter 4, the single head

Figure 6-13. Distribution of burials containing non-pottery grave goods, Trenches 1-K.

pot (Figure 4-14) and several pedestal pot fragments (cf. Figure 4-15) that came from this part of the site also probably are late Late Fort Ancient forms.

Bone and antler artifacts included weapons, tools, and ornaments (Figures 6-18a-c). All types listed in Table 6-5 as Late Fort Ancient horizon markers—arm bands, combs, shaft wrenches, harpoons, and rasps—were present. Not listed in Table 6-5 are bison bone artifacts, which would be later than 1450/1500. Some 60 fragments of beamers made from bison thoracic vertebrae were retained from the 1897-1911 excavations (Figure 6-18a), and at least one bison rib musical rasp and a few examples of other bones and teeth also have come from Madisonville (e.g., Cowan 1987:27; Tankersley 1981).

Also present, from general digging in Trench C, was a redstone pipe reworked from the notched prow of a typical post-1400/1450 Oneota disk pipe (Figure 8-25a; cf., Drooker 1992a: Fig. 15; Hamilton 1967:30; West 1934: Pls. 142.7, 142.9-12, 143.4, 145.1, 145.7).

Marine shell was present in many different forms. Besides the types illustrated in Figures 16-19a, 16-19b, and 16-19c, there were a very few marginella shell beads (e.g., HUPM Cat. No. 08-3-10/79635, with Burial D-7), some much smaller mushroom-shaped ornaments, and a variety of small pendant shapes. A number of the burials (D-86, E-29, E-30, F-10, F-17, F-23) contained matched sets of four to thirty or more small disk or cylindrical shell beads (Figure 6-21a, below) that resemble the Early Wampum found at protohistoric Seneca sites (Ceci 1989b; Sempowski 1989: Figs. 7-10; dates revised based on Saunders and Sempowski 1991), but that had started to develop as early as the late fifteenth-early sixteenth century.

None of the indigenous horizon markers present in Trenches 1-K except the head pot and the annular shell gorget are absent from collections made in the southwestern portion of the site. Two almost-complete examples of stemmed pedestal pots (Figure 4-15; Griffin 1943: Pl. LXVI.4) were recovered during the MLSS excavations (puzzlingly, the adult male in Block 1, No. 283, with which the first one was found is described as having a "small discoidal stone" underneath his head; Low 1880:132). Several additional time-sensitive artifacts came from pre-1897 excavations (cf. Figure 3-8). A damaged and reworked Citico rattlesnake marine shell gorget buried with a child was excavated during May 1882 (Figure 6-19a), probably on the eastern side of the site; it is a marker for the sixteenth–early seventeenth centuries. A redstone disk pipe engraved with the forked eye motif came from an adult burial (Figure 6-20; see also Figure 7-6). It and an effigy pipe of the same material are curated at the CMNH. They have not been chemically tested, but appear similar to known upper Mississippi Valley redstones.

European-Derived Artifacts

European materials and artifacts are the defining characteristic of the Late Madisonville Horizon. At the Madisonville site, over 460 small items of glass, iron, copper, brass, and other

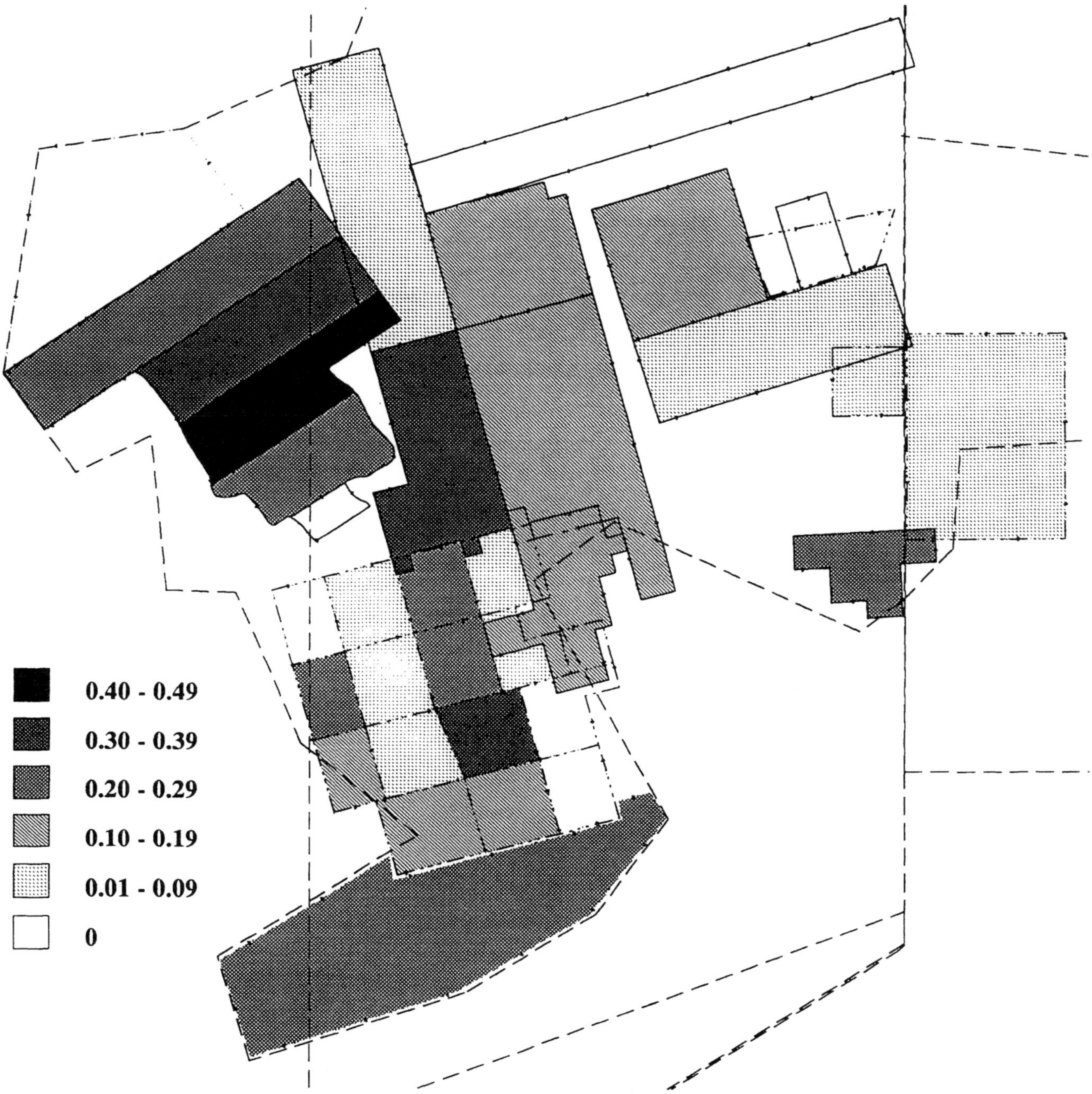

Figure 6-14. Densities of burials containing non-pottery grave goods (per 100 ft^2), by excavation block or trench. Keep in mind that in larger trenches burials were not necessarily located in all portions of the trench, and this undoubtedly holds true for Blocks 1-17 as well.

copper alloys were excavated from at least 45 burials and 97 refuse pits, as well as from midden deposits and general digging within trenches. From trace element analysis of a small sample of copper and brass artifacts from the southwestern portion of the site, it is known that native copper, European copper, and brass all were present (Drooker 1993b). Metallographic analysis of seven copper or brass items, including at least one probable European copper kettle fragment and a fragment of a tubular coil or ring, currently is underway (Nora Reber, pers. comm.). Scratch testing (Fitzgerald and Ramsden 1988) of all non-fragile metal items in the HUPM and CMNH collections has confirmed the presence of brass as well as copper in most classes of

Figure 6-15. Distribution of burials containing only ceramic vessels as grave goods, Trenches 1-K.

"copper" artifacts. A few small native-made ornaments consisting of copper-covered bone or wood might be prehistoric, and some of the smaller copper beads are similar in appearance to examples from predominantly early sites such as Feurt (e.g., Mills 1917: Fig. 61.6), but the great majority of metal and glass items can probably be traced ultimately to European sources, if not as manufactured items then as materials.

Table 6-6 lists the types and numbers of items present (see Drooker 1992b, 1992d, 1996b for detailed descriptions). All are relatively small, and only a few are unmodified European-made items. From information summarized in Chapter 3 (see Figure 3-8), time periods can be assigned to many of them.

The copper-covered objects from Madisonville (Figure 6-21a) undoubtedly were native-made, probably using native copper. They include at least two different forms. Three bone disks (1.5–2 cm diameter), first wrapped crosswise with fiber and then covered with copper, came from general digging in Trenches 1-5, a fourth from Burial C-9, and a fifth from Pit D-44. A copper-covered wood object was reported with Burial B-44, an adult male, but is no longer extant. Two bell-shaped small copper-covered wooden objects that might well be broken ear plugs were with a child burial excavated under the auspices of the MLSS for which the exact provenience is unknown (they were retained for awhile in Metz's collection, then acquired by the HUPM). Another small ornament, in the shape of a very short (1.5 cm), broad cone, might perhaps be wood covered with metal (Figure 6-21a, top). It was found with a richly endowed adult burial in Trench F (No. 23). The object appears to be seamless, with just a hole in its apex. It has different proportions and is much thicker than the typical conical sheet-metal tinklers described below. Although, from a scratch test, it definitely is yellowish-red metal (perhaps brass or gold rather than copper), it is quite light in weight.

Copper-covered wooden and bone objects are known from at least Hopewell times onward in this region, so one question with the Madisonville examples was whether they might be horizon markers for early components at the site. The answer seems to be "no." Not only have small copper-covered wooden earplugs with bell-shaped ends come from late prehistoric-protohistoric sites such as Rose Mound, Arkansas (Putnam 1973b: Fig. 22), Denton Mounds and Brooks, Missouri (O'Brien 1994: Pl. 1.c, Fig. 7.11), and Murphy, Indiana (Moorehead 1906: Figs. 23a, 23b), but also two of the Madisonville copper-covered items were excavated from features that also produced brass. The child burial in which two possible broken earplugs were found also included a brass spiral (Figure 6-21f, discussed below), and Pit D-43 contained at least 12 metal objects, most of them rolled beads, of which at least one is brass and another (from its thickness) is perhaps European kettle copper.

The greatest number of metal artifacts from Madisonville consist of simple shapes fashioned from sheet metal (Figure 6-21b), including cylindrical beads (analogous in shape to the bird-bone beads that are one of the common indigenous ornament types on the site); cylindrical rings (recognized as such by their

Figure 6-16. Densities of burials containing only ceramic vessels as grave goods (per 100 ft^2), by excavation block or trench. Keep in mind that in larger trenches burials were not necessarily located in all portions of the trench, and this undoubtedly holds true for Blocks 1-17 as well.

placement on fingers); conical tinklers (analogous to proximal deer phalanx ornaments common at Ontario Iroquoian sites [Fitzgerald 1990:501-4] and elsewhere, but not at Madisonville); clips with underturned edges made to fasten onto leather or textiles; small flat pendants in simple shapes (Figure 6-21c, top); and flat scrap, some of it cut to size and shape, ready to be fashioned into beads, rings, or tubular coils (Figures 6-21d, 6-21e). Many of these forms, such as rolled metal beads, continue a prehistoric tradition of ornaments made from native copper (Fox et al. 1995). However, at least a few examples from

TABLE 6-5
Numbers of Extant Horizon Marker Artifacts from Trenches 1-K

		WOOD-LAND	FORT ANCIENT			
			Early	Middle	E. Late	L. Late
JARS (vessels & sherds, N = 617)						
Thickened rim (Anderson)						
Completely cordmarked	18		X			
Smooth neck (dec./undec.)	178		x	X	x	
Thin rim (Madisonville)						
Decorated neck	10				X	
Undecorated neck						
Plain rim	106				X	x
Notched rim	224					X
Grooved-paddled surface	36					X
BOWLS (vessels & sherds, N = 75)						
Beaded rim	0				(X)	
Notched rim	40					X
PROJECTILE POINTS (N = 662)						
Notched or stemmed	29	X				
Type 2 triangular	40		X	x		
Type 3 triangular	0			(X)		
Types 4/5 triangular	338			x	X	x
Type 6 triangular	138				x	X
KNIVES (N = 74)						
Triangular	1		X			
Bipointed	52				X	X
ENDSCRAPERS (N = 339)						
Unifacial	56				X	X
Bifacial	271					X
DISCOIDALS	6		X			
PIPES (N = 99)						
Massive effigy	1		X			
Smaller sculpted effigies	9					
Ovoid	32			X	X	X
Vasiform	8				x	X
Large disk	1				X	x
Small disk	7					X
Keel	5					X
BONE						
Double-pointed pins	0			(X)		
Arm bands	4				X	X
Combs	5				X	X
Shaft wrenches	39				X	X
Harpoons	5				X	X
Rasps (fragments)	43					X
SHELL						
Annular gorget	1		x	X		
Maskettes	2				x	X
METAL (N = 228)						
Copper or brass	197	x	x	x	x	X
Brass	20					X
Iron	11					X
GLASS BEADS/fragments	27					X

Includes only artifacts still curated at HUPM. "N" designates size of total sample, including non-diagnostic items. "X" indicates the period(s) for which an artifact is a significant horizon marker; "x" indicates other period(s) when it may be present.

each category have been identified as brass rather than copper. All probably were made by native craftspeople. Native-made rolled brass beads were present in the Southeast before 1550. They and almost all of the other artifact types have been documented at late sixteenth-century Ontario and New York sites from 1570 onward, with European copper ornaments present in Ontario as early as 1550 (Drooker 1996b; Fox et al. 1995:282). However, these simple forms generally have too long a use period to be helpful as fine-grained horizon markers.

The brass clips present at Madisonville, like those at Hardin

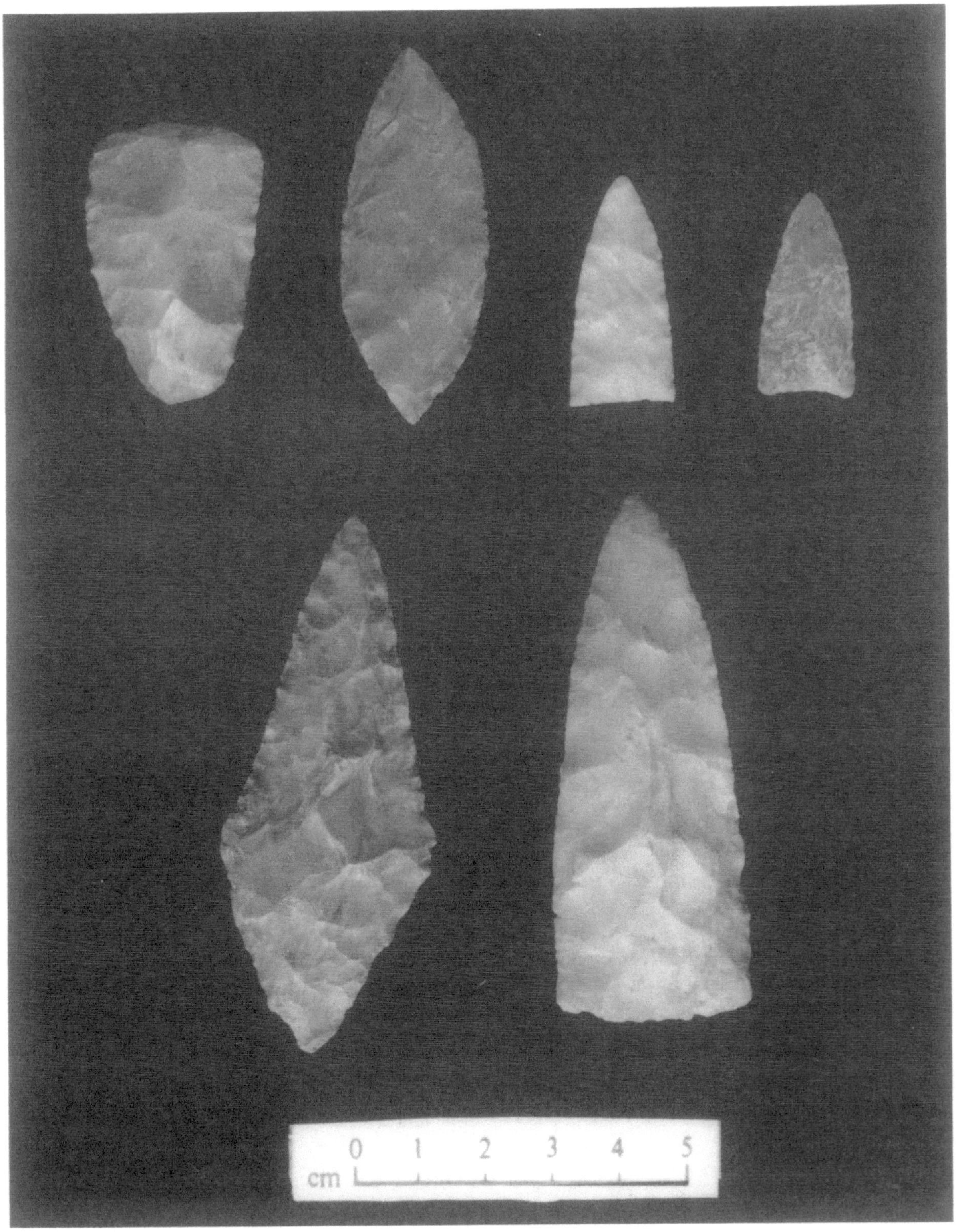

Figure 6-17a. Selected lithics from Madisonville. *Top*: bifaced endscraper (HUPM Cat. No. 08-3-10/79579), leaf-shaped knife (08-3-10/79579), projectile points, type 6 on right (07-610/78533 and 81-41-10/25235). *Bottom*: atypical knife, from Burial I-19 (11-10-10/A4046), pre-Madisonville Horizon point from Mound 1, Burial 4, beyond the village area to northeast (11-10-10/A4097). Photograph by Hillel Burger (HUPM Photo No. N33859). Copyright 1997 by the President and Fellows of Harvard College; used with permission.

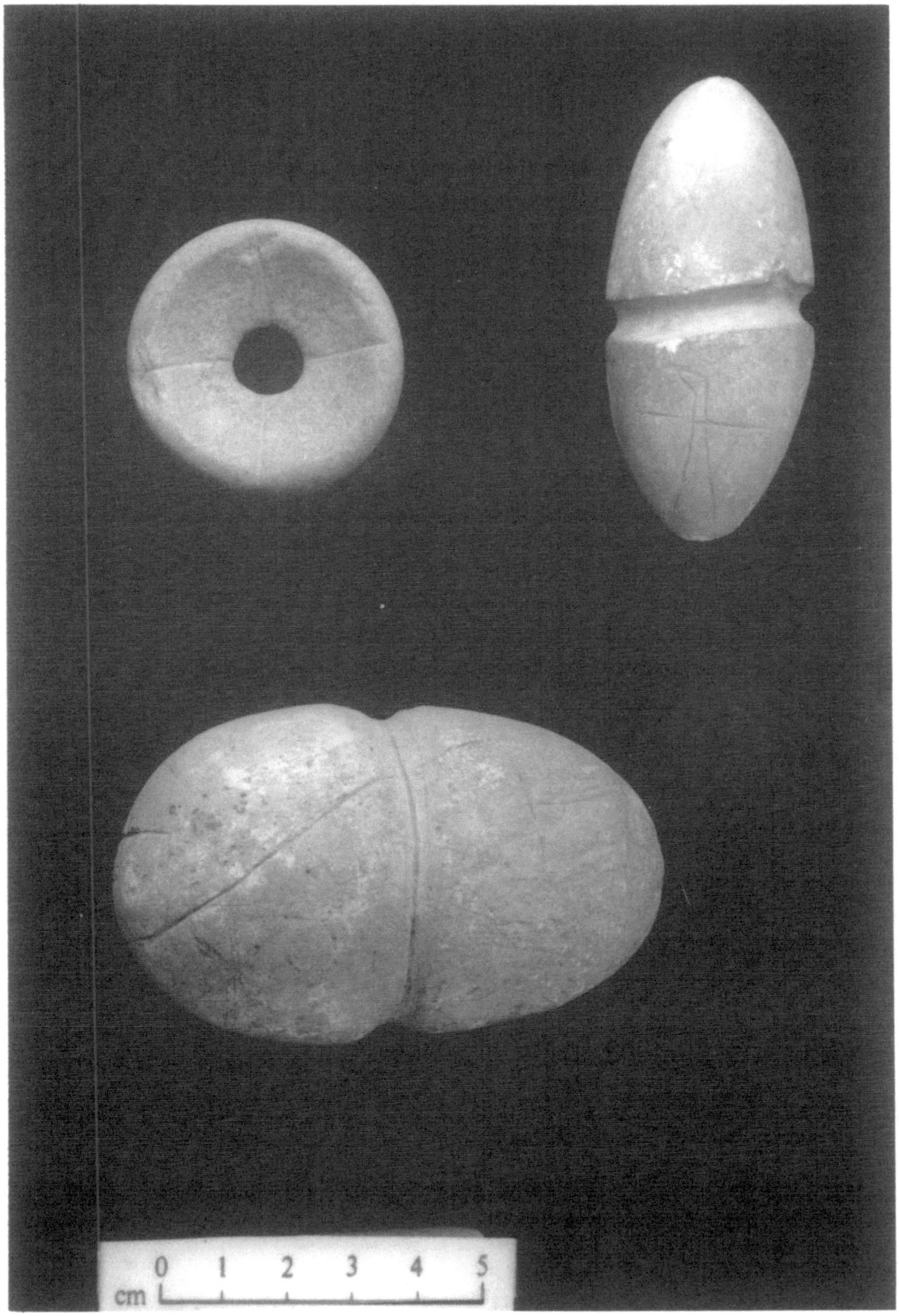

Figure 6-17b. Selected lithics from Madisonville. *Top*: discoidal with engraved "cross," Burial K-10 (HUPM Cat. No. 11-10-10/A4092), shaped stone club head with engraved thunderbird, from Pit F-31 (08-3-10/79415). *Bottom*: typical club head, grooved natural stone with engraved motifs including a "+" at each end, one of which is half-visible at left side (08-3-10/78892). Photograph by Hillel Burger (HUPM Photo No. N33860). Copyright 1997 by the President and Fellows of Harvard College, and used with permission.

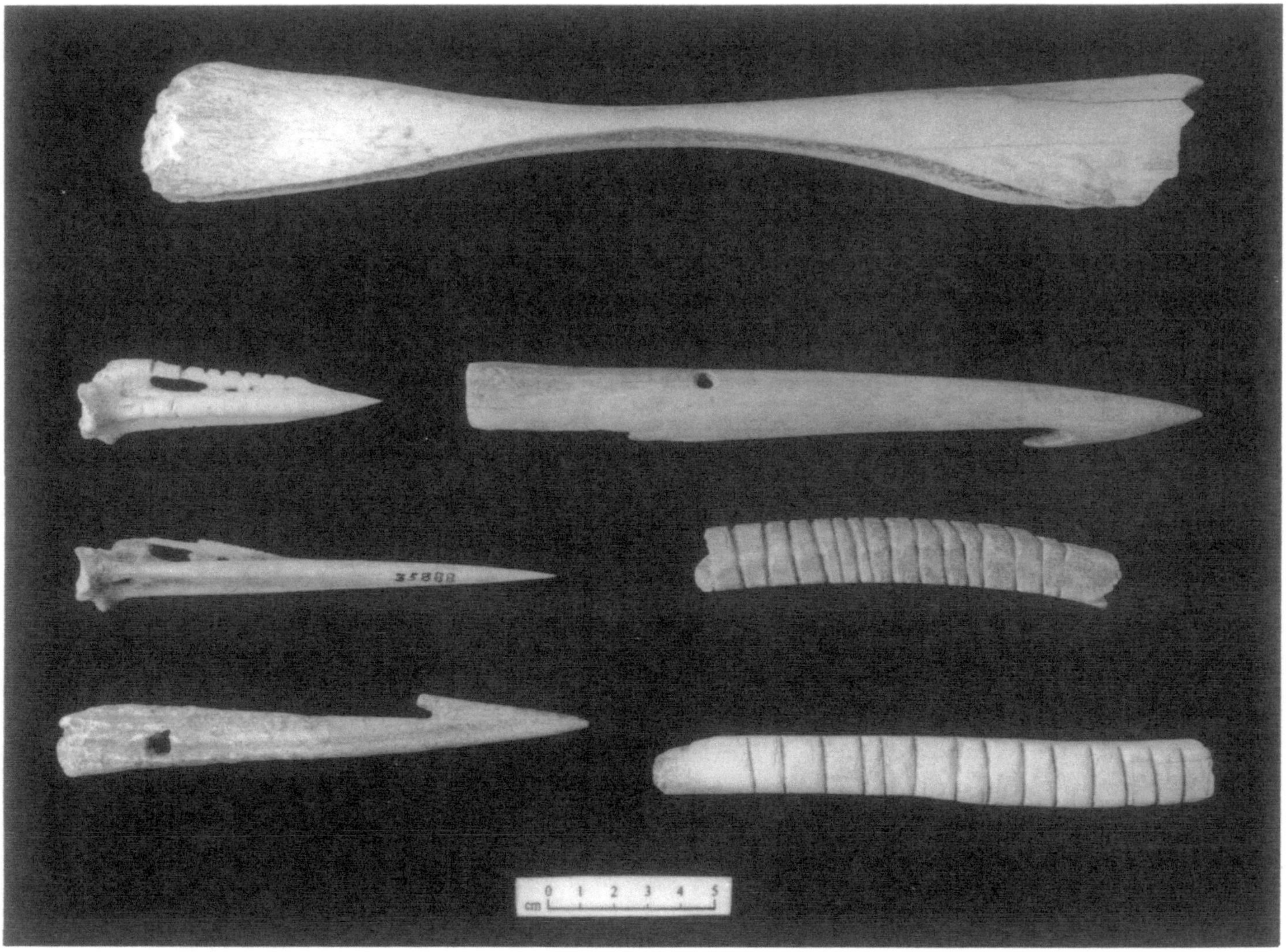

Figure 6-18a. Selected bone and antler artifacts from Madisonville. *From top to bottom, left to right*: "beamer" made from thoracic vertebra of bison (HUPM Cat. No. 01-38-10/67914), notched awl (08-3-10/71629), harpoon (84-68-10/35819), notched awl (84-68-10/35888), rasp fragment (01-38-10/69672), harpoon, from Burial I-19 (11-10-10/A4045), rasp fragment (84-68-10/35849). Photograph by Hillel Burger (HUPM Photo No. N33856). Copyright 1997 by the President and Fellows of Harvard College, and used with permission.

and Buffalo (Hanson 1966: Fig. 67, 1975: Fig. 63), are noncylindrical and much larger than most of those proposed as post-1630 horizon markers in the Southeast and elsewhere (see Chapter 3). They appear somewhat more similar to examples from the Susquehannock Washington Boro site, established around 1620 (Cadzow 1936:126; Sempowski 1994:61). The two from Madisonville are particularly large (3 × 3 cm and 3 × 2.5 cm, compared to maximum widths of 2 cm at the other two sites) and crudely made. One came from general digging in Trench E, and the other from Trench 1, Pit 55, in which a tubular copper serpent shape (probably pre-1625; see below) also was found. This was in the same part of the site as Burial 1-60, which had a set of even larger copper clips probably attached to a belt (Figure 6-21b, discussed below).

One copper tube was formed by a spiraling a thin, flat piece of metal rather than by rolling a rectangle (Figure 6-21c, bottom). Somewhat similar but much smaller-diameter examples were excavated at the Grimsby ossuary in Ontario (ca. 1630-1640) (Fitzgerald 1990; Kenyon 1982:51) and at the Seneca Tram and Cameron sites (Wray et al. 1991:76, 248), occupied between about 1580 and 1605 (Saunders and Sempowski 1991:23, 24). The most similar artifact I have found (the same diameter as the Madisonville example) came from a late prehistoric-protohistoric site in northeastern Iowa (Iowa Historical Society E.O. 1257).

The three "cross-shaped" flat metal pendants illustrated in Figure 6-21f are the largest metal artifacts from the site, with the possible exception of the copper or brass leg bands identi-

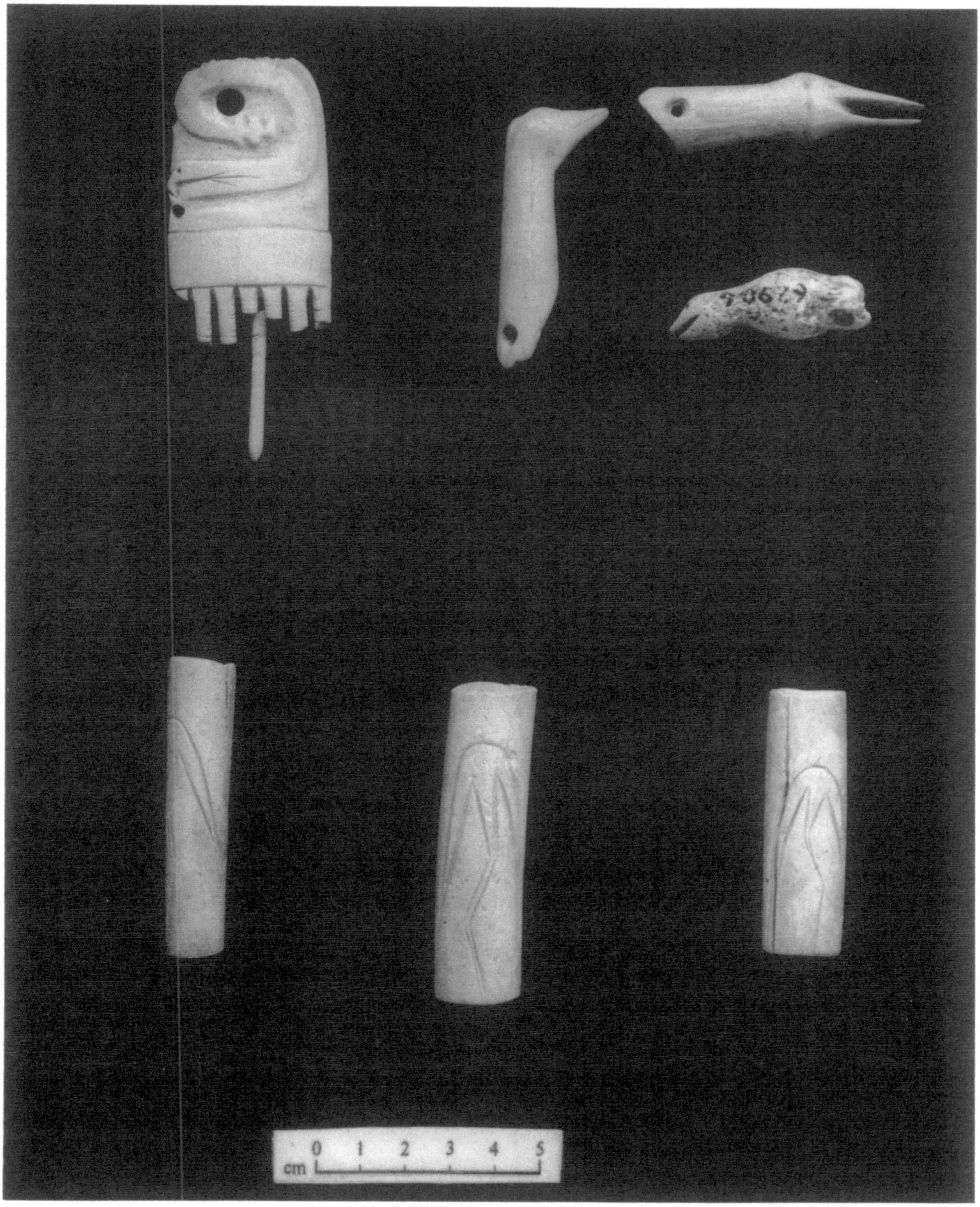

Figure 6-18b. Selected bone and antler ornaments from Madisonville. *Top*: comb with carved rattlesnake design, from Burial B-11 (HUPM Cat. No. 07-6-10/78587), bird head and bird effigies made from naturally shaped bone and antler, the bird from subadult Burial 3-16 (84-68-10/35827, 97-38-10/62941, 97-38-10/62906). *Bottom*: three bird bone beads from set of ten, seven of them engraved with "weeping eye" motif, from Burial 2-21 (97-38-10/62890). Photograph by Hillel Burger (HUPM Photo No. N33857). Copyright 1997 by the President and Fellows of Harvard College, and used with permission.

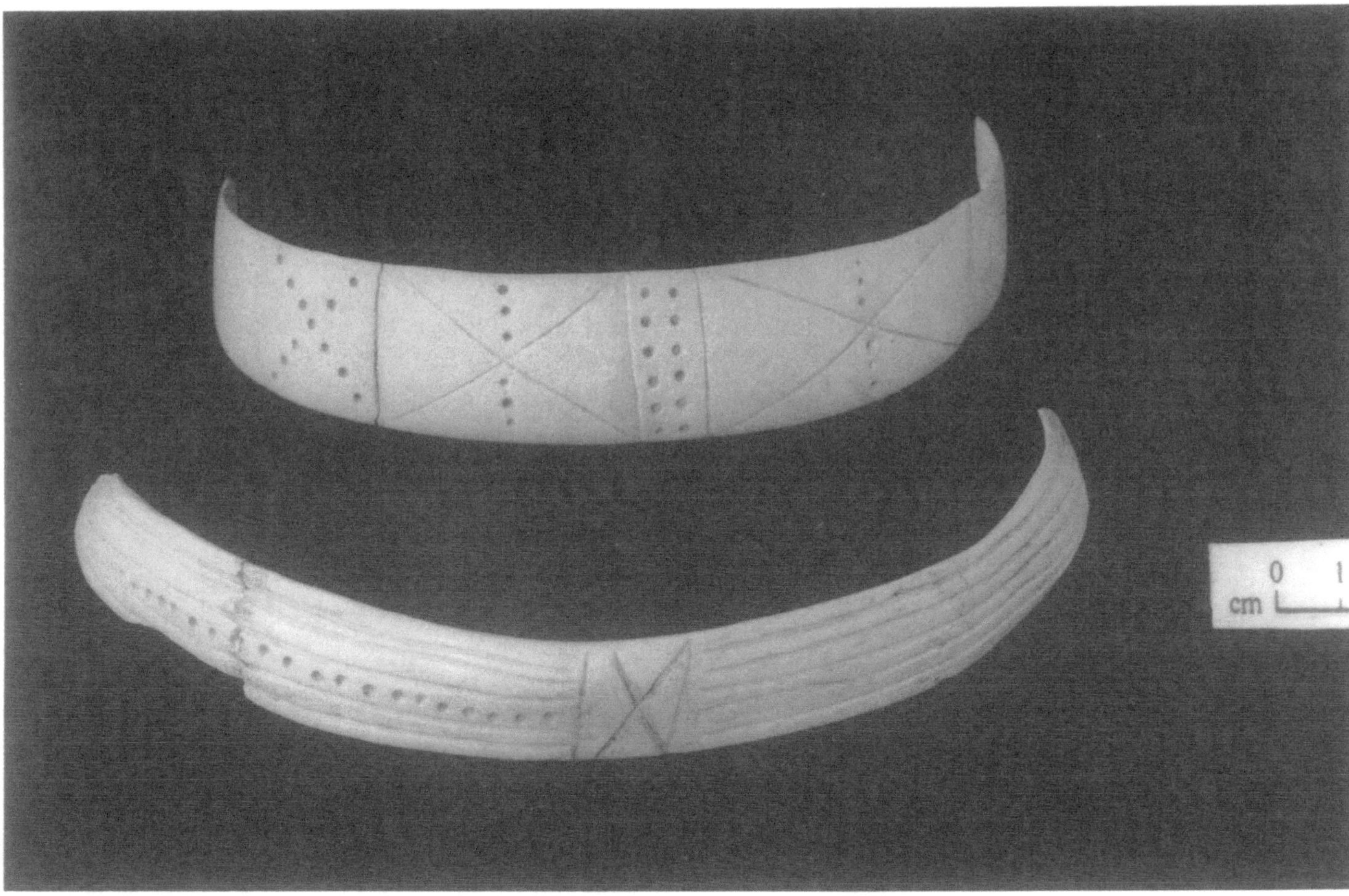

Figure 6-18c. Selected bone and antler ornaments from Madisonville. Two decorated arm bands, the top one from Burial B-9 (see also Figure 7-4, below) (HUPM Cat. Nos. 07-6-10/78583 and 11-10-10/A4087). Photograph by Hillel Burger (HUPM Photo No. N33858). Copyright 1997 by the President and Fellows of Harvard College, and used with permission.

fied only by large green stains on tibiae and fibulae of two adult male burials in Trenches 1 (No. 48) and B (No. 9). The two barred copper pendants came from adult male burials in Block 1 (No. 297) and Trench I (No. 19), while the brass one was buried with a child excavated during Putnam's visit to the site in May, 1882, but otherwise unprovenienced (Putnam 1973d:99-100). Similar pendants (Figures 7-31, 8-10) have come from both late prehistoric regions with no evidence for European contact (e.g., the vicinity of Nashville, Tennessee; Putnam 1973c: Fig. 1, 1973b:108), and sites and burials containing significant numbers of European-derived artifacts (e.g., Flynn cemetery, Allamakee County, Iowa (Bray 1961a: Pl. 2). Other Madisonville pendants include a variety of simple geometric shapes, such as the two examples in Figure 6-21c (Drooker 1996b).

The earliest dateable European object at Madisonville is a battered sheet brass Clarksdale bell, found with a child (No. 279) buried in Block 1 (Figures 6-21c, g; Low 1880:131). This is a type probably distributed by members of the de Soto expedition (1539-1543), but which has been found on Southeastern sites dating as late as 1630 (Brain 1975; Brown, 1979a; Drooker 1992b; Mitchem and McEwan 1988).

Distinctive large copper kettles with iron bands and lugs were traded by Basque fishermen on the Saint Lawrence from around 1580 to 1600 (Fitzgerald et al. 1993). Lugs, band fragments, and pieces cut from rims of these containers all have been excavated at Madisonville (Figure 6-21f, bottom; see also Hooton and Willoughby 1920: Pl. 18o-r). Most of the iron pieces—all found in pits and midden—had been beveled on one side to serve as tools. Eleven large copper rectangles (up to 6.4 × 5.7 cm, of dark red metal) cut from a kettle, as evidenced by rivets and rivet holes, were clipped or cinched around a leather belt or garment worn by a young adult buried in Trench 1 (No. 60) (Figure 6-21b, left; Hooton and Willoughby 1920: Pl. 18g).

An iron dagger guard (Figure 6-21f; see also Hooton and Willoughby 1920: Pl. 18t), placed on the chest of an adult burial in Block 12 (No. 20), identified as female, is a type common in Europe between about 1575 and 1625, probably from a left-handed dagger used in conjunction with a right-handed rapier

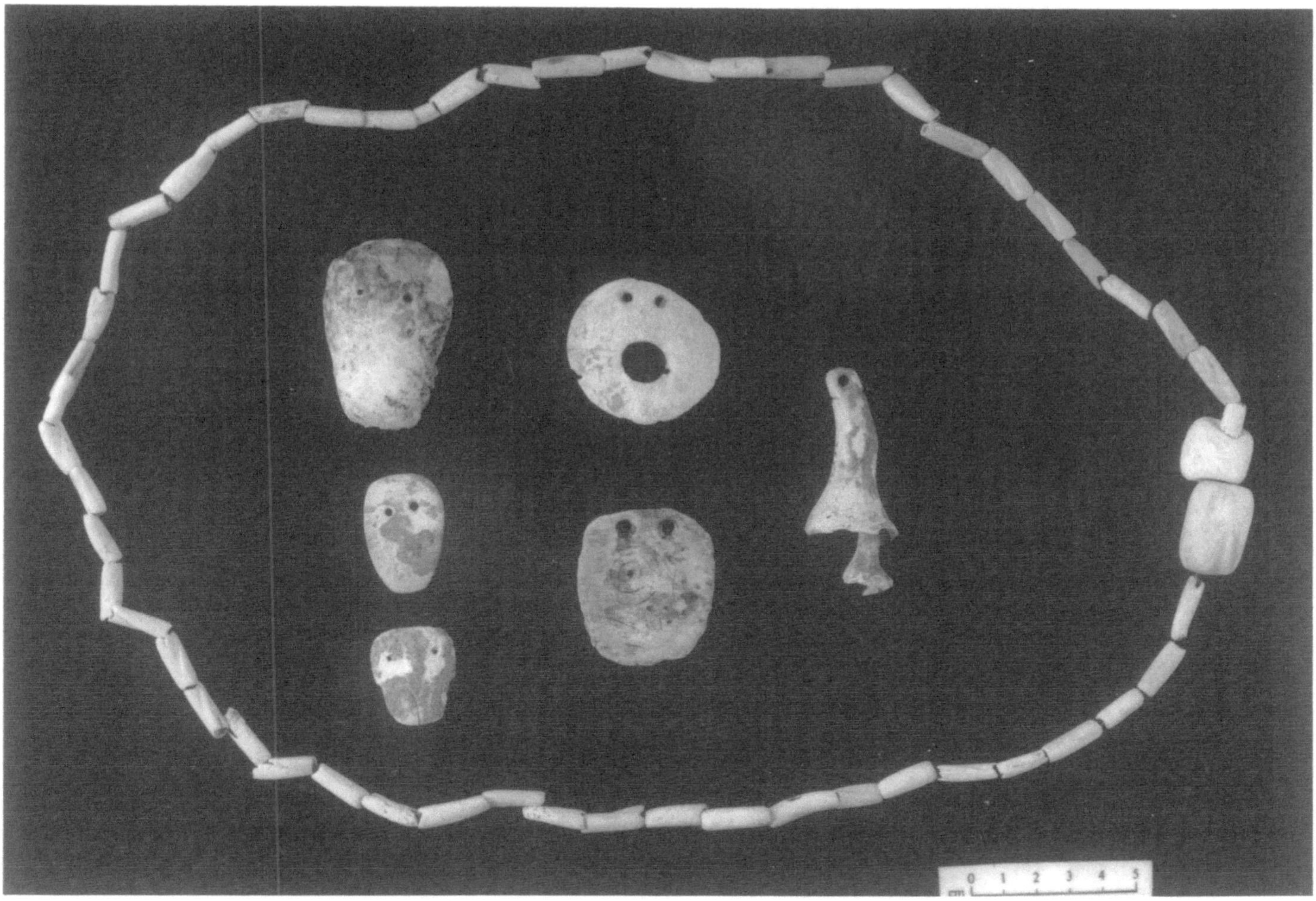

Figure 6-19a. Selected shell ornaments from Madisonville. Set of cylindrical beads from Burial 1-60 (HUPM Cat. No. 97-38-10/62871); three maskettes, the top one from Burial 1-61 and the middle one from a burial excavated in the 1880s (top to bottom: 97-38-10/62876, 84-68-10/35550,01-38-10/69641); annular gorget from Pit F-40 (08-3-10/79462); reworked fragment of Citico rattlesnake gorget from a child burial excavated in 1882 (82-53-10/28299); pendant from small univalve, from a burial excavated in the 1880s (84-68-10/35556). Photograph by Hillel Burger (HUPM Photo No. N33854). Copyright 1997 by the President and Fellows of Harvard College, and used with permission.

(Donald LaRocca, pers. comm.; see Drooker 1996b). It might once have had a side ring attached to the quillon block and perpendicular to it. A similar guard (on a rapier) has come from a sixteenth century burial in Nova Scotia that also contained iron-fitted Basque copper kettles (Harper 1956:19f), and others have come from two Seneca sites, Cameron and Factory Hollow, currently dated to around 1595-1625 (Saunders and Sempowski 1991; Wray et al. 1991:325; Martha Sempowski, pers. comm.).

A handful of translucent blue/green glass beads (Kidd Type IIa28/31) with weathered opaque, opalescent exteriors was excavated at Madisonville. They belong to a high-copper, low-calcium, very friable type that probably dates between 1580 and 1600 (Chafe et al. 1986; Drooker 1993a; Witthoft 1966:206). Most of the beads were with an infant buried in Trench 1 (No. 39), but two fragments came from an adult burial in Trench I (No. 12) and three from pits in Trenches 1 (No. 44) and 4 (No. 31).

Serpent shapes, coils, and a spiral made from thin copper and brass tubes (Figures 6-21c, 6-21e, 6-21f, 7-30b) are technologically congruent with metal spirals from Iroquoian sites occupied between 1550 and 1625 (Bradley and Childs 1991b; Childs 1994; Drooker 1992a, 1996b; Terry Childs, pers. comm.). The brass spiral (Figure 6-21f, top right) came from a child burial excavated under the auspices of the MLSS (exact provenience unknown), which also contained two ornaments of copper-covered wood (see above). Three copper serpents were with a highly endowed adult burial excavated in 1895 (No. 45), and one serpent, probably of brass, was with an unprovenienced subadult burial excavated during Putnam's visit to the site in May 1882 (Putnam 1973d:100-101). The remainder (at least two copper, one brass) came from pits in Trenches 1 (No. 55) and C (No. 2), and general digging in Trenches 1-5 (Figure 6-21f, 7-30b).

Spring-shaped coils made from thin metal tubes, plus circles, C-shapes, and other fragments of curved thin tubes, were ob-

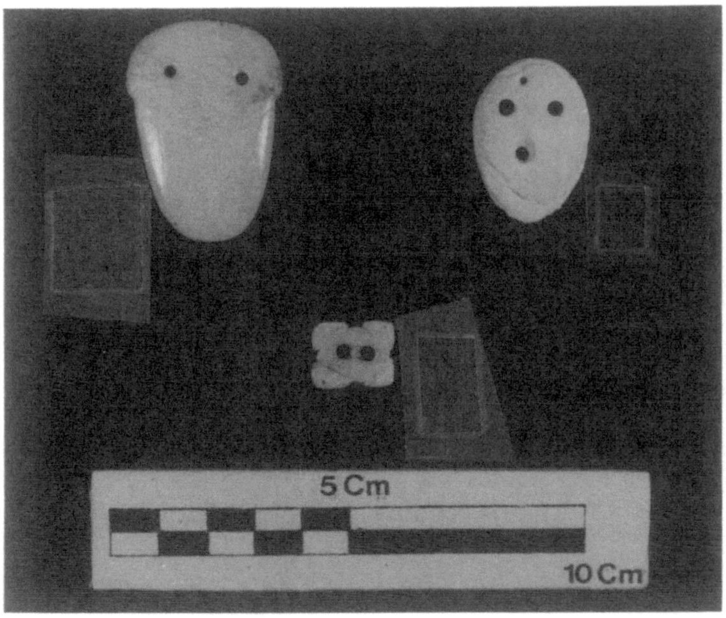

Figure 6-19b. Selected marine shell ornaments from Madisonville. *Top left*, maskette, found with Burial 16 in Block 6, a young child (CMNH Cat. No. 1918.831, gift of Harry Zerring); *top right*, pendant (CMNH No. A42215, excavated from midden in 1936); *bottom*, "button" from soil with previously excavated burial (A25587, gift of James Theler, excavated in 1962 or 1963). Photograph by William Collier, courtesy of the Cincinnati Museum Center.

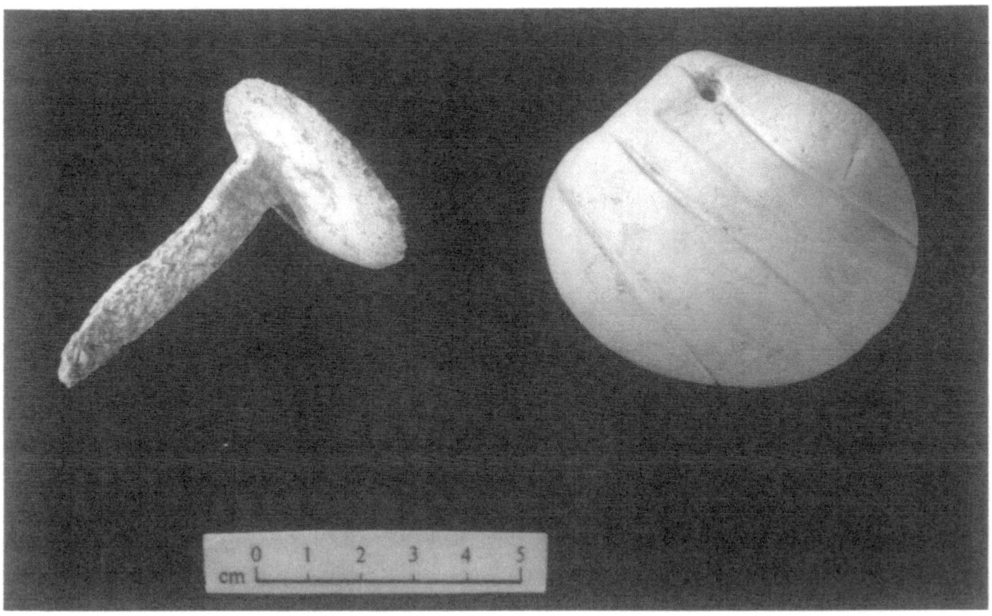

Figure 6-19c. Selected shell ornaments from Madisonville. Mushroom-shaped earplug from multiple burial, 11-15 in Trench 2 (HUPM Cat. No. 97-38-10/62883), pendant from infant burial D-7 (08-3-10/79634). Photograph by Hillel Burger (HUPM Photo No. N33855). Copyright 1997 by the President and Fellows of Harvard College, and used with permission.

Figure 6-20. Redstone small-disk pipe from Madisonville, with Burial 108 from Block 1 (CMNH Cat. No. 1908.1017, gift of Harry M. Levy). Weeping-eye symbol engraved on top of base, prow slightly pointed and notched. Photograph by William Collier, courtesy of the Cincinnati Museum Center. See also Figure 7-6.

TABLE 6-6
Types and Numbers of Metal and Glass Artifacts from Madisonville

	MINIMUM NUMBER*		
	With Burials	In Pits	Other
Copper-covered wood and bone ornaments	5	1	5
Copper and brass rolled beads	126	95	48
Copper and (mostly) brass rolled finger rings	5	4	
Copper and brass conical "tinklers"	7	3	2
Copper/brass "clips"	11	3	2
Copper and brass tubular coils, rings	16	7	15
Brass tubular spiral	1		
Copper and brass tubular serpents	4	3	1
Copper and brass flat pendants	4		2
Copper and brass scrap	5	36	32
Brass bell	1		
"German silver" ornament			1
Iron dagger guard	1		
Iron celt			1
Iron kettle lugs		1	2
Iron kettle band pieces		4	4
Other iron items (bead, rings)	1	2	
TOTAL METAL	187	159	115
Blue/green glass bead fragments	23+	4	

Summarized from Drooker 1996b:Table 1.

* Includes only specimens in museum collections, both items actually examined and documented accessions not located. Additional items, surmised from green stains on bone or mentioned in excavation reports but not included in collections, are not listed.

TABLE 6-7
Summary of Time Periods Associated with Madisonville Metal and Glass Artifacts

POSITIVE EVIDENCE (artifacts present) [a]

Clarksdale bell	ca. 1540-1630
Tubular metal spiral, coils, rings	ca. 1550-1625
Iron dagger guard	ca. 1575-1625
High-copper blue glass beads	ca. 1580-1600
Iron-banded kettle parts	ca. 1580-1630
Sheet-copper spiralling "bead"	ca. 1580-1640

NEGATIVE EVIDENCE (artifacts not present) [b]

- Post-1600 glass bead types
- Jesuit rings (e.g., Fitzgerald 1990:521-533)
- Brass wire with B-shaped cross-section (Drooker 1992a, 1996b)
- Solid brass or iron wire (e.g., Brain 1979:196; Bray 1978)
- Brass side-view animal effigy shapes (Waselkov 1989)
- Brass collars (Waselkov 1989)
- Non Clarksdale bell types, such as cast brass or Flushloop (Brown 1977, 1979a)
- Gun parts, ammunition (e.g., Wray 1985; Witthoft 1966:207)
- Catlinite elbow pipes (Brown 1989)
- Micmac-style pipes (Witthoft et al. 1953)
- True wampum (Ceci 1989b)

EVIDENCE YET TO BE REFINED [c]

- Cannel coal pendants resembling brass side-view animal effigies

[a] Datable metal and glass artifacts excavated at Madisonville.

[b] Examples of European-derived artifacts generally associated with post-1630 sites that are not found at Madisonville.

[c] Items that might or might not be associated with a post-1630 time period (see text for discussion).

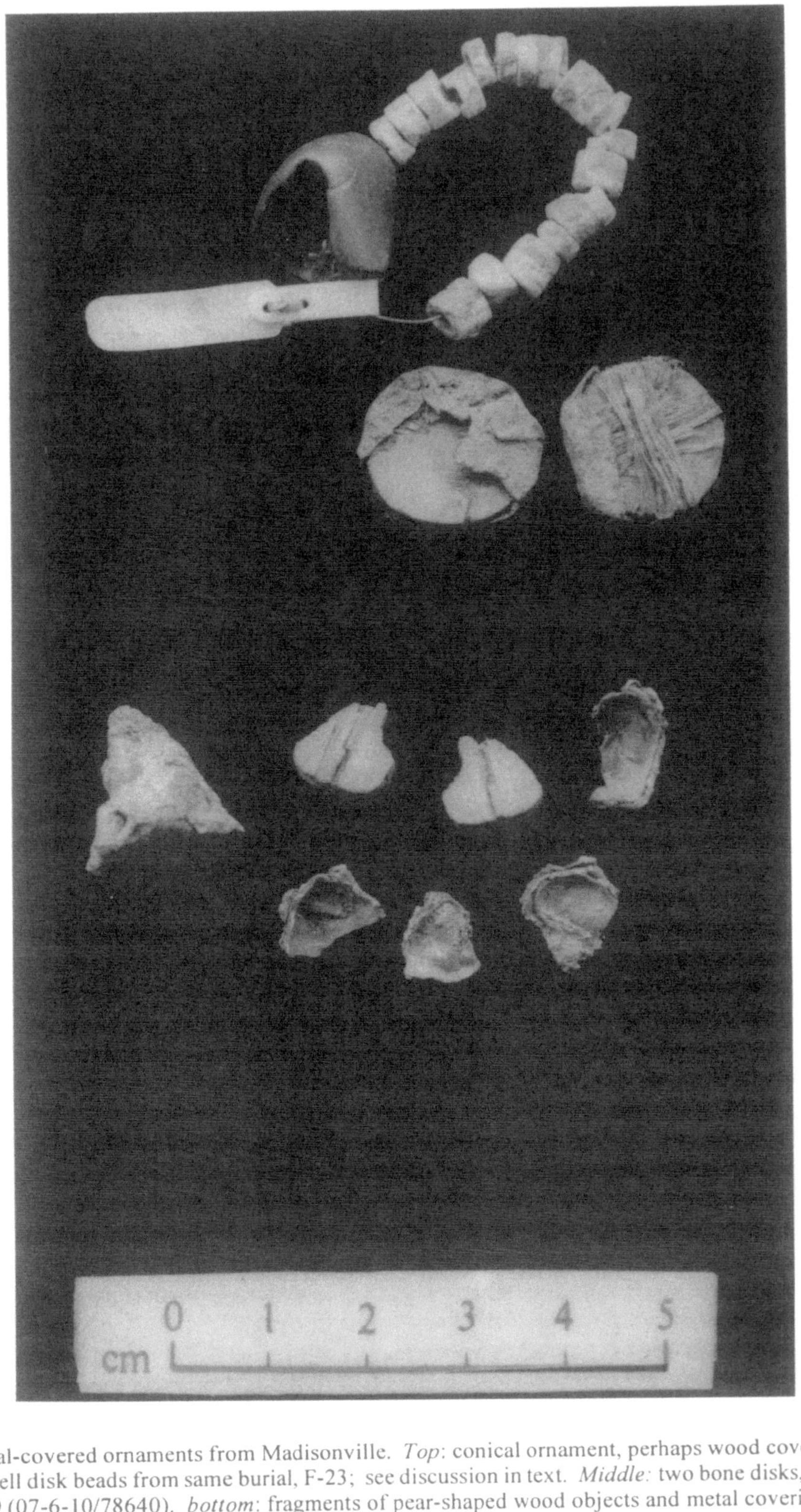

Figure 6-21a. Selected metal-covered ornaments from Madisonville. *Top*: conical ornament, perhaps wood covered with metal (HUPM Cat. No. 08-3-10/79712) with shell disk beads from same burial, F-23; see discussion in text. *Middle:* two bone disks, wrapped with fiber and then with metal, from Burial C-9 (07-6-10/78640). *bottom*: fragments of pear-shaped wood objects and metal covering, from burial excavated in 1880s (84-68-10/35562). Photograph by Hillel Burger (HUPM Photo No. N33861). Copyright 1997 by the President and Fellows of Harvard College, and used with permission.

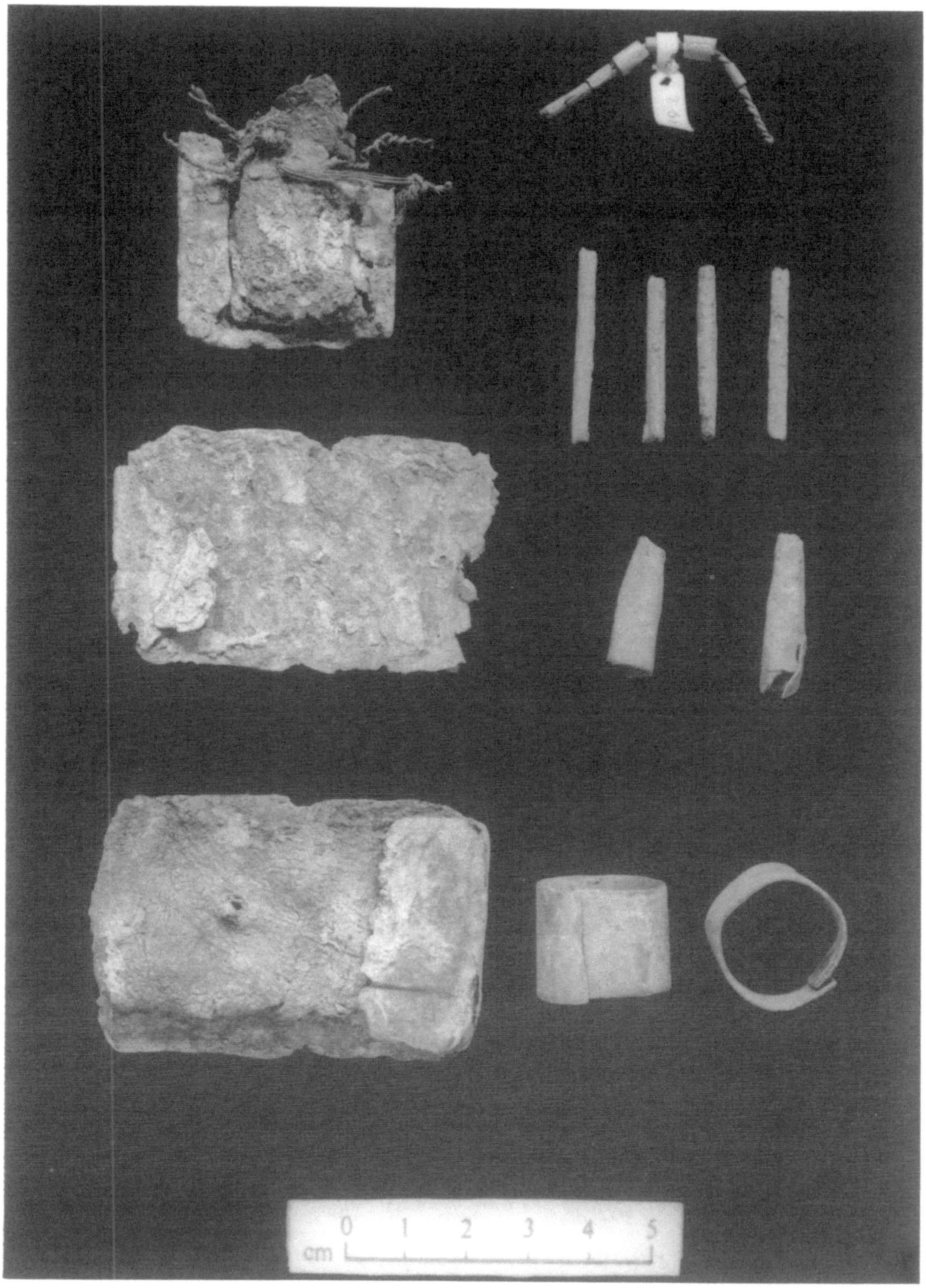

Figure 6-21b. Selected metal ornaments in simple shapes from Madisonville. *Left*: three copper clips from set of at least ten, secured to leather belt or garment (leather and cordage still present), from Burial 60 in Trench 1 (HUPM Cat. No. 97-38-10/62874). *Right, top to bottom*: small rolled metal beads on two-ply cord, from subadult burial excavated in 1882 (82-35-10/26611), four rolled copper beads from matched group of 22 found in Pit 1-50 (01-38-10/68201), two conical copper tinklers, from Burial 3-46 (97-38-10/62912), two brass rings of four with adult skeleton excavated in 1882 (82-35-10/26633,-34). Photograph by Hillel Burger (HUPM Photo No. N33862). Copyright 1997 by the President and Fellows of Harvard College, and used with permission.

Figure 6-21c. Selected metal artifacts from Madisonville in the collection of the Museum of Natural History and Science, Cincinnati: trianguloid brass pendant (Cat. No. 1992.1/A25560), ovoid copper pendant, photographed upside-down (1992.1/A25506), damaged "Clarksdale" brass bell (1990.33/1887.20658), thin tubular copper coil, photographed straight down, so that coiling is not visible (1992.1/A25501), spiraling copper(?) "bead" (1992.1/A25508), shield-shaped silver-colored copper alloy object (part of belt?) (1992.1/A25502). Proveniences discussed in text. Photograph by William Collier, courtesy of the Cincinnati Museum Center.

Figure 6-21d. Rolled metal beads and blank from Madisonville. *Left to right*: copper blank (CMNH Cat. No. 1992.1/A25529), copper bead (1992.1/A25511), brass bead (1992.1/A25509). Trace element analysis of the blank identified it as European copper (Drooker 1993b). All from Conover collection, excavated from nonmortuary contexts in southwestern portion of site, courtesy of the Cincinnati Museum Center.

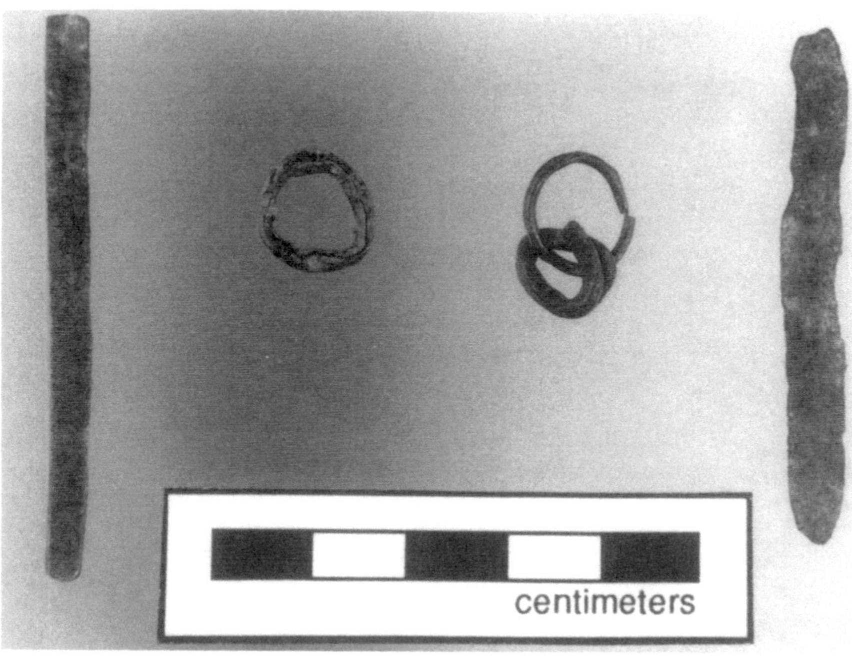

Figure 6-21e. Coils made from thin metal tubes and blanks for their production, from the Madisonville site. *Left to right*: copper blank (CMNH Cat. No. 1992.1/A25535), flattened copper coil (1992.1/A25550), linked copper (thinner) and brass (thicker) coils (1992.1/A25517), copper blank (1992.1/A25536). All from Conover collection, excavated from nonmortuary contexts in southwestern portion of site. Both coils came from midden deposits, the linked pair from a depth of 2-4 feet. Courtesy of the Cincinnati Museum Center.

0 1 2 3 4 5
cm

Figure 6-21g. Drawing of "Clarksdale" bell from the Madisonville site, with reconstruction at right. See Figure 6-21c, center, for photograph. Artist: Barbara Alexander, for the Museum of Natural History and Science, Cincinnati. Used with permission.

Figure 6-22a. Cannel coal objects from Madisonville: bison pendant, from general digging along the line between Trenches 1 and 2, near the southwest end of Trench 2 (HUPM Cat. No. 97-38-10/62935), piece of coal engraved with serpent, turtle, and horned monster (note "heartline") from Pit F-2 (08-3-10/79245; see Hooton and Willoughby 1920: Pl. 20 for drawings of engravings on both sides), geometric-shaped pendant, from kitchen midden, Trenches 4-5 (97-38-10/62934). Photograph by Hillel Burger (HUPM Photo No. N33852). Copyright 1997 by the President and Fellows of Harvard College. Used with permission.

Figure 6-21f. (*facing page*) Selected metal artifacts from Madisonville, most of them European-derived. *Top*: three copper serpent shapes (one possibly brass) (HUPM Cat. Nos. 01-38-10/69771, 84-68-10/35647, 01-38-10/68258) and brass spiral (84-68-10/35563), all made from thin metal tubes. *Second level*: barred copper pendant (84-68-10/35537), barred ("cross-shaped") brass pendant with copper rolled beads and copper and brass coils made of thin tubes (82-35-10/26620, 82-35-10/26618, 82-35-10/26619), barred copper pendant (11-10-10/A4042). *Directly below pendants*: iron dagger guard (82-35-10/26696), two iron kettle lugs (07-6-10/78487, 01-38-10/69776), two fragments of iron kettle band, each with a rivet at its narrower end (01-38-10/69777). *Below pendants, to right*: fragment of copper kettle rim (84-68-10/35553), iron kettle band fragment (01-38-10/67571), iron kettle band fragment fashioned into celt (84-68-10/35355). Note that the bottom segment of the broken brass "cross" pendant should have been turned onto its other side in order to fit together with the upper segment. Proveniences discussed in text. Photo No. N33205, Peabody Museum, Harvard University, by Hillel Burger (HUPM Photo No. N33205). Copyright 1993 by the President and Fellows of Harvard College, and used with permission. Previously published (Drooker 1996b: Fig. 5).

Figure 6-22b. Cannel coal objects from Madisonville: bearlike animal effigy, from Conover Burial 14 (CMNH Cat. No. A42213). Photograph by William Collier, courtesy of the Cincinnati Museum Center.

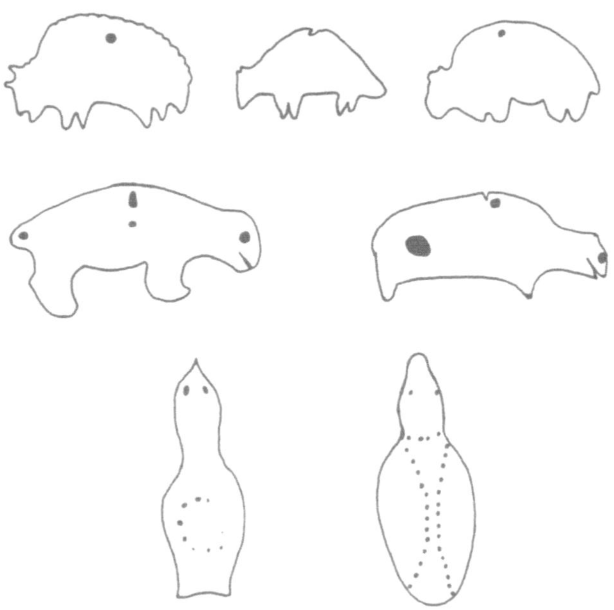

Figure 6-23. Animal effigies from Madisonville compared with effigies in other materials from elsewhere. *Top*: cannel coal bison effigy (see Figure 6-22a) and brass bison effigies (Fusihatchee and Coopers Farm, Alabama, ca. 1630-1700; after Waselkov 1989: Figs. 8a, c). *Middle*: cannel coal "bear" effigy (see Figure 6-22b; after Cowan 1992: Fig. 9) and brass "bear" effigy (Beale Mound, near Gallipolis, Ohio; W. Wertz collection). *Bottom*: antler/bone bird effigy (see Figure 6-18b) and shell bird effigy (Steele site, New York, ca. 1645-55; after Hayes 1989: Fig.11; dates from Saunders and Sempowski 1991:24). Not to scale.

tained from all parts of the site. The finest and most numerous group of coils was recovered during Putnam's visit in 1882, from the child burial containing the barred brass pendant (Figure 6-21f; for other examples, see Figures 6-21c and 6-21e). Of the 38 extant coils/rings, up to 19 came from the southwest portion of the site (3 from the Metz MLSS collection, 15 excavated by Conover and associates from midden areas and a pit, and 1 recovered during the recent CMNH excavations), 7 from Trenches 1-K (4 from adult burials of unknown sex—3-45, D-46, 2 with I-12—and the rest from two pits in Trenches 5 and E), and the remaining 12 from the child burial. At least 3 are brass and at least 25 are copper.

One artifact made from a silver-colored copper alloy was excavated from a midden in the southwestern portion of the site in 1938. It is a small shield-shaped item about two centimeters long with a horizontally oriented rectangular slot near its base, reminiscent of a metal tip from a modern leather belt (Figure 6-21c, bottom right; Drooker 1992d, 1996b). A high copper content is indicated by the green corrosion residue covering it. A likely material is German silver, a general name employed for high-nickel (>10%) copper alloys that also contain zinc, tin, and lead (Ellis 1948:45). The resemblance of German silver to genuine silver is deceptive enough that during the reign of William III (1672-1702 in the Netherlands, 1688-1702 in England) its manufacture was deemed a felony (Ellis 1948:131). Silver-colored high-tin copper alloys, the fabrication of which was discussed in print as early as 1540 (Biringuccio 1966:210), are another possibility. The closest counterpart for this item that I have yet found, described as part of a "brass belt buckle," came from a child burial at Brooks, Missouri, that also contained iron fragments, rolled and folded copper, and two copper-covered wooden ear plugs (O'Brien 1994: Fig. 7.11b). It seems to be

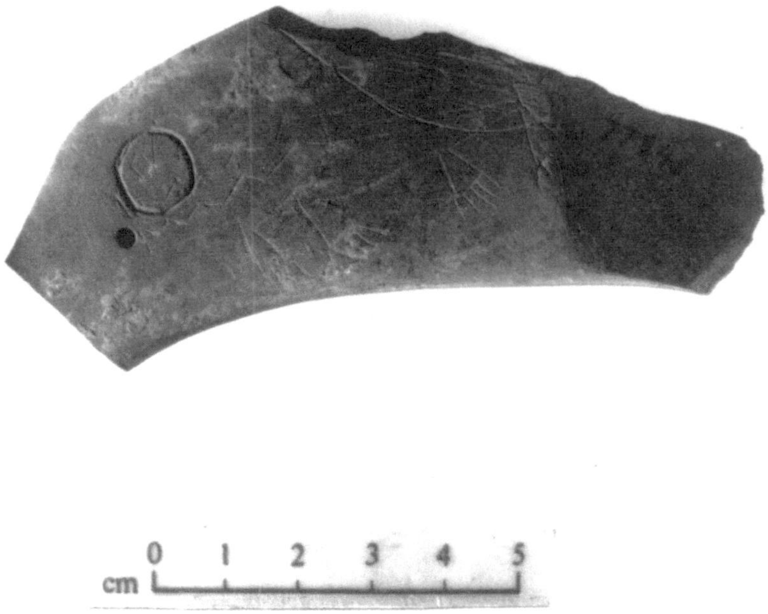

Figure 6-24. Engraved natural stone from Madisonville, Pit B-15 (HUPM Cat. No. 07-6-10/ 77945). Deep circle cuts into more lightly incised picture of horned and clawed monster (note "heartline"); reverse side depicts somewhat less detailed but similar monster. For drawings of engravings on both sides of stone, see Hooton and Willoughby 1920: Pl. 20. Photograph by Hillel Burger (HUPM Photo No. N33853). Copyright 1997 by the President and Fellows of Harvard College, and used with permission.

approximately the same size as the Madisonville artifact, but its slot has rounded rather than squared-off ends.

As summarized in Table 6-7, the vast majority of these materials and objects would have been available before 1600 (see also Figure 3-8). Table 6-7 also illustrates the point that many items common at post-1630 sites have not been found at Madisonville. Hypotheses that can account for this lack include: abandonment of the site soon after 1600, changes in exchange patterns that rendered European items unavailable, and a "broker" status for the settlement's residents such that later diagnostic European artifacts were not retained (cf. Ray 1978; Rogers 1990:162-63).

There is additional, albeit tenuous, evidence that might represent a somewhat extended occupation period for the settlement. Two carved cannel coal animal effigies have come from Madisonville, a bison, found in general digging in Trenches 1-2, and a bearlike creature, found with a detatched hand (assumed by the excavators to have been overlooked by pothunters) in the southwestern portion of the site in 1942 (Figures 6-22a, left, and 6-22b). Although significantly larger, they are otherwise remarkably similar to side-view brass animal effigies found at interior Southeastern sites dating between 1630 and 1700 (Figure 6-23, top) (Smith 1987:39-41; Waselkov 1989:124-28). A brass example that closely resembles the Madisonville bear came from a site in eastern Fort Ancient territory that was explored by amateurs, Beale Mound (Table 4-9), which also produced brass fish effigies and a very well-made Iroquoian-style tubular spiral, an artifact type that went out of use around 1625 (Bradley and Childs 1991a, 1991b). Which came first, coal or brass? It is impossible to know for sure. Although cannel coal tooth-, claw-, and forked-eye-shaped effigy pendants are well-known at Fort Ancient sites such as Fox Farm, Feurt, Clover, Orchard, and Buffalo (Graybill 1991: Table 14; Hanson 1975: Fig. 64h; Mayer-Oakes 1955: Pl. 107f-h; Mills 1917: Fig. 46; Smith 1910: Pl. xlix.1-xlix.7), as well as from Monongahela sites (e.g., Mayer-Oakes 1955: Figs. 25x, 25y), there appears to be no precedent for coal animal effigy pendants. The closest practice, perhaps, is that Madisonville residents and other Fort Ancient people did tend to collect and slightly modify natural stones and misshapen pieces of bone and antler that resembled animals and birds (e.g., Figure 6-18b, top right; Hooton and Willoughby 1920: Pls. 17e, 20f, 20h, 20i), and to engrave natural pebbles (including coal, sandstone, and other materials) with animal figures (Figures 6-22a, 6-24; Hooton and Willoughby Pl. 20a-c).

One of the Madisonville antler effigies, a bird pendant with a circle of small punctations on its back (Figures 6-18b, 6-23), closely resembles the small marine shell bird pendants that were popular on Seneca sites around 1640-1655 (Hayes 1989: Figs 1, 5, 11; Mackay 1989: Fig. 3; Sempowski 1989: Fig. 15; dates from Saunders and Sempowski 1991:24), except for the location of its hanging hole. Again, the question is: Which came first?

Mortuary Vessel Attributes

Although the nature of the sample precluded seriation or other statistical comparisons of ceramics from pit features, I had initial hopes of utilizing stylistic differences in mortuary vessels for identification of temporal components at Madisonville. I was particularly interested in distinguishing, if possible, ceramics associated with Early and Late Madisonville Horizon (prehistoric versus protohistoric) burials. As I discovered, the fairly tight constellation of attributes associated with Madisonville Horizon vessels at the site, which seems to represent a relatively short time frame, made it impossible to separate out precisely delineated groups of vessels, members of which could be assigned easily to successive time periods. The negative results do not warrant detailed discussion, so only a brief summary is included here (see Drooker 1996c:222-26 for a somewhat less abbreviated discussion).

Of 427 mortuary vessels with 424 burials recorded for the site, I have at least some information on 133 vessels that can be tied to particular burials. This includes detailed attribute data for 117, from personal inspection of whole vessels and sherds or from Griffin's published photographs, measurements, and trait lists (1943: Tables II-V), plus less detailed information on sixteen additional vessels from field notes, field photographs, or drawings. None of these vessels had the appearance of typical Anderson-like vessels (thickened, non-everted rim, neck plain or decorated with incised motifs, etc.), but a small minority of them had one or two early attributes, including castellations or "horns" above handles, loop handles, neck decoration, or thickened rims. Utilizing the 87 whole vessels of known provenience for which detailed attribute data were available (75 from Trenches 1-K and 12 from the remainder of the site), I carried out two types of analyses.

First, I attempted to use multidimensional scaling (Steponaitis 1983; Cowgill 1972), but ultimately rejected it as inappropriate for two reasons. First, too few gravelots at Madisonville included more than one vessel to allow seriation based on multiple vessels. Second, of the vessels in the sample, only a minority had attributes outside of the fairly narrow range of classic Madisonville Horizon pottery, and these attributes were diverse and idiosyncratic. For vessels with typical Madisonville Horizon attributes, MDS analysis did not result in any sort of linear pattern that could be interpreted as time-related—the attribute assemblages apparently were too interrelated to separate into clearly distinguished groups of vessels.

As an alternative, I applied K-means cluster analysis (a non-hierarchical iterative relocation procedure; Shennan 1988:226-28; Wilkinson et al. 1992:19-25) to the same group of whole vessels, using this procedure to cluster vessels together on the basis of similarity in selected nonmetric attributes. I did several sets of runs, each of which utilized a different group of attributes to derive different numbers of clusters, ranging from eight to eighteen. The attribute categories included as many traits as possible that had been suggested by other researchers as time-sensitive (e.g., grooved-paddling, lip notching, neck decoration), but were limited to attributes that occurred on at least five vessels and therefore did not include a number of other known time-sensitive attributes (e.g., thickened rims, loop handles).

In very general terms, these sets of runs gave similar results. In most cases there was one large cluster with a relatively large number of attributes shared among all or most of the vessels, a second smaller cluster with somewhat fewer attributes shared among all members, and many small clusters, most with only one or two members. Increasing the number of clusters generally led to the separating-off of additional individual vessels and some shifting of members between larger clusters, rather than to the formation of additional medium-sized clusters. The largest cluster in a given run tended to have vessels with four handles and very high frequencies of notched lips, plus relatively squat vessels (ratio of height to diameter < 1). Compared with vessels in the second-largest cluster, there were lower frequencies of smooth-surfaced vessels, higher frequencies of grooved-paddled surfaces, and higher frequencies of shoulder notching or punctation (e.g., Table 6-8). Since lip notching and grooved-paddling are among the attributes pinpointed by other researchers as most strongly associated with Late Madisonville Horizon vessels (Chapter 4), the constellation of attributes associated with the largest clusters probably is more recent than attributes associated with the second-largest clusters.

None of the provenienced burials with extant whole vessels contained metal or glass (although two did have copper-stained bone), so relative ages of vessels in the two clusters could not be checked by this means. Utilizing the two largest clusters from a 32-attribute, 18-cluster run (Table 6-8), there was a correlation between cluster group membership and burial depth in Trenches 1-K, with vessels from cluster 2 relatively more common with deeper burials (below 24 inches) and those from cluster 1 relatively more common with shallower burials, but the correlation was not statistically significant at the .05 level (Fisher's Exact Test, 3 df). Additional evidence for the relative ages of these attribute clusters will be developed below.

Locations of vessels from these cluster groups will be discussed further in the next section, but it is worth mentioning here that in all cases where vessels from the two largest cluster groups of a given run were mapped in Trenches 1-K, they appeared to be thoroughly intermixed, often found in adjacent burials, although there were some small areas where only vessels from the largest (probably most recent) cluster were present. The fact that vessels from the two cluster groups were not each associated with spatially separate groups of burials lends credence to the conclusion that the differences in form, surface treatment, and decoration between the groups were related to gradual temporal trends rather than to social differentiation.

Spatial Distributions and Stratigraphic Relationships of Horizon Markers

Besides the usefulness of horizon marker artifacts and practices in determining periods of occupation for the site as a whole, their positions within the site can be helpful in unraveling settlement occupation history. Although the Madisonville archaeological record is incomplete, enough information on provenience exists from Trenches 1-K to warrant further investigation. In addition, some gross similarities and differences in the presence of horizon markers can be detected between Trenches 1-K and Blocks 1-17. It must be kept in mind that lack of recorded presence for a particular trait does not necessarily mean that it was absent from the archaeological record.

TABLE 6-8
Attributes of Madisonville Mortuary Vessels
in Two Groups Identified by Cluster Analysis

	Cluster 1 (N = 45)	Cluster 2 (N = 21)
FORM	(relatively squat)	(less squat)
Height < diameter	91%	57%
Body diameter < lip diameter	58%	24%
Unusual form (e.g., oval, double, pedestal, etc.)	2%	0%
SURFACE TREATMENT		
Plain (smoothed)	27%	43%
Cordmarked	47%	43%
Grooved-paddled	27%	10%
LIP TREATMENT		
Notched	100%	0%
- around entire rim	78%	
- above handles	22%	
NUMBER OF HANDLES		
Four	98%	62%
Two	2%	24%
None	0%	14%
FORM OF HANDLES		
Strap	100%	100%
Loop	0%	0%
Cross section:		
- flat	100%	67%
- oval	0%	19%
Vertical shape:		
- tapered	71%	48%
- hourglass	20%	14%
- parallel sides	9%	24%
NECK TREATMENT		
Smoothed surface	100%	100%
Incised/punctated decoration present	0%	0%
Nodes present	0%	14%
SHOULDER TREATMENT		
Decoration present (notching, punctation)	22%	0%

Attributes of vessels in the two largest groups identified by K-means cluster analysis in a run utilizing 32 attributes and 18 clusters. The other 16 clusters ranged in size from one to three vessels. All vessels in Clusters 1 and 2 are jars. Percentages are of total number of vessels in each cluster group.

Trenches 1-K

Relatively detailed information on artifact types, styles, and proveniences, plus the development of a GIS map, made possible a more fine-grained consideration of spatial and stratigraphic relationships in Trenches 1-K than was possible for other portions of the site.

Stratigraphic Relationships. As observed by Hooton and Willoughby, a fair number of burials in the northern half of the site either cut through other features or were cut by other burials or pits. The distribution of recorded crosscutting features (Figure 6-25) implies that the northwestern part of the site was occupied for the shortest period of time; that is, people living there did not forget where earlier burials were located. This tentative conclusion should be taken with a grain of salt, however, as it is possible that the excavators of Trenches 1-5 simply did not begin to record this information until well into the excavation of Trench 3. Likewise, Trenches A-C had few recorded examples of crosscutting features, which could be due to the relative inexperience of the Harvard student in charge (Drooker 1996c:504-6).

Depths of burials might be roughly correlated with length of time since interment, as Hanson hypothesized was true at the Hardin site (Hanson 1966:71-73, 169). Distance from ground surface to "top of head" was recorded for most of the burials in Trenches 1-K. However, it is not clear exactly how this measurement was taken, nor whether excavators in different years were entirely consistent in method. Moreover, some time between 1897 and 1907 the site was heavily lumbered, undoubtedly compacting and otherwise altering the surface, so measurements from the surface in Trenches A-K might well differ from what they would have been prior to the timber cutting. Several of the excavators noted that a great many of the graves were just at or dug slightly into the hardpan layer, and some excavators frequently included measurements of burial depths relative to hardpan in their field notes. This would have been a very good benchmark for comparing burial depths, but unfortunately the information was not recorded consistently enough to make it useful for mapping purposes. Therefore, in mapping locations of burials at varying depths, I employed the recorded measurement from surface to top of head, but separated burials by arbitrary six-inch levels rather than making any finer-grained distinctions.

Figures 6-26a-d show the locations of burials at different levels. Almost 80% of the total were within 24 inches of the surface (Figures 6-26c, d). These graves were dispersed across most parts of Trenches 1-K. However, some areas of the site appear to have been more heavily used at particular levels. Many of the deepest burials were clustered together in Trench F at the north-central edge of the Harvard-excavated portion of the site, whereas there were few deep burials around the western, southern, and eastern edges (Figure 6-26a). The shallowest burials (Figure 6-26d) appear to have been least concentrated in Trench F, Trench 3, and adjacent portions of Trenches 2 and 4. Contrasts in burial depths are notable in two areas adjacent to the plaza, evident in comparisons between Figures 6-26b and d. The dense arc of burials in Trenches 2, 3, and 4 was concentrated between 30 and 18 inches beneath the surface. Directly across the open plaza, in Trenches E, F and D, was another densely packed group of burials, almost all at 24 inches and above.

I did find statistically significant differences in grave goods accompanying burials at different depths (Figure 6-27) that made it seem likely that the deepest interments probably were among the earliest. Only one burial below 36 inches had any grave goods, and none had mortuary vessels. None below 30 inches had classic Madisonville vessels, at least as far as can be determined from the extant sample. Although two burials between 30 and 36 inches below the surface contained copper, no Euro-

Figure 6-25. Distribution of crosscutting features, Trenches 1-K. Includes burials that cut through other burials or pits, burials over pits, and burials cut by other burials or pits. Pits that cut other pits generally were not possible to determine from the field notes.

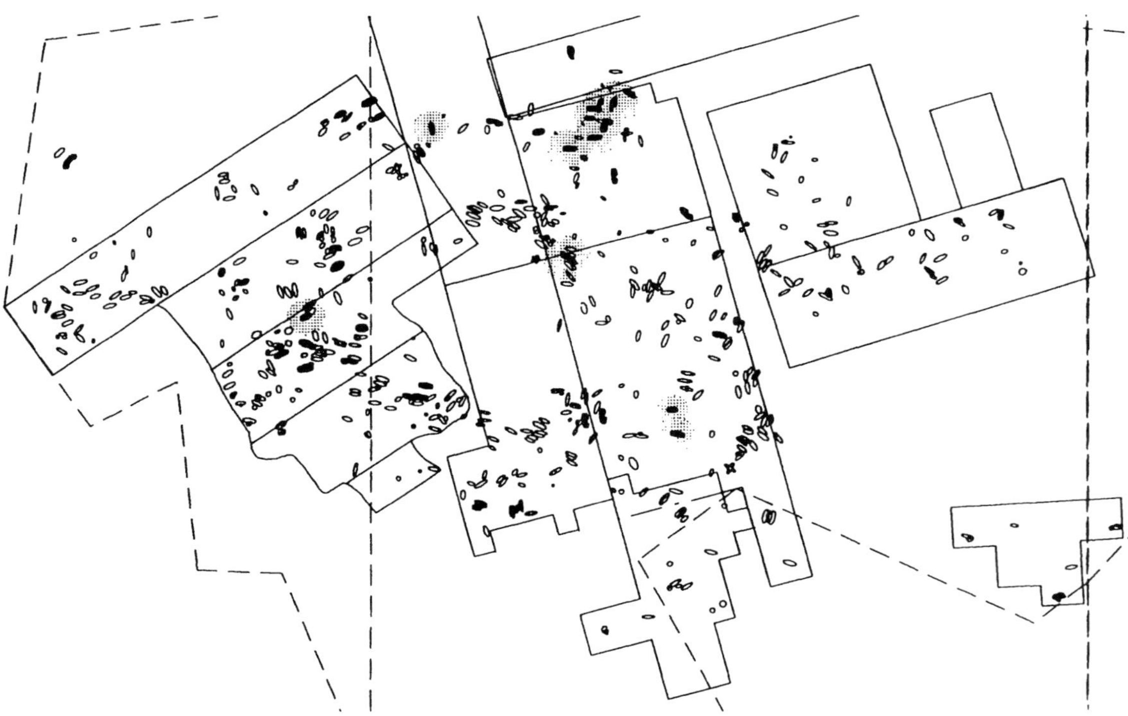

Figure 6-26a. Distribution of burials more than 30 inches below the surface, Trenches 1-K. Burials below 36 inches are highlighted.

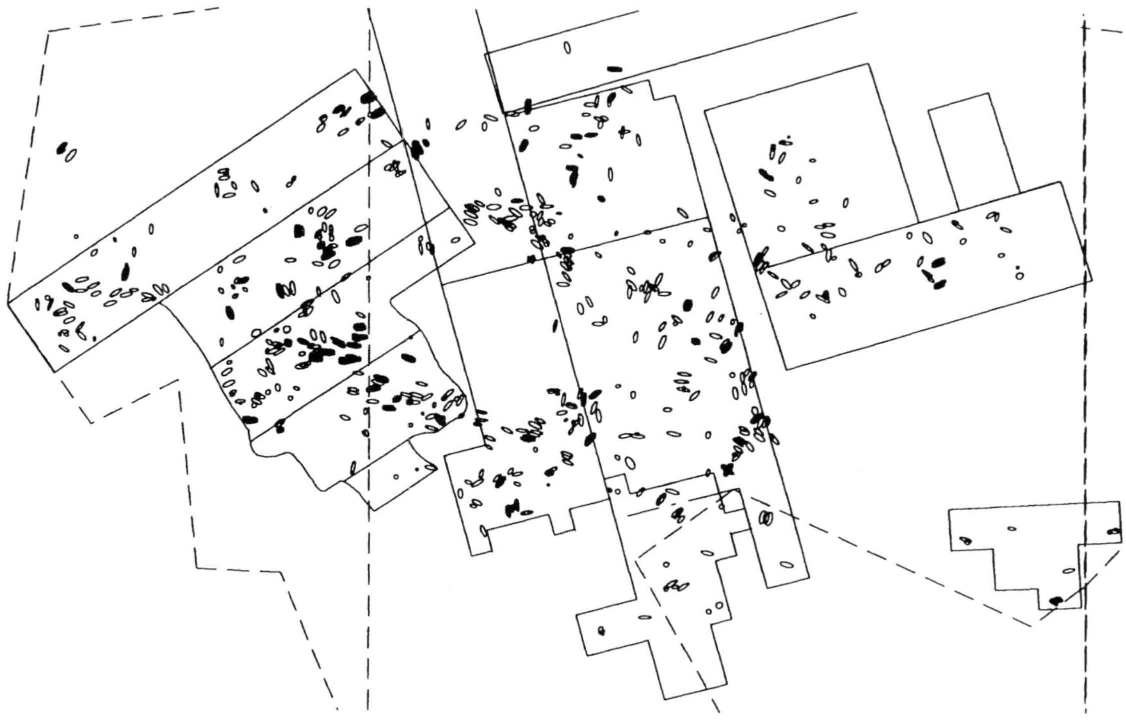

Figure 6-26b. Distribution of burials between 30 and 24.5 inches below the surface, Trenches 1-K.

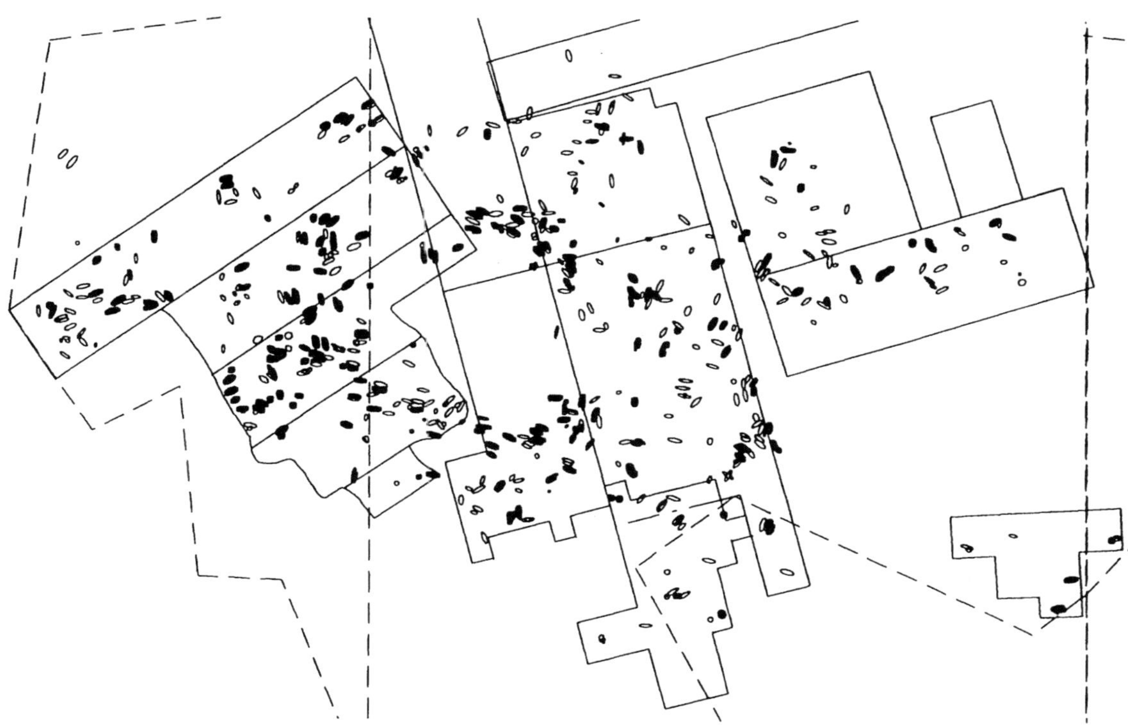

Figure 6-26c. Distribution of burials between 24 and 18.5 inches below the surface, Trenches 1-K.

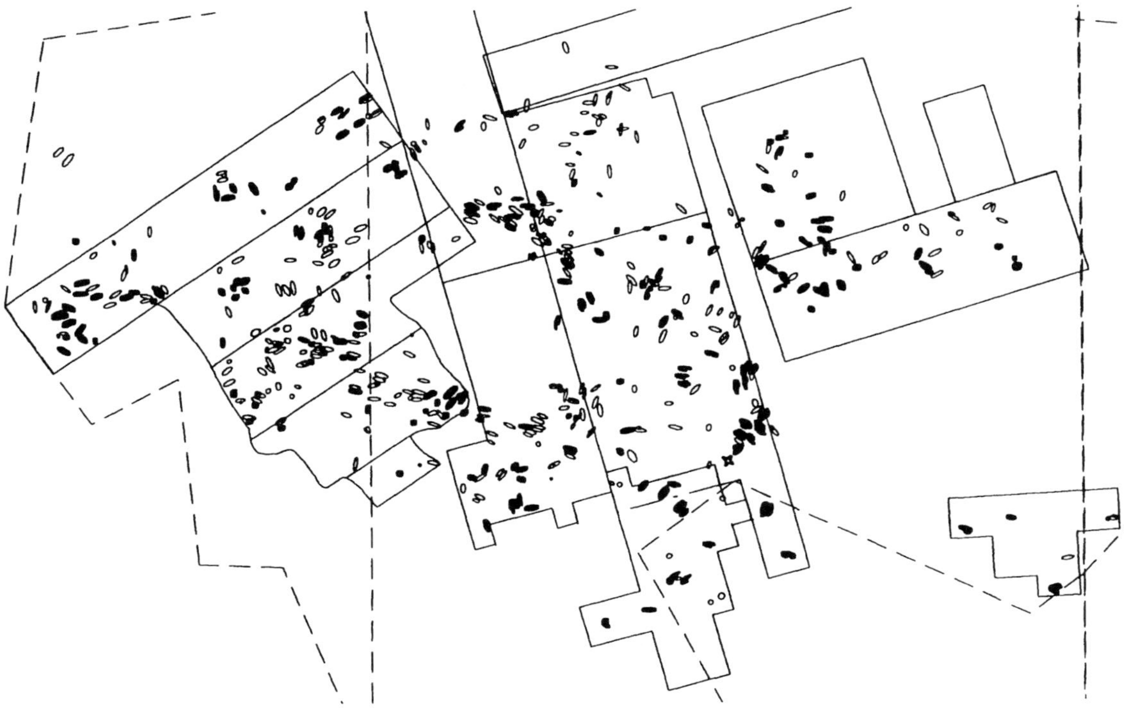

Figure 6-26d. Distribution of burials 18 inches or less below the surface, Trenches 1-K.

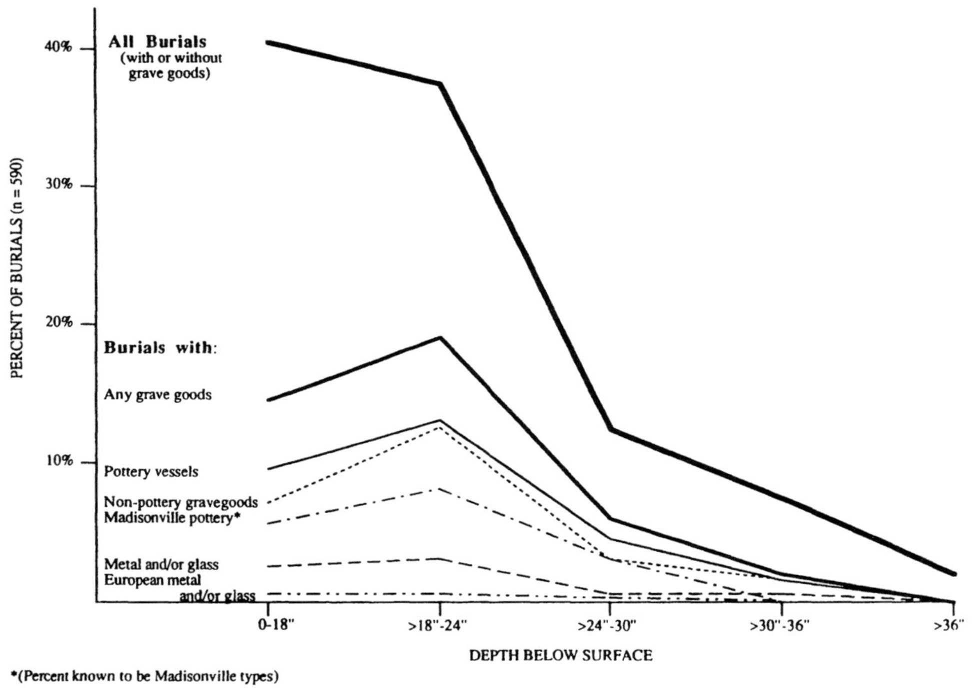

Figure 6-27. Frequencies of grave goods versus burial depths, Trenches 1-K.

pean-derived artifacts (e.g., of iron, brass, or glass) were found that deep. Only one burial known to have such materials (a special individual who will be discussed further in Chapter 7) was below 24 inches.

All grave goods occurred at lower frequencies with the shallowest burials than with burials in the second level (18 to 24 inches) (Figure 6-27). This raises the possibility that the frequency of grave goods might have declined with the most recent burials at the site. Of course, the observed differences might or might not be time-related. Burial depth also could be related to social factors, such as shallow disposal for individuals whose low status did not warrant much expenditure of energy (or particularly deep burial for high-status personages).

To investigate this further, I considered adult versus subadult burials at different depths. (Groups identified by sex and finer-grained age categories were too small to use for these purposes.) Indeed, there was a statistically significant preponderance of subadult burials within the shallowest level (chi square test, 1 df, $p = 0.05$). However, the interpretation of this occurrence is not simple. As illustrated in Figure 6-28, these subadults had a relatively high frequency of grave goods—not what would be expected if these were low-status burials. Adults buried within the shallowest level did have significantly fewer than expected grave goods. Probably these differences are related to both temporal and social factors. Numerous hypotheses are possible: for instance, that subadults always were buried at shallower depths than adults, so that many of those with grave goods in level 1 came from the same time period as adults with grave goods in level 2; or that during the final years of occupation there was both an excess of subadult deaths and an increased tendency to put grave goods with subadults rather than adults. Interpreting these data must also take into account an apparently high infant survivorship rate that probably is due to sample bias (Drooker 1996c:522-24, Fig. B1, Tables B2-B4).

Spatial Distribution of Horizon Marker Artifacts in Refuse Pits. Distribution of horizon marker artifacts also can be used to explore occupation history of the site. Because so many artifacts from pits (particularly ceramics) were left in the field or later deaccessioned, no fine-grained information can be sought through mapping their locations. However, if data limitations are kept in mind, distributions of certain nonmortuary artifacts still can be useful in obtaining generalized information about site occupation.

The great majority of pits in Trenches 1-K for which there are extant artifacts contained Late Fort Ancient horizon markers (Figure 6-29). Few are known to have contained Woodland artifacts, which in any case originally would have been deposited on the ground surface and only later redeposited in pits. Although CMNH archaeologists working in the southwestern portion of the site found few pits containing the early pottery that was associated with the lower levels of the stratified midden they excavated (Glowacki et al. 1993:4), Early and Middle Fort Ancient people are known to have dug deep storage pits (e.g., at the Haag, State Line, Incinerator, and Anderson sites: Essenpreis 1982:62, 68-69; Nass 1987:150-72; Oehler 1973:52; Reidhead and Limp 1974:15), so at least some pits at Madisonville might date to that period. Mapping locations of horizon marker items found in pits might shortchange the very earliest components, during which refuse was deposited in middens rather than refuse pits, but unfortunately no precise locations were recorded for items excavated from non-feature proveniences.

The distributions in Trench 1-K pits of different types of projectile points, which probably constitute a more complete collection than ceramics, illustrate the different scales of occupation during successive time periods and also give some indication of which parts of the site were being used. The few pre-Fort Ancient points found in pits were grouped together in small clusters across the flattest part of Trenches 1-K (Figure 6-30; cf. Figure 5-7). Somewhat more type 2 points than pre-Fort Ancient points are present in the HUPM Trench 1-K collection (Table 6-5), and a higher proportion of them were recovered from pits (Figure 6-31). They were found at wide intervals surrounding the plaza, with a definite presence in Trench F and adjacent areas, in a line along the rising ground toward the north and east. Although it is risky to read too much into an artifact's apparent absence, the lack of type 2 points in Trench 1, where many type 5 and type 6 points were found, is notable. Type 4 and type 5 points were most numerous, and covered the widest area (Figure 6-32). Type 6 points were found across much of that same area, but had far less of a presence in all trenches except 1 and H. They were more common at a distance from the plaza than close to its edges (Figure 6-33).

Early-Middle Fort Ancient ceramics were more broadly dispersed in pits (Figure 6-34) than were type 2 points (Figure 6-31). The decorated types probably were favored for retention in HUPM collections over the less-decorated Late Fort Ancient wares. In spite of this, though, almost twice as many pits containing Madisonville Horizon as pre-Madisonville Horizon ceramics are represented in the collection (Figure 6-35). More pits with early than late styles can be seen in Trench F, but later styles appear to have had a relatively greater presence in Trenches 1, B, and D.

A number of types of bone artifacts have been identified with Late Fort Ancient, the rasp being one that is thought to date to protohistoric times (Table 6-5). Rasp fragments were found in pits in a broad circle around the plaza but not immediately adjacent to it (Figure 6-36).

Spatial Distribution of Horizon Markers with Respect to Burials. Graves represent better time capsules than do refuse pits (Rowe 1962; Schiffer 1987:88). Because burials around the edges of plazas, rather than in and around houses, seem to have been more common at earlier Fort Ancient sites like Incinerator than at protohistoric sites like Buffalo (Chapter 4), I hypothesized that the earliest burials at Madisonville would be close to the open area and the later ones farther back. In actuality, occupation history appears to have been more complex. Although the most recent artifact types, European items, indeed were found in burials away from the plaza's edge, it was diffi-

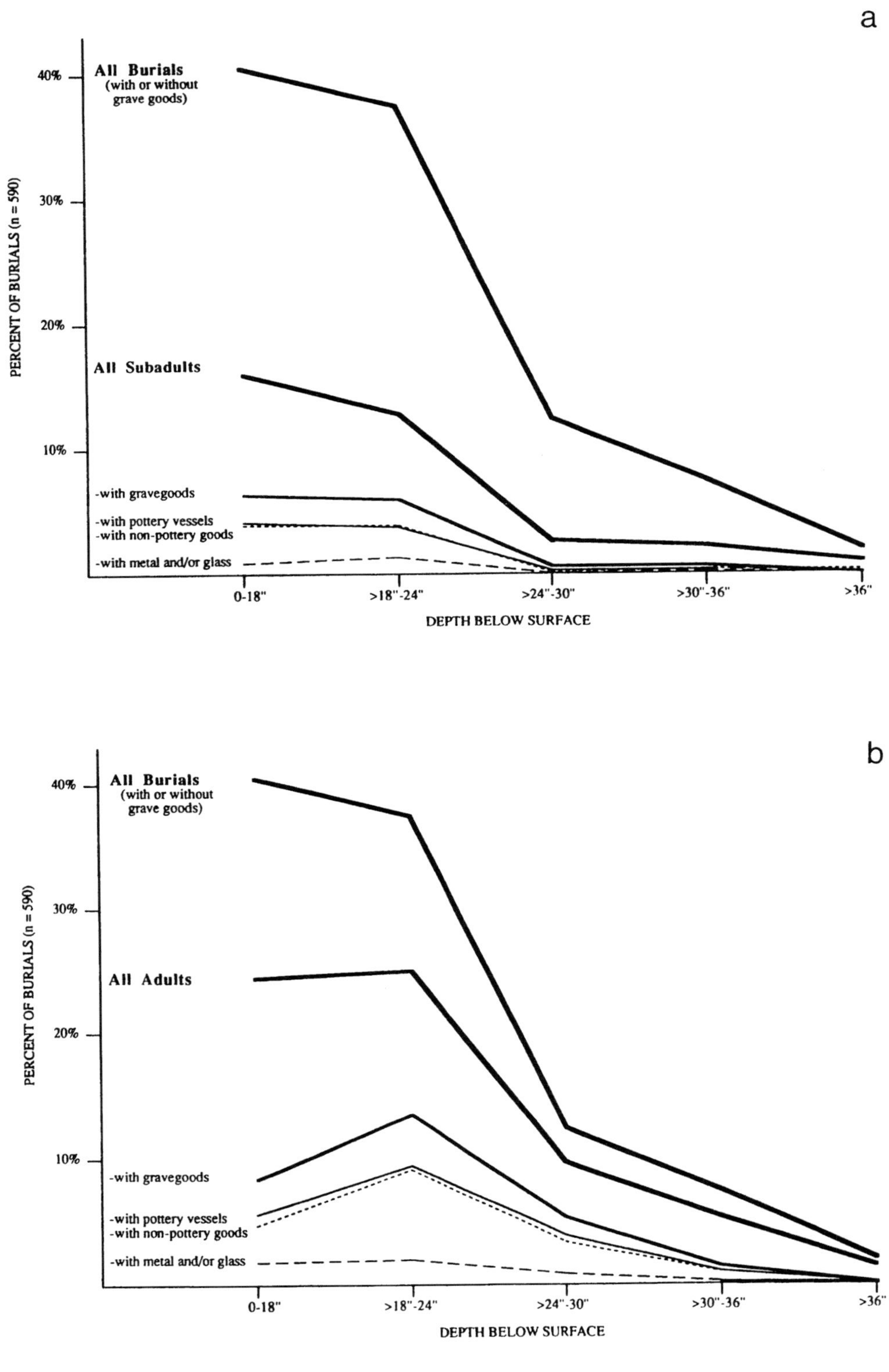

Figure 6-28. Frequencies of grave goods versus burial depths by age group, Trenches 1-K. *a*. With subadults. *b*. With adults.

Figure 6-29. Distribution of indigenous Late Fort Ancient (Madisonville Horizon) artifacts in pits at Madisonville, Trenches 1-K. Includes Madisonville jars and bowls, type 6 projectile points, leaf-shaped knives, endscrapers, bison bone beamers, rasps, combs, shaft wrenches, and vasiform, disk, and keel pipes that have been retained in the HUPM collection.

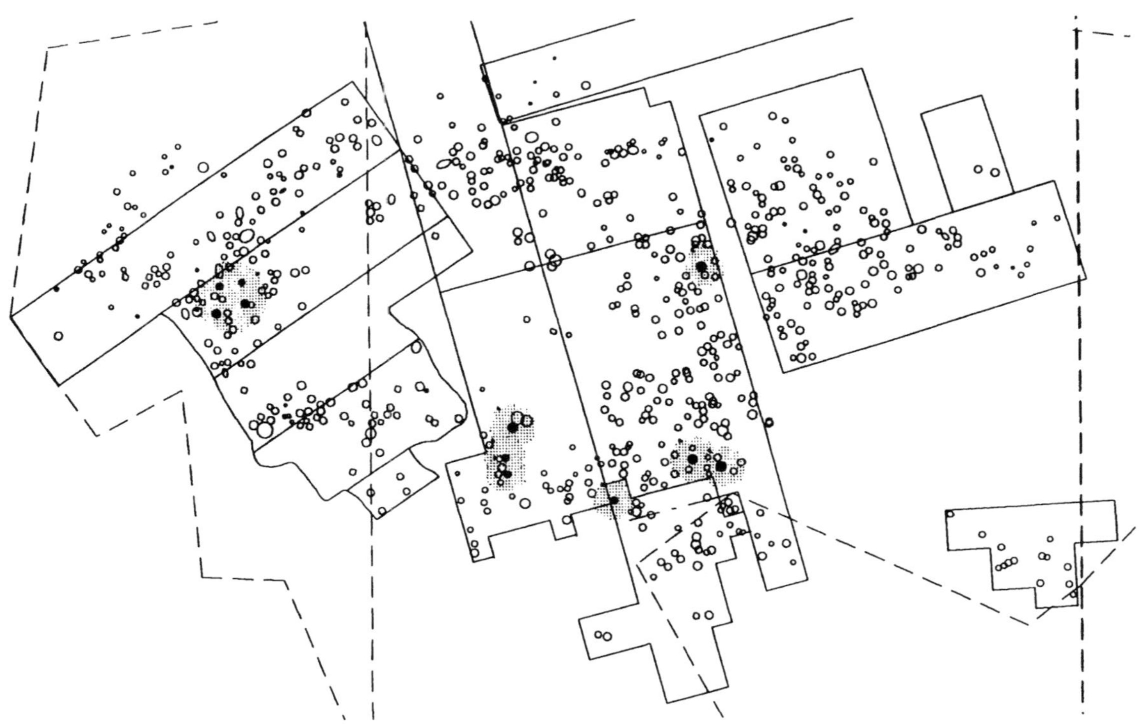

Figure 6-30. Distribution of notched and stemmed projectile points in pits at Madisonville, Trenches 1-K, based on artifacts retained in the HUPM collection.

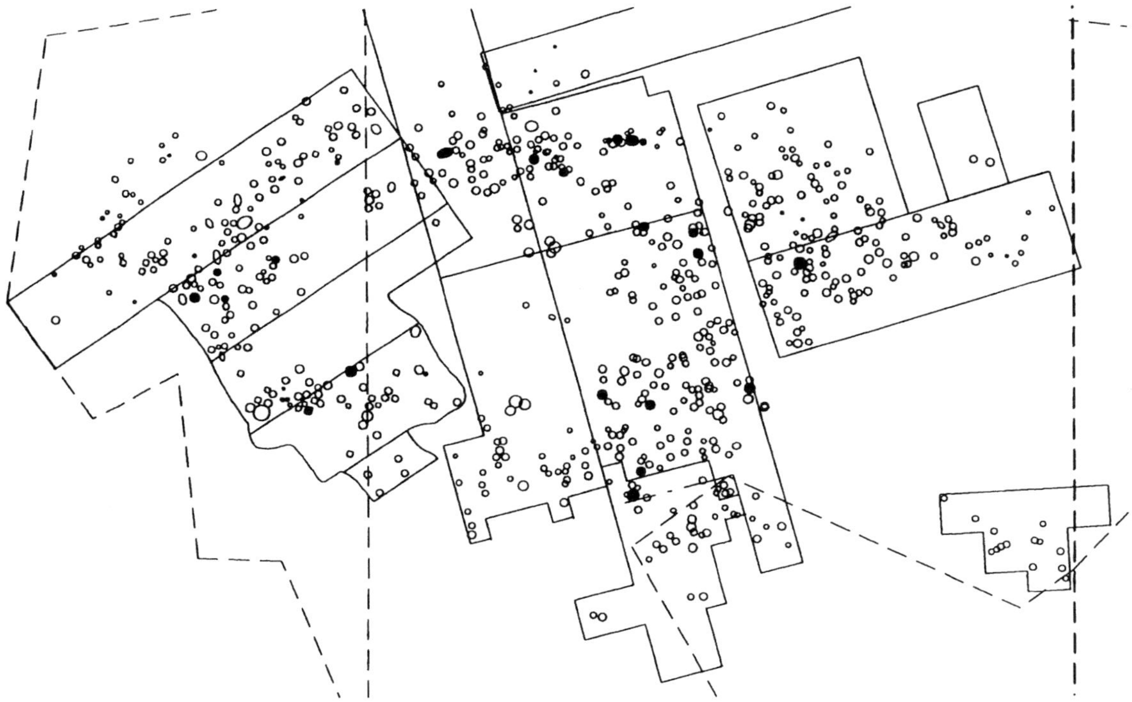

Figure 6-31. Distribution of type 2 triangular points in pits at Madisonville, Trenches 1-K, based on artifacts retained in the HUPM collection.

Figure 6-32. Distribution of types 4 and 5 triangular points in pits at Madisonville, Trenches 1-K, based on artifacts retained in the HUPM collection.

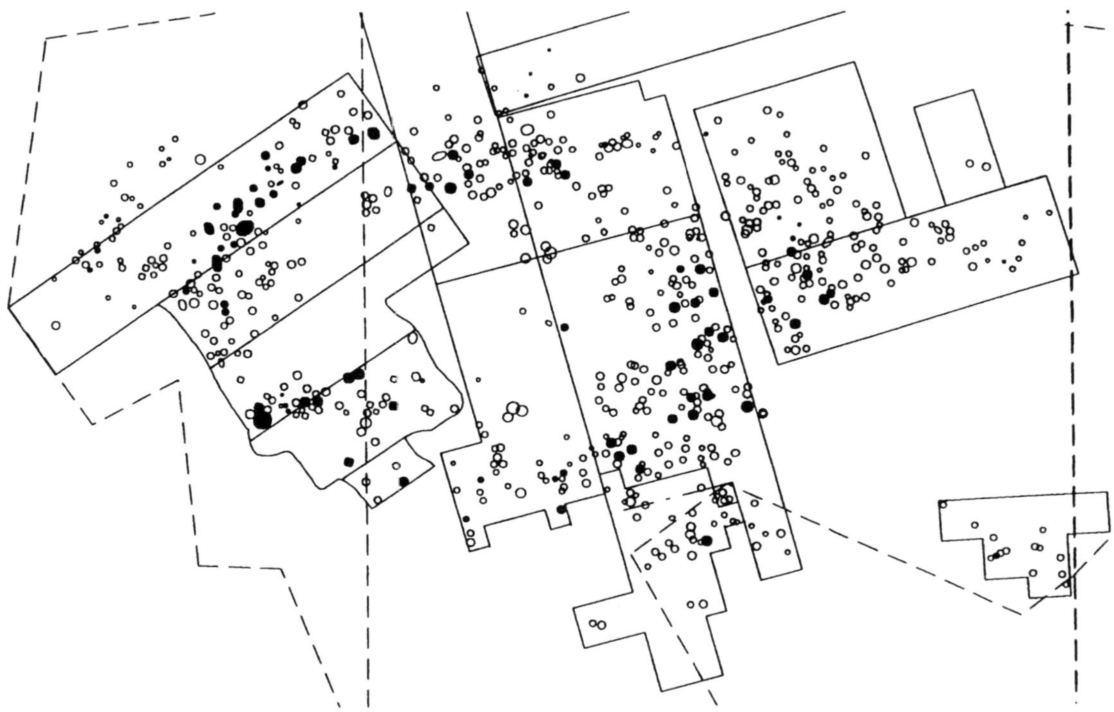

Figure 6-33. Distribution of type 6 triangular points in pits at Madisonville, Trenches 1-K, based on artifacts retained in the HUPM collection.

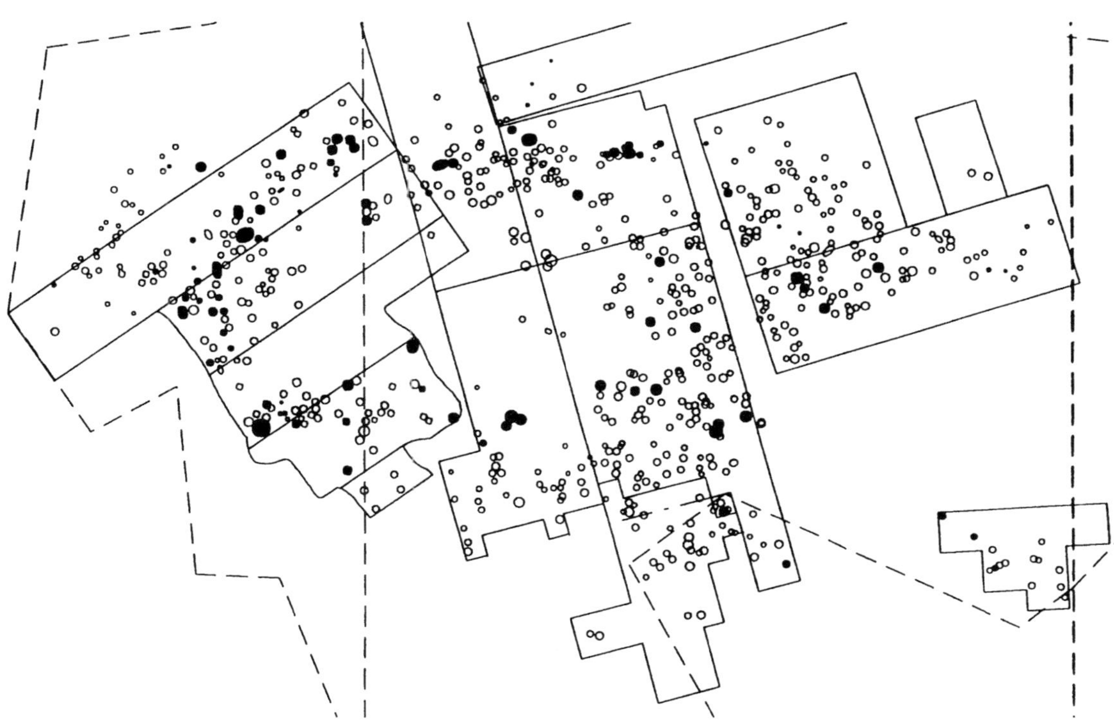

Figure 6-34. Distribution of Anderson Shell Tempered pottery in pits at Madisonville, Trenches 1-K, based on artifacts retained in the HUPM collection. All but eight of these pits had sherds with decorated necks or rim strips, which probably were selectively retained. The most common motifs were incised guilloche, square guilloche, or (more rarely) line-filled triangles over smoothed necks, sometimes with added punctation (see Figure 4-8). Eleven pits produced sherds with incised decoration over cord-marked necks.

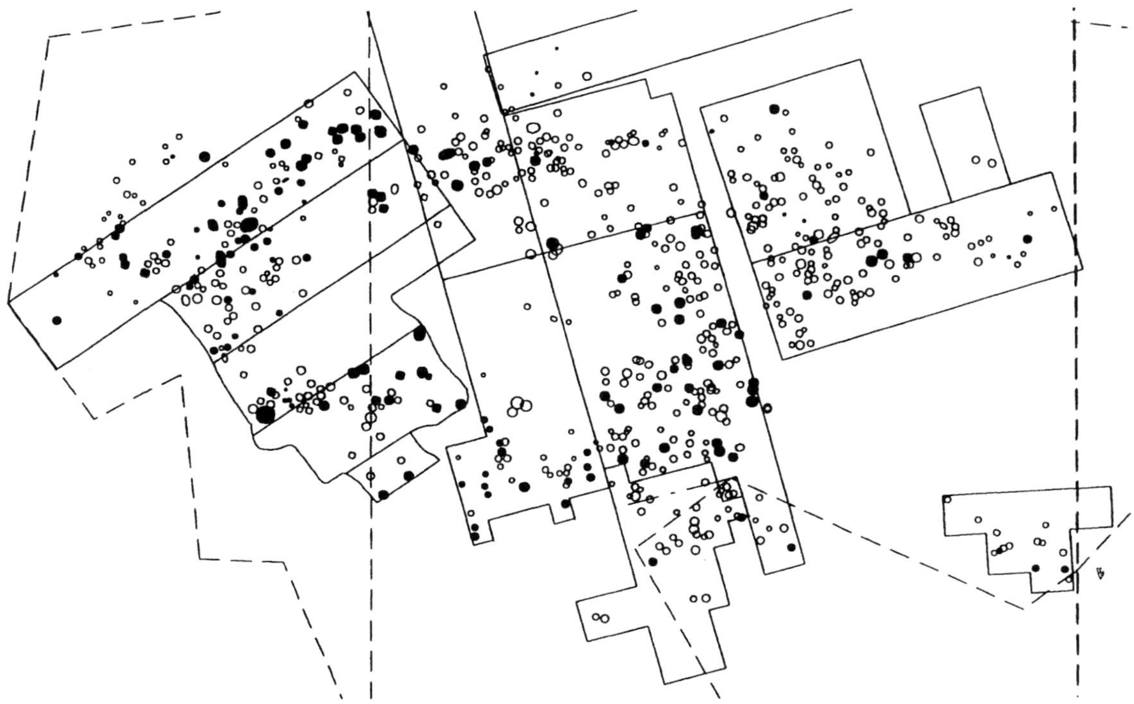

Figure 6-35. Distribution of Madisonville Horizon jars and bowls in pits at Madisonville, Trenches 1-K, based on artifacts retained in the HUPM collection.

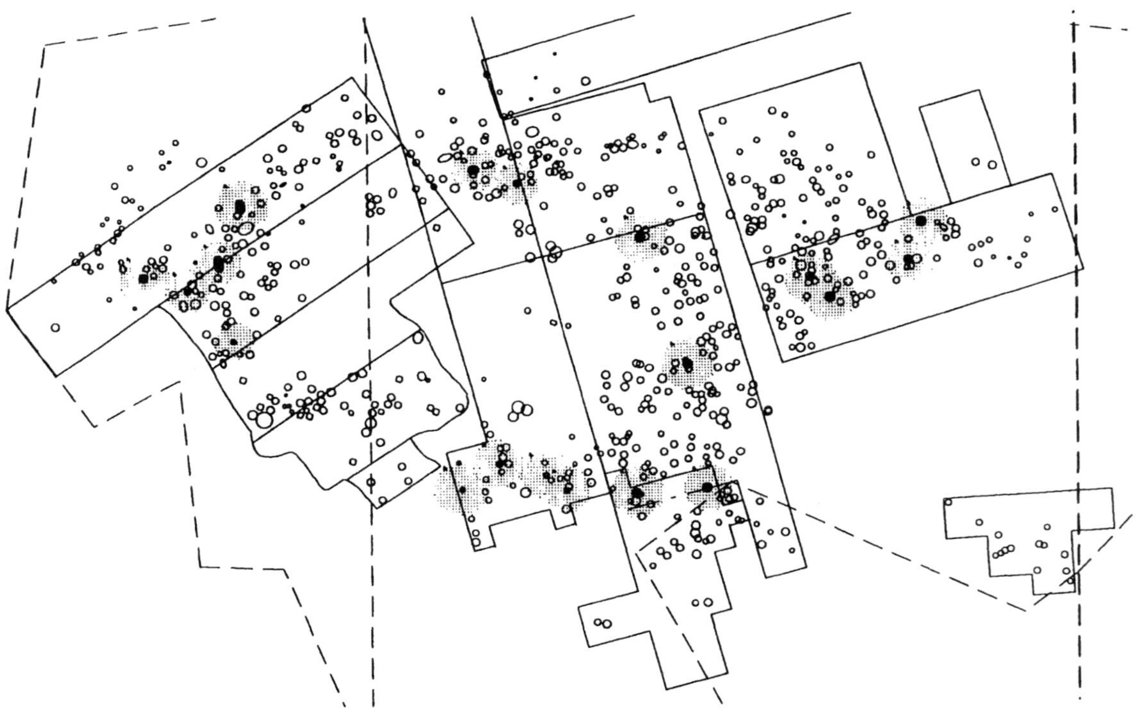

Figure 6-36. Distribution of pits containing bone rasps, Trenches 1-K, based on artifacts retained in the HUPM collection.

cult to discern any sort of gradual progression from center to periphery.

First of all, the very deepest burials, perhaps the earliest (Figure 6-26a, highlighted), were neither close to nor oriented around the plaza area. They may well predate it.

The very few extant mortuary vessels with pre-Madisonville Horizon attributes were found widely separated along a line following the edge of the rising ground to the northeast (Figure 6-37; cf. Fig. 5-7), with no strong relationship to the plaza. They form no coherent style group, and it is possible that some of them were foreign-influenced rather than early. (It is worth noting, though, that one-third of them were with burials deeper than 30 inches and two-thirds with burials deeper than 24 inches). All were more elongated and had less well-defined necks than typical Madisonville Horizon jars. Vessels with Burials E-29 and D-72 had broad castellations over their two handles, the vessel with Burial F-20 (Hooton and Willoughby 1920: Pl. 24a) had a decorated neck and no handles but not a thickened rim, the vessel with Burial D-70 had loop handles combined with a fingernail-notched shoulder (Hooton and Willoughby 1920: Pl. 23p), and the one with Burial K-1 (Figure 8-37c, below) had thickened rim and decorated neck with a cord-impressed rim perhaps similar to Oliver phase pottery (cf. Dorwin 1971: Fig. 6c).

Ninety-three of the 100 mortuary vessels in Trenches 1-K that could be typed were classic (smooth-necked) Madisonville Horizon jars and related styles, very similar to those in Figure 4-9. Many of the burials with such vessels were close to and oriented parallel to the edges of the plaza (Figure 6-38). There was no clear separation, however, between locations of Madisonville Horizon mortuary vessels that had earlier and later stylistic attributes. Both were found in burials close to and away from the plaza edge, and in burials oriented and not oriented to the plaza edge. Locations of earlier and later vessels distinguished on the basis of attribute analysis (Table 6-8) overlapped considerably, often being found in adjacent burials. However, vessels farthest from the plaza did tend to be ones with later attributes; for instance, in Figure 6-39, the vessels in Trenches 1, H, and I all had later attributes. Spatial intermixing also held true for Madisonville style vessels differentiated by individual earlier or later attributes, such as two versus four handles. This seems to demonstrate continuous, consistent use of space during Madisonville Horizon times over a time span long enough to allow gradual evolution of ceramic attributes.

Most, but by no means all, of the metal at the site probably dates to after 1540. Unlike the distribution of all burials accompanied by any metal, burials that definitely were associated with European items were not near the edge of the plaza (Figure 6-40). The difference probably is temporal, but could be social. Pits containing identified European materials are somewhat more widely distributed than burials with such items, but they, too, generally are not close to the plaza area (Figure 6-41; cf. Table 6-6). As can be seen, there are large portions of the site where no identified European items were found.

Figure 6-42 is designed to emphasize areas of the site where metal and glass were present or absent—a conservative indicator of areas that might have been in heavy use primarily after or before 1540. Of particular interest are the dense clusters of burials lacking metal/glass in Trench 3 and on the opposite side of the plaza, across Trenches E, F, and D. These two sectors also apparently lack bone rasps (Figure 6-36), so they might well have had most intensive use prior to the mid-sixteenth century. From burial depths, discussed above, the Trench 3 cluster might be the earlier of the two. Again, though, it must be noted that social differentiation might be at work here rather than, or in addition to, temporal differentiation. Also lacking metal are the very deep burials at the north end of Trench F (Figure 6-26a).

The burial that contained the greatest variety of European material, including items of European copper, brass, and iron (Trench 1, No. 60), also had the most marine shell, over 50 large columnella and barrel beads (Figure 6-19a). Since shell ornaments with burials are statistically correlated with both metal (chi square test, 1 df, $\alpha = 0.01$) and European materials (Fisher's Exact Test, 1 df, $\alpha = 0.05$), they, too might be generally associated with later burials. Only a few people with shell grave goods were interred close to the plaza (Figure 6-43).

The implications of these patterns, which do seem to indicate that the most recent residents of this portion of the Madisonville site were less strongly associated with the edge of the plaza area than were their immediate predecessors, will be explored further below.

Southern versus Northern Portions of Site

As mentioned previously, Hooton hypothesized that site occupation progressed from southwest to northeast. Does this hold up in light of the additional information now available on horizon marker artifacts?

The few extant artifacts associated with the house circles and one nearby burial mound on the high ground to the northeast appear to significantly predate the Madisonville Horizon, with no European artifacts or other protohistoric indicators known to have been present. This seems to be a completely separate component, minimally connected, if at all, with the Ancient Cemetery on the Ferris property.

The concentration of flexed burials without grave goods in the southwestern corner of the site probably also is pre-Madisonville Horizon, perhaps Late Woodland. Again, this very likely is a separate component, not part of a gradual shift in use of the site.

Both Woodland and Early-Middle Fort Ancient artifacts were present in the southwestern part of the site, but their relative frequencies are unknown. As noted above, virtually all types of pre-Fort Ancient, Early-Middle Fort Ancient, and Late Fort Ancient horizon markers present in Trenches 1-K also were present in Blocks 1-17. For artifacts associated with Late Fort Ancient, the fact that examples of many significant but rare forms

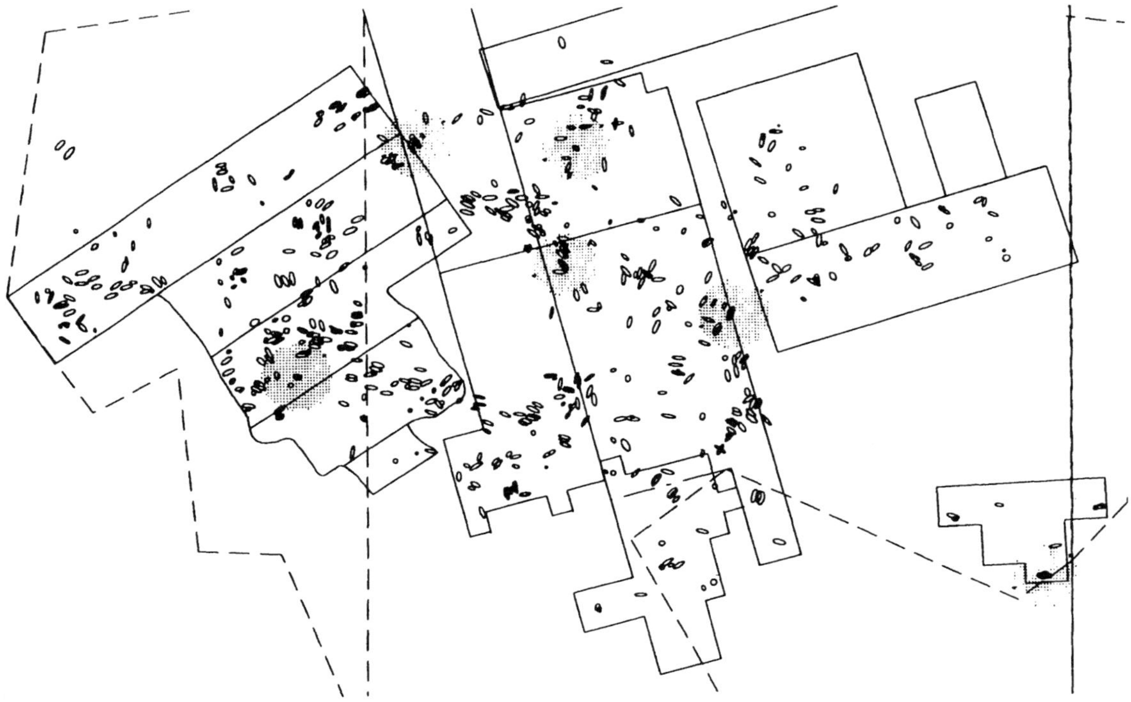

Figure 6-37. Burials known to have had mortuary vessels with pre-Madisonville Horizon or transitional attributes, Trenches 1-K. Includes jars with thickened rims, minimally everted rims, decorated necks, loop handles, or handles topped by castellations or "horns." Based on extant ceramics (74% of excavated mortuary vessels).

Figure 6-38. Burials known to have had mortuary vessels of classic Madisonville types and other Late Madisonville Horizon styles, Trenches 1-K. Includes plain, cord-marked, grooved-paddled, or net-impressed jars with smoothed necks, thin rims, and strap handles, and bowls with smooth or notched rims. Based on extant ceramics (74% of excavated mortuary vessels).

Figure 6-39. Distribution of mortuary vessels in Trenches 1-K belonging to the two largest clusters established by attribute analysis of 87 whole vessels (see Table 6-8). As a group, cluster 1 vessels have more late attributes than cluster 2 vessels.

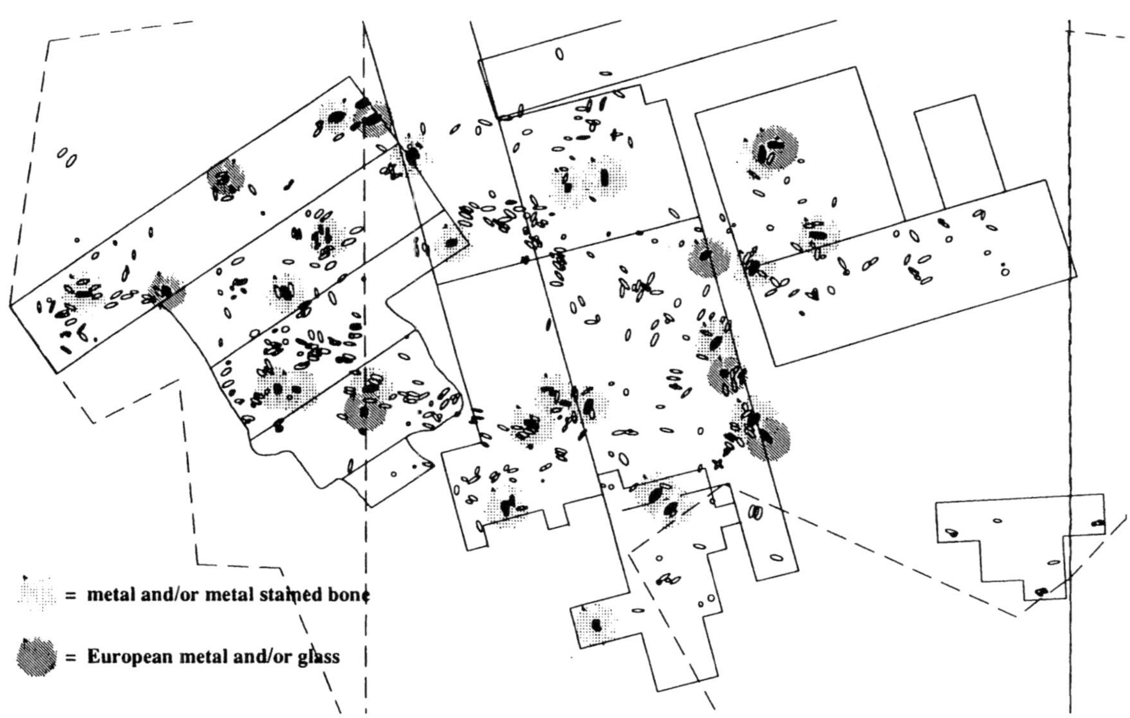

Figure 6-40. Distribution of burials with metal or metal-stained bone, Trenches 1-K. Highlighted features contained European metal or glass. Iron items, brass items (primarily identified by scratch tests), and European copper (visually identified by attributes such as the presence of rivets) represent a bare minimum of European metal present.

Figure 6-41. Distribution of all features containing European metal or glass, Trenches 1-K. Burials are highlighted.

Figure 6-42. Distribution of all features associated with metal or glass, Trenches 1-K: refuse pits containing glass, metal, or metal-stained material, burials with glass, metal, or metal-stained grave goods, and burials closely associated with them (e.g., in the same grave, or intruding into a pit). Shaded rectangles emphasize portions of the site where metal and glass are completely lacking.

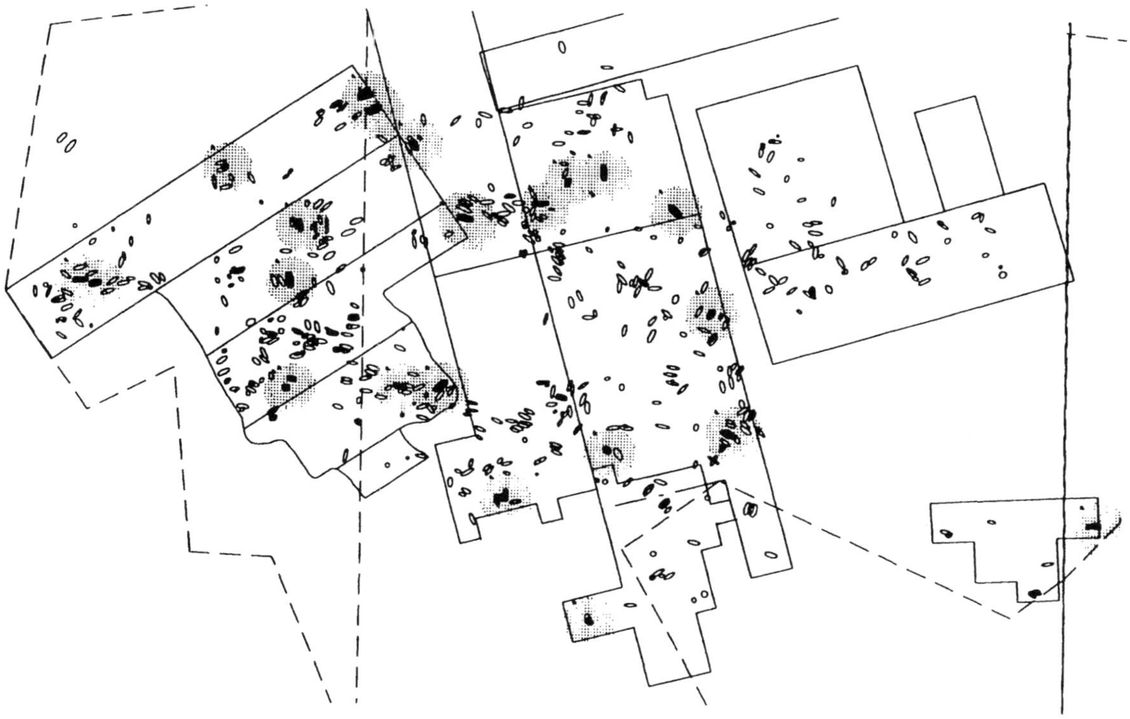

Figure 6-43. Distribution of all burials containing shell ornaments, Trenches 1-K.

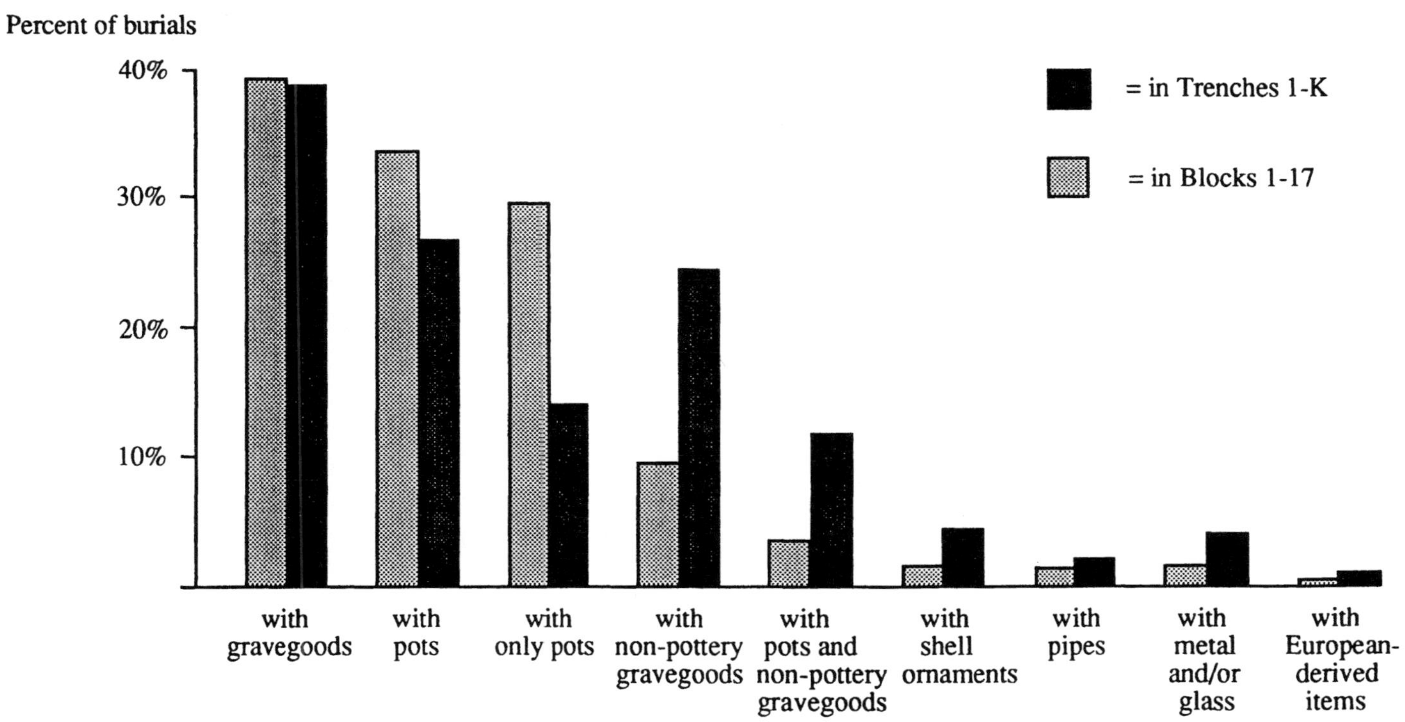

Figure 6-44. Frequencies of selected classes of grave goods, Blocks 1-17 versus Trenches 1-K. Differences between the two parts of the site in frequencies of burials containing mortuary vessels, only mortuary vessels, non-pottery grave goods, metal, and shell are statistically significant at the 0.05 level or better.

such as pedestal pots, vertical compound pots, oval bowls, jars with lizardlike appliqué, shell maskettes, coal animal effigies, iron kettle lugs, and copper cross-shaped pendants were found in both sections of the site (sometimes, as with the copper pendants, at extreme distances from each other) argues that the northern and southern sectors were roughly contemporaneous. However, quantitative differences in certain horizon markers (Figure 6-44) show that no simplistic, one-track hypothesis can account for the complete range of observed differences. Unfortunately, the deficiencies of the pre-1897 data base make it difficult to demonstrate definite answers to the many questions posed by available facts.

Judging from the presence of mortuary vessels (Table 6-4, Figure 6-11), a very large number of burials in Blocks 1-17 do seem to be associated with a Madisonville Horizon component. Were they generally contemporaneous with, earlier, or later than burials in the less densely populated northern portions of the site? It is difficult to tell from the vessels themselves because definite provenience is available for so few extant vessels, although the majority curated at the Smithsonian, the NMAI, the AMNH, and the CMNH, as well as most of the pre-1897 accessions at the HUPM, probably came from Blocks 1-17. From the small sample used for ceramic attribute analysis, 10 out of 87 of which were from the southern part of the site, some trends can be noted but no conclusions can be drawn. There are no statistically significant differences at an 0.05 level of significance or better between vessels in the sample from north versus south in surface treatment (smooth, cord-marked, grooved-paddled), lip notching, shoulder notching/punctation, number of handles (0, 2, 4, 8), or membership in cluster 1 versus cluster 2 (chi-square or Fisher's Exact Test as appropriate, 1 df). However, at an 0.06 level of significance, vessels from Trenches 1-K had higher than expected proportions of notched lips and four handles. These are later traits. There also were more vessels than expected in cluster 1 from Trenches 1-K compared with Blocks 1-17 (significant at $\alpha = 0.08$), again, a tie to later traits.

At first, this seems a puzzling development, considering the fact that the frequency of burials with mortuary vessels—supposed to be a late trait—is significantly higher in Blocks 1-17 than Trenches 1-K (Figure 6-44). However, evidence from other classes of artifacts allows the development of a possible scenario. Mortuary vessels in Trenches 1-K, but not Blocks 1-17, have a statistically significant association with metal and/or glass grave goods (chi square test, 1 df, $\alpha = 0.05$). In neither sector do known European goods have a statistically significant association with mortuary vessels. Considering these data along with the possible slight tendency toward later attributes associated with Trench 1-K mortuary vessels and the generally greater presence of metal, glass, and identified European goods in the northern part of the site (Figure 6-44), it is possible that the practice of including mortuary vessels with burials actually peaked and then declined during the Late Madisonville Horizon, so that it was less in evidence during the time when most metal and European items were coming into the settlement.

Just how great a difference is there in the amounts of metal excavated from Blocks 1-17 versus Trenches 1-K? This is one class of artifacts for which we do have good field records, because even the earliest excavators were well aware of the significance of its presence at the site. There are indeed differences between north and south, but they are by no means as pronounced as Hooton and Willoughby declared. From burial data alone, it seems that metal and definitely identified European items are most common in the northern portion of the site. The difference would be even greater if the four rich burials excavated during Putnam's visit to the site in 1882 (Drooker 1996c:600-601, "BX" burials), which probably were located in the northeastern portion of the site, were included. The 1895 excavations for the AMNH (location and exact number of burials unknown, but definitely north of Trenches 1-17) produced at least 52 metal artifacts, but no metal or glass came from Block M (east of Trenches 1-K), which contained at least 40 burials.

Differences between north and south are more ambiguous when metal and glass from nonmortuary proveniences are taken into consideration. Pits containing metal or glass are significantly more frequent in Blocks 1-17 than Trenches 1-K (Table 6-4); however, the possibility that this might be at least partly due to underrecording of pits during the earliest months of excavation in Block 1 is a very real one. The numbers of burials with metal/glass are lower in Blocks 1-17 than Trenches 1-K, but the proportion of metal/glass items in burials compared to the total number of such items excavated is higher (Table 6-9). This might well reflect the observed initial tendency of many Contact Period Native American groups to deposit a high proportion of newly acquired European items with their dead (e.g., Rogers 1990:153-211). Also higher than Trenches 1-K are the average number of metal items per burial for burials with metal, as well as the maximum number in one burial. Fewer people were buried with metal in Blocks 1-17, but many of those who did have it, had a lot.

In comparing numbers of metal items from all proveniences—burials, pits, and general digging in Trenches 1-K and Blocks 1-17, 22, L, and M (Figure 6-45)—it can be seen that they were found in most areas of the site, but were unevenly distributed. In the southern portion of the site, much more metal apparently came from excavation blocks closest to Trenches 1-K. It is possible that Blocks 1-6 might have been less intensely utilized during the period when most metal items reached the settlement. The earliest dateable object—the Clarksdale bell—was deposited there (see above), but other metal items are sparse, and burials and pits containing them are relatively few (4 burials, 7 pits; Figure 6-45, Table 6-3). This is in contrast to the very high densities and proportions of burials and of burials with ceramic vessels from this part of the site (Table 6-3, Figures 5-14, 6-11, 6-16).

The higher average numbers of grave goods per person in Trenches 1-K (Table 6-9), plus the significantly greater numbers of graves with marine shell items (Figure 6-43) also argue for a greater involvement of its residents in long-distance ex-

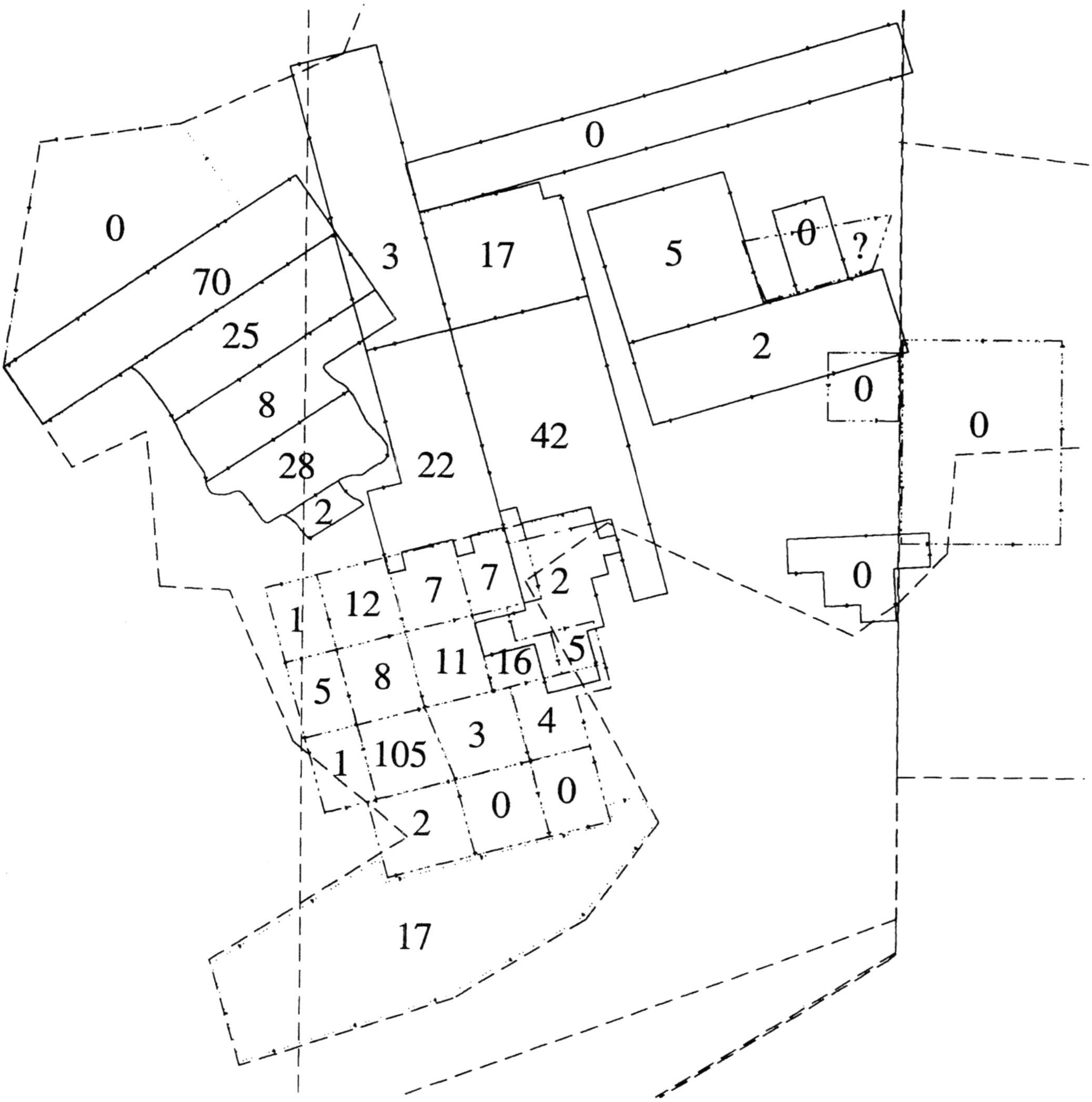

Figure 6-45. Numbers of metal artifacts per excavation block/trench excavated from all proveniences at the Madisonville site.

TABLE 6-9
Numbers of Gravegoods and Metal and/or Glass Items in Burials from Northern and Southern Portions of Site

	Blocks 1-17	Trenches 1-K
Number of burials	681	591
Number of burials with gravegoods	274	229
Number of burials with metal or glass (minimum)*	10	23
Number of burials with European-derived items (minimum)*	3	5
Total number of metal or glass items in burials (minimum)*	107	103
Total number of metal or glass items excavated (minimum)*	203	226
GRAVEGOODS		
Average number per burial		
- Considering all burials	0.67	1.23
- Considering only burials with gravegoods	1.72	3.18
Maximum number with a burial	92	69
METAL AND GLASS ITEMS		
Average number per burial		
- Considering all burials	0.16	0.17
- Considering only burials with metal/glass items	10.70	4.48
Maximum number recorded with a burial	88	18
Percentage of items in burials compared to total number excavated	52.7%	45.6%

* Numbers from extant items plus items reported in field notes and/or museum catalogs (total numbers not always given, and brass not always noticed). Does not include green-stained bone, (which *is* used in mapping metal occurrence), or items "from the leaf mold" in Blocks 1-17 (which might be modern).

change. Marine shell often was exchanged in the same early Contact Period interaction networks that brought European items inland (e.g., Bradley 1987a:89-103; Pendergast 1989; Sempowski 1989; Wray et al. 1991:393-95). Still, I must continue to sound a note of caution: It is possible that nonpottery grave goods (including marine shell), which apparently are much less frequent in Block 1-17 burials than Trench 1-K burials, simply were underreported by the MLSS excavators.

Temporal Relationships among Groups of Features, Trenches 1-K

Having defined some of the characteristics that can be used to identify pre-Madisonville Horizon, Early Madisonville Horizon, and Late Madisonville Horizon features, it is now possible to begin to unravel the relative ages of groups of features, and thus site use over time. The following paragraphs will consider the relative ages of the largest clusters of burials in Trenches 1-K and of the features that define the edge of the plaza. Even more could be done with this data set, but it is necessary to keep continually in mind the limitations and uncertainties that adhere to it, and refrain from overinterpretation.

Relative Ages of Large Burial Clusters

Possible pre-Madisonville Horizon burials, tentatively identified on the basis of depth below surface, grave characteristics, body position, and, in a very few instances, horizon marker grave goods, seem to be scattered around Trenches 1-K (Figures 6-4, 6-5, 6-26a, 6-37) rather than concentrated together. The largest groups that probably date to this period are in the north-central portion of the site, including two sets of burials associated with limestone slabs at the east end of Trench 3 and the southwest corner of Trench F (Figure 6-4), and the three flexed and six very deep burials at the north end of Trench F (Figures 6-5, 6-26a). Two small groups in Trench K (Nos. 1 to 5, 9 and 10) had early grave goods, including a discoidal and non-shell-tempered pottery somewhat similar to Anderson ware except that it had the nonlocal attribute of a cord-impressed design on the lip. Some percentage of burials without grave goods (Figure 6-6) also undoubtedly came from this time period, but identification of them is difficult if not impossible. Based on identifiable attributes, 40 to 50 burials, less than 10% of the total in Trenches 1-K, are possible candidates for this time period.

Among Late Fort Ancient burials in Trenches 1-K, there do not appear to be extreme contrasts and discontinuities in attributes of grave goods. For example, Late Fort Ancient ceramic styles present at Madisonville appear to have evolved gradually over time, with changing frequencies of attributes but no clear-cut types that can be assigned with certainty to earlier or later periods. However, there are still some differences that can be used to explore temporal relationships among groups of burials, as part of an effort to define areas that were used more heavily during different time periods.

In selecting groups of burials for comparison, I sought closely clustered graves with a high proportion of similarly-oriented individuals. After identifying thirteen possible groups (Figure 6-46), I eliminated those that were either too small or too variable (the latter probably because they consisted of subgroups buried at different times) to be amenable to statistical analysis. I was left with five groups (Nos. 2, 3, 5, 6, and 7) that seemed large and coherent enough to compare for relative age (for more details, see Drooker 1996c:239-40, Table 6.10). Each does contain individuals and smaller groups of burials that diverge from the general pattern in one or more attributes, and thus might have been buried at a significantly different time than most others in the group. It should be kept in mind that these are arbitrary groups for the purpose of general comparison, not necessarily exclusive, comprehensive social groups with members all dating to a particular, narrowly defined time period.

My working hypotheses, generated from the gross contrasts between grave goods in Blocks 1-7 versus Trenches 1-K (Figure 6-44), were that groups of burials with more mortuary vessels and higher proportions of vessels as the only grave good

Figure 6-46. Groups of burials considered for determination of relative ages. Dotted lines indicate groups eventually discarded from consideration due to small size or inconsistent attributes.

(and perhaps greater average depth) were earlier, while groups with more burials containing nonpottery grave goods, metal, European goods, and shell were later. I computed average depth, percentages of grave goods and important classes of grave goods, and ratios of burials with pottery, nonpottery grave goods, only pottery, only nonpottery grave goods, metal, and European materials to burials with grave goods for each cluster of burials, and made statistical comparisons among groups. I also looked at ceramic attributes, including presence/absence of both single attributes and jars assigned to cluster 1 (tentatively later) versus cluster 2 (tentatively earlier). No one measurement or ratio alone was sufficient to establish relative age, but consistent sets of characteristics were suggestive.

When general proportions of burials with grave goods and with different types of grave goods are considered, the burial groups do separate into some that seem to be earlier or later, but there are overlaps and ambiguities. It also seems clear that social differences are coming into play among some of the groups. The strongest time differences can be seen between burial groups 2, 6, and 7 versus burial groups 3 and 5, but evidence for relative time differences among 2, 6, and 7 and between 3 and 5 also is reviewed.

In considering percentages of burials in each group that had various grave good assemblage characteristics (Figure 6-47), it can be seen that group 7 has far more burials with grave goods and mortuary vessels than other clusters, although its general characteristics seem to parallel group 2 in many respects. Both, for example, have high ratios of pottery to nonpottery items. These seem to be "early" profiles, corroborated by the fact that these groups include only two burials with metal (one reported with "copper" beads, and one with green-stained bone), both in group 7. These similarities also are apparent in Figure 6-48 (which considers only burials with grave goods), but small-scale differences, such as a higher proportion of nonpottery grave goods in group 7 than group 2, also can be seen. That, along with the presence of metal, implies that group 7 might be later than group 2. However, mortuary vessel characteristics contradict that conclusion: burial group 2 shows a higher proportion of cluster 1 vessels and of vessels with notched lips (later indicators) (Table 6-10). Whatever the temporal relationships, the much higher proportion of burials in group 7 with grave goods of all kinds implies the possibility of some kind of difference in social status.

Group 6 is similar to group 2 in terms of the comparatively low proportion of its burials that had grave goods (Figure 6-47), but is more similar to group 7 than group 2 in terms of relative proportions of different kinds of grave goods (Figure 6-48). Considering burials with grave goods, group 6 has a lower proportion with mortuary vessels than either group 7 or group 2 (Figure 6-48). The characteristics of its mortuary vessels are earlier than those of group 7 (marginally smaller proportion of cluster 1 vessels, and far less lip notching). In fact, vessels with

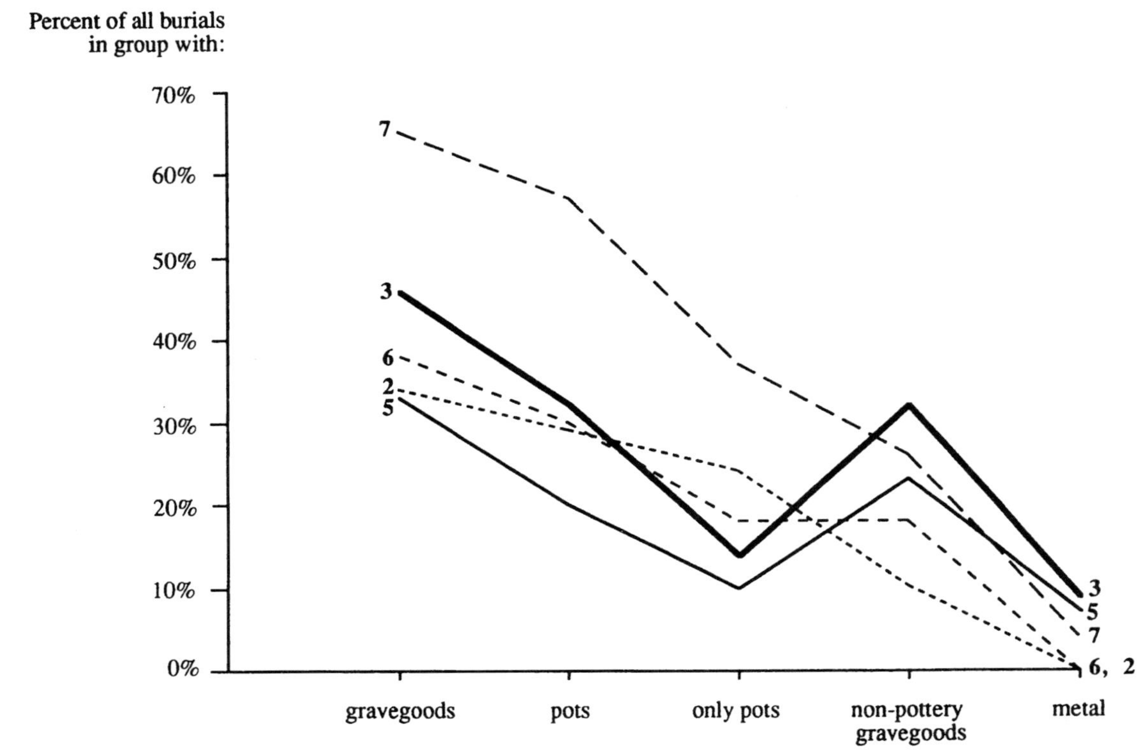

Figure 6-47. Burial groups with grave goods showing percentages of grave good types (see Table 6-10 for numbers of items).

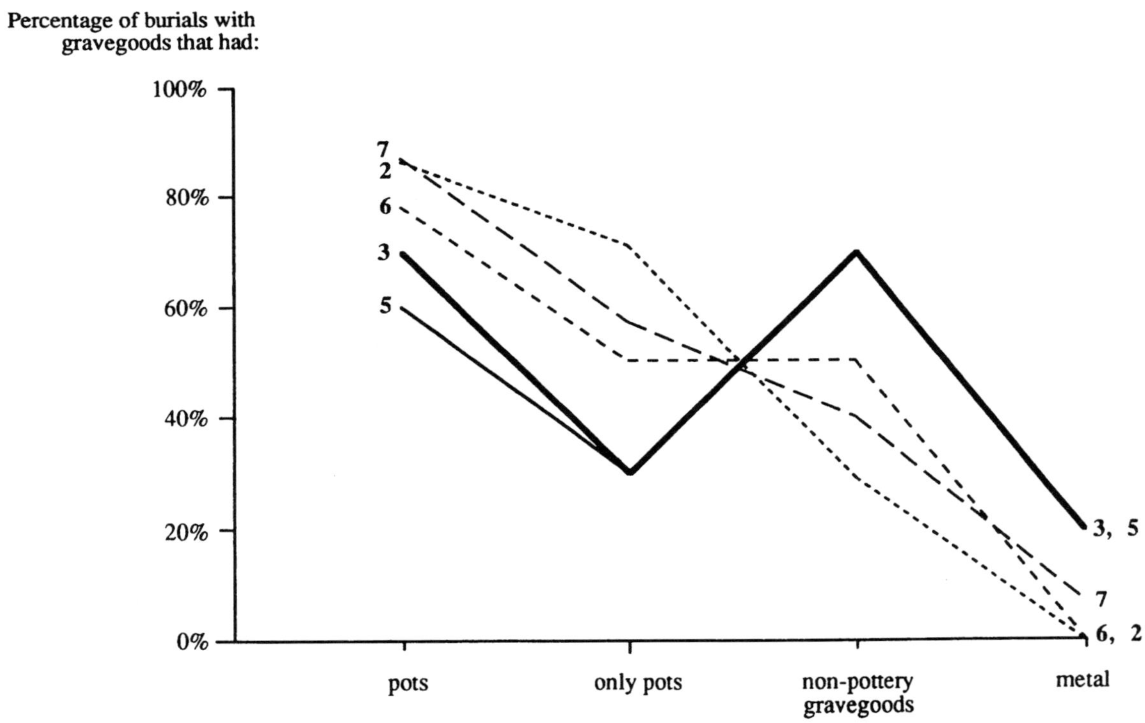

Figure 6-48. Types of grave goods present in burial groups into grave goods (see Table 6-10 for numbers of items).

TABLE 6-10
Attributes of Selected Groups of Adjacent Burials, for Consideration in Terms of Relative Age

	BURIAL GROUP NUMBER 2	3	5	6	7
Total number of burials	37	22	30	37	46
Average depth, inches [a]	19.7	27.3	17.9	25.6	22.2
Number with gravegoods	14	10	10	14	30
Number with mortuary vessels	12	7	6	11	26
Number with only ceramic vessels as gravegoods	10	3	3	7	17
Number with non-pottery gravegoods	4	7	7	7	12
Number with only non-pottery gravegoods	2	2	4	3	4
Number with pottery and non-pottery gravegoods	2	3	3	4	9
Number with shell ornaments	2	2	2	1	2
Number with pipes	0	0	0	0	3
Number with metal (includes metal-stained items)	0	2	2	0	2
Number with identified European-derived items	0	1	1	0	0
Number with vessels having identifiable attributes	9	3	3	9	24
Number with vessels assigned to Cluster 1 [b]	4/7	3/3	1/1	3/7	4/9
	(57%)	*(100%)*	*(100%)*	*(43%)*	*(44%)*
Number with vessels assigned to Cluster 2 [b]	1/7	0/3	0/1	3/7	4/9
	(14%)	*(0%)*	*(0%)*	*(43%)*	*(44%)*
Number with known notched-lip vessels [c]	8/9	3/3	3/3	4/7	14/17
	(89%)	*(100%)*	*(100%)*	*(57%)*	*(82%)*

[a] Excluding burials in pits.
[b] Number after slash indicates total number of vessels from that group included in the pottery cluster analysis.
[c] Number after slash indicates total number with identifiable lip characteristics.

plain lips seem to predominate in and near group 6 (Figure 6-49; cf. Figure 6-50), which may indicate a relatively early age for burials in this area compared to all Madisonville Horizon burials with mortuary vessels in Trenches 1-K. Group 6 also has relatively few burials with shell ornaments (1.6%, or 7.1% of burials with grave goods). Group 7 has proportionally more (4.3/6.7%), but group 2 has the highest proportion (5.4%, or 14.3% of its burials with grave goods), in spite of its very low proportion of nonpottery grave goods (Figures 6-47, 6-48).

The area around group 6 also had a concentration of burials with shell spoons in or near their mortuary vessels (Figure 6-51). This might be at least partially because excavators of Trenches A-K did not notice them (Drooker 1996c:578-79). When shell spoons are not decorated, they are easy to overlook. However, the apparent similarity in location of observed shell spoons and smooth-lipped mortuary vessels is notable. Inclusion of spoons with vessels might be a relatively early custom. Low notes shell valves (*Unio alatus*) as a common occurrence in vessels excavated under the aegis of the MLSS (1880:57, Fig. 21).

Vasiform pipes, markers for the entire Madisonville Horizon span, are concentrated along the southern edge of Trenches 1-K (as are all burials with pipes in this sector of the site) (Figure 6-52). Small-disk and keel-shaped pipes, which are characteristic of the Late Madisonville Horizon, were found with only two burials in Trenches 1-K, both of them at some distance from the plaza and not associated with any of the large burial groups. The only pipe in any of the large burial groups was in group 7. Since pipes are male status indicators (see Chapter 7), this again implies differences in social status between group 7 (and the area around it) and other more-or-less contemporaneous burial groups close to the plaza.

Groups 2, 6, and 7 certainly overlapped in time, but, from ceramic attributes and the proportions of burials with shell ornaments, group 6 (as a whole) might be earliest, then 7, and finally 2. If this is true, then the higher proportions of burials with ceramic vessels in groups 7 and 2 versus 6 (Figure 6-48) would represent a rise in the use of mortuary vessels during the pre-protohistoric Early Madisonville Horizon, when little metal and no European materials were reaching the site. This is in contrast with burial groups 3 and 5, the two groups that contain European-derived materials, which have comparatively low proportions of burials with mortuary vessels and comparatively high proportions of burials with nonpottery grave goods (Figure 6-48), including shell ornaments (Table 6-10).

While these two groups are consistent in their differences from the three groups that lack European goods, they differ between themselves with respect to amounts of grave goods. Rela-

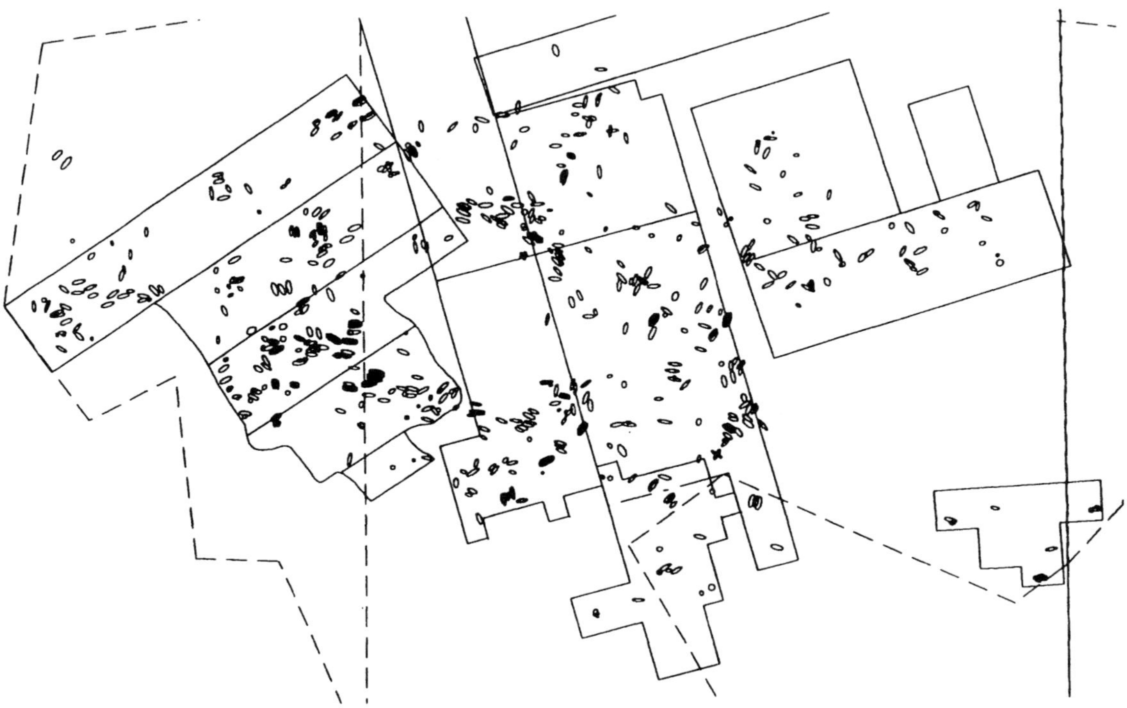

Figure 6-49. Burials known to have mortuary vessels with unnotched lips, Trenches 1-K.

tively more group 3 than group 5 burials contain grave goods (Figure 6-47). Group 3 not only has higher percentages than group 5 of burials with metal, European goods, and shell, but also has much higher total numbers of these types of items (17, 12, and 52, versus 3, 1, and 2). Groups 3 and 5 differ only slightly from each other in proportions of burials with different types of grave goods (Figure 6-48), and there appears to be no difference between them in mortuary vessel attributes, which are consistently later (Table 6-10). The incongruities in grave good numbers could be social or temporal (or both).

The differences between groups 2, 6, and 7 versus groups 3 and 5 in time-sensitive grave good characteristics do corroborate a more heavy use of the area close to the plaza during the earlier portion of the Late Fort Ancient occupation of the site. However, because groups of earlier and later burials overlap physically on the site (as I learned from my examination of all burial groups delineated in Figure 6-46), and because there are so many burials lacking grave goods, it is difficult to make blanket statements about overall use of the site during earlier and later periods. Prehistoric and protohistoric Madisonville residents might have been buried both close to the plaza and away from it. It does seem, though, that burials identifiable as protohistoric, from the European goods buried with them, tend to have been interred both farther from the plaza and in smaller groups rather than larger ones (Figure 6-40). I will examine possible reasons for this below.

The Plaza Revisited

The Madisonville plaza—an open space across Trenches 2, 3, 4, B, D, and E that apparently was almost devoid of features (Figure 5-9)—is quite small when compared with other measured Fort Ancient plazas (Table 5-9). However, considering evidence for the multicomponent nature of the site, it is possible that at least some of the features that intrude upon our archaeological perception of the open space might not have been in evidence during the time during which the plaza primarily functioned. Some of the graves and pits might have been dug by very early inhabitants of the site, and might not have been part of the visible scene when the plaza was in use. Others might postdate the major period of plaza use. Yet others might have been associated with the function of the plaza as special communal ritual space—for instance, pits associated with communal feasts, pits or burials associated with ritual functions, or burials of special-status individuals. In some well-mapped Fort Ancient sites (see Chapter 4), one or more special structures such as a sweat house or a council house intrude upon plaza space.

Now that the general distribution of important horizon marker artifacts and practices in Trenches 1-K has been reviewed, it is worth pausing to consider whether there is enough evidence to push back the edges of the plaza as it would have been perceived by its users. In fact, there are a number of features that

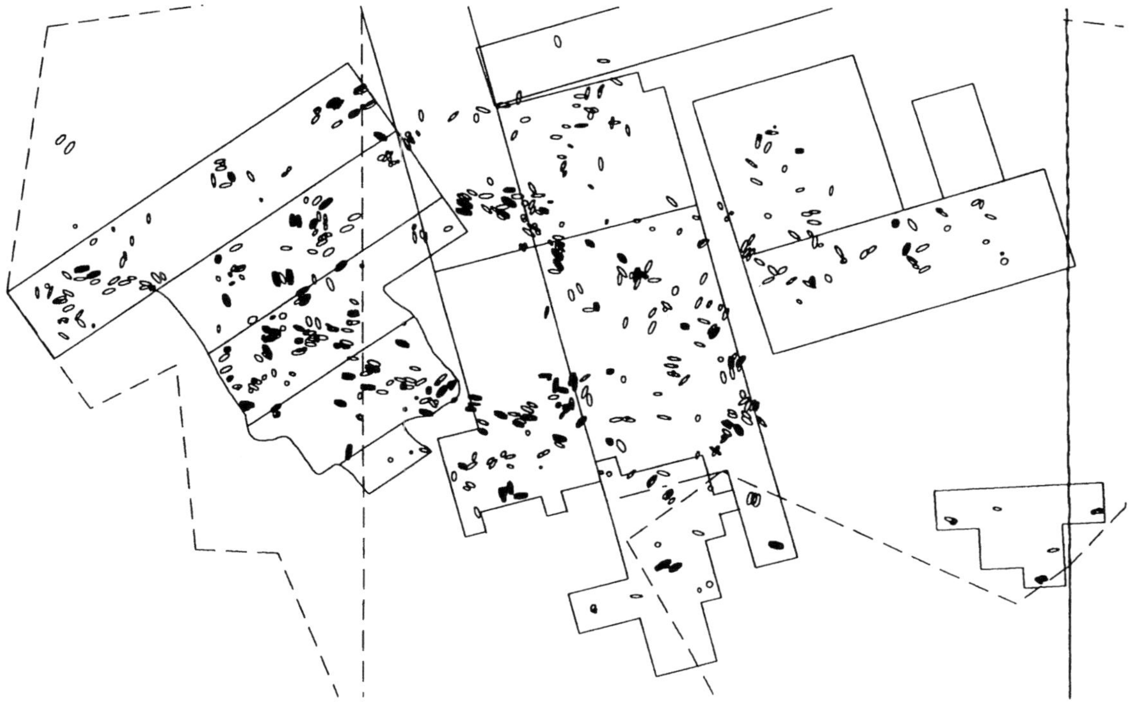

Figure 6-50. Burials known to have mortuary vessels with notched lips, Trenches 1-K.

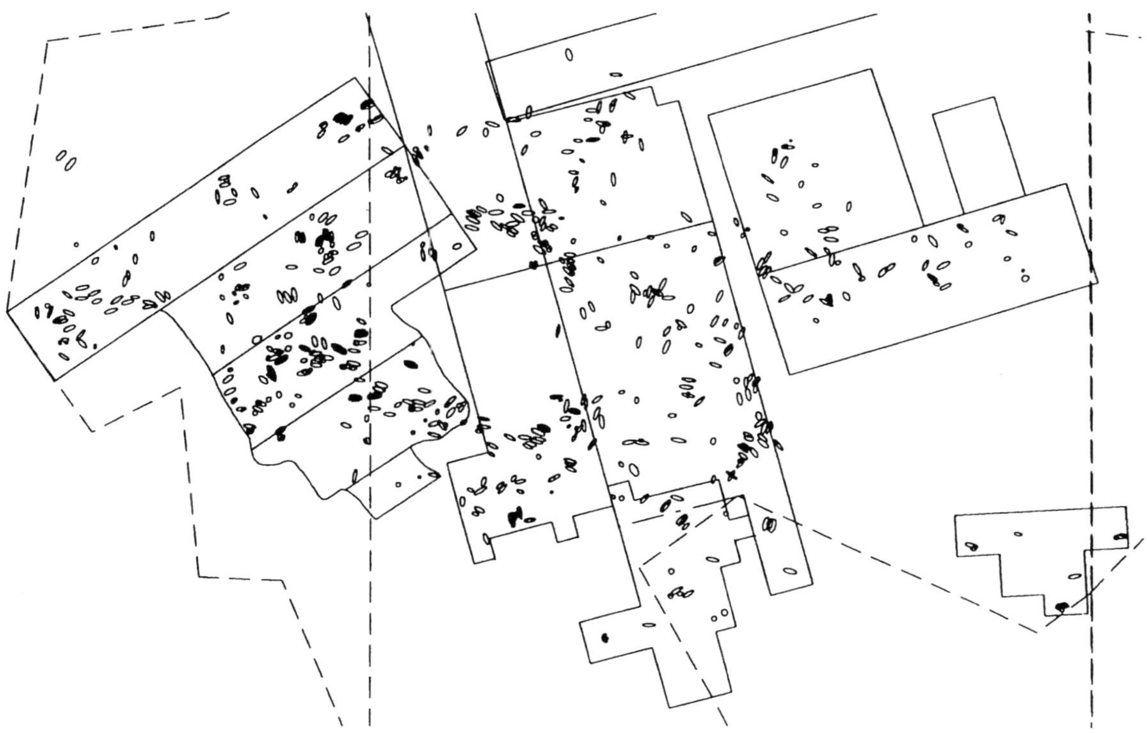

Figure 6-51. Burials known to have shell spoons in or near their mortuary vessels, Trenches 1-K.

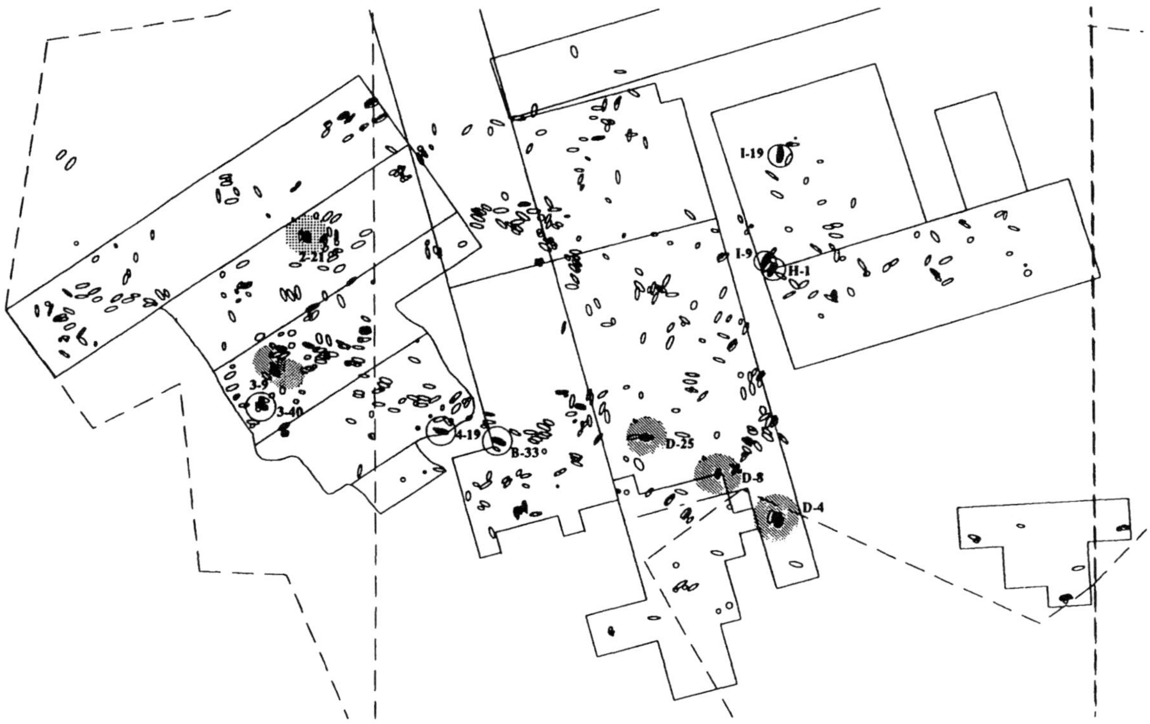

Figure 6-52. Burials with pipes, Trenches 1-K. Vasiform pipes, thought to span the entire Madisonville Horizon, are indicated by slanted lines. The small-disk pipe (dots) and keel pipe (horizontal dashed lines) are Late Madisonville Horizon forms. The remainder (circled) include a variety of forms, with several effigies.

inhabit the plaza space, but probably should not be used to define its boundaries.

Within the generally open oval space defined by the curved lines in Figure 6-53 is a scattering of features that I examined to see whether they might fit into any of the above categories. Burials 33, 35, and 36 in Trench 3, which are on limestone slabs and below the hardpan layer, could well predate the main period of plaza use, as could Burial 32, a foot below the hardpan layer and lacking grave goods. The adjacent Burial 39, a few inches closer to the surface than the others, might be considered a special individual: a child with copper-stained jaw surrounded by bits of copper and copper-stained bone. The large pit adjacent to these burials contained many stones, animal bones, and shells, plus a variety of artifacts. It, and the nearby large hearth in Trench 2, could conceivably be related to communal feasting.

The even larger hearth and pit in Trench 4 near Burials 66 and 25 probably were so related. The so-called fireplace consisted of a 12.5 × 14 foot, 7-inch-thick burnt layer, while the relatively shallow (2 ft, 8 in deep), large (5 ft, 7 in × 4 ft, 9 in) pit contained "two and a half baskets of bones" and "an abundance of ashes," along with "many ornamented pot handles," a "pot with a shell [spoon] in it like burial pots," a human frontal bone, and a variety of other artifacts (Swanton 1897). Burial 66 (to Trench 3) consisted only of skull fragments, similar to Burial 30, an infant "broken to bits" (Swanton 1897). Burial 25, an adult, which Hooton identified as a young male, with a projectile point in one vertebra, perhaps could be considered a special individual. His time frame was Madisonville Horizon, but probably not extremely recent: he was buried 30 inches below the surface, along with a two-handled, notched-lip Madisonville Cordmarked jar containing shell spoons. From field notes, the pit just south of him, close to a large hearth, contained mixed earth and ashes, a shell holding red ochre, and many other artifacts.

Certainly special was the large pit in Trench E containing Burials 9-14, which consisted of one articulated adult bent into a praying position with hands (tied?) in front of face, overlain by bones and crania of at least five individuals, including a child, two teenagers, and two adults, one probably female.

Burials 60 and 60A in Trench B, a young adult female with possible cutmarks on forehead and across femori, and a fetus, were only 17 inches below the surface, above a pit. The contents of the three pits near this interment are unknown. The five adjacent burials in Trench D all were at 24 inches or above, most of them extended and supine. Burial 59 had been disturbed along its right side, while 49 consisted of two charred cranial fragments in a five-foot grave. All but one lacked grave goods. Burial 58, a small child, was interred with a well-made adze, and a four-handled Madisonville Plain jar with notched lip and notched folded rim (Griffin 1943: Pl. LXX.4), a type with

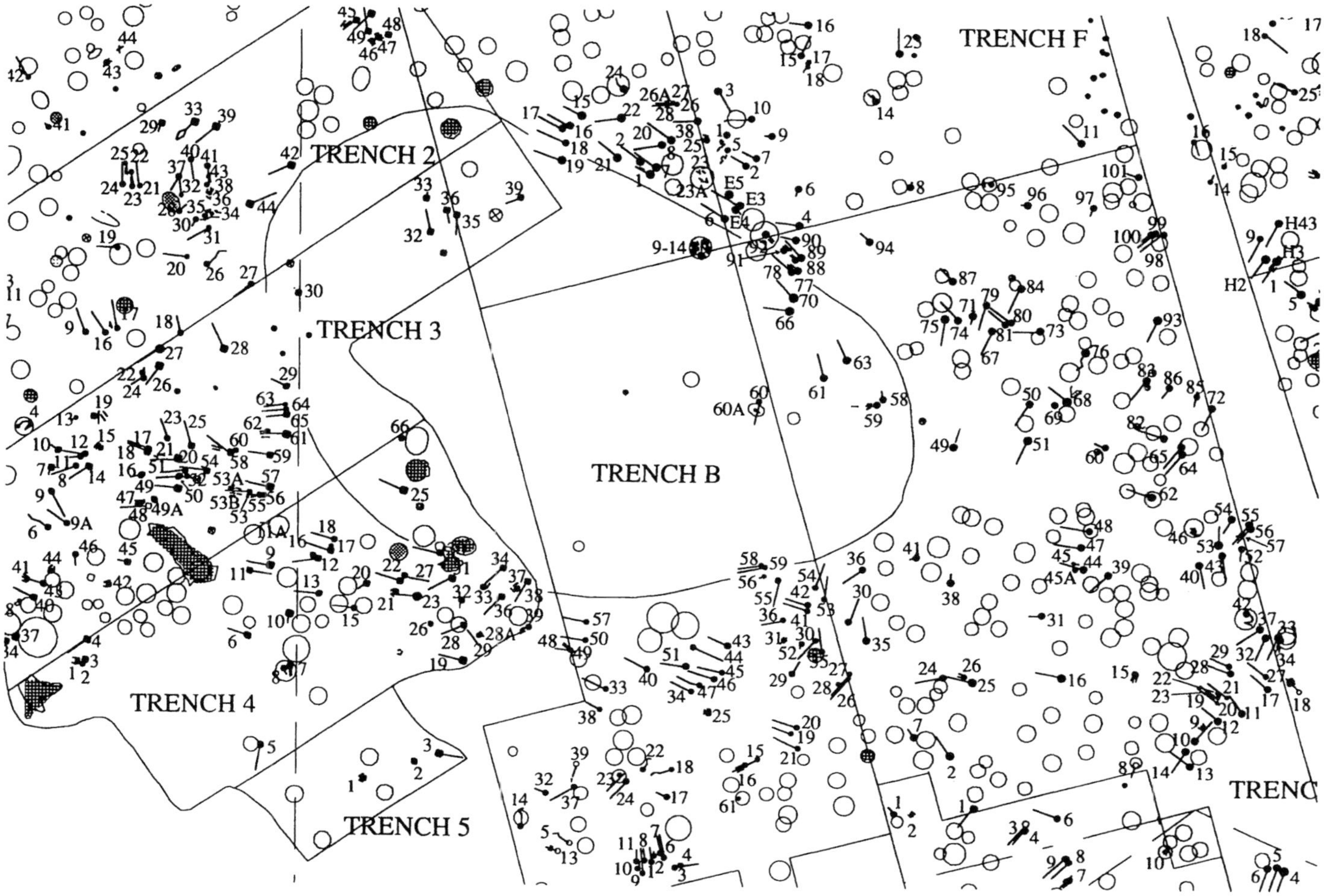

Figure 6-53. Features surrounding plaza area in Trenches 1-K.

connections to northern Ohio ceramics (see below). It is possible that many of these burials are late, encroaching upon space that earlier was reserved for a plaza function.

What, then, of the spurs of burials sticking into the plaza space as delineated in Figure 6-53 (e.g., the group extending north from Burial E-19, the group extending north from D-66, the group extending south from B-58 and B-59, the group extending south from 4-34, 4-37, and 4-38, and the group extending south of 3-29)? It is quite possible that these were family or lineage cemetery areas, originally associated with individual house structures or groups of structures, that gradually grew out toward the open area, similar to the situation at Incinerator, where a group of burials associated with House 2/1978 extended out from it into the plaza (Robertson 1984: Fig. 3). Other burial areas also might have developed out from the walls of structures, but alongside the open space rather than into it. The most obvious example, discussed in Chapter 5, is in Trench 3, where the L-shaped burial group 6 might well have been associated with a structure, first expanding along its walls, then perhaps growing eastward along the edge of the plaza into burial group 7 (cf. Figure 6-49). Burial group 2, which defines the corner of a rather open rectangular space in Trench F, also could have expanded in this way, both westward along the open space and southward out into the plaza. Some of the spurs extending out from burial group 7 could have been associated with smaller structures. The large spur just to the east of burial group 7 (cf. Figure 6-46) could have been associated with a structure farther east. Alternatively, such a structure might be defined by the burials with heads to the east and southeast in and near the eastern end of burial group 7 in Trench B (e.g., Burials 19, 20, 21, 34, 36, 41, 42, 43, 44, 45, 46, 47, 56, 57, 58), with southwest-northeast trending burials (which differed from the others in their grave goods profile) associated with a different component.

Many of the features in the southern half of Trench D could have been either earlier or later than most of the burials ringing the edge of the plaza. For example, Burials B-35, D-35, D-31, and D-16 were interred 34-50 inches below the surface and lacked grave goods; they could have predated the Madisonville Horizon. Burials D-39, D-44, D-45, D-45A, D-47, and D-48 lacked definitive grave goods, but the last five all were buried at 18 inches or above and Burial D-39 crosscut pit D-67, from which came a fifteenth century ^{14}C date (Table 6-1). In fact, all but one of these six burials crosscut earlier features (Figure 6-25). The pit at the feet of Burial D-47 contained a piece of copper and a grooved-paddled sherd with lip and shoulder notching (later attributes). It is possible that this small group of burials, plus many of the pits in their vicinity, postdated the larger clusters of burials, many with mortuary vessels, that surrounded them to the north, east, and west (cf. Figure 6-10). In this portion of Trench D was the densest concentration on the site of pits with bison bone (Figure 6-54), as well as many pits containing metal (Figure 6-42). Since pits with metal and pits with bison bone are significantly correlated (chi square text, 1 df, $p = 0.01$), the presence of bison bone very likely is a Late Madisonville Horizon indicator, postdating the most intense use of the plaza edge as a burial area. Utilization of this portion of the site during successive time periods also is indicated by its radiocarbon dates: Pit B-27, just east of Burial B-38 in group 7, and Pit D-75, between Burials D-48 and D-46, both contained corn kernels dated to the fifteenth and to the seventeenth centuries.

Functionally, then, the plaza in Trenches 1-K was at least somewhat larger than it appears from the archaeological record, probably toward the high end of the estimated range given in Table 5-9, or equivalent in size to the plaza at Anderson Village. The burials that defined its edge also encroached upon it, as did later features postdating the most intense use of the edge of the communal open space as a cemetery area and the most intense use of mortuary vessels as grave goods.

In the densely populated southern portion of the site, the lack of burials with mortuary vessels (or any grave goods) in Block 10, and their relative scarcity in Blocks 7 and 14 (Figures 6-9, 6-11; see also Figures 5-14 and 5-15) raise the possiblity that that portion of the site also served as a small plaza during Late Fort Ancient times, either concurrently with or prior to the establishment of the plaza area to its north. For instance, the very dense group of 55 burials with a high incidence of mortuary vessels in Block 6 (Figures 5-15, 6-11), adjacent to Blocks 7 and 10, might well be analogous to one of the large burial groups close to the plaza in Trenches 1-K. With respect to both burial density and grave good characteristics, it is much more similar to them than to burial groups 3 and 5. Its grave goods profile is very close to that of burial group 2 (Figure 6-55), but its relatively high percentage of burials with grave goods (56%) and relatively low proportion with shell ornaments (6.5% of burials with grave goods) plus the presence of copper in one burial (Table 6-3) align it with group 7.

As noted in Chapter 5, there also was an area of at least 40 × 60 feet in Block 1 that had very few features. This conceivably could have been a third small plaza.

Summary: Occupation Periods and Intrasite Temporal Components

To summarize, it seems likely that the Madisonville site was used repeatedly over a long period of time, until at least the early seventeenth century and perhaps later. Earlier occupations appear to have been smaller and more sporadic than Madisonville Horizon occupations.

The extreme southwestern part of the site probably was used as a cemetery during Late Woodland-Early Fort Ancient times, with flexed (contracted/doubled up/sitting) burials predominating. The two eleventh-century radiocarbon dates from this part of the site (Table 6-1, Figures 6-2, 6-3) might be associated with this occupation. Some or none of the few flexed and semi-flexed burials beyond the first-excavated portion of Block 1 might also be this early.

Above and northeast of the Madisonville site proper, the house circles and at least one nearby burial mound appear, from the few extant artifacts, to date to Early Fort Ancient times. Because this undoubtedly is a separate component, it will not be considered further in this study.

There might have been two Early-Middle Fort Ancient occupations in the Ancient Cemetery area. The sandy Anderson Shell Tempered pottery in the lowest levels of the stratified midden in the southwestern part of the site dates to the thirteenth-fourteenth centuries, as evidenced by its association with one of the two carbon samples dated to that period. Later, non-sandy Anderson Shell Tempered ware, some of it exuberantly decorated with incised and punctated designs on necks, rims, and handles (Figure 4-8), exists in collections from all parts of the site, but its relative frequency in different sectors cannot be determined. It might date as late as the early fifteenth century. People who made and used these types of pottery surely constitute some significant proportion of burials without mortuary vessels at the site (Figures 6-6, 6-7), but it is extremely difficult to single them out from later burials. In Trenches 1-K, the concentration of deep burials centered on the northern section of Trench F, at least some of the flexed and semi-flexed burials along the edge of the rising ground in Trenches F, H, and I, the burials with stone slabs, and some of the few additional flexed or very deep burials might well date to this pre-Madisonville Horizon period, but because most of them lack grave goods and few are clustered together, this is impossible to demonstrate with certainty.

The Madisonville wall-trench structure (Figure 5-17a) probably dates to the earlier of these components: in southwestern Ohio, settlements with non-semi-subterranean (above ground) wall trench structures have radiocarbon dates centered on the thirteenth century (Tables 4-1, 4-5). There probably were additional such structures at Madisonville, perhaps in the densely populated area excavated as Blocks 1-17, but their sizes, locations, and orientations are now irretrievably lost.

It seems likely that the largest numbers of Fort Ancient people who used the Madisonville site prior to the fifteenth century resided in the southern portion. This judgment is based on the locations of carbon samples that produced pre-fifteenth-century dates (Figure 6-3), the large midden containing sandy Anderson Shell Tempered ware, and the high densities of burials lacking grave goods in this portion of the site (Figure 6-7). At least one

Figure 6-54. Distribution of extant bison bone (mostly beamers made from thoracic vertebrae) in pits, Trenches 1-K. Highlighted pits also produced metal.

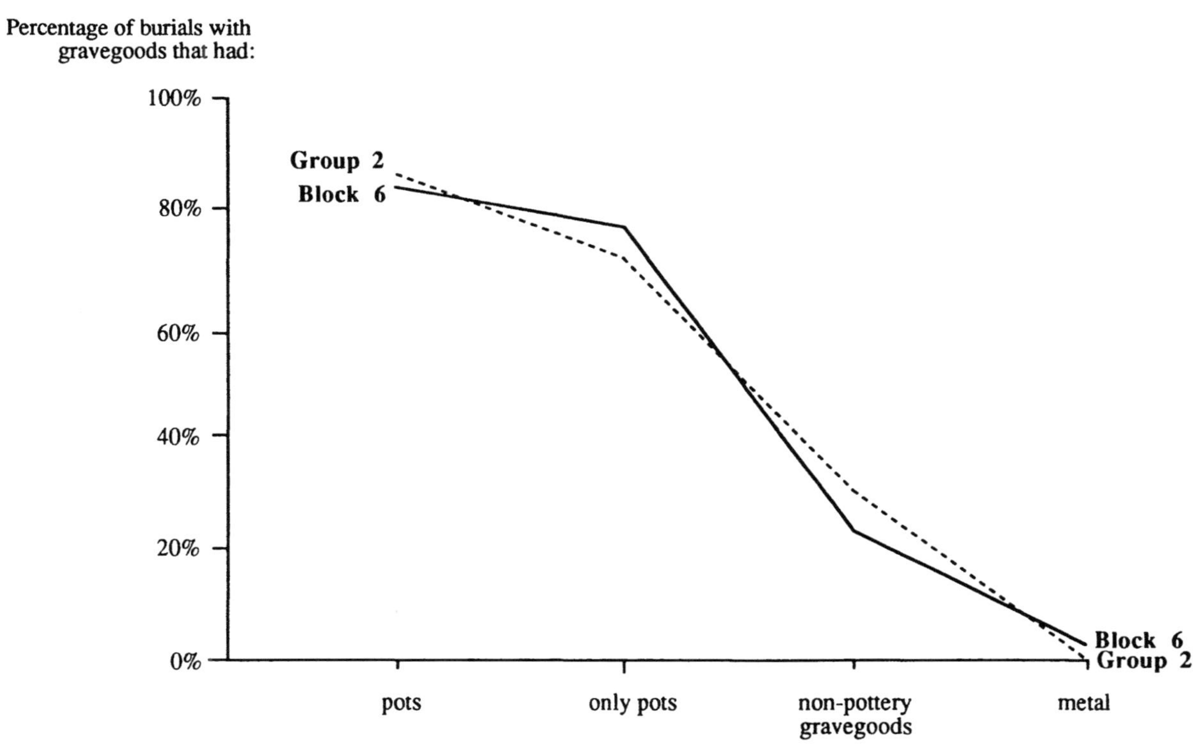

Figure 6-55. Comparison of burial group 2 and the burials in Block 6 with respect to types of grave goods present, for burials with grave goods.

household (Figure 5-17a), perhaps more, resided in the northern portion. A site pattern with a central plaza is a definite possibility, but impossible to prove. Considering the 47 flexed burials in Block 1 and the 40-50 burials in Trenches 1-K that have characteristics assignable to Early-Middle Fort Ancient, perhaps as many as 200 (14%) of the recorded 1450 burials from the site were people who used it before the Madisonville Horizon.

During the fourteenth century, site use might have been low or sporadic. This is evidenced by the pattern of radiocarbon dates (Figure 6-2) and the dearth of certain Middle Fort Ancient horizon marker artifacts such as double-ended bone pins and serrated (type 3) projectile points. Low-level occupation probably continued into the Early Madisonville Horizon, corresponding to the absence of beaded bowls and relatively small numbers of Todd Plain sherds and transitional Madisonville jars with decorated necks (Table 6-5), but the suite of radiocarbon dates shows a strong fifteenth-century representation (Figure 6-2), implying that the site began to see more intensive utilization not too many decades after 1400.

The settlement encompassed its greatest area during the Late Fort Ancient Madisonville Horizon period, for the first time making extensive, continuous use of the northern portion of the site. Most of the relatively flat area of the plateau (Figure 5-7) appears to have been included. In both Blocks 1-17 and Trenches 1-K, dense areas of related burials indicate intense use of certain portions of the site over a significant length of time, probably three generations or more (judging from ceramic style development coupled with a moderate amount of feature crosscutting). Different groups of burials appear to have been interred during overlapping but slightly different periods of time, implying a waxing and waning of subarea usage over time. These cemetery areas might have been associated with particular house structures and particular lineages. Their strong relationship with central open areas of common space implies a significant communal orientation. It seems likely that there were two or more such open areas, one across Trenches 3, 4, B, D, and E, and another centering on Block 10 (and perhaps one in Block 1). From their artifact assemblages and grave goods profiles, these portions of the site seem to be roughly contemporaneous. Unfortunately, it is impossible to track the formation and relative sizes of communal open spaces over time. For example, did one communal open area eventually fission into two or more? If so, was the first one in the north or in the south? Might it have been larger than later, multiple plazas? Again, these are questions to which we probably never will know the answers.

None of the pits and midden deposits from which came fifteenth-century radiocarbon dates (Figures 6-1, 6-2) are far from clusters of burials containing mortuary vessels, although their locations are only at the edges of the largest and densest burial groups adjacent to the plaza. The four fifteenth-century dates from Trenches 1-K came from Trench 4 south of burial group 6, Trench B at the southeastern edge of group 7, and Trench D, just west of burial group 11 (Figure 6-46; cf. Figures 6-10, 6-15). The three others came from Blocks 1-4 and the southern margin of the bluff (cf. Figures 6-11, 6-16). It is quite possible that the period of intense focus on plaza space and increase in mortuary vessel use originated during the late fifteenth century.

Somewhat later, as European artifacts started to reach the site (i.e., during the Late Madisonville Horizon), use of the margins of Trenches 1-K—Trench 1 and an arc across Trenches I and H—can be recognized. Concentrations of type 6 projectile points (Figure 6-33), cluster 1 (later) mortuary vessels (Figure 6-39), metal (Figures 6-40, 6-42), European materials (Figures 6-41, 6-42), shell ornaments (Figure 6-43), bison bone (Figure 6-54), and rasp fragments (Figure 6-36) occur both in Trenches 1, I, and H and elsewhere outside of the dense burial groups close to the plaza. Smaller burial groups (perhaps associated with smaller households or shorter occupancies) are evident for this period and these portions of the site, but the shift appears to have been gradual, not discontinuous: the extant mortuary vessels associated with them are closely related to those associated with the burials close to the plaza, although their stylistic attributes tend to be later. There also appears to have been a shift away from the inclusion of ceramic vessels with burials.

From relative amounts of European material and of extant bison bone and rasp fragments in Trenches 1-K (greater) versus Blocks 1-17 (lesser), the northern part of the site might have been used longer. However, from numbers and locations of definitely later burials, settlement occupation during protohistoric times might well have been less intense, involving discontinuous site use or smaller populations. At least in Trenches 1-K, residents did continue to maintain a central open area, but its extent or exact location may have differed from earlier times. Visually, it might or might not have included the densely placed earlier burial groups. The seven sixteenth-seventeenth century radiocarbon dates, which include four in the southwestern part of the site and three distributed equidistantly around the eastern and southern periphery of Trenches 2 to D (Figures 6-1, 6-3) support the idea of general contemporaneity between north and south.

Settlement Population and Lifeways over Time

Madisonville has been described as a late, large Fort Ancient settlement, populated by sedentary maize horticulturalists who came under increasing pressure from warfare or epidemic disease during the protohistoric period. From data now at our disposal, little of that description can be supported without qualification.

Population Size

The evidence discussed in this chapter points to a long-term site occupation by a moderate-sized population during the Late Fort Ancient period, rather than a single-generation occupation by a very large population. If approximately 1250 interments (see above) took place over 125 years (continuously or discontinuously) between the fifteenth and early seventeenth centuries, there would be an average of 10 per year. This is just within the range of burials per year estimated for the Early-Middle Fort Ancient Incinerator site (9.6-14), occupied for only a generation and estimated to have had a population of 250-300 (Drooker 1996a: Note 2; Essenpreis 1982:309; Evans 1994:2; Lileas 1988:51; Nass 1987:109). If the Late Fort Ancient occupation were continuous and longer, as might be inferred from the radiocarbon date range (Figure 6-2), average population could have been considerably lower. Population at Madisonville might have peaked during or previous to the sixteenth century, with fewer burials per year ascribable to the late sixteenth-seventeenth centuries, either by virtue of discontinuous site usage or a smaller group associated with the site, or both. In that case, the village population during the period of intense plaza usage could have been similar to or even somewhat higher than that of Incinerator, but it is unlikely ever to have exceeded it by much.

Subsistence

It does seem logical to connect the apparent change in site usage during the Late Madisonville Horizon with an increase in bison hunting. The significant presence of bison bone at Madisonville (Figure 6-54), probably does herald a significant change in subsistence and lifeways. Bison hunting requires group rather than individual action. In historically known horticultural groups with a significant involvement in bison hunting, a large proportion of a settlement's able-bodied residents were absent from home base during hunting season, which might include both early summer and late winter bison hunts. In fact, in the midwestern Prairie Peninsula area, the Illini, Sauk, and Osage moved among three venues during the yearly cycle: semi-permanent summer villages occupied during the planting and harvesting seasons, temporary camps for communal bison or bear hunting, and dispersed winter lodges used for individual hunting and gathering (Brown 1965:69). Tankersley has proposed that bison hunting by Madisonville residents took place at Big Bone Lick, Kentucky (Tankersley 1992; see Chapter 4). This is a good possibility, but not yet definitively corroborated by archaeological evidence. It also is possible that they went farther afield. In Chapter 8, I will be exploring the nature of long-term interactions between Madisonville residents and peoples living farther west, the probability that these intensified during the late prehistoric-protohistoric period, and the evidence of linkage to bison hunting.

A less sedentary way of life coupled with group subsistence activities organized in a new way might well lead to changes in burial practices and village layout. As early as the late prehistoric period in the Prairie Peninsula, rising emphasis on communal hunting that involved essentially the entire village probably led to de-emphasis of clan-centered cooperative units that formerly had organized horticultural pursuits (Brown 1965:74). Emphasis shifted to larger units (bands, phratries), and to individual households, composed of several related families. At Madisonville, the dense cemetery areas close to the plaza might be connected with subgroups such as lineages or clans that had important horticulture-related functions. As noted in Chapter 2, formal, bounded burial areas have been found to correlate under certain circumstances with corporate groups that control critical resources through lineal descent (Goldstein 1976:35-69, 1980:7-8; Saxe 1970:119, 233-34; Saxe and Gall 1977). Smaller burial groups away from the central space might be centered on households, operating in a time when horticulture was only one of several interrelated subsistence activities.

Venturing further into the realm of speculation, the apparent rise and fall in the custom of providing ceramic vessels for the dead—most of them with interior food lines or other evidence that they originally contained sustenance—might have coincided with, first, a rising concern with adequate nourishment during a period of less consistent climatic parameters when corn and locally available foodstuffs might not have been as reliable as hitherto, followed later by a lessening concern when bison became available as an important dietary supplement. These would have been relative differences, not any sort of food crisis. As discussed in Chapter 5, the lower Little Miami Valley had more than adequate resources to support a population of the size proposed for the Madisonville site. Even the relatively cool, moist conditions that probably prevailed after 1450 (e.g., Graybill 1981:57) should not have severely disrupted food production in this region (see Chapter 4). It is of note, however, that Myra Giesen found the sample of the Madisonville human remains that she studied to have been under less nutritional stress, with a "better pattern of dental health," than samples from Anderson, Incinerator, Buffalo, and Pearson, a northwestern Ohio site roughly contemporaneous with Anderson and Incinerator (Giesen 1992:202). Such a pattern would correlate well with people who were adding significant quantities of meat to an otherwise carbohydrate-dominated diet. Unfortunately, since much of Giesen's sample was drawn from the poorly provenienced southern portion of the site (Drooker 1996c:517-18), it is impossible to correlate particular well-nourished or poorly nourished burials with particular interment patterns or with earlier or later occupations of the site.

Greatly increased frequencies of projectile points per cubic meter of pit fill at Madisonville versus earlier occupied sites including Muir, Schomaker, Hine, and Campbell Island have been suggested as possible evidence of involvement in the seventeenth-century European-driven hide trade (Cowan 1992: Fig. 10, 19-20). Hide processing tools, such as bone beamers and chert endscrapers, also are much in evidence. However, they are found in significant numbers at both early and late Madisonville Horizon sites, and it is not clear whether any apparent increase in hunting and animal processing tools can be linked with certainty to protohistoric components alone. At Madisonville, in any case, any such increase might well be correlated with procurement of bison for subsistence rather than beaver or deer pelts for the European hide trade. Of course, bison meat and hides also had exchange value. I will return to this fact in Chapter 8.

Warfare

What of warfare? In his earlier works, Graybill hypothesized that warfare between eastern Fort Ancient people and their northern neighbors would have increased after about 1450, due to competition for hunting and gathering territories during a period of less favorable climatic conditions for horticulture (1981:169, 1986). He and others more recently proposed an upsurge of fighting during the protohistoric period, driven, after the first quarter of the seventeenth century, by the cogwheel of Iroquois "beaver wars" and "mourning wars," which are thought ultimately to have pushed Fort Ancient peoples from their central Ohio Valley homeland (Chapter 4). Evidence cited includes (1) palisades at at least some Late Fort Ancient sites (Graybill 1981:169), (2) increased numbers of secondary (disarticulated) burials and group burials (Cowan 1988:8-9, 1992:15), and (3) an influx of Riker/Wellsburg and/or Whittlesey refugees into eastern Fort Ancient sites after about 1550 (Baker 1988; Graybill 1986). Additional evidence would include an increase in warfare-related trauma, such as scalping or embedded projectile points. Is there any such evidence at Madisonville? If so, can it be tied to the most recent, protohistoric component at the site?

There is no direct evidence for palisades at Madisonville or any other lower Little Miami Valley site (Table 4-5; Drooker 1996a: Table 1). However, Madisonville was one of two sites in the area that were located on bluff tops (the other being Sand Ridge), which is another potential form of community defense. It is possible that periods during which these sites, rather than floodplain/terrace locations, were heavily used were times of increased warfare. Such periods were not restricted to the Late Madisonville Horizon.

There is no evidence that trauma exceeded that at earlier sites. For example, the approximately 6% frequency of fractures (including 1% head injuries) in 544 lots of human remains from Trenches 1-K and five known individuals with embedded projectile points (0.9%) (Drooker 1996c:518) seems not much different from the 6% trauma rate reported for the Early-Middle Fort Ancient Anderson site (Table 4-6). Individuals with embedded points, not all of whom died from their wounds, do include only adults, three of whom are known to have been male (Burials 1-38, 4-25, D-20, D-46, and I-19). One (Burial 4-25, interred within the plaza space and discussed above) was buried only with a Madisonville-style mortuary vessel and shell spoons, but the other four either themselves had or were associated with burials that had later grave goods: blue glass beads (with Burial 1-39, next to 1-38), two unusually shaped shell gorgets (Burial D-21, next to D-19), a small ring-shaped ornament made from a thin metal tube (just below D-46, which lay partially disarticulated in a pit), and a large copper pendant (I-19).

The distribution of all burials with projectile points (Figure 6-56), which included both possible injury-related artifacts (e.g., several found in the pelvic or chest cavity) and probable ceremonial grave goods (such as the matched set of six points under the crossed ankles of Burial B-49), seems to have clear social, as well as some possible temporal, implications. Members both of large burial groups close to the plaza lacking strong associations with either metal or European materials, and of smaller groups at some distance from the plaza having stronger associations with metal and European goods (cf. Figure 6-40), were buried with projectile points. Thus, points *per se* do not seem to be strongly associated with either earlier or more recent Late Fort Ancient burials at this site. However, there was a strong contrast, with social rather than temporal implications, between burial group 2 and burial groups 6 and 7. The latter, and the areas surrounding them, include far more burials with projectile points than burial group 2 and a wide area around it. It seems that burials on the southern side of the plaza were more strongly associated with weapons of warfare and hunting, just as they were more strongly associated with the male status indicators, pipes (Figure 6-52). People buried with projectile points in Trenches 1-K included 9 identified males, 1 identified female, 24 other adults, and 8 subadults (see Drooker 1997, in press: Databases 4 and 2). All twelve extant whole projectile points from burials are type 5 or type 6.

In considering body treatment, projectile points are statistically correlated (at the 0.05 level of significance) with articulated rather than disarticulated burials in Trenches 1-K. They were more likely to be found with people in groups rather than individual burials, but the correlation is not significant. Within group burials, projectile points were significantly less likely to be found with subsidiary burials (burials arranged in relationship to another, primary, individual; see Chapter 7) than with primary or equal-status burials. However, only eight percent of primary and ten percent of equal-status individuals in group burials had them. Thus, it might be that one way to gain nonsubsidiary status in a group burial was through association with warfare or hunting. However, it was by no means the only way.

A high proportion of disarticulated remains has been proposed as evidence of warfare during the Late Madisonville Horizon (e.g., Cowan 1988, 1992). At Madisonville, where there was a significantly higher proportion of disarticulated subadult than disarticulated adult remains (Table 7-5, Figure 7-8), this attribute does not seem to be a general indicator of warfare. Nor is there any strong indication of an increase of disarticulated burials over time. They were distributed across almost all of the excavation trenches (Figure 6-57), located both close to the plaza within large burial groups and far from it within smaller groups. The same is true for multiple burials. Although over 30% of those interred at Madisonville were consigned to a group burial (Figure 6-58), children and adolescents were far more likely to be members of such groups than were adults (Table 7-5, below).

However, there were a few large group burials consisting entirely of disarticulated skeletons that seem to be ritual in na-

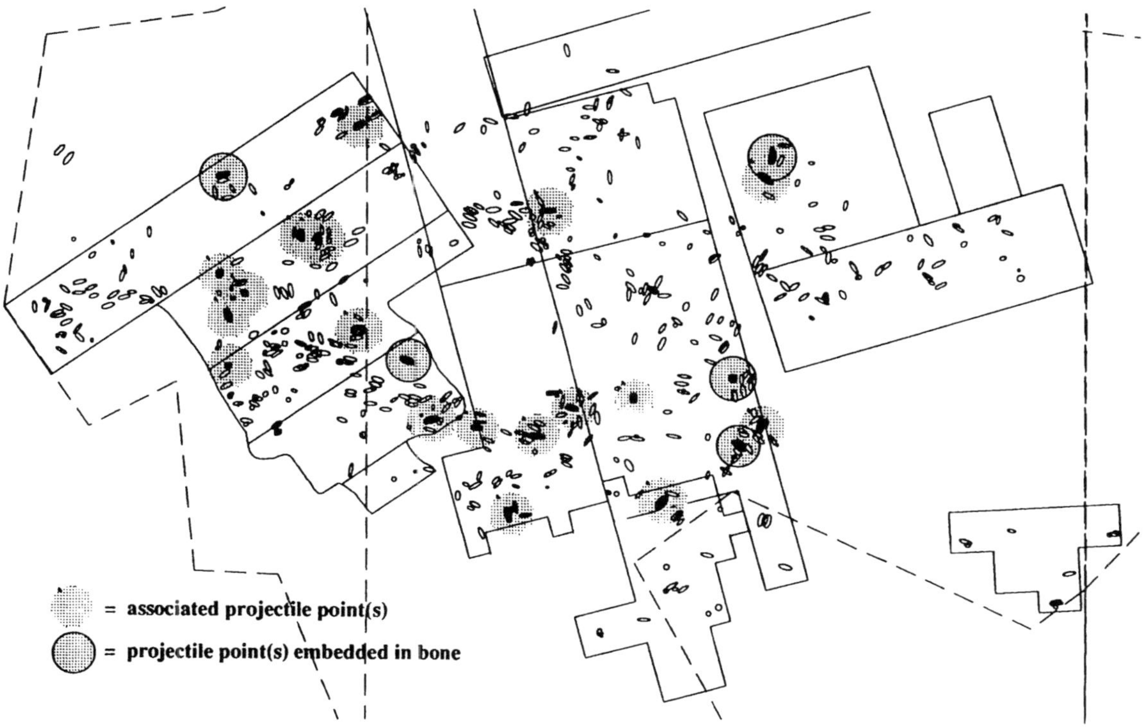

Figure 6-56. Distribution of burials associated with projectile points, Trenches 1-K. Circled burials had points embedded in their bones.

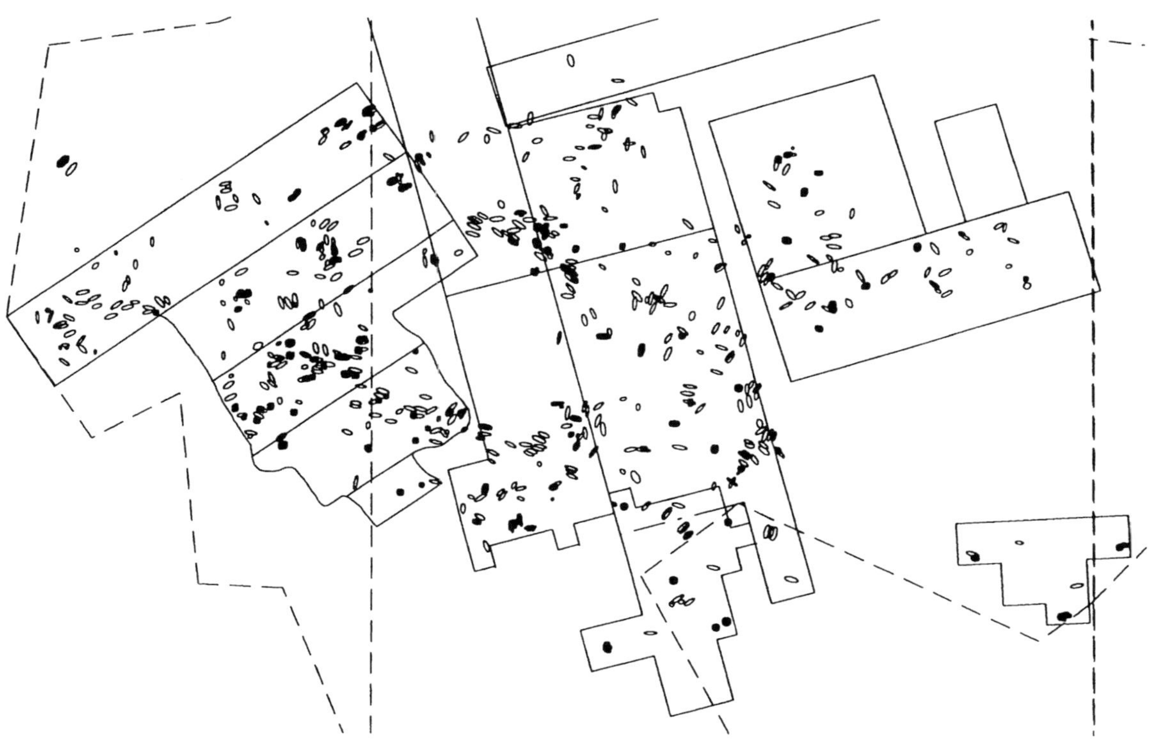

Figure 6-57. Distribution of disarticulated burials, Trenches 1-K.

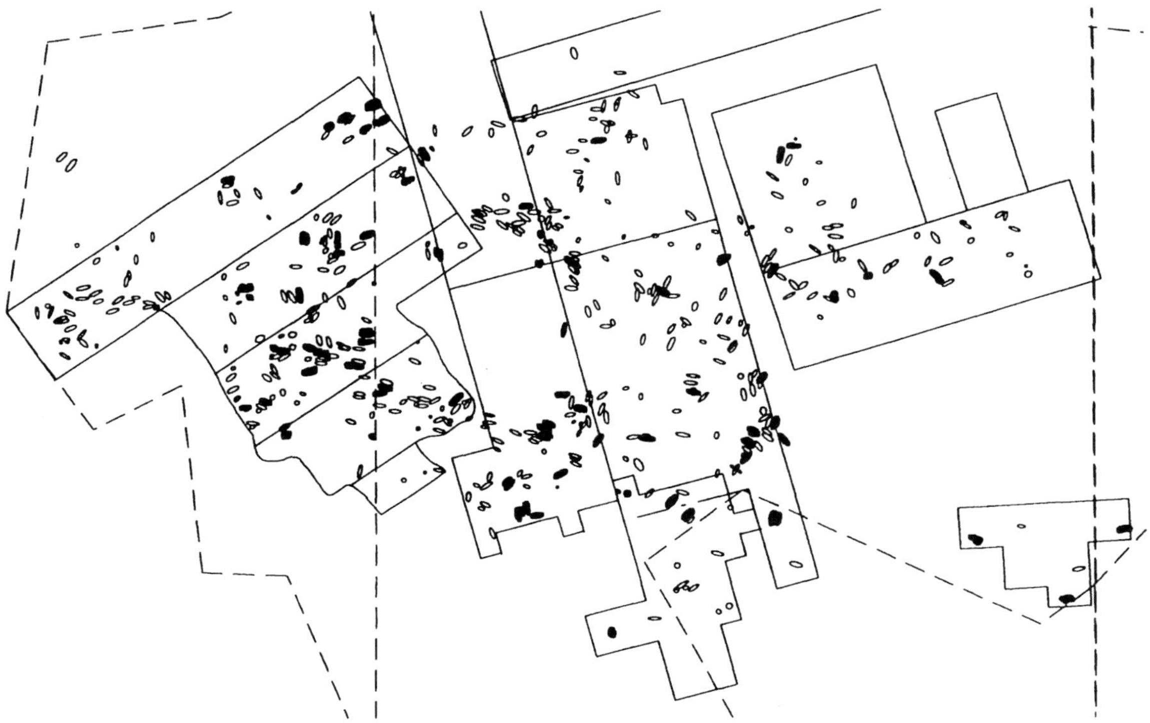

Figure 6-58. Distribution of multiple burials, Trenches 1-K.

ture. These might well have been related to warfare. Only one was associated with projectile points, and none included horizon marker artifacts. One group, consisting of Burials E-9 through E-14, was described above, under The Plaza Revisited. Another, Burials H-9 through H-24, was located within a depression associated with the wall trench house feature. It consisted of six skulls, an additional jaw, and a pile of other bones, in a space approximately 2 by 4 feet. Three of the crania were arranged along the southern edge of the pile, facing outward. At least three adults and one subadult were represented. A third mass burial, definitely related to warfare, was in Block 1. The bones of at least 22 individuals (Burials 51 through 72) were disposed in a space 3.5 feet in diameter and 4.5 feet deep, above a layer of unio shells. Directly above the shells were the postcranial remains, and above them the 22 crania. One sacrum and one skull had projectile points embedded in them. One additional burial, D-18, is worth noting in this connection. It consisted of the articulated leg bones of an extended, supine adult in a full-length grave, covered by a layer of fragmented, burnt bones from at least three adults plus a few artifacts that included a dozen rolled copper and brass beads. The sides of the grave, but not the bottom, were hardened by heat, implying that the bone fragments were added while still smoldering. Expert examination of the bone fragments might be able to distinguish between, for instance, cremation and cannibalism, but whatever the event that produced them, it was protohistoric rather than prehistoric.

From this body of evidence, it does seem that warfare and probably hunting were important social factors during Late Fort Ancient times. However, there is little to single out the protohistoric as a period during which which warfare increased significantly. Weapons and war-related death and ritual appear to have been present throughout the Madisonville Horizon. At no time did death by violence approach the magnitude of a site such as the fourteenth-century Oneota Norris Farms 36 Cemetery in Illinois, where 34% of the adults suffered traumatic death (Milner and Smith 1990:148).

Seventeenth-century refugees from northern Ohio might well have been present at Madisonville, but this is not the entire story. There *is* a strong northern Ohio presence at the site (which will be discussed further in Chapter 8), evidenced in ceramics, pipes, and other artifacts, but whether it was confined to the Late Madisonville Horizon is another question. It more likely was part of an ongoing pattern of interaction that had its roots much earlier.

Shell tempered and non-shell-tempered rim sherds decorated with appliqué notched strips below and parallel to the lip (see Figure 8-37a) are the most common extant nonlocal ceramic type at the site. They were found across Trenches 1-E (Figure 6-59), in pits in Block L and the pre-Block 22 1882 excavations, and in the upper levels of the midden in the southwestern part of the site excavated by the CMNH (Glowacki et al. 1993). This is a mode of decoration that occurs across all of northern Ohio (e.g., Fort Meigs Notched Appliqué, Reeve Filleted) dur-

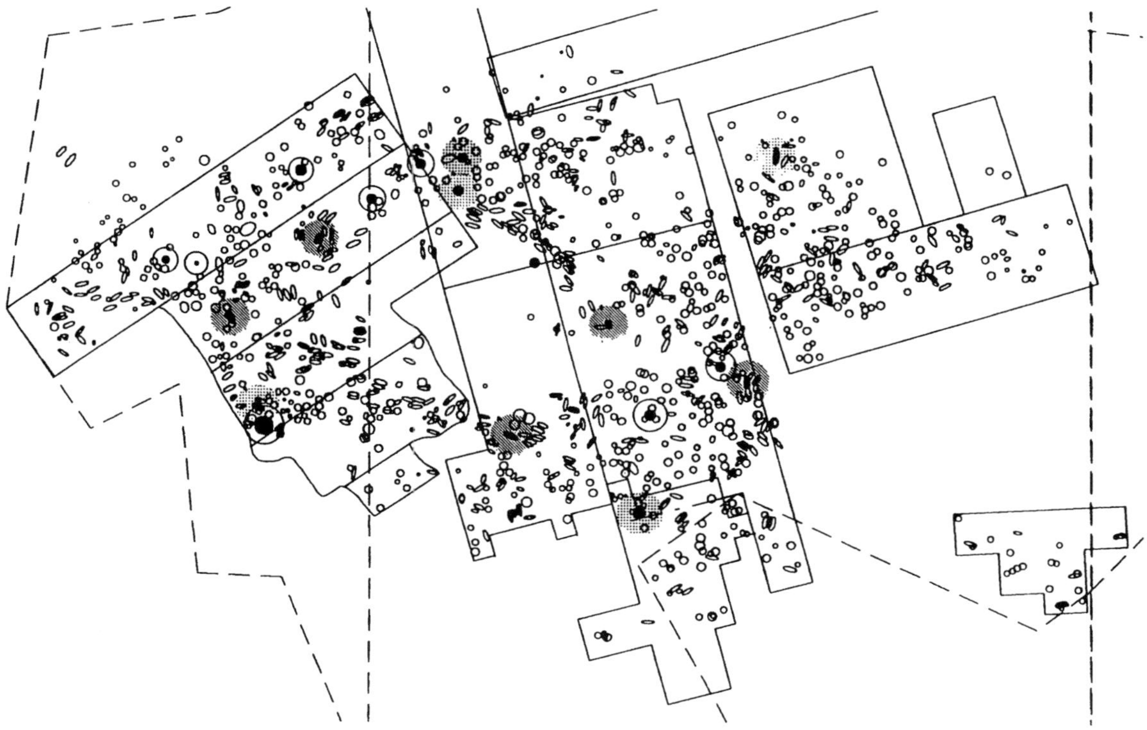

Figure 6-59. Distribution of extant ceramics and pipes with northern Ohio-related attributes, Trenches 1-K. They include rim sherds with notched appliqué strips in pits (circled), Indian Hills rim sherds in refuse pits (dots), mortuary vessels with notched collars or rim strips (slanted lines) and pipes in burials and pit E-3 made from crystalline quartzite or anorthosite with ties to the Reeve Village site (dashed slanted lines). See discussion in text.

ing late prehistoric-protohistoric times, as well as in northern Illinois (LaSalle Filleted), northern Indiana and southern Michigan (Moccasin Bluff Notched Appliqué Strip), southwestern Ontario, and northern West Virginia/western Pennsylvania (Wellsburg Simple Stamped, Wellsburg Cordmarked) (Baker 1988:42, 46; Brose 1994:73-79; Mason 1986:215-16; Murphy and Ferris 1990:223). A few sherds of Indian Hills ceramics, from northwestern Ohio (Figure 8-37c), were excavated from pits (Figure 6-59). At least one shell-tempered jar (Figure 8-37b) very close in formal attributes to Tuttle Hill Notched (David Stothers, pers. comm.), another with a notched appliqué strip (Figure 8-37a, bottom), and three more-refined local adaptations of notched collar vessels (Figure 6-60; see also Griffin 1943: Pl. LXX.2-4) that also have been noted as having similarities to Tuttle Hill Notched (Murphy 1971:40), were found with burials, by far the largest number of foreign-influenced mortuary vessels having any sort of common thread. Three were with subadults and two with adults, one of them female. They were not clustered together, although all came from the northern portion of the site, in Trenches 2, B, and D (Figure 6-59). (At least one rim sherd of this type, excavated before 1885, came from Metz's private collection, but its provenience is unknown.) Two vessels had teat lugs characteristic of the fifteenth-sixteenth century Riker series (James Morton, pers. comm.) combined with more familiar Madisonville Horizon characteristics (Figure 6-61). They were interred with Burials 2-40, a teenager, and 3-14, a young adult female, and both were associated with shell spoons (perhaps an earlier attribute). Similar jars have been reported from protohistoric eastern Fort Ancient sites (see Chapter 8), so this "northern" influence might well have come indirectly to Madisonville, via upriver Fort Ancient settlements. Another attribute of Riker series jars, a slightly incurvate rim, is present on a small number of Madisonville mortuary vessels, some with appliqué lizard effigies (e.g., Figure 4-13, Griffin 1943: Pl. LXVI.3, with Burial 34 from Block 6; see also Figures 6-65 and 7-4, below).

The locations of these vessels with "northern" attributes did not tie them definitely to earlier or later burials. However, all but one were at some distance from the edge of the plaza, and most were not within a large burial group. None was directly associated with metal or glass, but a few were close to features containing metal.

In addition to ceramics with northern Ohio affiliations, there are several pipes from Madisonville made of the white, crystalline anorthosite or quartzite very commonly used for pipes and blanks excavated at the Reeve Village site (also known as the Willoughby site), east of Cleveland (Ahlstrom 1979; Greenman 1935; AMNH Catalog Nos. 9/68, 9/87, 9/89). They include a very large claw effigy with Burial I-19 (which also had a double-barred copper pendant) and an ovoid with Burial 3-40 (Figures

Figure 6-60. Two vessels from Madisonville with notched collars (two views). *Left*: Madisonville Plain vessel, from Burial D-53 (HUPM Cat. No. 08-3-10/79655). *Right*: Madisonville Grooved-Paddled vessel with fingernail notching around shoulder, from Burial 2-2 (97-38-10/62880). Most of the rim strip has been broken off on the latter, but short portions are visible directly adjacent to the handle, which depends from the rim strip (for another view, see Griffin 1943: Pl. LXX.2). Photograph by Hillel Burger (HUPM Photo No. N33846A/B). Copyright 1997 by the President and Fellows of Harvard College, and used with permission.

Figure 6-61. Two vessels from Madisonville with paired nodes or teat lugs. *Left*: Madisonville Cordmarked vessel with four pairs of nodes, from Burial 2-40 (HUPM Cat. No. 97-38-10/62899). *Right*: Madisonville Plain vessel with two handles and two pairs of nodes, from Burial 3-14 (97-38-10/62905). Photograph by Hillel Burger (HUPM Photo No. N33844). Copyright 1997 by the President and Fellows of Harvard College, and used with permission.

7-5d and 7-5a), plus what appears to be a disk pipe blank from Pit E-3 (Figure 6-59).

The distribution of artifacts with northern Ohio associations at Madisonville does not have the flavor of a coherent group or groups of people fleeing seventeenth-century Iroquois aggression, but rather of long-term relationships involving interaction over an extended period of time. The locations of foreign-influenced vessels on the site, as well as the ceramic attributes, correspond to both Early (prehistoric) and Late (protohistoric) Madisonville Horizon time frames. Evidence for still earlier interaction between southwestern Ohio Fort Ancient and northwestern Ohio sites comes from grit-tempered Anderson- and Baum-like ceramics excavated at late thirteenth–early fourteenth century sites, such as Pearson, in eastern Sandusky County (Bowen 1994:2, Fig. 11). There may be late sixteenth century Madisonville-like ceramics from this region, as well (cf. Bowen 1994: Fig. 21). Anderson Incised, Baum Cordmarked, and perhaps Madisonville Cordmarked and Madisonville Plain sherds also have come from the late prehistoric Whittlesey South Park site in northeastern Ohio (Brose 1976:32, 1994:55, Fig. 5.2).

Epidemics

As discussed in Chapter 2, mass death by so-called virgin soil epidemics is a known effect of initial sustained contact between people from widely separated geographical locations. In addition to postulating an increase in warfare during the seventeenth century, some archaeologists have speculated that epidemic disease might have been instrumental in disrupting Fort Ancient society during the same time. There is no strong evidence for any such occurrence at Madisonville.

Multiple burials might indeed have been more common at Madisonville during protohistoric versus prehistoric time. For example, non-individual burials were significantly correlated with metal grave goods (chi square test, 1 df, $\alpha = 0.01$), as well as being correlated with European items, although not significantly (Fisher's Exact Test, 1 df, $\alpha = 0.065$). However, there is no positive evidence to tie this custom to an increase in epidemic disease. For example, there is nothing like the numerous mass graves containing dozens of individuals that have been excavated at seventeenth-century Spanish missions among the Apalachee, Guale, and Timucua (Milanich 1996:65). There are indeed large numbers of multiple burials at Madisonville (Figure 7-10, below), but the majority of them consist of only two or three individuals. Such burials often include both articulated and disarticulated remains, implying non-concurrent death. As discussed above, the few large mass graves that do exist at Madisonville are more evocative of warfare than of epidemic death. The disposition of remains (e.g., the 22 skulls arranged on top of postcranial remains in Block 1) was not done in hurried desperation, but in accordance with formal, recognized ritual. This also is true for smaller group burials, where subsidiary burials often were formally arranged around a central, primary burial.

Contemporaneous Southwestern Ohio Fort Ancient Sites

Was the village at Madisonville contemporaneous with any other settlements in its vicinity? If so, the relationships between or among them will be important in assessing regional settlement and interaction patterns, and larger patterns of Fort Ancient social organization.

Although there are over a dozen sites in the lower Little Miami Valley that have been identified as having a Fort Ancient component (Figures 4-6, 5-1), only a handful have been excavated or described to any useful extent in print. Settlement patterns for the densely occupied area across the river from Madisonville may be almost impossible to untangle at this late date, particularly since a significant number of sites probably have been destroyed without record over the past century and a half (Robert Genheimer, pers. comm.; see also quotations from nineteenth-century newspaper accounts in Metz 1878, 1881). Thus, the following discussion cannot claim to be definitive, merely to assess what the available evidence can tell us about relative ages of known sites. It will look briefly at the entire Fort Ancient time span, but will concentrate on Madisonville Horizon sites.

Radiocarbon Dates

Figure 6-62 diagrams the available radiocarbon dates from all lower Little Miami Valley Fort Ancient sites and all other southwestern Ohio sites that have a Madisonville Horizon component.

The late thirteenth-century occupation at Madisonville might have been contemporaneous with that of the Anderson site in the upper Little Miami Valley, and Horseshoe Johnson (Table 4-1) and Schomaker farther west. Locally, it perhaps overlapped slightly with the Turpin 1 component excavated by Oehler. The single Sand Ridge date falls within a thin period in the Madisonville radiocarbon sequence, during the late fourteenth-early fifteenth centuries. However, the carbon sample came from near the base of the stratified layers containing Fort Ancient materials (Riggs 1994), so Sand Ridge might have been occupied well into the fifteenth century, overlapping the earliest fifteenth century dates from Madisonville. Dates from Campbell Island in the central Great Miami Valley coincide with the lower range of Madisonville fifteenth-century dates, as does the single date from Carroll-Oregonia Road, in the upper reaches of the Little Miami.

Only two sites in addition to Madisonville have dates that calibrate later than the fifteenth century. One of the dates from the upper Little Miami South Fort (perhaps an outlier) calibrates to the sixteenth century, a period from which there are only a few Madisonville calibration intercepts. This also is the range covered by the samples from Hahn's Field, which overlap the sixteenth-seventeenth century Madisonville dates but have calibration intercepts centering on the sixteenth century, in the interval between the peaks of the bimodal Madisonville distribution of calibration intercepts.

Although the small numbers of radiocarbon dates from each of these sites are insufficient to define fully the ranges of time during which each one was occupied, they do indicate relative periods of use. For more fine-grained seriation, comparison of artifact (and feature) styles and types is necessary.

Horizon Markers

Of the few structures recorded from these sites, the wall trench feature from the Turpin 3 site (Table 4-5) was the closest in size and construction method to a Madisonville structure. Postholes were not recorded inside the Madisonville wall trenches as they were for the Turpin feature, but that does not mean they could not have been present. It is likely that this component was roughly contemporaneous with an Early-Middle Fort Ancient occupation at Madisonville.

No southwestern Ohio Fort Ancient site other than Madisonville has yet produced any European-derived materials. Two of the Turpin components did have copper (Table 4-7). This included pulley-shaped earplugs (Oehler 1973:32) and thin pins (HUPM 86-46-10/A4041) known from other Early-Middle Fort Ancient and contemporaneous Mississippian sites, plus a rolled bead and two scraps (CMNH 5/1131) that are comparable with Madisonville Horizon artifacts, but not necessarily from the protohistoric period. From this, it seems likely that none of these settlements was occupied to any significant extent during the Late Madisonville Horizon after about 1550.

None of them has a ceramics complex congruent with that of Madisonville. However, several do overlap portions of it.

Hahn's Field is the one site other than Madisonville with radiocarbon dates later than 1550. The AMS dates, on three carbonized corn kernels from two pits excavated by Metz in 1885, were obtained together with those from Madisonville. I had initially intended to include Hahn's Field as a significant segment of this project, but abandoned that idea when I found that many of the artifacts, including all of the complete vessels, were unprovenienced. In addition, producing an accurate map proved impossible, for the same reasons than hampered map production from data collected by Metz, Putnam, and the MLSS at Madisonville. However, I did examine all of the artifacts from this site curated at the HUPM. In spite of the late ^{14}C dates, the Madisonville Horizon ceramics fall toward the early end of the spectrum. Of the ten whole vessels (Griffin 1943: Pls. LXXXV-LXXXVII, one is a noded bowl. The nine jars include one with no handles and a piecrust rim, and eight with plain rims, seven of which had only two handles and one of which originally might

---

Figure 6-62 (*facing page*). Radiocarbon dates from selected southwestern Ohio sites (see Tables 4-1 and 6-1). Sites designated by boldface are located in the lower Little Miami Valley.

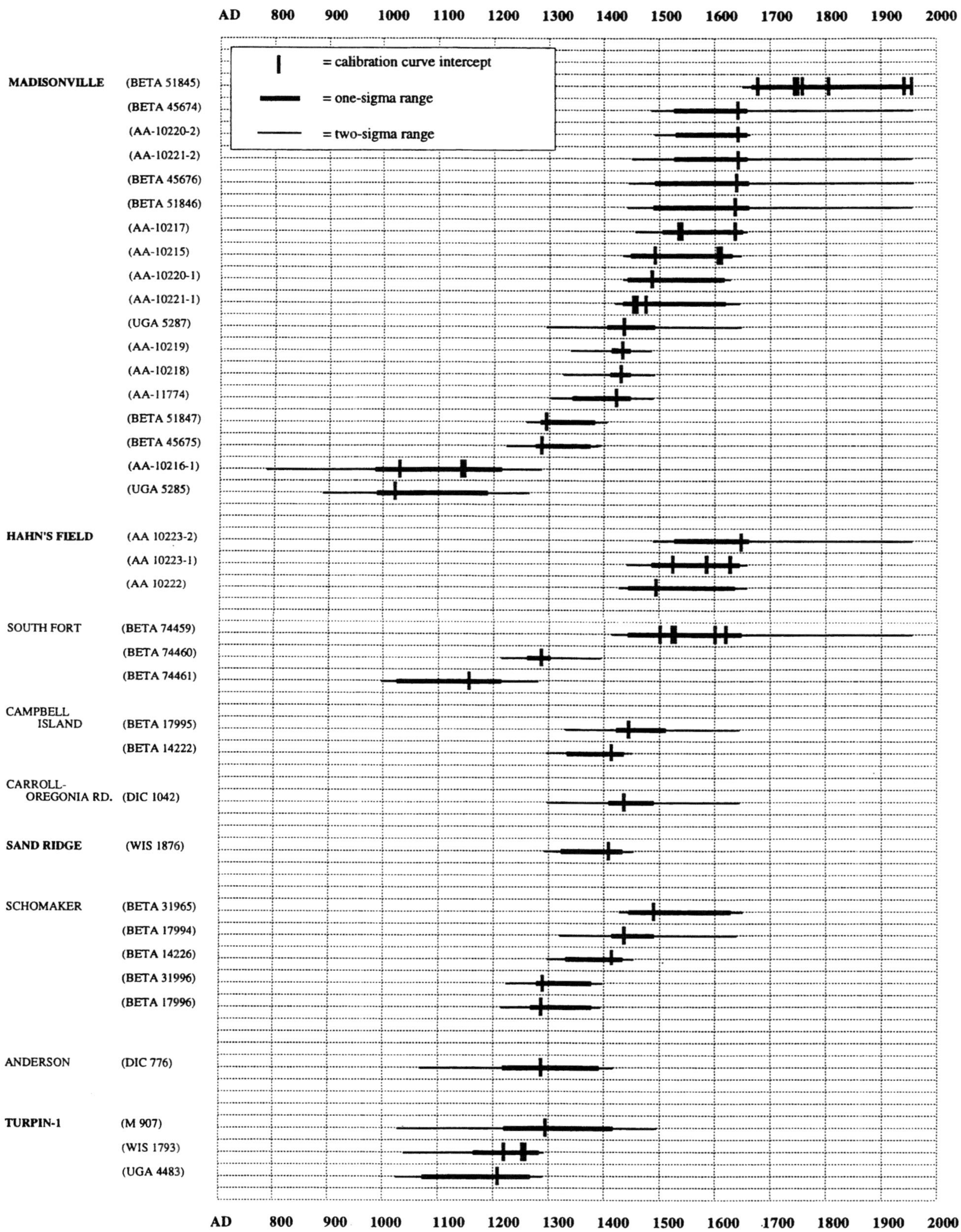
AD 800 900 1000 1100 1200 1300 1400 1500 1600 1700 1800 1900 2000
= calibration curve intercept
= one-sigma range
= two-sigma range
MADISONVILLE (BETA 51845)
(BETA 45674)
(AA-10220-2)
(AA-10221-2)
(BETA 45676)
(BETA 51846)
(AA-10217)
(AA-10215)
(AA-10220-1)
(AA-10221-1)
(UGA 5287)
(AA-10219)
(AA-10218)
(AA-11774)
(BETA 51847)
(BETA 45675)
(AA-10216-1)
(UGA 5285)
HAHN'S FIELD (AA 10223-2)
(AA 10223-1)
(AA 10222)
SOUTH FORT (BETA 74459)
(BETA 74460)
(BETA 74461)
CAMPBELL ISLAND (BETA 17995)
(BETA 14222)
CARROLL-OREGONIA RD. (DIC 1042)
SAND RIDGE (WIS 1876)
SCHOMAKER (BETA 31965)
(BETA 17994)
(BETA 14226)
(BETA 31996)
(BETA 17996)
ANDERSON (DIC 776)
TURPIN-1 (M 907)
(WIS 1793)
(UGA 4483)
AD 800 900 1000 1100 1200 1300 1400 1500 1600 1700 1800 1900 2000

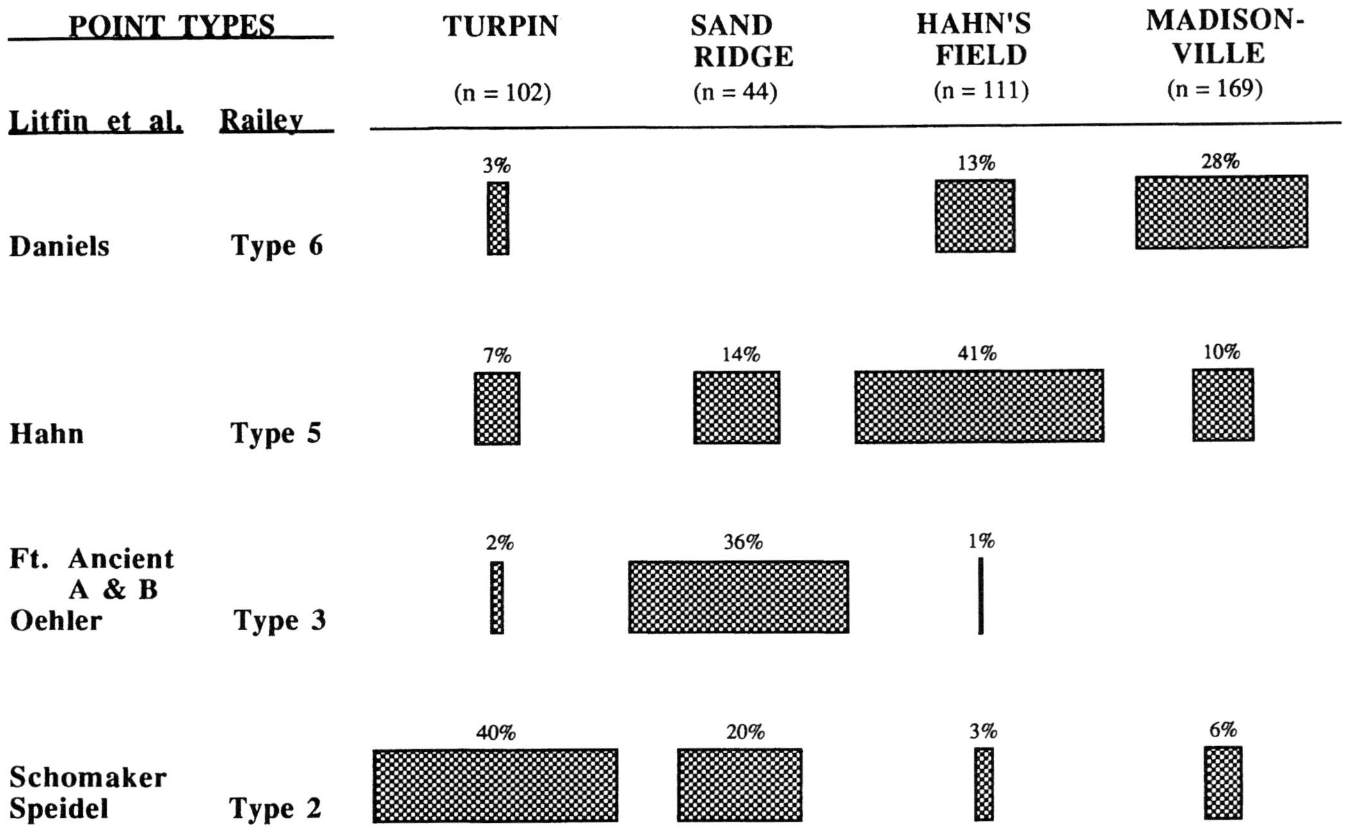

Figure 6-63. Frequencies of time-sensitive projectile point types at Turpin 1, Sand Ridge, Hahn's Field, and Madisonville. Data from Litfin et al., grouped by point types defined by Railey 1992. Data are from components excavated or collected by the CMNH.

have had four. None of the rims were thickened, but two were not everted. Surfaces were 40% smooth, 60% cord-marked. Of rim sherds from 88 vessels, six had decorated necks, three with thickened rims and three without; the remainder were consistent with the whole vessels. This appears to be a comparatively early Late Fort Ancient ceramics profile, overlapping with Late Fort Ancient mortuary vessels from the Madisonville site, but with a range that extends earlier. Consistent with the ceramics profile, three decorated shell spoons were excavated from Hahn's Field, a much higher frequency than Madisonville considering the relative sizes of the excavations.

Sand Ridge Fort Ancient ceramics include a significant amount of neck decoration, combined with both thickened and non-thickened rims (e.g., Griffin 1943: Pl. XCI). The large majority of sherds are shell tempered or shell-rock tempered, with everted rims. Riggs (1994) aptly calls this assemblage Middle-Late Fort Ancient, and demonstrates that it overlaps in time with pottery assemblages from three of the twelve pits at Madisonville included in his formal seriation (Pits 2-7, 2-8, and 4-30, all with high proportions of decorated Anderson Shell Tempered sherds).

Rigg's seriation found that Turpin 1 ceramics separated out as earlier than Sand Ridge, spanning Early-Middle Fort Ancient. Shell tempering, neck decoration, thickened rims, and everted rims all increase in frequency between the two periods that Riggs defines for Turpin, but still are less than at Sand Ridge. The Turpin 2 and 3 collection at the HUPM includes both whole jars with characteristics similar to those in the Turpin 1 sample (e.g., Griffin 1943: Pls. LXXXI, LXXXII.3) and whole jars and sherds with Early Madisonville Horizon attributes (e.g., Griffin 1943: Pl. LXXXII.5, HUPM 86-46-10/A4008): cord-marked bodies, plain necks, thin lips, slightly everted rims, and two handles. (Note that the Madisonville Horizon jars from Turpin in Griffin's Plate LXXXII.1, 2, and 4 come from the Johnson Turpin farm, rather than the Phil Turpin farm. I am unsure of the location of the former.) The HUPM Turpin collection also includes sherds of thick-rimmed, decorated-neck Anderson Shell Tempered ware (Figure 4-8), but I am uncertain what proportion came from the Phil Turpin farm. Both Turpin 1 and Turpin 2/3 span the Early-Middle Fort Ancient period, and Turpin 2/3 has an Early Madisonville Horizon component.

Campbell Island ceramics, too, appear to span more than one period (Griffin 1943:158-59, Pls. LXXXIX-CX). They include 20% grit-tempered wares, two- and four-handled Madisonville Cordmarked jars with plain necks and both notched and unnotched lips, and jars with decorated necks coupled with thin or (less frequently) thickened rims.

For four of these sites, seriation of projectile point types proved a useful adjunct to comparison of ceramics (Figure 6-63). Both major and minor temporal components indicated by ceramic types also are indicated in the projectile point seriation. Turpin 1 has the strongest Early presence, but also apparently a minor Middle-Late component. Sand Ridge comes next in time, and its sample contains no late Late Fort Ancient points. Hahn's Field is later, perhaps with a minor Early Fort Ancient component. Madisonville overlaps with the three other sites, but least with Sand Ridge. The samples used for Figure 6-63 came from CMNH collection at Hahn's Field and excavations at Turpin 1, Sand Ridge, and the southwestern portion of the Madisonville site. The Hahn's Field collection curated at the HUPM has similar point type frequencies to those in Figure 6-63, but the HUPM Madisonville collection includes a somewhat higher proportion of type 5 points than the CMNH collection.

Campbell Island (Shetrone 1926: Fig. 27), Hahn's Field (HUPM 86-46-10/91977, 92081), and Turpin 2 (HUPM 86-46-10/A4008) all have produced non-redstone disk pipes, corroborating the existence of at least minor early Late Fort Ancient components at each one. On the basis of its large disk size, the Campbell Island pipe probably is the earliest.

Summary: Settlement Patterns

Fort Ancient currently is characterized as never having had any hierarchical settlement patterns (e.g., Griffin 1992). In the lower Little Miami Valley this does appear to be true for at least the very Late Madisonville Horizon, when the Madisonville site seems to have been the only one occupied. Data for earlier periods are more ambiguous, particularly if the lack of hard information on most sites in this area is taken into account. The sites for which we do have data appear to have overlapped in time, but none seem to have had their largest occupations at exactly the same time.

Turpin 1 had a strong Early Fort Ancient presence. Turpin 2 appears to have overlapped with it (perhaps in space as well as time), and also to have had a minor early Late Fort Ancient component and perhaps a minor Middle Fort Ancient component. Anderson Shell Tempered ware defines Middle Fort Ancient components at Turpin 2 and the Johnson Turpin site, at Madisonville, and at Sand Ridge. Although it did overlap in time with the other two sites, Sand Ridge appears to have stood alone for at least a portion of Middle-Late Fort Ancient time. However, a single illustration of ceramics from the Waterworks site (Starr 1960:71) near the mouth of the Little Miami River (Figures 4-6, 5-1) hints that this site might have been contemporaneous with the major occupation at Sand Ridge. The Early Madisonville Horizon Hahn's Field site comes next, overlapping the early portion of the Late Fort Ancient occupation at the Madisonville site. (The Hahn's Field ^{14}C date range appears broader than that indicated by its artifact assemblage. Recent salvage excavation at this site (Genheimer 1994) may help to resolve this incongruence.)

Significant occupations on bluff-top sites appear to have occurred during the late fourteenth–early fifteenth century at Sand Ridge and from the mid-fifteenth century onward at Madisonville, with perhaps a short period during the early Late Fort Ancient when Hahn's Field, on the floodplain, was most in evidence. It is possible that this reflects periods of conflict and non-conflict in the region. The presence of early Late Fort Ancient components at other floodplain/terrace sites such as Turpin 2, the Johnson Turpin farm, and (farther afield) Campbell Island further marks this as a period perhaps less afflicted by warfare. The most recent components at Madisonville do reflect some emphasis on warfare, not only during the protohistoric period but prehistorically as well.

Known early Late Fort Ancient components farther north all appear to have been relatively small and probably short-term. Campbell Island is characterized as only one or two houses, not large enough to be called a village (Cowan 1986:54), while Carroll-Oregonia Road and South Fort might have been used sporadically as hunting camps (Brose and White 1983:19-22; Drooker 1996a). Late Fort Ancient large-village life appears to have been concentrated in the lower Little Miami Valley and, from the late sixteenth century onward, probably at Madisonville alone.

Madisonville's Place in Protohistoric Fort Ancient Relative Chronology

In previous overviews of protohistoric Fort Ancient (Chapter 4), Madisonville has been fit into relative chronological sequences with notable imprecision and inconsistency. Because its occupation history was not known in detail, it usually was treated as a single-component, very late protohistoric site. Now that more is known, it is possible to reconsider both how Madisonville fits into the chronological sequence for protohistoric Fort Ancient sites and how the new knowledge of Madisonville's occupation history might be useful in interpreting assemblages and features at contemporaneous Fort Ancient sites.

Figure 6-64 presents in graphic form the available radiocarbon dates from Fort Ancient sites with protohistoric components. It is evident that no site has produced a large enough suite of dates to fully define its occupation span. It also is evident that many of these sites included significant prehistoric components. Some of them, like Madisonville, might well have had multiple, separate occupations rather than completely continuous usage. Fox Farm, Clover, Neale's Landing, and Augusta all, like Madisonville, have produced at least two ^{14}C dates that calibrate to the fifteenth century. The relative importance of protohistoric components compared to late prehistoric ones, in terms of resident population and spatial use, has yet to be demonstrated for most of these settlements. For a number of

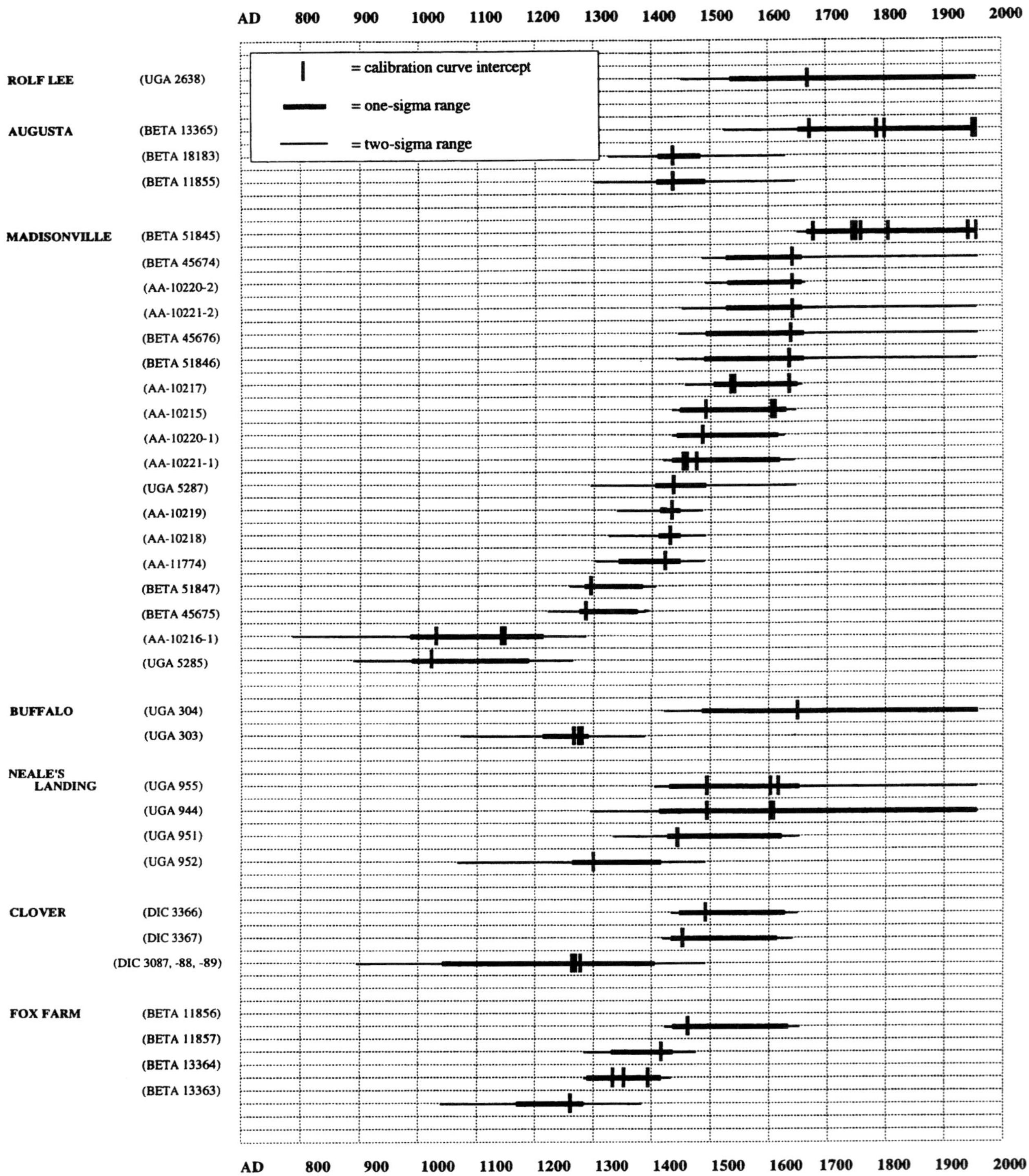

Figure 6-64. Radiocarbon dates from Fort Ancient sites with protohistoric components (see Tables 4-8 and 6-1).

TABLE 6-11
Important Metal and Glass Artifacts
Shared by Madisonville and Other Protohistoric Fort Ancient Sites

	Barred Copper Pendants	ITEMS MADE FROM THIN METAL TUBES		Friable Blue Glass Beads	Brass Clips (large)	Time Range of All Dateable European-Related Items
		Serpents	Coils, Rings			
Dunn	x					16th century
Fox Farm	x					16th century
Buffalo		?			x	1525-1625
Neale's Landing				x		1580-1630
Hardin	x		x		x	1550-1630
Madisonville	x	x	x	x	x	1540-1640
Augusta		?				1550-1670
Marmet				x		1580-1675?
Clover			x			1590-1700
Rolf Lee			x		x	1590-1700
Orchard						1630-1700?

Order determined by date range associated with most recent artifact reported from site.

them, areas of the site excavated non-methodically by amateurs appear to contain artifacts from time periods different from formally excavated areas. For example, the additional European items and large numbers of pipes reported from Hardin (Henderson et al. 1986:137-38; David Pollack, pers. comm.) and the European-derived artifacts from Fox Farm (Henderson et al. 1986:157-58; Turnbow 1992:51) point to later components than have been formally recorded.

The broad time frame for Madisonville European-derived artifacts, ca. 1540-1640 (Table 6-7), puts it within the same envelope as many of the other protohistoric Fort Ancient sites (Table 4-9). However, the fact that most of the Madisonville items could have been obtained prior to 1600 puts this site into a different category than Marmet, Hardin, Clover, Rolf Lee, and Orchard, which all produced at least some glass or metal artifacts probably not available until after that date (but see Note 1 to Table 4-9 for a caveat about the Orchard glass beads).

Few of the Madisonville European artifacts are duplicates of items at these other sites, raising the strong possibility that its residents functioned within different exchange networks than residents of many of the eastern Fort Ancient settlements. No other Fort Ancient site to date has been reported as producing iron kettle lugs, an iron dagger guard, a Clarksdale (or any other) brass bell, or a spiraling metal bead. Nor have any definitely produced a tubular metal serpent shape, although one has been reported from Augusta (Henderson et al. 1986:117) and one possible fragment did come from Buffalo (Hanson 1975: Fig. 71).

Madisonville does share friable blue glass beads with Neale's Landing and one of the Marmet components. Both contemporaneity and participation in the same interaction networks seems likely. This also seems extremely likely for Madisonville, Dunn, Fox Farm, and Hardin, all of which have produced large barred copper pendants as mortuary goods (Drooker 1994c, 1995, 1996a).

Table 6-11 summarizes the few metal and glass artifacts that Madisonville shares with other protohistoric sites. These mini-assemblages do not seriate in any satisfactory way. Considering the fact that few of these sites have been thoroughly and methodically excavated, this is hardly surprising. The table is organized by the date range assigned to the most recent metal or glass artifact reported from the site (Tables 4-9, 6-7). From this sparse evidence alone, Madisonville appears to have been roughly contemporaneous with Buffalo, Neale's Landing, and Hardin, to have been occupied longer than Fox Farm, and to have ceased functioning (or ceased aquiring European artifacts) before Marmet, Clover, Rolf Lee, and Orchard.

Madisonville does share several types of marine shell ornaments with eastern Fort Ancient protohistoric sites (Table 6-12, Figures 6-19a-c), including maskettes (of which it produced at least six), mushroom-shaped earplugs (at least four), and Citico rattlesnake gorgets (a single extremely worn and damaged example, with a child burial). However, it has produced none of the large mask gorgets that are in evidence at sites such as Rolf Lee (from which have come at least seven) and Marmet (at least four).

Numbers of metal, glass, and shell ornaments (and of burials with these artifact types) probably are a function of exchange spheres even more than of chronology at eastern versus western Fort Ancient sites. As such, they will be discussed in Chapter 8. However, a brief comparison among sites with at least some quantitative information can be useful.

TABLE 6-12
Important Marine Shell Artifacts at Madisonville and Other Protohistoric Fort Ancient Sites

	Citico Rattlesnake Gorgets	Maskettes	Mushroom Shaped Ear plugs	Time Range of All Dateable European-Related Items
Feurt	x			16th century
Fox Farm	x	x		16th century
Buffalo	x	x	x	1525-1625
Neale's Landing		x		1580-1630
Hardin	x	x		1550-1630
Madisonville	x	x	x	1540-1640
Augusta		x		1550-1670
Clover	x			1590-1700
Rolf Lee	x	x	x	1590-1700
Orchard		x	x	1630-1700

Order determined by date range of most recent European-derived artifact reported from site. Other sites with rattlesnake gorgets but not maskettes or mushroom-shaped earplugs include Pratt, WV, 15JS16, KY, Larkin, KY, and Henry Pyles, KY (Table 4-9).

At Madisonville, 2.6% of the burial sample (Drooker, in press: Databases 3, 4) had shell ornaments, and 0.9% of it was interred with known European items. These are far smaller proportions than occur at most of the protohistoric sites listed in Table 4-13. They might reflect, in part, a very large prehistoric burial population.

Looking at total numbers of metal, glass, and shell items excavated at particular sites (Table 6-13) gives a somewhat different picture. Shell ornaments are, indeed, significantly more common at eastern than western sites, undoubtedly reflecting a different source of supply. As at Madisonville, they seem to increase in amount over time; that is, sites known to have later European trade goods (Table 4-9) also have greater amounts of shell.

Total numbers of metal and glass items present, while certainly influenced by supply sources, might in addition reflect greater general availability of these items during later times. By this criterion, relative chronological placement of Madisonville would be similar to that based on types of metal and glass items present (Table 6-11). Neale's Landing and Buffalo appear somewhat earlier than Madisonville, Hardin somewhat later, and Rolf Lee significantly later. The anachronism is Orchard, with less metal reported (Moxley 1988a:40) than expected, given the size of the site and the reported presence of GBP 3 red tubular beads. However, the numbers of metal artifacts do omit those in at least one known private collection. Besides incomplete reporting or supply differences between Orchard and other sites, there are at least two other possible explanations. There might be a very large prehistoric component and only a small, idiosyncratic protohistoric component present at the site, or the red tubular beads (as noted in Table 4-9) might not have come from Orchard. Consideration of other artifacts will be helpful in tackling this problem.

Evidence from ceramics lends a bit more depth to the picture. This includes not only the matching of distinctive shared attributes that raise the likelihood of contemporaneity between Madisonville and other sites, but also the assessment of trends in ceramic vessel use.

The likelihood that mortuary vessel use peaked at Madisonville during the sixteenth century, rather than continuing to rise into the seventeenth century, is of interest in interpreting relative ages of protohistoric eastern Fort Ancient sites. However, exactly how to apply this information to eastern sites is debatable. They are too far from Madisonville to say with certainty that the same trends apply to both regions.

In any event, Orchard had a much higher frequency of mortuary vessels than any other eastern Fort Ancient site (Table 4-13). It is possible that this indicates intensive site use during the same period that Madisonville residents were putting mortuary vessels with high percentages of their burials, that is, during late prehistoric rather than protohistoric times. Other indicators favor this hypothesis. Of Orchard mortuary vessels with handles, approximately half had only two, and most vessels contained single unio shells, presumably spoons (Moxley 1988a:34, 39). At western Fort Ancient sites, both of these traits appear to have been associated with the Early Madisonville Horizon. Several special types of vessels found at Madisonville also were excavated at Orchard, including four jars with lizard effigy handles and a double, horizontally joined bowl (Moxley 1988a:34). At least one example of a vessel type common at Orchard but uncommon in western Fort Ancient was found with a burial at Madisonville: a cord-marked jar with four sets of two

TABLE 6-13
Shell and European Items from Selected Protohistoric Fort Ancient Sites

	Number of Burials in Sample	TOTAL NOS. OF ARTIFACTS Metal Items	Glass Beads	Shell Ornaments	NO. OF ARTIFACTS PER BURIAL Metal Items	Shell Ornaments
Madisonville (Trenches 1-K)	591	199	27 (frags.)	221	0.34	0.37
Neale's Landing	32	1	3	51	0.03	1.59
Buffalo	562	62	2	2810	0.11	5.00
Hardin	325	200(appr.)	3	1464	0.62	4.50
Rolf Lee (Kapp sample)	83	145	>2560	>6600	1.75	>30.9
Orchard	>300	37+	42	common	0.12+	high

Numbers of artifacts are those reported to have been excavated from all contexts (for Rolf Lee, no proveniences other than burials were reported). For comparison among sites, metal and shell have been normalized per numbers of burials at the site.

teat lugs instead of handles (Figure 6-61, left), virtually identical to one from Orchard (Moxley 1988:34, Fig. 7). Another Madisonville mortuary vessel had two handles paired with two sets of two teat lugs (Figure 6-61, right). Other indigenous horizon markers shared between Madisonville and Orchard include artifacts most strongly associated with the Late Madisonville Horizon, such as small-disk and keel-shaped pipes (Table 4-3) and marine shell maskettes and mushroom-shaped earplugs (Table 6-12), but the possibility does remain that there was a substantial early Late Fort Ancient component at Orchard. From indigenous artifacts, there certainly seems to have been at least some overlap in occupation periods at Madisonville and Orchard. The tubular red glass beads from Orchard remain anachronistic.

The Neale's Landing site, which shared a 1580-1600 glass bead type with Madisonville, has a ceramics assemblage that includes Wellsburg, Neale's Landing, and Madisonville series jars. The Madisonville types seem to have predominantly but not entirely later attributes: the ten reconstructed Madisonville jars were cord-marked or grooved-paddled, not plain, and all three of those illustrated had four handles; however, only three of the ten had notched lips (Baker 1988:45-46, Fig. 2). According to Baker, one of the mortuary vessels from the Madisonville site (Figure 6-65), found with Burial 153, Block 1, is very similar in form to Neale's Landing jars (1988:48).

Madisonville series jars from the Hardin site include attributes that in western Fort Ancient span the Early and Late Madisonville Horizon: at least some with decorated necks (usually incised guilloche motifs), relatively many with four handles but relatively few with notched lips, and a much higher proportion of cord-marked than plain vessels (Hanson 1966:76-101, 1968). Bowls with notched lips, but none with beading, were excavated. This assemblage certainly overlapped temporally with that at Madisonville, but it is difficult to say more than that. As at the Buffalo Downstream Village, Hardin burials were in and around houses, and few were accompanied by mortuary vessels (Table 4-13).

Not enough has been published about Buffalo ceramics to allow in-depth discussion of their time-sensitive attributes. The two Madisonville series jars illustrated in its site report (Hanson 1975: Fig. 53) and by Griffin (1943: Pl. CXXII.1) are cord-marked with notched rims. Earlier types also are present, including a beaded bowl (e.g., Griffin 1943: Pl. CXXII.4). So is at least one Neale's Landing series jar (Baker 1988: Fig. 2h). Burials in the Downstream Village, which is considered the later of the two components at this site, were found in and around houses, generally without mortuary vessels (Table 4-13). Considering the likely shift in Madisonville burials away from the plaza edge over time, it is frustrating that the plaza area at the Upstream Village, where burials were *not* found in or near houses, was not excavated. One can only speculate that burials there might have surrounded the plaza, and that many of them might have been interred with mortuary vessels.

Although Rolf Lee ceramics are said to be recognizable Madisonville series types, only a brief description of a few sherds has appeared in the literature (Youse 1965:16-17). Only one burial is known to have included a ceramic vessel, and that was a bowl (Ron Moxley, pers. comm.). Rolf Lee burials for which I have data differ from those at other protohistoric sites in their higher frequencies and quantities of grave goods and in the very high frequency of glass beads and shell ornaments present (Tables 4-13, 6-13). These differences might well be both temporal and social. In any case, from the limited information available to me, this site, of all Fort Ancient sites for which I have data, appears to have least in common with Madisonville.

Graybill's seriation of Buffalo, Orchard, and Rolf Lee triangular projectile points by base shape has Buffalo earliest, with the smallest proportion of concave-based points, then Orchard, and finally Rolf Lee (1981: Table 1), which seems consistent with Rolf Lee's temporal placement based on burial assemblage

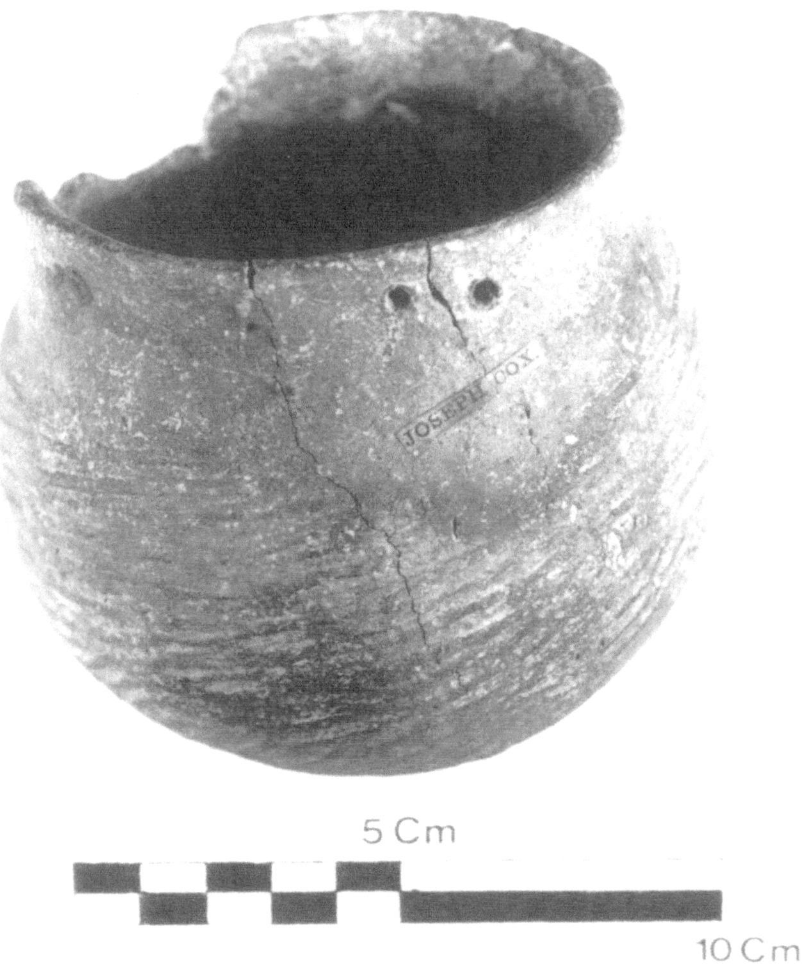

Figure 6-65. Grooved-paddled vessel with Neale's Landing-like form, from Madisonville Block 1, Burial 153 (CMNH Cat. No. 1888.698, gift of Judge Joseph Cox). Photograph by William Collier, courtesy of the Cincinnati Museum Center.

attributes. For all of these sites, the proportion of straight-based points is less than that of concave-based, which would seem to place their total occupation spans later than Madisonville. However, the sizes of the samples are given only as "ten or more," so it is difficult to know how important these differences are.

In the Fort Ancient region, rasps have been reported only from sites yielding European materials, with Madisonville producing far and away the greatest number. At least 52 fragments are still retained in the Harvard Madisonville collections, versus only two each reported from Buffalo and Hardin (Hanson 1966:153, 155, 1975:87). They also were present at Neale's Landing (Hemmings 1977:11-9, 11-10).

Besides Madisonville, Orchard is the only Fort Ancient site from which keel-shaped pipes have been reported (Table 4-3). Madisonville shares small-disk pipes with Orchard, Hardin, and a probable late component at Feurt (plow zone collection). The large-disk pipes from Fox Farm and Buffalo probably are prehistoric, roughly contemporaneous with the example from Campbell and earlier than the types of disk pipes found at Madisonville. All of the protohistoric Fort Ancient sites have vasiform and effigy pipes.

Differences among sites in total numbers of pipes present and numbers interred as grave goods probably are temporally significant, but data are not complete enough to make any definitive comparisons. Of all the sites, Orchard is reported as having the highest proportion of burials with pipes, some 15% (Table 4-13). For comparison, only 1.9% of Madisonville burials had pipes, in spite of the high frequency of pipes at the site (at least 99 excavated from Trenches 1-K, compared with only 22 from formal excavations at Hardin and 7 from Buffalo.) Social as well as temporal differences might well be in evidence here.

From these various lines of evidence then, Madisonville probably overlapped in time with most of the protohistoric eastern

Fort Ancient settlements. It probably was used longer than Fox Farm, but not as long as Marmet, Clover, Rolf Lee, and perhaps Orchard. Many of these sites, like Madisonville, appear to have had multiple temporal components, with significant pre-Contact period time depth. Interaction between them and Madisonville, both before and during the Late Madisonville Horizon, seems likely. Of particular interest are the non-normative Madisonville mortuary vessels with affinities to Neale's Landing and Orchard ceramics. In terms of types and numbers of metal and glass items present (Tables 6-11, 6-13), Madisonville shows greatest affinities with Hardin, which is intermediate in the relative chronological sequence among eastern Fort Ancient sites (Figure 4-9). Definitive comparisons are hampered by incomplete reporting from most of these sites, as are fine-grained assessments of which settlements were the latest occupied.

CHAPTER 7

Madisonville Internal Relationships

The general outlines of Madisonville settlement spatial organization and mortuary practices, and their evolution over time, were presented in Chapter 6. Significant to a consideration of local interaction patterns are: Madisonville's status as the only nucleated village in the lower Little Miami Valley during most of the Late Madisonville Horizon; the apparent lack of any hierarchical settlement pattern in the region throughout the Madisonville Horizon; Madisonville site organization around one or more plaza areas; a probable shift during Late Fort Ancient time from plaza-edge cemeteries to burials elsewhere on the site; differences in burial inclusions between groups on opposite sides of the plaza centered on Trench B; and a possible shift in subsistence over time to less horticulture. The social implications of these large-scale spatial and temporal patterns will be discussed further at the end of this chapter.

Finer-grained information on social organization is available through formal mortuary analysis. As described in Chapter 2, statistical comparison of biophysical, burial, and grave good attributes, combined with spatial analysis, can yield insight into vertical and horizontal status divisions and leadership roles within the community.

My ultimate goal in undertaking a mortuary analysis of Madisonville burials was to learn more about intersettlement and interregional interaction patterns. The results included a broad-brush determination of Madisonville social organization and its evolution over time, but particularly emphasized identification in the mortuary record of extra-settlement influences and ties. For example, I examined use and disposal patterns of exotic materials and artifacts in order to investigate the values placed on them, and also sought evidence that could be used to determine what individuals or social identities from this settlement might have been the agents of interaction and exchange.

This chapter summarizes the results of the mortuary analysis, and correlates them with information discussed in Chapter 6 (for additional details, see Drooker 1996c:278-358). The first section briefly discusses procedures used for the analysis, including input data, analytical methods, ethnographic models for particular status markers, and an initial assessment of high-value and low-value materials and artifacts at Madisonville. The second section summarizes mortuary relationships, including normative burial practices for the group as a whole and by age and sex, and the nature of subgroups and individuals associated with identifiable horizontal and vertical status divisions. The third section combines this information with the intrasite and intersite spatial relationships analyzed in Chapter 6 to consider social organization and change over time in the lower Little Miami Valley.

Mortuary Analysis Construction

The models and methods used in this analysis generally follow those of O'Shea (1984), discussed in Chapter 2. However, due to constraints and idiosyncracies of the Madisonville data set, there were procedural differences. Attributes and shortcomings of the data set, introduced in Chapter 5, are reviewed below. After that are short discussions of two special categories of potentially significant mortuary associations and practices: possible status markers as deduced from the ethnohistorical record, and high-value versus low-value materials and artifacts as deduced from the Madisonville archaeological record. The final portion of this section summarizes the assumptions and procedures followed in the Madisonville mortuary analysis.

Data Set

A minimum of 1450 burials were excavated at Madisonville under relatively controlled conditions (Table 5-6). Age, sex, burial treatment, grave goods, and other associated materials were determined for 591 burials excavated between 1897 and 1911, and for 802 burials excavated primarily before that time (Drooker 1997, in press, will contain downloadable tabulations of this data).

From extant remains, field notes, and photographs, it was possible to assign adult status to 774 individuals and subadult status to 439 (Table 7-1). Because almost none of the extant

TABLE 7-1
Demographic Data for Different Areas of the Madisonville Site

	Trenches 1-K		Block 1		Blocks 2-18		Conover Excavations		TOTAL Blocks 1-18 + Conover		1882 Excavations		Block M	
Subadults	197	33.3%	82	24.2%	139	38.8%	4	20.0%	225	31.4%	12	29.3%	5	12.5%
Adults	364	61.6%	140	41.3%	207	57.8%	16	80.0%	363	50.6%	26	63.4%	21	52.5%
Unknown age	30	5.1%	117	34.5%	12	3.4%	0	0.0%	129	18.0%	3	7.3%	14	35.0%
Total	591		339		358		20		717		41		40	
Identified females	62	45.3%	19	33.9%	90	56.25%	9	56.25%	136	58.6%	8	66.7%	0	
Identified males	75	54.7%	37	66.1%	90	56.25%	9	56.25%	136	58.6%	8	66.7%	0	
Percent immature *		34.5%		36.9%		41.0%		20.0%		38.7%		31.6%		19.2%

Data for burials outside of Trenches 1-K are from field notes, and should be considered with caution. The 1882 excavations include Block 22 and previous excavations during March and April (except for two burials probably from the Trench A area), Putnam's Block (Block L), the four rich burials that might or might not have come from Putnam's Block, and one burial from Stites property. At least 59 additional burials were excavated in 1895.
* Percent immature = subadults / (subadults + adults) x 100

TABLE 7-2
Age Category Data for Identifiable Burials from Trenches 1-K

	Female		Male		Unknown Sex		Total	
0-5 years					53	15.8%	53	15.8%
6-10 years					36	10.7%	36	10.7%
11-15 years					25	7.5%	25	7.5%
16-20 years	12	3.6%	3	0.9%	18	5.4%	33	9.9%
21-25 years	12	3.6%	8	2.4%	35	10.4%	55	16.4%
26-30 years	6	1.8%	10	3.0%	11	3.3%	27	8.1%
31-40 years	17	5.1%	26	7.8%	14	4.2%	57	17.1%
41-50 years	6	1.8%	21	6.3%	16	4.8%	43	12.9%
51- years	2	0.6%	2	0.6%	2	0.6%	6	1.8%
	55	16.5%	70	21.0%	210	62.6%	335	100.1%
Infants (0-2)					27	7.9%	27	7.9%
Children (3-11)					71	20.9%	71	20.9%
Adolescents (12-15)					21	6.2%	21	6.2%
Young adults (16-25)	24	7.1%	11	3.2%	53	15.6%	88	25.9%
Mature adults (26-40)	23	6.7%	36	10.6%	53	7.4%	84	24.7%
Older adults (41-)	8	2.4%	23	6.8%	18	5.3%	49	14.5%
	55	16.2%	70	20.6%	215	63.3%	340	100.1%

human remains excavated before 1897 now can be linked to particular burials, age and sex determinations were available solely from field judgments based on unknown criteria. Therefore, I used only "adult" and "subadult" categories for formal mortuary analysis. However, in considering particular, important burials I referred back to the field notes for tentative judgments on sex, and more fine-grained age categories. Table 7-1 does include statistics on identified males and females from these early excavations for comparison with burials from Trenches 1-K, but they must be viewed with great caution.

For extant remains excavated from Trenches 1-K, it was possible to determine sex for 62 females and 75 males, and to assign 340 individuals to six age categories (after Beck 1990:57-59 and Orser 1980:195, 200-201): 27 infants (aged 0-2), 71 children (3-11), 21 adolescents (12-15), 88 young adults (16-25), 84 mature adults (26-40), and 49 older adults (41^+) (Table 7-2). These individuals represent only 62% of the excavated burials (Table 5-8). The data probably are skewed toward the most recent burials, since less well-preserved specimens were discarded in the field. Infant remains, which often were de-

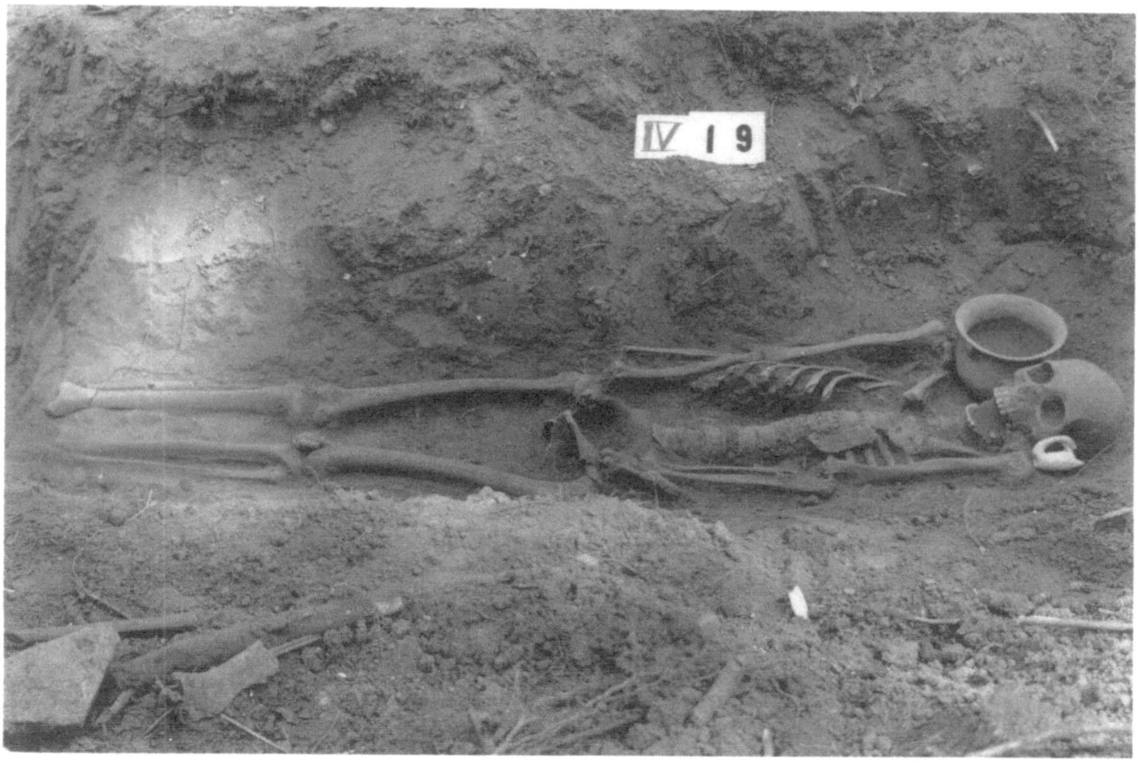

Figure 7-1. Example of individual burial in normative position, Madisonville cemetery. Burial 4-19, with pipe at left shoulder and jar at right shoulder. Harvard University Peabody Museum Photo No. N1635, copyright 1997 by the President and Fellows of Harvard College; used by permission.

scribed in field notes as fragmentary and probably deteriorated much more quickly than those of older people, almost certainly are underrepresented. Overinterpretation of survivorship curves (Drooker 1996c: Figs. B1, B2) would be unwise, because of the various problems associated with the extant sample of remains (e.g., poor preservation, incomplete recovery, multi-individual lots).

Burial treatments for which data were available include body posture and articulation (extended, flexed, disarticulated, and variations thereof), body parts present (whole, most parts present, only cranium, only postcranial bones, etc.), grave type (prepared unlined pit, stone-lined pit, refuse pit, bones scattered in soil, and variations thereof), depth below surface, compass orientation, individual versus multiple burial, and, for multiple burials, status within group and number of associated burials. To the extent possible, any prehistoric disturbances, such as refuse pits dug through burials, were noted.

Definitions of these categories, and associated problems, are provided elsewhere (Drooker 1996c:524-30). One that warrants extended discussion here is multiple burials, which were very much in evidence at Madisonville and have been the subject of varied interpretations.

The majority of people interred at Madisonville were in individual graves (Figure 7-1). Nonindividual burials took several forms: two or more articulated individuals (Figures 7-2, 7-3), two or more disarticulated individuals (or parts of individuals), and combinations of articulated and disarticulated individuals (Figure 7-4) (see also Hooton and Willoughby 1920: Pls. 3, 4). Sometimes multiple versus individual interments were clearly distinguished in the field notes, such as individuals described as "buried together" or as being eight inches apart but "not in the same grave." More often, such relationships only can be deduced from proximity, as with an infant "on the arm" of an adult or bones "scattered over the legs" of a complete skeleton. Very occasionally, the field notes allow finer interpretation of such burial relationships, as with one skeleton interpreted as being slightly disarranged when another was laid next to it, presumably after its bones were no longer articulated, or another skeleton described as being in the same grave but above and separated by dirt from an earlier burial.

In the published site report, disarticulated burials are implied to have been caused primarily by the disturbance of previous burials that actually were articulated when originally buried; for instance (preceding the description of a group interment of 22 individuals, with crania arranged on top of other bones): "In certain places a number of old burials may have been cleared away to make room for new ones and the disarticulated bones from the old graves buried in a common pit" and "Very commonly odd portions of a disturbed burial were found in a subsequent interment" (Hooton and Willoughby 1920:12). Similarly,

Figure 7-2. Example of group burial with no primary or secondary members. Burials D-5 and D-6, side by side at rear, were reported in field notes as "evidently buried together," with the left leg of B-6 perhaps having been moved during the later interment of D-4; if so, it still would have been articulated. Burial D-4, interred somewhat lower than the other two, was not interpreted as a member of the group. Note vasiform pipe at right shoulder and crushed pot to right of head. All three were adults of unknown age and sex. Harvard University Peabody Museum Photo No. N3590, copyright 1997 by the President and Fellows of Harvard College; used by permission.

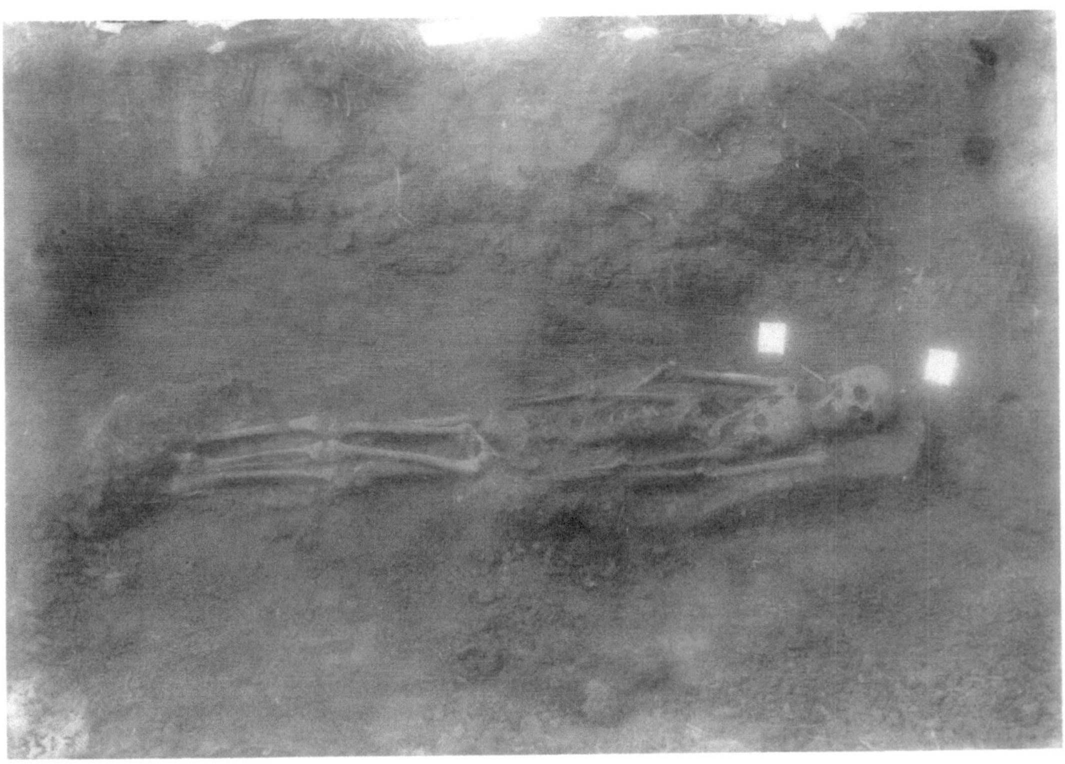

Figure 7-3. Example of group burial with two articulated individuals interpreted as primary and secondary members. Burial B-58, a mature adult female, lay on top of B-59, an older adult male, who was interpreted as the primary burial. Harvard University Peabody Museum Photo No. N3513, copyright 1997 by the President and Fellows of Harvard College; used by permission.

Figure 7-4. Example of group burial consisting of primary burial with articulated and disarticulated subsidiary burials. The primary burial, B-9, a young adult male, wore bone armbands (see Figure 6-18c) and metal legbands, and had two projectile points, one in the pelvic cavity and one to the left of the head. Disarticulated Burials B-8 and B-11, a young adult female and an adolescent, were arranged to the right and left of his legs, and B-10, an infant (originally articulated, but poorly preserved), lay on his left arm. Note unusual-shaped vessel with shell spoon adjacent to the right foot of B-9, and rattlesnake comb (Figure 6-18b), assigned by excavators to Burial B-11. Harvard University Peabody Museum Photo No. N3483, copyright 1997 by the President and Fellows of Harvard College; used by permission.

in his mortuary analysis of the protohistoric Hardin, Kentucky, site, Holmes reinterprets an earlier count of 164 single, 20 double, and 9 multiple (>2 individuals) burials (Hanson 1966:29-75) as 319 single and 8 double interments, reasoning that all or most disarticulated remains actually represented previous individual burials and thus should be counted as such (Holmes 1994:103-10). This may well be true in many cases, but other interpretations, such as deliberate exposure, defleshing, and joint reinterment of some burials, also are possible (e.g., Clay 1984; Galloway 1994:410-12; Kenyon 1982; O'Shea 1988; Swanton 1946:718-29).

At Madisonville, there were many reasonably certain instances of prehistorically disturbed burials, as when a storage pit was dug through the middle of a burial (Hooton and Willoughby 1920: Pls. 4a, d). However, a significant number of these were left in place, not gathered up and placed in another grave. Conversely, many disarticulated burials, individual and multiple, were located far from heavily populated areas where disturbance would have been likely to occur; for instance, in Trenches A, C, and K.

In any event, certain definite patterns associated with many of the multiple burials at Madisonville suggested they were entities, not simply a collection of overlapping single interments. These were cases where, even though exact temporal relationships might be in doubt, burials clearly were intended to be together, not thrown together accidentally and haphazardly. For example, there were a significant number of burials where a central extended, supine burial was closely surrounded by disarticulated burials, articulated or disarticulated, in a planned arrangement (Figure 7-4).

Thus, I identified to the extent possible both multiple burials—individuals buried together in the same grave, probably at the same time or within a short span of time (e.g., Figure 7-3 and Figure 7-2, Burials D-5 and D-6)—and associated burials, interred in separate graves but close together, parallel, and at about the same depth (e.g., Figure 7-2, Burial D-4). For the latter pattern to occur, exact knowledge of burial locations would have had to be maintained, so a given group of such burials may well have spanned less than a generation. Common burials of more than one articulated individual (e.g., Figure 7-3) might

TABLE 7-3
Occurrence of Different Types of Articles as Gravegoods, Trenches 1-K

Number of Burials in Which Article Type Was Found	Article Type
1	32 different types (see Tables 7-7 and 7-8)
2	animal claw bird skull ceramic bowl cannel coal, worked copper leg band (from staining on bones) copper/brass, piece glass bead(s) hammerstone shell, perforated - hoe? stone, worked whetstone
3	antler projectile point antler, worked bone, worked ceramic sherd flint knife
4	bone bead copper/brass coil copper/brass ornament/ pendant (all different) corn flint scraper mineral pigment (red ochre) stone celt
5	animal bones
8	animal skull and bones shell, function unknown
9	shell pendant
11	stone pipe
13	copper/brass bead copper staining (incl. on legs - see above)
17	shell bead
23	flint projectile point shell spoon (minimum number)
155	ceramic pot
(41	associated subsidary burials)

represent nearly simultaneous death and simultaneous burial, or sequential burial by carefully opening up a grave of known location. Multiple burials containing both articulated and disarticulated burials would most likely represent individuals who died at different times; they could have been interred together simultaneously or sequentially. If a central, focal burial could be identified (e.g, B-9 in Figure 7-4), I coded it as "primary" and burials arranged relative to it as "subsidiary." If not, burials were coded as "equal" (e.g., D-5 and D-6 in Figure 7-2).

Grave good types, numbers, special attributes, and object locations relative to the skeleton all were recorded (Drooker 1996c: Databases C1, C2). Information was compiled from extant artifacts, field notes, sketches, and photographs (Drooker 1996c: Tables A1, A2, A3; see Drooker 1997, in press), and published drawings, photographs, and descriptions (Griffin 1943; Hooton and Willoughby 1920; Low 1880). As discussed in Chapter 5, few grave goods excavated before 1897 now can be tied to particular burials, and many grave goods excavated between 1897 and 1911 no longer are extant. Sixty-six different types of items were included with burials in Trenches 1-K, only eleven of them with five or more individuals (Table 7-3).

To better allow comparisons among burials, artifacts were grouped into twelve functional categories (Drooker 1996c:581-86; cf. Rogers 1990). These included food containers (ceramic vessels), scoops (shell spoons), projectile points, tools (a very diverse category), animal and bird skulls (interpreted by excavators as possible "medicine bags"; ceremonial fans are an alternative possibility for the bird remains), charms (items such as quartz crystals, concretions, and engraved stones that probably functioned as talismans), smoking pipes, three categories of ornaments (metal or glass, shell, bone), and two categories for artifacts of unknown function (one for unique, large items, and the other for multiple small items). Subsidiary burials were included as a special category of mortuary offering associated with the primary burials around which they were arranged. A number of socioeconomically significant attributes that crosscut functional categories of artifacts also were noted: relative size, presence of decoration (representational or unidentifiable), and nonlocal source (indigenous or European). Large, decorated, or exotic items would require relatively high energy input, and might function as objects of wealth or status (see discussion below).

Because of their more extensive documentation, more accurate map, and more complete data base, burials from the Harvard-sponsored excavations of 1897-1911 (Trenches 1-K) were subjected to the most comprehensive analysis. Burials in other portions of the site were analyzed less quantitatively and in less detail, and are discussed primarily in relation to those in Trenches 1-K. The sketchy reporting of burial attributes for most pre-1897 work, the strong possibility that excavators did not recover or retain all grave goods, and the uncertainty of spatial relationships made me reluctant to include data from these burials in the statistical analyses.

As discussed in Chapter 6, the Madisonville site is multicomponent. The mortuary practices of its residents seem to have changed over time: burials reported as flexed or sitting probably were most strongly associated with a Late Woodland-Early Fort Ancient component; grave linings consisting of stone slabs with an Early-Middle Fort Ancient component; mortuary vessels and interment close to the plaza area with a prehistoric Early Madisonville Horizon component; and metal artifacts and interment in or around domestic structures away from the plaza with a protohistoric Late Madisonville Horizon component. However, because so many burials could not be put into a definite time slot (e.g., those without any grave goods or without horizon marker grave goods) and because of the lack of definitive data on house locations, it was impossible to clearly define separate groups of burials associated with each component. Because of this, the mortuary analysis was carried out on the entire data set. Burials with particular definitive horizon marker attributes (e.g., graves lined with stone slabs) were considered together as time-related groups, but never could be identified as the *only* burials associated with their time period. However, even though analyses could not be carried out on temporally separate groups of people, assemblages and burial characteristics of individuals identified as occupying vertically defined status positions were examined and time periods assigned if possible (e.g., where European artifacts were present). This information was used to consider change over time in leadership positions.

Ethnographic Models for Status Markers

When the mortuary practices of known groups are being analyzed, it is possible to set up a model of expected material correlates to their leadership positions and social divisions (e.g., O'Shea 1984:70-86). In the case of the Fort Ancient culture area, the ethnohistorical identity of its residents is uncertain (Chapter 4). During the seventeenth and eighteenth centuries, warfare, migration, heightened intergroup interaction, and alteration in subsistence patterns resulted in major demographic and socioeconomic changes across the Midwest (Chapter 3). Little firsthand information is available on candidate groups until after this period of significant change.

Working from early historical documents and linguistic evidence, Charles Callender, among others, has proposed the Shawnee, a Central Algonquian group, as late prehistoric residents of the middle Ohio Valley (Callender 1962, 1978f; Witthoft and Hunter 1955). As discussed in Chapter 4, other groups also have been proposed, based mostly on historical evidence. The Shawnee language (along with a suite of ritual concepts) is closely related to Fox, which in turn forms a close group with Sauk and Kickapoo (Callender 1962:1, 44, 1978f:622; Voegelin 1936:7-8). In traditional accounts, the Fox and Sauk separated from the Shawnee, moving north to the Saginaw Valley (Callender 1962:84); the Kickapoo, too, have a traditional tale that recounts their separation from the Shawnee (Trowbridge 1939:64).

There is general agreement among both ethnohistorians and archaeologists that Central Algonquian peoples, including those later known as Sauk, Fox, Kickapoo, and Mascouten, inhabited southern Michigan and northwestern Ohio during the late sixteenth century (e.g., Bauxar 1978:594; Brose 1994:179, 182; Callender 1962:1-3; Murphy and Ferris 1990:189; Stone and Chaput 1978:602; Stothers and Abel 1991:123; White 1991:1-49), with most of them migrating to Wisconsin during the mid-seventeenth century under threat of Iroquois depredations, after the defeat and displacement of the Winnebago at the hands of the Illini and allied groups (Figure 3-7). In these upper Mississippi Valley locations, many Central Algonquian groups are known to have had strong and enduring relationships with Siouan groups, including Menomini with Winnebago, Sauk and Fox with Ioway, and some southern bands of the Illinois Confederation (Tamaroa, Michigamea, and Cahokia) with Missouri (Callender 1962:2; Wedel 1986:13). Groups of Shawnee, first described by Europeans at widely separated locations in South Carolina (1674), Illinois (1683), and Maryland (1689), established long-term relationships with Creek, Delaware, and Seneca, among others (Callender 1978f:630, Fig. 1; Drooker 1991b: Fig. 3). Because of these dispacements and interactions, along with changes in subsistence patterns, nineteenth- and twentieth-century ethnohistorical data are only partially applicable to sixteenth-century Central Algonquian peoples, and must be used only with great caution.

Although direct evidence is extremely sparse, archaeological data do lend credence to a Central Algonquian affiliation for western Fort Ancient people. Several lines of archaeological evidence, touched upon in Chapters 3 and 6 and developed further in Chapter 8, indicate long-term positive interaction between Madisonville and northwestern Ohio peoples. They include the presence of southwestern Ohio ceramics at northwestern Ohio sites and vice versa, stylistic congruence in stone, bone, and antler tools (e.g., compare notched awls and single-barbed harpoons with attachment holes illustrated in Figure 6-18a and in Bowen 1994: Figs. 57, 64), apparent common usage of the uninhabited area between them as evidenced by distributions of artifacts such as endscrapers (J. Bowen, pers. comm.), and biological affinities among populations from thirteenth- through seventeenth-century southwestern and northwestern Ohio sites (Giesen 1992). This evidence seems strong enough to postulate a Central Algonquian affiliation for western Fort Ancient people and to utilize a Central Algonquian sociopolitical model to suggest the general nature of leadership positions and social divisions, plus possible material correlates, that might be visible among the Madisonville mortuary population. However, the presence of material culture probably related to Oneota/Siouan groups, such as disk pipes, also must be kept in mind.

Callender has summarized available ethnohistorical and linguistic evidence for the social organization of individual Central Algonquian groups around 1800, dividing them into three

TABLE 7-4
Recorded Patriclan Names from Central Algonquian Groups

Shawnee (1)	**Shawnee** (2)	**Miami** (1)	**Fox**	**Sauk**	**Kickapoo** (1)
Snake	Snake	Little Turtle	Bear	Bald Eagle	Berry
Turtle	Turtle	Snow Thaws	Fox	Bear	Eagle
Raccoon	Raccoon	Raccoon	Wolf	Bear Potato	Water
Turkey	Turkey	Turkey	Swan	Black Bass	Bear
Hawk	Deer	Moon	Partridge	Deer	War (or Man)
Deer	Bear		Thunder	Great Lake	Tree
Bear	Wolf		Elk	Panther	Raccoon
Wolf	Panther	**Miami** (2)	Black Bass	Ringed Perch	Elk
Panther	Horse (Elk)	Wolf		Stugeon	Buffalo
Elk	Turkey	Loon		Swan	
Buffalo	Buzzard	Golden Eagle		Thunder	
Tree	Owl	Turkey		Wolf	**Kickapoo** (2)
*Corn	Rabbit	Buzzard			Berry
*Wind	Loon	Panther			Eagle
*Night		Turkey			Water
*Cloud		Raccoon			Bear
*Moon		Snow			War (or Man)
*Water		Sun			Tree
*House		Water			Raccoon
*Fish					Elk
*Stone					Buffalo
*Dirt					Fox
*Big Fire	*Beaver				Wolf
*Skunk	*Swan				Turkey
*Squirrel	*Eagle				Thunder
*Rabbit	*Bald Eagle				
*Fox	*Pigeon Hawk				
*Otter	*Black Bird				

Shawnee and Miami lists recorded (1) by Trowbridge in 1824-25 (1939:16-17, 1938:18), and (2) by Morgan in 1859 (1959:44-47, 80). Fox and Sauk lists are from Callender (1978a:639, 1978e:649), based on work by Forsyth in the first quarter of the nineteenth century. Kickapoo lists are from Callender et al. (1978:660), after twentieth century work by (1) Dillingham and (2) others.
* Asterisked names no longer were in use at the time they were collected.

subtypes, "Prairie" (Sauk, Fox, Kickapoo, Potawatomi), "Woodland" (Menomini), and "Ohio Valley" (Shawnee, Miami, Illinois), which he compared and contrasted with north-central Algonquian (Ottawa, Ojibwa/Chippewa, Salteaux, Algonquin) and Chiwere Siouan groups, among others (Callender 1962, 1978b). His work included development of a model of late prehistoric (after about A.D. 1000) "Classical Period" Central Algonquian social organization (1962:74-84) suitable for providing guidance in anticipating and interpreting Madisonville mortuary data.

The proto-Central Algonquian kinship system involved cross-cousin marriage within relatively small, isolated population units. "Classical Period" Central Algonquians are projected to have lived in large village-bands, with lineage segmentation developing along with expanded population. Patrilineal, exogamous clans would have controlled intangible rather than tangible property, such as particular ritual powers and names derived from an eponymous founding ancestor. Historically known groups recognized from ten to thirty-four clans, named after animals, birds, fish, reptiles, plants, mythical beings, and other phenomena (Table 7-4), and clan members were given names with eponymic qualities. Dual divisions would have provided structured opposition. Historically recorded forms, which varied according to post-Contact history, included ranked Earth and Sky moieties (Menomini, Miami, probably Illini), Black-White divisions not based on descent groups (Kickapoo, Fox, Sauk, Potawatomi), opposed clans and/or villages (Shawnee, Illini), and peace-war dualism (Shawnee, Menomini) (Callender 1962, 1978a, 1978c; Clifton 1978; Ritzenthaler and Peterson 1956). Secret societies (such as shaman groups) and warrior associations would have crosscut clan memberships. Positions of civil leadership, concerned with organization of ritual and subsistence activities, would have been hereditary through particular clans or lineages, while war leadership would have been nonhereditary, based on achievement. From historical examples, civil offices might have included a council of elders, clan chiefs, village/band chiefs, and tribal or confederation chiefs. For the most part, their holders would have been mature adult males, but female chiefs were known historically among the Miami and Shawnee (Drooker 1991b:26-27; Trowbridge 1938:13-15, 1939:11-13). Shamans would have provided medicinal and ritual healing, prophecy, and social control through fear of sorcery. A vision quest during childhood or adolescence would have provided individuals (potentially both boys and girls, from historical practices) with personal guardian spirits. Historically, berdaches (regarded as manitous) and slaves were known among at least some of these peoples (e.g., Callender 1978c:675-76, 1978d:645).

The "Ohio Valley" variant that prehistorically probably included Sauk, Fox, Kickapoo, Shawnee, and perhaps Illini and Miami peoples, probably was more oriented toward village-centered than clan- or lineage-centered offices and rituals (Callender 1962). Among the historically known Shawnee, each village-band ("division") carried different responsibilities: two were concerned with political affairs (either could supply the tribal chief), one with warfare, one with medicine, and one with ritual. Group ritual at the village level, centering on sacred packs and related calendrical ceremonies and with roles of clans/clan members assigned based on eponymous qualities, would have provided a major avenue both of communication with the spiritual/natural world and of intracommunity integration.

In searching the historical and ethnohistorical literature, I have found very few material correlates of these social divisions and positions with potential to survive in the archaeological record. I include here examples noted by seventeenth through twentieth century observers. Recent ones, in particular, should be viewed with extreme caution, because practices do change over time. Formal differences, rather than particular attributes, might be more likely to persist.

Large council houses, used for both ritual and secular purposes, were significant features of eighteenth-century Shawnee and Miami towns (Callender 1978d:682, 1978f:625). Their presence emphasizes the village as basic organizational unit.

The red and white symbolism of war and peace was noted by a number of early writers. Seventeenth-century Illini peace pipes/calumets were decorated with white feathers and war pipes/calumets with red ones, while war captains/chiefs wore red scarfs (Shriver 1987:14). Eighteenth-century war party invitations were issued by sending a tomahawk daubed with red clay (Trowbridge 1939:17). Red-painted markers were set up at Sauk and Potawatomi warriors' graves (Voegelin 1944:369-370). In more recent times, the graves of Kickapoo and dwellings of deceased Shawnee civil chiefs were distinguished by white flags or white-colored poles (Ritzenthaler and Peterson 1956:64; Voegelin 1944:274).

Eighteenth- and nineteenth-century Miami chiefly insignia of power and of corporate tradition that were passed from generation to generation included belts made of bird bone beads (supplanted by wampum), medals, and pipes (Trowbridge 1938:10, 13). Nineteenth-century paintings and photographs of Central Algonquian chiefs only occasionally show them wearing outstandingly elaborate paraphernalia that sets them off from other men. For example, in fourteen portraits of thirteen Shawnee, Illini, Kickapoo, Fox, and Sauk chiefs or leaders (Bonvillain 1995: 12, 30, 56, 80, 85; Callender 1978a: Figs. 5-7, 1978c: Fig. 7, 1978e: Fig. 5; Callender et al. 1978: Fig. 12; Fundabark 1992: Figs. 168, 170, 268), there were no types of ornaments or insignia common to all. Nine wore turbans or wide headbands, six of these with feathers, two wore feathered roaches, and two sported very elaborate feathered headdresses. Twelve had ear ornamentation. Seven wore necklaces of tubular beads; five, most of them identified as bear clan members, wore elaborate bear claw necklaces. Five wore metal arm or wrist bands, four wore portrait medals, and one wore a bandolier adorned with circular metal ornaments. Two carried pipes; one (the famous Sauk leader Black Hawk), a ceremonial fan with attached bird (hawk?) body; one, a cane; one, a feathered staff; one, a shield; one, a bow and arrows; and three, hatchets (one adorned with red feathers). One, identified as a peace chief, was shown with a formidible "gunstock club" (Bonvillain 1995:30). It is worth noting that one young Fox chief in warlike regalia was portrayed twenty years later with a very different costume that appears more congruent with Bear Clan leadership (Callender, 1978a: 640-42, Figs. 5-7). Many of these chiefs were outshone by the costumes of warriors and dandies pictured in the same references, who wore larger quantities of beads, metal ornaments, and feathers. One Fox chief was dressed far less elaborately than his Ioway interpreter, as was a Sauk chief in comparison with the council members photographed with him. A Fox medicine man painted by Catlin is shown with extremely elaborate ear ornaments, necklaces, a crescent-shaped metal gorget, metal bracelets and armbands, a bow, and a feathered shield, but no headdress of any sort (Bonvillain 1995:34). In this small sample of references, male non-office holders were pictured with turbans, feathered roaches, beads, ear ornaments, metal and shell gorgets, metal arm- and wristbands, hatchets, spears, and stone clubs, and women were shown with beads, ear ornaments, and metal conchas.

Personal medicine bags, or bundles associated with individual guardian spirits, are known to have been used by members of at least some Central Algonquian groups (e.g., Callender 1978a:643). Among the late seventeenth-century Illini, they may have included literal representations of personal "manitous" in the form of "a serpent, a bird, or other similar thing" (Shriver 1987:14, quotations from Marquette). Early accounts of the Illini noted that "each warrior kept bird skins in a colored reed mat," perhaps comparable to birds of prey known from historically documented corporate war bundles (Callender 1978c:676). Such personal bundles or talismans would have been buried with their owners (e.g., Skinner 1913:65). It is very likely that shamanistic bundles, connected with even stronger spiritual power, also would have been. The well-known small-animal bags carried by members of the post-Contact Midewiwin or Medicine Society, and buried with them (Harrison 1989; Hickerson 1963, 1970; Skinner 1920), probably reflect this same tradition. Corporate sacred bundles or sacred packs associated with with lineages, clans, villages, or societies, or with group warfare or hunting, which are documented among almost all Central Algonquian groups, under ordinary circumstances would have been passed on to new human guardians rather than being buried with the old ones.

Although burial customs can change abruptly (e.g., Sempowski 1991; Speck 1907:97), a few notes are of interest.

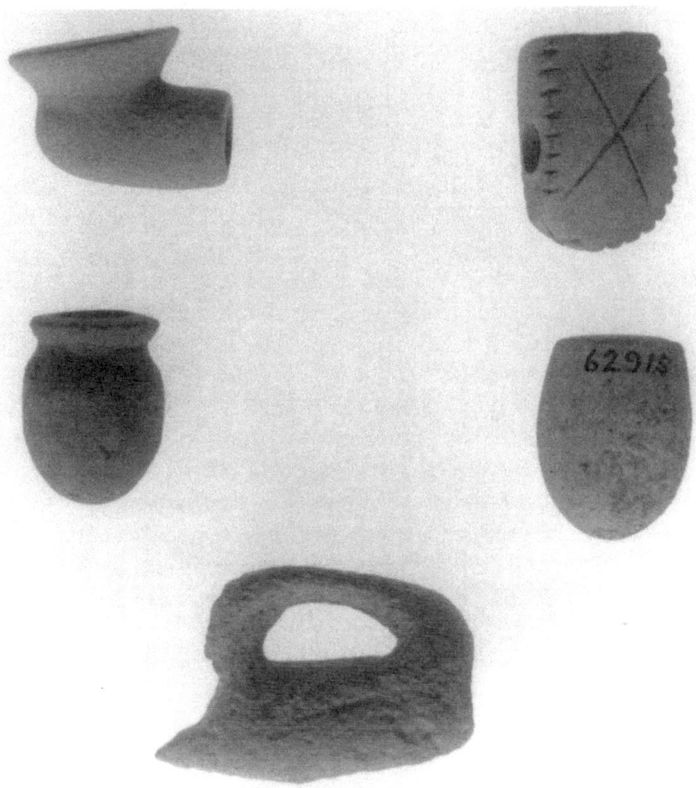

Figure 7-5a. Pipes found with burials in Trenches 1-4. *Top*: disk pipe, very light gray limestone (97-38-10/62888, Trench 2 Burial 21); "keel-shaped" pipe, notched edge, one side and base engraved with "+," other side engraved with "//," light gray limestone (HUPM Cat. No. 97-38-10/62902, Burial 3-8). *Bottom*: vasiform pipe, local tan sandstone (97-38-10/62903, Burial 3-8); globular pipe, pinkish gray crystalline stone (97-38-10/62915, Burial 3-40); two-headed "swan" effigy pipe with stem hole in bottom and bowl in breast, very light gray local limestone (97-38-10/6262971, Burial 4-19). Photograph by Hillel Burger (HUPM Photo No. N33980). Copyright 1996 by the President and Fellows of Harvard College.

In the nineteenth century, Menomini graves were grouped by clan, and Fox graves by clan and lineage (Callender 1962:36, 1978a:639). Most Central Algonquian groups marked graves with wooden posts. Some markers are documented as commemorating clan affiliation (Fox, Menomini, Potawatomi), age (Menomini), honors (Fox, Sauk, Potawatomi, Illinois), chiefly (Kickapoo, Illini) or warrior (Potawatomi, Sauk) status (Callender 1978a:639, 1978c:676; Clifton 1978:736; Ritzenthaler and Peterson 1956:64; Voegelin 1944:369-70). In several groups (Potawatomi, Menomini), warriors dedicated their slain enemies to accompany the dead, by marking the grave post (Skinner 1913:65-66; Voegelin 1944:369-70). From the seventeenth-century Illini documented by Joutel, to the twentieth-century Mexican Kickapoo studied by Ritzenthaler, food (alone or in a vessel) and tobacco were common burial gifts, and personal clothes and ornaments usually accompanied their owners to the grave. The Shawnee leader Blackhoof, buried in 1830, was laid out with his gun, tomahawk, and knife, and his pipe "at his side"; clothing, moccasins, and perhaps the pipe, but no weapons, were put in the grave (Harvey 1855:185-88). Clearly, nonperishable artifacts that survive with Central Algonquian burials would give only an incomplete picture of social status.

Several special treatments are noteworthy, as examples of the variety that could obtain even within a fairly standard burial program. Seventeenth-century Illini buried most of their dead, but chiefs were given scaffold burials (Stiles 1906:193). Most nineteenth-century Fox were interred in extended postures, but warriors could be sitting (Callender 1978a:639). In the nineteenth century, Potawatomi body position depended on the wishes of the deceased, and Miami also could request special treatments for themselves (Clifton 1978:736; Trowbridge 1938:32). Mexican Kickapoo buried those who had died away from the village at the location where they died, and provided no formal burials for suicides (Ritzenthaler and Peterson 1956:64).

High and Low Value Materials and Artifacts at Madisonville

Items valued highly within a particular culture might not be those that a modern researcher would instinctively choose. As discussed in Chapter 2, value might be ascribed on the basis of rarity, high inputs of energy or skill, and/or putative associations with power or spirituality. One way to approach emic values is to compare relative frequencies of a particular artifact excavated from mortuary versus nonmortuary contexts; those common in middens or similar contexts are assumed to have been less highly valued than those present only with burials (Braun 1977, 1979). At Madisonville, a number of items, by this defintion, appear to have been highly valued, although the incomplete retention of items from nonmortuary contexts means that such designations can be only tentative.

Materials and items occurring primarily as grave goods in Trenches 1-K include shell beads, pendants, and other ornaments (Figure 6-19), 90% of which come from mortuary contexts, glass beads (85%), quartz crystals (100%, but only one has been

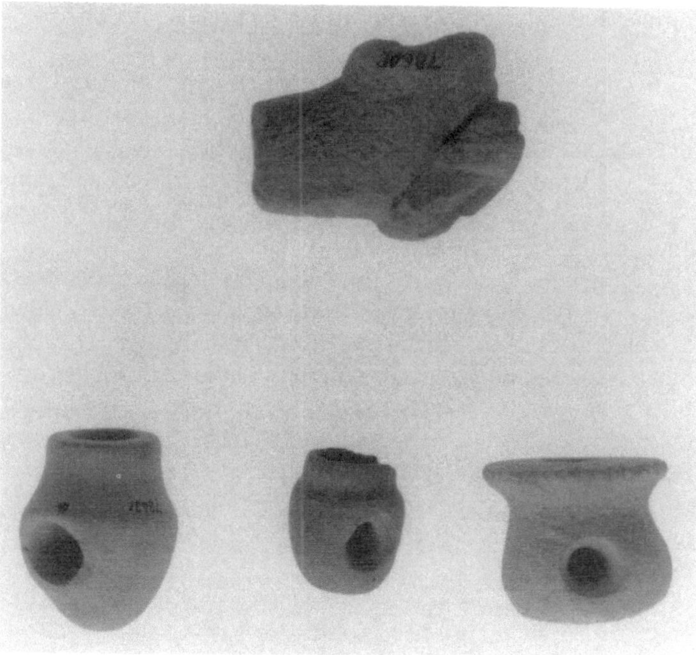

Figure 7-5b. Pipes found with burials in Trenches B and D. *Top*: effigy pipe, semi-elbow, humanoid head with "forked eyes" at front bottom, snake engraved around bowl, local tan sandstone (HUPM Cat. No. 07-6-10/77808, Burial B-33). *Bottom*: vasiform pipe, "+" engraved on bottom, pinkish gray stone (07-6-10/78631, Burial B-57); vasiform pipe, local dark reddish gray sandstone (08-3-10/79636, Burial D-8); vasiform pipe, notched rim, local light gray limestone (08-3-10/79646, Burial D-25). For vasiform pipe with Burial B-4, see Figure 7-2. Photograph by Hillel Burger (HUPM Photo No. N33983). Copyright 1996 by the President and Fellows of Harvard College.

Figure 7-5c. Pipe found with Burial I-9. Perching owl effigy, greenish-gray pipestone with tan streaks, speckled with black and white, "killed" (tail broken off) (HUPM Cat. No. 11-10-10/A4048). Photograph by Hillel Burger (HUPM Photo No. N33983). Copyright 1996 by the President and Fellows of Harvard College.

found), engraved bone beads (Figure 6-18b), 75% from burials, two out of three complete bone arm bands (Figure 6-18c), and a unique locally made head pot (Figure 4-14). Interestingly, metal does not appear primarily in mortuary contexts (only 32% of metal items from Trenches 1-K), although certain unique metal items, such as the brass bell, the tubular brass spiral, the iron dagger guard, the matched set of large copper clips, the two sets of large copper or brass leg bands, and four out of six flat metal pendants, including all three large barred copper/brass pendants, were found only with burials (Figures 6-21b, 6-21c, 6-21f, and 6-21g, Table 6-6). Marine shell maskettes (Figure 6-19a and 6-19b) are poorly provenienced, but only one out of five or six from the site definitely did not come from a burial. The single worn, reworked Citico rattlesnake gorget (Figure 6-19a) was with a burial. Two turtle-shell rattles reported from MLSS-excavated burials also appear to have no counterparts from nonmortuary contexts. Animal teeth were not valued as ornaments. Most of the extant examples were unaltered, and none of the eight drilled canines from Trenches 1-K were found in graves.

Pipes were not commonly deposited as grave goods: only 15 out of 99 pipes and pipe fragments excavated in Trenches 1-K were found with burials (Figure 7-5). However, there were a number of statistically significant differences between pipes deposited as grave goods compared with others in the sample (chi square test, $p \leq 0.05$). The average size was larger (mean maximum dimension = 5.6 cm versus 4.6 for nonmortuary pipes), and there was a higher-than-expected proportion of light-colored (white to light gray) to darker colored pipes. None of the mortuary pipes were unfinished, and significantly fewer were damaged than were statistically predicted. Those that *were* damaged (the two largest) appeared to have been deliberately "killed." Vasiform (5 out of a total of 8 excavated), keel-shaped (1 out of 5), and effigy (3 out of 10) pipes were significantly more likely than other types to be deposited as grave goods, as were pipes engraved with a "+" (3 out of 6). None of the four Iroquoian pipe fragments from this part of the site (see Figure 8-24) was deposited with a burial, nor are any known to have been elsewhere on the site. Disk pipes (1 out of 8) were present in approximately equal proportions in Trench 1-K mortuary and nonmortuary contexts. Elsewhere on the site, they appear to be overrepresented in burials (Figure 7-6; see also 7-30a, below), but there are too many pipes of unknown form to make a statistical evaluation. Other forms represented by five or more ex-

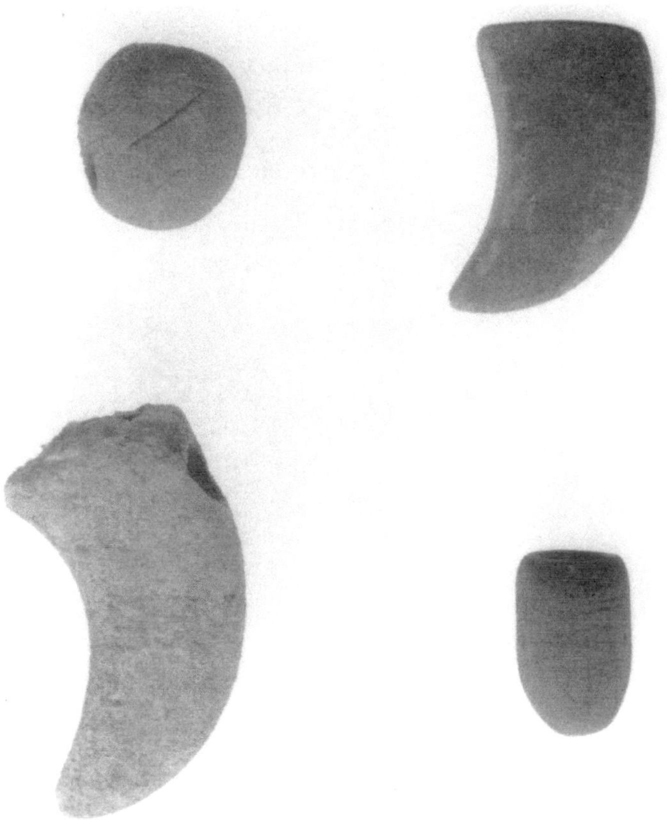

Figure 7.5d. Pipes found with burials in Trenches H and I and Block 22. *Top*: ovoid pipe, engraved with differently-finished diagonal lines on both sides (pipe motifs?), with older, rubbed-out turtle shape underneath on one side, also faint "lizard" "climbing" up front, very light gray limestone (HUPM Cat. No. 11-10-10/A4064, Burial H-1); claw effigy pipe, gray pipestone with light inclusions (82-35-10/26596, Block 22 Burial 5). *Bottom*: claw effigy pipe "killed" (top broken off), white crystalline anorthosite (11-10-10/A4043, Burial I-19); globular pipe, engraved with radiating and horizontal lines and "+" on bottom, local reddish brown sandstone (11-10-10/A4043, Burial I-19). Photograph by Hillel Burger (HUPM Photo No. N33982). Copyright 1996 by the President and Fellows of Harvard College.

amples in the Trench 1-K sample included ovoid (total $n = 32$), elbow (total $n = 9$), and semi-elbow (total $n = 5$), all of which were underrepresented as grave goods.)

Pipes made from exotic materials were no more or less likely to be deposited with burials in Trenches 1-K than those fashioned from local materials. However, there were some individual minerals—present in such small amounts that statistical evaluation was impossible—that were overrepresented among grave goods. They included a crystalline anorthosite probably from northeastern Ohio and a speckled pipestone, from which were fashioned the two largest pipes excavated in Trenches 1-K. At least two important disk pipes found with burials were made from exotic minerals: one of (Midwestern?) red pipestone from Block 1, and another of a (West Virginia?) golden chalcedony, excavated in 1895 (Figures 6-20, 7-30a). See Chapter 8 for further discussion of source locations for these nonlocal materials.

Marine shell is the largest category of exotic material that appears to have been valued in and of itself. Almost all of it is in the form of finished artifacts, so it seems unlikely that marine shell was crafted into ornaments at Madisonville on a regular basis. Glass and clear quartz—exceedingly rare at the site—appear to fall into the same high-value category. Metal does not. Although certain forms (including the largest copper/brass ornaments present) appear to have been valued as sociotechnic or ideotechnic items, metal *per se* was not. Over half of the metal items at Madisonville had been discarded or lost, not carefully guarded and deposited with burials. From the amount of scrap (Table 6-6) and the presence of blanks suitable for manufacturing rolled beads and thin tubes (Figures 6-21d, e), it seems likely that at least some copper/brass ornaments were fashioned on site, and most of the iron was modified into aboriginal-type tools.

High-value items in mortuary contexts can represent wealth or status. High energy inputs, either as transport costs for exotic goods or as time and skill necessary to craft a special item, commonly are characteristic of wealth items. "Wealth" indicators often are present in sets, with larger numbers indicating greater ostentation. Only a few types of grave goods are present in large sets (more than five items) at Madisonville. Small- to medium-sized copper/brass ornaments, particularly rolled beads, represent the most common examples of ostentatious wealth: at least eleven burials at Madisonville (five in Trenches 1-K, six in the remainder of the site) each contained six or more copper/brass items. The average was 20, the maximum 88. The only other exotic material that occurs relatively frequently in sets is marine shell: seven individuals at the site, all from Trenches 1-K, were buried with six to fifty shell beads (averaging 18), some of them with additional marine shell ornaments as well. Other sets of multiple items include two people each buried with a group of six projectile points, two each with sets of two large copper or brass legbands, and single individuals buried with ten large copper clips, at least ten glass beads, ten large bird-bone beads including eight decorated with forked-eye symbols, a necklace of eight deer horn tips, or eight solid bone cylinders.

Status items need only be present to be significant: a particular person will or will not be allowed to possess such items, depending on his or her social identity. Depending on the social distance over which symbolic messages are to be sent, emblemic items indicating a particular status may well be uniquely formed and relatively large in size (Wobst 1977). Grave goods that might have functioned as special status emblems at Madisonville include: large copper/brass pendants and leg bands; large and/or decorated shell ornaments; bone/antler armbands, engraved tubes/beads, and engraved combs; certain pipes, particularly large ones; and medicine bags. Unique assemblages of seemingly more mundane items also might signify special status. If present, these were expected to become apparent in the course of the mortuary analysis.

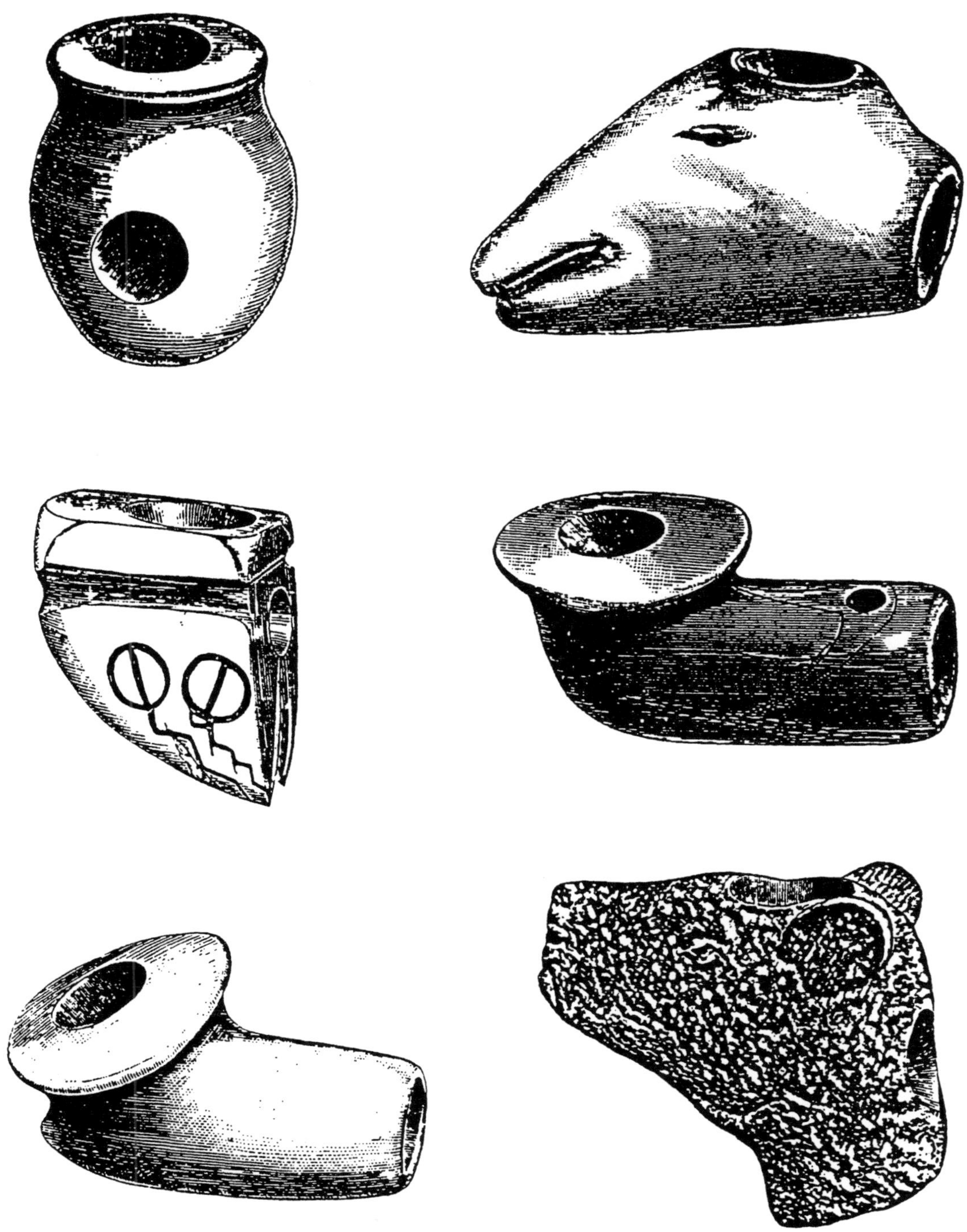

Figure 7-6. Drawings of pipes found with burials in Block 1, excavated by the MLSS in 1879 (Low 1880: Figs. 4, 5, 6, 11, 14, 28). *Top*: Burials 15 and 28-34; *Middle*: Burials 43 and 108; *Bottom*: Burials 127 and 297. The engraved disk pipe is redstone, perhaps catlinite (see also Figure 6-20). All others were described as made of limestone or (in the case of the smooth animal head) "stone."

Effigy representations have the potential to symbolize eponymous lineage/clan ancestors (Table 7-4), so all recognizable effigies in any material or artifact type were noted. They included carved or engraved pipes and ornaments of antler, bone, metal, and shell; animal and bird skulls probably functioning as parts of medicine bags, ornaments or talismans obviously identifiable as parts of particular animals (e.g., drilled bear canines), appliqué on ceramic pots, and carved wooden bowls or spoons.

Potential supralocal symbols at Madisonville include barred metal pendants, tubular metal serpents, marine shell maskettes, marine shell rattlesnake gorgets, certain pipe forms (such as disk pipes), the forked-eye motif, and perhaps lizard appliqué vessels and pedestaled vessels. Whether any of them functioned as high status indicators will be discussed below, on the basis of their mortuary contexts. Their distributions outside of Madisonville will be discussed further in Chapter 8. Those with distributions concentrated within Fort Ancient territory include barred metal pendants, marine shell maskettes, and lizard appliqué vessels.

Diversity within grave good assemblages is taken as representative of diverse social identities; that is, a complex social persona that probably incorporated achieved statuses. Two rough indicators of assemblage diversity were used: numbers of artifact types present and numbers of artifact functional categories present. If present, associated subordinate burials were taken as an additional indicator of diversity. Redundance in status emblems was expected to mark the highest leadership levels.

Among Madisonville burials, then, potential status indicators included: particular functional types of artifacts and particular styles within each type; special large and/or decorated items; supralocal symbols; and assemblage diversity. Whether a particular artifact or group of artifacts represented vertical or horizontal status is determined by how many and what sorts of individuals possessed it (cf. Tables 2-5 through 2-7). Social "meaning" of particular artifacts was conveyed not only by their own attributes but also by their location relative to the body (e.g., on a large headdress versus clasped in a hand, displayed on the chest versus hidden in a medicine bag). Potential wealth indicators included large numbers of exotic items (especially marine shell and copper/brass), decorated or finely crafted items, and unusually large items.

Analytical Methods

Formal procedures designed to aid in mortuary pattern recognition were carried out on all recorded burials from Trenches 1-K (Drooker 1996c:295-99). They included: determination of normative burial attributes for all burials and for burials by sex and age categories; preliminary determination of potentially significant attributes by means of exploratory data analysis (bivariate correlation) and exploratory spatial analysis (GIS mapping of individual attributes); construction of groups of individuals with comparable mortuary attributes by means of multivariate cluster analysis; determination of age and sex characteristics of cluster group members and of their relative burial locations; and comparison of group demographic and spatial characteristics with models of vertical and horizontal social differentiation (cf. Beck 1990; Brown 1987; Goldstein 1980; O'Shea 1984, 1985). Less comprehensive analyses were carried out on the remaining sample of burials. Because of data limitations, no complex statistical analysis was attempted. All computations were accomplished by means of SYSTAT 5.2 software.

Univariate analysis included determination of the most common modes of body treatment and grave type for the burial population as a whole, for adults and subadults, for each of the six age categories, and for identified males and females. Presence/absence (P/A) of normative body treatments, grave goods, artifact types, and artifact functional categories were noted for each category of age and sex, as were artifact types that appeared to be associated exclusively with one or a few age or sex categories. Frequencies of occurrence were calculated for all of these categories except artifact types, which were too diverse to make the calculation worthwhile (Table 7-3). For pottery vessels, the only artifact type that occurred with more than 5% of all burials, decorative attributes (surface finish, lip notching patterns, shoulder punctation, special forms) and location with respect to the person with whom they were buried also were compared by age and sex. Average, minimum, and maximum numbers of artifacts, of artifact types, of functional categories of artifacts, of subsidiary burials, of decorated artifacts, of large/unique artifacts, of representational artifacts (effigies), of exotic items, and of European items were determined for all burials and age/sex categories. All body treatments, grave types, artifact types, artifact functional categories, and pottery attributes present in more than five burials were mapped, as were effigy categories, to search for any obvious gross spatial patterns.

Bivariate analysis was carried out to determine the significance and strength of association between pairs of variables and to aid in choosing variables for multivariate analysis. For preliminary evaluation of strength of associations, correlation matrices utilizing the Jacquard coefficient were constructed (Shennan 1988:203-4), comparing presence/absence of normative body treatments, of grave goods, of subsidiary burials, and of artifact functional types. Tabular cross-correlations were carried out between each of these variables and three types of age/sex categories (adult-subadult, male-female, and the six age categories), with significance determined either by Pearson's chi-square test (for $n > 20$) or Fisher's Exact Test (for $n < 20$ or $E_i < 5$), probability ≤ 0.05. Some cross-correlations also were carried out between artifact functional types and other nondemographic variables.

Two types of multivariate analysis commonly are used in mortuary studies, often discussed as "R-mode," which includes principal components analysis and factor analysis, and "Q-mode," which includes a variety of cluster analysis techniques. All have advantages and drawbacks, depending on the data set and analytical intent (e.g., Braun 1979; Brown 1987; O'Shea 1985; Peebles 1972; Shennan 1988:212-32, 241-88). Because

TABLE 7-5
Frequencies of Normative Burial Treatments, Trenches 1-K.

	Unknown Age (n = 30)	Subadults (n = 197)	Adults (n = 364)	TOTAL (n = 591)	Females (n = 62)	Males (n = 75)
Individual burials (not multiple)	50.0% (30)	65.5% (197)	69.7% (363)	67.3% (590)	61.3% (62)	69.3% (75)
Extended, supine	24.1% (29)	**67.0%** (191)	**77.7%** (363)	71.5% (583)	80.6% (62)	77.3% (75)
Articulated	31.0% (29)	**69.3%** (192)	**81.5%** (363)	75.0% (584)	85.5% (62)	82.7% (75)
Whole [a]	27.6% (29)	**71.1%** (194)	**81.3%** (364)	75.3% (587)	85.5% (62)	84.0% (75)
Head east [b]	57.1% (14)	**66.4%** (146)	**75.7%** (309)	70.5% (474)	64.5% (62)	61.3% (75)
Prepared grave [c]	96.0% (25)	93.8% (179)	94.9% (359)	95.4% (563)	96.7% (61)	91.8% (73)
Gravegoods NOT present	76.7% (30)	62.9% (197)	59.1% (364)	61.3% (591)	51.6% (62)	50.7% (75)
	Infants (n = 27)	**Children (n = 71)**	**Adolescents (n = 21)**	**Young Adults (n = 88)**	**Mature Adults (n = 84)**	**Older Adults (n = 49)**
Individual burials (not multiple)	**85.1%** (27)	**60.6%** (71)	**47.6%** (21)	**65.9%** (88)	**64.3%** (84)	**77.6%** (49)
Extended, supine	**88.5%** (26)	**68.1%** (69)	**57.1%** (21)	**76.1%** (88)	**84.5%** (84)	**83.7%** (49)
Articulated	**88.9%** (27)	**69.6%** (69)	**61.9%** (21)	**83.0%** (88)	**84.5%** (84)	**89.8%** (49)
Whole [a]	**85.2%** (27)	**66.7%** (71)	**71.4%** (21)	**81.8%** (88)	**85.7%** (84)	**91.8%** (49)
Head east [b]	37.0% (27)	54.9% (69)	52.4% (21)	62.5% (88)	64.3% (84)	69.4% (49)
Prepared grave [c]	100.0% (21)	95.45% (66)	85.7% (21)	95.4% (87)	97.5% (81)	93.9% (49)
Gravegoods NOT present	67.7% (27)	60.6% (71)	66.7% (21)	50.0% (88)	56.0% (84)	53.6% (49)

n = total sample size. Number (in parentheses) represents sample size with missing data omitted. **Boldface** indicates significant differences between/among age/sex groups (Pearson's Chi Square for $n > 20$ and $E_i > 5$ or Fisher's Exact Test for $n < 20$ or $E_i < 5$; probability ≤ 0.05).
[a] All major body parts present when buried.
[b] NE, E, or SE: 22.5°-157.5° from N.
[c] Not in refuse pit or scattered in soil layer.

of the highly diverse, non-covarying grave goods assemblages at Madisonville, use of R-mode analytical techniques was not feasible, so I relied completely on cluster analysis, choosing the iterative, nonhierarchical divisive K-means procedure (Kintigh and Ammerman 1982:38-50; O'Shea 1985:106; Shennan 1988:225-28; Wilkinson et al. 1992:25, 34-35). As O'Shea demonstrated by controlled experimentation, hierarchical procedures only function well when the data set is characterized by "strongly redundant and exclusive marker attributes," deteriorating rapidly when nonessential or nonexclusive attributes are employed (1985:105). Nonexclusive, nonredundant markers are exactly what can be expected in societies where status is largely achieved and individuals are marked by multiple social identities, each shared with a different group of people. Thus, the K-means procedure, which can be used to explore overlapping suites of variables, was the method of choice.

Five types of runs utilizing different suites of variables were carried out, three oriented toward detecting large-scale horizontal groupings, and the others more toward vertical status groupings. Burial locations of members of cluster groups resulting from these analyses were mapped, to see if they exhibited spatial clustering (or some other significant pattern) in addition to attribute clustering. Demographic characteristics of each cluster group were determined and compared with the theoretical model (Tables 2-5 through 2-7) to see whether they conformed to any predicted pattern for horizontal, vertical, or special-status social distinctions. Cluster analysis procedures and results are presented here in summary form only (for details, see Drooker 1996c).

Mortuary Patterns

Results of these formal analyses are presented below. Only those that appear to have significant socioeconomic correlates are discussed at any length. Unless otherwise specified, all statistical information is for burials in Trenches 1-K.

Normative Practices and Variation of Attributes by Age and Sex

Mortuary treatments that vary from the norm, whether representing honored leadership, dishonored deviation, or some other difference, can only be determined if "usual" burial treatments are known for comparison. Thus, determination of the most common burial practices and the associated range of differences is an essential first step in any mortuary analysis.

Since all known societies make at least some distinctions among members on the basis of sex and age, normative practices for males, females, adults, subadults, and six socially significant age categories also were determined. For each age/sex category, significant correlations with individual attributes were sought, to help determine whether any of them might be signifiers of age/sex status. Conversely, age/sex distributions were determined to the extent possible for attributes characteristic of more than five percent of the population.

Body Treatment. Grave preparation, body treatment, compass orientation, and number of individuals buried together all varied within the Madisonville cemetery. Table 7-5 summarizes this variation with reference to normative treatments, and Figures 7-7 through 7-10 graphically represent the categories of variation encountered. The average burial in Trenches 1-K was single (67%), extended and supine (71.5%), articulated (75%) with no significant body parts missing (75%), interred in a prepared but non-stone-lined pit (88%), with head oriented easterly (70% of those with known orientation, but only 56% of the total). The preference for easterly head orientation (Figure 7-9) was constrained but not obscured by evident preferences for orientation parallel to the plaza or parallel to sides of buildings (Figure 5-10).

There were no statistically significant differences in dichotomous burial treatment attributes between males and females, but subadults were significantly less likely than adults to be extended and supine, articulated, whole, and with head easterly (Table 7-5). Greater-than-expected numbers of subadults were disposed in refuse pits and in miscellaneous ways that included scattered bones in the soil layer (Figure 7-7). The lower-than-expected easterly orientation of subadults (Figure 7-9) undoubtedly was connected with their disproportionately high rates of disarticulation and of disposition as subsidiary members of group burials (Figure 7-10). Although members of group burials most often paralleled each other, subsidiary burials of subadults frequently were positioned at a significant angle to the primary burial in the group, for example, lying on and across the chest, or at the feet and perpendicular to the primary burial. Almost all primary burials were adults (Figure 7-10). Males and females were equally likely to serve as primary burials (13% of identified males, 14% of identified females), but males were more likely to have two or more associated subsidiary burials: 40% of primary males but only 22% of primary females had more than one subsidiary burial. No identified females were among the five individuals with three or more subsidiary burials. The person with the greatest number was an older adult male.

When finer-grained age categories were compared among the 340 burials for which they could be determined, there were significant differences among them with respect to some attributes (Table 7-5). Several cautions apply in interpreting these figures. As a group, these burials (which include most of the 137 for which sex could be determined) were more likely (and burials of unknown age were less likely) to conform to normative treatments than the total burial population of 591. This might well be a time-related phenomenon, since the human remains that were saved and that could be aged and sexed were those that were better preserved. In addition, infants, whose fragile bones are most likely to deteriorate quickly, undoubtedly are underrepresented in the sample.

Infants and older adults were more likely than the norm to be buried alone, whereas children and adolescents were more likely to be buried with others. Adults and infants were more likely to be whole, articulated, extended, and supine, whereas children and adolescents were less likely than expected to conform to this treatment. In general, normative treatment seems to have been more important for adults—fully operational members of society—than for subadults.

Non-normative grave attributes, including the presence of limestone slabs (a time-related attribute), the presence of a special layer (e.g., ashes, burnt soil) above or below a burial, or disposal in a refuse pit rather than in a prepared grave, showed no significant variation by age or sex. However, pits were significantly more likely than prepared graves to contain flexed burials, disarticulated remains, and portions of skeletons.

Grave Goods. More than half of the burials in Trenches 1-K (61%) had no surviving grave goods (Table 7-5). Many of these people could have been interred with perishable wooden, leather, or textile items such as carved dishes or spoons, or decorated clothing, bags, baskets, or mats, but only a handful of fragments from such artifacts survived the soil conditions at Madisonville (Hooton and Willoughby 1920: Pls. 21a-e). The average number of surviving grave goods per burial was 1.2. Only 19% of the burials had two or more items, and only 9% had three or more. There were no statistically significant differences in presence/absence of grave goods by age or sex (Table 7-5-). In other words, all people of whatever age or sex were roughly equally likely (or unlikely) to have been buried with *something*.

Grave good assemblages were diverse and idiosyncratic. Only one artifact type, ceramic vessels, was found with more than 5% of the burials, and only a few additional types occurred with more than 1% of burials (Table 7-3). It is not surprising, then, that few statistically significant correlations with age or sex were apparent, even when artifacts were grouped into categories of functional types (Table 7-6).

Tables 7-7 and 7-8 summarize types of articles present with adult versus subadult burials in Trenches 1-K and in the remainder of the site. The most significant difference is that a greater variety of artifact types was interred with adults than with subadults (65 versus 43, considering all burials). This would be expected if grave goods reflect social personae (Table 2-4) that were largely achieved: individuals who lived longer would have more chance to accumulate a variety of social identities, for which different types of grave goods would be appropriate. Fewer items were found exclusively with subadults than with adults, and most of those were ornaments rather than tools. Since most of these articles were found with only one or a few individuals, their presence has no statistical significance. Differences between the two groups that appear to be notable, including a higher association of projectile points, pipes, and animal

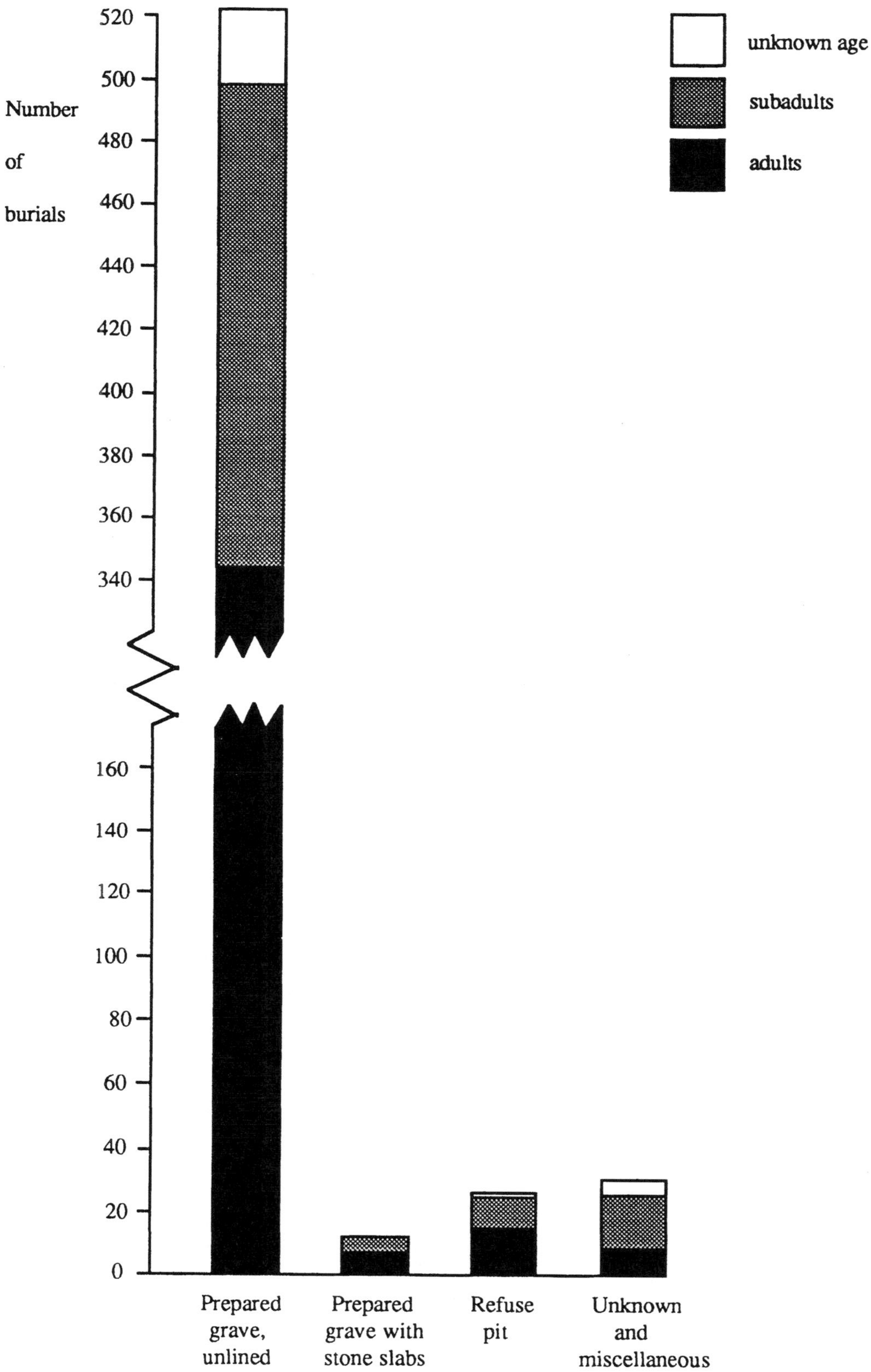

Figure 7-7. Grave types, Trenches 1-K ($n = 591$).

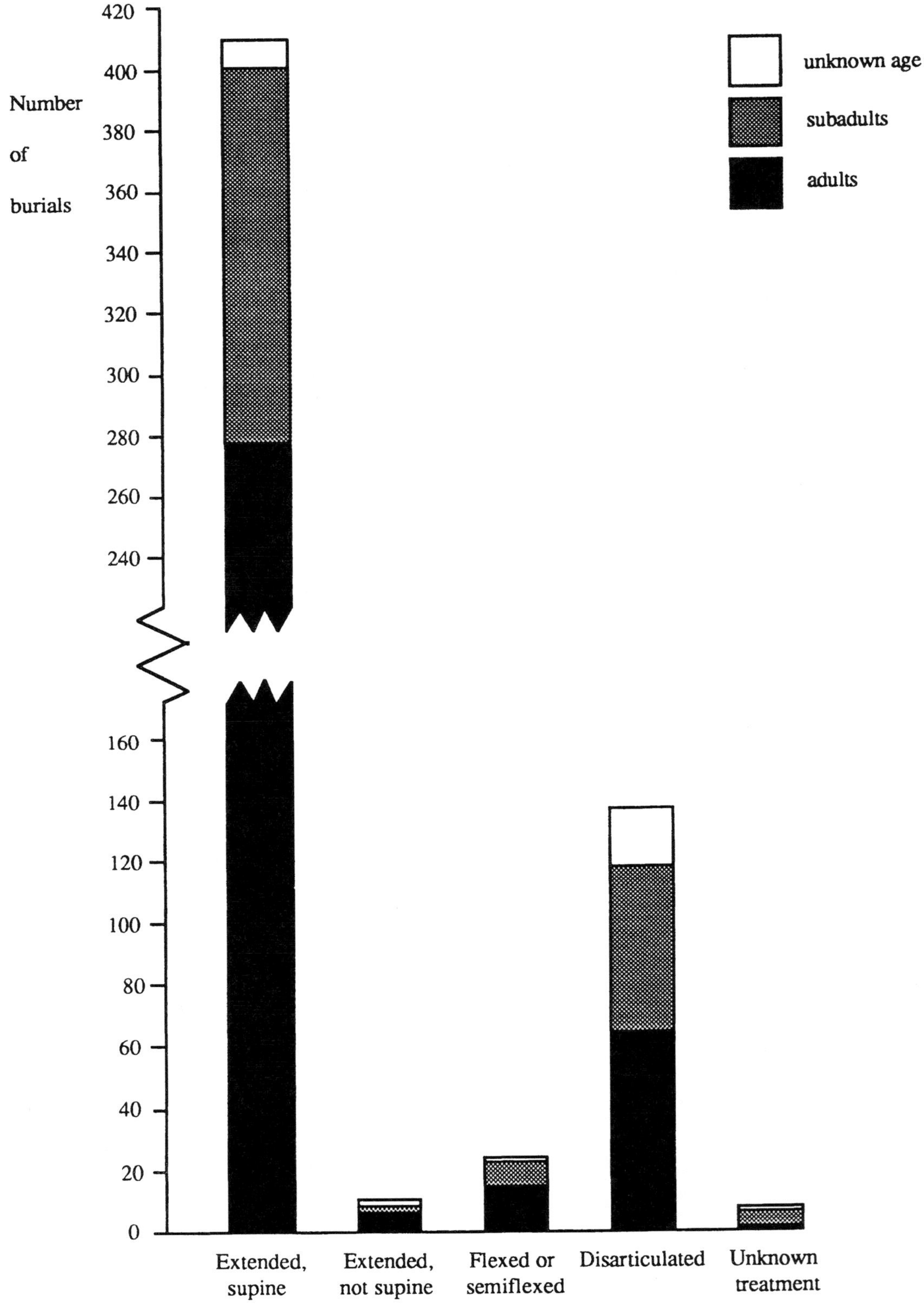

Figure 7-8. Body positions, Trenches 1-K ($n = 591$).

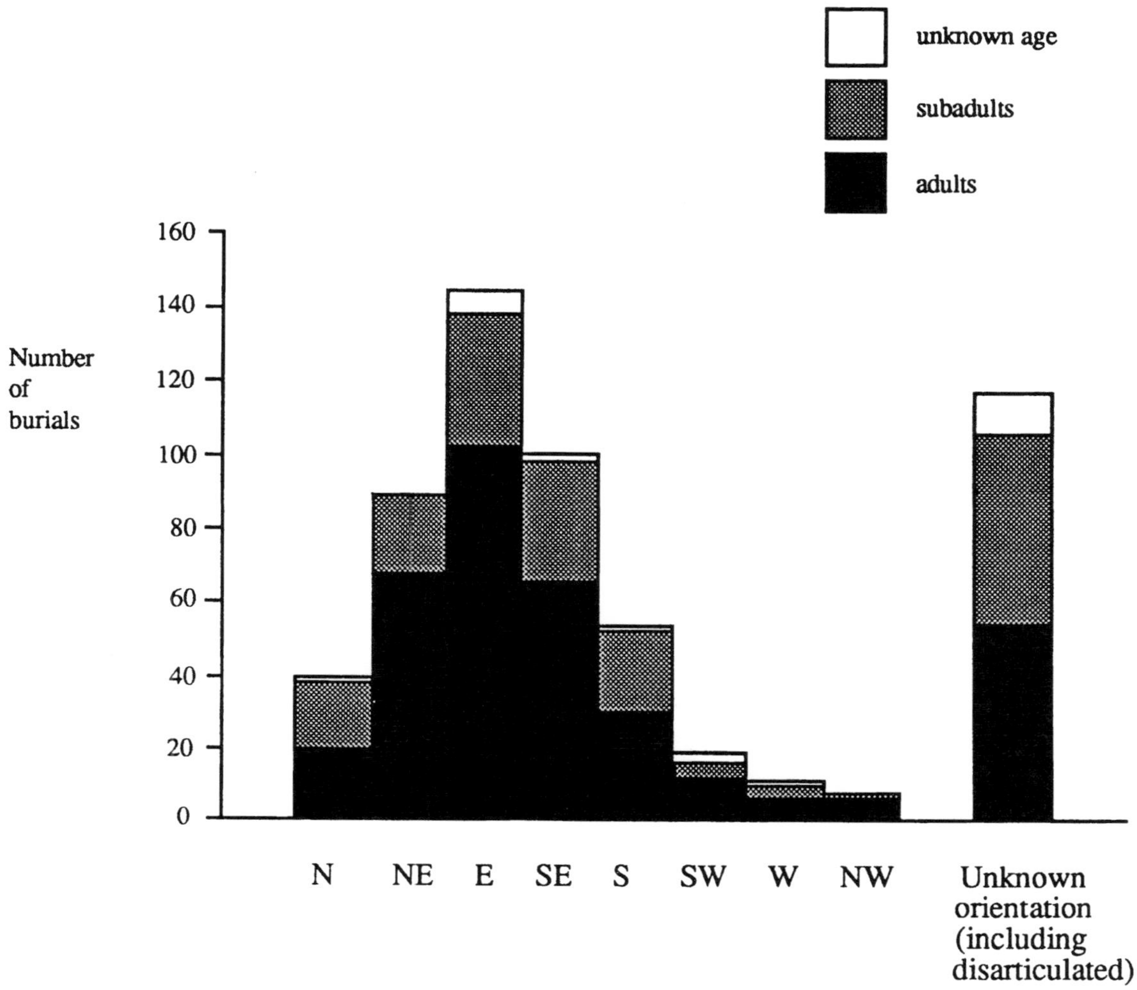

Figure 7-9. Compass orientations of burials (heads), Trenches 1-K ($n = 591$).

skulls with adults, will be examined below in the context of artifact functional categories. The differences in numbers of artifact types between burials in Trenches 1-K (Table 7-7) and the rest of the site (Table 7-8) could be related to differences in occupation time periods or to differences in excavation procedures.

Table 7-9 lists artifacts associated with burials in Trenches 1-K that could be assigned to more fine-grained age groups. Unlike types of artifacts associated with adults and subadults, the apparent discrepancy in numbers of artifact types among groups is directly proportional to the number of people assigned to each age category, with one exception: older adults are associated with more artifact types than expected, given their numbers. Again, this finding is congruent with status attained largely by achievement. All items that appear to be unique to a given age group (highlighted in the table) occur with only one or two burials, so none of them can be suggested as badges of age group membership.

Table 7-10 lists artifact types associated with identifiable males and females in Trenches 1-K. In this sample of burials, a much greater variety of extant artifacts was associated with males than with females. More males had ornaments (antler, bone, brass, copper or shell), pipes, projectile points, and animal or bird skulls. Females were much more often associated with tools than with ornaments. In this sample, only females were buried with flint scrapers, hammerstones, or hoes. They were more likely than males to have shell spoons and more than one ceramic jar. These associations reflect historically recorded female tasks of food production/preparation and hide preparation, and male domination of hunting, warfare, and diplomacy.

Table 7-6 summarizes frequencies of occurrences of ten functional categories of artifacts, plus subsidiary burials, by age and sex. Figure 7-11 diagrams the relative numbers of different types occurring with adults, subadults, and people of unknown age.

The most common grave good type, present with 26% of the burials in Trenches 1-K, was ceramic vessels, most with interior

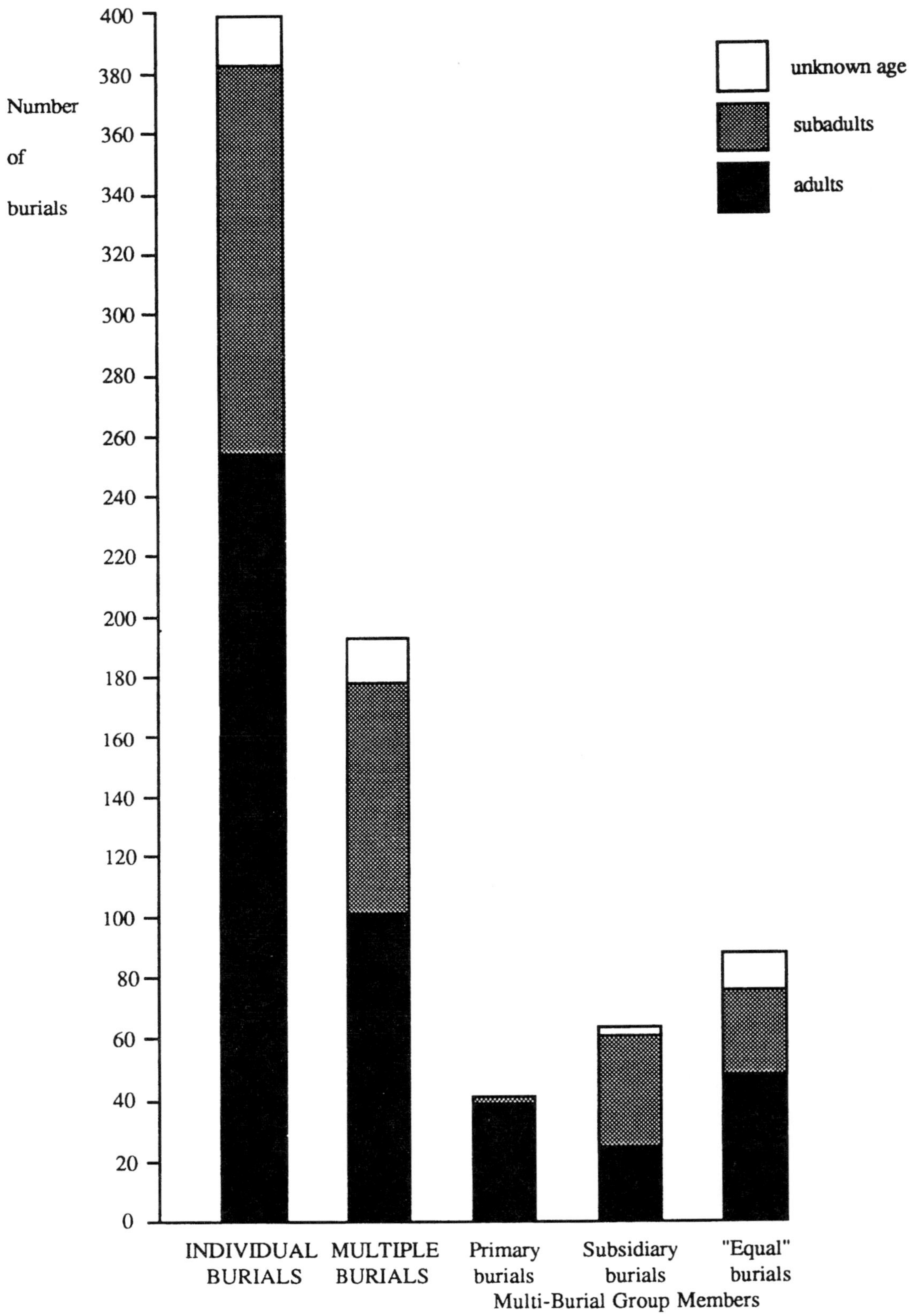

Figure 7-10. Individual and group burials, Trenches 1-K ($n = 591$).

TABLE 7-6
Frequencies of Occurrence of Gravegood Functional Types with Burials, Trenches 1-K

	Unknown Age (n = 30)	Subadults (n = 197)	Adults (n = 364)	TOTAL (n = 591)	Females (n = 62)	Males (n = 75)
Any gravegoods	23.3%	37.1%	40.9%	38.7%	48.4%	49.3%
Associated subsidiary burials	0.0%	**1.0%**	**10.7%**	6.9%	14.5%	13.3%
Ceramic vessels	20.0%	23.9%	28.0%	26.2%	38.7%	34.7%
Shell spoons	10.0%	2.5%	4.1%	3.9%	6.5%	5.3%
Projectile points	0.0%	3.6%	5.2%	4.4%	1.6%	8.0%
Tools	0.0%	2.0%	3.8%	3.0%	8.1%	1.3%
Metal or glass (mostly ornaments)	3.3%	5.1%	6.3%	5.8%	3.2%	9.3%
Shell ornaments	0.0%	5.6%	3.8%	4.2%	3.2%	6.7%
Bone/antler ornaments	0.0%	1.5%	1.6%	1.5%	0.0%	4.0%
Charms	0.0%	3.0%	3.6%	3.2%	3.2%	6.7%
Animal/bird skulls	0.0%	1.0%	2.5%	1.9%	**0.0%**	**6.7%**
Pipes	0.0%	**0.0%**	**3.0%**	1.9%	**0.0%**	**5.1%**

	Infants (n = 27)	Children (n = 71)	Adolescents (n = 21)	Young Adults (n = 88)	Mature Adults (n = 84)	Older Adults (n = 49)
Any gravegoods	33.3%	39.4%	33.3%	50.0%	44.5%	46.9%
Associated subsidiary burials	**0.0%**	**0.0%**	**4.8%**	**12.5%**	**8.3%**	**14.3%**
Ceramic vessels	25.9%	26.8%	19.0%	37.5%	33.3%	30.6%
Shell spoons	0.0%	1.4%	9.5%	9.1%	2.4%	4.1%
Projectile points	0.0%	4.2%	0.0%	6.8%	7.1%	6.1%
Tools	3.7%	1.4%	0.0%	3.4%	2.4%	8.2%
Metal or glass (mostly ornaments)	11.1%	8.5%	0.0%	9.1%	2.4%	8.2%
Shell ornaments	7.4%	8.5%	0.0%	6.8%	3.6%	0.0%
Bone/antler ornaments	0.0%	1.4%	4.8%	3.4%	0.0%	2.0%
Charms	0.0%	2.8%	0.0%	3.4%	3.6%	2.0%
Animal/bird skulls	0.0%	1.4%	4.8%	0.0%	4.8%	4.1%
Pipes	0.0%	0.0%	0.0%	2.3%	4.8%	4.1%

Boldface indicates significant differences between/among age/sex groups (Pearson's χ^2 for n > 20 and E_i>5 or Fisher's Exact Test for n<20 or E_i<5; probability $\leq$0.05).

rings indicating the presence of food (for frequency of occurrence elsewhere on the site, see Table 6-3 and Figure 6-44). There was no statistically significant difference in occurrence between adults and subadults, males and females, or the six age categories. Neither did I find significant differences by age or sex in terms of vessel placement or stylistic attributes. As discussed in Chapter 6, burials with ceramic vessels did tend to occur close to the "plaza" (Figures 6-10, 6-15), probably a time-related phenomenon.

Second only to pots as mortuary associations were subsidiary burials, which were found with 9% of Trench 1-K interments, significantly more often with adults than subadults. None were found with identifiable infants or children. This does appear to be an age-related practice.

The most common surviving ornaments (nonclothing items that appear to have been worn) with burials were fashioned from metal, the next most common from shell, then from bone or antler, and two people were buried with glass beads. Although there were differences in occurrence of ornaments by age and sex (for instance, no identifiable females in Trenches 1-K had bone ornaments, and few had any ornaments), none were statistically significant.

In the case of projectile points, their more frequent occurrence with adults than subadults, and males than females, was not significant.

The association of tools with women (versus men) was significant at the 0.055 level. However, they did occur with at least one male, an older adult (Burial I-19). The total distribution included four subadults, four female adults, one male adult, and eight adults of unknown age or sex.

Animal and bird skulls were not found with identifiable females, a statistically significant occurrence. Most of them were buried with adults (two with older adults, three with mature adults, one with a young adult, and three with adults of unknown age), but one was found with a 12-15 year-old adolescent and another with an 11-12 year-old child (Burials C-8 and B-38). A mature adult male and a young adult (Burials E-19 and 1-61) each had two animal skulls, two of them identified in the field as otter and sable or marten, and one older adult (E-32) had three long-billed bird skulls. No one was reported as possessing both animal and bird skulls. The placement of many of the skulls and associated materials, which often included additional animal or bird bones, relative to burials (e.g., between arm and upper body) makes it very likely that they represent the equiva-

TABLE 7-7
Gravegoods buried with adults and subadults, Trenches 1-K

Adults (n = 365)	Subadults (n = 196)
(animal) bone arm band (1)	animal bones (2)
animal bones (3)	animal skull and bones (2)
animal claw (1)	animal (bear) claw (1)
animal skull and bones (6)	**antler comb** (1 adolescent)
animal (beaver) tooth scraper (1)	**antler pendant** (1)
antler cylinders (1)	antler projectile point (1)
antler harpoon (1)	antler, worked (1)
antler projectile point (2)	bone bead (1)
antler shaft wrench (1)	brass clip (1)
antler, worked (3)	ceramic bowl (1)
bird wing bones (1)	ceramic pot (45)
bird skull and/or beak (2)	ceramic sherd (2)
bird bone whistle (1)	**ceramic pot, "toy"** (1)
bone bead(s) (3)	copper/brass beads (4)
bone pendant (2)	copper, piece (2)
bone, worked (3)	copper staining (3)
brass bead (1)	corn (1)
ceramic bowl (1)	flint point tip (poss. broken knife) (1)
ceramic pot (102)	flint projectile point (7)
ceramic sherd (1)	flint (2)
charred material (1)	glass beads (1)
cannel coal (3)	red ochre staining (2)
copper/brass beads (9)	shell beads, incl. 1 marginella (6)
***copper/brass coils** (4)	**shell (busycon) ornament** (1)
copper or copper-covered pendants/ornaments (unique) (5)	shell pendant (6)
copper staining (10)	shell spoon (5)
copper, worked pieces (1)	shell, unknown function (4)
corn (3)	**shell, worked** (1)
flint drill (1)	stone celt (2)
flint knife (2)	***stone club** (1)
flint projectile point (22)	***stone discoidal** (1)
flint scraper (4)	**stone, notched** (1)
flint (3)	stone, natural (1)
glass bead (1)	**tooth, burnt** (1)
iron bead (1)	
red ochre (2)	
shell beads (11, incl. 1 with marginellas)	
shell pendant (3)	
***shell pendant, maskette** (1)	
shell spoon (12)	
shells, unio, perforated - hoes? (2)	
shell, unknown function (4)	
stone celt (2)	
stone, hammerstone (2)	
***stone pipes** (11)	
stone, natural	
stone whetstone (2)	
stone, worked (2)	

Boldfaced items were never found with identified members of the opposite age group (although they might be found with people of unknown age). Numbers of burials that had each type of item are given in parentheses.
* Asterisks indicate items that do occur with burials of the opposite age group in other areas of the site (see Table 7-8).

TABLE 7-8
Gravegoods Buried with Adults and Subadults, from Excavations Other than Trenches 1-K

Adults (n = 244)	Subadults (n = 406)
antler harpoon (1)	**animal tooth pendant** (1)
antler implement, perforated (1)	**antler "arrow flakers"** (1)
antler tip (deer) necklace (1)	antler implements (1)
bone beads/cylinders (10)	bone bead(s) (2)
bone cylinders, solid (2)	***brass coils** (1)
bone fishhook (1)	**brass pendant, barred** (1)
bones, "a few small" (1)	**brass bell** (1)
bone, worked (1)	***ceramic bowl ("flat dish")** (1)
brass finger rings (1)	ceramic pot (81)
ceramic pot (160)	copper/brass beads (4)
cannel coal, circular piece (1)	**copper pendant, oval** (1)
cannel coal pendant (1?)	copper, piece (5)
copper/brass bead(s) (4)	copper serpent, tubular, small (1)
copper, flattened fragments (1)	flint projectile point (1)
copper pendant, double-barred (1)	***shell beads** (3)
copper serpents, tubular (1)	shell pendant/ornament (4)
***corn, charred** (2)	***shell pendant, maskette** (1)
"flint chippings" (1)	shell spoon (1)
flint knife (2)	stone celt (1)
flint projectile point(s) (8)	stone club (2)
iron dagger guard (1)	stone pipe (2)
***shell disks w/center perforation** (3)	stones, round - hammerstones?(1)
shell pendant, cylindrical (1)	
shell spoon (4)	
shell, unio, perf. - hoe? (1)	
shells, unio, function unknown (2)	
stone celt (7)	
stone club/hammer (1)	
***stone discoidal** (2)	
stone, fossil bivalve shells (1)	
stone (slate) ornament (1)	
stone pipe (12)	
stones, "pestle-like" (1)	
stone implements (1)	
stone, round- hammerstone? (1)	
stone, worked (1)	
tortoise shell rattle (2)	

Boldfaced items were never found with identified members of the opposite age group (although they might be found with people of unknown age). Numbers of burials that had each type of item are given in parentheses.
* Asterisks indicate items that do occur with burials of the opposite age group in Trenches 1-K (see Table 7-7).

lent of historically documented medicine bags. (A possible alternative for bird remains is a ceremonial fan, but their locations and orientations with respect to burials seems more congruent with the medicine-bundle interpretation.) Because of their comparative scarcity, I think it more likely that such bags were associated with shamanism than with individual vision quests (two possibilities from ethnohistorical analogy). There also do not seem to be enough examples to postulate any large-scale "medicine society." The presence of medicine bags with younger as well as older people would be consistent with the start of shamanistic training at a relatively early age, perhaps initiated though a vision quest during early adolescent years. No animal or bird skulls were recorded as grave goods outside of Trenches 1-K, but this does not necessarily mean that they were not present.

Pipes seem to be a male marker. In Trenches 1-K, none occurred with subadults or identified females; the positive correlations with adults and males were statistically significant. One older adult male (Burial I-19) and one mature adult male (Burial

TABLE 7-9
Gravegoods Interred with Persons of Known Age Category, Trenches 1-K

Infants (n = 27)	Children (n = 71)	Adolescents (n = 21)	Young Adults (n = 88)	Mature Adults (n = 84)	Older Adults (n = 49)
bone chisel/scraper (1)	antler, worked (1)	**antler comb** (1?)	antler projectile point (1)	animal bones (1)	animal skull &bones (1)
ceramic pot (5)	claw, bear (1)	animal skull and bones(1)	antler, worked (2)	animal skull and bones(3)	animal bone (1)
ceramic pot, "toy" (1)	animal skull and bones(1)	ceramic pot (4)	**(animal) bone arm bands** (1)	bird skull/beak (1)	**antler harpoon** (1)
glass beads (1)	bone bead (1)	flint piece (1)	**(bird) bone beads, engraved** (1)	bone, worked (1)	bird skull/beak (1)
shell beads (2)	**brass clip** (1)	shell spoon (2)	bone (1)	ceramic pot (30)	**(bird) bone flute** (1)
shell pendant (1)	ceramic pot (19)		brass bead (1)	claw, animal (1)	**bone ornament** (1)
shell, unio, fragments (1)	ceramic sherd (2)		ceramic bowl (1)	cannel coal, worked (1)	ceramic pot (17)
	copper or brass beads (2)		ceramic pot (31)	**copper-covered wood ornament** (1)	copper/brass bead (1)
	copper pieces (2)		ceramic sherd (1)	copper leg bands (1)	**copper pendant, cross-shaped** (1)
	copper staining, head (1)		cannel coal (2)	copper staining, arm (1)	copper staining (2)
	corn, charred (1)		**copper-covered belt** (10 clips) (1)	flint projectile point(s) (9)	copper-stained animal/bird bones(1)
	flint knife tip, broken (1)		**copper-covered bone disk** (1)	shell beads (1)	corn (1)
	flint projectile point(s) (3)		copper/brass leg bands(1)	shell pendant (1)	flint (1)
	shell beads (4)		copper staining, skull/fingers (2)	shell pendant,maskette(1)	flint knife (1)
	shell gorget/earplugs (3)		corn (1)	shell spoon (2)	flint projectile point(s) (4)
	shell spoon (2-3)		flint (1)	stone celt (1)	**shell valves, perforated, hoes?** (2)
	shell, worked (1)		flint projectile point(s) (5)	stone hammerstone (1)	shell spoon (2)
	stones (1)		**iron bead** (1)	stone pipe (4)	stone celt (1)
			red ochre, in shell (1)	stone, **quartz crystal** (1)	stone pipe (2)
			shell beads (5)	stone, worked (1)	**stone whetstone** (1)
			shell pendants (4)	stone, unworked (1)	stone, worked (1)
			shell spoons (8-11)		
			stone pipes (2)		

Boldfaced items were never found with identified members of any other age categories (although they might be found with persons of unknown age). Numbers of burials that had each type of item are given in parentheses.

3-9) each had two pipes. In the remainder of the site, two burials with pipes (of at least 16) were described as subadults. One of them (Burial 12 in Block 8) was an adolescent with age given as about 15 years. The other, described simply as a "child," was buried on the "lower extremities" of an adult, with the pipe at its feet and probably also on top of the adult; both of them lay above a second adult, described as a male (Burials 19-21, Block 11). It is quite possible that the pipe attributed to the child by the excavators was actually associated with an adult. It is of interest that both the adolescent and one of the two young adults with pipes in Trenches 1-K (Burial 2-21, a male in his early 20s) had their pipes between their thighs, whereas older adults most commonly had pipes laid next to their heads (e.g., Figures 7-1, 7.2), clasped in one hand, or on or alongside an arm.

Attributes of artifacts that crosscut functional categories were also evaluated with respect to age and sex of the burials with which they were associated (Table 7-11). The only statistically significant differences were the association with males (versus females) of large or unique artifacts and of representational artifacts/effigies. Although they are not statistically significant, the distributions of exotic materials and artifacts are worth noting: greater proportions with subadults than adults, with males than females, and with young adults than mature or older adults. The message is mixed, with no clear monopoly or hierarchy of acquisition.

Not only presence/absence but also numbers of artifacts with particular attributes were compared by age/sex occurrence. On average, adults had greater numbers of grave goods, artifact types, functional types, exotic items, large/unique artifacts, decorated artifacts, and subsidiary burials than subadults (Table 7-11). However, adults had no monopoly on these attributes. Although the three individuals with the largest numbers of grave goods were adults (Figure 7-12), 11 out of 37 of the burials with four or more artifacts were subadults, a proportion roughly the same as their frequency in the population. Likewise, although the highest artifact diversity, measured by numbers of artifact types and functional types, was achieved by an adult (Burial I-19, an older adult male), not only adults had diverse assemblages. At least two subadults (12.5% of a total of 16) had four or more artifact types among their grave goods, and one of them (Burial 3-4, a young child) had grave goods of four functional types (Figure 7-13). The one category of mortuary offering

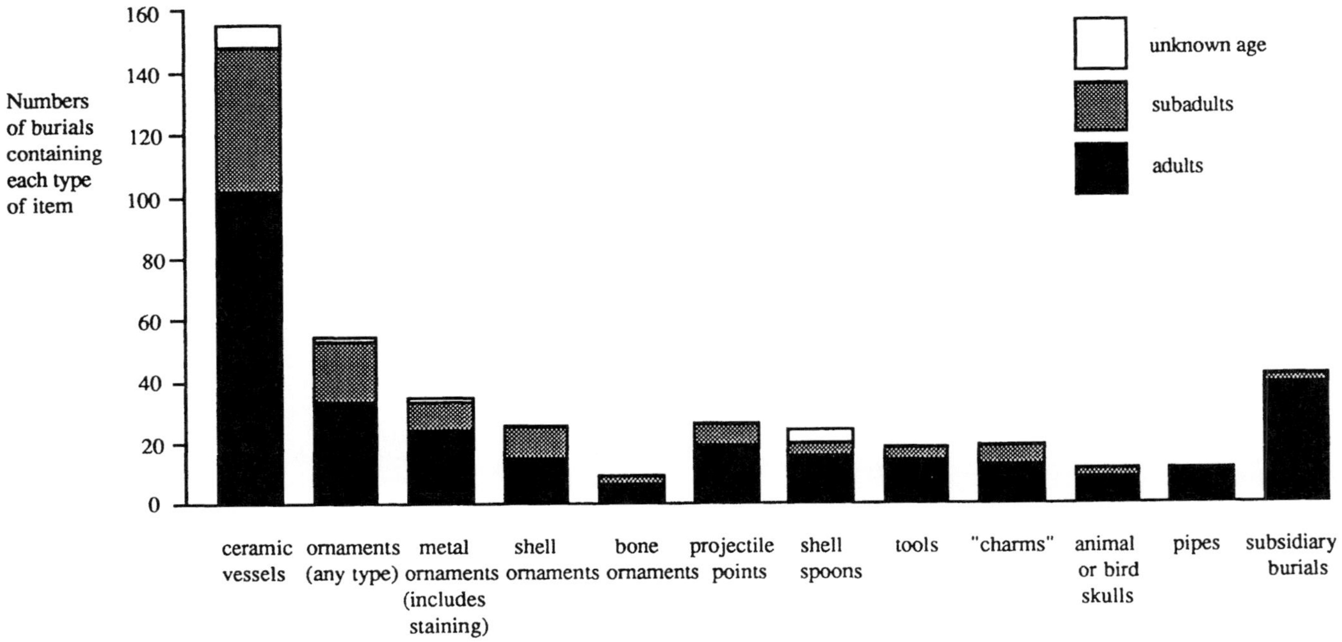

Figure 7-11. Numbers of burials with the most common functional types of mortuary offerings, Trenches 1-K.

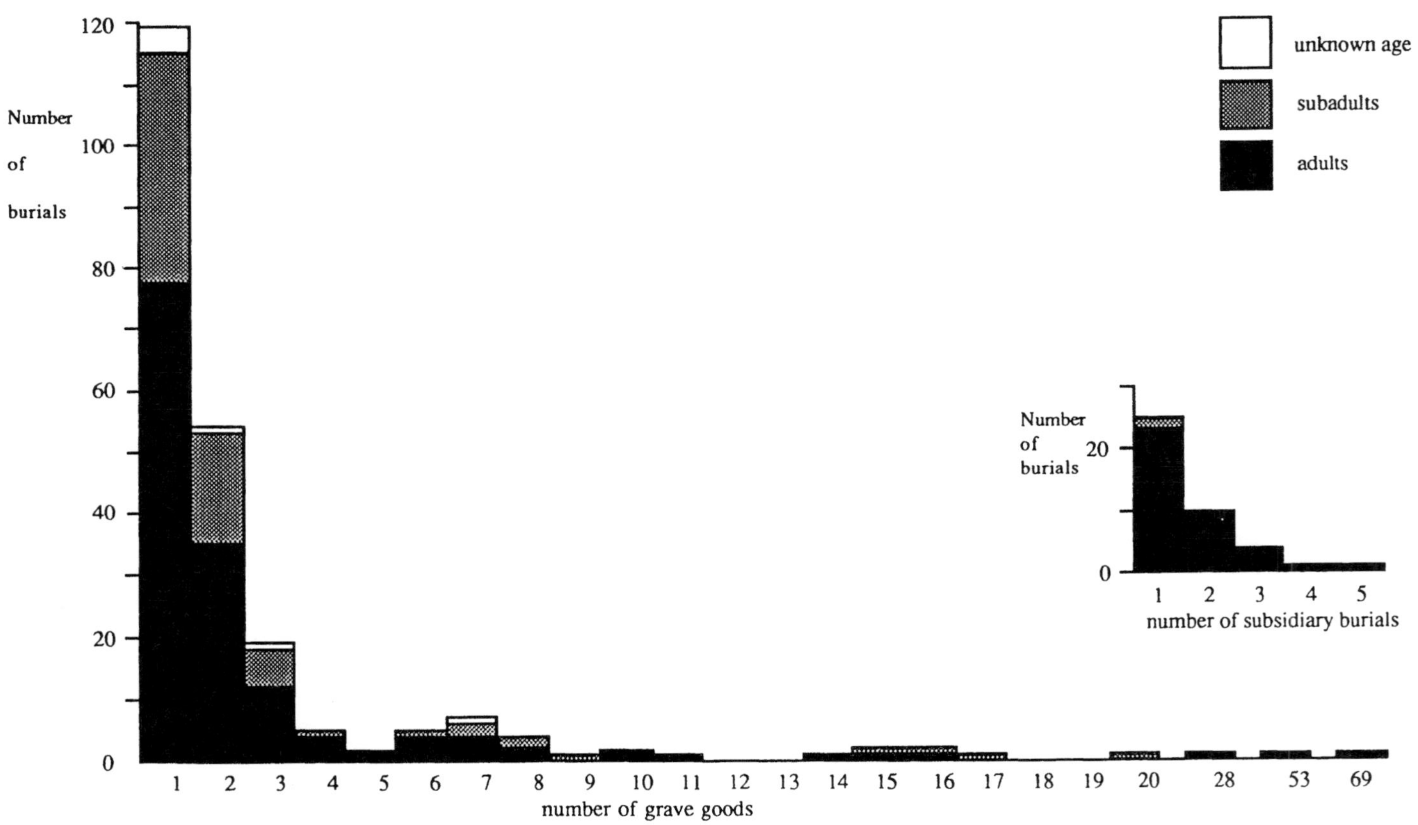

Figure 7-12. Numbers of grave goods and subsidiary burials per burial, Trenches 1-K ($n = 591$). Not charted are the 362 burials with no grave goods, including 215 adults, 124 children, and 23 of unknown age.

TABLE 7-10

Gravegoods Interred with Identified Males and Females, Trenches 1-K

Males (n = 75)	Females (n = 62)
(animal) bone arm band (1)	antler, worked (1)
animal bones (1)	bone, animal (1)
animal claw (1)	**cannel coal** (2)
animal skull and bones (5)	ceramic jar (24, incl. 3 with 2 jars)
antler comb (1--adolescent male)	**copper-covered bone disk** (1)
antler harpoon (1)	copper stains (on hair, bark, etc.) (1)
antler, worked (1)	flint (1)
(bird) bone beads (1)	flint projectile point (1)
bird skull and/or beak (1)	**flint scraper** (2)
bird wing bones (1)	shell beads (1)
bone ornament (1)	**shell valve, probably hoe** (1)
ceramic jar (26 -- none with >1 jar)	shell spoon (6)
copper beads (1)	shell, unknown function (2)
copper/brass cone-shaped ornament (1)	**stone celt** (1)
copper-covered wood ornament (1)	**stone hammerstone** (1)
copper leg bands (from stained leg bones) (2)	**stone, worked** (1)
copper pendant, cross-shaped (1)	
copper stains (on mastoids, humerus, ilium) (4)	
corn	
flint (1)	
flint knife (1)	
flint projectile point(s) (9)	
red ochre, in shell valve (1)	
shell beads (4)	
shell pendant (1)	
shell pendant, maskette (1)	
shell spoon (3)	
stone pipe(s) (7)	
stone, "special" (2)	

Boldfaced items were never found with identified members of the opposite sex (although they might be found with adults of unknown sex). Numbers of burials that had each type of item are given in parentheses.

where numbers clearly favored adults was subsidiary burials: no subadult had more than one.

In considering finer-grained age categories, young adults had highest average numbers of grave goods, artifact types, functional types, large/unique artifacts, and decorated artifacts, and averaged almost as many subsidiary burials as older adults (Table 7-12). Considered as a group, people dying in their physical prime clearly were valued members of society, as evidenced by markers of both status and wealth. Young adults were exceeded in average numbers of exotic grave goods only by infants, who also had the second-highest average number of grave goods; identified infants thus appear to have correlations with wealth indicators. After young adults, older adults had the highest average numbers of artifact types, while mature and older adults shared second place in average numbers of functional types. In general, these two age groups were comparatively high in potential indicators of achieved status, but not in indicators of wealth. Adolescents, with the lowest average numbers of grave goods, artifact types, functional types, and exotic items, nevertheless had the highest average number of effigies. The small number of people in this age group make interpretations hazardous, but this does correspond with Braun's suggestion that in a society with largely achieved status, deceased infants and young children might be "gifted" according to their family's status, whereas teenagers would not, and because they would be just beginning to acquire their own social identities (Table 2-4), they would have few grave goods (Braun 1979:72).

On average, males had greater numbers of grave goods, artifact types, functional types, exotic items, large/unique artifacts, decorated artifacts (including representational decoration), and subsidiary burials than females (Table 7-12). There does seem

TABLE 7-11

Frequencies of Occurrence of Gravegoods with Special Attributes, Trenches 1-K

	Unknown Age (n = 30)	Subadults (n = 197)	Adults (n = 364)	TOTAL (n = 591)	Females (n = 62)	Males (n = 75)
Exotic artifacts/materials	0.0%	10.2%	8.8%	9.0%	4.8%	14.7%
European artifacts/materials	0.0%	2.0%	1.4%	1.5%	0.0%	0.0%
Large/unique artifacts	3.3%	3.1%	2.8%	2.5%	**0.0%**	**8.0%**
Decorated artifacts	0.0%	4.6%	3.9%	3.4%	1.6%	6.7%
Representational artifacts (effigies)	0.0%	4.1%	5.2%	4.6%	**1.6%**	**13.3%**
	Infants (n = 27)	**Children (n = 71)**	**Adolescents (n = 21)**	**Young Adults (n = 88)**	**Mature Adults (n = 84)**	**Older Adults (n = 49)**
Exotic artifacts/materials	14.8%	15.5%	0.0%	13.6%	6.0%	8.2%
European artifacts/materials	7.4%	2.8%	0.0%	1.1%	0.0%	2.0%
Large/unique artifacts	0.0%	4.2%	4.8%	4.6%	4.8%	2.0%
Decorated artifacts	0.0%	2.8%	4.8%	4.6%	4.8%	2.0%
Representational artifacts (effigies)	0.0%	5.6%	9.5%	4.6%	7.1%	6.1%

Boldface indicates significant differences between/among age/sex groups (Pearson's χ^2, probability ≤ 0.05).

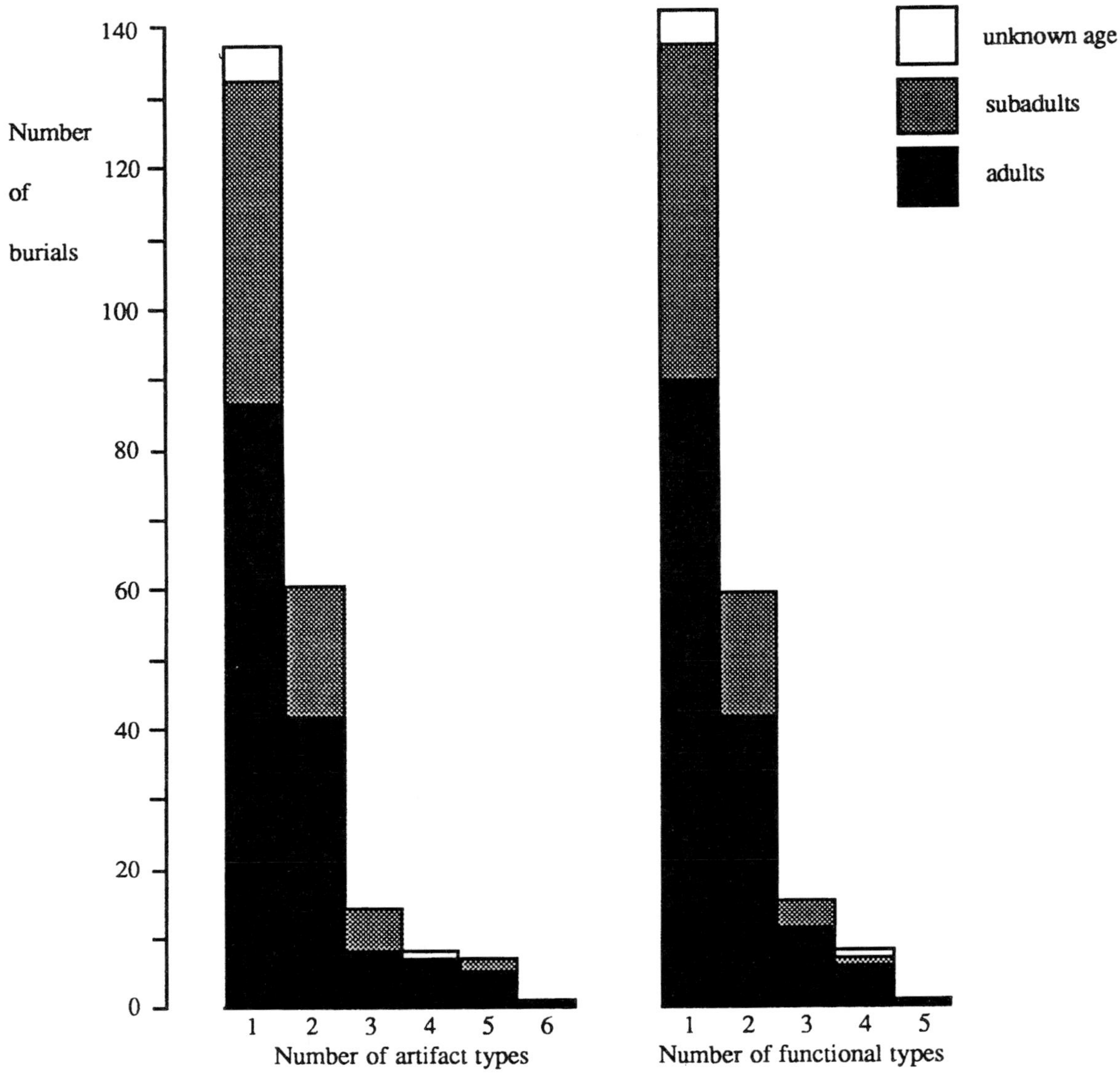

Figure 7-13. Numbers of artifact types per burial and functional categories of artifacts per burial, Trenches 1-K, for the 229 burials with grave goods.

to have been an imbalance of nonperishable mortuary offerings with males.

In addition to cross-correlations by age and sex, (dichotomous) cross-correlations were carried out between burial attributes, including artifact functional types and burial treatments, as a preliminary step in choosing attributes for multivariate analysis. The artifact functional types with significant correlations to age/sex categories correlated significantly with very different types of attributes.

Burials with animal or bird skulls correlated significantly with "charms," with metal, shell, and bone ornaments, with subsidiary burials (but not with two or more), and with reasonably diverse grave good assemblages (three or more functional types). None included projectile points or shell spoons, although the negative correlation was not statistically significant. One of the nine lay with head to northwest and two with heads to south, outside the most common compass orientations (Figure 7-9). Exotic goods, charms, and non-normative burial orientation would not be out of place for people associated with shamanistic activities. My tentative conclusion is that animal and bird skulls can be recognized as one marker for this role.

Burials with pipes (the strongest male marker) correlated significantly with two other artifact functional categories, projectile points and bone/antler ornaments, and also with three or more subsidiary burials, decorated artifacts, large/unique artifacts, and highly diverse grave good assemblages (four or five functional types). Both burials interred with two pipes were males older than 30. These associations are appropriate for

TABLE 7-12
Average Numbers per Burial of Gravegoods, Gravegood Categories, and Gravegoods with Special Attributes, Trenches 1-K

	Unknown Age (n = 30)	Subadults (n = 197)	Adults (n = 364)	TOTAL (n = 591)	Females (n = 62)	Males (n = 75)
Gravegoods	0.53	**1.06**	**1.38**	1.23	**0.95**	**1.47**
Artifact types	0.30	**0.57**	**0.69**	0.67	**0.69**	**0.93**
Functional types	0.30	**0.51**	**0.64**	0.63	**0.69**	**0.89**
Exotic artifacts	0.33	**0.51**	**0.57**	0.52	0.13	0.24
Large/unique artifacts	0.00	**0.04**	**0.07**	0.06	0.00	0.16
Decorated artifacts	0.00	0.05	0.04	0.04	**0.02**	**0.09**
Representational artifacts (effigies)	0.00	**0.05**	**0.08**	0.07	**0.02**	**0.17**
Associated subsidiary burials	0.00	**0.01**	**0.18**	0.11	**0.18**	**0.24**
	Infants (n = 27)	Children (n = 71)	Adolescents (n = 21)	Young Adults (n = 88)	Mature Adults (n = 84)	Older Adults (n = 49)
Gravegoods	**1.82**	**1.23**	**0.52**	**2.42**	**1.00**	**1.06**
Artifact types	**0.56**	**0.69**	**0.38**	**0.91**	**0.68**	**0.78**
Functional types	**0.52**	**0.59**	**0.33**	**0.82**	**0.67**	**0.69**
Exotic artifacts	1.48	0.58	0.00	1.31	0.10	0.12
Large/unique artifacts	**0.04**	**0.08**	**0.05**	**0.22**	**0.06**	**0.06**
Decorated artifacts	0.04	0.04	0.05	0.06	0.05	0.04
Representational artifacts (effigies)	0.00	0.06	0.19	0.05	0.11	0.14
Associated subsidiary burials	0.00	0.00	0.05	0.21	0.12	0.25

Based on minimum numbers known to be present. **Boldface** indicates significant differences between/among age/sex groups (Pearson's χ^2, probability ≤ 0.05).

people having recognized status associated with multiple social identities. Since there appears to be no redundant, exclusive set of high-status markers (with the one statistically nonsignificant exception that both of the double-barred cross-shaped copper pendants occurred with burials that had pipes), individualistic achievements, rather than rote ascription, would seem to have been the most likely avenue to nonritual leadership at Madisonville. Pipes appear to mark one social identity associated with such leadership roles. Judging from ethnohistorical analogy, this probably was an identity related to external interaction, including diplomatic relations. Such an identity would not be out of place in individuals associated with projectile points, considering warfare is another (often related) form of external interaction. Pipes as symbols of external interaction would be congruent with the significant presence of nonlocal styles and materials in pipes deposited as mortuary offerings, as discussed above.

Graves with stone slabs (an Early-Middle Fort Ancient attribute) had a significant positive correlation with only one artifact functional type, shell ornaments. There also was a statistically significant negative correlation to ceramic vessels. None of the thirteen burials with slabs contained bone ornaments, metal ornaments, tools, subsidiary burials, large/unique or decorated artifacts, five or more artifact types, or four or more functional types of artifacts.

Spatial Distributions of Individual Attributes, Trenches 1-K

As discussed in Chapter 2, spatial clustering of burials is predicted to express the broadest and most important social relationships within a group, such as classes, moieties, clans, or families. As a preliminary step in recognizing markers that might signify these important social relationships, all burial attributes characterizing five percent or more of the mortuary population in Trenches 1-K were mapped. In these preliminary, exploratory distribution maps, I looked for groupings of burials with a particular attribute that could not be explained simply by their coincidence with higher densities of burials. I was particularly interested in finding any attributes that clustered together on (roughly) half of the site, which might be indicative of dual divisions such as moieties.

Human Remains and Burial Treatments. Adults and subadults do not appear to have been buried separately at Madisonville, nor do members of any of the six age groups, although subadults might be somewhat less common than adults immediately adjacent to the plaza edge (Figures 7-14 and 7-15). Identified males and females generally coincide in location, although there are several portions of the site that appear to have an excess of either males or females (Figures 7-16 and 7-17). However, since persons of identified sex represent only 38% of identified adults, these spatial differences probably are

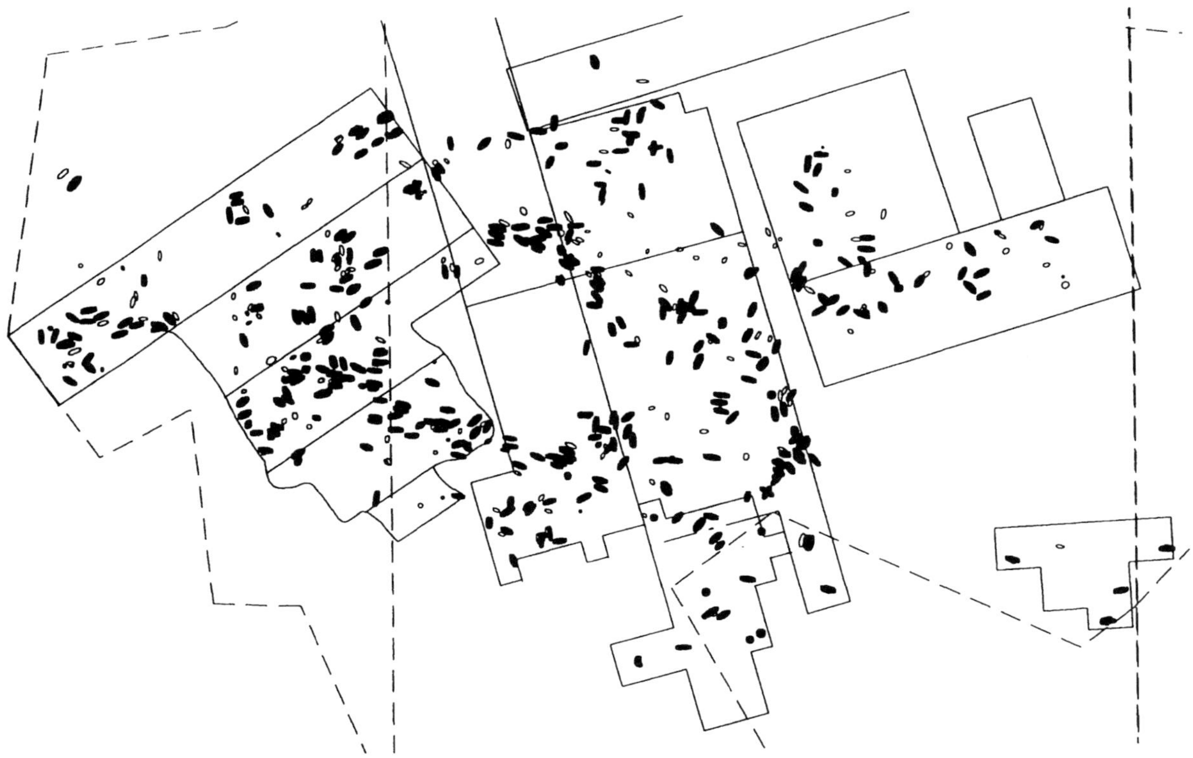

Figure 7-14. Distribution of identified adults, Trenches 1-K.

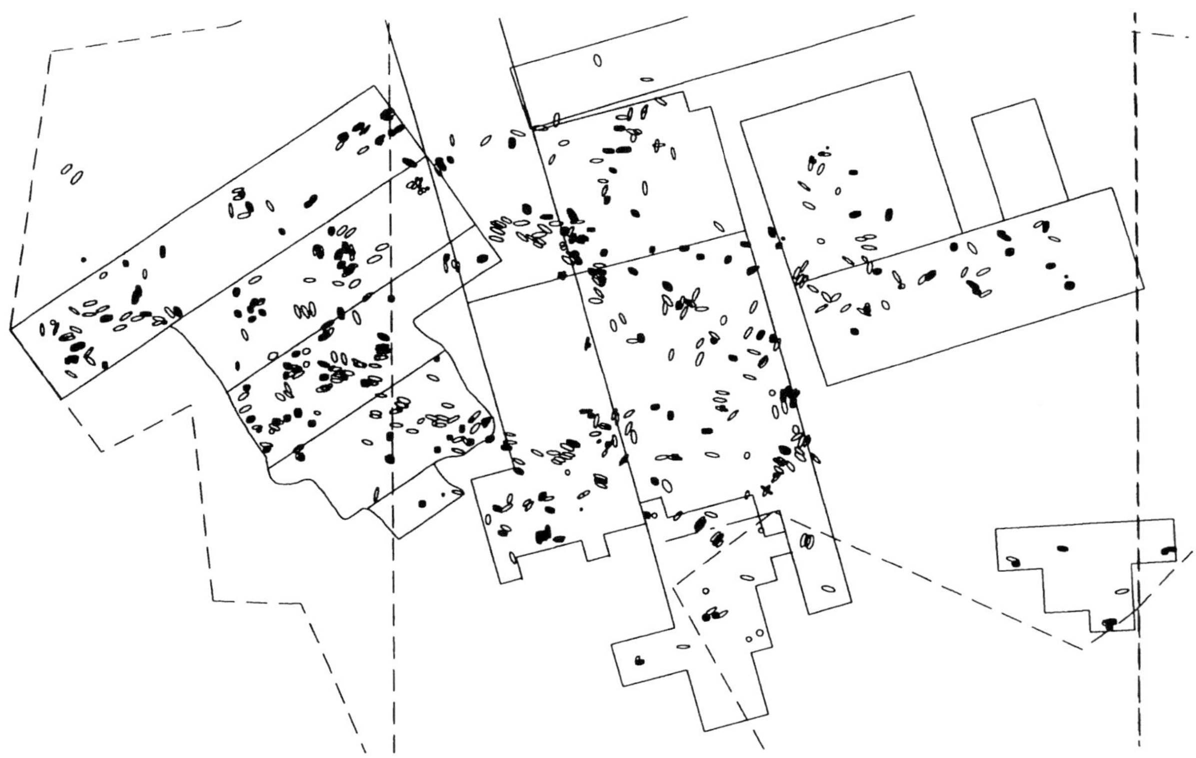

Figure 7-15. Distribution of identified subadults, Trenches 1-K.

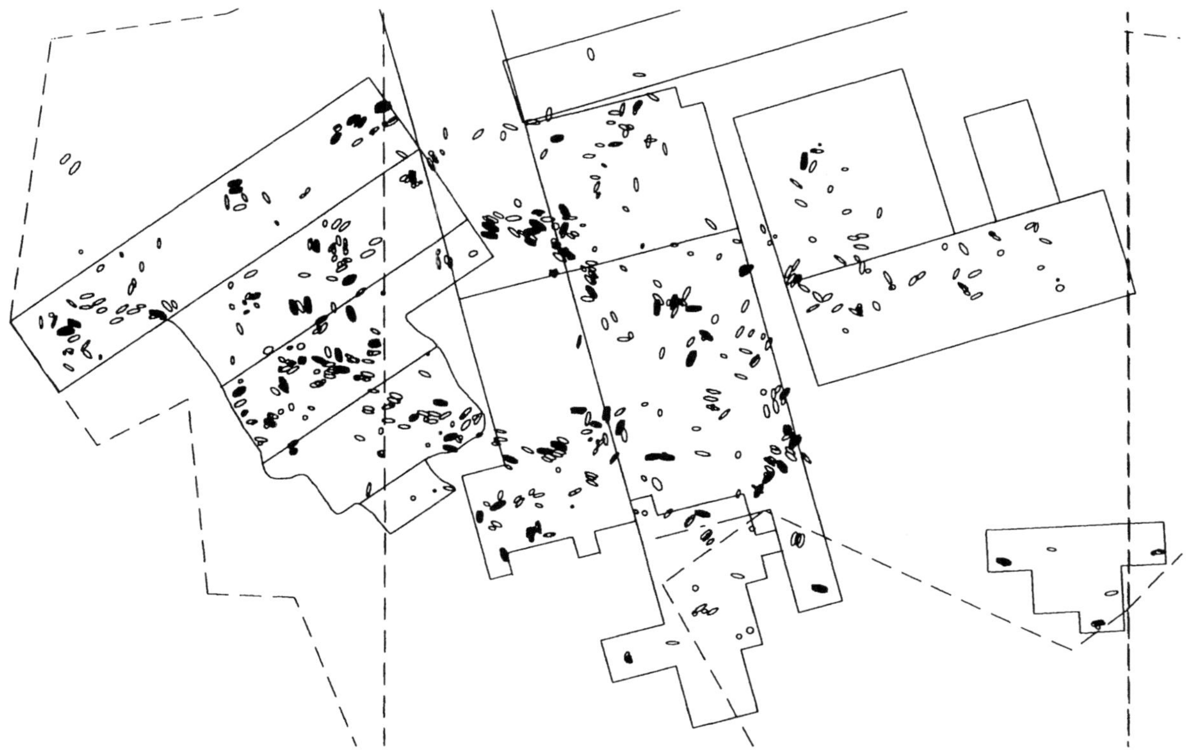

Figure 7-16. Distribution of identified males and probable males, Trenches 1-K.

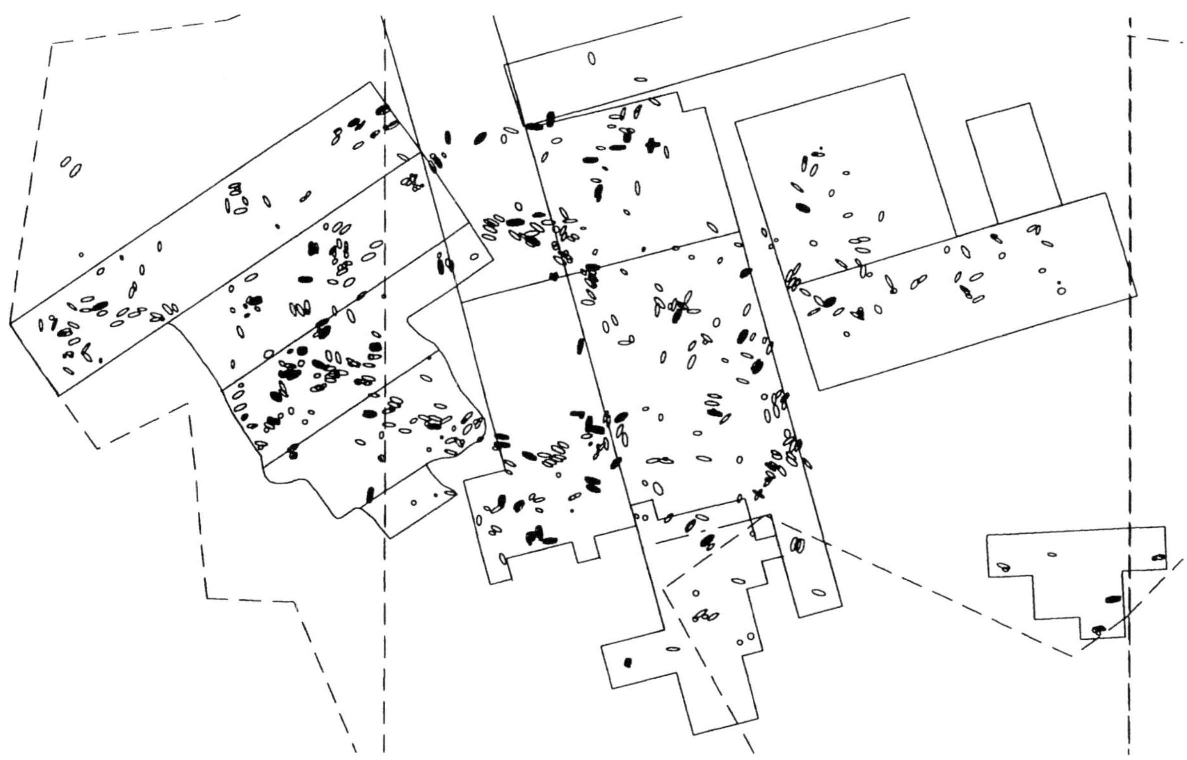

Figure 7-17. Distribution of identified females and probable females, Trenches 1-K.

more apparent than real. The three near-plaza burial groups discussed in Chapter 6 (Figure 6-46) all included a range of ages and both sexes.

Normative burial attributes including individual graves (Figure 6-58, unhighlighted burials), extended and supine posture (Drooker 1996c: Fig. 7.15), and easterly head orientation (Drooker 1996c: Fig. 7.16) are pervasive across Trenches 1-K. The distributions of rare non-normative treatments such as graves lined with stone slabs (Figure 6-4) and flexed and semi-flexed postures (Figure 6-5) that probably are typical of earlier time periods have been discussed in Chapter 6.

Human remains found in refuse pits that excavators recognized as "burials" are mapped in Figure 7-18. A wide variety of body treatments are represented—articulated and disarticulated, flexed, sitting, and extended—so they probably do not represent a single type. With the exception of two multiple interments in Trench E (Burials 9 through 14, 23, and 23A), at least one of which probably was ceremonial (see Chapter 6), these dispositions are not close to the plaza's edge. Quite a few of them are in or close to the midden areas that filled ravines (cf. Figure 5-7). Individual human bones also were reported from at least 20 other pits in Trenches 1, 2, 4, B, C, and G.

Disarticulated burials are scattered across Trenches 1-K, both close to and distant from the central plaza (Figure 6-57). The densest groupings coincide with some of the relatively dense burial groups, such as Burial Groups 2 and 6 north and south of the plaza (Figure 6-46). There does not appear to be any significant spatial separation of adult versus subadult disarticulated remains.

Multiple burials (Figure 6-58) occur in most portions of Trenches 1-K. Individuals with associated subsidiary burials (Figure 7-19) are concentrated in and around the northeastern end of Trench 1, the center and western end of Trench 2, and the southern ends of Trenches B and D. This is a significant adult marker (Figure 7-12), with male primary burials averaging larger numbers of associated subsidiary burials than female primary burials. Primary burials with three or more subsidiaries were fairly evenly disposed around the plaza, no two of them in close association. Almost all were some distance from the plaza edge and associated with additional burials (Figure 7-19). If lineages occupied separate areas on the site, each of these people likely would be associated with a different lineage.

Grave Goods. As discussed in Chapter 6, some types of grave goods exhibited distribution patterns probably at least partially tied to change in site use over time. These included ceramic containers (Figures 6-10, 6-15, 6-39), perhaps shell spoons (Figure 6-51), metal and European goods (Figure 6-40; see also Figures 6-41, 6-42), perhaps shell ornaments (Figure 6-43), and grave goods *per se* (Figure 6-8). The distribution patterns of many of these items undoubtedly have social dimensions as well. The following paragraphs examine the distributions of individual artifact functional types deposited as grave goods in Trenches 1-K, as well as crosscutting characteristics possibly indicative of wealth or status, including exotic grave goods, numbers of items, of exotic items, and of functional types per burial, and grave goods that were special in terms of size or decoration.

Ceramic vessels are most common close to the plaza (Figure 6-10). This is by far the largest extant class of grave goods, the only one large enough to consider the possibility of a correlation between decorative attributes and socially recognized groups such as lineages, clans, or moieties, as has been postulated for the Early-Middle Fort Ancient Incinerator and Gartner sites (Heilman 1988; Mills 1904:35; Robertson 1984). As discussed in Chapter 6, smooth-rimmed (Figure 6-49) versus notched-rimmed (Figure 6-50) pots probably are time-related attributes, as are trends in surface treatments (plain, cord-marked, grooved-paddled, net-impressed), and handle shapes and numbers.

For possible nontemporal patterns, I looked at distributions of shoulder marking (plain, notched/punctated), lip-notching patterns (entire rim, over handles, between handles), and special, rare decorative attributes. Pots with and without shoulder decoration largely overlap on the site, with the latter far more numerous than the former. Lip notching does give some indication of a dichotomous spatial pattern. Lips known to be completely notched ($n = 35$) show no particular clustering, but lips known to have been notched only over handles ($n = 16$) and lips known to have been notched only between handles ($n = 11$) were excavated mainly on the east and west sides of the site, respectively (Drooker 1996c: Fig. 7.19). Each of the two groups with these pots includes subadults and adults, males and females, in proportions roughly similar to the population at large, so they might represent some sort of horizontal dual division. However, since spaced notching is present on so few extant pots, and since many mortuary vessels no longer are extant, this idea cannot be more than a suggestion. Only five effigy pots are known to have been used as mortuary vessels in Trenches 1-K. All were with burials to the east of the plaza area, the head pot (Figure 4-14) with Burial D-64, a young adult female, and four jars with lizardlike appliqué (including those in Griffin 1943: Pls. LXIX.1 and LXIX.3) with Burials C-12, D-41, D-87, and F-11, an adult, a subadult, a child, and a young adult. The one vertical compound pot known to have accompanied a burial in Trenches 1-K (Figure 4-12) was with Burial 2-17, a young adult male. At least one more vertical compound vessel, three more lizard pots, and a pedestaled pot can be provenienced with particular burials excavated between 1879 and 1882: Burials 1-10 (small child), 6-33, 7-1, and 22-5 (two adults reported as female and one probable adult), and 1-283 (an adult reported as male), respectively (cf. Griffin 1943: Pls. LXIII.3, LXVI.1, LXVI.3, LXVI.4, LXIX.2). With special vessels outside of Trenches 1-K, there was no apparent spatial pattern.

I also examined pot location relative to body: at head (by far the most common placement, e.g., Figure 7-1) versus below shoulders, at left side versus right side, and smaller-scale variations. There do seem to be some spatial differences between right-side and left-side placement (Drooker 1996c: Figs. 7.20, 7.21), with left less common than right along the northeastern

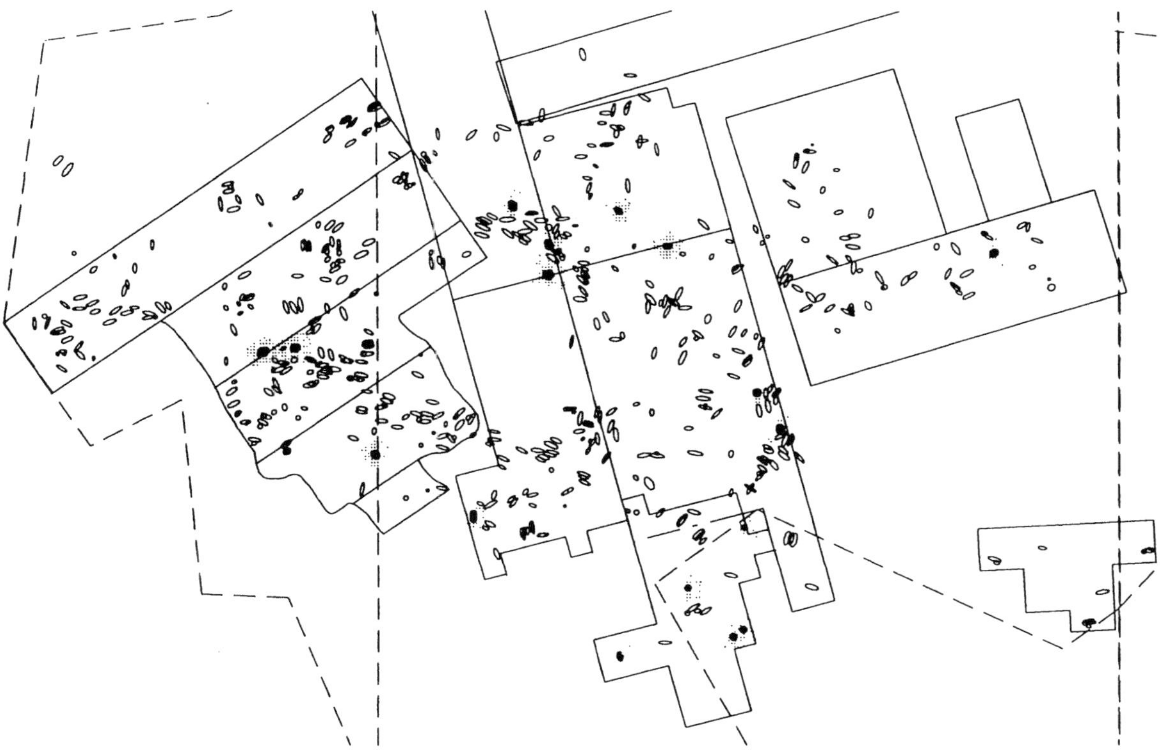

Figure 7-18. Distribution of burials in refuse pits, Trenches 1-K.

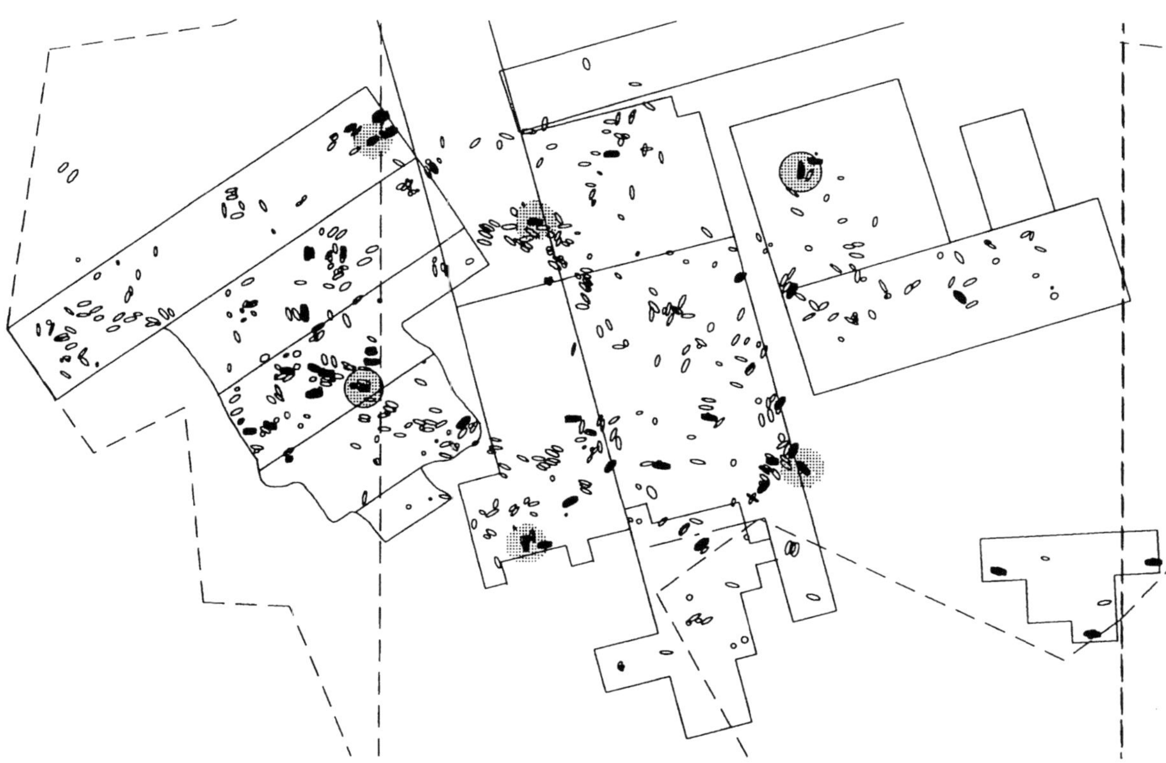

Figure 7-19. Distribution of burials with associated subsidiary burials, Trenches 1-K. Those with three or more subsidiary burials are highlighted, with circles around those with four or five.

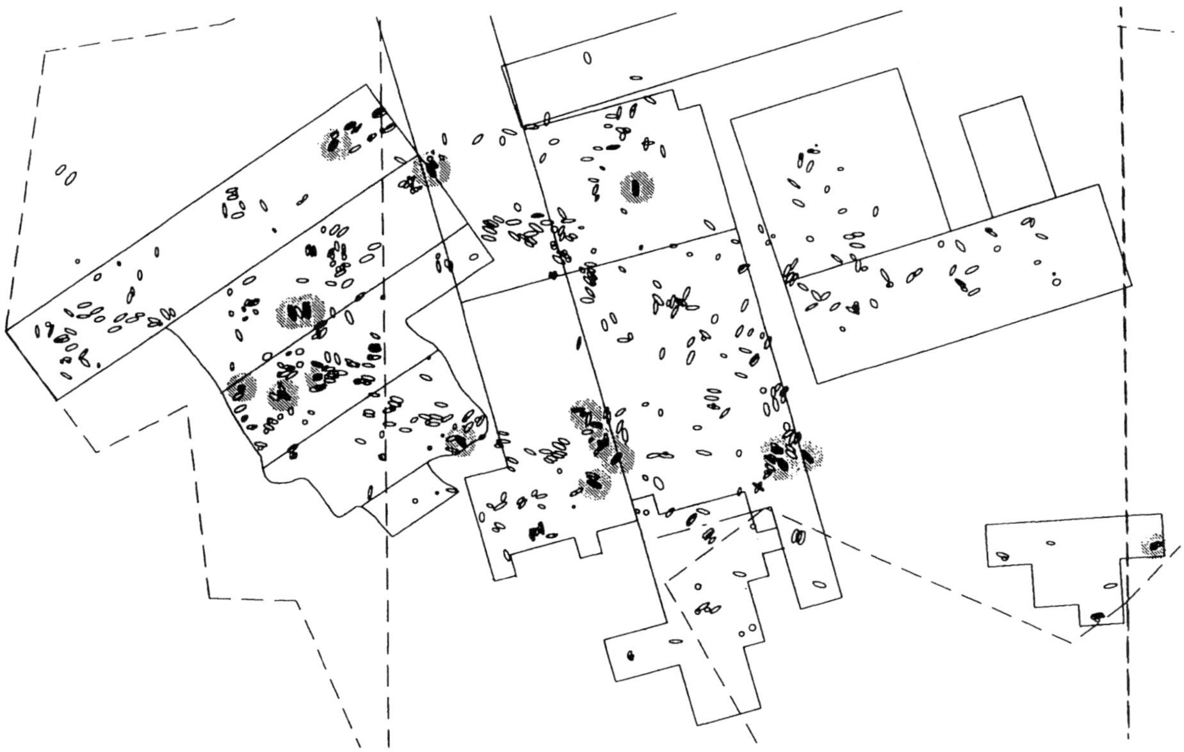

Figure 7-20. Distribution of burials with charms, Trenches 1-K.

edge of the plaza and more common in Trenches H and I, and also concentrated in some small burial groups such as the south end of Trench B. However, there is no clear-cut spatial dichotomy, nor are there any large-scale exclusive groupings.

Burials with non-pottery grave goods are found across most of the site, but are sparser to the north and east of the plaza area (Figure 6-6). They accompany few burials right at the edge of the plaza in that area of the site.

Burials with ornaments ring the plaza area, but very few of them are found near its edge. Metal ornaments were widely spaced, occurring with burials in most parts of the site except along the northeastern edge of the plaza and in Trench K and most of Trench H (Figure 6-40). European items were found with burials generally at the far west and far east of the site (Figure 6-41). Blue glass beads were found with Burials 1-39 and I-12, at the far northwestern and northeastern edges of the site. Shell ornaments were interred with burials in most excavation trenches except H, I, and J (Figure 6-43). They are not particularly common close to the plaza, but are least concentrated to its east. Bone/antler ornaments, found with only eight burials in Trenches 1-K, were concentrated to the west and south of the plaza, away from its edge.

Charms of various sorts were recognized with burials mostly in the west and south of the site, back from the plaza edge (Figure 7-20). Only one burial northeast of the plaza (F-23) included charms. It should be noted that many of the artifacts categorized as ornaments because they incorporated holes or other means of suspension probably also functioned as charms, so this distribution is incomplete.

Projectile points were concentrated in an arc from the northeast end of Trench 1, around the southern part of the site to the southeast portion of Trench D (Figure 6-56). Only one was found with a burial anywhere close to the northeastern edge of the plaza. The five people who definitely had suffered injuries (points embedded in bone) were not concentrated in any one area, but those who were buried with caches of six or more points (Burials B-45, B-49, and D-32, including a young adult, a child, and an older adult male) were confined to the southern ends of Trenches B and D.

Tools were found with burials on the west and south sides of the site, and with two in Trench H (Figure 7-21). Few of these burials were close to the plaza edge, so tools as mortuary offerings might be more strongly associated with later than with earlier burials.

The distribution of pipes has been discussed in Chapter 6. They were found with burials in the west, the south and the northeast of Trenches 1-K (Figure 6-52). The majority of them in Trenches 1-K were located along an east-west line at the south side of this part of the site. However, the four burials with pipes in the northern portion of this part of the site included the two largest pipes (Burials I-9 and I-19), one of only two burials with two pipes (I-19), the only burial with both pipe and bird/animal

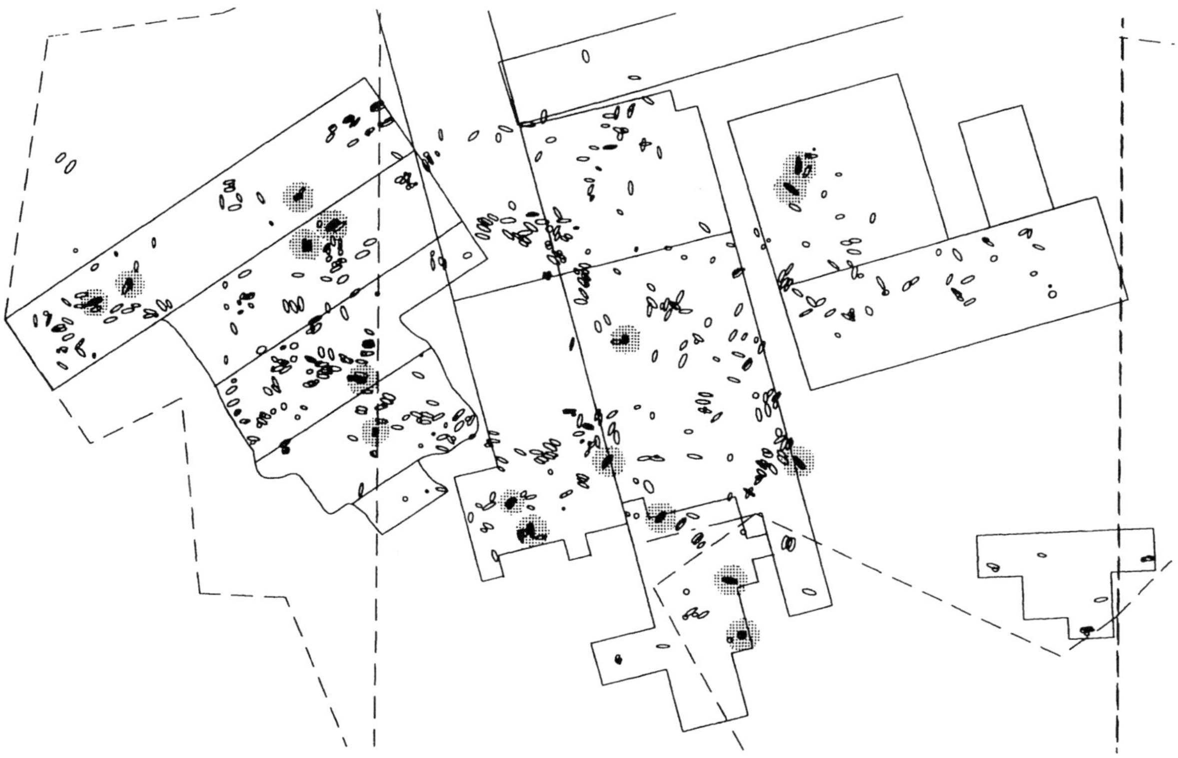

Figure 7-21. Distribution of burials with tools, Trenches 1-K.

Figure 7-22. Distribution of burials with animal or bird skulls, Trenches 1-K. (Burial B-38 might have had a bird rather than an animal skull; reports were conflicting.)

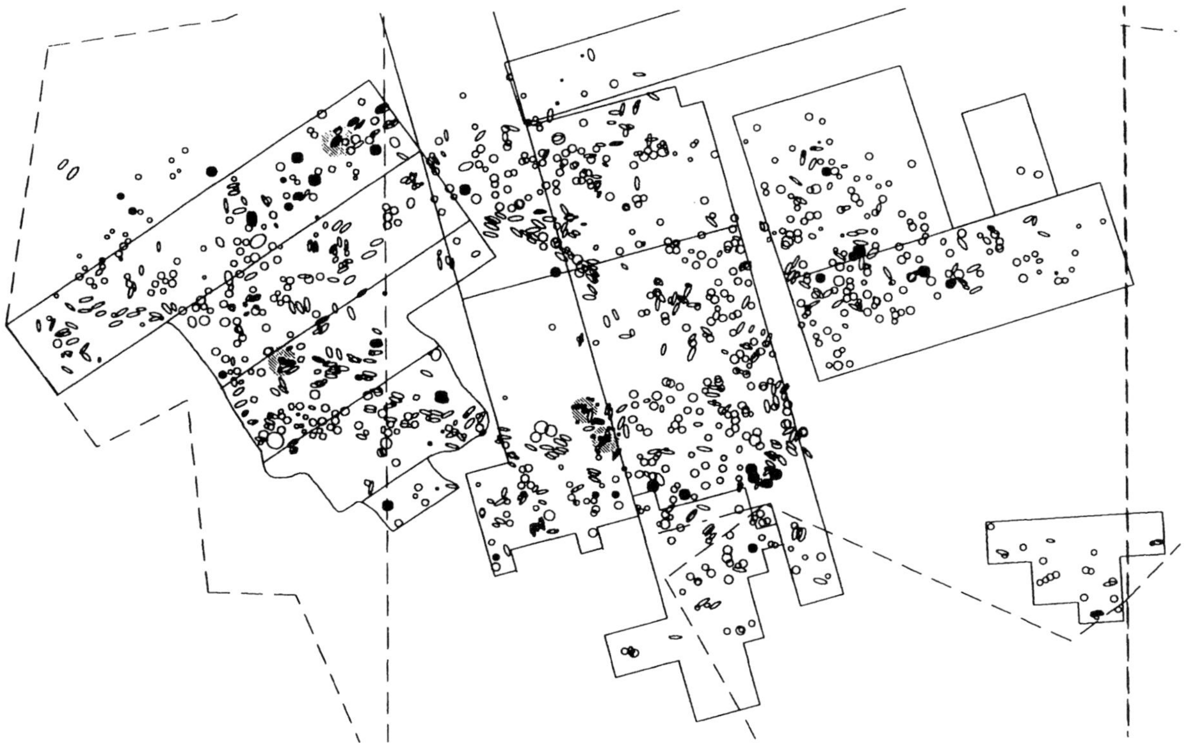

Figure 7-23. Distribution of burials and pits containing red ochre, Trenches 1-K. Burials are highlighted.

skull (H-1), and the only three burials with pipes that also contained three or more artifact functional types (Burials H-1 and I-19 with four, and 2-21 with five). Compared to other people buried with pipes, the social personae associated with these four individuals have the earmarks of higher status.

Burials with reported animal and bird skulls were most common at the northeastern end of Trenches 1-3 and the southern portion of Trench B (Figure 7-22). The three burials in the former location were the only ones with multiple skulls. As with pipe occurrences, assemblages with aspects of higher status—larger numbers of skulls, larger numbers of artifact functional categories—were far more common for individuals with "medicine bags" who were buried in the north than in the south of Trenches 1-K (see Table 7-18, below).

Red ochre was noted with only four burials, so could not be considered a separate type of mortuary offering. However, its distribution in both burials and pits (Figure 7-23) is worth looking at, always remembering that a very large proportion of artifacts excavated from pits were not retained (Table 5-5). Occurrences of red ochre with burials included large lumps in a unio shell valve (Burial 1-45, a young adult male), stains in a mortuary vessel (Burial 3-10, a subadult), and stains on human bones (Burials B-30 and B-56, adult and subadult). Known locations occur in clusters along a broad arc around the west, south, and east of Trenches 1-K.

Exotic grave goods (mostly metal and marine shell ornaments) are widely dispersed about Trenches 1-K, with no remarkable clusters (Figure 7-24). However, burials with large numbers of exotic items—a potential indicator of wealth—are not so evenly distributed. Small clusters occur, for example, in Trench F, in Trenches 3 and 4, and near the northeastern end of Trench 1.

Burials containing large, unique, or decorated items—potential indicators of wealth or status, depending on their numbers and total assemblages—almost completely circled the plaza area, but generally were not located close to its edge (Figure 7-25). Decorated artifacts of antler, bone, clay, shell, and metal were most common on the east side of Trenches 1-K, although several were concentrated together at the west end of Trenches 2 and 3. Large/important artifacts were most common on the west side of this part of the site (with one tight grouping at the northeastern end of Trenches 1 and 2), but the largest pipe and the largest metal pendant occurred in Trench I. Burials with both decorated and large/important artifacts were fairly evenly spaced around the site, but somewhat more concentrated at the west end of Trenches 2 and 3 and less concentrated directly north of the plaza. There are almost no duplicates among these items, so their spatial distributions would not have been correlated with any one social identity.

Diverse grave good assemblages—possible indicators of achieved status—were found with burials in many parts of Trenches 1-K (Figure 7-26), with concentrations to the south of the plaza in and around the southern end of Trench B, to the west of the plaza in Trenches 2 and 3, to the north of the plaza in Trenches E and F, and to the northeast in Trenches H and I.

Figure 7-24. Distribution of burials with exotic artifacts, Trenches 1-K.

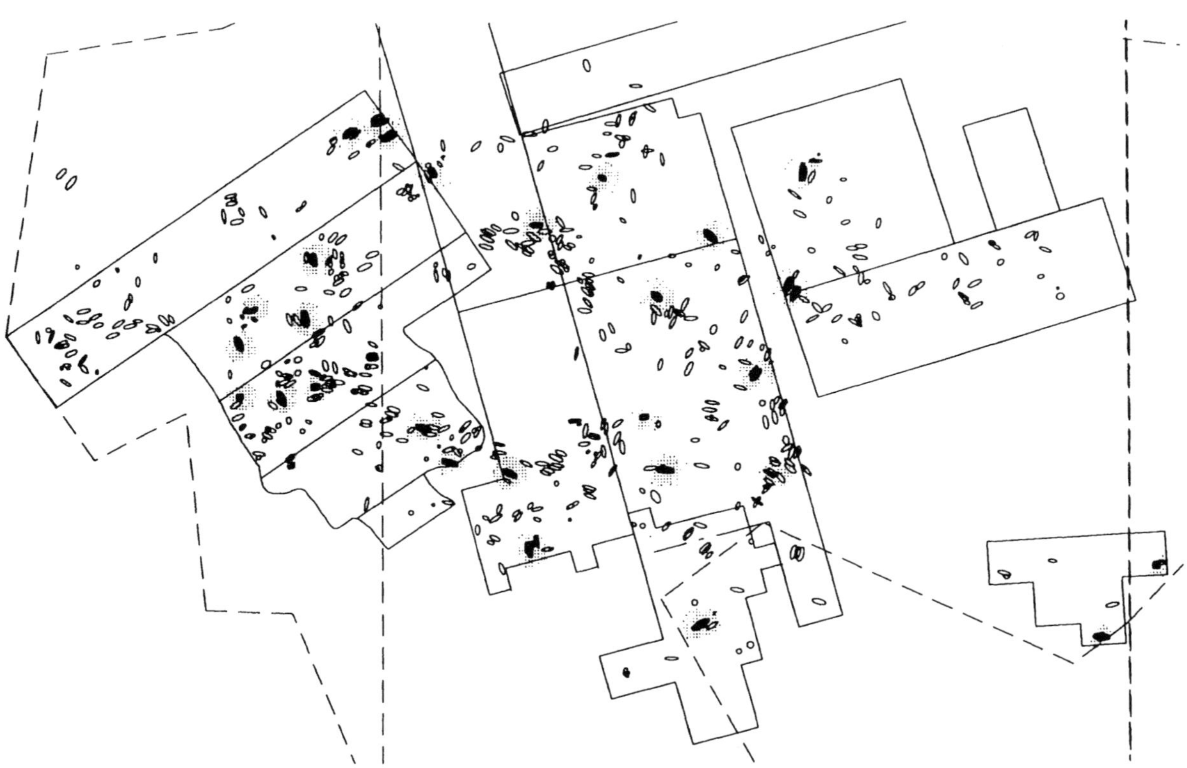

Figure 7-25. Distribution of burials with decorated or large/important artifacts, Trenches 1-K.

Figure 7-26. Distribution of burials with diverse artifact assemblages, Trenches 1-K.

Assemblages of highest diversity (four or five functional types), few of which were with subadults, were located within at least four different spatially separated burial groups. At least some of these individuals might be associated with lineage or clan leadership roles.

The distributions of recognizable representations ("effigies") were examined for possible clues to clan or moiety spatial patterns (Table 7-13). This effort was hindered by the absence of important perishable items such as feathers, and by the fact that few examples could be identified at a lower level than animal (mammal), bird, or reptile. Even then, an emic correlation solely with sky, land, or water could not be assumed; for example, otters and snakes inhabit both land and water, and water birds are at home in both sky and water. Bird, reptile, and animal representations partially overlapped in Trenches 1-K, with birds not found in the southeast, non-humanoid mammals not found in the northeast, and reptiles not found in the northwest (Figure 7-27). No clear earth-sky spatial dichotomies could be recognized.

It is of interest that no important grave goods with ties to large mammals were noted in Trenches 1-K, such as the bear tooth necklaces worn by Bear Clan members among historically known Central Algonquian groups. (Of groups with historically recorded clan names [Table 7-4], only the Miami are not known to have incorporated a Bear Clan.) Actually, there were few exclusively land-dwelling mammals represented—water and sky, rather than land and sky, were the large-scale categories most in evidence. The remainder of the site was slightly more productive of large mammal-related grave goods, including bear and deer (Table 7-13).

As can be seen from the maps of single artifact categories, the area north of the plaza in Trenches E, F, and D appears to have been deficient in many types of grave goods (cf. Figure 6-13), including metal and bone ornaments, projectile points, pipes, and tools. It was also deficient in large/unique grave goods, and in group burials that included primaries and subsidiaries (Figure 7-19). Only ceramic vessels (Figure 6-10) and, to a lesser extent, shell ornaments (Figure 6-43) were relatively common. Vessels most often were placed on the right side of the body (Drooker 1996c: Fig. 7.20). Burials with high numbers of exotic grave goods and one with animal skulls (a possible shaman or ritual specialist) did occur in this area (Figures 7-24 and 7-22), but the lack of pipes (a male marker), projectile points (related to hunting and war), and red ochre (a color related to war) raise the possibility that people buried in this portion of the site did not include war leaders. Either an ascribed peace-war dual division or ascribed and separate clan/subgroup responsibilities related to war, civil leadership, and shamanistic ritual (found historically among Central Algonquian groups) would be congruent with spatial patterns of this sort.

TABLE 7-13
Gravegoods with Recognizable Representational Aspects (Effigies)

Trenches 1-K	Excavation Blocks 1-17 and Southwestern Part of Site	Remainder of Site
ANIMAL (MAMMAL) Small animal skulls/medicine bags, including identified otter and marten/sable (with burials 1-21, 1-61, B-44, B-54, C-8, D-11, E-19) [a] Claw, bear (1-17) Claw, animal (2-17)	ANIMAL (MAMMAL) Small animal skulls/medicine bags (??) [b] Cannel coal pendant, bear-shaped (CN-14) Deer horn tip necklace (1-127) Pipe - animal head (8-12) Pipe - bear? head (1-297)	ANIMAL (MAMMAL) Deer tooth, perforated (1895 excavations, Burial 14)
BIRD Bird skulls or beaks/medicine bags, including identified raven (2-17, E-32, H-1) [a] Bird wing bones (probably deposited as wings) (F-23) Beads, very large tubular - bird bone, engraved with forked eye motifs (2-21) Deformed antler, engraved to represent bird (3-16) Pipe - probably bird claw (but perhaps animal claw) (I-19) Pipe - engraved with possible feather representations (I-19) Pipe - owl effigy (I-9) Pipe - two-headed swan/goose effigy (4-19) Whistle, made from bird bone (E-32)	BIRD Beads, very large tubular - probably bird bone (1-1, 1-98, 1-272, 1-280) Pipes - engraved with forked eye and related motifs (1 - 43, 1-108)	BIRD Brass pendant, barred - perhaps representing bird tail (1882 excavations) Pipe - probably bird claw (but perhaps animal claw) (22-5) Pipe - eagle (M-25) Pipe - owl (1895 excavations, Burial 45)
REPTILE/FISH Comb, carved with rattlesnake (B-11) Jars with lizard-like appliques or handles (C-12, D-41, D-87, F-11) Pendant, copper, two cross bars (probably represents rattlesnake tail) (I-19) Pipe - engraved turtle and lizard, smoothed over and over-engraved with unidentifiable motif (H-1) Pipe - snake plus humanoid face (B-33) Turtle bone (4-29)	REPTILE/FISH Tortoise shell carapaces, probably rattles (3-15, 3-17) Jars with lizard-like appliques or handles (6-33, 7-1) Pendant, copper, two cross bars (probably represents rattlesnake tail) (1-297)	REPTILE/FISH Copper tubular serpents (1882 excavations, 1895 excavations Burial 45) Jar with "lizard" appliques or handles (22-5)
HUMANOID Cut deer tibia, engraved with figure of man (3-4) Individual human bones in patterned arrangement (H-1) Jar - "face pot" (D-64) Pipe - humanoid face plus snake (B-33) Shell ornament - engraved maskette (1-61)	HUMANOID Jar with humanoid face on top of handle (4-1) Pipe - engraved with stylized face (6-26) Shell ornament - engraved maskette (6-16)	

[a] One probable medicine bag, with Burial B-38, was described in different records as a bird skull and as an animal skull and bones, so could not be categorized.
[b] Animal and bird skulls were not noted as gravegoods by excavators outside of Trenches 1-K, but it is unlikely that that they were entirely absent.

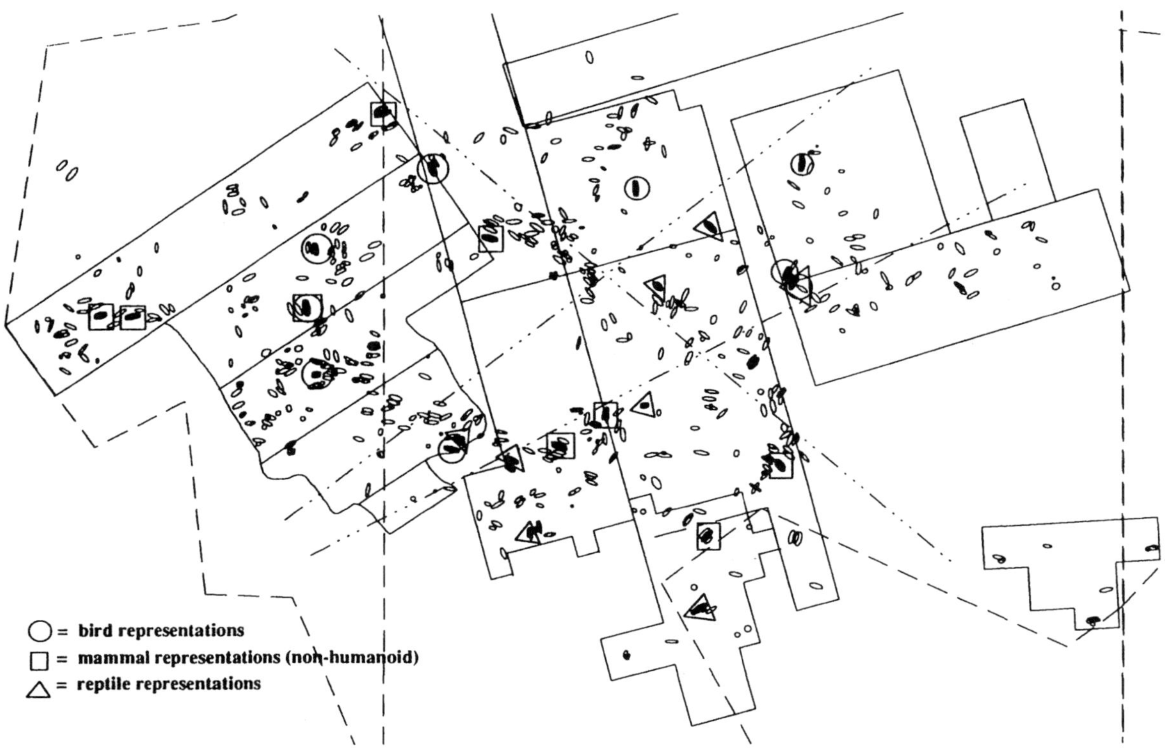

Figure 7-27. Distribution of burials with artifacts having recognizable representational decoration or form (effigies), Trenches 1-K.

Multivariate Clustering of Mortuary Attributes

The initial exploratory data analysis and spatial analysis procedures generated a great deal of useful information. They also reinforced my growing awareness that available mortuary data sets were sparse and incomplete, yielding the most useful results when examined from many different analytical directions. K-means cluster analysis, followed by demographic and spatial analysis of cluster group members, was employed to further explore covariation among mortuary attributes, that is, to see what artifacts and attributes tended to occur together with individuals, and what individuals might be grouped together on the basis of similar grave goods and burial treatments.

Burials in Trenches 1-K. Using burials within Trenches 1-K, a series of runs was carried out with different sets of attributes and numbers of cluster groups (Drooker 1996c:318-40). Some used attributes of grave goods and of body treatments, and others included only grave good characteristics. None of them can be taken to reveal "the social organization" at Madisonville, but they did provide additional insight into a variety of aspects of social relations. Here, I will briefly describe the results of a run designed to highlight individuals of wealth and status, some of whom might have served in leadership roles. For baseline comparisons see Table 7-14, which contains summaries of demographic and mortuary assemblage characteristics for the entire Trench 1-K population.

This cluster analysis was carried out on all burials with mortuary associations (grave goods and associated subsidiary burials), using presence/absence of all functional categories of artifacts (ceramic vessels, metal ornaments, shell ornaments, bone ornaments, projectile points, tools, charms, animal and bird skulls, pipes, subsidiary burials, and the two categories of grave goods of unknown function), and large/unique artifacts, decorated artifacts, more than two subsidiary burials, more than ten grave goods, more than ten exotic items, more than four artifact types, and more than three artifact functional categories. The use of crosscutting variables was designed to add emphasis to grave good assemblages reflecting wealth (via large numbers and complexity of artifacts) or status (via diversity and symbolic significance of artifacts), and to allow ranking of persons who appeared likely to have served in leadership roles.

Figure 7-28 and Table 7-15 show the results of a 15-cluster run, performed only on burials that had either grave goods or associated subsidiary burials. For completeness, they include, as cluster 16, all burials lacking mortuary associations. The cluster groups are ordered first by group size, then by average number of artifact function types, then by average number of artifact types. Because many categories of mortuary associations were included and individual burial assemblages were so idiosyncratic, upper-tier groups were far more fragmented than in cluster analyses employing fewer variables: half of the "clusters" consisted of only a single individual. There was one large

TABLE 7-14
Summary of Demographic and Mortuary Assemblage Characteristics for Trenches 1-K

	ENTIRE POPULATION			BURIALS WITH GRAVEGOODS AND/OR SUBSIDIARY BURIALS		
	Number	Percent of Total		Number	Percent of Total	
Unknown age	30	5.1%		7	2.8%	
Subadults	197	33.3%		75	30.1%	
Adults of unknown sex	227	38.4%		91	36.5%	
Identified females	62	10.5%		34	13.6%	
Identified males	75	12.7%		42	16.9%	
TOTAL	591	100.0%		249	99.9%	
Subadult : adult ratio			0.54			0.45
Female : male ratio			0.83			0.55
Single (not multiple) burials		67.3%			63.1%	
Extended and supine		71.5%			85.9%	
Articulated		75.0%			85.9%	
Any gravegoods		38.7%			92.0%	
Associated subsidiary burials		6.9%			16.1%	
Ceramic vessels		26.2%			61.8%	
Metal or glass (mostly ornaments)		5.8%			13.7%	
Shell ornaments		4.2%			10.0%	
Bone/antler ornaments		1.5%			3.6%	
Projectile points		4.4%			10.4%	
Tools		3.0%			7.2%	
Pipes		1.9%			4.4%	
Animal/bird skulls		1.9%			4.4%	
Charms		3.2%			7.6%	
Exotic artifacts		9.0%			21.3%	
Identified European artifacts		1.5%			3.6%	
Large/unique artifacts		2.5%			6.0%	
Decorated artifacts		3.4%			8.0%	
Representational artifacts		4.6%			10.8%	
More than 10 gravegoods		1.9%			4.4%	
More than 10 exotic gravegoods		1.4%			3.2%	
More than 4 artifact types		1.7%			4.0%	
More than 3 artifact functional types		2.0%			4.8%	
More than 2 subsidiary burials		1.0%			2.4%	
Average number of gravegoods			1.23			2.92
Average number of artifact types			0.67			1.49
Average number of artifact functional types			0.63			1.37
Average number of exotic artifacts			0.52			1.24
Average number of associated subsidiary burials			0.11			0.27

group with 168 members, four groups with fifteen to sixteen members, one each with seven and three members, and eight consisting of one person. At first inspection, group sizes do not appear to be congruent with those expected for dual divisions, clans, or ranked classes (cf. Tables 2-5 through 2-7). It is unlikely that any of these cluster groups represents a real social group, although several of the single individuals and people within small cluster groups probably filled leadership roles. It is notable (and expected from exploratory data analysis) that the ratios of subadults to adults and of females to males are both lower among burials with mortuary associations than in the population as a whole (Table 7-14).

The largest group in Figure 7-28, cluster 16, includes 342 burials with no reported mortuary associations. It represents 58% of all burials in Trenches 1-K. Age and sex distribution were similar to the Trench 1-K population as a whole. Although this fact, coupled with the lack of mortuary associations, raises the possibility that these burials represent the lower level of a ranked social system (cf. Table 2-7), the fact that these burials are competely interspersed on the site with burials that do have mortuary associations (Figure 7-29a) argues against any such interpretation. As discussed in Chapter 6, there may be a time-related element here, with both the earliest and some of the latest burials on the site having fewer grave goods. However, from the composition of many of the tightly-clustered small burial groups, it is clear that burials both with and without nonperish-

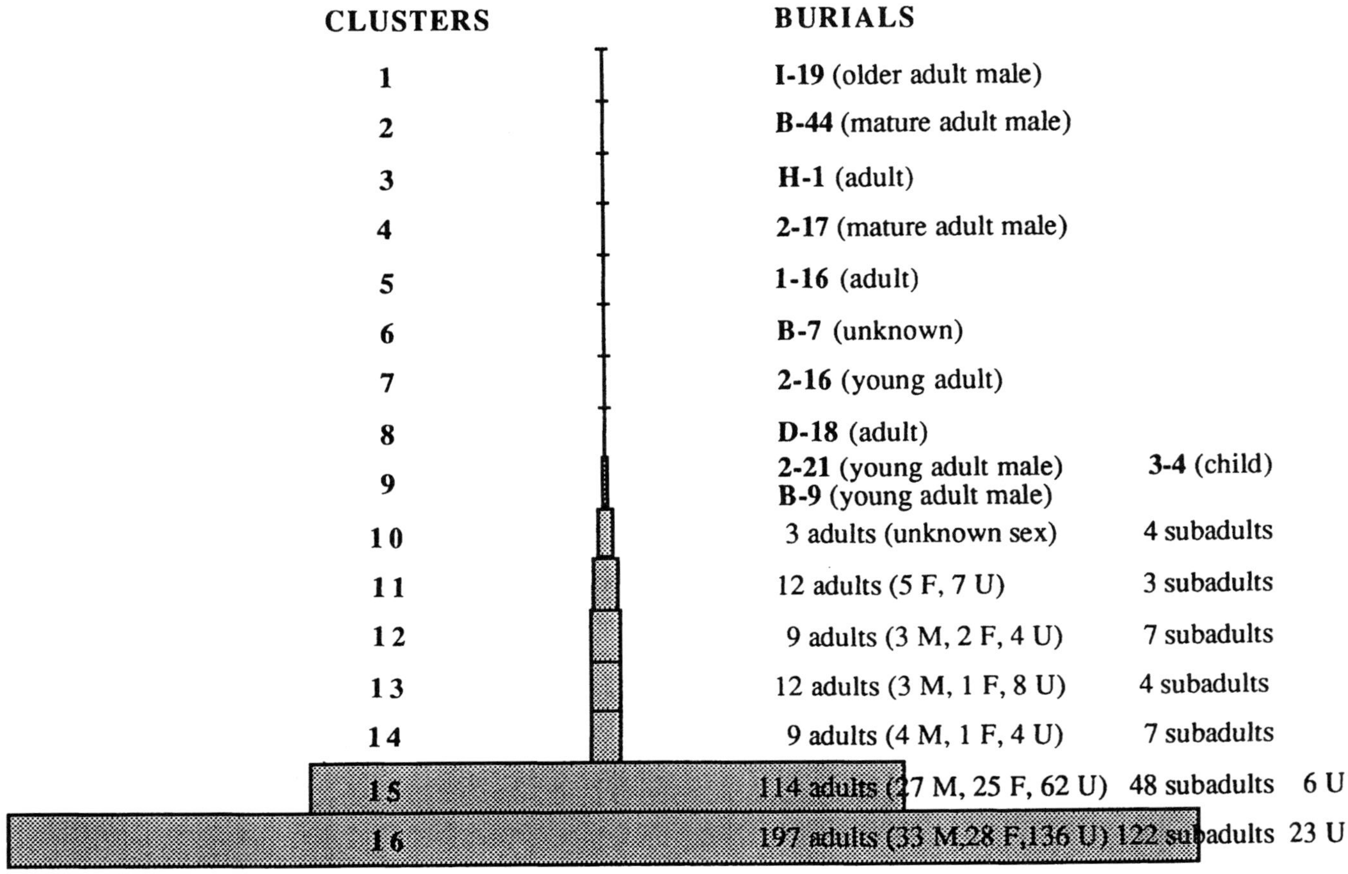

Figure 7-28. Group sizes and demographics from a K-means cluster analysis based on all functional categories of mortuary associations plus crosscutting indicators, Trenches 1-K (see Table 7-15).

able grave goods and subsidiary burials were being interred contemporaneously.

Cluster group 15, like group 16, includes age and sex distributions consistent with those of the general Trench 1-K population, although the ratios of females to males are considerably higher than in the entire population with mortuary associations (0.94 versus 0.55). Half the size of group 16, cluster group 15 includes people who had at least one mortuary offering (most of them no more than that), but there is no common attribute shared by all. There is a relatively high proportion of mortuary vessels (Table 7-15). Virtually no indicators of wealth or high status were present. Five people had animal/bird skulls (including the two youngest interred with "medicine bags," Burials B-38 and C-8), and two were buried with pipes. Three of the former (B-38, B-54, D-11) and one of the latter (D-4) also had a pot, putting them above the group norm for diversity. All seven were located in the southern portion of Trenches 1-K (Figure 7-29b). The spatial distribution of people in this cluster group reflects that of all burials with mortuary vessels (Figure 6-10), including lesser representation in the northeasterly portion of Trenches 1-K.

Most members of clusters 1 through 14 had multiple mortuary associations. Many of these clusters had unbalanced age or sex distributions (Table 7-15). Cluster 11 had a preponderance of females and no identified males. In cluster 12, the female-to-male ratio (0.67) was above that for all people with grave goods. Cluster groups 13 and 14 had very low female-to-male ratios, and no identified females occurred in groups 1 through 10 (although the unidentified individual in cluster 6 might perhaps be one). Subadults were very well represented in clusters 12 and 10, but do not appear to be associated with clusters 1 through 8 (but see discussion of cluster 6). Thus, there is a strong adult male association with the diverse grave good assemblages in the nine smallest clusters. The five largest of the small cluster groups (10-14) were examined to see whether they had any characteristics consistent with societies, age-grades, or other special statuses. Most of them showed no strong spatial clustering, and there were no clearly "opposed" group locations that might argue for inherited statuses.

The sixteen-member cluster 14, which included only one identified female and no people with animal/bird skulls, was characterized by decorated artifacts, but shared no one artifact type

TABLE 7-15
Summary of Demographic and Mortuary Assemblage Characteristics for Cluster Groups 1 - 16, Trenches 1-K

CLUSTER GROUP	16	15	14	13	12	11	10	9	8	7	6	5	4	3	2	1
Group size	342	168	16	16	16	15	7	3	1	1	1	1	1	1	1	1
Unknown age	6%	3%	-	-	-	-	-	-	**100%**	-	**100%**	-	-	-	-	-
Subadults	34%	29%	**44%**	25%	**44%**	20%	**57%**	33%	-	-	-	-	-	-	-	-
Adults of unknown sex	40%	37%	25%	50%	25%	47%	43%	-	-	**100%**	-	**100%**	-	**100%**	-	-
Identified females	9%	15%	6%	12.5%	**33%**	-	-	-	-	-	-	-	-	-	-	-
Identified males	10%	16%	**25%**	19%	19%	-	-	**67%**	-	-	-	-	**100%**	-	**100%**	**100%**
Subadult : adult ratio	.62	.42	.78	.33	.78	.25	1.33	.50	0	0	?	0	0	0	0	0
Female : male ratio	.85	.94	.25	.33	.67	high F	?	0	?	?	?	?	0	?	0	0
Any gravegoods	-															
Associated subsidiary burials	-	15%	13%	-	19%	20%	14%	33%	**100%**	-	-	-	**100%**	**100%**	-	**100%**
Ceramic vessels	-	**71%**	**69%**	6%	**56%**	**40%**	14%	**100%**	-	**100%**	**100%**	**100%**	**100%**	-	**100%**	-
Metal or glass (mostly ornaments)	-	4%	-	**75%**	19%	-	**71%**	33%	**100%**	**100%**	**100%**	**100%**	-	**100%**	**100%**	**100%**
Shell ornaments	-	-	-	-	**100%**	-	**86%**	33%	-		-	-	**100%**	**100%**	-	-
Bone/antler ornaments	-	1%	**13%**	-	-	-	-	**67%**	-	**100%**	-	**100%**	-	**100%**	-	-
Projectile points	-	10%	6%	**19%**	-	7%	14%	**100%**	-	-	-	-	-	-	-	-
Tools	-	-	-	-	-	**100%**	14%	-	**100%**	-	-	-	-	-	-	**100%**
Animal/bird skulls	-	1%	**31%**	-	-	-	-	**33%**	-	-	-	-	-	**100%**	-	**100%**
Pipes	-	2%	-	6%	**13%**	-	-	-	-	-	-	-	**100%**	**100%**	**100%**	-
Charms	-	2%	13%	**44%**	6%	7%	14%	33%	**100%**	-	-	-	**100%**	-	-	-
Unknown function (Category 1)	-	10%	-	6%	-	7%	-	33%	-	-	**100%**	-	-	-	-	-
Unknown function (Category 2)	-	4%	-	-	-	13%	14%	-	-	-	**100%**	-	-	-	**100%**	-
Large/unique artifacts	-	1%	**31%**	-	**31%**	-	14%	**100%**	-	-	-	-	-	-	-	**100%**
Decorated artifacts	-	-	**100%**	-	13%	-	-	**100%**	-	-	-	-	-	**100%**	-	**100%**
More than 10 gravegoods	-	-	-	-	-	-	**100%**	33%	**100%**	**100%**	-	-	-	-	**100%**	-
More than 10 exotic gravegoods	-	-	-	-	-	-	**100%**	-	**100%**	-	-	-	-	-	-	-
More than 4 artifact types	-	-	-	-	-	**20%**	14%	**67%**	-	-	-	-	-	-	**100%**	**100%**
More than 3 artifact functional types	-	-	-	-	-	-	-	**100%**	-	-	**100%**	**100%**	**100%**	**100%**	**100%**	**100%**
More than 3 subsidiary burials	-	1%	-	-	-	7%	-	**33%**	-	-	-	-	-	-	-	**100%**
Average number of artifact types	0	1.1	1.4	1.8	2.1	2.3	**3.3**	**4.7**	**3**	**4**	**4**	**4**	**4**	**4**	**5**	**5**
Average number of function types	0	1.1	1.4	1.6	1.9	1.7	2.3	**4.3**	**3**	**3**	**4**	**4**	**4**	**4**	**4**	**4**
WEALTH indicators significant	-	-	-	-	-	-	X	+	X	x	-	-	-	-	+	-
STATUS indicators significant	-	-	x	-	+	+	+	X	-	-				X	+	X

Boldfaced attributes were present in notably higher frequency than in the total population of Trenches 1-K buried with gravegoods and/or subsidiary burials (cf. Table 7-14).
X, x, and + indicate, respectively, very high, moderately high, and moderate significance of status or wealth indicators for the group as a whole.

(Table 7-15). Mortuary vessel possession was slightly above the average for people with grave goods (cf. Table 7-14). There were high proportions of people with pipes (31%), bone ornaments (13%), and large/unique items (31%), but grave good numbers and diversity were low. Group members were spaced at fairly equal intervals around all sides of the plaza except the northwest (Figure 7-29c). Most were not right at the edge of the open area, but about one-third were close to it and oriented parallel to it. The one female identified (Burial D-64, a very young adult) was interred with the unique locally made face pot (Figure 4-14). The five people with pipes did not cluster together, although four of them were located south of the plaza area. Burial 3-9, a mature adult male, was one of only two burials with two pipes reported from the site, and also had a mortuary vessel and shell spoon; the pipes were a vasiform and an engraved keel-shape (Figure 7-5a). Burial D-25, an older adult male, had a vasiform pipe with notched edge (like a miniature Madisonville jar; Figure 7.2b), a pot, and a subadult subsidiary burial on his right. Burial 4-19, a young adult male, had a mortuary vessel and a pipe in the shape of a two-headed swan or goose (Figures 7-1, 7-5a). The two burials lacking additional grave goods possessed pipes of very high quality and interest (Figures 7-5b, 7-5c), including a carved human head with forked-eye decoration and encircling snake (with B-33, a mature adult male) and a very large perching owl fashioned of exotic pipestone (with Burial I-9, a young adult male, who also had part of a human jaw near the right shoulder). It is appropriate to correlate this cluster group with male status, but not with wealth.

Cluster 13, another group of sixteen, had both low female and low subadult representation (Table 7-15). Average numbers of grave goods (2.6 per person), artifact types, and artifact function categories were higher than in Cluster 14, but, in contrast, there were no decorated, large, or unique grave goods. There was no one artifact category common to all, but metal ornaments, projectile points, and charms were present in high proportions. The lack of subsidiary burials and dearth of pots contrasts with the similar-sized clusters 14, 12, and 11. Only one burial with a "medicine bag" (E-32, an older adult with three long-billed bird skulls, copper-stained animal or bird bones, and a bird-bone whistle) and none with pipes were included in the group. There was some spatial clustering among members of this group, with three people to the northwest of the plaza, three to the northeast, and the remainder to the south and east (Figure 7-29d).

The sixteen-member cluster 12 had high proportions of subadults, and there were two identified females (versus only one each in clusters 13 and 14). All members were buried with shell ornaments, and there were high proportions of subsidiary burials, pots, metal, animal skulls, and large/unique artifacts (Table 7-15; cf. Table 7-14). Both of the adults with animal/bird skulls, Burials 1-61 and E-19, had two of them, along with a variety of other associations (Burial 1-61, a young adult male, was interred with two or three disarticulated subsidiary burials, two animal skulls identified as otter and sable on his chest, and a marine shell maskette on his right shoulder, while E-19, a mature adult male, had a small pot, two small animal skulls, and shell beads, all to the left of his head). Between them in the northwestern segment of the site, a young adult female and child with a variety of grave goods, Burials E-29 (with two subsidiary burials, two pots, four shell beads, and copper-stained hair) and E-30 (with eight shell beads and a shell gorget), were adjacent to E-32 (of cluster group 13), another person with "medicine bags." Five burials were north of the plaza, with the remainder were in a band south of the plaza from the far west to the far east of this portion of the site (Figure 7-29e).

Cluster 11, with fifteen members, had the highest association with females of any group in this run (five identified, with no identified males). On average, members had more artifact types than members of the similar-sized clusters 12, 13, and 14 (Table 7-15). All had tools, and a high proportion had more than four artifact types. None were buried with exotic, decorated, or large/unique artifacts—that is, there was no association with wealth. The person in this group with the most diverse assemblage was Burial I-18, an older adult who had a bundlelike group of tools on the left humerus, including two flint scrapers, two whetstones, a celt, and a worked stone, plus a flint point under the pelvis. This skeleton was measured in the field as 72 inches. Although Burial I-18 was in Trench I, burials in cluster group 11 were most common in Trenches 1 and 2 and the area around Trench C and the southern portion of Trench B (Figure 7-29f). Few were in the dense cemetery areas near the plaza edge.

Cluster 10, with only seven members, had a very high ratio of subadults to adults, and none were older than their mid-twenties. Artifact assemblages were more diverse than those of previous groups. No artifact category was shared by all, but the majority had metal (71%) and shell (86%) ornaments. All cluster group members had more than ten grave goods and more than ten exotic items buried with them, which gives the group as a whole a definite association with wealth. Included in the cluster group was the very young adult (Burial 1-60, in the late teens) who had the largest numbers of artifacts and of exotic artifacts of anyone buried in Trenches 1-K, but only two artifact functional types: metal ornaments (including a leather belt with large copper clips around the thighs illustrated in Figure 6-21f, a brass and an iron bead, and three metal tinklers) and shell ornaments (at least one marginella shell and at least fifty shell beads "made from the inner whorls of univalves"). This was the only member of cluster group 10 interred with subsidiary burials: a partially disarticulated child at the feet and a subadult at the right side. Burial F-23, a young adult male with a bone projectile point in his knee, had three bird wing bones arranged on his pelvis and at his jaw, and wore at least 42 shell beads, 7 copper/brass beads, and a unique cone-shaped metal or metal-covered ornament (Figure 6-21a). At least three members of cluster 10 possessed European artifacts. However, one very early interment also was included: Burial F-10, a very young adult, was in a grave paved with limestone slabs, with a pit dug through the lower body and upper legs (Hooton and Willoughby 1920: Pl.

4a). Mortuary associations included a reportedly large number of shell beads probably in a necklace, an antler projectile point, and large pieces of cannel coal scattered in the grave. This was the richest early burial on the site. All but one of the cluster group members were north of the plaza, and none was close to it (Figure 7-29g).

Artifact assemblages and demographic characteristics of clusters 10-14 were too diverse to postulate coherent social groups. Each one had its own flavor, however, giving insight into types of artifact assemblages associated with fairly well-endowed people of differing ages and sexes. Of particular interest were high-tool assemblages associated with females in cluster 11, the high-wealth (but not high-status) assemblages associated with subadults and very young adults in cluster 10, and the status but not wealth associations of the male-dominated cluster 14. Neither the cluster with the highest male representation (cluster 14) nor the one with the highest female representation (cluster 11) included people with animal or bird skulls, yet cluster 14 had five members with pipes. The remaining nine cluster groups (mostly individuals) were characterized by diverse and varied grave good assemblages and a preponderance of adults and males. Their mortuary associations are summarized in Table 7-16.

The three people in cluster 9 included two young adult males and a child. As a group, they were characterized by higher grave good assemblage diversity than any but the two individuals in clusters 1 and 2 (Table 7-15). All had pots, projectile points, decorated artifacts, large/unique artifacts, and more than three functional categories of artifacts. The actual mortuary goods, however, differed considerably (Table 7-16). The young adults, Burials 2-21 and B-9, both were buried within very close, parallel family-sized groups at some distance from the plaza (Figures 5-13, 7-29h). The engraved bone beads with the former and the engraved bone armband and large metal legbands worn by the latter were among the most impressive ornaments from any burial. It is also of note that one of the subsidiary burials with B-9, Burial B-11, included a unique antler comb engraved with a carved rattlesnake (see Figures 6-18b, 7-4, and 7-32). The engraved deer tibia accompanying the child was among the most impressive non-ornamental mortuary offerings.

Although there is some element of wealth in the numbers and large sizes of the ornaments accompanying the adults in cluster group 9, status is even more strongly evident, but not necessarily the same status for all three members. A warrior status is possible for the two young men. Besides the projectile points with them, the forked eye motif of the bone beads is associated with warfare throughout the Southeast and Midwest (e.g., Brown 1985; Smith and Smith 1989), and the "X" prominent in the armband design (Hooton and Willoughby 1920: Pl. 17b) is a motif strongly associated with club heads found at the site.* The burials in cluster group 9 were not located close together, but all three were to the west or south of the plaza and at some distance from its edge (Figure 7-29h).

The individuals in "clusters" 1-8 were interred with comparatively large and highly varied mortuary assemblages (Table 7-16), which of course is why they were singled out by the clustering algorithm. Some assemblages are merely idiosyncratic, but others undoubtedly objectified important social identities (Table 2-4).

"Cluster" 8, Burial D-18, was an extremely unusual interment, unlike any other described from the site. It occupied a grave of the normal size and shape for an adult, but consisted of burnt and unburnt fragments of human bone from at least three individuals in a mass over a pair of undisturbed, unburned adult leg bones. The portion of the grave where the trunk and head associated with the legs should have been was empty. Scattered among the bone fragments were a variety of artifacts (Table 7-16).

Grave goods associated with burials in cluster groups 5, 6, and 7 (Table 7-16) were remarkable for their diversity, but do not appear to mark the status associated with leadership roles. Where age is known, these individuals were young, and they might have included one female (Burial B-7 is listed as of unknown age and sex because bones from at least three individuals, including a young adult female and an adolescent, are stored together under this label; either one might fit the description in the field notes, but the best fit probably is with the younger individual). Burial 2-17 ("cluster" 4), with important but not numerous mortuary associations, was adjacent to and almost parallel with Burial 2-16 from "cluster" 7, at the same depth.

The three adults in "clusters" 1-3 include Burial B-44, a mature adult male buried at the south edge of the plaza with "medicine bag," pot, and copper-covered wooden object, Burial H-1, the only person known to have been interred with both a "medicine bag" and a pipe, and Burial I-19, an older adult male with a very diverse grave goods assemblage and five subsidiary burials, the most with any individual on the site. The last-mentioned was one of only two men known to have possessed two pipes (the other being Burial 3-9, a mature adult male) and also one of only two men found with a large, double-barred copper pendant, an emblem badge with supralocal associations (see discussion below). Burials I-19 and H-1 were arguably the highest status burials in Trenches 1-K, while B-44 combined elements of modest wealth with moderate status, and also was set apart by non-normative burial treatment: his skull (like that of Burial D-11, who also was interred with an animal skull) was reported to have been crushed before burial, and his northwesterly orientation was opposite that of the adolescent buried about a foot away in the same grave, and to those of the surrounding burials.

---

*Of the seven extant decorated grooved club heads from Trenches 1-K, five were engraved with "X" or "+" on one or both ends, and one of these also was decorated with a thunderbird (Figure 6-17b; see also Hooton and Willoughby 1920: Pl. 10c). The other two decorated clubs had designs like feathers or flames strongly reminiscent of the bottoms of three-pronged forked-eye motifs. The X motifs also are engraved on some pipes—a male-associated artifact—from the site.

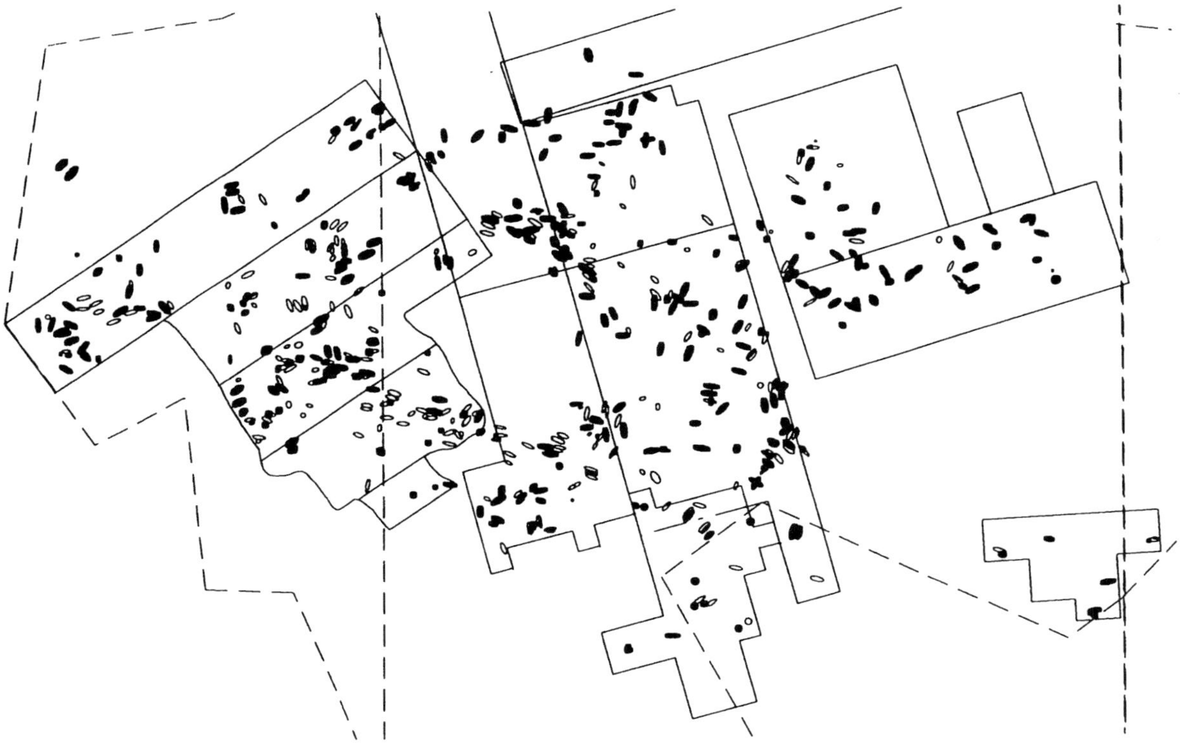

Figure 7-29a. Distribution of burials assigned to cluster analysis group 16, Trenches 1-K (see Figure 7-28, Table 7-15). Includes all burials with no grave goods or susidiary burials.

Figure 7-29b. Distribution of burials from cluster analysis group 15, Trenches 1-K (see Figure 7-28, Table 7-15).

Figure 7-29c. Distribution of burials from cluster analysis group 14, Trenches 1-K (see Figure 7-28, Table 7-15).

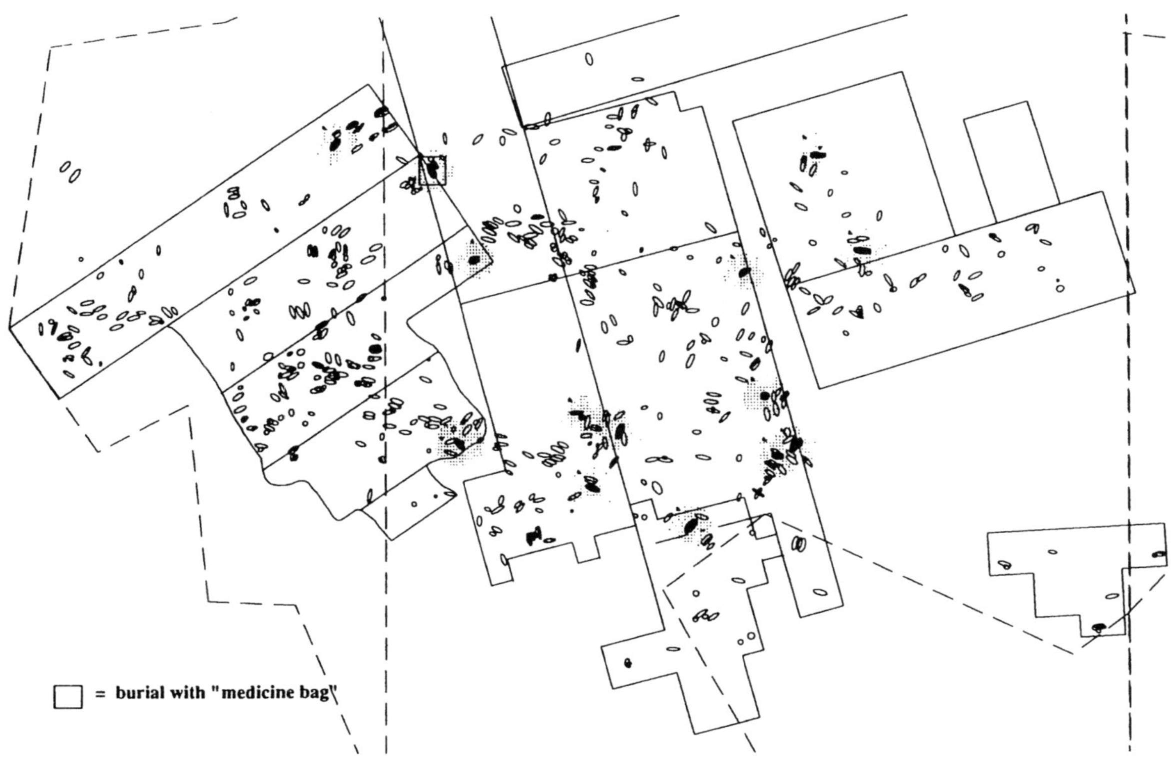

Figure 7-29d. Distribution of burials from cluster analysis group 13, Trenches 1-K (see Figure 7-28, Table 7-15).

Figure 7-29e. Distribution of burials from cluster analysis group 12, Trenches 1-K (see Figure 7-28, Table 7-15).

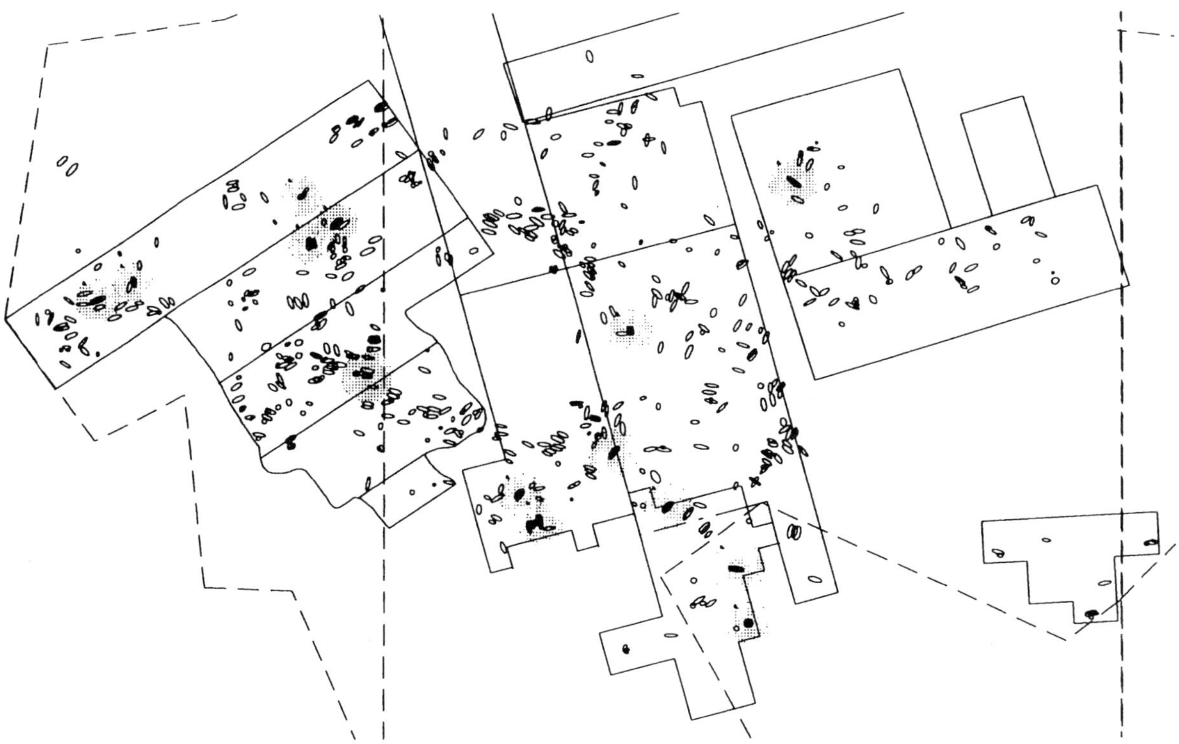

Figure 7-29f. Distribution of burials from cluster analysis group 11, Trenches 1-K (see Figure 7-28, Table 7-15).

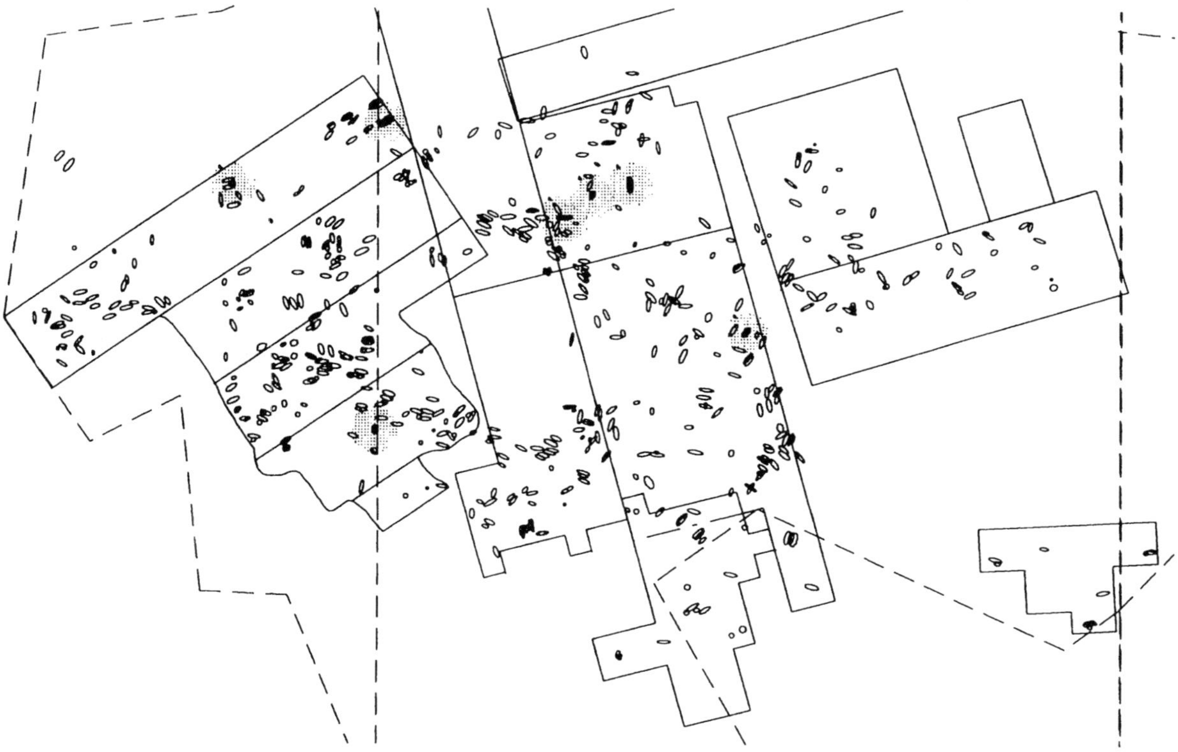

Figure 7-29g. Distribution of burials from cluster analysis group 10, Trenches 1-K (see Figure 7-28, Table 7-15).

Figure 7-29h. Distribution of burials from cluster analysis groups 1-9, Trenches 1-K (see Figure 7-28, Table 7-15). Dashed slanted lines indicate members of group 9. Individuals in "groups" 1-8 are highlighted with slanted lines.

TABLE 7-16
Mortuary Associations with Individuals in Cluster Groups 1-9, Trenches 1-K

Cluster Group	Burial	Age/ Sex	Associated Object(s)	Location	See Figure
1	I-19	OA-M	Large double-barred copper pendant	On left shoulder	6-21f
			Large claw-shaped stone pipe, crystalline rock	On right humerus	7-5d
			Globular pipe, red standstone, engraved with feather-like motifs and "+"	Above knees, among bones	7-5d
			Bone harpoon	Near left humerus	6-18a
			Flint knife or "spear point," large and fine (obsidian-like material)	At left knee	6-17a
			Flint projectile point	Embedded in frontal, betw. eyes	
			Flint projectile point	On ribs of right side	
			Subsidiary burial (I-20): disarticulated adult, MA-M	Near left foot	
			Subsidiary burial (I-21): disarticulated adult	Near right foot	
			Subsidiary burial (I-22): disarticulated child	Over leg, just below knee	
			Subsidiary burial (I-23): cranium, adult	At right of right knee	
			Subsidiary burial (I-24): disarticulated child	Cranium at right of right tibia	
2	B-44	MA-M	Ceramic jar	At left of head	
			Wooden object covered with sheet copper	With	(6-21a, for similar)
			Small animal skull and bones, copper-stained	Over left humerus	
			12 animal bones	Beside left hand	
			Copper staining	On left humerus, under animal skull	
			(In same grave with B-43, teenager, with head in opposite direction)		
3	H-1	A	Globular white limestone pipe, engraved w/turtle and lizard	In left hand	7-5d
			2 small pieces worked copper	In and under left hand	
			2 tubular bone beads	Near right elbow	
			Bird skull	Under right hand	
			Subsidiary burial (H-3): disarticulated young adult male - arm bones	On right and left sides of pelvis	
			- 5 other bones	Encircling head	
4	2-17	MA-M	Grooved paddled Madisonville vertical compound vessel, notched lip, 8 H	At right of head	4-12
			Shell ornament, eye-shaped, one hole	On ight shoulder	
			Bird beak, raven	Under right hand	
			Animal claw	Under right arm	
			Subsidiary burial (2-17A): partially disarticulated young adult female	Along and over left side	
5	1-16	A	Ceramic jar	At right of head	
			2 copper beads, in "armlet"	Upper left arm	
			Marginella shell, in "armlet"	Upper left arm	
			Small bone, in "armlet"	Upper left arm	
6	B-7	U	Cord-marked Madisonville vessel, notched lip, 4 handles	At head	
			Copper bead	At left of head	
			Fragments of small animal bones	Near lower jaw at back of skull	
			Small unio shell	In right hand	
			Small unio shell	Distal end right humerus	
			Flat natural stone	Distal end left humerus	
			Large natural stone	At left of head	
			(In double burial with B-6, mature adult,female, adjacent to and parallel with group that included B-9)		
7	2-16	YA	Cord-marked Madisonville jar	At left of head	
			2 copper beads, in string	Upper left arm	
			2 bone beads, in string	Upper right arm	
			2 copper beads, in 15" string,	Semi-circle over pelvis	
			2 bone beads, in 15" string,	Semi-circle over pelvis	
			Other small objects, in 15" string,	Semi-circle over pelvis	
8	D-18	A	12-13 copper beads	Among burnt bones	
			Natural stone, peculiar form	Among burnt bones	
			Worked antler (broken "shaft wrench")	Among burnt bones	
			Subsidiary burials: fragmented, burnt bones of 2 or 3 individuals (D-18A&B)	Over legs	

TABLE 7-16 (cont.)
Mortuary Associations with Individuals in Cluster Groups 1-9, Trenches 1-K

Cluster Group	Burial	Age/ Sex	Associated Object(s)	Location	See Figure
9	2-21	YA-M	Cord-marked Madisonville jar, notched lip, 4 handles	At right of head	
			Small-disc pipe, gray limestone	Betw. legs, claspedin both hands	7-5a
			10 large bird-bone beads, 7 engraved with forked eye motif, in 2 rows	From each side of mouth, running to arms and down them	6-18b
			Carved bead, shell or bone	Against mouth	
			Flint projectile point	With	
			(Buried in close group with 2-22, -23, -24, and -25, not ness. contemporaneous)		
9	B-9	YA-M	Ceramic vessel, unusual form, cord-marked, notched lip, 4 handles	To right of feet	7-4
			Shell spoon	In vessel	7-4
			Large copper or brass legbands (from staining on leg bones)	On lower right and left legs	
			Bone arm band, engraved	On upper right arm	6-18c, 7-4
			Bone arm band, plain	On upper left arm	7-4
			Flint point	Under right hand, on pelvis	
			Flint point	In pelvic cavity	
			Subsidiary burial (B-8): disarticulated mature adult female	At right leg	7-4
			Subsidiary burial (B-10; poorly-preserved infant	On left arm	7-4
			Subsidiary burial (B-11): disarticulated teenager, probably male	At left leg	7-4
9	3-4	Ch	Cord-marked Madisonville jar, notched lip, handles	At left leg, between thighs	
			Fragment of perforated shell	With	
			Cut deer tibia, engraved with picture of man wearing legbands	At right of head	
			2 worked antlers	With	
			Flint point, "reject"	With	

I=infant, Ch=child, T=teenager, MA=mature adult, OA=older adult, A=adult, age unknown, M=male, U=unknown age and sex
All 11 burials were extended and supine. None had any significant missing parts except D-18, where only the legs were present (see text). B-7 was somewhat disarranged. It is described as probably having been moved and crushed when B-1 and B-2 were buried above it.

Several of the eleven well-endowed burials in Clusters 1-9 probably were the remains of people who occupied positions of authority while living. However, there was no consistent, co-occurring, redundant set of artifacts or symbols that strongly signaled any particular status, or high status in general. The adults with the most diverse mortuary offerings (Burials I-19, H-1, B-9, B-44, 2-17, and 2-21) and with significant large, unique or decorated artifacts (Burials I-19, H-1, B-9, and 2-21) probably were recognized as high-status individuals, with the oldest among them (Burials I-19, 2-17, B-44, and perhaps H-1) the best candidates for leadership not associated with warfare. The three people with animal/bird skulls (2-17, B-44, H-1) probably functioned as important ritual specialists. Among them, Burial H-1, the only person with both "medicine bag" and pipe, who also was buried with very carefully arranged human bones, may have been particularly powerful. At least two of the young adults, Burials 2-21 and B-9, might have been prominent warriors. Burial I-19, the oldest male in the group, possessing five subsidiary burials, a healed war wound, extremely diverse and high-status (but not ostentatiously wealthy) grave goods, and one of only a few artifacts with supralocal symbolism from the site, is an excellent candidate for highest-level civil leadership.

These eleven diversely endowed burials were located to the west, south, and east of the plaza area (Figure 7-29h), with a few of them forming small spatial clusters. Burials 2-16, 2-17, and 2-21 not only were close together but all had heads oriented south and southeast (cf. Figure 5-13). Burials B-7 and B-9 lay within the same dense family-sized grouping, all with heads southerly. In the northeastern sector, Burial I-19 also was buried with head to south, whereas H-1 and the nearby but deeper I-9 (with the very large owl pipe and human jaw) were oriented northeasterly.

An area of the site that contained no members of clusters 1-9, near the northeastern ends of Trenches 1-3, appears to have a rather high number of individuals associated with "medicine bags" (Burials 1-61, E-19, and E-32 from clusters 12 and 13, all with two or more animal/bird skulls) and with relatively large numbers of exotic items (e.g., Burials 1-39, 1-60, F-17, and F-23 from cluster 10; see Figures 7-29e-g).

It is notable that wealth and high status generally did not occur together within any one cluster group (Table 7-15). A few unique exotic items, but never large numbers of exotic items, were associated with high-status burials, including older people who probably were important figures of authority. In contrast, wealth was most strongly associated with younger people. For example, Burial 1-60, who had a very large assemblage of shell and metal items, including a variety of European materials, was the most "wealthy" individual reported from Trenches 1-K, but probably died before the age of 20. In the early stages of my research I hypothesized that this person might have been an incipient Big Man, seeking to gain power through ostentatious display and lavish gifts, but the age seems far too young. As an alternative hypothesis, such items might have been obtained though long-distance travel undertaken as a vision quest or similar rite of passage. It is of interest that a large amount of metal was discarded in refuse pits in this part of the site (Figures 6-41 and 6-42). The area in which this young man was buried was between two possible shamans from cluster groups 12 and 13 (Burials 1-61 and E-32).

"Knowledge quest" behavior—searching for power through difficult journeys to distant places—is often associated with shamans (cf. Helms 1988). There are indications that individuals from Madisonville might fit such a characterization. Not only were animal/bird skulls significantly associated with exotic items within the same burial (see above), but also in several cases, younger people (possible relatives?) with important or relatively large numbers of exotic items were buried adjacent to, or in the same grave with, people who had "medicine bags" (e.g., Burials 1-60 and 1-61, Burials 2-16 and 2-17, Burials D-21 and D-11, Burials E-29, E-30, and E-32, and Burial 1-16 not far from 1-21).

Burials Outside Trenches 1-K. Some limited cluster analysis was carried out on the burials from the remainder of the site. Because of pronounced deficiencies in excavation procedures, reporting, and data retention for these burials, no definitive conclusions can be drawn. Here I will very briefly discuss the results of one run intended to highlight burials of status and wealth, for comparison with those noted in Trenches 1-K.

Variables were similar but not identical to those utilized for burials in Trenches 1-K. This was because some grave goods present in that part of the site (e.g., animal/bird skulls) were not reported from other excavations (Tables 7-7, 7-8), and because grave good assemblages, on average, were smaller outside of Trenches 1-K (Table 6-9). Cluster analysis variables included presence/absence of ceramic vessels, metal ornaments, shell ornaments, bone ornaments, projectile points, pipes, tools, and subsidiary burials, plus crosscutting indicators (large/unique artifacts, decorated artifacts, more than ten grave goods, more than ten exotic items, more than two artifact types, more than two artifact functional types, and more than two subsidiary burials). The results discussed below are from a 16-cluster run carried out on all 800 burials excavated between 1879 and 1891 (Drooker 1997c: Database B1; Drooker 1997, in press), not just those with grave goods. (The 59 or more burials from the 1895 excavations were omitted because information about them was so very limited, but two interments from that group with extant grave goods are included in the discussion below because of their very impressive grave goods.)

One very large group (cluster 16) of 651 burials included few people with grave goods except for 31% with ceramic vessels, and none with subsidiary burials. The 42 individuals in the next largest cluster (group 15) all had subsidiary burials, but only one person had more than two. Sixty percent of the members had mortuary vessels; none were buried with shell ornaments, pipes, or projectile points, and no other type of grave good was included with more than one interment. An eleven-member cluster (group 14) included 91% with decorated items, 73% with pots, and 64% with pipes, three of which are illustrated in Figure 7-6. The characteristics of this cluster group are notably congruent with those of cluster 14, Trenches 1-K (Table 7-15). The adult with the redstone disk pipe (Figure 6-20), Burial 108, Block 1, was the only person from this cluster group who had a subsidiary burial. The other mortuary offering was a "transitional" Madisonville pot with decorated neck (incised and punctated design), unthickened rim, notched lip, and pairs of nodes around the shoulder (Figure 4-10a). Five burials clustered together (group 13) because all had large/unique items, but no type was common to all members. The largest categories were tools (60%) and shell ornaments (40%). A group of four burials (cluster 12) all had pots, tools, more than two artifact types, and more than two functional types; none had pipes or metal or shell ornaments. This is congruent with the female-oriented cluster 11 from Trenches 1-K (Table 7-15).

Another cluster of four (group 11) all possessed metal ornaments, with three people each buried with large/unique items, more than ten grave goods, and/or more than eleven exotic items—the only multimember cluster from this part of the site associated with wealth. Its analog in Trenches 1-K would be cluster group 10 (Table 7-15). All members were subadults. Unfortunately, only one of them (Burial 279 from Block 1, gifted with the brass Clarksdale bell illustrated in Figures 6-21c and 6-21g) was provenienced. The others were three extremely rich burials excavated during Putnam's visit to the site in May 1882 that averaged 18 grave goods each, including the barred brass pendant, the largest number of tubular metal coils from any one burial, and a small tubular metal serpent (Figure 6-21f) (Drooker 1996c: Database C1).

The thirteen remaining burials included the most diverse grave good assemblages (Table 7-17). Their clusters consisted of one group of three, one of two, and eight individuals, all extended and supine. The human remains were identified in the field as including three subadults, seven females, three males, and one adult of unspecified sex. This female-to-male ratio is far different from that of the people with the most diverse grave goods in Trenches 1-K. Moreover, females were reported with artifacts, such as pipes, that were statistically correlated with males in Trenches 1-K. It is highly probable that at least some of these females were misidentified, so the male and female designations included in Table 7-17 should be taken lightly.

Cluster 10 included three people, all with pipes and subsidiary burials but no other accompaniments. Their locations, in Blocks 6, 8, and 15 (Figure 5-8), were to the southeast, south-

TABLE 7-17
Mortuary Associations with Individuals in Cluster Groups 1-10, Outside Trenches 1-K

Cluster Group	Burial	Age/ Sex*	Associated Object(s)	Location	See Figure
1	B1-127	A-M	Limestone small-disk pipe	At right of head	7-6
			2 fossil bivalve shells (*Orthis lynx* and *Orthis occidentalis*)	At left of head	
			8 deer horn tips (probably in necklace)	Near neck	
			2 polished bone cylinders (cf. "Cluster" 9)	Near neck	
			"Numerous" flint points and chips		
2	B7-1	A-F	Ceramic vessel with "lizard" handles	Near "lower extremities"	4-13
			88 copper or brass beads and tubular coils	Along the spine and chest	
			2 bone beads (cf. "Cluster" 9)	At neck	
			Handful of charred corn	Around cranium	
3	B12-20	A-F	Iron dagger guard	On chest	6-21f
			6 rolled copper beads	At hands	
			3 bone beads	At neck	
			Subsidiary burial: "very young child"	At right side of pelvis	
4	B1-96	A-F	Ceramic vessel	Near head	
			Jasper or flint spear head	In right hand	
			Stone celt	At side	
			Subsidiary burial: "small skeleton"	Head on pelvis	
5	B1-297	A-M	Ceramic vessel	Right side of head	
			Limestone pipe, bear or wolf head effigy	At left side of head	7-6
			Large double-barred copper pendant	At right side of neck	6-21f
6	BX-3 (Putnam 1882)	A	4 brass rings	On fingers of both hands	6-21b
			Fragments of bone bead	From surrounding leaf mold	
			Charred corn (cf. "Cluster" 2 above)	From surrounding leaf mold	
7	B11-20	Ch/I	Pipe	At feet	
			Shell beads	At feet	
			Strip of copper	At feet	
			(This burial was subsidiary to an adult, "lying over the lower extremities," with heads in opposite directions. Some/all gravegoods might belong to adult.)		
8	B1-134	Ch	Ceramic vessel		
			3 shell ornaments, including triangular pendant	On neck and chest	
			2 bone beads	On neck and chest	
			(Buried "in a group" with 2 adults, each with a pot; all 3 were oriented to SE)		
9	B1-272	YA-F	2 polished hollow bone cylinders, about 2" long	Each side of neck	
			5 subsidiary burials: disarticulated children, aged "8-12"	On and around legs	
			(B1-272 was pregnant)		
9	B1-280	A-F	2 polished hollow bone cylinders, about 2" long	Each side of neck	
10	B6-26	A-M	Ovoid stone pipe engraved with stylized face	At the right hand	
			4 subsidiary burials: children, arranged with feet toward B6-26	2 at right shoulder, 2 at right thigh	
10	B8-12	T-M	Animal effigy pipe, elaborately carved and polished	Between thighs	
			Subsidiary burial: small child	At right side and parallel	
10	B15-4	A-F	Pipe	At left hand	
			Subsidiary burial: infant	On thighs w/head on pelvis	
			(Buried alongside another adult. 2 pots were with group, ascribed to other burials: 1 to right of infant's head and beside B15-4's right hand, and 1 at left tibia of other adult.)		

*Age and sex are as reported from the field, based on unknown criteria, and cannot be considered totally reliable.

west, and northwest of the plaza area postulated to have been centered on Block 10 (cf. Figure 6-52). The two reported females in cluster 9 probably lay close to each other in Block 1 — at least, they were excavated within a period of three days. (The child with the Clarksdale bell was excavated on the day between the excavations of these two adults.) Both were buried with two polished hollow bone cylinders on each side of the neck but no other grave goods, although one of them also was interred with subsidiary burials.

It is worth noting that at least seven people in Trenches 1-K were described as buried with one or two cylinders or tubes of bone or antler at or near their necks. However, since few examples were available for examination and descriptions rarely were in detail, it was difficult to know whether they should be grouped together as a single artifact type. The burials included one child (Burial 3-4), three adults of unknown sex (2-33, D-28, F-23), a young adult female (B-3), and a young adult male (D-30), spaced widely apart around the northwestern portion of the site. Burial 2-21 (not far from 2-33), the young adult male with the set of large engraved tubular bone beads arranged from mouth down along the arms, should probably also be included.

The individuals in "clusters" 8 to 5 all were interred with grave goods of three functional types and no subsidiary burials. "Clusters" 3 and 4 each reported a female adult with three functional types of artifacts and one subsidiary burial. The adult "female" in "cluster" 2 was lying directly over another adult, but oriented in the opposite direction. Her mortuary assemblage was among the "wealthiest" from the entire site. The adult male in "cluster" 1 had the largest number of artifact functional types of any burial in the southern portion of the site. This definitely was a status burial, as was the "cluster" 5 adult male buried with double-barred copper pendant and effigy pipe.

Surpassing both those burials and the highest status burials from Trenches 1-K (clusters 1, 3, and 9, Table 7-16) was a very highly endowed adult excavated by Metz in 1895 (Burial Q-45). This person was described as having a pipe in the left hand, three copper serpent-shaped tubular pendants at either side of the head and at the right shoulder, and a pot at the right shoulder. The pipe was one of the two largest from the site (10.8 cm long), of a golden-colored chalcedony and unique in form: a bird with folded wings (probably an owl) with a disk on its back (Figure 7-30a). Like the still larger (13.1 cm) perching owl pipe found in the left hand of Burial I-9, the owl/bird-disk pipe was missing a portion of the tail, probably ceremonially broken. (The serpent pendant on the shoulder of Q-45, Figure 7-30b, also was missing a portion.) Listed in the AMNH catalog as additional grave goods with this burial were a 9-inch (23-cm) worked bone, two polished stone celts and four other stone implements at least two of them adze-like, eight natural stone pestle-like objects (hammerstones?), three pieces of worked(?) stone, a unio shell valve, and a piece of stone arrow point (Figure 7-30c). According to a letter from Metz to Putnam (June 25, 1895, on file at the AMNH), this burial was located in the Ferris Woods, that is, within the Harvard Tract property line, and it also would have been north of Blocks 1-17, which had been completely excavated by 1880. Unfortunately, nothing more is known of its provenience. This burial personified both status and wealth, an unusual combination at Madisonville.

Burials excavated in 1895 also included one (Q-14) with at least 29 rolled copper beads, seven shell beads, and a perforated deer tooth (congruent with the two burials in clusters 2 and 3), and a child burial with six shell ornaments.

Exotic Artifacts and Supralocal Symbols in Madisonville Mortuary Contexts, and Implications for Signifying Status

Burial Q-14 and the other individuals outside of Trenches 1-K with more than a few exotic items (e.g., cluster groups 6 and 11) are consistent with individuals in wealthy clusters from Trenches 1-K such as cluster 10 in that many were subadults or reported as female, and none were identified as old or male. Most of the glass beads excavated at the site, along with at least seven shell beads, were with an infant in Trench 1(1-39, interred at the right shoulder of a mature adult male, 1-38, who had a remodeled hole and a flint flake in his left parietal). The heavy association of European-derived items with subadults, younger adults, and reported non-males outside of Trenches 1-K (e.g., iron dagger guard, brass bell, brass coils, brass spiral, brass pendant) underscores their non-association with older males buried within Trenches 1-K. European copper might have been acceptable as mortuary offerings with older males, but glass and metal, having no indigenous counterpart, seem not to have been. Only singular, relatively large, symbolically important artifacts of exotic materials (metal, stone, shell) seem to be associated with the highest positions of male authority at Madisonville, not the wealth of large numbers of relatively small nonlocal objects such as multiple copper or shell beads, nor the power of entirely foreign materials such as blue glass or brass.

Wealth in exotic items, which seems most strongly associated with younger people, may have several connections. It might in some cases be the product of vision-quest type travels (which might or might not be related to the development of shamanistic powers) or, drawing on historical analogy, of treks by aggressive young "trading captains." It might have been appropriate for the adornment of young, nubile women or young warriors (as it was historically), or it might have been given as gifts to children and young people related to older persons of consequence. In any case, except for an apparent negative association with mature and older adults, it does not seem to have been concentrated in any one location, age grade, or gender.

Although neither one of them was reported to have been accompanied by subsidiary burials, the adult "male" Burials 297 and 127 of Block 1 ("clusters" 1 and 5) had grave goods congruent with types found with very high-status males in Trenches 1-K, including pipes plus a diverse variety of artifact functional types (but no large numbers of exotic artifacts). Of particular interest were the co-occurrence of pipes and large double-barred copper pendant at shoulder in Burial I-19 and Burial 297 of

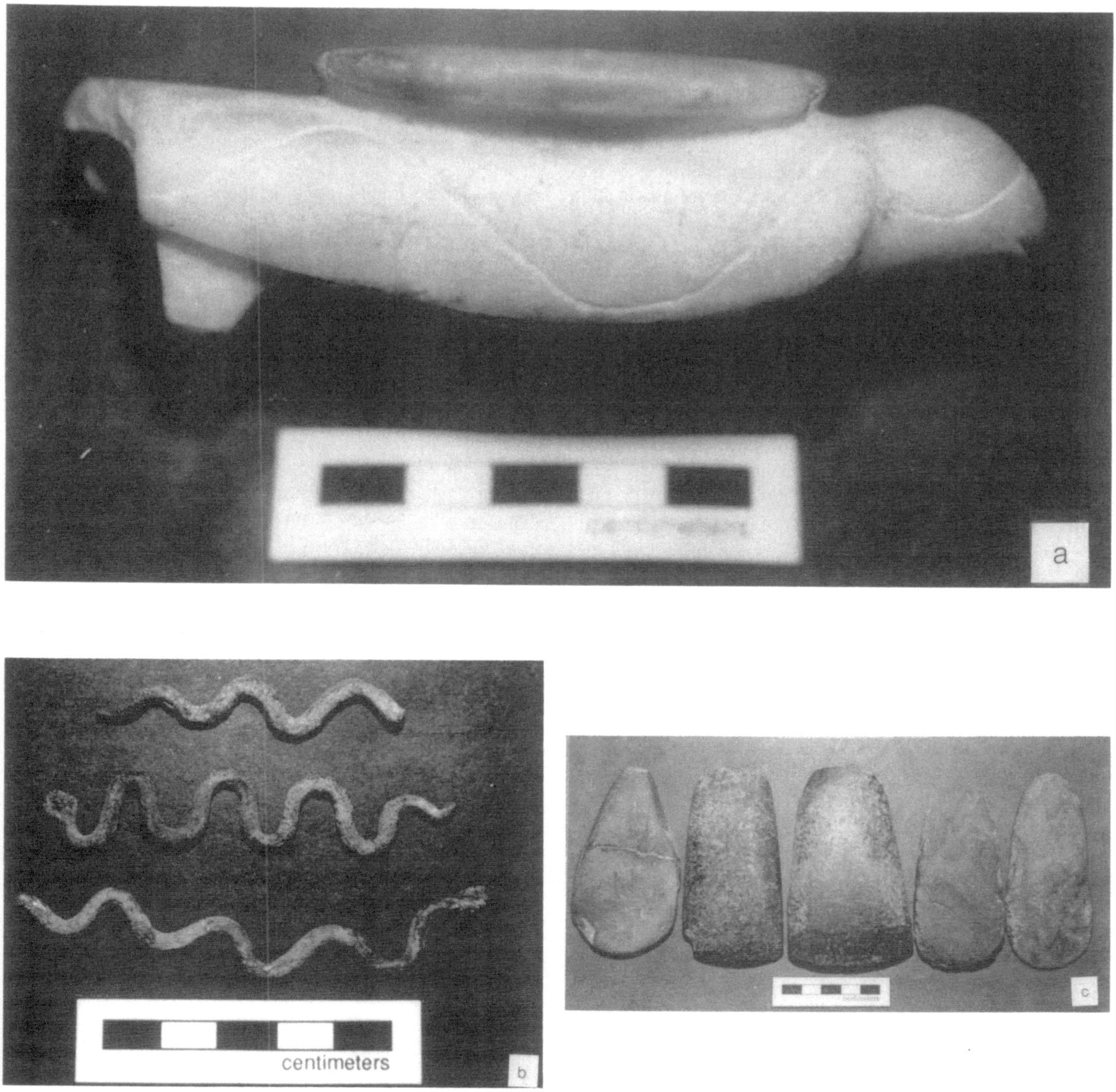

Figure 7-30. Some of the grave goods from Burial 45, excavated in 1895. *a*. Chalcedony bird/owl-disk pipe (AMNH Cat. No. 1895-29/1414). *b*. Three serpent pendants made from thin copper tubes (1895-29/1366). *c*. Stone tools (1895-29/3704-3708).

Block 1. I take these co-occurrences to represent redundant symbols of male authority. Since the pendants have supralocal connections, I would propose that at least some aspect of social identity symbolized by them was related to external interaction.

Anticipating the discussion in Chapter 8, I will note that although barred copper pendants are known from diverse locations including sites in Tennessee, Arkansas, and Iowa, the majority have come from burials at four Fort Ancient sites in Ohio and Kentucky: Madisonville, Dunn, Fox Farm, and Hardin (Figure 7-31). Of them all, only the brass example from Madisonville is known to have been associated with a child rather than an adult. These large metal pendants may well represent ties among high-status leaders from these sites. Since no one site has a monopoly on them, they probably symbolize leadership at roughly the same level, not the apical level of an hierarchical system such as in a complex chiefdom. What might they symbolize? The double- and multi-barred pendants are so similar in shape to the depiction of the tail of a rattlesnake engraved into a comb found with Burial B-11 (in the same cemetery group as Burial B-9) and other depictions of rattlesnakes from the Ohio Valley (Figure 7-32) that I would identify them as such with no hesitation. Although the double-barred examples might perhaps be interpreted as quadrupeds, analogous to brass "lizard" effigies from other sites; as discussed in association with Figure 8-13, the resemblance is not as great as to the rattlesnake tails. Additional examples of stylized serpents with multi-barred tail tips include two engraved on redstone disk pipes, one found in Union County, Ohio, not far from the highest point in Ohio at the upper reaches of the Great Miami drainage system, and the other excavated from above the level of a house floor at the Angel site in southwestern Indiana (Black 1967: Fig. 148; Converse 1995a). The single-barred pendants, particularly those with a pendulous diamond-shaped base, strongly resemble the foot and tail sections of Oneota and Mississippian bird/hawk-shaped symbol badges (Drooker 1994c; Hall 1962:141-46, Pl. 80; Williams 1980: Figs. 1, 2) and the motifs on Oneota pottery that have been taken as hawk symbolism (e.g., Benn 1989). My interpretation is that the multi-barred and single-barred variations of the cross-shaped metal symbol badge might represent opposing or interlocking symbolism, and might have had dual division significance (cf. Emerson 1989 for some possible connections between bird/Thunderer motifs and serpent/water motifs in Mississippian art). See Chapter 8 for further discussion of their geographical distributions and the significance for interregional interaction.

Burial 45 from the 1895 excavations also was adorned with supralocal symbols—three tubular serpent pendants—and held a pipe (Figure 7-30). The extreme diversity of the grave good assemblage (greater than any other reported from the site), the very large and exquisitely fashioned pipe of exotic stone, and the multiple metal serpent pendants argue for association with a position of very high authority. The supralocal ties, however, are not primarily eastward, toward other Fort Ancient settlements, but westward, toward Oneota territory. As will be discussed further in Chapter 8, the tubular serpents have been found at many more Oneota than Fort Ancient sites, including locations in Michigan, Indiana, Illinois, and Iowa, plus Arkansas and Alabama (Figure 8-7, below). At the Anker site in Illinois, where five burials with copper serpents were found among many people with extremely diverse and highly ceremonial grave good assemblages, excavators suggested a connection between snake symbolism and ritual healing, as there was in the historically known Midewiwin ceremony (Bluhm and Liss 1961:96-99; Herold et al. 1990:90-91). Although the largest number of tubular metal serpents from any one location was excavated at Madisonville, only half of them came from burial contexts, three from Burial 45 of 1895, and one minuscule example from a child excavated in 1882. Only one more example is known from a Fort Ancient interment, a serpent reportedly obtained from a burial context during an uncontrolled excavation at the Augusta site (Henderson et al. 1986:117). The bird/owl-disk pipe, too, has a westward connection, even beyond the simple fact that it is a disk form. The most congruent example that I have seen is a much smaller white limestone disk pipe with bird- or owl-shaped base in the same position as the Fort Ancient example, from the Caborn-Welborn Slack Farm site (Pollack et al. 1996:21). Thus, in spite of the significant status and wealth embodied in "his" grave good assemblage, it seems unlikely that Burial 45 occupied a position within a singularly Fort Ancient system of authority. The assemblage seems to have more affinity to those of shamanistic burials than to those associated with civil leadership at Madisonville, in spite of the presence of the pipe.

Another artifact type with supralocal symbolism, the marine shell maskette, occurred in burial contexts that might connect it

---

Figure 7-31. (*facing page*) Examples of barred metal pendants or symbol badges from late prehistoric and protohistoric sites: three from burials (one child [*left*], two adult males) at Madisonville, Ohio (Hooton and Willoughby 1920: Pl. 18; see also Figure 6-21f); two from Fox Farm, Kentucky, one of them (*left*) from the chest of a burial (after Henderson et al. 1986: Fig. 24A; William Wertz collection); one from an adult burial at Zollicoffer Hill, near Nashville, Tennessee (Putnam 1973d: Fig. 10; see also Figure 8-10); one from an adult burial at Rose Mound, Cross County, Arkansas (Putnam 1973d: Fig. 11, 1973e; Peabody Museum accession ledger); one from an adult burial at Flynn Cemetery, Allamakee County, Iowa (after Bray 1961a: Pl. 2); one from another site in northeastern Iowa (Iowa Historical Society Cat. No. E. O. 1269); one from the Tremaine site near LaCrosse, Wisconsin (after Boszhardt 1989: Fig. 2.9G); and a large, non-perforated specimen described as a mace, from Wythe County, Virginia (after Dye and Wharey 1989:343). Other examples include three reported from burials at the Hardin site, Greenup County, Kentucky, and one from the Dunn site, Campbell County, Kentucky (Henderson et al. 1986:137, 123), and one reported from Dwyer Rockshelter in western Wisconsin (Boszhardt 1989:67), plus a double-barred flint mace from a stone box grave in Humphreys County, Tennessee, west of Nashville (Ganier 1948:8, Fig. 2k). All drawn to approximately the same scale. Illustrations from Hooton and Willoughby 1920 and Putnam 1973d, courtesy of the Peabody Museum of Archaeology and Ethnology, Harvard University.

Madisonville, OHIO

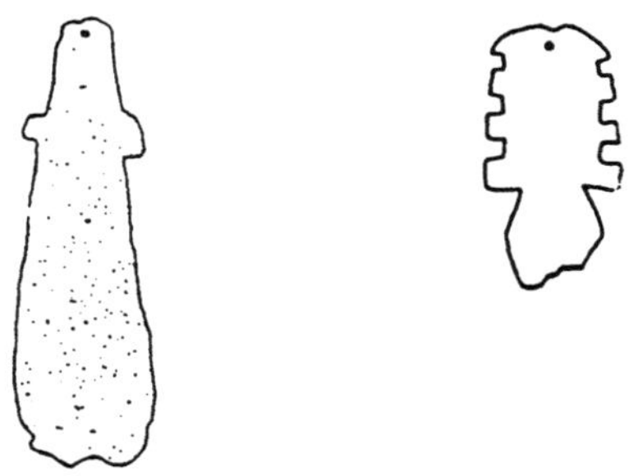

Fox Farm, KENTUCKY

Wythe County, VIRGINIA

near Nashville, TENNESSEE

Rose Mound, ARKANSAS

Flynn Cemetery, IOWA

northeastern IOWA

Tremaine, WISCONSIN

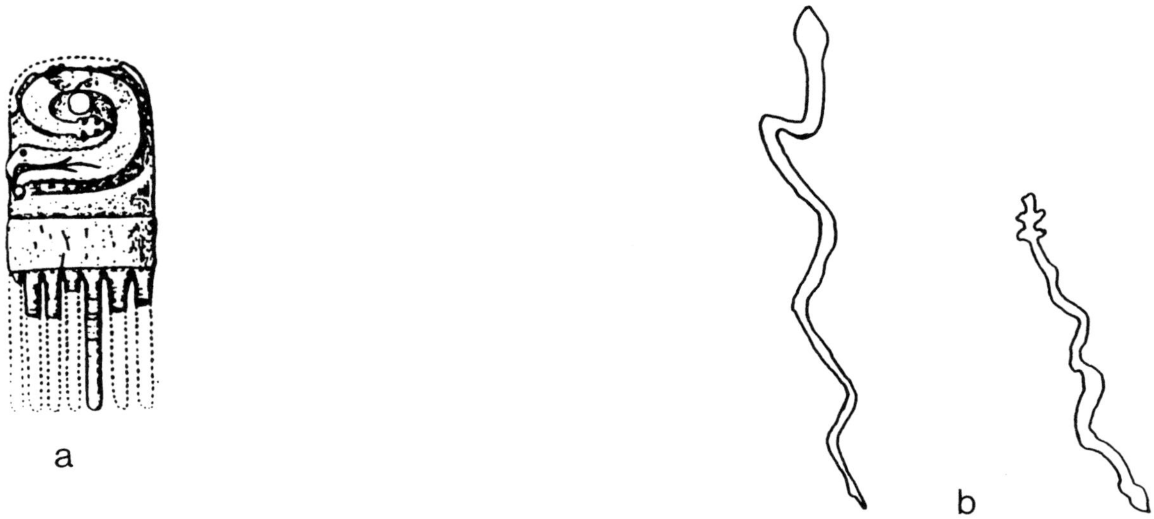

a b

Figure 7-32. Depictions of rattlesnakes with double-barred tails. *a*. Antler comb with engraved rattlesnake, from Burial B-11 at Madisonville (Hooton and Willoughby 1920: Pl. 17k; see also Figures 6-18b and 7-4). Courtesy of the Peabody Museum of Archaeology and Ethnology, Harvard University. *b*. Snake petroglyphs from the upper Ohio Valley, Venago County, Pennsylvania (after Swauger 1974: Pl. 7).

with leadership authority: one was on the right shoulder of Burial 1-61, an adult male who also possessed two animal skulls, and another, with engraved forked eyes, was reported to have been found "near the lower jaw of an adult" (Hooton and Willoughby 1920:64, Pl. 16f, g; see also Figure 6-19a). However, maskettes also occurred with children. Examples without forked eyes were found with at least two subadult burials (Hooton and Willoughby 1920: Pl. 16d; Low 1880: Fig. 36; see Figures 6-19a, b). Like the barred copper pendants, but unlike larger mask gorgets, which are centered in eastern Tennessee, the distribution of these artifacts is most concentrated within Fort Ancient territory. They are known from at least five Fort Ancient sites and are very strongly represented at Madisonville, from which a half-dozen examples are known; they also occur more rarely in Tennessee, northern Ohio, Illinois, and Iowa (see Figure 8-16, below). Unfortunately, most maskettes from Fort Ancient sites are poorly provenienced, so no generalizations can be made about their burial associations. Hanson reported four large masks (two engraved) and "five small 'faceless' specimens" from Hardin, all with burials (1966:161). Holmes listed six: a large engraved mask with an adult male, and five other "masks" with subadults (Holmes 1994:127). The impression is that the maskettes might have been primarily with subadults. Mask gorgets *per se*, particularly those with forked-eye motifs, have been associated with males, warfare, and hunting (Smith and Smith 1989).

Small-disk pipes are another category of supralocal symbol with strongest concentrations in Oneota, rather than Fort Ancient, territory, although they are not uncommon at Fort Ancient settlements (Table 4-3), particularly Madisonville. At least four out of twenty-four people buried with pipes at Madisonville possessed disk pipes, including the three individuals with the most diverse grave good assemblages (Burials 21 from Trench 2, 127 from Block 1, and 45 from the 1895 excavations). The redstone disk pipe with engraved forked-eye motif (Figure 6-20) (undoubtedly an import and not a local copy, from its stem attachment hole, which is uncharacteristic of Fort Ancient pipes) was found "near the head" of Burial 108 in Block 1. In this, it echoes the at-shoulder placement of all the important artifacts with supralocal symbolism (copper cross-shaped and serpent-shaped pendants, marine shell maskette) buried with adults. I would argue that such placement of any important artifact underlines its significance as status symbol, and that if a person were buried with multiple symbols of status or personal identity, this would be the chosen location for the objects symbolizing highest-level or most-preferred status. Pipes were found at this location with at least eight adults (Burials 3-9, with one at each side of the head, 4-19, D-4, and D-25 in Trenches 1-K, Burials 108, 127, and 297 in Block 1, and CN-1 in the southwestern portion of the site; see Figures 7-1 and 7-2), for whom they might have functioned as the equivalent of symbol badges. The larger of the two pipes with Burial I-19 was on the humerus, just below the level of the copper symbol badge on the shoulder. Burial 127 of Block 1 had two fossil bivalves on the opposite side of his head from his disk pipe.

Besides the shell maskette with Burial 1-61, at least one other male burial (2-17) had a shell ornament at his shoulder, an oval disk. Both of these men also possessed animal/bird skulls, placed elsewhere. Although "medicine bags" often were placed along-

Figure 7-33. Distribution of burials displaying symbolically significant items at the shoulder, Trenches 1-K.

side an arm, there were at least two instances of animal/bird skulls placed at the shoulder: Burial E-19 had two bird skulls and E-32 an animal skull at the left side of the head. Burial D-11 had an animal skull "in front of the jaw," which perhaps also should be included. Burial I-9 (who held the large perching owl pipe in his left hand) had a human jaw near his right shoulder. For Burial H-1, whose "medicine bag" and pipe were located under and in the left hand, the human bones circling the head might have signaled the dominant identity.

Mapping the positions of the people in Trenches 1-K with symbolically significant artifacts positioned at their shoulders gives an interesting result (Figure 7-33). Those displaying shell objects (two) or "medicine bags" (two) are in the northwest, those privileging pipes (four) are in the south, and the two with human bones most in evidence are close together in the northeast, not far from the individual with the copper symbol badge on his shoulder. It is conceivable, but unprovable, that different types of status, symbolized by these different objects, were most prominent within lineages or clans occupying these different sectors of the site.

Also falling into this category might be the pairs of bone tubes/cylinders placed at either side of the neck in a number of burials noted above. However, these do not appear to cluster together on the site. On a much larger scale, a position adjacent to the head or shoulder was the preferred location for mortuary vessels (at least 80% of all those with pots), even for some people who also had pipes, animal/bird skulls, or other significant objects (Figures 7-1 and 7-2). Whether this signaled social identity, accessible nourishment on the path to the Land of the Dead, or some other meaning, the position was not chosen randomly.

Table 7-18 summarizes grave goods and subsidiary burials for all people buried with pipes or "medicine bags." Individuals are listed roughly in order of number of grave goods and functional types of artifacts present, and separated on the basis of whether they had pipes or bags. Burials with multiple pipes, multiple animal/bird skulls, or examples of both were given priority. This information illustrates why it proved difficult to rank probable leaders at Madisonville in a consistent hierarchical pattern. Not only was there too much variation in types and numbers of mortuary associations (no exclusive, redundant sets), but emic concepts of the significance of each particular inclusion were unknown. Using location of apparently symbolically significant objects to help prioritize their importance in the identity of these people is a useful concept that should be explored further. Theoretically, this can be done by means of multivariate analysis. In practice, however, that only leads to further fragmentation of an already fragmented and disparate set of grave good assemblages.

Also of importance is the time factor. It is difficult to know which of these "status" people coexisted. None was buried with definitely European objects, although the presence of metal suggests a later date. Also suggestive of more recent interment are lack of mortuary vessel and Trench 1-K burial location away from the plaza edge. However, neither is definitive. Neither

TABLE 7-18
Mortuary Associations of People with Pipes and/or "Medicine Bags"

	No. of "Bags"	No. of Pipes	Pipe Shape/Decoration	No. of Pots	Group Burial, Size	No. of Subsidiary Burials	Other Gravegoods, Comments
BURIALS IN TRENCHES 1-K							
I-19 (OA-M)		2	claw ovoid/"feathers"		6	5	Large **double-barred copper pendant,** 2 proj. points, harpoon, knife
3-9 (MA-M)		**2**	keel/"X"+"//"+ntchng vasiform	1			Shell spoon
2-21 (YA-M)		1	disk	1	3?	2?	10 bone tubes, 8 engraved with forked eye motif (**2**), shell bead, proj. point
D-25 (OA-M)		**1**	vasiform/ntchd rim	1	2	1	
D-4 (A)		**1**	vasiform	1			
4-19 (YA-M)		**1**	2-headed swan	1			
I-9 (YA-M)		1	owl		2	**1** (jaw)	
B-33 (MA-M)		1	elbow/human+snake				
3-40 (YA-M)		1	ovoid				
["near" D-8 (A)		1	vasiform]				
H-1 (A)	1	1	ovoid/turtle+lizard		2	**1**	2 copper pieces, 2 bone beads
E-32 (OA)	3 (**1**)						Copper-stained animal/bird bones, bird bone whistle
1-61 (YA-M)	**2**				6-7	2-3	**Shell maskette**
E-19 (MA-M)	**2**			1			Shell beads
B-44 (MA-M)	1			1	2	0	Copper-covered wood object, copper stained bones
2-17 (YA-M)	1			1	2	1	**Shell disk**, (pot is vertical compound)
B-54 (OA-M)	1			1			
D-11 (A-M)	1			1			
B-38 (Ch)	1			1			
1-21 (A)	1						
C-8 (T)	1				2	0	
BURIALS SOUTH OF TRENCHES 1-K							
B1B127 (A-M)		**1**	disk				**2 fossil shells, 8 deer horn tips, 2 bone cylinders**, several proj. points, flint chips
B1B297 (A-M)		**1**	bear or wolf	1			Large **double-barred copper pendant**
B1B108 (A)		**1**	disk/forked eye	1	2	1	
B11B20 (Ch?)*		1	?	1	3	0	Copper strip, shell beads, unio shell (spoon?)
B15B4 (A)		1	?	1	3	1	
CNB1 (A)		1	semi-elbow	1			
CNB16 (A)		1	ovoid/lines				Knife
B6B26 (A-M)		1	ovoid/face		5	4	
B8B12 (T)		1	animal head				
B1B28-34 (?)		1	animal (deer?) head				
["near" B1B15		1	vasiform]				
["near" B1B43		1	keel/forked eye?]				
BURIALS IN REMAINDER OF SITE							
BQB45 (A)		1	owl-disk	1			3 **copper serpents**, 2 axes, 4 other stone implements, natural stones, unio valve, worked bone
B22B5 (A?)		1	claw	1			(Pot has lizard decoration)
BMB4 (A)		1	?				
BMB14 (A)		1	animal				
BMB25 (A?)		1	eagle				

"B" burials were in Blocks 1-22, "C" burials were excavated by Conover and associates, "BQ" burials were excavated in 1895, "BM" burials were in Block M.
Ch= child, T=teen/adolescent, YA=young adult, MA=mature adult, OA=older adult, A=adult, age unknown, M=male or reported as male
Items in **boldface** were positioned at the neck/shoulder. Underlined pots were beside head.
*In group with two adults; pipe might well have belonged to one of them.

pipes nor extant mortuary vessels can be seriated with any certainty. For example, considering the individuals listed in Table 7-18, of eleven with mortuary vessels, the five with vessels that were included in the attribute analysis (Burials 2-17, 2-21, 3-9, 4-19, E-19; see Figure 6-39) had jars in cluster 1, thought to be the later of the two largest clusters. In addition, one person (Burial B-54) was buried close to an individual with a cluster 1 jar, but two (Burials E-32 and D-11) were adjacent to individuals with cluster 2 jars.

It is even more difficult to know which individuals might actually have held office contemporaneously. The two men with double-barred copper pendants probably were very close in time, but whether they were contemporaneous or one succeeded the other is impossible to establish. One (I-19) was interred close to a group burial (I-11 and I-12) associated with a fragmentary blue glass bead; this would date to the late sixteenth century. The other (Block 1, Burial 297) was not close to anyone else with metal, glass, or other horizon marker artifacts, but was the eighteenth burial excavated after the child with the brass Clarksdale bell (Block 1, Burial 279) a month earlier; this might put him closer to the mid-sixteenth century. As previously discussed, the high status and high wealth burials in the northeast (I-19) and northwest (e.g., 1-60, 1-61, E-29, E-32) probably postdated most of the burials close to the plaza edge. However, it is uncertain which burials in the southern part of Trenches 1-K were contemporaneous with them, so it is difficult to propose a complete synchronic leadership structure and changes over time.

Social Organization and Change at Madisonville

Several different lines of evidence have been pursued in hopes of elucidating social organization at Madisonville and any obvious changes over time. Chapters 6 and 7 laid out evidence pertaining to local settlement patterns, intrasite organization, and mortuary treatments. Here I will attempt to present a coherent overview by summarizing the conclusions of these efforts. This should not be taken as a definitive assessment—there are too many uncertainties and assumptions involved—but it nevertheless may serve to advance discussion of Late Fort Ancient social relationships.

Individual Social Identities and Social Personae at Madisonville

No ranked class divisions were recognized in the Madisonville mortuary analysis. There were no redundant, exclusive markers crosscutting age and sex categories that analytically isolated any groups as owning ascribed high status. To the contrary, there was much evidence to support a system of achieved status with multiple, overlapping social identities. Although wealth, in terms of fairly large numbers of small exotic objects, often was invested on children and very young adults, it was almost entirely adults who accumulated the assemblages of diverse grave goods and symbolically important large objects that would seem to mark them as persons of accomplishment and authority.

As predicted for societies where achievement was the road to personhood (Braun 1979:72), adolescents, on average, possessed the least impressive mortuary associations, although there were some exceptions (see below). Subadults, on average, had fewer grave goods and were less likely to have any grave goods than adults. However, infants and children were more likely than any other age category to be buried with nonlocal items, including European objects of unfamiliar materials like brass and glass. A few of them were gifted with the wealth of fairly large numbers of exotic artifacts. This might well have been in honor of their families, not themselves as individuals. However, particular age-related practices, such as preferential adornment of younger people, or beliefs, such as the desire to lure back the spirit of a loved child for rebirth, also probably came into play.

Female authority could not easily be recognized on the basis of the archaeological record at Madisonville. From extant nonperishable grave goods, workaday tools related to agriculture, food preparation, and hide preparation were the mark of the accomplished woman. Grave goods with identified females included far fewer types than with males, and no large/unique objects that might have symbolized significant status. No identified older adult females were pinpointed as having mortuary associations that would set them off from the crowd as potential leaders or figures of authority. The older adult Burial I-18, accompanied by a diverse, high-tool grave good assemblage and located close to the important older adult male, Burial I-19, would be perhaps the best candidate if "her" measured length of 72 inches did not eliminate "her" from consideration; however, berdache status is a possibility. Some young adult females and reported females (e.g., Burials D-21, E-29, 1 from Block 7, and 20 from Block 12) were interred with exotic ornaments and multiple pots that put them above the norm, and there were more identified adult females than identified males accompanied by subsidiary burials. In general, though, surviving male burial accouterments outshone those of females. I am of the belief that it is impossible to fully assess female (or, for that matter, male) social identities at Madisonville without having access to the perishable record of wood, basketry, bags, quillwork, feathers, fabrics, and leather.

Male-associated grave good categories, including pipes (statistically significant), projectile points, large copper ornaments, and bone ornaments, underline the importance of men as hunters, warriors, and diplomats. Pipes were strongly correlated with male identity, and probably signaled a particular adult male social identity or leadership role, very likely including ritual greeting and external interaction. As noted earlier, pipes with burials were more likely than other pipes to be large and light-colored (white being associated with peace, versus the war-associated red). Some richly adorned young adult males were identified as possible war leaders (e.g., Burials 2-21 and B-9). A number of older men, former warriors as indicated by healed wounds, might have survived to become civil leaders (e.g., Burial I-19) or to be honored at death (e.g., Burial I-38, with the infant I-39, wearing glass bead and shell wealth, lying on his upper right arm).

Shamanistic activity probably was symbolized by "medicine bags" (indicated by small animal or bird skulls), which in turn were correlated with exotic materials and charms, and also connected in a few cases with non-normative burial practices. Of course, these probably were not the only marks of shamans or ritual specialists, but they do form a coherent set. Across North America, pipes and smoking were associated with spiritual communication (Paper 1988; von Gernet 1992), so pipe possession might well have been associated with shamanistic powers as well as diplomatic ritual. The two teenagers with "medicine bags" provide evidence that training began young, perhaps initially through power achieved during a vision quest. No identified females had animal/bird skulls. Ritual specialists with a different or broader focus might perhaps be represented by the human bones arranged around the head of Burial H-1 or the copper tubular serpents worn by Burial 45 from the 1895 excavations, both of whom also carried important pipes. Burial H-1 is the only burial known to have both a pipe and an animal/bird skull, although the large number of fine tools with Burial 45 from 1895 might be interpreted as a "bundle."

Highest status or authority is postulated for adults with evidence of multiple important social identites, signified by mortuary associations of high diversity and high visibility (e.g., large ornaments), or double or triple inclusions of artifacts associated with particular significant statuses (e.g., animal/bird skulls, pipes). Several such people are listed in Table 7-18, none of whom have been identified as females. Although a group of very high-status individuals can be separated out, any sort of ranked hierarchy is difficult to achieve, due to the extreme variety of assemblages and the difficulty of determining contemporaneity.

Spatial Organization and Group Identities at Madisonville

Like virtually all well-mapped Fort Ancient sites, Madisonville spatial organization focused on a communal open area or plaza. Two, possibly three, small plaza areas have been recognized on the site, one centered around the eastern portion of Trench 3 and the northern portion of Trench B (cf. Figure 5-9), another centered around Block 10 (cf. Figure 6-16), and a third possibly located within Block 1. Some of them might have been in use concurrently. As reconstructed with the aid of ceramic analysis and horizon marker artifacts including European goods, usage of the northern and of the southern portions of the site appear to have somewhat differing histories. Both sectors probably were used concurrently during at least part of the sixteenth century, but occupation of the southern part of the site seems to have the most time depth, while occupation of the northern portion appears to have lasted somewhat later. It is difficult to tell whether this represents a shift in focus from a southern to a northern plaza area, or the simultaneous vigorous usage of both (or even of more than two). Concurrent, long-term organization around more than one well-developed communal space would imply recognizable, significant social division within the settlement.

Evidence for the social reality and nature of such a division is tenuous, because the extant material and documentary evidence for the area south of Trenches 1-K is grievously incomplete. Two apparent structural oppositions might perhaps characterize the southern versus northern parts of the site. First, large mammal representations (e.g., deer, bear) appear to be more common with burials in the south than the north, and representations of birds and perhaps reptiles more common with burials in the north. For example, the pipe in the same grave as the double-barred copper pendant in Block 1 was carved in the shape of a bear's head (Figure 7-6), while the two pipes interred with the second such pendant, in Trench I, had avian associations: one was engraved with featherlike motifs, and the other perhaps represented a bird's claw (Figure 7-5d). Second, small-animal skulls, bird skulls, and bird beaks, probably the remains of medicine bags, are a significant grave good in the northern portion of the site but were not reported with burials from the south. Such differences (if real) might signal an earth-sky or earth-sky/water distinction coincident with a moiety, phratry, or other large-scale community division, in which members of different divisions had different, ascribed functional specialties.

The burials close to and aligned with the plaza edge in Trenches 1-K probably represent a late prehistoric occupation with subsistence centered on maize horticulture and a strong communal focus. Both the burial locations and the apparent upsurge of mortuary vessels as grave goods—vessels remarkably similar in size, form, and muted, small-scale decoration, and often the sole grave good—would be congruent with a strongly integrative whole-group focus. People in positions of ritual and civil authority during this period might have included individuals such as Burials E-19 and B-38, interred close to the plaza edge with both "medicine bags" and pots but lacking metal, and Burials 3-9, 4-19, and D-25, buried close or reasonably close to the plaza with both pipes and pots but lacking metal. Of these, Burials E-19 and 3-9, buried on opposite sides of the plaza and interred with two small animal skulls and two pipes, respectively, might have had the most dominant social personae. Based on the absence, or virtual absence, of projectile points, pipes, red ochre, and metal from burials near the northern edge of the plaza, a war-peace functional division is tentatively proposed.

In the portion of the site excavated by Trenches 1-K, there seems to have been a shift during Late Fort Ancient time from plaza-edge cemeteries to burials in small groups farther back from the open area. This implies a shift away from a strong whole-group-centered focus, and might (as discussed in Chapter 6) be related to a change in subsistence from primary dependence on maize horticulture to diversification into big game (bison) hunting plus horticulture. Besides probable changes over time in burial locations, mortuary inclusions seem to have changed from primarily mortuary vessels to more diverse and (on average) larger assemblages of grave goods. That an open communal area was maintained through this probable shift in food acquisition strategy and mortuary program implies at least some continuity in group relationships, in spite of the fact that plaza boundaries might not have been maintained in exactly the same locations.

It is truly unfortunate that structure locations, orientations, and sizes cannot be determined, as such information would allow more detailed and reliable time-related and status-related comparisons among smaller social groups. However, from average posthole sizes, at least some houses probably were quite large, very likely sheltering extended families or lineages. The smaller burial groups that exist toward the margins of the site might perhaps represent smaller, less permanent households in existence near the end of the site occupation.

It was anticipated that if power (important leadership roles) clustered in one lineage, then high-status adults should be buried near each other, perhaps also with family members whose mortuary offerings would reflect the status of their relatives. There were no notably large, coherent groups of this sort. However, there were some instances of people with important similarities being buried in the same general area of Trenches 1-K, enough so to postulate lineage, clan, or dual-division specialties—preferred leadership in certain activities coming from particular ascribed groups. Here are the strongest examples, with particular reference to Figure 7-33 and Table 7-18.

The northeast (in and near Trench I), although relatively sparsely occupied, contained the highly endowed Burial I-19, probably a civil leader of great authority, Burials I-9 and H-1 with their special arrangements of human bone, their important pipes, and (in the case of H-1) also a "medicine bag," and the high-tool Burial I-18. (Also very likely on this side of the site was the enigmatic Burial 45 excavated in 1895, the adult with the most diverse grave good assemblage found at Madisonville—including highly visible trappings of both status and wealth, some perhaps associated with shamanistic curing, plus a notably large assemblage of tools.) This was indeed a locus of power, but it is not clear whether there is great time depth to the occupation of this part of the site by powerful figures. Although the "small pieces of worked copper" with H-1 and the large copper pendant with I-19 have not been identified as either European or non-European, a burial very close to I-19 was one of only two that contained friable blue glass beads, so the time frame might have been late sixteenth century. However, one factor makes me inclined to place Burial H-1 earlier in time than Burial I-19. As the only person at Madisonville with both pipe and "medicine bag" (plus other ritual objects), this person is strongly reminiscent of the individuals identified as possible shamans at the Early-Middle Fort Ancient Anderson and Incinerator sites, both of whom possessed pipes as well as ritual paraphernalia, including, at the Anderson site, a human jaw bone (Essenpreis 1982:219). It is possible that in later times it became more common to separate the social functions objectified by pipes and bundles, instead of concentrating the entire spectrum of authoritative social identities in one person.

The area near the eastern ends of Trenches 1-3, to the north and west of the plaza, was the locus of burial for the only three individuals with multiple animal/bird skulls (Burials 1-61, E-32, and E-19) and for the two adults with "medicine bags" who also had marine shell ornaments as probable social identity indicators at their shoulders (Burials 1-61 and 2-17; Figure 7-33). There seems to be a strong connection with high-level shamanistic authority in this area. Also in this sector were: the richest burial in Trenches 1-K (Burial 1-60, whose belt was decorated with large clips probably cut from a Basque copper kettle); much discarded copper and brass (Figures 6-43, 6-44); a fragment of an iron band from a Basque kettle (in Pit 66, Trench 1); and the infant burial (1-39) gifted with the largest number of glass beads found together at the site (again, friable blue ones). These associations not only help to date many of the burials in this part of the site to the late sixteenth century but also imply a connection with interaction networks reaching up to the Saint Lawrence Seaway—conceivably associated with knowledge/power quest activities of some of its shamanistic residents (cf. Helms 1988). There appears to be more time depth here than among the important burials in the northwestern sector. For example, as discussed above, Burial E-19 might well have been associated with the burial group along the northern edge of the plaza, an area hypothesized to have been used earlier, before much metal came into the settlement. If so, this possible shaman was one of the few people from this cemetery group (group 2) with any grave goods in addition to a mortuary vessel, and might well have been its most authoritative member.

Although people with other strong identities were buried in the area directly south of the plaza, this part of the site seems to have been a significant locus over time for the interment of people with pipes (Figures 6-52, 7-33), including the three older or mature adult men and an additional adult, whose pipes were placed at their necks, perhaps indicating a particularly strong social identity objectified in them. Civil leadership (perhaps below the very highest level) might well have been centered here. Analogously, from the early excavations, it is Block 1 in the far southern portion of the site (well south of the postulated plaza centered in Block 10) in which all examples of pipe placement at neck were located (Burials 108, 127, and 297, plus Conover Burial 1 in the same general area). South-of-the-plaza might be equated with civil leadership in both portions of the site.

Other smaller-scale dual or multiple divisions, such as those hinted at by differences in placement of lip notching on mortuary vessels (Drooker 1996c: Figure 7.19), by the left-right placement of mortuary vessels (Drooker 1996c: Figures 7.20, 7.21), or by the locations of extant, recognizable effigy representations (Figure 7-27) probably were important to the living residents of Madisonville, but cannot be untangled at this late date. It does seem that there were identities being expressed here, but they were multiple and crosscutting—impossible to sort out completely from the fragmentary archaeological record. Again, this is what would be expected from a society where social personae and leadership positions were achieved, built up from multiple social identities over time, but anchored in an inherited system of clan (or similar group) membership that brought with it certain ascribed qualities or opportunities.

Settlement Patterns and Community Alliances as Seen from Madisonville

Throughout the Madisonville Horizon, there seems to have been no settlement hierarchy in the lower Little Miami Valley. Some villages, including Madisonville, seem to have overlapped in time with others, but there is no evidence that any one of them functioned as a major center in conjunction with outlying minor centers or smaller settlements. There may have been an alternation over time of village locations, due to agricultural requirements (for example, shifting production away from temporarily depleted soils to a different portion of the floodplain). Or village sites might have shifted due to cycles of warfare (for instance, preferential location on blufftops versus floodplains for defensive purposes). Still another contributor might have been subsistence changes (to sites favoring long-term storage during seasonal absences for big-game hunting, versus other sites during periods when maize agriculture was the primary dietary mainstay).

It must be emphasized that a number of known village locations in the lower Little Miami Valley (Figures 4-6, 5-1) were never explored well enough to define their sizes, periods of occupation, or intrasite organization, so that construction of a complete picture of local area occupation is, and will remain, impossible. In spite of these information gaps, Madisonville appears to be firmly established as the only nucleated village in this subregion during the protohistoric Late Madisonville Horizon, following a series of earlier, smaller-scale occupations of the site. It does not appear to have had a population at any one time much greater than Early-Middle Fort Ancient sites of short-term occupation such as Incinerator, but does appear to have been utilized over a much longer period and, toward the end of that period, to have supported a more complex social system.

During protohistoric times, the village's size and importance appear to have been roughly matched by a cohort of settlements spaced upstream along and close to the Ohio River, including Dunn, Augusta, possibly Fox Farm, Hardin, Clover, Rolf Lee, Orchard, and Buffalo, among others (Figures 4-2, 4-5). A few of these, such as Buffalo, probably had larger populations than Madisonville, but, like Madisonville, none has afforded evidence that it acted as a major center in a hierarchy of sites. Approximately equivalent, independent, moderate-sized villages separated by relatively short buffer zones appear to represent the typical protohistoric Fort Ancient settlement pattern.

This is consistent with a nonhierarchical regional social organization, and a good match for a peer polity model. If there were formal ties among Fort Ancient settlements, they would be expected to exist in approximate equality. The barred metal pendants excavated from burial contexts at four western to central Fort Ancient sites (Madisonville, Dunn, Fox Farm, and Hardin) have been postulated as signifying just such a relationship, perhaps a multisettlement alliance or even a longer-lasting confederacy. The two adult males at Madisonville buried with these symbol badges on their shoulders, and perhaps some additional adult with whom the richly endowed child wearing the cross-shaped brass pendant was associated, are likely to have been the individuals through whom intersettlement contacts were maintained.

Such ties seem to have been a late development, coinciding with the protohistoric Late Madisonville Horizon. At Madisonville, the cross-shaped brass pendant and the close proximity of one of the double-barred copper pendants to a burial with a fragmentary blue glass bead show that these symbol badges probably were in use during the decades surrounding 1600. The third pendant might have been in use somewhat earlier. This time frame will be revisited in Chapter 8, with discussion of the distribution of all such pendants both inside and outside Fort Ancient territory.

Chapter 8

Madisonville External Relationships

It does seem to be true that, as James Griffin put it, Fort Ancient people had no class (Griffin 1992). Nonetheless, it is abundantly clear from the archaeological record that they *did* have connections. They participated in exchange networks that extended northeast to the lower Saint Lawrence region, southeast to chiefdoms like Coosa, and northwest to the redstone quarries of the upper Mississippi Valley. As must already be apparent from discussions of temporal horizon markers and exotic grave goods at Madisonville, its residents were intimately involved with these networks. In previous chapters, we have seen that different types of exotic artifacts reached Madisonville at different times from different directions and were used by different people in different ways. What does this imply for the relationships between Madisonville residents, residents of other Fort Ancient settlements, and people from outside the Fort Ancient region? What, if any, changes might have been precipitated in the interaction patterns of this interior region by the gradual penetration of Europeans into the continent?

This chapter first looks at geographical distributions, sources, and quantities of exotic items present at Madisonville, to get an idea of the directions and redundance of interaction networks through which its residents obtained them. Also considered are locally made items with clear inspiration from foreign objects. After that, the strength of links between Madisonville and the various culture areas with which its residents interacted, including Fort Ancient, are evaluated on the basis of types, numbers, and usage of these items, and on the time depth behind the interactions.

Geographic Distributions and Sources of Madisonville Imports over Time

Earlier chapters have introduced some of the important nonlocal materials and artifacts excavated at Madisonville, including metal and glass, marine shell, pipes, and ceramics. Spatial distributions and sources were alluded to, but not usually described in detail. Here, maps allow direct visual comparison of interaction networks through which different types of items traveled.

European Goods and Related Materials

Madisonville residents obtained European goods from at least two directions, northeast and south. Most items probably were acquired indirectly, through native intermediaries. The question is, which ones? Through whom did European items reach Madisonville? Were there long-established exchange relationships through which these items passed from hand to hand, or did new ones spring up with the advent of new opportunities?

The distributions of two types of items illustrate the north-south geographical range of Madisonville's sixteenth-century connections to far-flung regions. Sheet brass Clarksdale bells are found throughout the Southeast in a pattern that ties them to the 1539-1543 de Soto entrada and other early Spanish expeditions (Brain 1975; Mitchem and McEwan 1988). They have been excavated at sites occupied through the first quarter of the seventeenth century (Smith 1987:44-47). Madisonville is the northernmost site from which one has been recovered (Figure 6-23), with a considerable distance between it and the closest example at another site (Figure 8-1). Did the bell reach the settlement from the southeast, or from the southwest? From the map, either seems possible. This question will be considered further below, in conjunction with presence or absence of other artifacts originating from these two interior southeastern regions.

Large copper kettles with iron fittings were brought into the Saint Lawrence estuary by Basque traders during the late sixteenth century (Fitzgerald 1990; Fitzgerald et al. 1993; Turgeon 1990). Whole kettles and parts have been found at Micmac and Iroquoian sites in New Brunswick, Nova Scotia, Ontario, and New York (Figure 8-2). The copper used in these kettles is often very pure, over 99.5% (Fitzgerald et al. 1993: Table 3), which can lead to confusion between it and native copper. Madisonville, which has produced the largest number of iron kettle lugs recorded from any site (cf. Fitzgerald et al. 1993:Table

4), is the southernmost site—and apparently the only Fort Ancient site—at which Basque kettle parts have been found (Figure 6-22).

Two other European-derived artifacts excavated at Madisonville might also have come from this direction. The iron dagger guard (Figure 6-21f) is similar to examples, including both dagger and sword guards (which were made in matching sets) from the Seneca Cameron and Factory Hollow sites in New York, and from a Micmac grave in Nova Scotia that also contained nine whole Basque kettles (Figure 8-3) (Harper 1956:Appendix A; Wray et al. 1991:325; Rochester Museum and Science Center Exhibition; Martha Sempowski, pers. comm.). An iron dagger blade was found at the Onondaga Sheldon site (Bradley 1987:Pl. 7). Sword guards from the Southeast often are more elaborate in design than these (e.g., Hally 1988: Fig. 1.3; Morrell 1965: cover, Pl. 7).

The friable high-copper, low-calcium blue glass beads are chemically and physically similar to beads from the late sixteenth-century Huron Molson site, Kleinburg Ossuary (Huron-Petun?), and Seneca Adams site (Chafe et al. 1986; Drooker 1993a; Kenyon and Kenyon 1983:59-60; Wray 1983:42; Wray et al. 1987:114-15). Greenish-blue beads from the Saint Lawrence Valley Chicoutimi site also appear to fall within this chemical range (Moreau 1993). Friable blue glass beads have been excavated at the GBP1 Neutral Carton Ossuary (Kenyon and Kenyon 1983:59-60) and at sixteenth-century sites across New York state, including the Erie(?) Ripley site (Harvard University Peabody Museum Cat. No. 04-3-10/65188), the proto-Susquehannock Englebert site and related sites across the border in Bradford County, Pennsylvania (Kent 1984:213; Stewart 1973:4), and two protohistoric Mohawk sites, England's Woods and Barker (Rumrill 1991). Farther south, they have been reported from the Keyser complex in western Virginia and from Monongahela sites of southwestern Pennsylvania (Witthoft 1966:206), and are known from at least two eastern Fort Ancient sites, Marmet and Neale's Landing (Barnett and Paxton 1955; Hemmings, 1977:12.2–12.3). They also were excavated at at least one Caborn-Welborn site and the O'Regan site in northeastern Iowa (Cheryl Munson, pers. comm. 1991; M. Wedel 1959:77, 162; personal examination of Iowa Historical Society Cat. Nos. Ae12-461, Ae12-609), and are present in the Southeast, for instance at the Period C Bradford Ferry site in Alabama (Marvin Smith, pers. comm.).

Because descriptions of the physical condition and exact hue of blue glass beads in the literature are often vague, and undoubtedly also because these beads tended to disintegrate under archaeological conditions, the complete geographical distribution is difficult to determine. Figure 8-4, which maps the distribution of definite cases of friable "early blue" beads, must be considered partial and approximate. From it, there appear to be two possible source areas and several different avenues through which these beads could have reached Madisonville. One *entrepôt* does seem to be the Saint Lawrence estuary, but a Chesapeake Bay distribution point also appears to be a real possibility. As Pendergast has been at pains to remind the archaeological community, "it would be incorrect to attribute to the Saint Lawrence River axis a[n]...overwhelming, even dominant, role in the movement of European goods to the interior in the sixteenth century....[O]ther major riverine routes to the hinterlands were used by Europeans from the outset" (Pendergast 1994:14). From Chesapeake Bay, glass beads could have been transported up the Susquehanna River to New York Iroquoians, up the Potomac to the Monongahela-Allegheny river system, or up the James or Roanoke to the New-Kanawha system (Figure 3-1; cf. Rountree 1993a: Fig. 1.3). However, the glass bead sequence from the Chesapeake Bay region itself commences only well after 1600 (Miller et al. 1983). According to Marvin Smith, the Southeast also should be considered a possible source of friable blue glass beads (pers. comm.).

The spirals, coils, and serpents made from thin metal tubes undoubtedly shared the same indigenous technology, but have significantly different distributions. The spirals are almost exclusively associated with Iroquoian sites (Figure 8-5, Table 8-1), and seem emblematic of Iroquoian identity (see Bradley and Childs 1991 for a thorough discussion of distribution over time, contexts of disposition, and manufacturing techniques). They are most in evidence at New York Iroquois and Susquehannock settlements, although nine have come from the Monongahela Ingraham/Spragg site (Johnson 1994: Table 10). Both smelted European copper (including some very pure samples) and brass were used, but the sophisticated craftwork appears to be native. Sempowski has proposed that Seneca spirals were manufactured primarily by Susquehannock craftspeople, since they disappeared from Seneca sites at the beginning of the seventeenth century, at a time when Seneca-Susquehannock exchange networks apparently were broken (Kuhn and Funk 1994:81-82; Sempowski 1994:52, 61). Bradley and Childs note that while the largest source of European copper in the sixteenth century was Basque mariners in the Saint Lawrence, brass probably came to Susquehannocks (and hence to interior peoples) from Norman traders plying the mid-Atlantic coast from at least 1559 onward (1991:14-15).

The small, unspectacular Madisonville brass spiral is consistent with some of the more modest Seneca specimens (e.g., Wray et al. 1987:60). It could have been acquired from external sources or made locally, as a copy of a spiral seen elsewhere. The only other spiral from Fort Ancient territory, reported to have come from a location near Gallipolis, Ohio (William Wertz, pers. comm.), along with a brass animal effigy (Period D, ca. 1630-1670), was far better made and seemingly unconnected with the one from Madisonville. Thus, there is no strong evidence—except its brass, rather than copper, material—to suggest a southern derivation (Susquehannock, Monongahela) over a northern derivation (Seneca, Erie, Neutral) for the latter. Madisonville is the westernmost site from which a tubular metal spiral has come.

The distribution of tubular metal coils and rings (Figure 8-6, Table 8-1) does not extend far into Iroquoian territory, but does encompass a broad band across the Midwest and into the mid-south that almost completely encircles the settlement at Madisonville. More coils/rings have been counted there than at any other site (38, including at least 3 brass and 25 copper), but many of them are fragmentary. The largest number (12) and some of the finest examples were buried with a child, together with the barred brass pendant (Figure 6-21f). Although copper and brass tubular rings and coils are reported from eight Neutral and Huron sites (4 of GBP1, 3 of GBP2, 1 of GBP3) and two early Seneca sites, their quantities are not great. The largest number, 2 coils and 3 rings, came from the Seneca Adams site. The Fort Ancient Hardin site produced nine fragmentary brass coils and two pieces of "wire," probably all from a single item (Hanson 1966:168). The Indian Hills site in northwestern Ohio produced what might be as many as sixteen tubular metal artifacts (or as few as none): 10 beads and 4 earrings of "coiled strip and coiled wire" and 2 other items described as "wire," along with two types of GBP2 glass beads (Stothers, in press ; Stothers and Abel 1991: Fig. 2).

Although Mildred Wedel reported only 1 or 2 coils from most of the protohistoric sites clustered in and near northeastern Iowa, the exception being 7 from Lane (1959: Table 1), I examined 7 from Burke, 9 from Woolstrom, and 10 from O'Regan at the Iowa Historical Society. I observed both copper (at least 18) and brass (at least 4), consistent with the results of Wedel's spectrographic analysis of 2 examples (1 brassy copper, 1 interpreted as native copper; 1959:63-76). Almost all were tubes, but one might have been solid. Wedel suggested that the small diameter and regularity of tubes in some of the O'Regan examples might indicate French manufacture.

Another site that produced a significant number of coils, perhaps surpassing Madisonville but incompletely described, was the Caborn-Welborn Murphy cemetery (Moorehead 1906:62-86). All were excavated from burial contexts. One, analyzed by Wedel, was interpreted as native copper (1959:70). The single example that I have examined (Robert S. Peabody Museum Cat. No. 38/171-15211) was very well made, similar to examples from both Madisonville and Iowa. At least five disk pipes, including one with a notably large disk, came from burials at this site (Moorehead 1906: Fig. 22). All were made of white-light gray limestone (Malinda Blustain, pers. comm.), with forms similar to limestone and redstone examples from four Fort Ancient sites: Buffalo, Fox Farm, Campbell, and an unspecified site in Butler County, just north of Cincinnati (Glass n.d.:30; Hanson 1975:89; Shetrone 1926:454, 459; West 1934: Pl. 53). The sixth pipe excavated at the site was a vasiform of the same light-colored limestone (Moorehead 1906: Fig. 22; Malinda Blustain, pers. comm.).

The only other locations with relatively large numbers of coils were on the Tennessee River in northern Alabama, including the isolated burial of a male with a large-disk redstone pipe at the right side of the skull and six coils in each ear (one analyzed by electron microprobe was interpreted as native copper because of its purity; Jolly 1969), and three adult burials at the Lu86 site with coils in their ears (two with three in each ear, one with an unknown number; Webb 1939:28-29). One of the two males with coils at the latter site had a tubular metal serpent on his "right breast" and a limestone small-disk pipe inside his left elbow; the other had an animal-head effigy pipe that was topped by a small disk.

Unlike the spirals, then, coils appear to be most strongly associated with Madisonville and Oneota-related locations.

As with coils, Madisonville has produced more tubular metal serpents than any other site, of both copper and brass and in a variety of sizes, including the greatest number (three) with any single burial (Figures 6-21a, 7-30). However, the site lies near the eastern limit of distribution (Figure 8-7). There are only two possible examples from other Fort Ancient sites, Buffalo (a fragmentary undulating tube, not certainly a serpent shape) and Augusta (reported from a burial context by a collector) (Hanson 1975:71; Henderson et al. 1986:117). They are most strongly represented at Oneota sites, particularly Anker, where five (of "flattened sheet copper") were with five well-endowed burials, including a child (Bluhm and Liss 1961:96-99). Single serpents were found with burials at Blood Run in northwestern Iowa and O'Regan and New Galena in northeastern Iowa (Harvey 1979:138; M. Wedel 1959:72), the Lu86 site in Alabama (see above), Hoxie Farm, Illinois, and Dumaw Creek, Michigan, including adults and at least two children, and at a number of other sites (Table 8-1). Spectrographic and special-element analysis of a serpent from the Lane site in northeastern Iowa revealed 99+% copper content, interpreted as native copper (M. Wedel 1959:70).

All of the serpents that I have examined (from Madisonville and Orr phase sites) were made from thin tubes, many of them flattened. The vast majority of published examples probably were made the same way, but the overlapping seam is difficult to see unless the examiner is looking for it, and descriptions and illustrations in the literature often are ambiguous. This is unfortunate, because chubbier non-tubular serpent shapes also were made, with a pedigree reaching back in time to Cahokia and Spiro (Brown 1976: Fig. 63; Pustmueller 1950). They have come from Oneota, Caborn-Welborn, Mississippian, and Fort Ancient sites that were occupied up to protohistoric times, but cover a significantly deeper time span than the tubular serpents (Table 8-2). Their distribution, from West Virginia to Wisconsin to Alabama, echoes that of the tubular serpents, without extending to very recent sites such as those in northeastern Iowa.

All examples that might be tubular are included in Table 8-1 and Figure 8-7. Tabulated but not mapped are a late prehistoric example known to have a solid square cross-section (Carter Mound Group, Illinois), and a jagged "serpent" probably made from an awl (Summer Island, Michigan). The latest known thin serpent pendant, from the historical Zimmerman site, was fashioned of European brass wire with a B-shaped cross-section (Brown 1975:Pl. 7), a material that is a marker for the late seventeenth–early eighteenth century and that has been found at several sites in New York, Illinois, and Missouri occupied around

TABLE 8-1
Sites with Ornaments Made from Thin Copper or Brass Tubes

		Serpent Shapes	Coils, Rings	Spirals	References
Lu/0 86	AL	x	x		Webb 1939
Seven Mile Is.	AL		x		Jolly 1969, 1973
near N. Little Rock	AR	(x)			M. Wedel 1959
Mt. Royal	FL	(x)			Moore 1894, 1920
Anker	IL	(x)	x		Bluhm and Liss 1961; Herold et al. 1990
Carter Mound	IL	*			Ctr. for Amer. Arch., K. Farnsworth, pers. comm. 1995
Hoxie Farm	IL	(x)			Butkus 1973; Herold et al. 1990:88-7; Dausman 1990
New Lenox	IL		x		Lurie 1994
Palos	IL		x		Munson and Munson 1969a,1969b
Zimmerman	IL	*			M. Brown 1975
Fifield	IN	(x)*			Faulkner 1972; Herold et al. 1990
Murphy	IN		x		Moorehead 1906; M. Wedel 1959
Blood Run	IA	x	x		Harvey 1979
Burke	IA		x		M. Wedel 1959
Dixon Village	IA	(x)			Harvey 1979
Hogback	IA		x		M. Wedel 1959
Lane	IA	x			M. Wedel 1959
New Galena	IA	x			M. Wedel 1959
O'Regan	IA	(x)	x**		M. Wedel 1959
Woolstrom	IA		x		M. Wedel 1959
northeastern Iowa	IA	x			Iowa Historical Soc., #E.O. 1250
Fanning	KS		x		W. Wedel 1959
Augusta	KY	(x)			Henderson et al. 1986
Hardin	KY		x		Hanson 1966
Slack Farm	KY		x		C. Munson, pers. comm. 1991
Dumaw Creek	MI	(x)			Quimby 1966a
Summer Island	MI	*			Brose 1970
Cooper	MN		x		Birk and Johnson 1992
Hogback	MN		x		M. Wedel 1959
Utz	MO		x**		Bray 1978
Adams	NY		x	x	Wray et al. 1987
Bach	NY			x	Bradley and Childs 1991
Cameron	NY			x	Bradley and Childs 1991
Chase	NY			x	Bradley and Childs 1991
Culbertson	NY		x	x	Wray et al. 1987
Diable	NY			x	Bradley and Childs 1991
Englands Woods	NY			x	Bradley and Childs 1991
Genoa Fort	NY			x	Bradley and Childs 1991
Pompey Center	NY			x	Bradley and Childs 1991
Ripley	NY			x	Bradley and Childs 1991
Smith-Pagerie	NY			x	Bradley and Childs 1991
Spragg	NY			x	Bradley and Childs 1991
Tram	NY			x	Wray et al. 1991
Beale Mound	OH			x	Wm. Wertz, pers. comm. 1993
Indian Hills	OH		x		Stothers 1994
Madisonville	OH	x	x	x	Hooton and Willoughby 1920
Brantford area	ON	*			Fox 1991:6
Dwyer	ON			x	Bradley and Childs 1991
Fonger	ON			x	Fitzgerald 1990
Graham-Rogers	ON		x		Fitzgerald 1990
Green Lake	ON		x	x	Fitzgerald 1990
Grimsby	ON			x	Bradley and Childs 1991
Hood	ON		x		Fitzgerald 1990
Kleinburg	ON		x		Fitzgerald 1990
Sault Ste. Marie area	ON	*			Fox 1991:6
Snider	ON		x		Fitzgerald 1990
Warminster	ON		x	x	Fitzgerald 1990
Foley Farm	PA			x	Bradley and Childs 1991
Ingraham/Spragg	PA			x	Johnson 1994
Overpeck	PA			x	Bradley and Childs 1991
Schultz	PA			x	Bradley and Childs 1991

TABLE 8-1 (cont.)
Sites with Ornaments Made from Thin Copper or Brass Tubes

		Serpent Shapes	Coils, Rings	Spirals	References
Shenks Ferry	PA			x	Bradley and Childs 1991
U.Susquehanna sites	PA			x	Bradley and Childs 1991
WashingtonBoro	PA			x	Bradley and Childs 1991
46HM73	WV			x	Bradley and Childs 1991
Buffalo	WV	(x)*			Hanson 1975
Herriott Farm	WV			x	Bradley and Childs 1991
La Poe	WV			x	Johnson 1994
Pancake Island	WV			x	Brashler 1987; Johnson 1994
State Road Coulee	WI		x		Boszhardt 1989
Valley View	WI		x		Boszhardt 1989

(x) indicates ambiguously-described examples that probably are tubes, but might be flattened tubes or flat cut-outs.
* Sites that produced non-tubular or otherwise aberrant thin metal serpent shapes. The Carter Mound example is solid, with a square cross-section, the one from Zimmerman was made from brass wire with a B-shaped cross-section, and the Summer Island artifact is a non-undulating shape perhaps formed by folding a copper awl. The Fifield serpent is described as "somewhat square in cross section," but this shape could result from a flattened tube. The Buffalo example is a fragmentary undulating tube, not certainly a serpent shape. I have been unable to check out the morphology of the Ontario examples.
** Wedel suggests that the small diameter and regularity of the tubes might signify that they were French-made. Some Utz rings were tubular, but coils are reported as "wire."

TABLE 8-2
Sites wth Flat Copper Serpent-Shaped Pendants or Related Artifacts

		ARTIFACT TYPE		PROVENIENCE		
		Pendant(s)	Other	Mortuary	Unknown	References
Charlotte Thompson Place	AL	x		x		Moore 1899:Fig. 50
Cahokia	IL	x		x		Pustmueller 1950
Charles W. Cooper	IL	x			?	Conrad 1996a:Fig. 40
Norris Farms 36 Cemetery	IL	x		x		Santure et al. 1990:Fig. 10.6i, j
Hovey Lake	IN	x			?	C. Munson, pers. comm. 1991
Spiro	OK		x	x		Brown 1996:Figs. 2-115, 2-117
Buffalo	WV	x *			?	Hanson 1975:Fig. 71
Rolf Lee	WV	x			?	Anon. 1982; R. Maslowski, pers. comm. 1993
Grand River focus	WI	x			?	Jeske 1927:Pl. XXXI.12, Hall 1962:143, Pl. 80F
Glen Oaks	WI	x			?	Hall 1962:143, Pl. 80E
Walker-Hooper	WI	x			?	Hall 1962:143, Pl. 80G

* Fragmentary pendant from Buffalo is described as of brass.

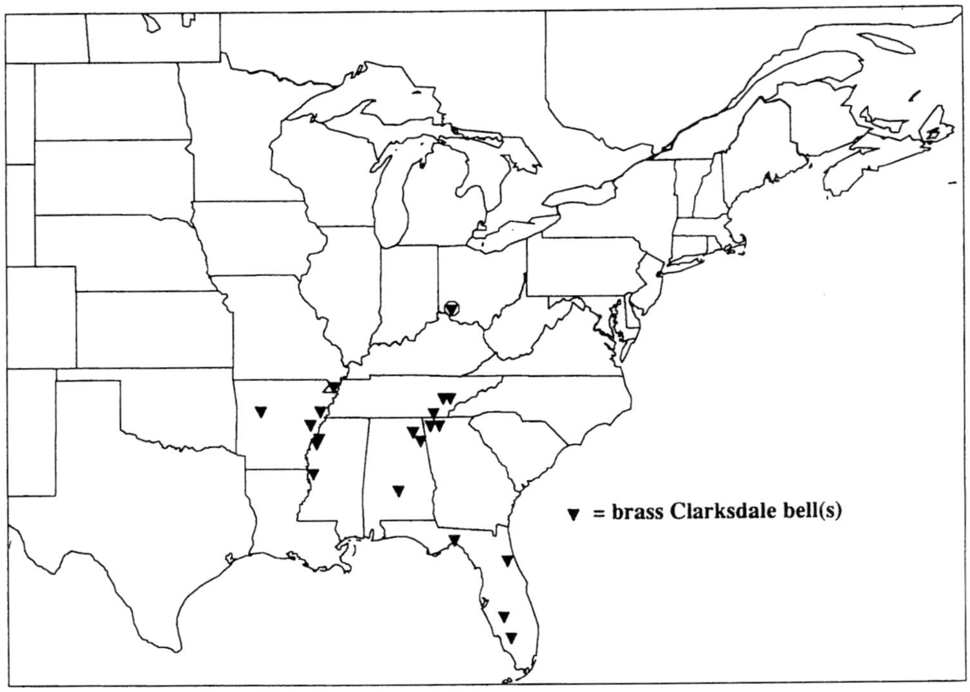

Figure 8-1. Geographical distribution of sheet brass Clarksdale bells (see Mitchem and McEwan 1988: Table 3 for sites).

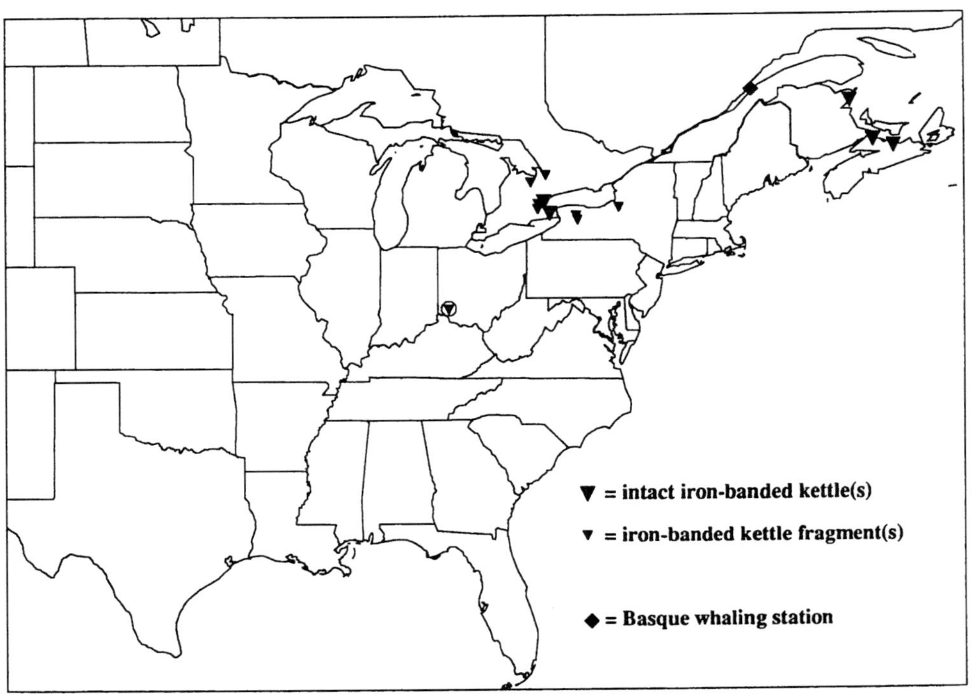

Figure 8-2. Geographical distribution of Basque iron-fitted copper kettles and parts (after Fitzgerald et al. 1993: Fig. 2).

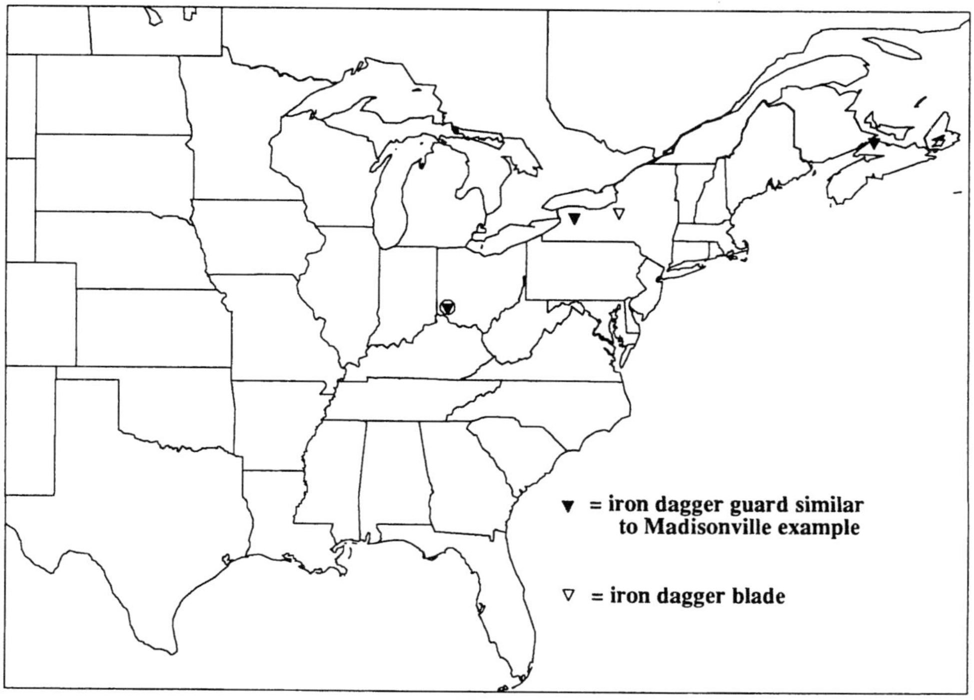

Figure 8-3. Geographical distribution of iron dagger guards similar to the example from Madisonville (see text for sites).

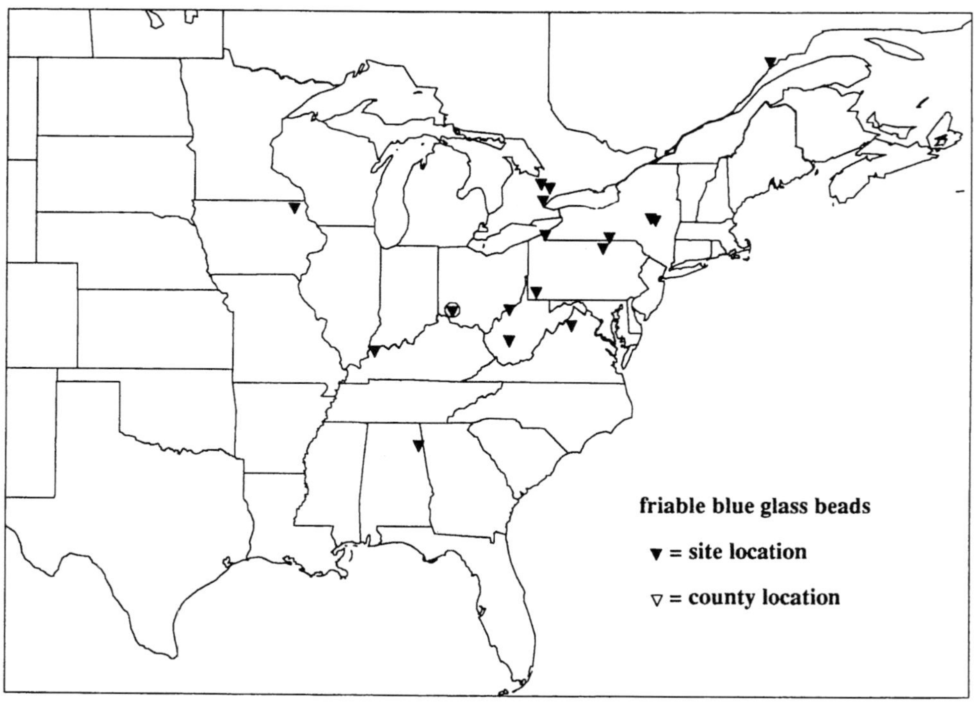

Figure 8-4. Geographical distribution of friable blue glass beads. They undoubtedly were present at many more sites, but descriptions in the literature are not detailed enough to include any more with certainty (see text for sites).

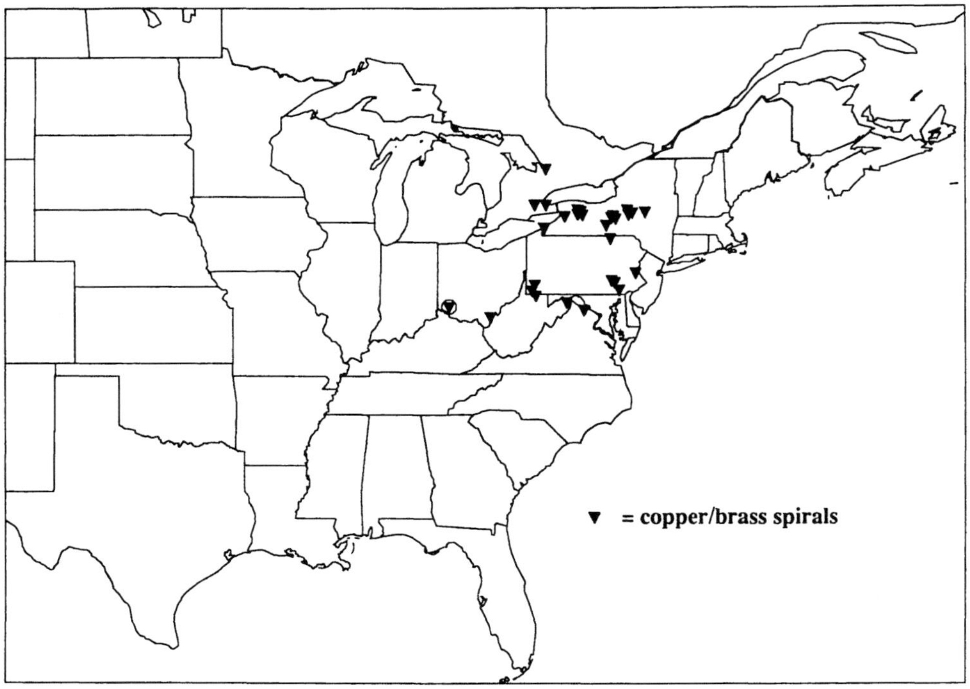

Figure 8-5. Geographical distribution of copper and brass spirals made from thin metal tubes (see Table 8-1 for sites).

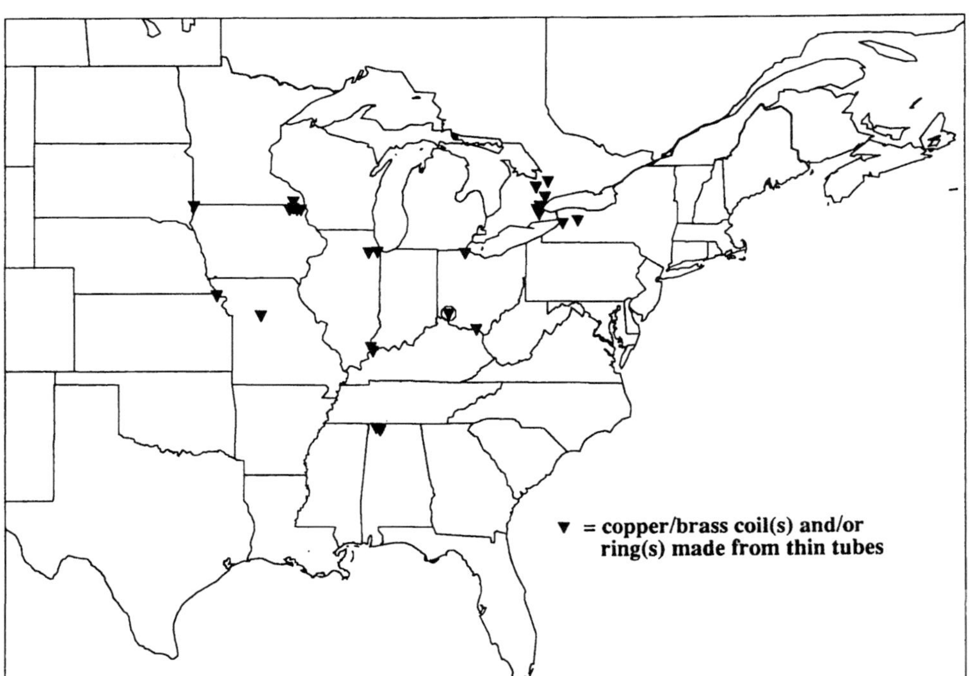

Figure 8-6. Geographical distribution of copper and brass coils made from thin metal tubes (see Table 8-1 for sites).

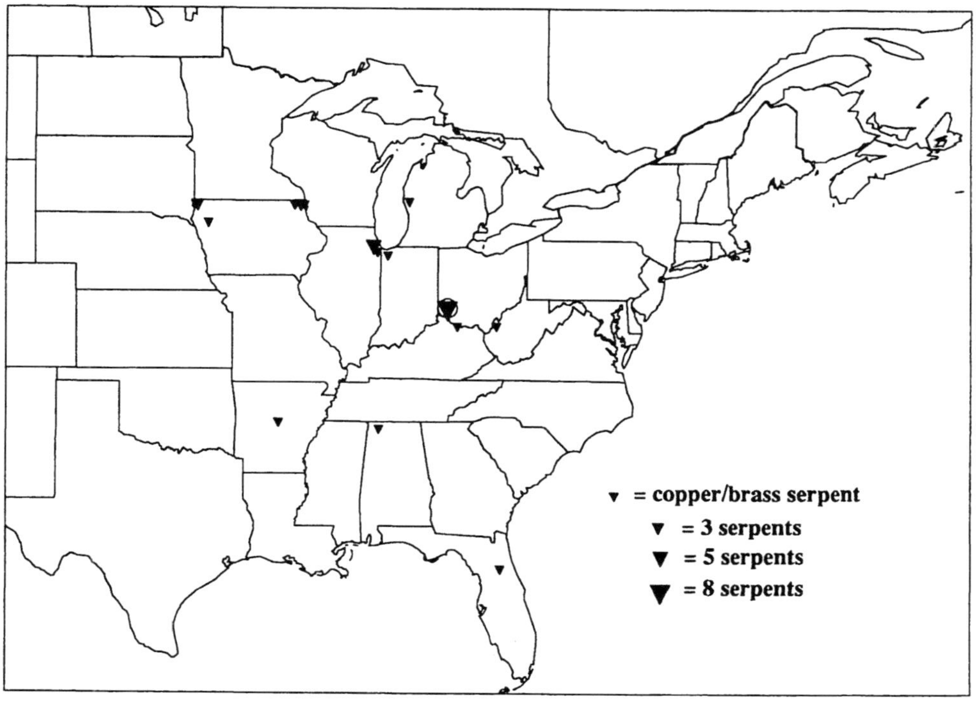

Figure 8-7. Geographical distribution of thin, elongated copper and brass serpents, most of which probably were made from thin metal tubes (see Table 8-1 and discussion in text).

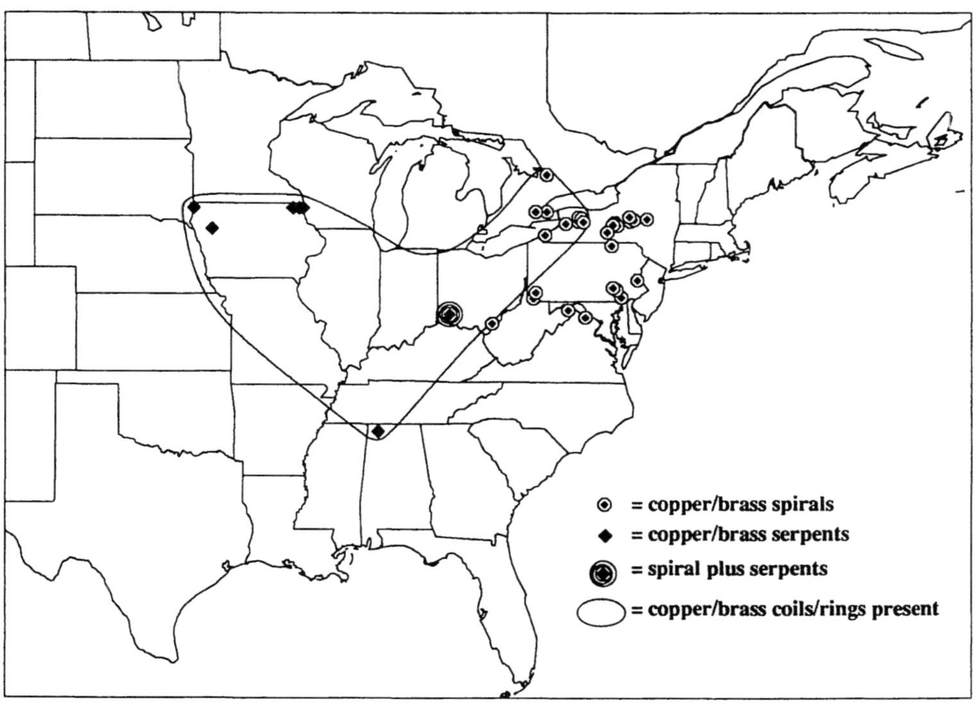

Figure 8-8. Geographical distribution of ornaments made from thin metal tubes. Only serpents known to have been tubular were included (cf. Figure 8-7). Madisonville is the only site that has produced examples of all three types

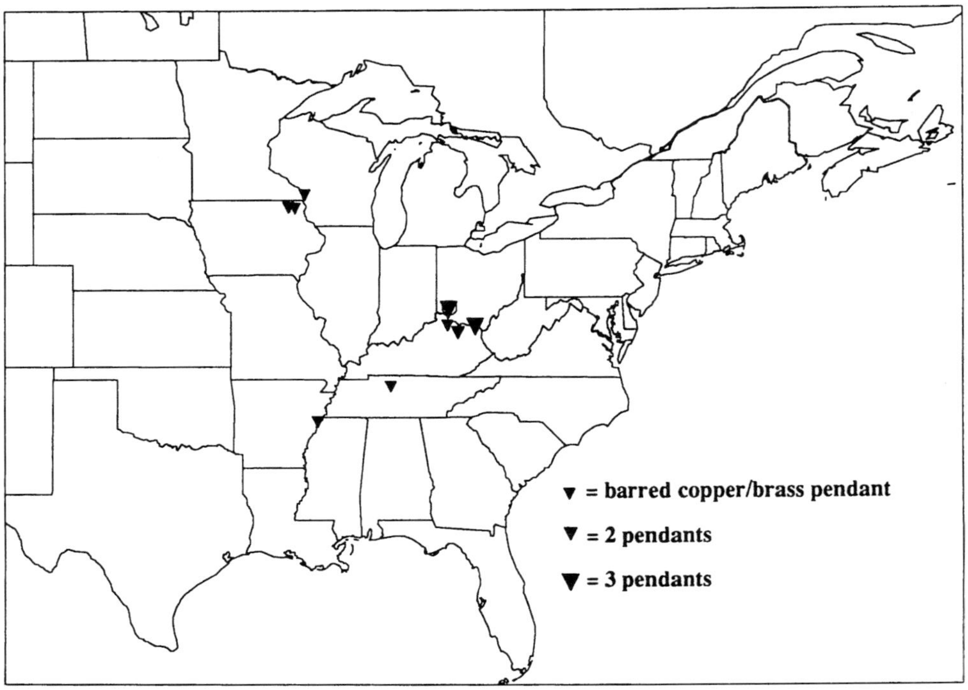

Figure 8-9. Geographical distribution of barred metal pendants (see Figure 7-31 for sites).

1680-1720 (Bray 1978:1-7, 32-34, 50-53; J. Brown 1961:61-62; M. Brown 1975:30, 32-33; Drooker 1992a:22-23, Fig. 13; Herold et al. 1990:83; Munson and Munson 1969a, 1969b; Rochester Museum and Science Center Exhibition). Tubular serpents do not appear to have been made after the mid-seventeenth century, perhaps even earlier.

As can be seen in Figure 8-8, Madisonville occupies a central position in the wide area over which ornaments made from thin copper and brass tubes have been excavated, and is the only site that has produced coils, serpents, and a spiral. From the relatively large numbers of tubular artfacts and fragments in nonmortuary contexts (Table 6-6) and the presence of long, thin "blanks" of the correct size and shape to make these ornaments (Figure 6-21e), it seems very likely that craftspeople were fashioning them at Madisonville.

The late prehistoric and protohistoric barred pendants illustrated and described in Figure 7-31 are mapped in Figure 8-9. They are concentrated in Fort Ancient territory, with the largest numbers coming from Hardin and Madisonville. All provenienced examples are from burials, with placement that makes it likely that they acted as symbol badges. Among metal ornaments found on Fort Ancient sites, they are surpassed in size only by the large brass armbands found mainly at Rolf Lee. The only non-single-barred examples are from Madisonville and Fox Farm. The only precedent I have found for the use of a double-barred shape as symbol badge is a flint mace from a stone box grave near Nashville (Ganier 1948:8, 2k). Since the middle Cumberland valley was almost completely depopulated after the mid-fifteenth century (Smith 1992:413-25), it is unlikely that either the flint mace or the single-barred metal pendant from the same vicinity (Figure 8-10) date after that time.

Protohistoric single-barred pendants have earlier precedents in Wisconsin. For example, Hall (1962: Pl. 80) illustrates "mace shapes" from the tenth through twelfth century Metro-Diamond Bluff and Walker-Hooper sites (Gibbon 1986:317-318; Jeske 1927; Lawshe 1947) that are remarkably similar to the crosslike shapes from Flynn Cemetery, Iowa, and Rose Mound, Arkansas, as well as a combination serpent-mace from Walker-Hooper that provides a visual link in a virtual continuum from cross-shape to flat serpent shape. In Chapter 7, I postulated that single-barred protohistoric examples might represent the feet and tails of birds (cf. Hall 1962: Pl. 79E), in contrast to double/multi-barred examples that seem to represent rattlesnake tails. This may be so, but, judging from the full variety of available examples, the distinction might well be ambiguous rather than sharp.

However, there is no ambiguity about the large, fully formed bird/hawk symbol badges that Williams proposed as a marker of his protohistoric Markala Horizon. He and Hall illustrate eight complete and partial examples from Tennessee, Arkansas, and Wisconsin, the locations of which are mapped in Figure 8-11 (Hall 1962: Pl. 79; Williams 1980: Fig. 2). Hawk locations are completely separate from Fort Ancient and Orr phase barred pendants (Figure 8-9), although it is of interest that one metal bird symbol badge, one single-barred metal pendant, and the double-barred flint mace all came from near Nashville, Tennessee. The larger size and comparative intricacy of the birds/hawks might reflect usage by personages of importance in social sys-

Figure 8-10. Barred metal pendant from an adult stone box grave burial at Zollicoffer Hill, near Nashville, Tennessee (HUPM Cat. No. 77-57-10/11831). It was positioned on the chest of the individual, and a short piece of cord was found in the suspension hole (Putnam 1973c:39-40). Photograph by Hillel Burger (HUPM Photo No. N3363). Copyright 1997 by the President and Fellows of Harvard College, and used with permission.

tems of greater complexity. Still more complex repoussé copper "falcons" and "falcon warriors" have come from very high-status burials in Mississippian mound centers such as Etowah (Strong 1989).

Since no copper ornaments that might have served as symbol badges are known from Early or Middle Fort Ancient contexts, the historical precedent for the Fort Ancient pendants appears to be Mississippian/Oneota. The large size of the Madisonville examples makes European kettle copper and brass the most likely sources of materials, but the craft technology was well within local capabilities (S. Terry Childs, pers. comm.).

For completeness in later discussion, I include here distribution maps of three types of metal artifacts that have only peripheral connection to the Madisonville site. Sheet brass side view animal effigies that probably originated in Spanish Florida are mapped in Figure 8-12. To sites listed by Waselkov (1989: Table 5) are added the Beale Mound and Clover sites in Fort Ancient territory and the Monongahela Varner/John Lapping site (Johnson 1994: Table 10; Maslowski 1991: Fig. 7.16; Mayer-Oakes 1955: Pl. 107; W. Wertz, pers. comm.). These ca. 1630-1670 artifacts might perhaps be echoed or previewed by two cannel coal effigies at Madisonville (Figures 6-22, 6-23). Another "bearlike" cannel coal effigy is in the Stahl Collection at the Blennerhassett Museum, presumably from Blennerhassett Island where the Neale's Landing site is located.

Slightly overlapping the side view effigies geographically, but extending no farther south than West Virginia, are top view metal lizard or beaver effigies (Figure 8-13). Locations include the Seneca Cornish and Feugle sites, four Monongahela sites, some of which have produced multiple examples, the Luray Complex Barton site in West Virginia, and the Fort Ancient Marmet, Clover, and Hardin sites (Henderson et al. 1986:137; Johnson 1994: Table 10). Since Feugle dates to ca. 1610-1620 (Saunders and Sempowski 1991:24), these effigies might slightly predate those shown in Figure 8-12.

The large brass armbands tabulated by Waselkov for seventeenth-century sites south of southeastern Tennessee (1989:Table 4) also were found on an individual buried at the Overhill Cherokee Chota-Tanasee site and at two Fort Ancient sites: on a child burial at Orchard, and thirteen examples generally from the forearms of adult burials at Rolf Lee, as many as four per individual (Figure 8-14) (Kapp 1961-1968; Moxley 1988a:40; Schroedl 1986:170-72; Everett Schwartz, pers. comm.). The two sets of large metal legbands at Madisonville, known only from green-stained bones, might be related to the same interaction sphere. If these large metal artifacts had disintegrated, they probably dated much earlier than the Rolf Lee examples, but another possibility—that they were removed sometime after burial—should not be overlooked.

Madisonville metal artifacts differ in numbers and materials from other protohistoric Fort Ancient sites (Table 8-3). Comparisons give a more complete picture of the nature and source of metal supply at this site. The number of copper/brass items from Madisonville is far greater than from any other Fort Ancient site. However, standardization by burial population size reveals a different picture. The lowest numbers are for Buffalo, undoubtedly reflecting an early occupation period. The incomplete reporting for Orchard makes its metal assemblage difficult to assess, but my impression is that its numbers per total burial population size are indeed lower than Madisonville or Hardin. Rolf Lee, a later site, has the highest standardized value,

TABLE 8-3
Copper and Brass Excavated at Protohistoric Fort Ancient Sites

	Madisonville (1)	(2)	(3)	Hardin	Buffalo	Orchard	Rolf Lee
Total number of copper/brass items	225	461	13	200 ±	62	37+	145
Number of burials	591			335	562	>300	83
Copper/brass items, standardized (divided by number of burials)	.38			.60	.11	.12+	1.75
Number of items known to be brass	20	59	3	66			
Percent known to be brass	9%	13%	23%	33%			
Number of items in burials	77			190 ±	most?	?	entire
Percent in burials	34%			± 95%			sample

Data are for sites with reasonably large quantitative samples (Hanson 1966, 1975; Kapp, 1961-1968; Moxley 1988a). Rolf Lee includes only gravegoods, from 83 burials excavated by Kapp. Orchard includes all reported artifacts, but list probably is incomplete; for example, numbers from the Paxton collection are not known. Madisonville listings are (1) for Trenches 1-K, not including metal-stained bone, (2) all metal artifacts in field notes and museum collections, and (3) for the sample of 13 artifacts subjected to neutron activation analysis (Drooker 1993b). See also Table 6-13.

as would be expected. However, Hardin has half again as much metal per person as does Madisonville. This probably is not a time-related factor. From its other European-related goods, the site is roughly contemporaneous with Madisonville, perhaps even earlier. Since almost all metal artifacts excavated there were grave goods, Hardin residents do not appear to have been on familiar terms with copper/brass—they regarded it as far more valuable than did Madisonville residents. Both there and at Buffalo and Orchard, very little scrap was reported, only small finished ornaments.

One relevant factor in the differences between Hardin and Madisonville probably was different sources of supply. Considering the relatively high proportion of brass at Hardin (Table 8-3), metal very likely was reaching that location from the mid-Atlantic region, where late sixteenth-century Norman traders provided much more brass than did Basque traders in the Saint Lawrence (Bradley and Childs 1991a:14-15). In contrast, Madisonville people probably were obtaining much of their metal from the northeast, through the same network that brought them Basque copper kettle parts (Figure 8-2). If they were making and exporting finished artifacts, relatively fewer metal items might have been retained for disposal as grave goods (cf. Ray 1978).

Shell Ornaments

As we have seen, marine shell was rarer and more highly valued at Madisonville than was metal (Chapter 7). The settlement had both much lower numbers and much lower numbers per person of shell items than other protohistoric Fort Ancient sites (Table 6-13), and most of these items were found with burials, not discarded in nonmortuary contexts. The types of artifacts that were present indicate that shell reached Madisonville from several different directions.

Engraved Citico style rattlesnake gorgets have been proposed as a marker of the Coosa polity, where they were found with subadult and adult female burials (Hally et al. 1990:133-34). Fort Ancient territory shows the second greatest concentration of sites from which these artifacts have come (Figure 8-15; see Tables 4-9 and 6-12 for names of Fort Ancient sites), although few if any Fort Ancient settlements have produced more than one or two (e.g., Brashler and Moxley 1990). At Madisonville, a single worn and reworked example was excavated from a child's grave (Figure 6-19a). Aside from a reworked fragment from the Neutral Sealey Village site (Fitzgerald 1992), Madisonville is the northernmost location from which has come a rattlesnake gorget.

Engraved mask gorgets appear to have a similar, though more dispersed, distribution than rattlesnake gorgets (Figure 8-16). They have been found in nineteenth-century Plains Indian war bundles, and in burials as far north as Manitoba. The three largest concentrations of sites from which they have come include eastern Tennessee, northeastern Arkansas, and Fort Ancient territory (Smith and Smith 1989: Table 1; Table 4-9). Caborn-Welborn, Oneota, and lower Great Lakes sites include Murphy, Indiana; Utz, Missouri; a northeastern Iowa highway cut; Anker,

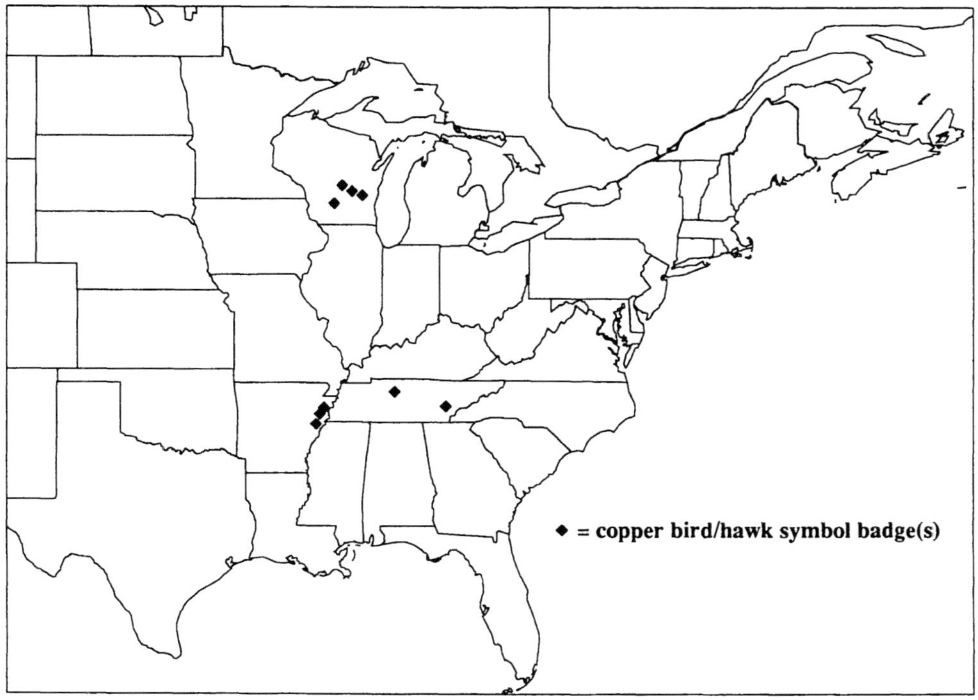

Figure 8-11. Geographical distribution of bird/hawk symbol badges (after Hall 1962: Pl. 79 and Williams 1980: Fig. 1).

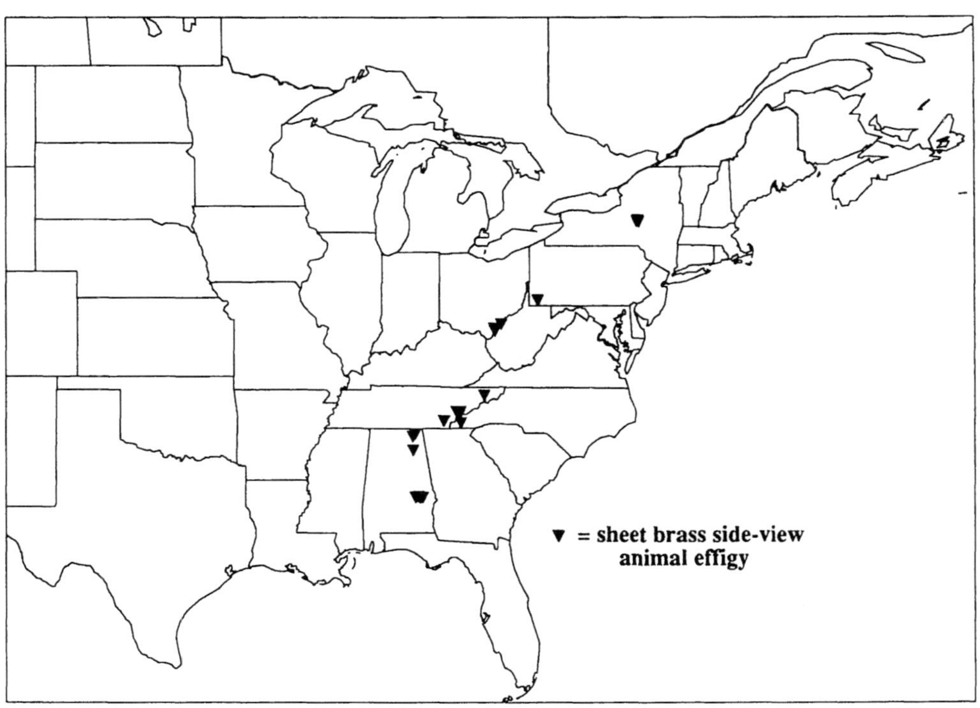

Figure 8-12. Geographical distribution of side-view sheet brass animal effigies (after Waselkov 1989: Fig. 7; see text for additional sites).

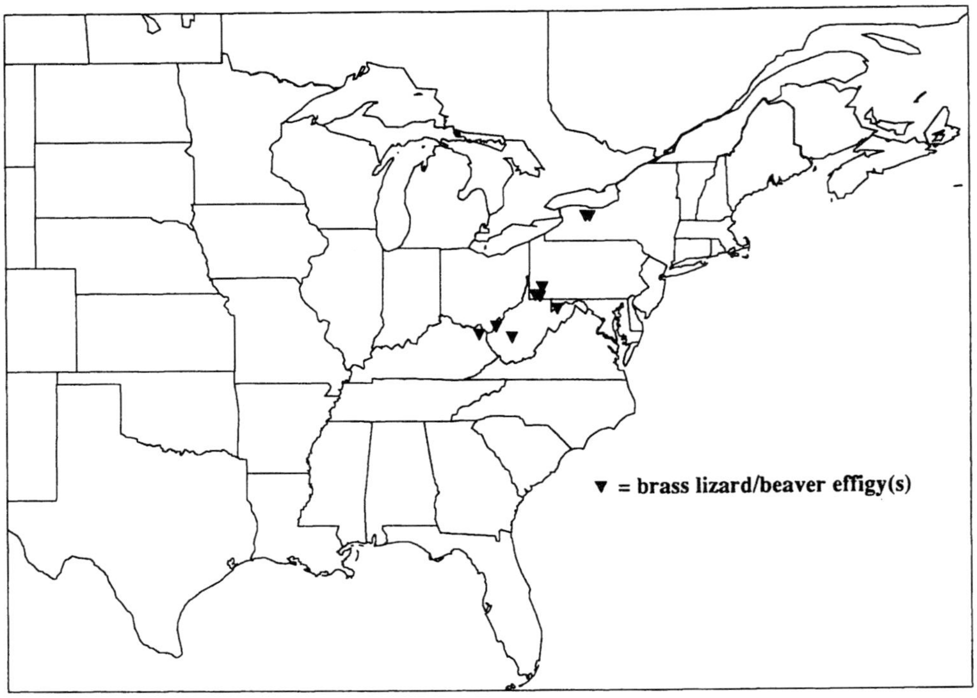

Figure 8-13. Geographical distribution of top-view brass lizard/beaver effigies (most data from Johnson 1994; see text for list of sites).

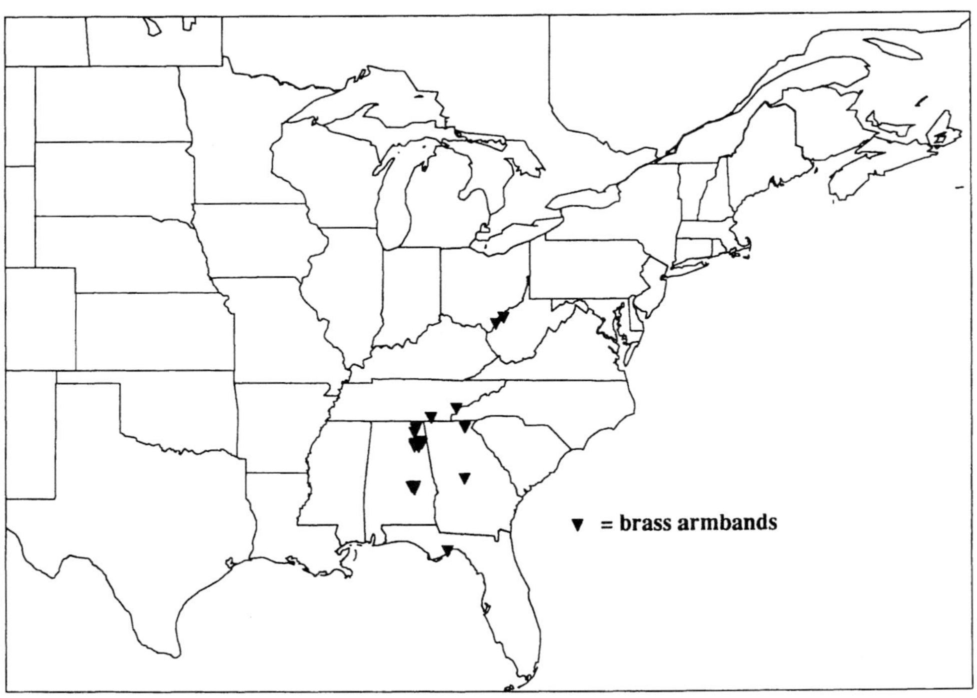

Figure 8-14. Geographical distribution of brass armbands (after Waselkov 1989: Fig. 6; see text for additional sites).

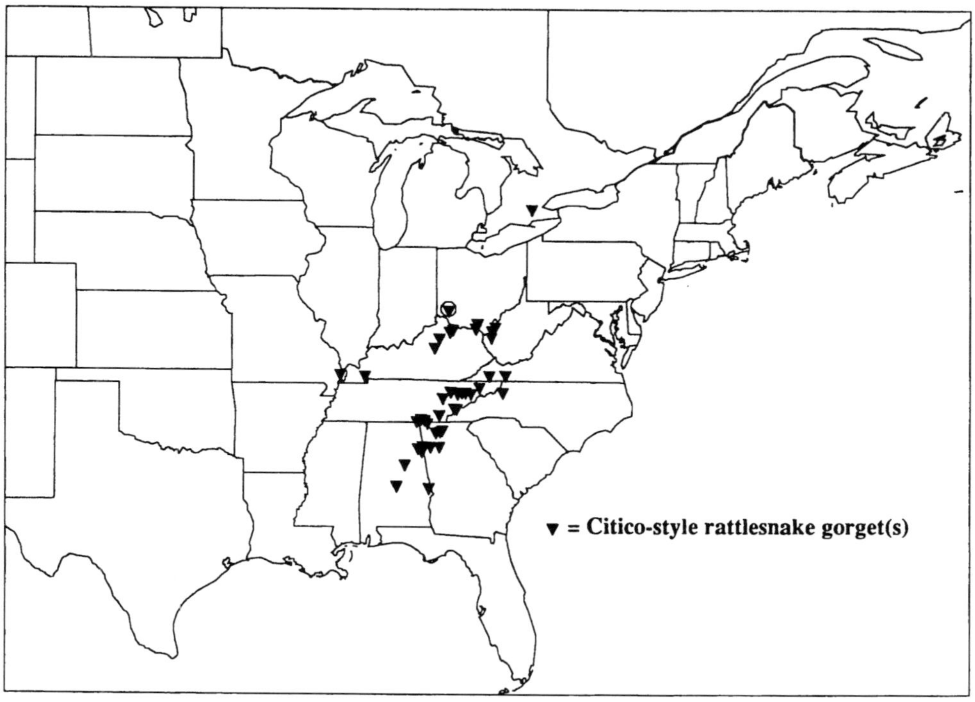

Figure 8-15. Geographical distribution of marine shell Citico rattlesnake gorgets (after Hally et al. 1990: Fig. 9-3). See Table 4-9 for Fort Ancient sites. Ontario site is the Neutral Sealey Village (Fitzgerald 1992, pers. comm.).

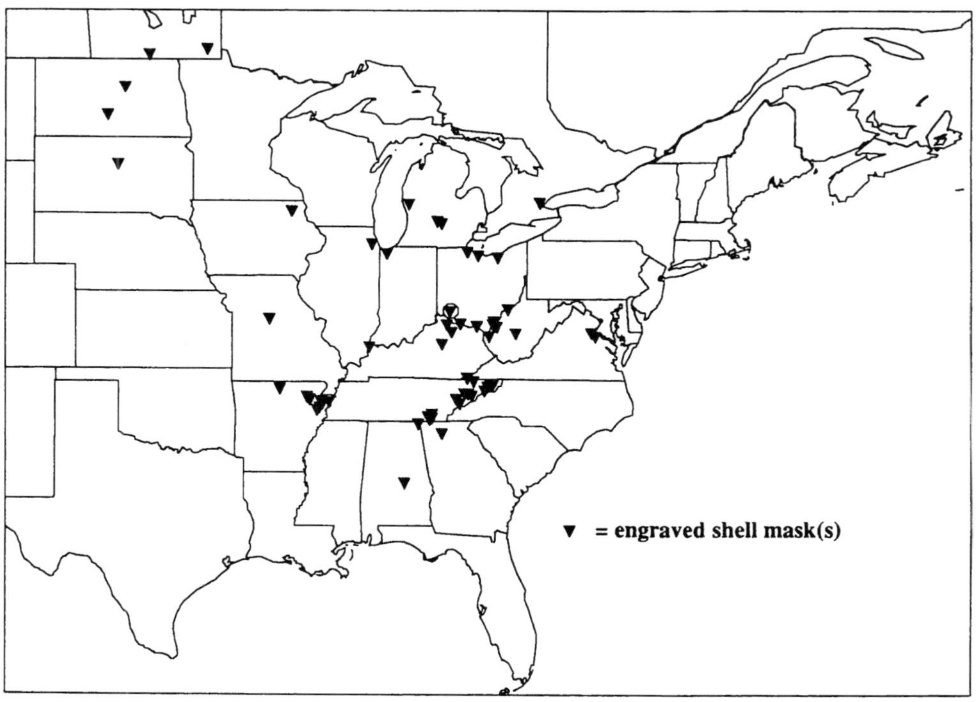

Figure 8-16. Geographical distribution of engraved marine shell mask gorgets (after Smith and Smith 1989; see Table 4-9 for Fort Ancient sites, plus text for additional non-Fort Ancient sites). Includes both large and small (maskette) examples, and two made from materials other than marine shell: freshwater clam from the Yetter locality in northern Ohio, and a ceramic sherd from Fifield, Indiana (Bowen 1994: cover; Faulker 1972:131).

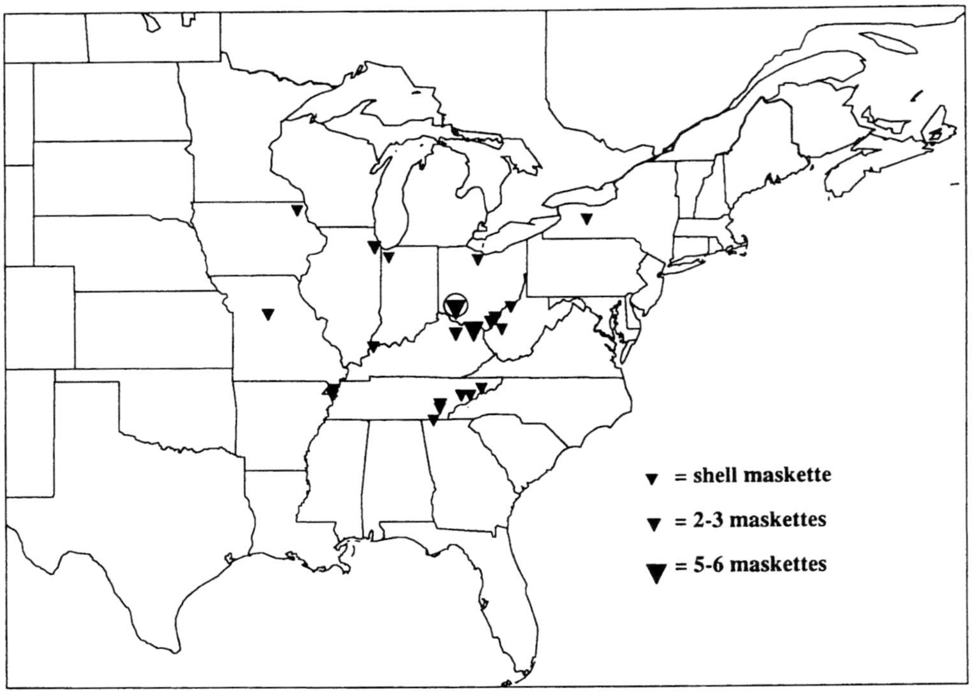

Figure 8-17. Geographical distribution of shell maskettes (see text for sites and discussion).

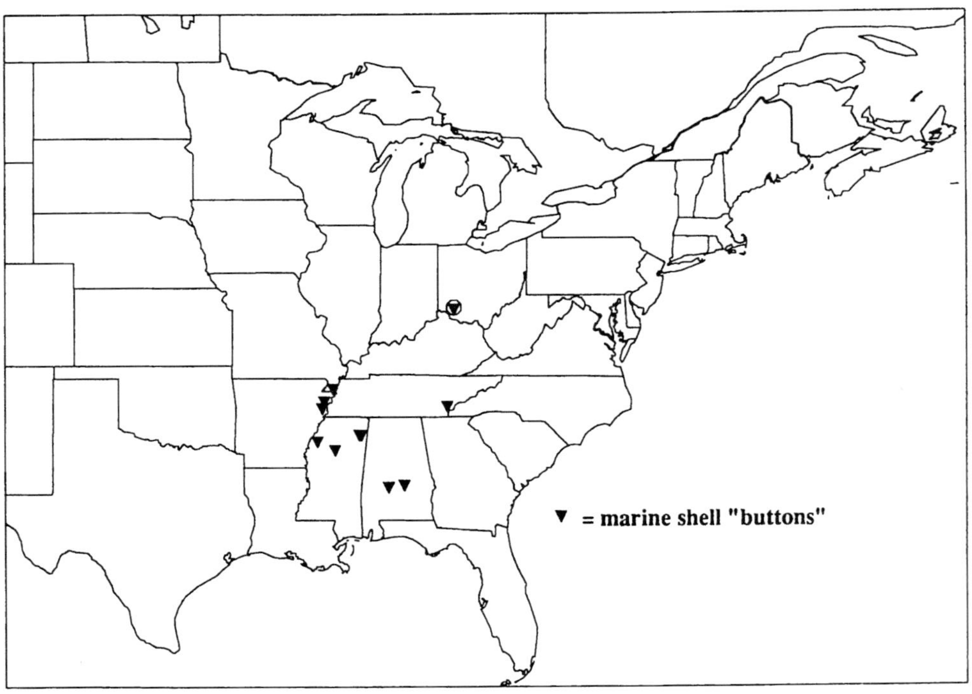

Figure 8-18. Geographical distribution of engraved rectangular shell "buttons" (after Williams 1980). In addition to sites on the map, these artifacts have come from Frenche's Island, on the Tennessee River (MacCurdy 1917b: Fig. 16).

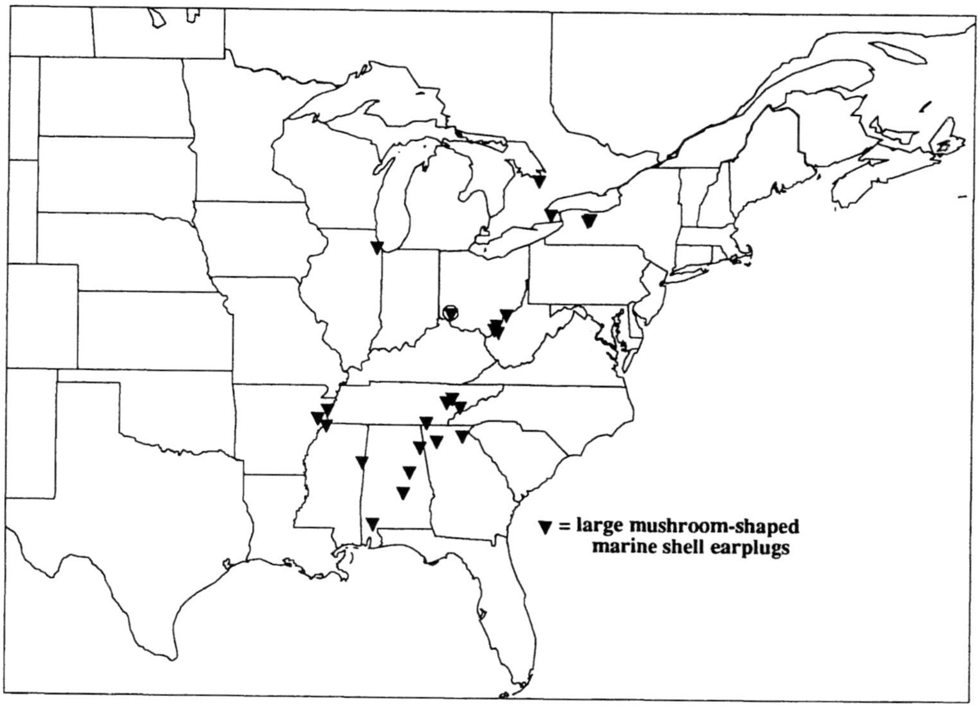

Figure 8-19. Geographical distribution of large mushroom-shaped marine shell earplugs. Does not include small or rectanguloid examples, or hatpinlike shapes. See text for site list.

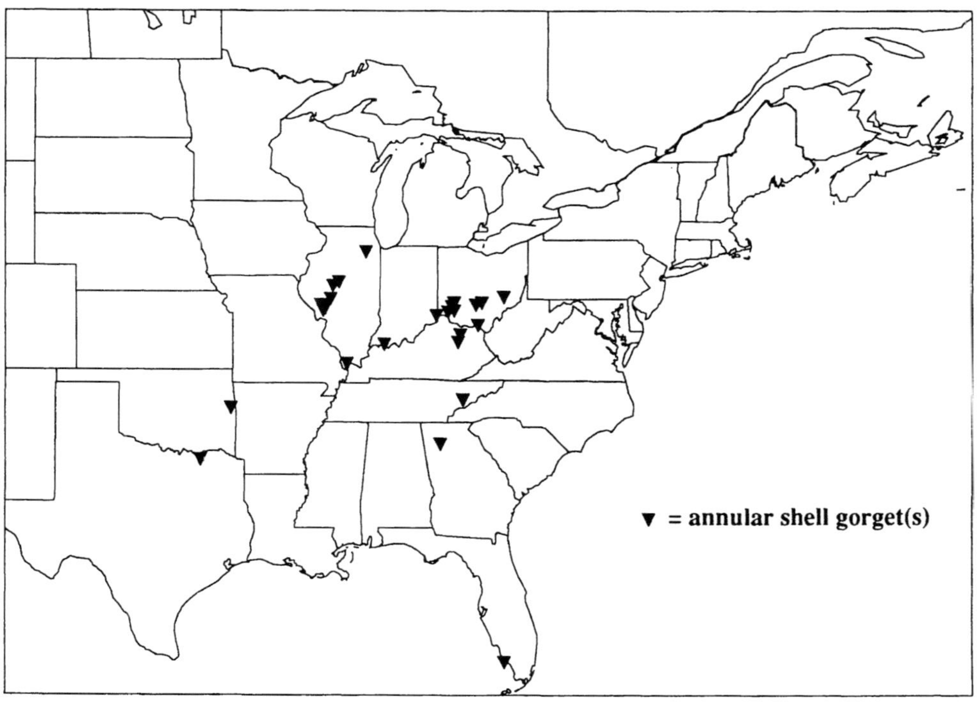

Figure 8-20. Geographical distribution of annular shell gorgets. See text for references and site names.

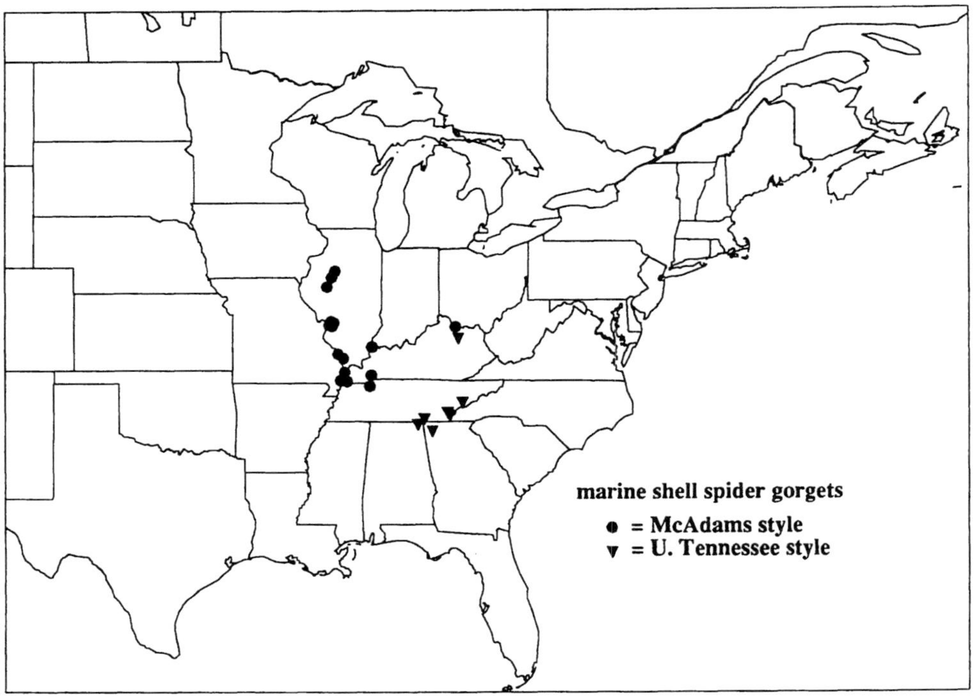

Figure 8-21. Geographical distribution of spider marine shell gorgets of the McAdams (Illinois and surrounding area) and U. Tennessee (eastern Tennessee and surrounding area) styles. Non-Fort Ancient sites from Esarey 1990; Fort Ancient sites from Wagers 1993 and Glass n.d.:7.

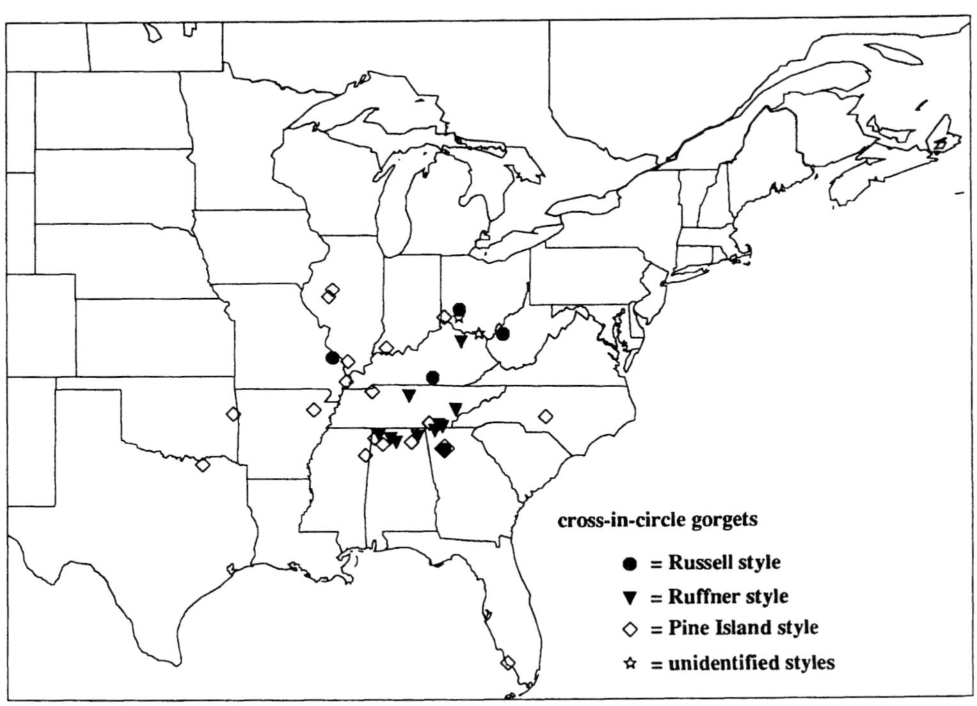

Figure 8-22. Geographical distribution of cross-in-circle marine shell gorget styles found within Fort Ancient territory (Brain and Phillips 1996:28-33; Moore 1907: Fig. 10; see text for Fort Ancient sites and references).

Illinois; Fifield, Indiana (on a shaped ceramic sherd); Dumaw Creek and two Grand River Valley sites (20IA51 and "near Lansing") in Michigan; Muddy Creek, Vetter locality (a freshwater clam), and Eiden, Ohio; and Robertson Village, Ontario (Bettarel and Smith 1973:145, Pl. 82; Bluhm and Liss 1961; Bowen 1994; Bray 1963; Collins 1994; Faulkner 1972; Fitzgerald 1992; McKenzie 1973; Cheryl Munson, pers. comm.; Pollack et al. 1996:26; Quimby 1966a). Three of those sites, Anker, Fifield, and Dumaw Creek, also produced thin metal serpent pendants. The greatest number of mask gorgets from any one area has come from Tennessee, where they may often have been placed over the faces of the dead (Kneberg 1959:27). Their burial association is with males, and Smith and Smith consider them symbols of hunting and war (1989:14-16). They propose the square-jawed style as primarily representative of Fort Ancient, where it has been found at at least six sites, including Madisonville (although examples also have come from Tellico and Dallas, Tennessee, and Anker, Illinois). The greatest numbers of large masks in Fort Ancient territory have come from eastern sites, with Rolf Lee producing at least five large and two small examples (Brashler and Moxley 1990: Table 1).

Many Fort Ancient mask gorgets, including all five or six from Madisonville, actually are maskettes (Figures 6-19a, 6-19b; see also Hooton and Willoughby 1920: Pl. 16; an additional example with three-pronged forked eyes from Madisonville, very similar to a larger mask from Site 20IA51 in central Michigan, is curated at the National Museum of the American Indian, Cat. No. 21/9275). These small-sized masks, less than about six centimeters maximum dimension, are in fact concentrated in Fort Ancient territory (Figure 8-17), with at least five from Hardin (none engraved, but one with a carved nose), three from Orchard (two engraved with forked-eye motifs), two or three forked-eye examples from Fox Farm, two from Rolf Lee (one with carved nose reworked from a Citico gorget, and one with forked eyes), two from Buffalo (one with forked eyes), and one with forked eyes from Neale's Landing (Brashler and Moxley 1990; Glass n.d.:8, 51; Griffin 1943: Pl. cxxi; Hanson 1966:161, 613, Fig. 63, 1975:79; Hemmings 1977:5-18, 9-9, Fig. 64). Maskettes from Tennessee (Cox Mound, Fain's Island, Hiwassee Island, Lisle Mound, Williams Island) are all unengraved (Brain and Phillips 1996; Lewis and Kneberg 1946: Pl. 83B). Campell and McCoy (the only two Pemiscot County, Missouri, sites from which have come catlinite disk pipes) produced unengraved shell maskettes with carved noses; from McCoy has also come a pecked stone example (O'Brien 1994:242, 302-3). A "small mask" came from the Caborn-Welborn Murphy site (Cheryl Munson, pers. comm.). Most Fort Ancient sites with maskettes (Table 4-9, and above) have at least one engraved with the forked-eye motif. This is true also of maskettes from the Vetter vicinity, northern Ohio (freshwater shell); Fifield, Indiana (ceramic); Anker, Illinois; Allamakee County, Iowa; and Utz, Missouri (see previous paragraph for references). The greatest numbers of maskettes have come from Madisonville and Hardin. At least one unengraved maskette comparable to those found farther south was excavated in Seneca territory (Sempowski 1989: Fig. 18), plus a variety of others, in both shell and other materials, rendered in a uniquely Iroquoian style related to their large false face masks (e.g., Mackay 1989: Figs. 1, 4, 6, 7; Rochester Museum and Science Center exhibit).

Rectangular shell "buttons" with two holes and engraved diagonals across each corner have been proposed by Williams as one of the primary markers of his protohistoric Markala Horizon (Williams 1980:106-8). One was excavated at Madisonville (Figure 6-19b), the northernmost example of its type (Figure 8-18; CMNH Cat. No. A25587). It is of interest that of the ten sites listed by Williams as producing these artifacts, half have also produced Clarksdale bells (Mitchem and McEwan 1988: Table 3; cf. Figure 8-1).

Another type of marine shell artifact with strong southern associations has been found at Madisonville and a number of eastern Fort Ancient sites (Buffalo, Neale's Landing, Orchard, Rolf Lee, and a Mason County, West Virginia site), as well as quite a few Northeastern ones (Figure 8-19). It is a large, asymmetrical mushroom-shaped ear ornament made from intersecting planes of large conch shells (Hanson 1975:86; Moore 1899:295). Madisonville has produced only one pair from a provenienced location (Figure 6-19a), but at least one additional example has been reported from the site (CMNH Cat. No. 1918.830). Three pairs were reported from both Buffalo and Orchard (Hanson 1975:86, 87, Fig. 68; Moxley 1988a:38-39). Johnson has proposed that these ornaments reached Iroquoian settlements through Fort Ancient peoples (Johnson 1994). Two examples were found at the GBP2-3 Grimsby site in Ontario, while the Seneca sites from which examples have come, Power House and Dann, date to as late as the 1660s (Hayes 1989:41, Fig. 7; Kenyon 1982: Pls. 69, 70; Saunders and Sempowski 1991; Sempowski 1989:94, Fig. 18), a time period when many researchers believe that Iroquoian groups were raiding the Ohio River valley for captives. Farther south, these earplugs are known from many sites, including at least one sixteenth-century settlement that also produced a Clarksdale bell, Parkin, Arkansas (Morse 1981), plus sites with European goods that date them at 1565-1630, such as ICE308, Alabama, and Brakebill Mound and Williams Island, Tennessee (Little and Curran 1981: Table 3, Pl. 3; MacCurdy 1917a: Fig. 13, 1917b: Fig. 18; Smith 1987: Table 3.4).

As discussed in Chapter 4, marine shell was a valued material even at very early western Fort Ancient sites (see, for instance, Table 4-7). Prehistorically, this region may have obtained shell ornaments via people living both to the west and to the south of it, with sources shifting over time as a reflection of shifting centers of population, power, and alliance within the Southeast (Drooker 1994c). At any rate, it has shared different gorget styles with different geographical areas over time.

Annular gorgets (Figure 6-19a) appear to objectify a strong relationship between Early-Middle Fort Ancient settlements mainly in Ohio and settlements in the central Illinois River valley that date to around 1100 or 1200 to 1450 (Figure 8-20). Within Fort Ancient territory, they have been excavated at Anderson, Baum, Clay, Feurt, Fox Farm, Gartner, Madisonville, Richards, State Line, and Taylor, with many sites producing multiple examples and at least two sites, Fox Farm and Gartner, producing large specimens fashioned from the whorled tops of *Busycon* valves (Carskadden 1994; Glass n.d.:6; Griffin 1943: Pls. XLIV, XLVII, XCVIII, CXX, CXXI; Mills 1904: Figs. 12, 13, 54, 1906: Figs. 58, 59; H. Smith 1910: Pl. L; Vickery and Genheimer 1994; OHS Cat. No. 161/45; HUPM Cat. Nos. 86-46-10/A3679, 86-46-10/A3681, 08-3-10/79462). Both large and small central holes and notched and unnotched edges are present in Fort Ancient examples. Outside Fort Ancient territory, locations of annular gorgets are as reported by Conrad (1991:148-49, 154, 1996b) and Phillips and Brain (1996:125). Only one has been reported from the eastern Tennessee region that was an important producer of many of the later styles, coming from a surprisingly early site (Smith and Hodges 1968: Pl. VI).

In the case of spider gorgets, which have a time frame of around 1200 to 1500 (or perhaps later, in the case of one example from Toqua, Tennessee), Esarey has demonstrated that there are two distinct style zones, one centered on southern Illinois and the other on eastern Tennessee (Esarey 1990). One gorget of each style has been found within a small area in northern Kentucky (Figure 8-21), at Fox Farm and a Bracken County site (Glass n.d.; Wagers 1993), unfortunately not from controlled excavations. Where provenience is known, spider gorgets have been found buried almost exclusively with infants, children, and females (Esarey 1990:17-18).

The styles of cross-in-circle gorgets recognized at Fort Ancient sites, which include Brain and Phillips's Pine Island (simple cruciform defined by four triangular or quarter-circle fenestrations), Ruffner (unfenestrated, with incised cross surrounded by concentric circles), and Russell (fenestrated cross incorporating an engraved filfot motif), may, as a group, date somewhat later. They have only weak connections to central Illinois, being found mainly southward from the latitudes of the Ohio River (Figure 8-22). The only two certainly identified examples from the central Illinois River valley are from sites that date from 1300 to 1450, Larson and Crable (Conrad 1996b). Fort Ancient cross-in-circle gorgets do not all fit easily into Brain and Phillips's categories. The "Pine Island" example, from State Line, has a circle engraved around its border area, so might mark a transition with Ruffner (Vickery and Genheimer 1994). If so, interregional connections would be more southerly than apparent from Figure 8-22. An elaborate incised and punctated gorget from Hardin with triangular "sun rays" surrounding concentric circles and the central cross (Hanson 1966: Fig. 65), is described by Brain and Phillips as "unique," with some relationship to the triskele (1996:36), but it can be viewed as an elaboration of Ruffner. The description of the fenestrated cross-in-circle gorget from Anderson is not detailed enough to allow classification (Essenpreis 1982:229). Other examples mapped in Figure 8-22 are from Taylor, Fox Farm, and Somers Farm (Brashler and Moxley 1990: Fig. 13; Funkhauser and Webb 1928:103-4; Griffin 1943: Pl. XLVII).

Fox Farm is the one Fort Ancient site that has produced examples of all three of the types mapped in Figures 8-20, 8-21, and 8-22. Both its spider and its cross-in-circle gorgets are close in style to examples from the region centering on southeastern Tennessee. The spider gorget is completely congruent with one from Etowah, Georgia (Esarey 1990: Fig.2a), and the Ruffner style cross-in-circle gorget (Funkhouser and Webb 1928:104) is identical to an example from Hixon, Tennessee (Kneberg 1959: Fig. 3). Fox Farm is rich in marine shell (Smith 1910; Glass n.d.; Griffin 1943: Pls. CXX-CXXI). Shell beads and ornaments are particularly common with mound burials from the site's earlier component (American Museum of Natural History Catalog 20, Vol. I, Accession No. 1895-36). Although absolute numbers of shell artifacts are not available for this or most other pre-1450 Fort Ancient sites, the relative numbers of burials with shell are highest at centrally located Early-Middle Fort Ancient sites (Figure 8-23), consistent with a significant southern entry point at Fox Farm during that time period (Essenpreis 1982; Griffin 1943; Metz 1885b; Mills 1904, 1917; Oehler 1973; Riggs 1977).

Although very little marine shell has been reported from prehistoric eastern Fort Ancient sites, protohistorically there was far more shell at eastern than at western Fort Ancient sites (Figures 8-24a, b), as discussed above. By 1500, very likely it was entering Fort Ancient territory almost entirely from that direction.

However, at least some marine shell excavated at Madisonville may well have reached the site during the late sixteenth century via a more circuitous route, from the Northeast. At Northeastern sites, where protohistoric increases in marine shell quantitites often accompanied a growing input of metal and glass, marine shell morphology has been used as evidence in tracing changing interaction networks (specifically, to indicate a Chesapeake Bay source of supply to certain groups during certain periods). Whereas large sinistrally whorled *Busycon,* as well as smaller dextrally whorled shells, are known from sixteenth and very early seventeenth century Ontario Iroquoian sites (Pendergast 1989:98-99), only dextrally whorled shells have come from Seneca sites of this period (Martha Sempowski, pers. comm.). It is of interest that the 50 marine shell beads accompanying the individual at Madisonville, who had a belt adorned with large clips made from kettle copper (Burial 1-60), included examples of both small-diameter dextrally whorled and large-diameter sinistrally whorled columellas (Figure 6-19a; noted by Sempowski, 1995). They might well have been acquired together with the copper, via an Ontario Iroquoian interaction network.

Pipes and Pipestones

Because pipes were used by men who often traveled widely for both peaceful and non-peaceful purposes, and pipe bowls

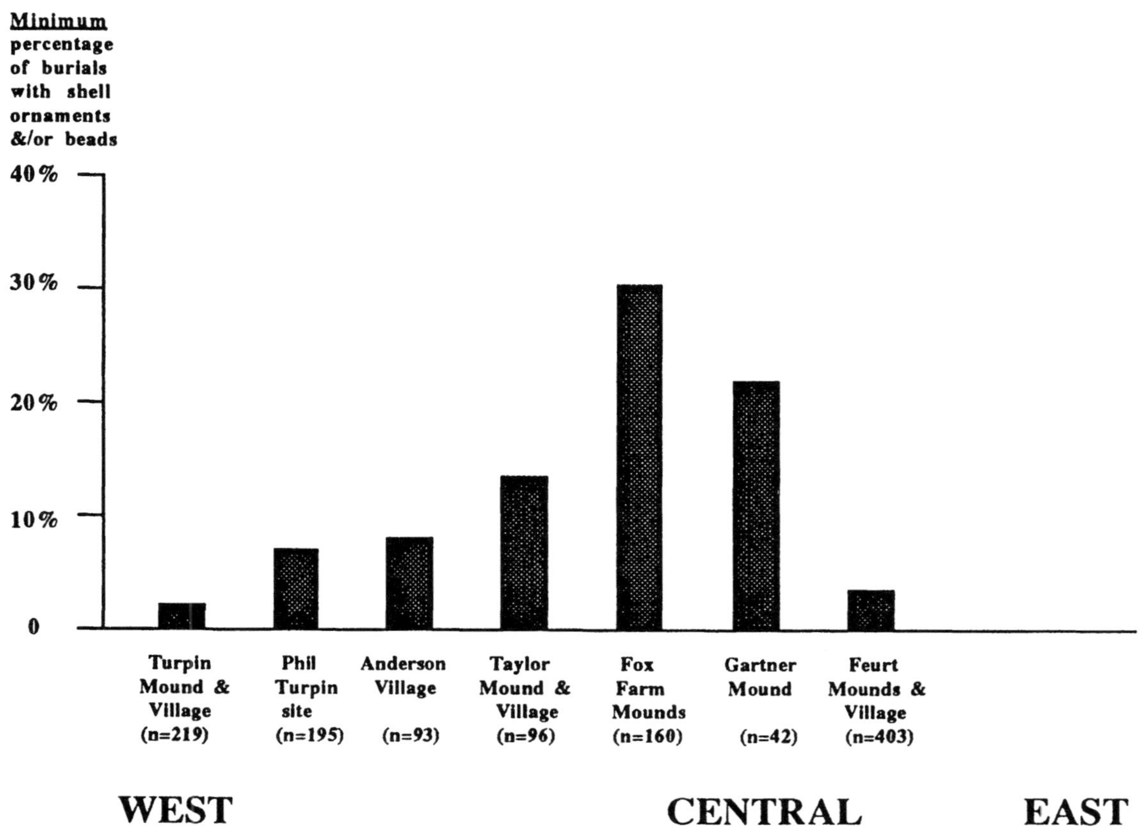

Figure 8-23. Frequencies of burials with shell ornaments and/or beads at earlier Fort Ancient sites (twelfth through fourteenth centuries) (Metz 1885b; Mills 1907, 1917; Griffin 1943; Oehler 1973; Riggs 1977; Essenpreis 1982). The *n* refers to total number of burials.

frequently were exchanged in formal greeting and alliance-making rituals (Chapter 3), these artifacts are excellent markers for broad interregional interaction patterns. Particularly valued or spiritually powerful pipes were likely to be included as grave goods with their owners. Unfortunately, no one has yet "written the book" on late prehistoric and protohistoric North American pipe style distributions (the closest thing being George West's monumental but atemporal 1939 compendium), so comparative material of wildly varying pedigree is scattered far and wide throughout the literature and museum collections.

Madisonville pipes objectify the interactions its residents enjoyed with peoples from an extremely broad surrounding area. Much remains to be done in order to accomplish a complete identification of the collection via all possible avenues of analysis, including stylistic, mineralogical, and trace element determinations. Here, I will summarize the best-documented directions of interaction, using the information gathered so far. In addition to the burial pipes illustrated in Figures 7-5, 7-6, and 7-30, selected examples that either originated or were inspired by examples from outside Fort Ancient territory are shown in Figures 8-25, 8-26, and 8-27.

As already discussed in Chapter 7, the most common pipe form with nonlocal connections—and one of the few exotic types found with burials—is the disk. Madisonville has produced more disk pipes than any other Fort Ancient site: at least ten percent of 157 pipes that definitely have come from the site. At least four examples came from burials. In Trenches 1-K there were eight disk pipes from both mortuary and nonmortuary contexts, four of which are illustrated in Figures 7-5a and 8-25. Examples from other parts of the site are shown in Figures 7-6, 7-30, and 8-26. The most common style is compact with a small disk, similar to pipes from protohistoric Orr Focus sites in northeastern Iowa (M. Wedel 1959: Fig. 11; West 1934: Pl. 257). Few at Madisonville have the notched prow that often is found on examples from Wisconsin (one exception being the foreign-made redstone disk pipe in Figure 6-20), although one redstone pipe was fashioned from a cut-off notched prow (Figure 8-25). Only three of the Madisonville disk pipes were made from red stone. Many were fashioned from local materials, very likely locally made. The broken, poorly shaped sandstone example in Figure 8-25, which might have had an effigy prow, has a larger disk than most examples from the site, perhaps an early local imita-

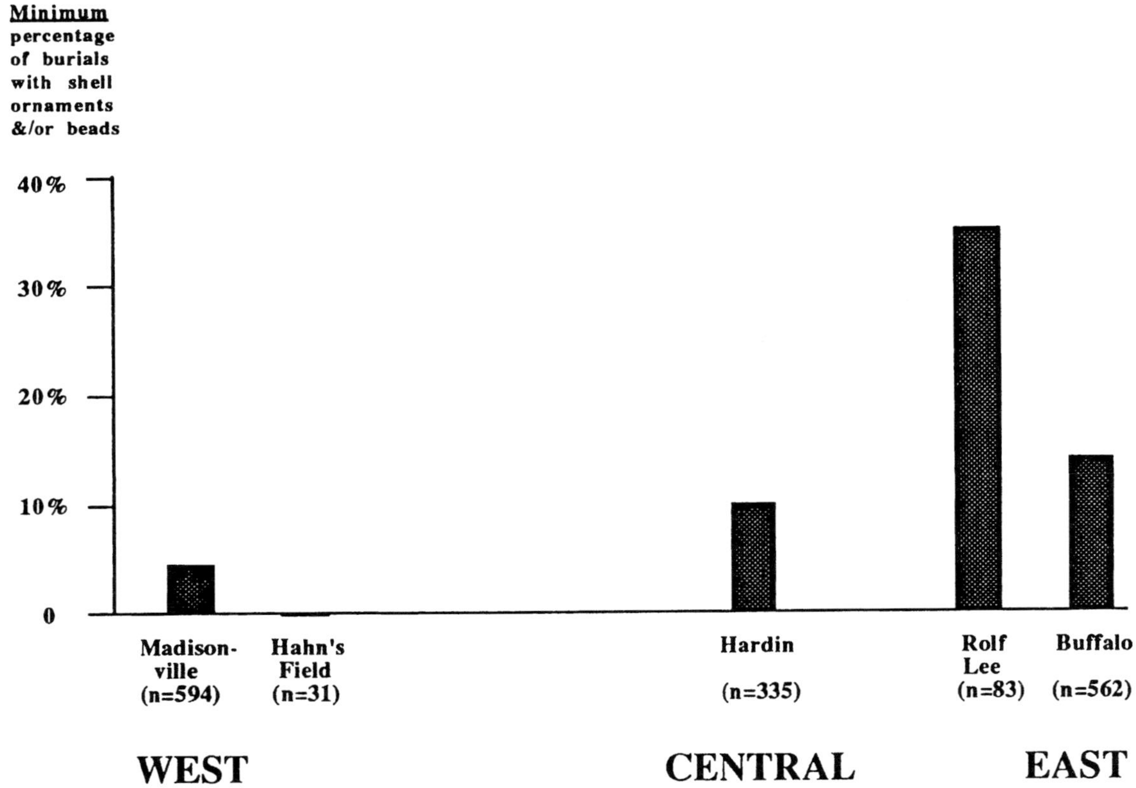

Figure 8-24a. Marine shell at protohistoric Fort Ancient sites (fifteenth and sixteenth centuries): frequencies of burials with shell ornaments and/or beads (Metz 1885a; Griffin 1943; Kapp 1961-1968; Hanson 1963, 1966, 1975).

tion of a pipe seen elsewhere. At any rate, its material is a local stone, the light brown Waverly sandstone. In addition to these disk pipes, Madisonville also has produced pipe forms that often are called "disk" in the literature (they are found associated with disk pipes in the upper Mississipi Valley), but in which the disk itself has shrunk to minuscule proportions (e.g., Figure 8-26, bottom right, and Figure 8-42; see also Hooton and Willoughby 1920: Pl. 19.l; cf. Hamilton 1967: Figs. 3A, 3E, 4A, 4B, 4F; M. Wedel 1959: Figs. 11h, 11i). Some of them may be transitional to later elbow/"calumet" forms.

Many other Fort Ancient sites produced one or two disk pipes (Figure 8-28, Table 4-3). Forms that apparently were earlier, with larger disks and longer prows but otherwise fairly simple in design, are known from Campbell Island (one of white limestone), Fox Farm (two of redstone, with a burial), Buffalo (one of redstone), and a site in Butler County, where Campbell Island is located (one of redstone) (Glass n.d.:30; Hanson 1975:81; Shetrone 1923:454, 459; West 1934: Pl. 53). They are very similar in form to five white limestone examples from the Caborn-Welborn Murphy site (Moorehead 1906: Fig. 23). East of Fox Farm they are not reported from burials, although at least two at Orchard, where "most [pipes] were found with burials" (Moxley 1988a:35), might well have been mortuary offerings. Unlike the interior Southeast, no large, fine, elaborately shaped catlinite "war bundle" disk pipes (e.g., Brown 1989: Fig. 3b, 3d, 3e, 3f, 3h, 3i) have come from formally excavated Fort Ancient sites. The few of which I am aware have no firm provenience (Brown 1989: Fig. 3b, "from Kentucky"; Vietzen 1974: Pl. following p. 48, "from Holmes County, Ohio," said to be of "Ohio pipestone," but of typical Midwestern form; West 1934: Pl. 151, "from Ohio"; and HUPM 67-30-10/682, "from a mound," Columbus?, Ohio; the last carried an incised human figure with many similarities to the one incised on a deer bone that accompanied Burial 3-4 at Madisonville).

The homeland for redstone disk pipes appears to have been Wisconsin (Figure 8-29). The far-ranging distribution of these artifacts—particularly the largest, finest examples—may well be associated with late prehistoric diplomatic interactions (cf. Brown 1989).

A better indicator of artifact origin than style is mineralogical or trace element analysis and comparison to mineralogical or chemical profiles from stones of known source (e.g., Gundersen 1992a, 1992b; Murphy 1996). As part of a much larger study, Sigstad (1973) used neutron activation analysis to

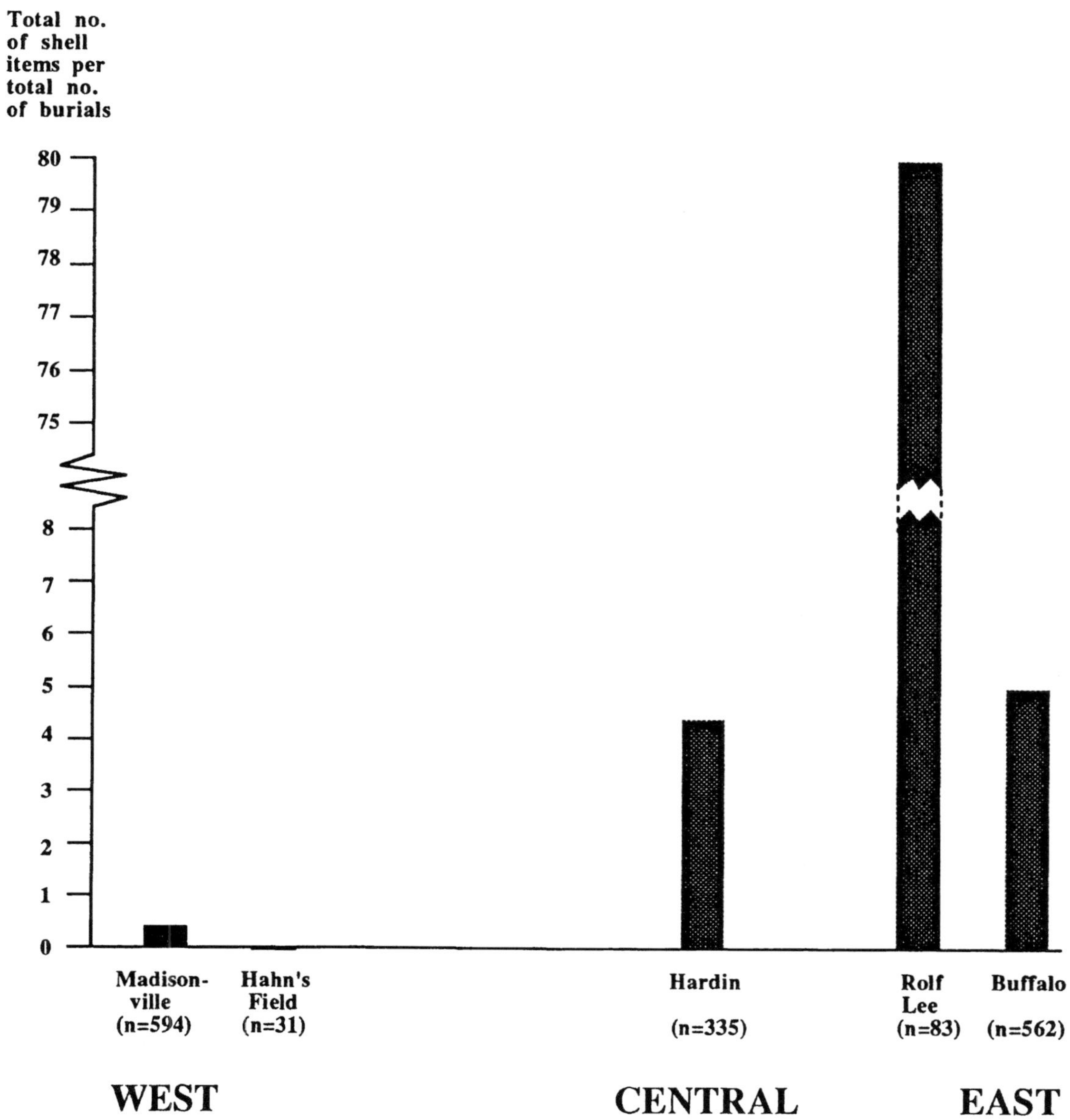

Figure 8-24b. Marine shell at protohistoric Fort Ancient sites (fifteenth and sixteenth centuries): numbers of shell ornaments and beads at protohistoric Fort Ancient sites, standardized on a per burial basis. The *n* refers to total number of burials.

test redstone pipes and raw material from Fox Farm, Hardin, and Feurt, finding that the Fort Ancient samples came from at least five different Midwestern sources (Drooker 1992a:25-35). His results should be employed with caution, however, until they are corroborated by more modern analytical techniques (cf. Gundersen 1993).

Madisonville redstones have not been chemically sourced, but it is likely that they contain at least a few examples from upper Mississippi Valley quarries. At least five redstone pipes (three disk pipes and two probably made from parts of disk pipes) and three pieces of shaped redstone have come from Madisonville (Low 1880: Figs. 7, 11; Wachtel 1952:10-11; HUPM 07-6-10/78481, 07-6-10/78511, 07-6-10/78572, 84-68-10/35660, 97-38-10/62960; CMNH 1908.1017). Visually, at least three different types of stone seem to be present, ranging in color from deep, bright red (Munsell 7.5R 3/6) to reddish gray (10R 4/3 to 5/4) to grayish red (5R 4/1), with differing streak colors. It is of interest to note that Madisonville produced more redstone disk pipes than the formally excavated portion of the Hardin site (from which came only one), but fewer total redstone artifacts and fragments (Hanson 1966:139-40; Sigstad 1973: Pl. 4).

The three largest Madisonville pipes all have foreign connections. All were mortuary offerings, and thus were discussed in Chapter 7. The largest disk pipe from the site, the bird/owl effigy (Figure 7-30a), is exceptional in size, material, and form.

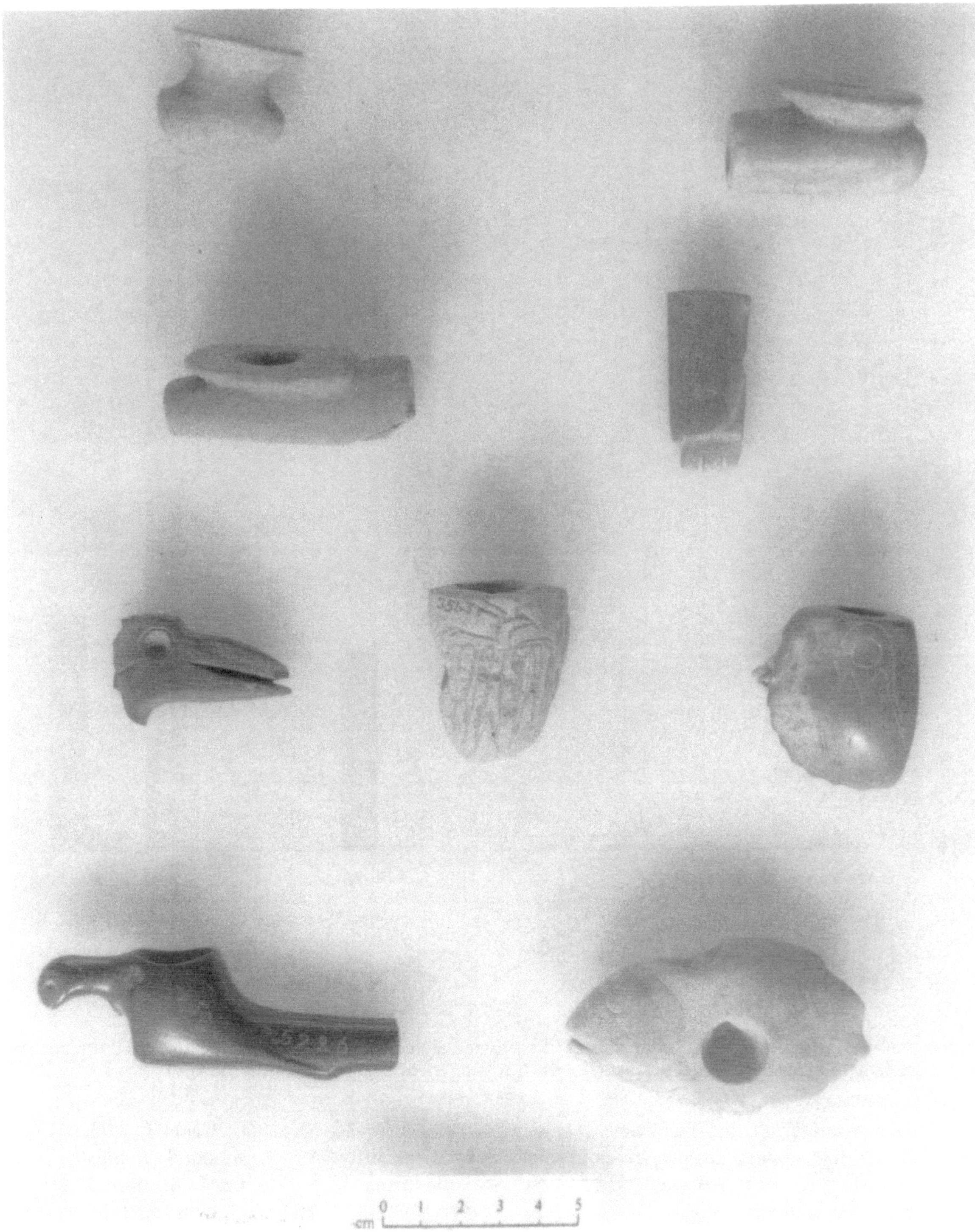

Figure 8-25. Selected pipes of nonlocal design or material from nonmortuary contexts at Madisonville. *First row:* small-disk pipe, light brownish gray pipestone (97-38-10/62953, Trenches 1-5, general digging); small-disk pipe, brown pipestone, "+" on tip of prow (97-38-10/62952, Trenches 1-5, general digging). *Second row*: large-disk pipe, local sandstone, bottom engraved, broken (97-38-10/62927, Trench 2, Pit 19); redstone pipe made from notched prow of disk pipe, "turkey track" engraved on front (07-6-10/78511). *Third row*: fragmentary bird head effigy pipe bowl (raven? kingfisher?), very dark gray shale (?) (08-3-10/78973, probably Trench E, Pit 2 or 3); cast of keel-shaped pipe with engraved thunderbirds each side (84-68-10/35637, surface 1880s); keel-shaped pipe with engraved "forked eye" motif both sides, notched edge, highly polished dark gray stone with light inclusions (08-3-10/71957, Trench D, Pit 93). *Fourth row*: turkey effigy black steatite elbow pipe (82-35-10/25226, "ash pits," 1881); fish effigy pipe, polished gray pipestone with lighter inclusions (08-3-10/71475, Trench D, Pit 39). Photograph by Hillel Burger (HUPM Photo No. N33985). Copyright 1996 by the President and Fellows of Harvard College.

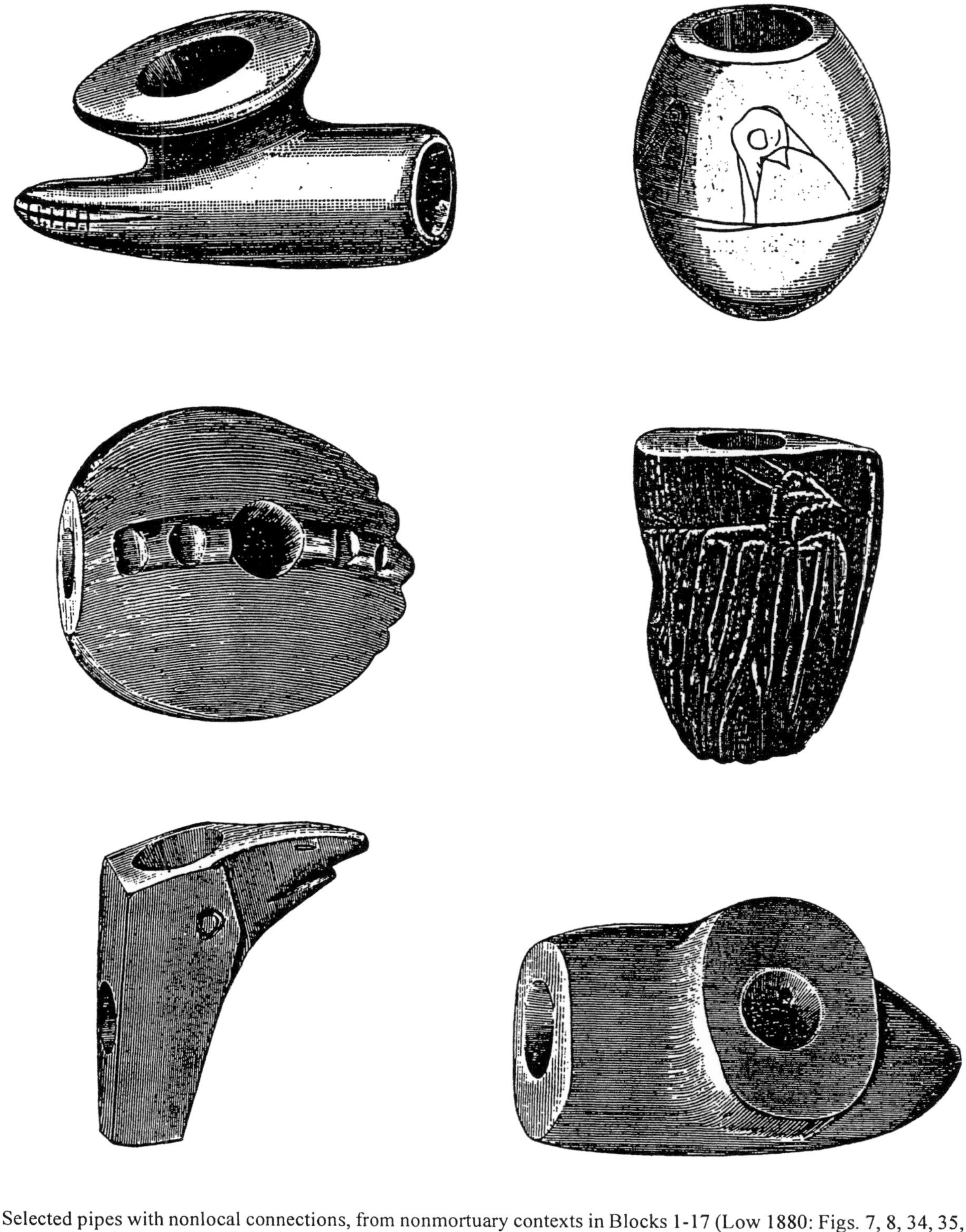

Figure 8-26. Selected pipes with nonlocal connections, from nonmortuary contexts in Blocks 1-17 (Low 1880: Figs. 7, 8, 34, 35, 37, 40). The effigy disk pipe was described as of "catlinite," the keel pipe with thunderbird (cf. cast, Figure 8-24a) and the pipe at lower right were identified as sandstone, and the others were described as limestone or "stone."

Figure 8-27a. Iroquoian or Iroquoian-inspired pipes from nonmortuary contexts at Madisonville. *Top*: ceramic trumpet pipe bowl fragments with decorated rims (08-3-10/71346, Trench D, Pit 22, upside-down; 83-48-10/32527, "ash pits," 1880s), has two rows of punctates separated by a horizontal line around the rim. *Center*: two ceramic pipe stems, ceramic humanoid effigy pipe bowl fragment (all 97-38-10/62959, Trenches 1-5, general digging). *Bottom*: stem fragment of carved stone elbow pipe, showing rear leg and tail of "lizard," the head of which would have been at top front of bowl, polished gray stone with white inclusions (08-3-10/79597, Trench D, general digging); gray stone square collared pipe bowl fragment (08-3-10/79443, Trench F, Pit 33). Photograph by Hillel Burger (HUPM Photo No. N33984). Copyright 1996 by the President and Fellows of Harvard College.

Figure 8-27b. Iroquoian ceramic pipe bowl and pipestems (CMNH Cat. Nos. A42217, A42214, and A42216). The bowl fragment and one stem were excavated in 1946 and 1941 from refuse pits in the southwest portion of the site. Photograph by William Collier, courtesy of the Cincinnati Museum Center.

The closest form that I have found was a much smaller white limestone pipe from the Caborn-Welborn Slack Farm site, with a medium-sized disk riding on the back of a bird/owl (Pollack et al. 1996:21). A possible related example was excavated at Utz, an odd bird effigy of catlinite that might once have had a disk on its back (Hamilton 1967: Fig. 6A). Another pipe with similarities is a large (13.5 × 5.7 cm) "pipestone" duck head effigy with a disk riding on its neck, from Greenup County, Kentucky, where the Hardin site is located (West 1934: Pl. 147). The yellowish-tan agatelike chalcedony from which the Madisonville bird/owl-disk pipe was made was used for at least one other pipe from the site, a broken ovoid (11-10-10/A4072, from Trench H, Pit 10), and also was found as an oblong fragment, probably from a pipe (84-68-10/35669, in an MLSS-excavated refuse pit). Three pipes or fragments from the Thomas Cleneay collection curated at CMNH (possibly, but not certainly, from Madisonville) also were made of this material (an ovoid, a semi-elbow, and a broken-off disk: Cat. Nos. 1887.15127, 1887.15126, 1887.11531). I also discovered this or very similar material in a perching owl pipe from a cave burial near Shinnston, West Virginia (National Museum of Natural History Cat. No. 289345), and it may perhaps be the "banded tan calcite of stalagmite or stalactite origin" found in a subrectangular pipe from Neale's Landing, and the "marbled, honey and cream-colored translucent calcite" (ascribed to an unknown cave source) of a bison effigy pipe fragment from Rolf Lee (Baker 1994:8; Hemmings 1976:58).

A West Virginia source for the Madisonville bird/owl-disk pipe material seems to be a good possibility. This is a spectacular artifact, clearly intended to strongly impress anyone, humans or spirit beings, to whom it was displayed. The disparate sources of its form and material imply that it might be a Fort Ancient-made hybrid.

The very large perching owl pipe with Burial I-9 (Figure 7-5c) is of a form that is most common east and north of Madisonville (Figure 8-30). Perching bird effigy pipes found in and around Ohio tend to be reasonably naturalistic in form. Farther east, they tend to be more blocky and stylized, and to have a suspension hole in the claw area.

The material from which the Madisonville pipe was made, a black-and-white-speckled, variegated-matrix (greenish gray with tan banding) pipestone, has been found in at least three other

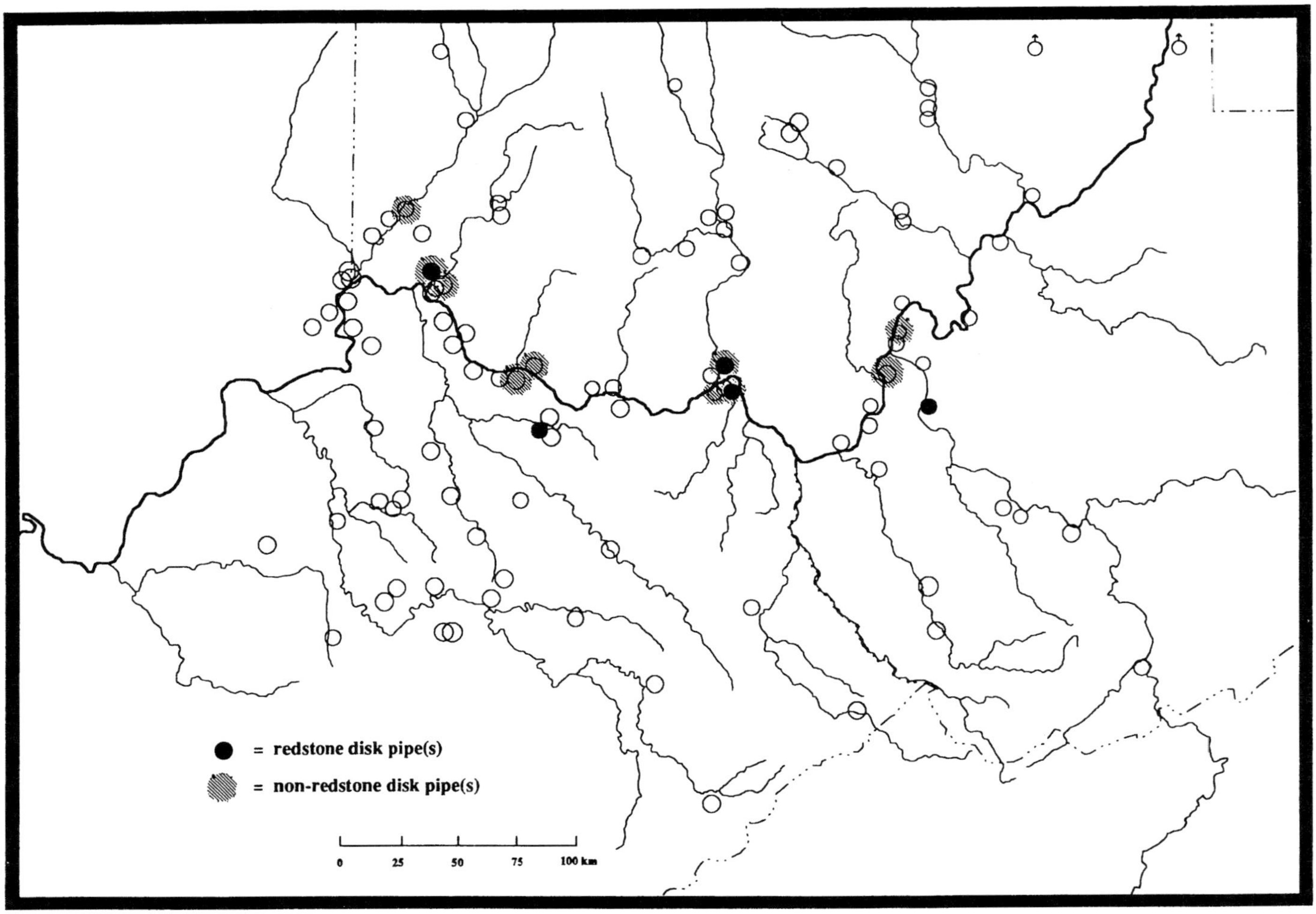

Figure 8-28. Fort Ancient sites with disk pipes (see Table 4-3; additional sites include Madisonville, Augusta, Bentley, Eagle Creek, and an unnamed site in Butler County) (Pollack and Henderson 1984:13; Snider 1991; Webb 1955; West 1934: Pl. 53).

pipes from the site, including: a deliberately damaged semi-elbow ovoid or vasiform identified in the HUPM catalog (Cat. No. 82-35-10/26986) as coming from the leaf mold over the central hearth in House Circle No. 2, but not mentioned in Putnam's enumeration of artifacts from there in his field notes; a semi-elbow vasiform from Burial 1 excavated by Conover (original number 438M, curated at the CMNH); and two battered fragments, perhaps from a disk pipe, excavated during the 1880s (84-68-10/35365 and 35366).

The source of this material is problematic. It has been identified in print as "Ohio pipestone" (Cowan 1987:7), but a catalog entry on a pipe that appears to be the same material, curated at the CMNH (1888.463, a frog effigy with missing head from the "Cincinnati vicinity"), gives the following information.

> Curatorial information: 1975, stone identified by Geology Dept., University of Cincinnati as altered sedimentary rock—a pisolithic rock which is a bauxitic soil altered by weathering under tropical conditions and consolidated, all solubles except aluminum oxide leached out and then partially silicified; this kind of rock is found in the Lower Mississippi valley, specifically Arkansas in the coastal plain of an ancient tropical inland sea.

In seeking information on the range of appearance of so-called Ohio pipestone, I have failed to locate any that is specked in this way (which does not mean that none exists). The name often is used as if it refers to one material from a single source, but this does not appear to be so.

Material from the Feurt Hill quarry in Scioto County near the Fort Ancient Feurt site (of which I have examined samples, courtesy of Robert Converse) has a cream to yellowish to pink to maroon matrix with tannish gray inclusions (Converse 1995b, pers. comm.; Holzapfel 1995). A local "fireclay" industry centered in the city of Portsmouth manufactured vast numbers of bricks out of Scioto County materials until the large quarries were exhausted around 1923 (Holzapfel 1995:4). Witthoft, Schoff, and Wray describe Portsmouth fireclay as "a distinctive

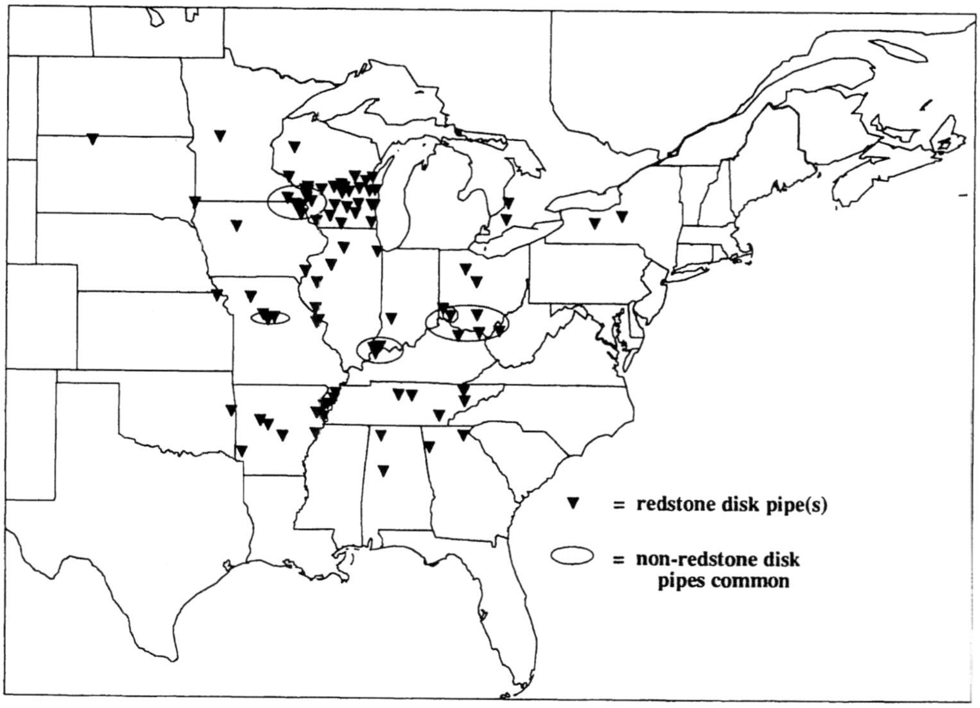

Figure 8-29. Geographical distribution of catlinite and other redstone disk pipes, plus areas where disk pipes made from other materials are common (after Brown 1989: Fig. 2; Salter 1977: Fig. 5; West 1934). Most Wisconsin and Illinois icons are by county; most others are by site. Additional examples from Plains sacred bundles are known. Non-red-stone disk pipe areas are preliminary, and probably can be expanded.

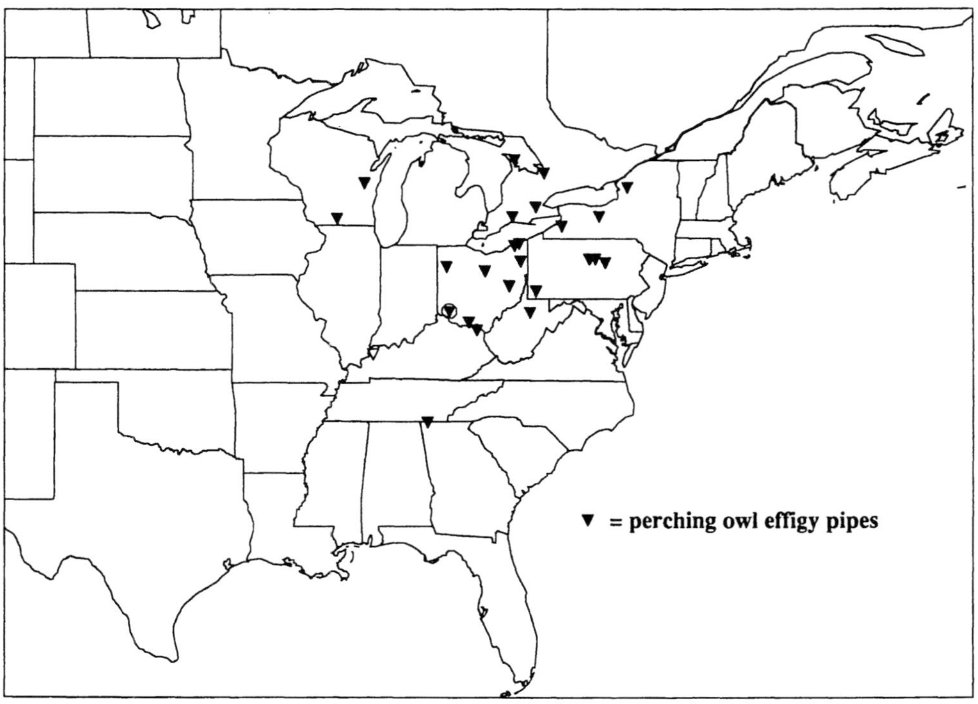

Figure 8-30. Geographical distribution of perching owl effigy pipes (data from Ahlstrom 1979; Anonymous 1968; Fox 1990:464; Laidlaw 1903, 1913, 1916; MacCurdy 1917b; Meuser 1954; Morgan and Ellis 1943:18, 19; Vietzen 1974; West 1934; Witthoft et al. 1953; museum collections including American Museum of Natural History, Museum of the American Indian, and Smithsonian Institution). Not complete, but does show general areas of concentration.

light grey shale of almost as fine a grain as serpentine...with an attractive mottled grey pattern," that can vary in color "from white through grey and brown to reddish" and takes a high polish, citing it as a material used for Late Archaic period bannerstones and Adena birdstones and tube pipes, as well as later pipes with bowls (Witthoft et al. 1953:93). They mention one other similiar fireclay, from Clearfield County in central Pennsylvania; this is harder than the Portsmouth material and "much darker in color..., with coarser mottling and large lense-like masses of dark grey and brown color up to a half-inch in diameter" (1953:93).

The Ohio pipestone used in Hopewell pipes in general does not have the same appearance as the material from which the Madisonville owl effigy was fashioned (N'omi Greber, pers. comm.), and Converse believes that at least some Hopewell pipes might have been made from a pipestone outcropping in Gallia County, Ohio, east of Portsmouth. The collection of the Orton Geological Museum, Ohio State University, contains specimens of Sciotoville flint clay, a light gray, very fine-grained material from near Logan, in Hocking County. E. Thomas Hemmings, in discussing pipes from Blennerhassett Island, mentions another pipestone source area: "fireclays...outcropping along the upper Ohio River in the [West Virginia] panhandle area," specifically a location "at Pipe Creek on the right bank of the Ohio River below Moundsville, West Virginia" (Hemmings 1976:58). Recently, researchers in northern Illinois have found a pipestone source there that visually is almost identical to stone used in Hopewell pipes previously thought to have been made from Ohio pipestone (Berres et al. 1993).

The Madisonville perching owl pipe, with its fine black speckling, does not appear to me to have been made from Feurt Hill pipestone. Without full-scale mineralogical or trace element analysis and comparison with a variety of appropriately chosen source materials, there is no way to be certain of the origin of its material. In any case, even if the stone did come from Arkansas (which would be *very* interesting), it seems unlikely that the pipe was made there, considering the distribution of similar forms (Figure 8-30). Its naturalistic style seems congruent with known examples from Ohio sites like Reeve Village and Riker (e.g., Ahlstrom 1979:86, Pipe No. 93; Vietzen 1974:109) rather than pipes from farther east and north, so it might well have been made within the state. Only one other possible perching owl effigy was excavated at Madisonville (in 1895), a pipe blank of fine-grained, light gray stone (AMNH 20/3760). Perching owl pipes are rare from other Fort Ancient sites. I know of only two: a small one from Hardin with shell disk bead eyes that was fashioned from "dark gray-green pipestone probably from a local source" (Anonymous 1968b), and one from Scioto County in the NMAI collection, perhaps of red Feurt Hill pipestone (Cat. No. 4/6573). A few non-owl perching bird pipes are known from Neale's Landing, Orchard, and Buffalo, including a "vulture" and a raptor with a human head in its talons (Hanson 1975:87, 89; Hemmings 1976: Fig. 1; Moxley 1988b: Fig. 17). The closest site with any large number of perching bird pipes and pipe blanks is Reeve, with some two dozen recorded examples (Ahlstrom 1979: Pls. XIV, XV).

The third large, "killed" mortuary pipe at Madisonville was the claw effigy with Burial I-19 (Figure 7-5d). Its material is a crystalline anorthosite (sometimes identified as quartzite) that is very common among the large collection of pipes and pipe blanks from the Reeve or Willoughby site near Cleveland, and occurs there in several claw effigies (Ahlstrom 1979: No. 106; AMNH Cat. Nos. 9/87, 9/89). This material also was used for several other pipes at Madisonville, including an ovoid with Burial 3-40 (Figure 7-5a), an ovoid blank and possibly an elbow blank (CMNH Conover Nos. 622M, 670M, from the southwestern portion of the site), and a disk pipe blank (07-6-10/78986, from Trench E, Pit 3). Three additional claw effigy pipes from Madisonville included a smaller, stylized one "near" Burial 5 from Block 22 (Figure 7-5d), and two examples with engraved beaks and eyes (one of them also with forked-eye surrounds) that turned the claw shapes into bird's heads (Figure 8-26, plus 84-68-10/35638, excavated in the 1880s, which has a pointed bottom). Like perching owls, the distribution of claw effigies is mainly to the east and north of Madisonville (Figure 8-31).

A related form is exemplified in the two-headed swan effigy pipe of local white limestone interred with Burial 4-19 (Figures 7-1, 7-5a) and a similar pipe illustrated by Hooton and Willoughby that I never located (1920: Pl. 19p, said to be "from a cache pit"). Both Madisonville examples clearly represent floating water birds preening their tail feathers, but they resemble a fairly well-known type of perching bird effigy in having the pipestem hole in the lower part of the pelvis and the bowl in the breast area, just under the neck, which means that they would not be upright when smoked. West illustrates a similar water bird from Mineral County, West Virginia (1934: Pl. 95.3), adjacent to Hampshire County where the early Susquehannock Pancake Island and Herriot Farm sites are located (Brashler 1987; MacCord 1952; Manson and MacCord 1941, 1944). These sites, both of which have produced metal spirals, postdate proto-Susquehannock sites on the upper Susquehanna River near Binghamton, New York, and immediately predate late sixteenth century Susquehannock sites on the lower Susquehanna. At least one additional site in the vicinity is reported to have produced what Gerard Fowke called "Venetian polychrome" glass beads (Brashler 1987:3), which would date it to the early seventeenth century, and another very recently excavated site in Hardy County has produced a variety of early seventeenth-century European-derived artifacts (Patrick Trader, pers. comm.), so the local Susquehannock occupation might have persisted longer than Brashler hypothesized. Laidlaw calls the two examples he illustrates, from northern Pennsylvania just south of Binghamton, New York, and from just north of Toronto, cranes or herons (Laidlaw 1913:46, 47, 59, 1914:77-78). An almost identical "heron" probably came from the vicinity of Tobermory, Ontario, at the tip of the Bruce Peninsula (Fox 1990:464, Fig. 14.11). Interestingly, Laidlaw also shows a similar example from New Athens, Illinois, "not far from the old settlement of Kaskaskia"

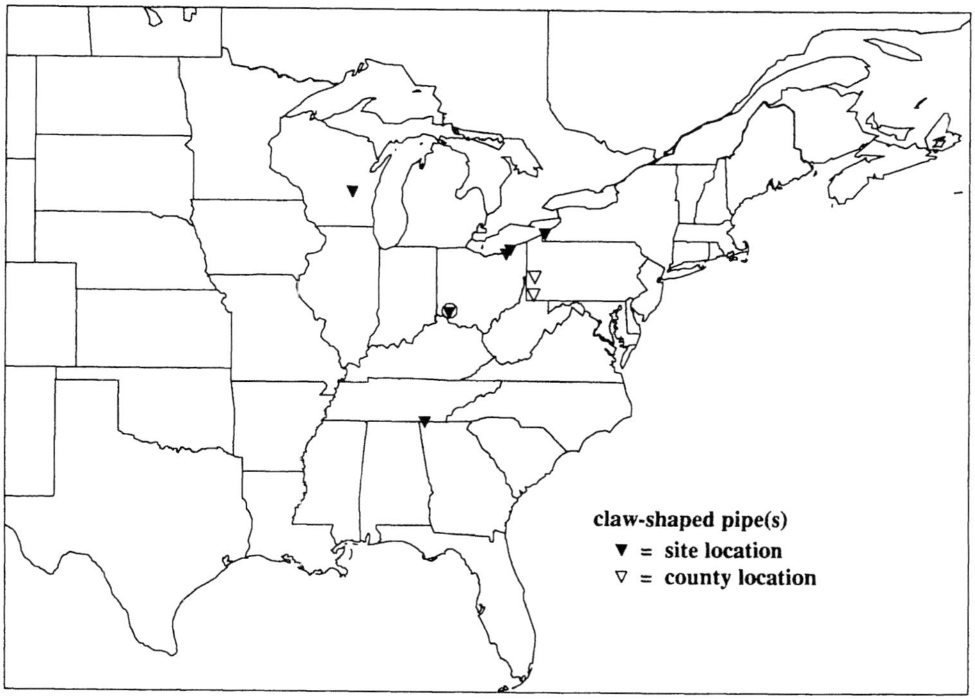

Figure 8-31. Geographical distribution of claw effigy pipes, probably incomplete (Ahlstrom 1979:35, 36; Greenman 1937:363; Mayer-Oakes 1955:223; Moore 1915: Fig. 84; West 1934: Pls. 134.1, 162.3; see also Parker 1916:489, 501).

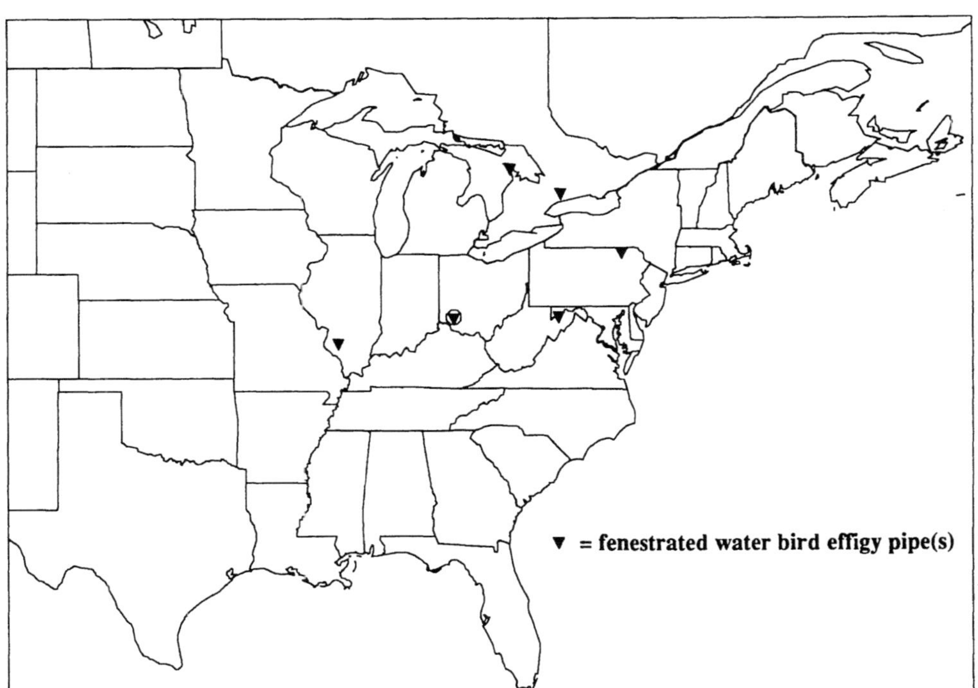

Figure 8-32. Geographical distribution of fenestrated water bird effigy pipes (see text for references).

that was occupied by an Illini subgroup during the early eighteenth century (Laidlaw 1924:72-73); however, no pipes even close to this form are reported from excavations at the actual village site (Good 1972). Like the Madisonville swan, these effigy pipes have open spaces between beak-head-neck and body, but they appear to be bending forward, with beak touching feet, so that they would be upright when smoked. Witthoft and colleagues speak of this as a "major" Northeastern type, but illustrate only one unprovenienced Pennsylvania example (1953:94, Pl. 1.18). In spite of its two heads (unique within Fort Ancient territory), the swan pipe does not resemble Iroquoian multiheaded clay elbow pipes (Mathews 1981) or other two-headed forms (e.g., West 1934: Pl. 105, a two-headed perching owl pipe from Ontario). The two Madisonville pipes might well have been locally made from a Northeastern (Susquehannock?) model, but additional provenienced examples are needed before any firm opinion can be offered (Figure 8-32).

After disk pipes, with their strong Oneota affiliations, the largest geographical representation of pipes at Madisonville is Iroquoian. Iroquoian pipes make up about six percent of pipes excavated at the site. Ceramic pipe fragments included trumpet, acorn, and effigy forms (Figures 8-27a, b). Three out of four extant stem fragments from HUPM and CMNH collections exhibited the bulbous ends found on pipes from at least one late sixteenth-century Erie or Neutral site in western New York and from some of the same early seventeenth-century (GBP2 and 3) Neutral sites that also produced Basque kettle parts (Fitzgerald 1982:153-54; Lennox 1981: Figs. 18, 42; M. White 1978: Fig. 4; cf. Fitzgerald et al. 1993: Tables 1, 4). A ceramic humanoid effigy pipe fragment (Figure 8-27a) might also have ties to Ontario. One of the pipes at the early seventeenth-century Neutral Christianson site is described thus: "An elbow fragment...contained the representations of the arms, backbone and buttocks of a sitting or crouching individual" (Fitzgerald 1982:160). Examples of stone pipes with crouching humans, from sites in New York and Pennsylvania, can be seen in Laidlaw 1913:68-70.

Both of the trumpet fragments (Figure 8-27a) have plain outer bowls but rims decorated with a horizontal line and tiny punctates, which I have not traced to a definite locale. They are similar in some ways to Saint Lawrence Iroquois examples, but not completely congruent (Pendergast 1992, pers. comm.). The larger one resembles examples from the Ripley site in southwestern New York and the Nichols site in Jefferson County, northeastern New York, except that the rims of the plain-surfaced New York pipes are decorated with only a single row of punctates, not a more elaborate pattern as on the Madisonville pipe (Parker 1922: Pl. 95.6; Rutsch 1973: Fig. 134).

The closest published example to the ceramic owl head effigy fragment (Figure 8-27b) that I have found came from the late sixteenth–early seventeenth century Susquehannock Schultz site, but the Madisonville example also resembles an unprovenienced pipe in the Royal Ontario Museum (Kent 1984: Fig. 26, bottom center; Mathews 1980: Fig. 2; for Schultz dates, cf. Sempowski 1994:61). A crude acorn or "round-topped" (Noble 1992:43) form from the CMNH collection that probably came from Madisonville (1918.847) is decorated with vertical lines above a single horizontal line encircling the bowl. I have not yet found a close counterpart. A "round-topped" or "bulbar ring" ceramic pipe was collected from the Hardin site, which had the horizontal encircling lines that are more typical of Neutral and Huron-Petun forms—plus an engraved lizard clinging to the bottom (Henderson et al. 1986:138, Fig. 33A). Hardin is the only other Fort Ancient settlement from which an Iroquoian pipe bowl has been reported, although the Huntington Art Museum collection from the Clover site does contain one shell-tempered ceramic straight-ended pipe stem (Cat. No. 80.206.823).

The stone elbow pipe stem with carved lizard (Figure 8-27a), plus another stem fragment with a long carved tail curated at the AMNH (20/1456), are similar but not identical in form to examples from a number of Ontario Iroquoian sites, and to one found under a copper kettle in Nova Scotia (Laidlaw 1914:56, 62-67). Both Madisonville stems were fashioned from a gray stone with lighter colored inclusions similar to the stone used for a number of other Madisonville pipes, including the fish effigy illustrated at the bottom right of Figure 8-25 and examples in Figure 8-42. The square "collared" gray stone pipe bowl (Figure 8-27a) is reminiscent of an inept copy of a Neutral "coronet trumpet" type (cf. Noble 1992: Fig. 4.8).

None of the Madisonville Iroquoian-style pipes were whole, and all of the fragments came from refuse pits or middens, not mortuary contexts. Although smoking was important in Iroquoian ritual and everyday life, pipe bowls were not typically exchanged by individuals, in contrast to upper Mississippi Valley/Great Lakes customs (e.g., Fenton 1953; Paper 1992:163-65). Thus, the presence of Iroquoian pipes implies the presence of Iroquoian people, not long-distance, down-the-line exchange.

Various unique pipes from nonmortuary contexts point toward additional areas of contact. The scratched and battered long-beaked bird head fragment (Figure 8-25, third row) is stylistically close to a "woodpecker or kingfisher" effigy pipe from Dumaw Creek, west-central Michigan (Quimby 1966a:52-53). The finely made fish effigy pipe (Figure 8-25, bottom row) is unlike any other that I have seen, but does very much resemble fish effigy vessels from northeastern Arkansas, northwestern Mississippi, and Tennessee (e.g., Brown 1926: Figs. 286, 287; Hathcock 1976:130-33; Thruston 1897: Pl. VII). Likewise, a turtle effigy pipe with ridged shell (Figure 8-26; Cowan 1987: Fig. 30) is surprisingly similar to a snapping turtle effigy vessel from Mississippi County, Arkansas (Hathcock 1976: Fig. 360).

The steatite turkey effigy elbow pipe in Figure 8-25 also is unique at Madisonville, and I have found few comparable examples. Mayer-Oakes shows a drawing of this general shape and color of elbow pipe, but without any effigy, as a typical Monongahela artifact (Mayer-Oakes 1955: Fig. 26I); the original was excavated at the Speidel site in the West Virginia panhandle (Mayer-Oakes 1954: Fig. 8D). A plain black steatite elbow pipe with sloping bowl came from the Fort Ancient Mann site (see map, Figure 4-2), and a similar one with a brass insert came from Orchard (Moxley 1985:46, 1988a: Fig. 13). According to Swanton (1946:Map 13), steatite is common in the eastern slope of the Virginia Appalachians, but of course that is not the only source for this mineral. The pipe that I have found with the greatest overall resemblance to the Madisonville example was excavated from a flexed burial at Mt. Carbon, West Virginia, on the upper Kanawha River. It was a gray limestone elbow pipe with a bird's head projecting from the front of the bowl (McMichael 1962: Pl. 8). The component was identified as A.D. 1200-1300 Fort Ancient, although a child burial there included twelve rolled copper beads.

There is no way to trace Fort Ancient pipe forms found outside the central Ohio region back to a particular site, such as Madisonville. To give an idea of general trends, I will note that outside Fort Ancient territory, stone vasiforms, probably the most typical Late Fort Ancient form (Table 4-3, Figures 7-2, 7-5a, b), have been mapped by George West from eastern New York and northeastern Pennsylvania, across southern Ontario and northern Ohio, southern Michigan, and northern Indiana, to Wisconsin, western Illinois, and down the Mississippi Valley as far as southeastern Missouri (1934: Map 9). They are not uncommon in Oneota territory (e.g., West 1934: Pl. 160; personal inspection of Milwaukee Public Museum collection), and have been found in limited numbers at sixteenth and early seventeenth century Ontario and New York Iroquoian sites, more in the west than the east (Rutsch 1973:85-91; Witthoft et al. 1953: Pl. 1). The Iroquian examples tend to be more elongated than Fort Ancient forms (more similar in shape to Iroquoian pottery) and, unlike Fort Ancient pipes, to have attachment holes for stems (Rutsch 1973:85-91; personal examination of examples from Seneca sites curated at the Rochester Museum and Science Center). At Seneca sites, stone pipes first appear, in the form of sandstone ovoids, at the mid-sixteenth century Richmond Mills site, with stone vasiforms first present at the Adams site around 1580, and in evidence up to around 1640 (M. Sempowski, pers. comm.). In intermediate territory, stone vasiforms are common at the eastern and northeastern Ohio Riker and Reeve village sites, and "typical" of southwestern Pennsylvania Monongahela sites (Ahlstrom 1979:30-31; Mayer-Oakes 1955:222-23; Vietzen 1974:102-13).

"Ohio pipestone (Sciotoville flintclay)" was reported from the late prehistoric Reeve site in northeastern Ohio (Greenman 1935:9). Portsmouth fireclay from Feurt Hill and vicinity has been visually identified in artifacts from a number of sites in western and northwestern Pennsylvania (Witthoft et al. 1953:92-94, 100-101), and chemically identified in a disk fragment from the Utz site in Missouri (Figure 8-33) (Sigstad 1973:39-40). The pipes in Monongahela territory identified as being made of Ohio pipestone include a repaired disk pipe with effigy animal face from Lawrence County, a vasiform from the John Lapping/Varner site (where blue glass beads and a brass fish effigy also were found), and a perching owl effigy pipe from a grave near Waynesburg (Johnson 1994: Table 10; Witthoft et al. 1953:92-93, Pls. 1.9, 1.19). From early sixteenth century Quiggle-McFate sites in north central Pennsylvania came Portsmouth fireclay raw material, pendants, and pipes in the form of a perching owl, a long spike shape, and an ovoid human face effigy (Johnson 1994:24; Kent 1984:118-24, 307-10; Witthoft et al. 1953:93-94, n. 14, Pls. 1.13, 1.16, 1.21). Although visual identification of Ohio pipestones might not always be reliable, this early sixteenth-century spate of trading activity in Portsmouth fireclay does seem to correlate with a shift to shell-tempered ceramics by West Branch Susquehanna River people, which Witthoft proposed came about by influence from Allegheny-Ohio Valley Monongahela peoples, through whom the pipestone presumably was being acquired (Witthoft 1959:27, 50-51; cf. Kent 1984:309-10). The chemically analyzed Utz fragment points to exchange activity between protohistoric Fort Ancient and Oneota peoples, although current research indicates that Sigstad's work may require reanalysis.

Bone and Antler

Several types of bone and antler implements provide connections between Madisonville and regions to its north and west.

Two workaday tools at the site occur in styles with only thin or nonexistent connections to other protohistoric Fort Ancient sites. Turkey bone awls with transverse notching along their spines make up five percent of extant bone awls from Trenches 1-K (Figure 6-18a; see also Griffin 1943: Pl. LXXIX, bottom left, and Hooton and Willoughby 1920: Pl. 12h). Among Fort Ancient sites, I have seen similar examples only from Hardin (Hanson 1966: Fig. 57), the pre-Madisonville Horizon Gartner site (Mills 1904: Fig. 42), and Mound 1 at the Fox Farm site (Smith 1910: Pl. LIII.1). However, notched awls *are* reported from three sixteenth–early seventeenth century components in the Sandusky River area (Bowen 1994:11, Fig. 57), as well as from the Whittlesey late prehistoric South Park, Tuttle Hill, and Reeve Village sites farther east (Greenman 1935: Fig. 15, 1937:357).

Five out of six extant harpoons from Madisonville were simple single-barbed antler harpoons with attachment holes (Figure 6-18a); the sixth had a bifurcated barb and attachment hole (Hooton and Willoughby 1920: Pl. 11; Cowan 1987: Fig. 28). Unlike almost all other categories of functional tools, half of the Madisonville harpoons were found with burials, all of them adult males (Burials I-19, 323 from Block 1, and 7 from Block 15). The only identical artifact that I have located in the literature, complete with attachment hole, came from an early sixteenth century context in eastern Sandusky County (Bowen 1994:12, Fig. 64). Bowen reports "similar" harpoons from two nearby sites, Indian Hills and Edwards, but does not state whether they include attachment holes.

The only antler harpoon I have found from another Fort Ancient site was like the Madisonville examples except that it had no hole. It came from a burial at the eighteenth-century, multi-

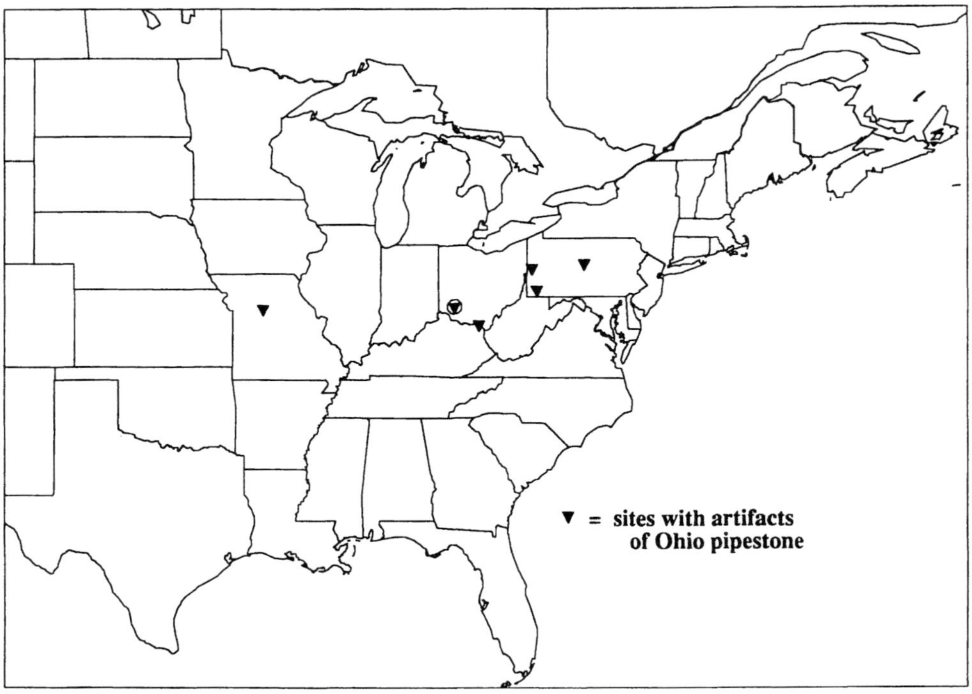

Figure 8-33. Locations of some sites with pipes reportedly made from Ohio pipestone (Portsmouth fireclay) from the vicinity of the Feurt site. See text for discussion.

component Bentley site, which also contained a vasiform pipe and a piece of copper or brass (Pollack and Henderson 1984:21-22). At least three Iroquoian sites also have produced single-barbed antler harpoons with no holes, Reed Fort/Richmond Mills (mid-sixteenth century) and Adams (GBP1), New York, and Grimsby (GBP2-3), Ontario, as have the prehistoric Oak Forest site and early historical, multicomponent Zimmerman site in Illinois (Bluhm and Fenner 1961:160; Brown 1975:49, Pl. 11; Kenyon 1982: Pl. 186; Parker 1918: Fig. 10B; Wray et al. 1987:3-10b).

The relatively large amount of bison bone at Madisonville—a material not identified at any other Fort Ancient settlement—was discussed in Chapter 6. Only selected bones were retained at Madisonville, mostly thoracic vertebrae used for hide-scraping beamers (Figure 6-18a, 6-54). Potential sources (discussed at more length in Chapter 6, and in the last section of this chapter) include Big Bone Lick, Kentucky, or prairie environments farther west.

Robert Boszhardt has proposed musical rasps made from animal ribs as a late prehistoric-protohistoric marker of interaction across the Great Plains, with their origins in the southwest and southern Plains but occurring from Pecos Pueblo, New Mexico, across Texas, Oklahoma and Kansas to Oneota sites during the sixteenth century (Figure 8-34) (1993, pers. comm.). Madisonville is the easternmost site at which they appear in any numbers: there are at least 45 extant complete and fragmentary examples from Trenches 1-K (Figure 6-18a; Hooton and Willoughby 1920: Pl. 15), plus at least one made from a bison rib bone (Cowan 1987: Fig. 29). Within Fort Ancient territory, two fragments have been reported from the Buffalo site and at least one has come from Neale's Landing (Hanson 1975:87; Hemmings 1977:11-10). A few fragments have come from Whittlesey sites: at least three from South Park, and at least one from Fairport Harbor (Brose 1994: Fig. 8.1B; Greenman 1937:343, Fig. 20, 1943:57). In southwestern Michigan, Moccasin Bluff has produced at least two (Bettarel and Smith 1973: Pl. 65).

Stone Implements

Sources of chert/flint for Madisonville projectile points and knives, analyzed by Litfin et al. (1993), were reported in Chapter 5. Three varieties from Kentucky and four from Ohio, including Flint Ridge flint, could have been obtained by human transport or from local river deposits. Two varieties from southeastern and south-central Indiana would have had to have been carried.

Clubs or mauls made from bilaterally symmetrical oval stones with a central groove are another fairly common artifact at Madisonville that, to my surprise, I did not find reported from other Fort Ancient sites. There are thirty extant examples from Trenches 1-K (Figure 6-17b; Hooton and Willoughby 1920: Pl. 10a-c), twenty percent of them decorated with a "+" at one or both ends. More elaborate decoration on some examples includes concentric rings around the +'s, one with featherlike designs, and one finely-made example with an engraved thunderbird motif in addition to +'s.

The only similar grooved maul I found that might have come from another Fort Ancient site is in the Stahl Collection (Blennerhasset Museum, Parkersburg), much of which was collected from Blennerhasset Island, West Virginia, where the Neale's Landing site is located. Somewhat similar grooved specimens drilled for hafting, which probably date to around 1800, have been reported from three northern Ohio locations (Holzapfel and Converse 1995). Eight "Grooved Stone War Club Heads" are listed for the mid-sixteenth century Seneca/Cayuga Reed Fort/Richmond Mills site (where a redstone large-disk pipe was excavated), and one is illustrated from the early protohistoric Seneca Adams site, but none from its immediate successors, Tram and Cameron (Parker 1918:31; Wray et al. 1991; Wray et al. 1987: Fig. 3-120b, Burial Index 1028).

Grooved clubs are much more common west of Madisonville, appearing as early as the Mill Creek phase (ca. A.D. 900-1300) in northwestern Iowa (Laird 1989: Object 8-32, from the Wittrock site) and at the eleventh-twelfth century Aztalan site in southeastern Wisconsin (Freeman 1986: Fig. 7-6.40). In fact, I suspect that they are so common in the west that they often aren't illustrated in archaeological reports, so the distribution map in Figure 8-35 is undoubtedly far sparser than the archaeological reality. In a rapid survey, I found examples reported from as far south as Clarksdale, Mississippi (Brown 1926:233) and as far west as Blood Run in northwestern Iowa (Harvey 1979:150; Laird 1989: Objects 11-11, 11-12, 11-24). They were "common" at the Utz site, thought to have been the principal village of the Missouri Indians during the late seventeenth century (Bray 1961b:221, 1991:126-28). During the nineteenth century, grooved mauls were used by many groups inhabiting areas west of the Mississippi, as witnessed by contemporaneous artists such as George Catlin and Karl Bodmer. A few examples include Catlin's famous painting, "Scalp Dance," depicting Teton Sioux around 1835, a Catlin portrait of three Osage men, around 1834 (Wilson 1988:12 shows an engraved version), and Bodmer's "Buffalo Dance of the Mandan Indians" (Hail 1983:156). Even after guns became available, these weapons were retained as important symbols, being used as coup sticks, as badges of office for some military societies, and as highly decorated "dance clubs" (Hail 1983:157). Numerous nineteenth century Plains mauls or clubs are curated in museum collections (e.g., Hail 1983:157-66).

Ceramics

Across eastern North America, ceramics were made and used for cooking almost entirely by women. Thus, when foreign ceramics turn up on a site, the tendency has been to ascribe them to the presence of foreign women, as willing or captive brides, as refugees, as adoptees, or as slaves. However, such extrapolations may be hazardous, particularly when based on the presence of only a few nonlocal sherds. Martha Latta has enumerated other possibilities, including (1) travel by potters, who returned home to copy styles or motifs observed elsewhere, or (2) the movement of pots rather than potters, as containers for exchanged foodstuffs or for food consumed by travelers (Latta 1991). She particularly notes a new style of pot among Iroquoians during the early sixteenth century, with a smaller size, squat shape, constricted neck, and "useless" tiny handles that would make a vessel very well suited for canoe travel when secured by a rope around the neck and under the handles. While large numbers of whole foreign vessels at a settlement *would* very likely signal a significant influx of nonlocal people, a few exotic sherds at a site might well be more likely to signify a short-term visitor.

The only vessel type at Madisonville with possible Iroquoian connections is the much-discussed stemmed, pedestaled form (Figure 8-36). Although it often has been discussed as if it were a typical Madisonville type, no more than three or four have come from the site. Figure 4-15 depicts the most nearly complete example; another, with no handles, is missing most of the pedestal (CMNH 1937.677, unknown provenience). HUPM collections contain a nearly complete pedestal that includes part of the bottom of the bowl (01-38-10/69724, from Trench 1-5 general digging), plus four possible pedestal fragments.

The largest number of stemmed, pedestaled vessels reported from any one site is five, from the Monongahela GBP1-2 Foley Farm site, and one has come from the nearby Vesta site, which had no European artifacts (Johnson 1994: Tables 9, 10). Not far away, a small Indian Hills Stamped vessel with a short stem but no pedestal recently was excavated at the protohistoric Cullison site in northeastern Ohio (Table 4-9) (James Morton, pers. comm.). Latta gathered data on pedestaled vessels from four Huron and five Neutral sixteenth-seventeenth century sites. She, like John Griffin before her, attributed them to copying by indigenous potters of French goblets or chalices, perhaps associated with Catholic religious services, but Peter Ramsden and William Fitzgerald disputed this, based (among other things) on a fifteenth–early sixteenth century occupation of one of the sites, long before any Europeans reached the area (Griffin 1945; Latta 1987, 1990; Ramsden and Fitzgerald 1990). That site, however, did produce two pieces of brass, indicating that residents might have seen Europeans using similar-shaped vessels elsewhere. Three whole ceramic stemware vessels were excavated from three mid-sixteenth century Titus phase sites in Texas (two of them from burials), along with a ceramic spoonlike artifact, and have been attributed to copying of goblets carried by members of the de Soto entrada (Perttula 1992:27, 103, 248; Turner 1978:98-103). The most recent known example, a castellated vessel (Kent 1984: Fig. 105), came from the third-quarter seventeenth century Susquehannock Byrd Leibhart site, occupied during a time period when English Catholics were well established in nearby Maryland (Table 3-1, Figure 3-6).

Since the bowls of stemmed vessels from different areas have different forms, all congruent with local jar or bowl shapes, these do seem to be instances of local potters copying objects that they had seen or had had described to them. The disposition of many of them, including two from Madisonville, with burials

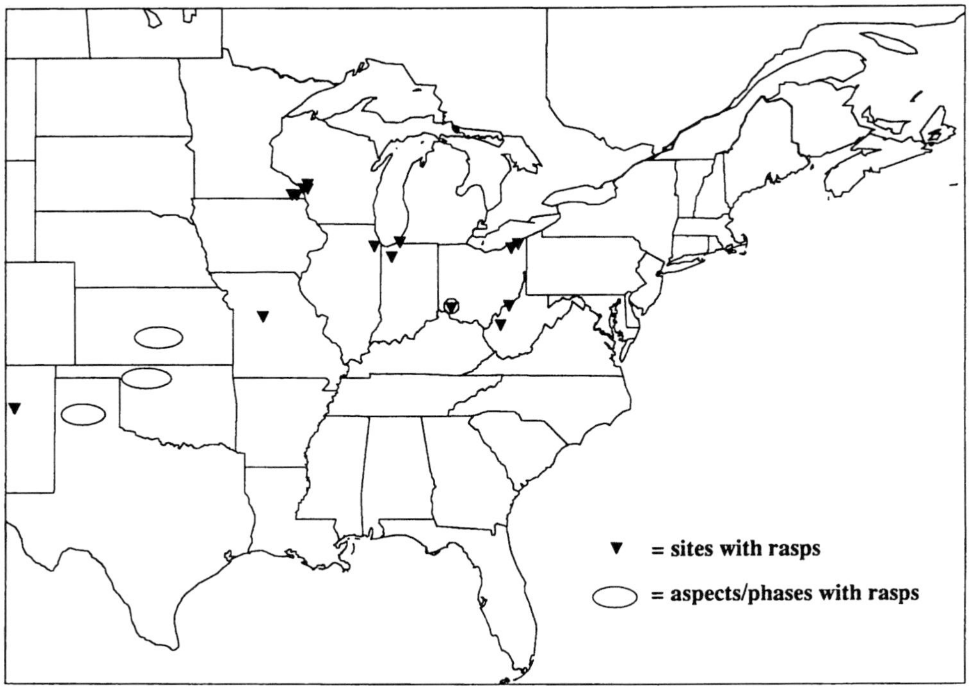

Figure 8-34. Geographical distribution of animal rib rasps at late prehistoric-protohistoric sites and regions (after Boszhardt 1993 and pers. comm., with Fort Ancient and Whittlesey additions discussed in text). Sites include Pecos Pueblo, New Mexico; Utz, Missouri; Farley Village and Yucatan/Riceford Creek, Minnesota; Farley Village, Valley View, and State Road Coulee, Wisconsin; Hoxie Farm, Illinois; Fifield, Indiana; Moccasin Bluff, Michigan; South Park, Fairport Harbor and Madisonville, Ohio; and Buffalo and Neale's Landing, West Virginia. Regions include the Texas Panhandle Aspect/Antelope Creek phase, the Oklahoma Washita River phase, and the Kansas Great Bend Aspect.

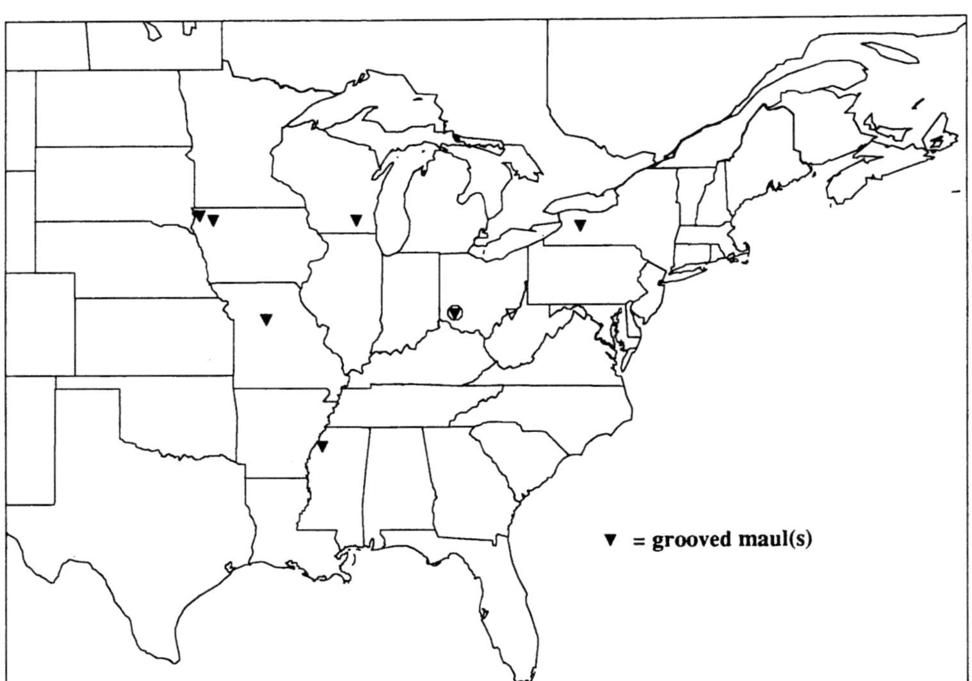

Figure 8-35. Geographical distribution of grooved mauls (partial; see text for discussion).

does imply that they were thought to have some special, important qualities. Vessels used by Catholic priests to celebrate communion, as postulated by Latta, would seem to be a very good possibility. French Catholics in Iroquoian territory would not have been the only available sources of inspiration. Besides Spanish expeditions through the interior Southeast and Southwest, the mid-sixteenth century saw attempts by Spaniards to colonize as far north as Chesapeake Bay (Table 3-1), and English Catholics began to populate the Baltimore area in 1633.

I have jumped the gun by already discussing the most numerous class of pottery at Madisonville that has nonlocal connections, ceramics with strong relationships to northern Ohio (see Chapter 6). In particular, these include shell-tempered and non-shell-tempered sherds and whole vessels with notched rims or rim strips, which are very common across northern Ohio and surrounding areas to the west, north, and east, plus some Indian Hills sherds from northeastern Ohio. Figures 6-60 and 8-37a-c illustrate just a few examples. I cited the presence of both numerous sherds and whole mortuary vessels, distributed around the site (Figure 6-59) in arguing for intimate and fairly frequent interaction between Madisonville residents and their nearest northern neighbors. In addition, the presence of Anderson-like and Madisonville-like ceramics at northern Ohio sites was cited as evidence of long-term interaction patterns. To this evidence might be added a few cord-impressed rim sherds at Madisonville (e.g., Figure 8-37c) perhaps similar to Indiana Oliver phase cord-impressed lip decoration (e.g., Dorwin 1971: Fig. 6c), that together with Anderson-like ceramics at Oliver phase sites might extend this pre-Madisonville Horizon interaction pattern toward the northwest.

Also described in Chapter 6 were several mortuary vessels with attributes perhaps derived ultimately from late prehistoric upper Ohio Valley types. These include teat lugs, perhaps related to late fifteenth-century Riker series pottery from western Ohio (James Morton, pers. comm. citing Whitman 1975), and grooved paddling (also called simple stamping), typical of Wellsburg ceramics (e.g., Figures 4-12, 6-61, 6-65). Eastern Fort Ancient archaeologists have noted the strong presence of Wellsburg and Riker-like pottery at protohistoric eastern Fort Ancient and related sites such as Neale's Landing, Orchard, Buffalo, and Bosman, as well as hybrid forms between them and Madisonville ceramics (e.g., Baker 1988:46-50, Figs. 2-3; Carskadden et al. 1992:60; Moxley 1988a: Figs. 5-7; James Morton, pers. comm.; cf. Brose 1994:177), which they generally link to interaction precipitated by sixteenth-century Iroquois incursions into the upper Ohio Valley—first mixed bands with recognizably separate pottery types, followed in some cases by blending within vessels of originally separate ceramic traits. At least one handleless, almost shoulderless grooved-paddled jar from a Madisonville burial (Figure 6-65) has a shape like Wellsburg Simple Stamped vessels and vessels that Baker has designated Neale's Landing Cordmarked (cf. Baker 1988: Figs. 2d, g). Other vessels from Madisonville (e.g., Figures 4-13, 7-4) have incurvate rims that might be linked to Wellsburg forms.

As noted in Chapter 4, there are at least two four-handled, notched-rim jars (Figure 4-19) from the Seneca Dann site (ca. 1655-1670) with similarities to notched rim examples at Madisonville. However, they are not identical to any particular Madisonville jars. One of them is very squat, and the other is globular but hardly has a shoulder. The former characteristic probably marks that jar as later than jars at the Madisonville site, while the latter characteristic may signal an eastern Fort Ancient rather than a western Fort Ancient connection (e.g., shapes associated with Neale's Landing ceramics; cf. Baker 1988).

In at least two instances, links can be shown between Madisonville pottery with northern and northeastern Ohio connections and pottery excavated at and near the Zimmerman site in Illinois. Caution must be used in interpretation, however, because of the multicomponent nature of the sites involved. As noted in Chapter 6, two Madisonville mortuary vessels had teat lugs characteristic of the Riker series, combined with more familiar Madisonville Horizon characteristics such as smoothed neck surfaces (Figure 6-61). (A third vessel combined typical Madisonville Horizon form with teat lugs and a decorated neck; see Figure 4-10a.) At Orchard, fourteen of over one hundred excavated vessels had lugs or nodes rather than handles (Moxley 1988b:4). At least one cord-marked mortuary vessel from Orchard with eight teat lugs grouped in pairs was virtually identical to the Madisonville vessel at left in Figure 6-61 (Moxley 1988a: Fig. 7). At least one similar large cord-marked cooking pot with paired teat lugs has been excavated at Rolf Lee (photograph in possession of Ronald Moxley), as have rim sherds with paired teat lugs from Neale's Landing (Hemmings 1977: Fig. 42g).

These vessels, in turn, appear to be almost the same as a four-lugged Danner Cordmarked jar (reclassified as Keating Cordmarked) from an early component at Zimmerman, Illinois (Brown 1961: Fig. 8D; cf. Brown and Willis 1995:7-8). There also was at least one "unique," squat Danner Grooved Paddle vessel at Zimmerman (Brown 1961: Fig. 13A; quotation from Brown and Willis 1995:7) that approaches late style Madisonville notched-rim/notched-collar vessels in morphology and surface treatment, and also shows similarities to the two mid-late seventeenth century vessels from the Seneca Dann site (Figure 4-19) . As a group, they might represent late derivations from early–mid-seventeenth century Central Ohio Valley forms. The "Madisonville Grooved Paddle" vessel with handles from the Hotel Plaza site near Zimmerman (Schnell 1974: Fig. 10) has a non-everted rim reminiscent of Wellsburg rather than Madisonville jars, although its form is similar to at least one poorly provenienced four-handled vessel excavated during the 1880s at Madisonville (Griffin 1943: Pl. LXVIII.5).

A few more vessels and sherds at Madisonville have connections toward the northwest. A Huber-like heavy, incised handle (Figure 8.37d, bottom) compares well with late ceramics from the Chicago area (cf. Herold et al. 1990: Fig. 2.7f; Michalik and Brown 1990: Fig. 10.2b). Another abruptly everted rim with

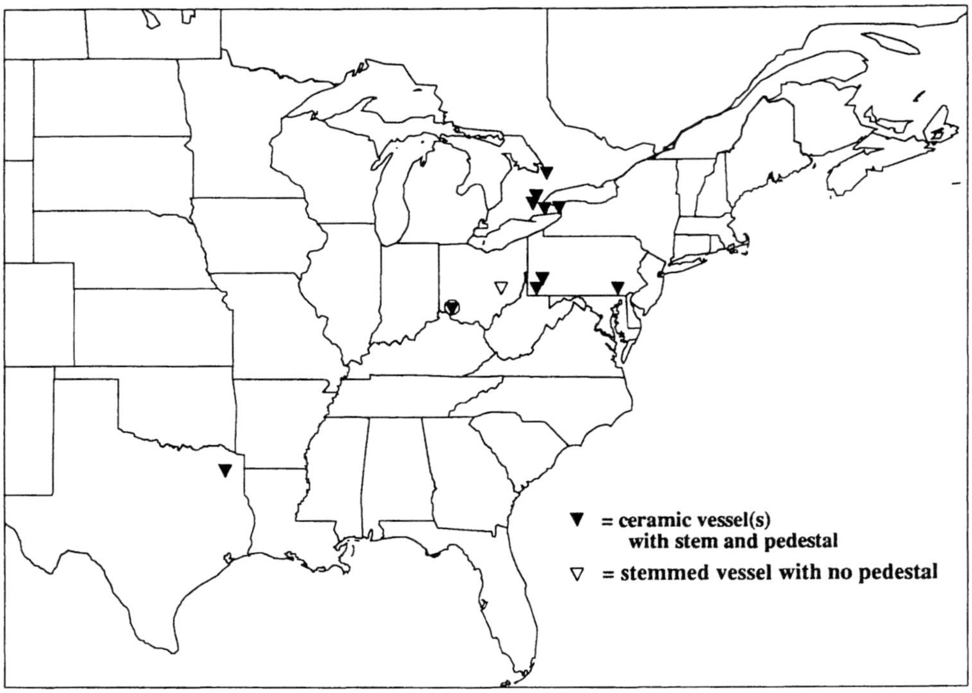

Figure 8-36. Geographical distribution of stemmed ceramic vessels (see text for discussion).

finely incised shoulder decoration (Figure 8.37d, center right) also appears to have Oneota-like attributes. Not illustrated is a body sherd with deep, broad vertical and diagonal shoulder trailing (HUPM 01-38-10/69711) in an Oneota style that is not dissimilar to some examples of Allamakee Trailed from northeastern Iowa (e.g., Griffin 1943: Pl. CXLIV.3; M. Wedel 1959: Fig. 29b).

The 1980s CMNH excavations at Madisonville unearthed an almost complete large globular, constricted-mouth plain-surfaced vessel (Figure 8-38) that is described as "comparable to those commonly found in Mississippian sites in the Lower Ohio and Cumberland drainages" (Glowacki et al. 1993). It came from a stratified midden in the southwestern portion of the site, 162 cm below the surface.

Looking farther southward, toward the Central Mississippi Valley, two sherds from the same vessel (one shown in Figure 8.37d, center left) are reminiscent of Campbell Appliqué with unnotched appliqué strips (cf. O'Brien 1994:41-43, Figs. 6.12, 6.13; Phillips 1970:61-62; see also Mainfort 1996). A vessel with very similar rim came from Durand's Bend, Alabama (Moore 1899: Fig. 28), which also produced engraved shell "buttons" like the example from Madisonville (Figure 6-19b). It is worth noting that arcaded Campbell Appliqué vessels resemble typical thin, V-shaped Madisonville strap handles. A probable fish effigy bowl (Figure 8.37d, top, one of at least two such vessels from Madisonville) also has congruencies with Middle Mississippi vessels (cf. O'Brien 1994: Fig. 7.4f). Hooton and Willoughby figured a shallow bowl with a painted black cross-in-circle inside (1920: Pl. 24b), similar in concept to Carson Red on Buff interior-painted bowls from northeastern Arkansas (cf. Morse and Morse 1983: Fig. 13.4g; Phillips 1970:63). It was described as being in the "Cincinnati Museum," but no one alive today remembers seeing it.

Unlike sites such as Fox Farm and Clover (e.g., Griffin 1943: Pl. CXIX.11–CXIX.18; Mayer-Oakes 1955: Fig. 104A), Madisonville has produced no Mississippian-like bird effigy heads from bowls, or at least, I have seen none. Effigy heads generally seem to have topped jar handles rather than forming one end of an effigy bowl with head and tail as was common at Tennessee and central Mississippi Valley sites. Examples of Madisonville effigy heads from the Harvard collections include eared "bears" (97-38-10/62939, Trenches 1-5 general digging; 08-3-10/78451, Trench B general digging; identical to Thruston 1897: Fig. 51, second from right) and a crested humanoid (01-38-10/69721, Trenches 1-5 general digging). The National Museum of the American Indian collection from Madisonville includes a deerlike effigy head (with possible forked-eye surrounds) and a flat human head topping a handle (21/9270). Only one related nearly-complete vessel is extant. It has flat humanoid effigy heads affixed to the tops of two handles peering over the rim of a typical Madisonville cord-marked jar (Figure 4-13). A sherd with similar effigy head also came from Hahn's Field (HUPM, from Metz's 1885 excavation), and Griffin illustrates another possible example from Buffalo (1943: Pl. CXXV.6). At the HUPM, there is one extant sherd with an appliqué leg plus a separated leg appliqué, similar to appliqué frog effigies on bowls from the central Mississippi Valley (01-38-10/69720,

Figure 8-37a. Selected sherds with notched appliqué strips from Madisonville, with affinities to northern Ohio types. Shell tempered unless otherwise noted. For related whole vessels with notched rim strips, see Griffin 1943: Pl. LXX. *Top*: 82-35-10/26749, Block L, Pit 15. *Center*: 07-6-10/78455, Trench B, general digging, note deep trailing below strip; 01-38-10/67761, Trench 1, Pit 22; 08-3-10/71907, Trench D, Pit 89, sand tempered. *Bottom*: 01-38-10/69589, Trench 2, Burial 27. Photograph by Hillel Burger (HUPM Photo No. N33986). Copyright 1996 by the President and Fellows of Harvard College.

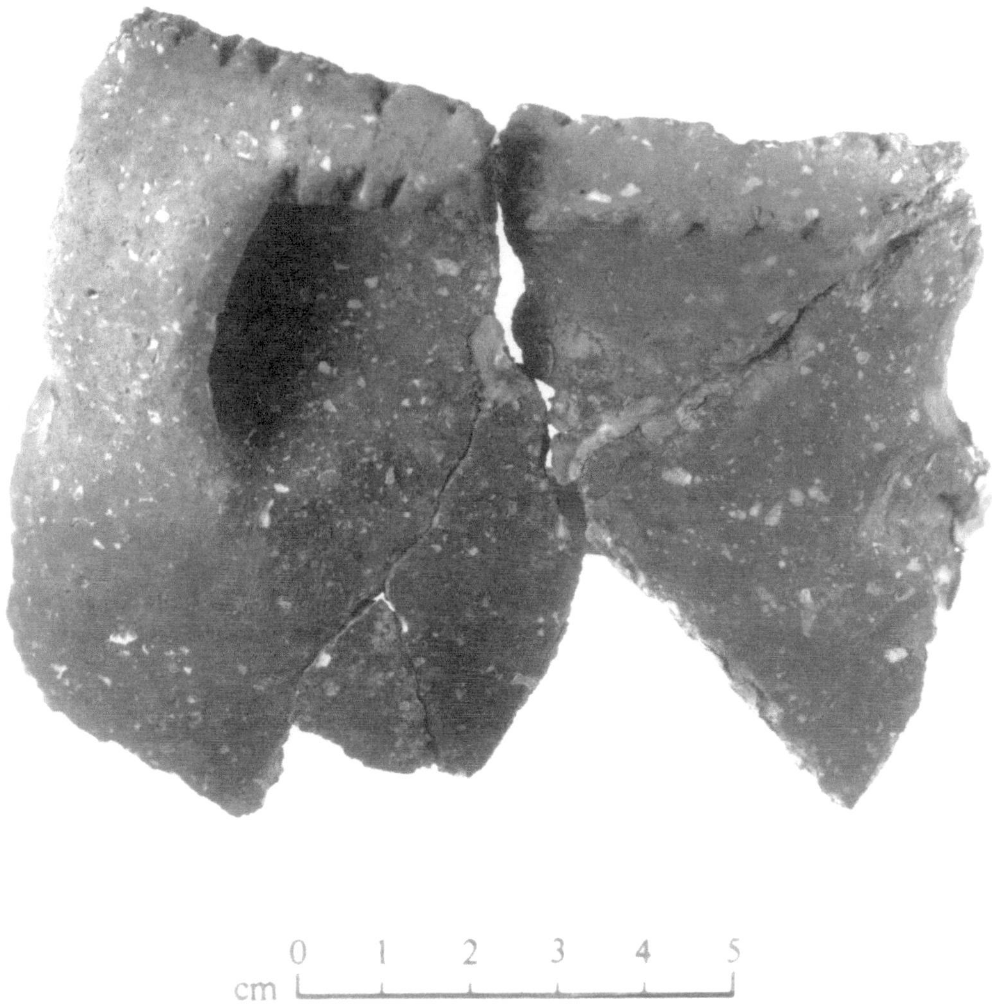

Figure 8-37b. Madisonville vessel with notched rim strip, similar to Tuttle Hill Notched (HUPM Cat. No. 07-6-10/78613, from Burial B-40). Photograph by Hillel Burger (HUPM Photo No. N33847). Copyright 1997 by the President and Fellows of Harvard College.

Trenches 1-5 general digging; 08-3-10/78532, Trench C general digging).

The well-known Madisonville head pot, interred with Burial D-64, is the only mortuary vessel with foreign traits at the site besides jars with connections to northern Ohio ceramics. The vessel was fashioned from local paste in typical Madisonville Plain ceramic style, but the skillful modeling of the face on this unique jar argues that its maker had had previous experience in creating face effigies. The face on the jar, with its sharp nose, horizontally molded eyelids and mouth, and pointed, receding chin, has general resemblances to a number of well-known head pots from southeastern Missouri (e.g., O'Brien 1994: Pls. 7a, b, e). I found a particularly close match of facial features with a water bottle from a "Missouri mound" in the HUPM collection (Figure 8-39); similarly made features can be seen on head pots from northeastern Arkansas (e.g., Hathcock 1976).

Missouri potters, too, might have been imitating Madisonville jars. A "Neeley's Ferry Plain" vessel with tapered strap handles and notchlike decoration around rim and shoulder, from a burial at the Murphy site (O'Brien 1994: Fig. 5.17b), is a remarkably close match, in a stiff, non-Fort Ancient way, for Madisonville jars and decorated handles such as illustrated by Griffin (1943: Pls. LXIII.1 and LXVII.5) and Cowan (1987: Fig. 17).

To the Madisonville ceramics can be added evidence of westward interaction from other somewhat earlier western Fort Ancient sites. These include a restored constricted-mouth Oneota-like jar from Campbell Island (Griffin 1943: Pl. XC.1) and from Hahn's Field a piecrust-type rim identified by Griffin with Fisher Focus (northwestern Indiana-southwestern Michigan) ceramics and a partially restored vessel with vertical trailed shoulder decoration reminiscent of vessels from Anker and northeastern Iowa (Griffin 1943: Pl. LXXXVIII.9 and 10; cf. Bluhm and Liss 1961:

Figure 8-37c. Selected nonlocal and related sherds from Madisonville. Shell tempered unless otherwise noted. *Top*: Indian Hills sherds (07-6-10/78225, Trench C, Pit 2; 08-3-10/79091, Trench E, Pit 19). *Bottom*: cord-impressed rims, similar to Oliver phase motifs (11-10-10/A4743, Trench K, Burial 1, sand tempered, incised and punctate design; 07-6-10/78455, Trench B, general digging). Photograph by Hillel Burger. Copyright 1996 by the President and Fellows of Harvard College.

Figure 8-37d. Selected nonlocal and related sherds from Madisonville, all shell tempered. *Top*: rim sherd from fish effigy bowl (01-38-10/69721, Trenches 1-5, general digging), upsidedown. *Center*: sharply everted rim with thinly incised design (soot-covered) (08-3-10/71313, Trench D, Pit 13); sharply everted rim with vertical appliqué and nodes (84-68-10/35615, excavated 1880s). *Bottom*: sharply everted rim with massive handle, similar to Huber (08-3-10/71207, Trench D, Pit 8). Photograph by Hillel Burger (HUPM Photo No. N33988). Copyright 1996 by the President and Fellows of Harvard College.

Fig. 54c; M. Wedel 1959: Figs. 28a, 29b). Of course, the Early Fort Ancient Turpin site is known for vessels with so-called Cahokia shoulders and for one with Ramey Incised-like decoration (Griffin 1943: Pls. LXXXI.1, LXXXII.3; Cowan 1987: Fig. 8), carrying these westward ties back to much earlier times. I have not seen Oneota-like sherds from any Fort Ancient sites east of the Little Miami Valley.

As with pipes, it is impossible to pinpoint Fort Ancient vessels excavated outside of Fort Ancient territory as having come from any one particular site. Here are a few examples, to add to those already mentioned from northern Ohio.

Elongated Madisonville Plain-like vessels with four tapering strap handles have come from northern Indiana and a rockshelter in Fentress County, northern Tennessee (Griffin 1943: Pl. CL; Lewis 1947). A squat, four-handled Madisonville Plain-like jar is in the R. S. Peabody Museum collection from the Caborn-Welborn Murphy site in southwestern Indiana (Cat. No. 38/73-1552).

Vessels with appliqué lizards or lizard effigy handles are a Fort Ancient type for which there is some limited evidence of copying and perhaps transport. Madisonville, with at least nine extant examples curated at four different institutions, and Orchard, with at least four extant examples, are the only two sites from which complete vessels certainly have come, although one in the Stahl Collection probably came from Blennerhassett Island, on which the Neale's Landing site is located (Cowan 1987: Figs. 18, 19; Griffin 1943: Pls. LXIII.3, LXVI.3, LXIX.1-3; Hemmings 1977:6-24; Hooton and Willoughby 1920: Pls. 23r, 23t; Low 1880: Figs. 38, 39; Mayer-Oakes 1955: Pl. 103F; Moxley 1988a: Table 2). Where provenience is known, such vessels have accompanied burials, including some notably wealthy ones such as Burial 1 from Block 7, an adult female whose grave goods also included 88 copper/brass beads and coils.

Two forms are seen: the typical Madisonville series everted-rim jar, with two of the four handles rendered as lizard/animal effigies peering over the rim, or, in a few examples including two from Madisonville, a bowl/jar with inverted rim, cord-marked up to the lip, that ordinarily has two lizard- or salamanderlike appliqué figures on the body of the vessel between two loop handles (Figure 4-13, bottom). Although a few incurvate-rim cord-marked non-effigy bowls have been reported from Fort Ancient sites such as Buffalo and Hardin (Hanson 1966: Fig. 32, 1975: Fig. 60B), handles on them are virtually unknown. The one exception to this is an example with four parallel-sided strap handles from an important Madisonville burial (Figure 7-4), a vessel that Griffin describes as an "unusual application of handles to a Fox Farm Bowl" (Griffin 1943: Pl. LXIX.6). One of the lizard effigy vessels from Orchard has this same form, but with four appliqué lizards alternating with four handles (Figure 8-40a). The only other vessel I have seen with four appliqué lizards and four handles is one reportedly excavated from a mound near Nodena, in northeastern Arkansas, but that one had an everted rim (Figure 8-40b). Incurvate-rimmed bowls appear to be a minority form in both Tennessee (northern and eastern) and the central Mississippi Valley (e.g., Brown 1926: Fig. 332; Thruston 1897: Pl. VII; Griffin 1943: Pls. CXXVIII.2, CXXXI.4). Less globular constricted-rim, nearly shoulderless jars (slightly gourd shaped) are common at the Neale's Landing site, upstream from Orchard (Baker 1988:48, Fig. 2d).

Broken-off appliqué figures and lizardlike handles also have come from Madisonville pits and middens (nine of the former and six of the latter from Trenches 1-K, at least eleven total from other parts of the site), mostly long-tailed reptilians usually interpreted as lizards or salamanders, but a few with ears. The figures on one nearly whole jar have been interpreted as flying squirrels (Cowan 1987:15, CMNH A8104). At least six other late prehistoric-protohistoric Fort Ancient sites have produced one or two broken-off lizardlike pieces of appliqué or handles, including Gartner, Augusta, Fox Farm, Feurt (described as a "raccoon"), Hardin, and Clover (Hanson 1966:95, Fig. 41; Mills 1904:36-37, 1917:360, 365, Figs. 32, 34; Smith 1910: Pl. LIV.9; Roland E. Barnett collection from Orchard, West Virginia; Huntington Art Museum collection from Clover, West Virginia). No mention of lizard effigy vessels was made in the Buffalo site report (Hanson 1975:69). Effigy handles in the form of eared animals are known from northern Tennessee (e.g., Thruston 1897: Fig. 51), the Glass site in northwestern Mississippi (Brown 1926: Fig. 336), and a mound burial on a bluff opposite East St. Louis, St. Clair County, Illinois (HUPM 83-76-10/38879, collected in 1883 by William McAdams; the vessel contained a unio shell spoon). Of the Glass site jar, Brown quotes Clarence Moore as saying: "There were presented to us here fragments of a vessel which we were told had washed from a bank. This vessel is of very coarse shell-tempered ware, and entirely unlike that found by us in the mound. On each of two opposite sides of the vessel is modeled in relief a long-bodied quadruped somewhat similar to the lizard-like figures present on a vessel found at Madisonville, Ohio" (1926:342). Although coarse shell tempering certainly applies to Madisonville series ceramics, the straight-necked shape and incised and punctated neck decoration of this vessel do not.

Figure 8-41 shows the geographical distribution of lizard effigy jars and bowls, and related examples. The center of gravity is Madisonville, with its large number of complete vessels and effigy fragments, followed in quantity by Orchard. However, the impression is not of diffusion from a central originating Fort Ancient location, but of influences in vessel form and decoration running back and forth among regions, starting probably in the late prehistoric period when the Cumberland Valley still was occupied, but continuing into the protohistoric.

A number of researchers have drawn a parallel between Madisonville Horizon lizard effigy vessels and Iroquoian vessels with full-figure lizard, snake, and humanoid appliqués. The Iroquoian examples (e.g., Kent: Figs. 21, 24) appear much later than the Fort Ancient ones, in the mid-seventeenth century, at Susquehannock and Seneca sites (Witthoft 1952:250). Although they might have been at least partially inspired by Fort Ancient

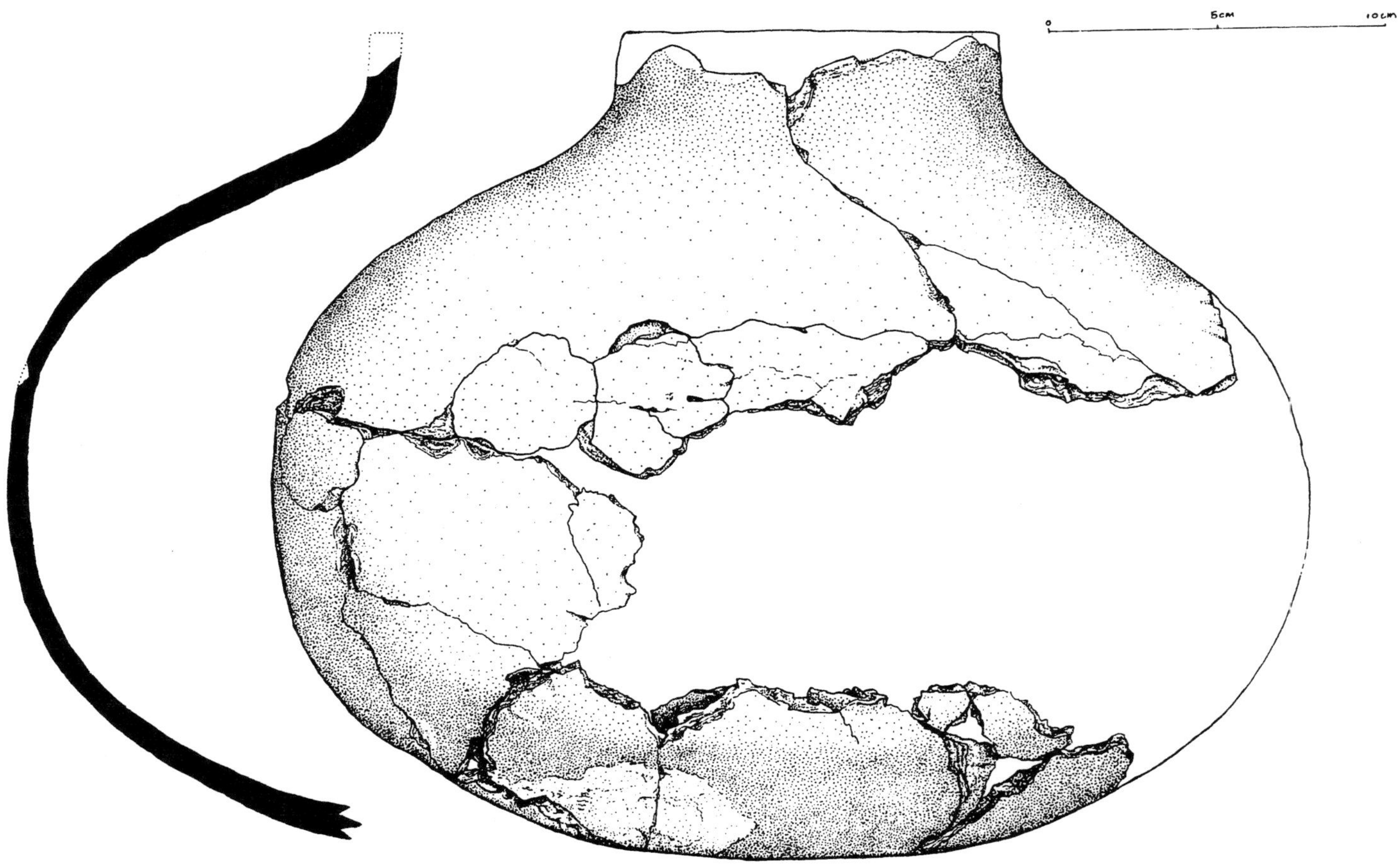

Figure 8-38. Mississippian-like vessel from stratigraphically excavated midden at Madisonville (CMNH Cat. Nos. A15797/1- A15797/32). Drawing by Barbara Alexander, courtesy of the Cincinnati Museum Center.

examples (with or without the intervention of Fort Ancient "captive potters"), their form and style are, like the Seneca maskettes, uniquely Iroquoian.

In discussing Fort Ancient lizard effigy vessels, I cannot forbear mentioning the so-called "Alligator Mound" or "Opossum Mound" near Granville (just east of Columbus), the only nonserpent Ohio effigy mound (Romain 1992:39, Figs. 1, 2; Squier and Davis 1848). Its shape is a perfect match for many of the creatures that crawled up Late Fort Ancient vessels. If it dates to Late Woodland-Early Fort Ancient times, as apparently does at least one of the several Ohio serpent mounds (Glotzhober and Lepper 1994), as well as the effigy mounds in Oneota territory (Goldstein 1995:102; Hall 1993:51, 65), this would indicate a symbolic continuity expressed in different media over time (cf. DeBoer 1991) that I believe also is reflected in the serpent mounds *vis-à-vis* the snakelike intertwining of the guilloche motifs that decorate ceramic vessels during Early-Middle Fort Ancient times and in the serpents engraved in stone (Figure 6-22a), carved in antler (Figures 6-18b, 7-32), and formed of metal (Figures 6-21f, 7-30a) during Late Fort Ancient times. In other words, I think these two liminal water-earth creatures were important symbols to both pre-Fort Ancient and Fort Ancient peoples in the central Ohio Valley. The snake, but not the lizard, salamander, or opossum, has been listed as a clan name for at least one historically documented Central Algonquian group (Table 7-4).

Intraregional and Interregional Interaction

Madisonville residents participated in many different, overlapping interaction networks. Some of these networks remained relatively constant over long periods of time, cemented by many different tokens. Others were more short term and less intensive. Some—but only some—of these spheres of interaction included other settlements that modern archaeologists call Fort Ancient. In the following sections, I trace these interactions region by region.

Unfortunately, due to various factors, including incomplete formal excavation or reporting of sites, and long-term or repeated short-term occupation of sites (sometimes unrecognized

Figure 8-39. Head pots from Madisonville and from a Missouri burial mound (HUPM Cat. Nos. 08-3-10/79660, 95-21-10/48692). Photograph by Hillel Burger (HUPM Photo No. N33843B). Copyright 1997 by the President and Fellows of Harvard College.

by excavators), it is frustratingly difficult to fine-tune chronologies so as to be able to analyze late prehistoric to protohistoric events sequentially. Particularly difficult is separating movements and interactions during the late fifteenth–early sixteenth century that probably were due at least in part to climatic change (connected with such fifteenth-century events as the movement of most Fort Ancient settlements closer to the Ohio River valley and the depopulation of central Indiana and the middle Cumberland Valley), from movements and interactions during the mid- to late sixteenth century that might have been precipitated, at least in part, by European influences of various sorts. Thus, I often have had to blend these periods in my discussion, and have found it difficult to define clearly changes "due to" the increasing presence of Europeans in North America. I hope that in future, these efforts can be refined and expanded as more data become available, and as archaeologists familiar with other regions critique my interpretations of their data.

The available data are most useful if considered by means of a range of approaches. Broad-scale regional distributions of key artifacts, quantitative comparisons of them among sites, contexts of disposition, and variations in style and material all can contribute in different ways to our view of interpersonal and intergroup interaction in and around the protohistoric central Ohio Valley.

Madisonville Interaction with Other Fort Ancient Settlements

Ceramics always have loomed very large in the definition of Fort Ancient territory. In particular, the ceramic complex of the late prehistoric-protohistoric Madisonville site and Madisonville Horizon, with its predominant and clearly recognizable plain-necked, everted-rim, two- or four-handled jar form, not only appeared internally coherent but also contrasted in form and decoration with the decorated shoulders and sharply everted rims of Oneota jars, the decorated castellations of Iroquoian jars, and the much greater variety of form and decoration in Mississippian ceramics farther south. Although attributes were not uniform west to east (and eastern Fort Ancient pottery assemblages included different types and proportions of non-Fort Ancient forms than western assemblages), Madisonville potters certainly appear to have been attuned to the same design template as their sisters farther east, probably through both intermarriage and regular visiting. This kind of frequent, familiar interaction does appear to have increased throughout the central Ohio Valley after ca. 1450 (and I think it is important to visualize it in terms of temporary and permanent movements of individuals and groups of people, rather than as vague "diffusion" of material traits).

This does not mean, however, that people in this region became homogenized after the mid-fifteenth century. Of particular note are apparent persistent differences in burial customs and personal adornment between western and eastern Fort Ancient communities, some traceable to long-term differences in customary practices and some due to differences in external contacts, including material exchange and intermarriage. At Madisonville, low percentages of flexed burials, high percentages of mortuary vessels, pipes as important male grave goods, low numbers of shell ornaments, the absence of barrel-shaped deer bone beads, and the virtual absence of ornaments made from animal teeth, animal claws, and cannel coal contrast strongly with burial customs and grave goods at most protohistoric eastern Fort Ancient sites (Tables 4-12, 4-13, Figure 8-24; for illustrations of eastern Fort Ancient grave goods, see references given in Table 4-10).

Evidence for external contacts at eastern Fort Ancient sites that differ from those apparent at Madisonville includes the following. These artifacts reflect both northerly and southerly interaction, as recognized by Graybill (1986, 1987). Significant percentages of recognizable upper Ohio Valley Wellsburg ceramics occur at sites such as Neale's Landing and Orchard, interpreted as reflecting the presence of Wellsburg people at Fort Ancient sites. Burials with large numbers of barrel-shaped deer bone beads probably attached to skirts, which have been described as an important type of protohistoric Monongahela adornment (Davis 1984), have been excavated at Orchard, Buffalo, Hardin, and Feurt (Holmes 1994:158; Moxley 1988b:5). The apparent movement of Portsmouth fireclay through the upper Ohio and into the west branch of the Susquehanna during the late sixteenth century (Figure 8-33), the early presence of brass at Hardin perhaps from a Chesapeake Bay source, and the presence of bead types at Rolf Lee that also have been found at early seventeenth century Susquehannock sites (Table 4-9) might trace a continuing relationship with peoples directly east whose shifting settlement patterns reflected a growing European presence in the Chesapeake region. Large numbers of marginella beads and other marine shell beads and ornaments accompanying eastern Fort Ancient burials (Table 4-13, Figure 8-24), particularly the Citico style rattlesnake gorgets associated in death with women and subadults of the Coosa polity (Figure 8-15) and the large mask gorgets also associated with eastern Tennessee peoples (Figure 8-16), indicate significant interaction to the south, persisting well into the seventeenth century as evidenced by distributions of brass side-view animal effigies and large brass armbands (Figures 8-12, 8-14). This is the period when eastern Tennessee populations were shifting their settlement locations southward (Smith 1987), and the increasing distance between occurrences of horizon marker artifacts in Fort Ancient and the interior Southeast (e.g., Figure 8-15 versus Figure 8-14) reflects that shift while objectifying a continuing relationship between eastern Fort Ancient and proto-Creek peoples.

At Orchard, the presence of high percentages of burials with mortuary vessels, including lizard effigy forms, and the importance of pipes, including at least two disk pipes, provide definite links to western Fort Ancient peoples, even though other traits, such as percentages of flexed burials, some types of adornment, and the total ceramic assemblage, differ. Orchard (perhaps) has produced a few mid-seventeenth-century glass beads, but appears to have have been occupied for a significant period prior to that time. The chronology of the Madisonville-Orchard relationship will be difficult to decipher without access to Orchard field notes, which are currently unavailable.

Besides certain special types of pottery such as lizard effigy jars (Figures 4-13, 8-40), two symbolically significant artifacts—engraved marine shell maskettes and barred metal pendants—have distributions that center on Fort Ancient territory.

Unfortunately, provenience is unknown or not reported for many of the Fort Ancient maskettes, which are associated with the entire geographic range of protohistoric sites, from Neale's Landing and Buffalo at the east to Madisonville at the west. At Madisonville, one (perhaps engraved) was on the shoulder of an adult male thought to be a shaman, another, engraved with forked-eye surrounds, was said to have been with an adult, and two minimally engraved examples were buried with children. At Hardin, where Hanson reported four large masks, two of them engraved with forked eyes, and "five small 'faceless' specimens," all with burials, Holmes reported only six masks (of unspecified size), including one engraved specimen with an adult male, four examples with small children, and one with a teenager (Hanson 1966:161-63; Holmes 1994:164, Table 7.7). From the field notes (on file at the University of Kentucky William S. Webb Museum of Anthropology), it can be ascertained that the teenager had the second engraved mask, and that one of the remaining large masks was with a child. It would seem, then, that at least two of the unengraved maskettes were with children, but whether any were buried with adults is unknown. The forked-eye maskette from Neale's Landing was with a child of about three years who also had a perching vulturelike effigy pipe, shell beads, and a Madisonville-style ceramic vessel (Hemmings 1977:9-9, Fig. 64). Also among the Neale's Landing burials was a mature adult male interpreted as a shaman, whose grave goods included a fisher "medicine bag" and a vasiform pipe engraved with a "+" on the bottom (Hemmings 1977:5.9–5.11, 9.7, Fig. 53b). The forked-eye maskettes outside Fort Ancient territory, at Anker and in Allamakee County, Iowa, were all with burials. At least one of the two or three engraved masks from Anker was small enough to be called a maskette, but it is not clear with which burial it was interred. Two people (at least one a probable adult) with mask gorgets (size unspecified) were among the eight at the site with "medicine bags," and a mask (size unspecified) also was reported with an infant burial (Bluhm and Liss 1961:98, 99, 131, 133, Fig.

70a). The Iowa example was with an infant (Collins 1994:251-53).

The strongest Fort Ancient association seems to be with subadults, but there are too many Fort Ancient maskettes of unknown provenience, including at least nine or ten from sites such as Orchard, Rolf Lee, and Buffalo, to make any definitive statement.

The barred copper pendants, strongly associated with adult burials, have been proposed as symbol badges marking high-status individuals engaged in external interaction, perhaps even objectifying an alliance or confederacy among the western and central Fort Ancient settlements at which they have been found (see Figures 7-31 and 8-9, and associated discussions). Since the closest probable prehistoric example came from the Nashville region, it seems possible that the first Fort Ancient manifestation of these symbol badges might have been at Fox Farm, which might well have been the prehistoric gateway through which most interaction took place with Tennessee (see Figures 8-21, 8-22, and 8-23, and associated discussion). It is notable that a number of the western Fort Ancient sites included in Figure 8-23 (Anderson, Taylor, and Fox Farm, plus Incinerator) had large proportions of stone box graves, probably signaling significant Middle Fort Ancient connections southwestward to the Cumberland Valley heartland of this burial practice, perhaps via the upper Cumberland River (Tables 4-6 and 4-12, Figure 3-1; cf. Brown 1981: Fig. 3).

From this brief discussion, it should be apparent that late prehistoric-protohistoric Fort Ancient settlements were separate polities with continuing interactions on many levels, from casual visiting to intermarriage to semiformal alliance. Individuals within different settlements appear to have had different types of emblemic ornamentation, asserting locally important identities. Settlements and subregions also differed in external interaction patterns, with long-term prehistoric relationships apparently carrying over into protohistoric times. There also were commonalities, such as Madisonville Horizon ceramics, vasiform pipes, and marine shell maskettes, that crosscut the entire region. At some times, within some subregions, there might have been formal diplomatic ties among settlements, on a peer polity basis. However, "Fort Ancient" never was a homogenous, monolithic culture area. Rather, it was more like a fluid, heterarchical, loosely related continuum.

As the westernmost protohistoric Fort Ancient settlement, what was Madisonville's place in that continuum? After summarizing its relationships with various non-Fort Ancient regions, I will return to consider further its position in protohistoric Fort Ancient interaction networks.

Western Fort Ancient Interaction with Non-Fort Ancient Peoples

Northern Ohio

Interaction with northern Ohio appears, from the two-way movement of ceramics, to have been in place before Madisonville Horizon times, and to have continued into the late prehistoric-protohistoric period. Indian Hills sherds at the Madisonville site, for instance, definitely mark interaction between Madisonville residents and people from near the southern Lake Erie shore, as do antler harpoons with attachment holes and notched turkey bone awls. Mortuary vessels at Madisonville with northern Ohio and upper Ohio Valley attributes such as notched rim strips, grooved paddling/simple stamping, and teat lugs could be due to direct interaction northward and northeastward, or (in the case of upper Ohio Valley traits) to indirect interaction through eastern Fort Ancient settlements. Direct interaction with northeastern Ohio seems to be indicated by crystalline anorthosite pipes and pipe blanks with strong associations to the Reeve Village site (see Figure 8-31 and associated discussion). The large, "killed" anorthosite claw effigy pipe with Burial I-19 apparently was considered a powerful and important object, so interaction in this direction might well have had significant social meaning. The imposing perching owl pipe with Burial I-9 also implies interaction in this general direction (Figure 8-30 and associated discussion).

During the protohistoric period, northwestern Ohio settlements (but apparently not northeastern Ohio settlements) had access to European goods. Might some of the metal and glass items at Madisonville have reached there through those settlements? The northwestern Ohio European assemblages do have some similarities to Madisonville items, but are not completely congruent in time frame, types of items, or disposition of items. As of 1994, 109 European-derived items (6 glass, 11 iron, 14 definitely brass, and the remainder of copper or brass) had been excavated from seven Indian Hills phase and one Sandusky River Period 1 sites: Indian Hills (69), Farnsworth Park (1), LaSalle Ossuary (19), Petersen (12), Edwards (1), Muddy Creek (2), Bear Fort (2), and Sandusky Avenue (3) (Stothers, in press; Stothers and Abel 1991; Bowen 1994).

The glass beads all are dissimilar to those from Madisonville. The four from the Indian Hills site include one GBP1 striped gooseberry type and three GBP2 beads (two polychrome flush eyes and one white ovoid), all from within or close to a single pit feature. The two glass beads from an extended adult male burial at Petersen (which also included a small piece of sheet iron and seven shell beads) are called "early blue," but their color, given as Kidd type II55a, makes them darker than the Madisonville examples, they are not described as fragmentary or friable, and their appearance in a slide is not the same as those from Madisonville.

Some of the metal from these sites is similar to that at Madisonville, some different. The Indian Hills assemblage included seven copper and one brass "wire" item, including five coils and two rings, some of which might conceivably have been fashioned of thin metal tubes. Thirty-three percent of the copper/brass at the eight sites consisted of scrap or unidentifiable fragments, compared with 18% in Madisonville Trenches 1-K (16% overall). At most of the sites, metal appears to have been more valued than at Madisonville, since it was much more likely

Figure 8-40. Lizard effigy vessels with four appliqué animals and four handles. *Above:* cord-marked, with two lizard effigy handles and two non-effigy handles, from a burial at Orchard, West Virginia (collection of Roland E. Barnett; used with permission). *Left:* from a mound near Nodena, Arkansas (Thruston 1890:146, Fig. 53).

to have been disposed of as grave goods. The proportion of copper/brass with burials at the seven sites with the smallest numbers of items was 64%, compared with 34% in Trenches 1-K at Madisonville (Tables 6-6 and 8-2). I do not know the proportion for the Indian Hills site (Stothers 1981, in press; Stothers and Abel 1994); the fact that none of the glass beads were in burials implies that copper and brass might have been treated similarly, but the description of five items as "ear" or "nose" rings implies that they were found with human remains.

All in all, it seems possible that some European metal might have traveled to Madisonville via northwestern Ohio, but the differences in bead assemblages indicate that the two regions were not acting in lock step. In particular, the Indian Hills site artifact assemblage, which includes a brass kettle lug and iron knife blade segments in addition to GBP2 beads, appears later in time than that at Madisonville.

Oneota

Interaction between Madisonville/western Fort Ancient and Oneota peoples appears to have had significant time depth and to have had many-faceted connections. Late prehistoric-protohistoric artifacts whose geographic distributions mark these relationships include marine shell maskettes (Figure 8-17), disk pipes (Figures 8-28 and 8-29), rasps (Figure 8-34), grooved clubs/mauls (Figure 8-35), bison bone, tubular metal coils and serpents (Figures 8-6, 8-7, 8-8), and barred copper symbol badges (Figure 8-9). Although minor amounts of Oneota pottery were present at Madisonville, this medium (with its putative female associations) does not appear to be a strong marker of interaction. The strongest markers relate to probably male-dominated activities, including diplomacy, shamanism, and hunting.

Just as the strongest (female-related) nonlocal ceramic ties at Madisonville are to eastern Fort Ancient and northern Ohio types, the strongest (male-related) smoking pipe ties, aside from those to eastern Fort Ancient settlements, are to Oneota territory, particularly to people of far-distant northeastern Iowa. Small-disk pipes are the single largest category of foreign-related pipe styles to be found in mortuary contexts at Madisonville, objectifying significant, high-level diplomatic ties between the two territories. Madisonville produced far greater numbers of disk pipes than have been documented from any other Fort Ancient settlement, from both mortuary and nonmortuary contexts. In addition, several pipes of non-disk form were engraved with forked eyes, featherlike designs, thunderbirds, or thunderers, beings with strong Oneota connections (e.g., Figures 7-5d, bottom right, 7-6b, 8-25, 8-26; see also Hooton and Willoughby 1920: Pl. 20e; additional examples with engraved thunderbirds include one made of local Waverly sandstone from the Ohio Historical Society (806/15-2) and two curated at the AMNH (Cat. Nos. 20/1417, 20/1420)). Another high-status artifact that might reflect the same ties is the barred copper pendant, concentrated in Fort Ancient territory but known from at least two protohistoric Iowa sites (Figures 7-31, 8-9).

Considering all the evidence, I believe that the interaction signaled by disk pipes was connected with late prehistoric-protohistoric bison hunting, evidenced by significant numbers of selected bison bones and bison bone tools at Madisonville (Figure 6-54), by the presence of western-type grooved clubs (Figure 8-35), including one with an engraved thunderbird (Figure 6-17b), and by the relatively large numbers of rasps, also more common farther west (Figure 8-34). Either or both of two scenarios are possible. Groups of Madisonville people might have traveled west periodically or on a regular seasonal basis to hunt bison. As discussed in Chapter 6, the presence at Madisonville of large storage pits to conceal stored food and other prized items might be evidence in favor of this scenario. Alternatively, Oneota groups might have carried bison products to Madisonville for exchange. I will consider this question further in the last section of this chapter.

A closer source of bison products, the saline hunting area at Big Bone Lick, has been discussed. One argument in favor of that, more local, source, is the prediliction of Madisonville folk for beamers (hide scrapers) made from bison thoracic vertebrae. I have not seen this from any other site or region—leg bone beamers are most often employed—and it seems like the sort of usage that might have developed in isolation from other bison-hunting groups. Of course, both local and distant bison ranges might have been exploited at different times, as Kenneth Tankersley has pointed out (1992). I endorse many of the general concepts in his analysis, but not all of the details. For example, it does not seem necessary to postulate an all-or-nothing removal of the entire Madisonville population to Illinois to hunt bison there—back-and-forth movement of smaller groups is a reasonable alternative, at least initially. Such movements might, of course, have been a prelude to larger scale migration (cf. Sutton 1995). The travel distances that I am proposing might seem long, but they are no farther than recorded historically for numerous war, hunting, and trading parties traveling by foot and canoe (Little 1987; Ray 1974; Rountree 1993b). For example, in 1673-74 Gabriel Arthur traveled for five months with a group of Tomahittan Indians from a starting point probably in the lower Kanawha Valley, and covered over 2000 miles (Rountree 1993b:25), and middleman groups in the seventeenth-eighteenth century fur trade made annual canoe trips to Hudson's Bay trading posts of 800 or more miles one way (Ray 1978:28-29).

Other artifacts at Madisonville of nonlocal materials—marine shell maskettes and tubular serpent pendants (Figures 8-17 and 8-7)—show connections to people identified with shamanism at Oneota sites such as Anker, where one individual with a "medicine bag" was adorned with a copper serpent and a metal coil, and two with "medicine bag" assemblages each had an engraved mask or maskette (Bluhm and Liss 1961:96-99), analogous to Burial 1-61 at Madisonville, who had a maskette and two "medicine bags." The highly endowed Burial 45 from the 1895 excavations at Madisonville, with large bird/owl-disk pipe, three copper serpents (more than any known individual from any site), ceramic vessel, and fourteen or more stone implements (Figure 7-30), was much closer in "his" lavish grave good assemblage to the Anker high-status burials than to any other individual at Madisonville. "He" might well have been someone with strong ties to powerful shamans in Oneota territory, although the material and form of the pipe bespeak a complex identity. The ostentatious display of copper and extraordinarily large, finely wrought disk pipe also bring to mind the adult male at Seven Mile Island, Alabama (Figure 8-6), who was buried with six tubular copper coils in each ear and a large redstone war bundle–type disk pipe, said to be identical to an example from the Utz site in Missouri (Jolly 1969).

Single burials at Neale's Landing, Buffalo, and Hardin have been noted as accompanied by small-animal skulls that probably were associated with medicine bags (e.g., Hemmings 1977:5-11) or by grouped objects including charms (e.g., Broyles 1970; Hemmings 1977:5.9–5.11; Holmes 1994:164-65). Madisonville is the only Fort Ancient site from which a significant number of "medicine bags" has been recognized, artifacts that appear completely congruent with examples from Oneota sites such as Anker, Illinois, and Flynn, Iowa, and from Arikara and other Plains Indian sites yet farther west (Bray 1961a; Ubelaker and Wedel 1975). The shamanistic interaction network in which Madisonville people participated might have had tendrils extending to eastern Fort Ancient sites such as Neale's Landing, but it appears to have been weighted most heavily northwestward, far beyond Fort Ancient territory.

Although the buffer zone between Madisonville Horizon western Fort Ancient and contemporaneous Caborn-Welborn sites was significantly greater than existed in Early-Middle Fort Ancient times (cf. Anderson 1991: Figs 3, 4, 5), this might be related primarily to subsistence change due to climatic variation, and would not necessarily have precluded interaction. Tubular metal coils, large-disk pipe styles including at least one bird/owl-disk specimen from Slack Farm and a limestone example from Murphy identical to one from Campbell Island, plus the presence of a vasiform pipe with a burial at the Murphy site (Mills 1926: Fig. 27; Moorehead 1906: Fig. 23; Pollack et al. 1996:21; Robert S. Peabody Museum Cat. Nos. 38/171 5211, 38/143 15019) imply at least minimal relationships between the regions. There might be ceramic ties as well. At least, the two squat, plain-surfaced, handled, coarsely shell-tempered jars that I have examined from Murphy could have passed without notice as local if excavated at Madisonville (Robert S. Peabody Museum Cat. Nos. 38/30 15071, 38/73 15502).

Archaeologists currently working in Caborn-Welborn territory are skeptical about sustained interaction between this region and Fort Ancient territory upriver, due, for instance, to a lack of Fort Ancient ceramics at recently excavated Caborn-Welborn sites (Pollack and Munson 1995; Pollack et al. 1996:25; David Pollack, pers. comm.). I prefer to not to shut this door quite yet, pending additional data such as from current excavations at the Murphy site by Cheryl Munson.

Central Mississippi Valley

Interaction with central Mississippi Valley peoples involved some significant artifacts, including the Madisonville head pot (Figure 8-39), probably made locally by an artisan with previous experience elsewhere, other pottery such as fish effigy bowls (Figure 8-37d, top) and lizard effigy vessels (Figures 4-13, 8-40, 8-41), the shell "button" and earplugs (Figures 6-19b, 6-19c, 8-18, and 8-19), and probably the Clarksdale bell (Figures 6-21c, 6-21g, 8-1). Rather than being imports, the fish and turtle effigy pipes (Figures 8-25, 8-26) appear to have been inspired by central Mississippi Valley ceramic forms. Barred copper pendants (Figures 7-31, 8-9) also might be indicative of interaction. These varied artifacts might represent a continuation of earlier western Fort Ancient interaction with Mississippi Valley peoples (cf. Figures 8-20, 8-21) or with middle Cumberland Valley peoples, some of whom (judging from similarities in pottery and other indicators) probably moved westward during very late prehistoric times. Considering the variety, types, and disposition of these artifacts, contacts between the central Ohio Valley and the central Mississippi Valley seem to have been at more than a casual level, but the strength and constancy of interregional ties is difficult to judge. The artifacts at Madisonville from this region are redundant, but not numerous. They might represent repeated interaction by many individuals—for instance, they are widely scattered around the Madisonville site, from Block 1 to Trenches 1 and D—or a single trip, since their time frame is fairly tight.

South and Southeast

As discussed above, late prehistoric and protohistoric eastern Fort Ancient people probably interacted to a significant degree with the people of eastern Tennessee. Marine shell ornaments provide particularly good evidence for this relationship (e.g., Figures 8-15, 8-16, 8-24), which probably was ongoing from earlier times (cf. Figure 8-21). It is very unlikely that Madisonville people carried on direct interaction in that direction. What shell reached them from the southeast (e.g., the single reworked Citico gorget, the minuscule number of marginella shell beads) probably passed through the hands of Fort Ancient people farther east. In spite of relatively high numbers of large engraved mask gorgets at eastern Fort Ancient sites like Rolf Lee and Marmet, apparently not a single one reached (or at least remained at) Madisonville.

Monongahela and Susquehannock

Most interaction between Madisonville residents and Monongahela and Susquehannock peoples also probably would have been indirect, via eastern Fort Ancient settlements in more frequent contact with groups farther east. However, there are a few indicators suggesting that a small number of people from Madisonville might have traveled eastward through and beyond Fort Ancient territory, and/or that the settlement might have received some visitors from the Allegheny, Potomac, or Susquehanna River drainages. One such indicator is the fragment of a ceramic "owl" effigy pipe bowl similar to one illustrated from a late sixteenth century Susquehannock site on the lower Susquehanna River (Figure 8-27), which most likely betokens a nonlocal visitor to Madisonville. Another indicator would be the two water bird pipes, which might have connections to mid-sixteenth century Susquehannocks on the upper Susquehanna and upper Potomac rivers. At least one of them, the two-headed swanlike bird (Figure 7-5a), seems very likely to be a local interpretation of an artifact seen elsewhere.

Also perhaps fitting into that category is the Madisonville brass spiral (Figure 6.17), a form and material strongly—but by no means exclusively—associated with Susquehannock groups during the late sixteenth century (Bradley and Childs 1991a, 1991b). Since no examples of spirals have been found at any contemporaneous Fort Ancient sites farther east (the Beale Mound example being later), down-the-line exchange is unlikely. Either direct long-distance transport or manufacture at Madisonville based on an example seen elsewhere seem more probable. The form of the ornament, with tapering "tail" to the outside rather than the inside of the spiral (a "serpent" rather than "panther" model), might best support the latter scenario. Of course, such artifacts also could have been seen at southwestern Pennsylvania Monongahela, western New York Iroquois, or Ontario Iroquoian settlements (Figure 8-5).

No great variety of glass beads, such as probably was available to Rolf Lee people through Susquehannock connections during the second quarter of the seventeenth century (Graybill 1981:126-27), reached Madisonville even through down-the-line exchange. Any direct contact between western Fort Ancient and Susquehannock people, if it did take place, undoubtedly occurred well before that time, and seems to have been of short duration.

Iroquois

Direct contact with Iroquoian sources, including Neutral and perhaps Erie, Seneca, and/or Saint Lawrence Iroquois, does seem likely. There are at least two "smoking guns." One is the parts from Basque iron-fitted copper kettles. The large assemblage, apparently unique in Fort Ancient territory, undoubtedly traveled to Madisonville from the Saint Lawrence Valley (Figure 8-2). The dagger guard and friable blue glass beads also might have come from that direction (Figures 8-3, 8-4). From the bulbous ceramic pipe stems and punctate-rim ceramic trumpet fragments excavated at Madisonville (Figure 8-27), it is extremely probable that Ontario and perhaps New York Iroquoians themselves visited the site—a second "smoking gun" for direct contact rather than down-the-line exchange via intervening groups. The disposition of many comparatively large pieces of kettle copper and perhaps shell beads obtained via northern sources with a single young adult burial (1-60) raises the possiblity that this individual was involved in bringing these items to the site. Other items with northeasterly connections, including blue glass beads and iron kettle fittings, were excavated from a variety of locations around the site, from the extreme southwest (kettle lug) to the extreme northeast (beads), as were the more-common copper artifacts and scrap (Figures 6-40, 6-41, 6-42) that might well have reached Madisonville from the same direction. Although some copper did reach the Lower Great Lakes via the Saint Lawrence as early as the 1530s, its availability became widespread only after about 1580, when Basque kettles also appear to have been most available (Fitzgerald 1990:542-63; Fitzgerald et al. 1993). Kettles and other metal artifacts probably were cut into pieces by Saint Lawrence and Ontario Iroquoians, and/or Northern Algonquians also involved in the Saint Lawrence trade axis, for gift-giving or exchange with peoples farther inland. For example, a "gift pack" of four large pieces of metal tied with a cord was excavated at the GBP3 Neutral Hood site, a practice that Fitzgerald suggests was common during the previous century (1990:546). Differences in total quantity, metal composition, and disposition of copper and brass at Madisonville versus the roughly contemporaneous Hardin site (Table 8-2) suggest the possibility of a different and separate source of supply rather than only a down-the-line feeder from eastern to western Fort Ancient sites. By what route(s) might this material have reached Madisonville?

Looking at the artifact distribution maps and at the physiographic map (Figure 3-1), several possibilities are apparent. One is westward through extreme southwestern Ontario (a largely abandoned buffer zone during the early historic period; Murphy and Ferris 1990), around the western end of Lake Erie, and south via the Maumee, Great Miami, and Little Miami drainages. However, archaeologists working in northwestern Ohio are adamant that the historically observed hostilities between Neutrals and local Central Algonquian (Assistaeronon or Fire Nation) populations during the 1630s and 1640s were of long-standing duration (e.g., Stothers 1991, in press; Stothers et al. 1994; but see Murphy and Ferris 1990:271-77 for an alternative view), precluding the use of such a route. Stothers has proposed a waterborne exchange route, via Lakes Erie and Ontario, between the southwestern Lake Erie basin sites and Northern Algonquian "kinsmen" northeast of Iroquoian territory (Stothers and Abel 1991: Fig. 1). It is quite possible that some metal ultimately

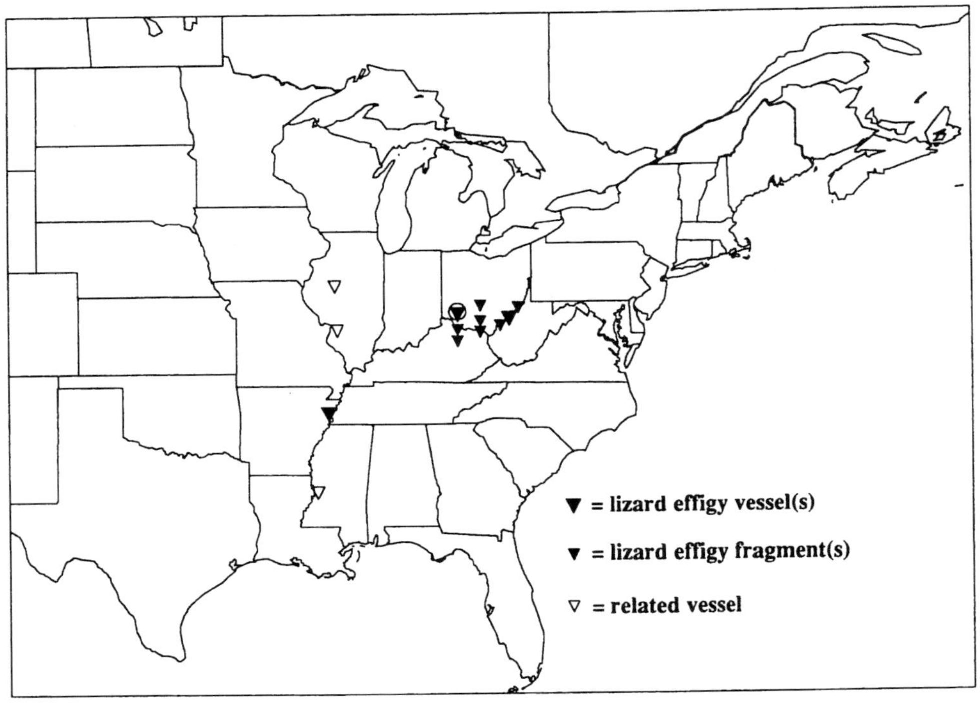

Figure 8-41. Geographical distribution of Fort Ancient lizard effigy vessels, and related forms (see text for discussion).

from the Saint Lawrence region reached Madisonville via these northwestern Ohio settlements, but the horizon markers at Indian Hills, the only site with large numbers of European-derived artifacts, appear to postdate those at Madisonville (see above).

I would propose, as another possibility, a cross-country route along the divide between the Ohio and Great Lakes drainages, to the upper reaches of the Miamis (Figure 3-1). Where would its northern terminus have been? One possibility is the Reeve site in northeastern Ohio, marked by its extremely large pipe assemblage (which included ceramic elbow pipes in trumpet, barrel, bulbous, conical and collared ring forms, and stone ovoids, vasiforms, perching bird effigies, keel shapes, and even two small-disk pipes; Ahlstrom 1979) as a possible multi-ethnic meeting site. However, the absence or near absence of European goods (cf. Greenman 1935:93) and of sixteenth-seventeenth century radiocarbon dates (Brose 1994:168), suggests this settlement was not a protohistoric center of exchange. The multicomponent Ripley ceremonial site in southwestern New York is a better possibility for the late sixteenth century. It has produced iron, copper, and brass objects including, among other things, a metal spiral and seven to eleven rolled sheet metal rings, identical to those adorning four fingers of an adult buried at Madisonville (Figure 6-21b), and probably to one worn by an individual buried at the Petersen site (Stothers 1994:9), as well as examples from nine GBP 1-3 Neutral and Huron-Petun sites (Fitzgerald 1990:Table 33), but not reported from any other Fort Ancient sites. Also found were friable blue glass beads, shell-tempered pottery in non-Iroquoian styles, and at least one disk pipe, engraved with a pantherlike creature, similar to an engraved example illustrated from "Flamboro township, about two miles southwest of the famous Neutral stronghold at Lake Medad" (Fitzgerald 1991; Skinner 1926; Sullivan et al. 1995:122-23; beads and pipe are HUPM Cat. Nos. 04-3-10/65188 and 65225). One or more of the Neutral settlements west of Niagara Falls, where so many Basque kettles and kettle fragments have been excavated (Figure 8-2) is perhaps a stronger possibility. Direct travel all the way between Basque traders in the lower Saint Lawrence and Madisonville in southwestern Ohio seems extremely unlikely, not only because of the distances involved but also because of the efforts of intervening Iroquoian and Algonquian groups to monopolize trade routes, with fierce warfare and raiding along the Saint Lawrence Valley until the early 1600s (Trigger 1978a:344-47, 1986:141-63).

The apparently peaceful contact between Madisonville residents and Ontario/New York Iroquoians appears to have been a short-lived phenomenon, perhaps initiated during the last quarter of the sixteenth century and lasting no more than a decade into the seventeenth. I have found no material evidence at Madisonville or elsewhere in the central Ohio Valley of prehistoric interaction with Iroquoians. One indirect indicator, the presence of a ceremonially "killed" large-disk redstone pipe in a burial at the mid-sixteenth century Seneca/Cayuga Richmond Mills (Reed Fort) site (Hamilton 1967:24; Parker 1918; Witthoft et al. 1953:92, 101) might correlate with the few unprovenienced large-disk pipes reported from central Ohio (see above) and signal the start of an attempt at long-distance diplomatic bridge-building through Fort Ancient territory. Richmond Mills was

Figure 8-42. Pipes of mottled gray stone. *Top left*: animal effigy pipe, from kitchen midden excavated in 1897 (HUPM Cat. No. 97-38-10/62933). *Bottom left*: modified disk pipe, from general digging, Trenches 1-5 (97-38-10/62954). *Right*: keel pipe with engraved forked eyes on both sides, from Pit D-93 (08-3-10/71957). Photograph by Hillel Burger (HUPM Photo No. N33851). Copyright 1997 by the President and Fellows of Harvard College. For additional examples, see Figures 7-5d (top right), 8-25 (bottom right) and 8-27a (bottom left).

the earliest Seneca site to produce stone ovoid pipes (Martha Sempowski, pers. comm.), similar to Fort Ancient forms.

Madisonville as a Protohistoric Exchange Center

What was Madisonville's place in the post-1492 world of eastern North America? It seems very likely that the residents of this strategically positioned settlement, located at the western edge of the densely populated central and upper Ohio River valley with access, through established diplomatic contacts with Oneota peoples, to the broad hunting grounds of the Prairie Peninsula and points west, expanded their activities into yet wider interaction spheres for a period of a few decades during the late sixteenth and early seventeenth centuries. The key to this expansion may well have been European metal. The key to my interpretation of it is Native American pipes.

It is well known that in protohistoric western North America there was a network of semipermanent villages and established rendezvous locations that together made up an interaction sphere reaching from the Pacific to the Mississippi, facilitating the transport of Northwest Coast dentalia shells to the Dakotas, southwestern turquoise to Missouri, and bison products to sedentary horticultural groups (e.g., Spielmann 1991; Swagerty 1988, 1991). Trading centers often were located at the edges of environmental zones along natural corridors of communication, forming interfaces, or gateway cities, between regions of differing products and needs (Hirth 1978; Swagerty 1991:478-84). One of the easternmost centers noted by trans-Mississippi researchers was the Grand Village of the Missouri, located until the early eighteenth century at the Utz site (Bray 1961b, 1963, 1978, 1991; Hamilton 1967). Another was the Dakota Rendezvous, located just west of the extensive Blood Run site (Harvey 1979:135-233) in northwestern Iowa and the catlinite quarries of southwestern Missouri (Swagerty 1988: Fig. 1, 1991: Fig. 24.2). Utz and Blood Run are characterized by early European trade goods including tubular copper artifacts and blue glass beads, unworked catlinite, and many pipes. They are among the westernmost sites included within the range of my distribution maps (e.g., Figures 8-6, 8-7, 8-16, 8-29).

Madisonville exhibits a number of these characteristics, including a large number of pipes indicative of interregional interaction. It might well have served as a gateway community between Fort Ancient territory and points west. How might this have worked during the short protohistoric period when interaction seems to have been at its height?

As discussed above, Madisonville residents seem to have acquired at least one good source of metal during the late sixteenth century, perhaps more. Unlike the residents of the roughly contemporaneous Hardin site, they did not utilize most of their copper and brass as ornaments and dispose of it primarily as grave goods (Tables 6-6, 8-3). Rather, as evidenced by their casual discard of scrap and fragmentary thin tubes and by the presence of prepared blanks (Figure 6-21d, 6-21e), they seem to have been making metal ornaments, probably including tubular coils and serpents and flat metal pendants, as well as more mundane beads and tinklers. These products undoubtedly were displayed by important Madisonville leaders and given to their children, but they might also have been useful ceremonial presentations to visiting dignitaries, dignitaries who might bring with them desirable products from their own regions, or desirable alliances for future benefit. These are the kinds of people whose remains have been found west and south of Madisonville at sites like Murphy, Indiana, Anker, Illinois, and Seven Mile Island, Alabama, adorned with many tubular ear coils and/or with prominently displayed copper serpents (Figures 8-6, 8-7).

Madisonville people also apparently were making pipes for exchange with known interaction partners of differing tastes. This is the most parsimonious explanation for the broad variety of pipe forms found at the site that were made from a single, distinctive type of stone, a gray limestone with white inclusions (probably small fossils) that could be buffed to a high polish. Only one of these pipes, a stylized claw effigy (Figure 7-5d, top right) was found with a Madisonville burial (actually, its position was described in Putnam's field notes as "near the skeleton," so its inclusion as a grave good was an arbitrary decision on my part). Other forms included two modified disk pipes, one of them an animal effigy (Figure 8-42, left), the finely finished fish effigy perhaps inspired by a central Mississippi Valley effigy vessel (Figure 8-25, bottom right), and two long "Iroquoian" elbow pipe stems with clinging lizardlike effigies (Figure 8-27a, bottom left, and AMNH Cat. No. 20/1456, excavated in 1895). A keel pipe with forked-eye motifs engraved on both sides (Figures 8-25, third row, right, and 8-42, right) was of similar but darker stone with more diffuse inclusions.

Fairly large amounts of bison products seem to have been making their way to Madisonville. It may well be that some of them were obtained from farther west in exchange for (or in exchanges involving the presentation of) pipes and metal ornaments. Judging from the numbers of bone beamers and flint endscrapers at the site, Madisonville women were processing significant quantities of hides, undoubtedly including bison. Were they all for the use of local family members and friends? A few clues suggest that they might have been exchanged farther afield. No bison bone has been reported from any Fort Ancient site east of Madisonville, but two pipes from West Virginia sites provide visual representations of bison: a massive, polished gray and red pipestone effigy (visually similar to the red variety of Feurt Hill pipestone), emphasizing horns and cloven hooves, that was found in the hand of an adult male burial at a lower Kanawha Valley site not far downstream from Buffalo, and a broken full-figure bison effigy of golden "calcite" from Rolf Lee (Baker 1994), a material that sounds very much like that of the Madisonville bird/owl-disk pipe. The presence of such representations in far eastern Fort Ancient territory hints that bison products, too, probably reached the area. It is possible that they traveled even farther. According to Rountree, "buffalo hides were reported in the possession of the people of Roanoke Island in the 1580s," although the animals themselves were unknown from anywhere in the Virginia–North Carolina region (Rountree 1993b:45). It is not inconceivable (though admittedly unlikely) that the route by which they reached Abemarle Sound went through the central Ohio Valley (cf. Figures 3-1 and 3-4).

Located in the same county as the two sites with bison effigy pipes, the Orchard site is known for its large assemblage of pipes, most of them (unlike Madisonville's) interred with burials. I can speculate that Orchard and Madisonville peoples—who shared the custom of placing mortuary vessels with their dead—might have been closely related in this internal and external Fort Ancient exchange activity. Unfortunately, however, available documentation from the West Virginia site is not detailed enough to pursue this possibility.

Except for an apparently new direction of interaction to the Northeast, or at least an extension beyond the people in northern Ohio with whom they already were in contact, Madisonville entrepreneurs at the turn of the seventeenth century seem to have been making use of well-established relationships and exchange partners. The vigor, magnitude, and ultimate extent of these in-place interaction networks appear to have blossomed with the advent of a new source of desirable metals, but that particular flower was short-lived. From the lack at Madisonville of distinctive European goods postdating the early seventeenth century, exchange contacts toward the northeast might have been cut off during the turmoil surrounding the establishment of Dutch Hudson Valley trading centers and the initiation of Seneca-Susquehannock hostilities during the 1610s, well before the legendary all-out external warfare conducted by the Iroquois League from the 1640s onward.

Beginning in the first quarter of the seventeenth century, groups of Madisonville people might gradually have established their primary residences elsewhere, either at eastern Fort Ancient settlements such as Orchard that were closer to intermediary groups (Susquehannock, proto-Creek) who were trading with Chesapeake Bay and La Florida settlements (Figure 3-5), or toward the western prairies near Oneota allies, who were closer to rich sources of bison hunting. Ultimately, there would be both the push of ever-widening Iroquois League hostilities and the pull of new European settlements with no established middlemen groups surrounding them, such as Green Bay, Fort St. Louis, and Charles Towne (Figure 3-6), to induce Fort Ancient people to travel even farther from their central Ohio Valley homeland.

References Cited

Adair, James
1930[1775] *History of the American Indians.* Watauga Press, Johnson City, Tennessee.

Adams, Robert, McC.
1974 Anthropological Perspectives on Ancient Trade. *Current Anthropology* 15:239-58.

Ahlstrom, Richard M.
1979 *Prehistoric Pipes: A Study of the Reeve Village Site, Lake County, Ohio.* Lake County County Chapter, Archaeological Society of Ohio,

Albers, Patricia C.
1993 Symbiosis, Merger, and War: Contrasting Forms of Intertribal Relationship among Historic Plains Indians. In *The Political Economy of North American Indians,* edited by John H. Moore, pp. 94-132. University of Oklahoma Press, Norman.

Allen, Kathleen M. S., Stanton W. Green, and Ezra B. W. Zubrow (editors)
1990 *Interpreting Space: GIS and Archaeology.* Taylor and Francis, London.

Alvord, Clarence W., and Lee Bidgood (editors)
1912 *The First Explorations of the Trans-Allegheny Region by the Virginians, 1650-1674.* Arthur H. Clark, Cleveland.

Anderson, David G.
1990 Stability and Change in Chiefdom-Level Societies: An Examination of Mississippian Political Evolution on the South Atlantic Slope. In *Lamar Archaeology: Mississippian Chiefdoms in the Deep South,* edited by Mark Williams and Gary Shapiro, pp. 187-213. The University of Alabama Press, Tuscaloosa.
1991 Examining Prehistoric Settlement Distribution in Eastern North America. *Archaeology of Eastern North America* 19:1-22.
1994 *The Savannah River Chiefdoms: Political Change in the Late Prehistoric Southeast.* University of Alabama Press, Tuscaloosa.

Anonymous
1968 Fort Ancient Artifacts in the James Miller Collection. *Ohio Archaeologist* 18:60-61.

Anonymous
1982 *West Virginia Archaeologist* 34:cover.

Anonymous
1994 Monongahela Village Site Donated. *The Archaeological Conservancy Newsletter* Spring 1994:1, 4.

Anthony, David W.
1990 Migration in Archeology: The Baby and the Bathwater. *American Anthropologist* 92(4):895-914.

Ashmore, Wendy
1981 Some Issues of Method and Theory in Lowland Maya Settlement Archaeology. In *Lowland Maya Settlement Patterns,* edited by Wendy Ashmore, pp. 37-69. University of New Mexico Press, Albuquerque.

Atwater, Caleb
1820 Description of the Antiquities Discovered in the State of Ohio and Other Western States. *Archoelogia Americana* 1:105-267.

Baart, Jan
1988 Glass Bead Sites in Amsterdam. *Historical Archaeology* 22:65-75.
1973 A Multivariate Analysis of European Death Ritual. *Ethnologia Europea* 7:111-28.
1982 A Historical Review of Ethnological and Archaeological Analysis of Mortuary Practice. *Journal of Anthropological Archaeology* 1:32-58.

Baden, William W.
1995 The Impact of Fluctuating Agricultural Potential on Coosa's Sociopolitial and Settlement Systems. Paper presented at the Southeastern Archaeological Conference, Knoxville, Tennessee.

Bailey, Amy
1993 An Analysis of Triangular Projectile Points from the Clampitt Site. In *Current Research in Indiana Archaeology and Pre-*

history: 1991-1992. Abstracts of Papers Presented at the Annual Meeting of the Indiana Historical Society, 1991 and 1992, edited by Brian G. Redmond, pp. 4-7. Research Reports No. 14. Indiana University, Glenn A. Black Laboratory of Archeology, Bloomington.

Baker, Brenda J., and Lisa Kealhofer (editors)
1996 *Bioarchaeology of Native American Adaptation in the Spanish Borderlands.* University Press of Florida, Gainesville.

Baker, Stanley W.
1984a Blennerhassett Island: People Participating in Archaeology. *Ohio Archaeologist* 34(2):18-21.
1984b An Iron Trade Axe from the Neale's Landing Site, 46WD39, on Blennerhassett Island. *West Virginia Archaeologist* 36-(2):50-53.
1986 Early Seventeenth Century Trade Beads from the Upper Ohio Valley. *Ohio Archaeologist* 36(4):21-24.
1988 Neale's Landing Site Ceramics: A Perspective on the Protohistoric Period from Blennerhasset Island. *West Virginia Archaeologist* 40(2):40-53.
1994 Upper Ohio Valley Bison Art and Bison Archaeology. *Ohio Archaeologist* 44(2):5-11.

Bamann, Susan, Robert Kuhn, James Molnar, and Dean Snow
1992 Iroquoian Archaeology. *Annual Review of Anthropology* 21:-435-60.

Barnett, Roland E., and C. L. Paxton
1955 Notes on Glass and Shell Beads from 46-KA-9 (Marmet). *West Virginia Archaeologist* 7:31-33.

Bartel, Brad
1989 Acculturation and Ethnicity in Roman Moesia Superior. In *Centre and Periphery,* edited by Timothy C. Champion, pp. 173-85. Unwin Hyman, London.

Barth, Fredrik
1969 Introduction. In *Ethnic Groups and Boundaries: The Social Organization of Culture Difference,* edited by Fredrik Barth, pp. 9-38. Little, Brown, and Company, Boston.

Bauxar, J. Joseph
1978 History of the Illinois Area. In *Handbook of North American Indians: Northeast,* edited by Bruce G. Trigger, pp. 594-601. Smithsonian Institution, Washington, D.C.

Beck, Lane A.
1990 *Redefining Copena: A Regional Analysis of Mortuary Patterns in "Southern Hopewell."* Ph.D. dissertation, Northwestern University. UMI, Ann Arbor, Michigan.
1995 Regional Cults and Ethnic Boundaries in "Southern Hopewell." In *Regional Approaches to Mortuary Analysis,* edited by Lane A. Beck, pp. 167-87. Plenum, New York.

Bell, Robert E.
1947 Trade Materials at Spiro Mound as Indicated by Artifacts. *American Antiquity* 12(2):181-84.

Benn, David W.
1989 Hawks, Serpents, and Bird-Men: Emergence of the Oneota Mode of Production. *Plains Anthropologist* 34(125):233-60.

Berres, Thomas, Kenneth Farnsworth, and Randall Hughes
1993 Northern Illinois Pipestone and Hopewellian Exchange Systems. Poster presented at the Society for American Archaeology Annual Meeting, St. Louis, Missouri.

Bettarel, Robert L., and Hale G. Smith
1973 *The Moccasin Bluff Site and the Woodland Cultures of Southwestern Michigan.* Anthropological Papers No. 49. University of Michigan Museum of Anthropology, Ann Arbor.

Binford, Lewis R.
1962 Archaeology as Anthropology. *American Antiquity* 28:217-25.
1971 Mortuary Practices: Their Study and Their Potential. In *Approaches to the Social Dimensions of Mortuary Practices,* edited by James A. Brown. *Society for American Archaeology Memoirs* 25:92-112.

Biringuccio, Vannoccio
1966 *The Pirotecnhia of Vannoccio Biringuccio,* translated by Cyryl S. Smith and Martha T. Gnudi. M.I.T. Press, Cambridge, Massachusetts.

Birk, Douglas A., and Elden Johnson
1992 The Mdewakanton Dakota and Initial French Contact. In *Calumet & Fleur-de-Lys: Archaeology of Indian and French Contact in the Midcontinent,* edited by John A. Walthall and Thomas E. Emerson, pp. 203-40. Smithsonian Institution Press, Washington, D.C.

Black, Glenn A.
1934 Archaeological Survey of Dearborn and Ohio Counties. *Indiana History Bulletin* 11(7).
1967 *Angel Site: An Archaeological, Historical, and Ethnological Study.* Indiana Historical Society, Indianapolis.

Blair, Emma H. (editor)
1911-1912 *The Indian Tribes of the Upper Mississippi Valley and Region of the Great Lakes, as Described by Nicolas Perrot, French Commandant in the Northwest; Bacqueville de la Potherie, French Royal Commissioner to Canada; Morrell Marston, American Army Officer; and Thomas Forsyth, United States Agent at Fort Armstrong.* Arthur H. Clark, Cleveland.

Blakely, Robert L
1971 Comparison of the Mortality Profiles of Archaic, Middle Woodland, and Middle Missisippian Skeletal Profiles. *American Journal of Physical Anthropology* 34:43-53.
1977 Sociocultural Implications of Demographic Data from Etowah, Georgia. In *Biocultural Adaptation in Prehistoric America,* edited by Robert L. Blakely, pp. 45-66. University of Georgia Press, Athens.

Blakely, Robert L., and David S. Mathews
1990 Bioarchaeological Evidence for a Spanish-Native American Conflict in the Sixteenth-Century Southeast. *American Antiquity* 55(4):718-44.

Blakeslee, Donald J.
1981 The Origin and Spread of the Calumet Ceremony. *American Antiquity* 46:759-68.

Blanton, Richard, and Gary Feinman
1984 The Mesoamerican World System. *American Anthropologist* 86:673-82.

Blitz, John H.
1993 *Ancient Chiefdoms of the Tombigbee.* University of Alabama Press, Tuscaloosa.

Bloch, Maurice
1981 Tombs and States. In *Mortality and Immortality: The Anthropology and Archaeology of Death,* edited by S. C. Humphreys and Helen King, pp. 137-47. Academic Press, New York.

Blom, Jan-Petter
1969 Ethnic and Cultural Differentiation. In *Ethnic Groups and Boundaries: The Social Organization of Culture Difference,* edited by Fredrik Barth, pp. 74-85. Little, Brown, and Company, Boston.

Bluhm, Elaine A., and Gloria J. Fenner
1961 The Oak Forest Site. In *Chicago Area Archaeology,* edited by Elaine A. Bluhm, pp. 138-61. Illinois Archaeological Survey, Carbondale.

Bluhm, Elaine A., and Allen Liss
1961 The Anker Site. In *Chicago Area Archaeology,* edited by Elaine A. Bluhm, pp. 89-137. Illinois Archaeological Survey Bulletin 3, Carbondale.

Bohannan, Paul
1955 Some Principles of Exchange and Investment among the Tiv. *American Anthropologist* 57:60-70.

Bonvillain, Nancy
1995 *The Sac and Fox.* Indians of North America. Chelsea House, New York.

Borque, Bruce J.
1994 Evidence for Prehistoric Exchange on the Maritime Peninsula. In *Prehistoric Exchange Systems in North America,* edited by Timothy G. Baugh and Jonathon E. Ericson, pp. 23-46. Plenum, New York.

Borque, Bruce J., and R. H. Whitehead
1985 Tarrentines and the Introduction of European Trade Goods in the Gulf of Maine. *Ethnohistory* 324:327-41.

Boszhardt, Robert F.
1989 Ceramic Analysis and Site Chronology of the Pammel Creek Site. *The Wisconsin Archeologist* 70(1-2):41-94.
1993 Turquoise, Rasps, and Heartlines: the Oneota Bison Pull. Paper presented at the Midwest Archaeological Conference, Milwaukee.

Bowen, Jonathan E.
1994 *The Sandusky River Area of North-Central Ohio: 1300-1600.* Sandusky Valley Chapter, Archaeological Society of Ohio, Upper Sandusky.

Boyd, C. Clifford, Jr., and Donna C. Boyd
1991 A Multidimensional Investigation of Biocultural Relationships among Three Late Prehistoric Societies in Tennessee. *American Antiquity* 56(1):75-88.

Bradley, James W.
1987a *Evolution of the Onondaga Iroquois: Accommodating Change, 1500-1655.* Syracuse University Press, Syracuse.
1987b Native Exchange and European Trade: Cross-Cultural Dynamics in the Sixteenth Century. *Man in the Northeast* 33:31-46.

Bradley, James W., and S. Terry Childs
1991a Basque Earrings and Panther's Tails: The Form of Cross-Cultural Contact in 16th Century Iroquoia. In *Metals in Society: Theory Beyond Analysis,* edited by Robert M. Ehrenreich, pp. 7-17. MASCA Research Papers in Science and Archaeology, vol. 8, pt. II. MASCA, The University Museum of Archaeology and Anthropology, University of Pennsylvania, Philadelphia.
1991b Basque Earrings and Panther's Tails: The Form of Cross-Cultural Contact in 16th Century Iroquoia. Paper presented at the annual meeting of the Society for American Archaeology, New Orleans.

Bradley, Richard
1991 Ritual, Time and History. *World Archaeology* 23(2):209-19.
1995 Forward: Trial and Error in the Study of Mortuary Practices: Exploring the Regional Dimension. In *Regional Approaches to Mortuary Analysis,* edited by Lane A. Beck, pp. v-ix. Plenum, New York.

Brain, Jeffrey P.
1975 Artifacts of the Adelantado. *The Conference on Historic Site Archaeology Papers* 8:129-38.
1979 *Tunica Treasure.* Papers of the Peabody Museum of American Archaeology and Ethnology No. 71. Harvard University Press, Cambridge, Massachusetts.
1988 *Tunica Archaeology.* Papers of the Peabody Museum of American Archaeology and Ethnology No. 78. Harvard University Press, Cambridge, Massachusetts.

Brain, Jeffrey P., and Philip Phillips
1996 *Shell Gorgets: Styles of the Late Prehistoric and Protohistoric Southeast.* Peabody Museum of Archaeology and Ethnology, Harvard University, Cambridge, Massachusetts.

Brashler, Janet
1987 A Middle Sixteenth Century Susquehannock Village in Hampshire County, West Virginia. *West Virginia Archaeologist* 39(2):1-31.

Brashler, Janet G., and Ronald W. Moxley
1990 Late Prehistoric Engraved Shell Gorgets of West Virginia. *West Virginia Archaeologist* 42(1):1-10.

Braun, David P.
1977 *Middle Woodland-(Early) Late Woodland Social Change in the Prehistoric Central Midwestern United States.* Ph.D. dissertation, University of Michigan, Ann Arbor.
1979 Illinois Hopewell Burial Practices and Social Organization: A Reexamination of the Klunk-Gibson Mound Group. In *Hopewell Archaeology: The Chillicothe Conference,* edited by David S. Brose and N'omi Greber, pp. 66-79. Kent State University Press, Kent, Ohio.
1981 A Critique of Some Recent North American Mortuary Studies. *American Antiquity* 46(2):398-416.

1986 Midwestern Hopewellian Exchange and Supralocal Interaction. In *Peer Polity Interaction and Socio-Political Change,* edited by Colin Renfrew and John F. Cherry, pp. 117-26. Cambridge University Press, Cambridge.

Braun, David P., and Stephen Plog
1982 Evolution of "Tribal" Social Networks: Theory and Prehistoric North American Evidence. 47:504-25.

Braund, Kathryn E. Holland
1993 *Deerskins and Duffels: Creek Indian Trade with Anglo-America, 1685-1815.* University of Nebraska Press, Lincoln.

Bray, Robert T.
1961a The Flynn Cemetery, an Orr Focus Oneota Burial Site in Allamakee County. *Journal of the Iowa Archaeological Society* 10(4):15-25.
1961b The Missouri Indian Tribe in Archaeology and History. *Missouri Historical Review* 15(3):213-25.
1963 Southern Cult Motifs from the Utz Oneota Site, Saline County, Missouri. *Missouri Archaeologist* 25:1-40.
1978 European Trade Goods from the Utz Site and the Search for Fort Orleans. *The Missouri Archaeologist* 39:1-87.
1991 The Utz Site: An Oneota Village in Central Missouri. *The Missouri Archaeologist* 52:1-146.

Breitburg, Emanuel
1992 Vertebrate Faunal Remains. In *Fort Ancient Cultural Dynamics in the Middle Ohio Valley,* edited by A. Gwynn Henderson, pp. 209-41. Monographs in World Archaeology No. 8. Prehistory Press, Madison, Wisconsin.

Broida, Mary
1984 An Estimate of the Percents of Maize in the Diets of Two Kentucky Fort Ancient Villages. In *Late Prehistoric Research in Kentucky,* edited by David Pollack, Charles D. Hockensmith, and Thomas N. Sanders, pp. 68-82. Kentucky Heritage Council, Frankfort.

Brooks, S., and Judy M. Suchey
1990 Skeletal Age Determination Based on the Os Pubis. *Human Evolution* 5(3):227-38.

Broom, Leonard, Bernard J. Siegel, Evon Z. Vogt, and James B. Watson
1954 Acculturation: An Exploratory Formulation. *American Anthropologist* 56:973-1000.

Brose, David S. (editor)
1976 *The Late Prehistory of the Lake Erie Drainage Basin: A Symposium.* Scientific Papers. Cleveland Museum of Natural History, Cleveland.

Brose, David S.
1970 *The Summer Island Site.* Studies in Anthropology No. 1. Case Western Reserve University, Cleveland.
1978 Late Prehistory of the Upper Great Lakes Area. In *Handbook of North American Indians: Northeast,* edited by Bruce Trigger, pp. 569-82. Smithsonian Institution, Washington, D.C.
1983 Rethinking the French Presence in the Upper Great Lakes. In *Lulu Linear Punctated: Essays in Honor of George I. Quimby,* edited by Robert Dunnell and D. Grayson, pp. 209-52. Anthropological Papers No. 72. Museum of Anthropology, University of Michigan, Ann Arbor.
1990 Toward a Model of Exchange Values for the Eastern Woodlands. *Midcontinental Journal of Archaeology* 15(1):100-136.
1994 *The South Park Village Site and the Late Prehistoric Whittlesey Tradition of Northeast Ohio.* Prehistory Press, Madison, Wisconsin.

Brose, David S., and Nancy Marie White
1983 Recent Data on Fort Ancient Occupation in the Caesar Creek Valley, Southwestern Ohio. *West Virginia Archaeologist* 35(2):3-39.

Brown, Calvin S.
1926 *Archeology of Mississippi.* Mississippi Geological Survey, University.

Brown, Ian W.
1977 Historic Trade Bells. *The Conference on Historic Site Archaeology Papers* 10:69-82.
1979a Bells. In *Tunica Treasure,* edited by Jeffrey P. Brain, pp. 197-205. Harvard University of Press, Cambridge, Massachusetts.
1979b Functional Group Changes and Acculturation: A Case Study of the French and the Indian in the Lower Missisippi Valley. *Midcontinental Journal of Archaeology* 4:147-65.
1979c Historic Artifacts and Sociocultural Change: Some Warnings from the Lower Mississippi Valley. *The Conference on Historic Site Archaeology Papers 1978* 13:109-21.
1981 A Study of Stone Box Graves in Eastern North America. *Tennessee Anthropologist* 6(1):1-26.
1989 The Calumet Ceremony in the Southeast and Its Archaeological Manifestations. *American Antiquity* 54(2):311-31.

Brown, James A. (editor)
1961 *The Zimmerman Site: A Report on Excavations at the Grand Village of Kaskaskia, La Salle County, Illinois.* Report of Investigations, No. 9. Illinois State Museum, Springfield.

Brown, James A.
1965 *The Prairie Peninsula: An Interaction Area in the Eastern United States.* Ph.D. dissertation, University of Chicago, Chicago.
1971 The Dimensions of Status in the Burials at Spiro. In *Approaches to the Social Dimensions of Mortuary Practices,* edited by James A. Brown, pp. 92-112. Society for American Archarology, Washington, D.C.
1975 Spiro Art and Its Mortuary Contexts. In *Death and the Afterlife in Pre-Columbian America,* edited by Elizabeth P. Benson, pp. 1-32. Dumbarton Oaks Research Library and Collections, Washington, D.C.
1976 *Spiro Studies: The Artifacts.* Stovall Museum of Science and History, University of Oklahoma, Norman.
1981 The Search for Rank in Prehistoric Burials. In *The Archaeology of Death,* edited by Robert Chapman, Ian Kinnes, and Klavs Randsborg, pp. 25-37. Cambridge University Press, Cambridge.
1982 What Kind of Economy Did the Oneota Have? In *Oneota Studies,* edited by Guy E. Gibbon, pp. 107-12. Publications in Anthropology, No. 1. University of Minnesota, Minneapolis.
1983 Spiro Exchange Connections Revealed by Sources of Imported Raw Material. *Oklahoma Archaeological Survey Studies in Oklahoma's Past* 11:129-62.

1985 The Mississippian Period. In *Ancient Art of the American Woodland Indians*, edited by David S. Brose, James A. Brown, and David W. Penney, pp. 94-140. Harry N. Abrams, New York.
1987 Quantitative Burial Analysis as Intrassemblage Comparison. In *Quantitative Research in Archaeology: Progress and Prospects*, edited by S. Aldenderfer, pp. 294-308. Sage Publications, Newbery Park, California.
1990 Ethnohistoric Connections. In *At the Edge of Prehistory: Huber Phase Archaeology in the Chicago Area*, edited by James A. Brown and Patricia J. O'Brien, pp. 155-60. Center for American Archaeology, Kampsville, Illinois.
1991 The Falcon and the Serpent: Life in the Southeastern United States at the Time of Columbus. In *Circa 1492: Art in the Age of Exploration*, edited by Jay A. Levenson, pp. 529-34. National Gallery of Art, Washington, D.C.
1993 From Mounds to Cemeteries: Continuity and Change in Oneota Mortuary Practices. Paper presented at the Midwest Archaeological Conference, Milwaukee.
1995 On Mortuary Analysis—with Special Reference to the Saxe-Binford Research Program. In *Regional Approaches to Mortuary Analysis*, edited by Lane A. Beck, pp. 3-26. Plenum, New York.
1996 *The Spiro Ceremonial Center: The Archaeology of Arkansas Valley Caddoan Culture in Eastern Oklahoma*. Memoir No 29. University of Michigan Museum of Anthropology, Ann Arbor.

Brown, James A., David L. Asch, Laura K. Michalik, Rochelle Lurie, Nancy Asch Sidell, Sarah W. Neusius, and Robert Jeske
1990 The Oak Forest Site: Investigations into Oneota Subsistence-Settlement in the Cal-Sag Area of Cook County, Illinois. In *At the Edge of Prehistory: Huber Phase Archaeology in the Chicago Area*, edited by James A. Brown and Patricia J. O'Brien, pp. 121-308. Center for American Archaeology, Kampsville, Illinois.

Brown, James A., Richard A. Kerber, and Howard D. Winter
1990 Trade and the Evolution of Exchange Relations at the Beginning of the Mississippian Period. In *The Mississippian Emergence*, edited by Bruce D. Smith, pp. 251-80. Smithsonian Institution Press, Washington, D.C.

Brown, James A., and Patricia J. O'Brien (editors)
1990 *At the Edge of Prehistory: Huber Phase Archaeology in the Chicago Area*. Center for American Archaeology, Kampsville, Illinois.

Brown, James A., and John Willis
1995 Re-Examination of Danner Pottery from the Starved Rock Area. Paper presented at the Midwest Archaeological Conference, Beloit, Wisconsin.

Brown, Margaret K.
1975 *The Zimmerman Site: Further Excavations at the Grand Village of Kaskaskia*. Reports of Investigations, No. 32. Illinois State Museum, Springfield.
1979 Cultural Transformations Among the Illinois: An Application of a Systems Model. *Michigan State University Publications, Anthropological Series* 1(3):217-67.

Broyles, Bettye J.
1970 Burial of a Medicine Man. *Wonderful West Virginia* 34(4):12-13, 27.

Broyles, Bettye J, and E. Thomas Hemmings
1978 Blennerhassett Island: Preserving the Past. *Wonderful West Virginia* 39(1):8-12.

Brumfiel, Elizabeth M., and Timothy K. Earle (editors)
1987 *Specialization, Exchange, and Complex Societies*. Cambridge University Press, Cambridge.

Buikstra, Jane E.
1972 *Hopewell in the Lower Illinois River Valley: A Regional Approach to the Study of Biological Variability and Mortuary Activity*. Ph.D. dissertation, University of Chicago, Chicago.
1979 Contributions of Physical Anthropologists to the Concept of Hopewell: A Historical Perspective. In *Hopewell Archaeology: The Chillicothe Conference*, edited by David S. Brose and N'omi Greber, pp. 220-33. Kent State University Press, Kent, Ohio.
1981 Mortuary Practices, Paleodemography and Paleopathology. In *The Archaeology of Death*, edited by Robert Chapman, Ian Kinnes, and Klavs Randsborg, pp. 123-32. Cambridge University Press, Cambridge.

Buker, William E.
1968 The McKees Rocks Site: A Late Prehistoric Village. *Pennsylvania Archaeologist* 38:1-49.

Burghardt, A. F.
1971 A Hypothesis about Gateway Cities. *Annals of the Association of American Geographers* 61:269-85.

Butkus, E.
1973 The Hoxie Farm Site, Cook County, Illinois. *Central States Archaeological Journal* 20(2):66-70.

Byers, Stan
1995 Arapaho Assimilation and Distinction. Paper presented at the symposium, Expressions of Ethnicity: Evolutionary and Historical Persectives on Plains Indian Art, Knoxville, Tennessee.

Cadzow, Donald A.
1936 *Archaeological Studies of the Susquehannock Indians of Pennsylvania*. Safe Harbor Report No. 2. Pennsylvania Historical Commission, Harrisburg.

Caldwell, Joseph R.
1964 Interaction Spheres in Prehistory. In *Hopewellian Studies*, edited by Joseph R. Caldwell and R. Hall, pp. 134-43. Scientific Papers No. 12. Illinois State Museum, Springfield.

Callender, Charles
1962 *Social Organization of the Central Algonkian Indians*. Publications in Anthropology. Milwaukee Public Museum, Milwaukee.
1978a Fox. In *Handbook of North American Indians: Northeast*, edited by Bruce G. Trigger, pp. 636-47. Smithsonian Institution, Washington, D.C.
1978b Great Lakes-Riverine Sociopoligical Organization. In *Handbook of North American Indians: Northeast*, edited by Bruce G. Trigger, pp. 610-21. Smithsonian Institution, Washington, D.C.
1978c Illinois. In *Handbook of North American Indians: Northeast*, edited by Bruce G. Trigger, pp. 673-80. Smithsonian Institution, Washington, D.C.

1978d Miami. In *Handbook of North American Indians: Northeast,* edited by Bruce G. Trigger, pp. 681-89. Smithsonian Institution, Washington, D.C.

1978e Sauk. In *Handbook of North American Indians: Northeast,* edited by Bruce G. Trigger, pp. 648-55. Smithsonian Institution, Washington, D.C.

1978f Shawnee. In *Handbook of North American Indians: Northeast,* edited by Bruce G. Trigger, pp. 622-35. Smithsonian Institution, Washington, D.C.

Callender, Charles, Richard K. Pope, and Susan M. Pope

1978 Kickapoo. In *Handbook of North American Indians: Northeast,* edited by Bruce G. Trigger, pp. 656-67. Smithsonian Institution, Washington, D.C.

Carniero, Robert L.

1977 A Theory of the Origin of the State. *Science* 169:733-38.

Carr, Christopher, and Robert F. Maslowski

1995 Cordage and Fabrics: Relating Form, Technology, and Social Processes. In *Style, Society, and Person: Archaeological and Ethnological Perspectives,* edited by Christopher Carr and Jill E. Neitzel, pp. 297-343. Plenum Press, New York.

Carskadden, Jeff

1992 The Bosman Site, Muskingum County, Ohio. *Field Notes: The Newsletter of the West Virginia Archaeological Society* 34(3):3-4.

1994 Fort Ancient in the Central Muskingum Valley of Eastern Ohio: A View from the Philo II Site. Paper presented at Cultures Before Contact: A Conference on the Late Prehistory of the Ohio Region. Ohio Archaeological Council, Cincinnati.

Carskadden, Jeff, Larry Edmister, and James Morton

1992 Scenes from the Bosman Site Excavation, Muskingum County, Ohio. *Ohio Archaeologist* 42(1):60-63.

Carskadden, Jeff, and James Morton (editors)

1977 *The Richards Site and the Philo Phase of the Fort Ancient Tradition.* Occasional Papers in Muskingum Valley Archaeology, Nos. 1-9. Muskingum Valley Archaeological Survey, Zanesville, Ohio.

Cassidy, Claire Monod

1984 Skeletal Evidence for Prehistoric Subsistence Adaptation in the Central Ohio River Valley. In *Paleopathology at the Origins of Agriculture,* edited by M. N. Cohen and G. J. Armelagos, pp. 307-45. Academic Press, New York.

Ceci, Lynn

1977 *The Effect of European Contact and Trade on the Settlement Pattern of Indians in Coastal New York, 1524-1665: The Archaeological and Documentary Evidence.* Ph.D. dissertation, City University of New York, New York.

1982 The Value of Wampum among the New York Iroquois: A Case Study in Artifact Analysis. *Journal of Anthropological Research* 38(1):97-107.

1988 The Anthropology of Shell Beads: Subsistence, Systems, and Symbols. In *Proceedings of the 1986 Shell Bead Conference: Selected Papers,* edited by Charles F. Hayes III, Lynn Ceci, and Connie Cox Bodner, pp. 1-5. Rochester Museum and Science Center, Rochester, New York.

1989a The Anthropology of Shell Beads: Subsistence, Systems, and Symbols. In *Proceedings of the 1986 Shell Bead Conference,* edited by Charles F. Hayes III and Lynn Ceci, pp. 1-5. Rochester Museum and Science Center, Research Records No. 20, Rochester, New York.

1989b Tracing Wampum's Origins: Shell Bead Evidence from Archaeological Sites in Western and Coastal New York. In *Proceedings of the 1986 Shell Bead Conference,* edited by Charles F. Hayes III and Lynn Ceci, pp. 63-80. Rochester Museum and Science Center, Research Records No. 20, Rochester, New York.

Chafe, Anne, Ron Hancock, and Ian Kenyon

1986 A Preliminary Report on the Neutron Activation Analysis of Early Historic Blue Glass Trade Beads. Manuscript on file, Rochester Museum and Science Center, Rochester, New York.

Champion, Timothy, C. (editor)

1989a *Centre and Periphery: Comparative Studies in Archaeology.* Unwin Hyman, London.

1989b Introduction. In *Centre and Periphery,* edited by Timothy C. Champion, pp. 1-21. Unwin Hyman, London.

Chang, K. C.

1958 Study of the Neolithic Social Groupings: Examples from the New World. *American Anthropologist* 60:298-334.

Chang, K. C. (editor)

1968 *Settlement Archaeology.* National Press, Palo Alto, California.

Chapman, Anne C.

1957 Port of Trade Enclaves in Aztec and Maya Civilizations. In *Trade And Market in the Early Empires,* edited by Karl Polanyi, Conrad M. Arensberg, and Harry W. Pearson, pp. 114-54. Henry Regnery, Chicago.

Chapman, Lynn

1996 Shell Mask Gorget from Ionia County. *The Michigan Archaeologist* 42(2):79-85.

Chapman, Robert

1981 The Emergence of Formal Disposal Areas and the "Problem" of Megalithic Tombs in Prehistoric Europe. In *The Archaeology of Death,* edited by Robert Chapman, Ian Kinnes, and Klavs Randsborg, pp. 71-81. Cambridge University Press, Cambridge.

1995 Ten Years After: Megaliths, Mortuary Practices, and the Territorial Model. In *Regional Approaches to Mortuary Analysis,* edited by Lane A. Beck, pp. 29-51. Plenum, New York.

Chapman, Robert, and Klavs Randsborg

1981 Approaches to the Archaeology of Death. In *The Archaeology of Death,* edited by Robert Chapman, Ian Kinnes, and Klavs Randsborg, pp. 1-24. Cambridge University Press, Cambridge.

Charles, Douglas K.

1995 Diachronic Regional Social Dynamics: Mortuary Sites in the Illinois Valley/American Bottom Region. In *Regional Approaches to Mortuary Analysis,* edited by Lane A. Beck, pp. 77-99. Plenum, New York.

Cherry, John F., and Colin Renfrew
1986 Epilogue and Prospect. In *Peer Polity Interaction and Socio-Political Change,* edited by Colin Renfrew and John F. Cherry, pp. 149-58. Cambridge University Press, Cambridge.

Childs, S. Terry
1994 Native Copper Technology and Society in Eastern North America. In *Archaeometry of Pre-Columbian Sites and Artifacts,* edited by David A. Scott and Pieter Meyers, pp. 229-53. The Getty Conservation Institute, Los Angeles.

Church, Flora
1987 *An Inquiry into the Transition from Late Woodland to Late Prehistoric Cultures in the Central Scioto Valley, Ohio, circa A.D. 500 to A.D. 1250.* Ph.D. dissertation, Ohio State University.

Clay, R. Berle
1984 Styles of Stone Graves. In *Late Prehistoric Research in Kentucky,* edited by David Pollack, Charles D. Hockensmith, and Thomas N. Sanders, pp. 131-44. Kentucky Heritage Council, Frankfort.

Clayton, Lawrence A., Vernon J. Knight Jr., and Edward C. Moore (editors)
1993 *The de Soto Chronicles: The Expedition of Hernando de Soto to North America in 1539-1543.* University of Alabama Press, Tuscaloosa.

Cleland, Charles E. (editor)
1971 *The Lasanen Site: An Historic Burial Locality in Mackinac County, Michigan.* Publications of the Museum, Anthropological Series, vol. 1, no. 1. Michigan State University, East Lansing.

Cleland, Charles E.
1992 *Rites of Conquest: The History and Culture of Michigan's Native Americans.* The University of Michigan Press, Ann Arbor.

Clifton, James A.
1978 Potawatomi. In *Handbook of North American Indians: Northeast,* edited by Bruce G. Trigger, pp. 725-42. Smithsonian Institution, Washington, D.C.

Cobb, Charles R.
1989 An Appraisal of the Role of Mill Creek Chert Hoes in Mississippian Exchange Systems. *Southeastern Archaeology* 8(2):79-92.

Collins, James M.
1988-89 The Des Moines Rapids and Western Oneota Socio-Political Patterns. *Journal of the Steward Anthropological Society* 18(1-2):165-86.
1995 A Shell Mask Gorget from Allamakee County, Iowa. *Plains Anthropologist* 40(153):251-60.

Conover, J. Donald
n.d. Notes on file, Cincinnati Museum of Natural History, Cincinnati.

Conrad, Lawrence A.
1991a *Recovering a Heritage: Prehistoric Art of West Central Illinois.* Western Illinois University, Macomb, Illinois.
1991b The Middle Mississippian Cultures of the Central Illinois Valley. In *Cahokia and the Hinterlands: Middle Mississippian Cultures of the Midwest,* edited by Thomas E. Emerson and R. Barry Lewis, pp. 119-56. University of Illinois Press, Urbana.
1996 Another Look at the Late Prehistoric Gorgets from the Central Illinois River Valley. Paper presented at the Southeastern Archaeological Conference, Birmingham, Alabama.

Converse, Robert N.
1995a A Catlinite Pipe from Union County, Ohio. *Ohio Archaeologist* 45(4):17.
1995b A Turtle Effigy Pipe. *Ohio Archaeologist* 45(4):25.

Cook, Della C.
1981 Mortality, Age Structure and Status in the Interpretation of Stress Indicators in Prehistoric Skeletons: a Dental Example from the Lower Illinois Valley. In *The Archaeology of Death,* edited by Robert Chapman, Ian Kinnes, and Klavs Randsborg, pp. 133-44. Cambridge University Press, Cambridge.

Cowan, C. Wesley
1986 *Fort Ancient Chronology and Settlement Evaluation in the Great Miami Valley, Volume II: Excavations and Chronology.* Manuscript on file, Ohio Historic Preservation Office, Cincinnati.
1987 *First Farmers of the Middle Ohio Valley: Fort Ancient Societies, A.D. 1000-1670.* Cincinnati Museum of Natural History, Cincinnati.
1988 From Pithouse to Longhouse, from Community to Chaos: Late Prehistoric and Proto-historic Developments in the Middle Ohio Valley. Paper presented at the Midwest Archaeological Conference, Champaign-Urbana, Ilinois.
1992 The Dawn of History and the Demise of the Fort Ancient Cultures of the Central Ohio Valley. Paper presented at the annual meeting of the Society for American Archaeology, Pittsburg, Pennsylvania.

Cowan, C. Wesley (editor)
in press *Recent Research at the Madisonville Village Site, Hamilton County, Ohio.* Occasional Papers in Anthropology, No. 1. Cincinnati Museum of Natural History, Cincinnati.

Cowan, C. Wesley, Sandra Dunavan, John P. Nass Jr., and Susan Scott
1990 The Schomaker Site, A Middle Period Fort Ancient Town on the Great Miami River, Hamilton County, Ohio. *West Virginia Archaeologist* 42(1):11-35.

Cowgill, George L.
1972 Models, Methods and Techniques for Seriation. In *Models in Archaeology,* edited by David L. Clarke, pp. 381-424. Methuen, London.

Crane, Verner W.
1929 *The Southern Frontier, 1670-1732.* University of Michigan Press, Ann Arbor.

Creamer, Winifred, and Jonathan Haas
1985 Tribe versus Chiefdom in Lower Central America. *American Antiquity* 50(4):738-54.

Creel, Darell
1991 Bison Hides in Late Prehistoric Exchange in the Southern Plains. *American Antiquity* 56(1):40-49.

Crosby, Alfred W., Jr.
1972 *The Columbian Exchange.* Greenwood Press, Westport, Connecticut.

Crumley, Carole L.
1995 Heterarchy and the Analysis of Complex Societies. In *Heterarchy and the Analysis of Complex Societies,* edited by Robert M. Ehrenreich, Carole L. Crumley, and Janet E. Levy, pp. 1-5. Archaeological Papers No. 6. American Anthropological Association, Washington, D.C.

Crumley, Carole L., and William H. Marquardt (editors)
1987 *Regional Dynamics: Burgundian Landscapes in Historical Perspective.* Academic Press, New York.

Crumley, Carole L., and W. H. Marquardt (editors)
1987 *Regional Dynamics: Burgundian Landscapes in Hisorical Perspective.* Academic Press, New York.

Darlington, William M.
1893 *Christopher Gist's Journals with Historical, Geographical and Ethnographical Notes and Biographies of His Contemporaries.* Arthur H. Clark Co., Cleveland.

Dausman, Raymond J.
1990 The Hoxie Farm Site, Ck4, Cook County, Illinois. In *At the Edge of Prehistory: Huber Phase Archaeology in the Chicago Area,* edited by James A. Brown and Patricia J. O'Brien, pp. 113-15. Center for American Archaeology, Kampsville, Illinois.

Davis, Christine E.
1984 A Mortuary Pattern for Monongahela. *Pennsylvania Archaeologist* 54(1-2):1-11.
1993 A Unique 17th Century Settlement Pattern and Exchange Newwork in Western Pennsylvania: The Sony Site. Paper presented at the annual meeting of the Society for American Archaeology, St. Louis.
1996 Results of the Sony Site in Westmoreland County, Pennsylvania. Paper presented at the Eastern States Archeological Federation annual meeting, Huntington, West Virginia.

Deagan, Kathleen A.
1983 *Spanish St. Augustine: The Archaeology of a Colonial Creole Community.* Academic Press, New York.

DeBoer, Warren R.
1981 Buffer Zones in the Cultural Ecology of Aboriginal Amazonia: An Ethnohistorical Approach. *American Antiquity* 46:364-77.
1988 Subterranean Storage and the Organization of Surplus: The View from Eastern North America. *Southeastern Archaeology* 7(1):1-20.
1990 Interaction, Imitation, and Communication as Expressed in Style: The Ucayli Experience. In *The Uses of Style in Archaeology* edited by Margaret W. Conkey and Christine A. Hastorf, pp. 82-104. Cambridge University Press, Cambridge.
1991 The Decorative Burden: Design, Medium, and Change. In *Ceramic Ethnoarchaeology,* edited by William A. Longacre, pp. 144-61. University of Arizona Press, Tucson.

DePratter, Chester B., and Marvin T. Smith
1980 Sixteenth-Century European Trade in the Southeastern United States: Evidence from the Juan Pardo Expeditions (1566-1568). In *Spanish Colonial Frontier Research,* edited by Henry F. Dobyns, pp. 67-77. Center for Anthropological Studies, Albuquerque.

Deutchman, Haree L.
1980 Chemical Evidence of Ceramic Exchange on Black Mesa. In *Models and Methods in Regional Exchange,* edited by Robert E. Fry, pp. 119-33. Society for American Archaeology Papers No. 1, Washington, D.C.

Dexter, Ralph
1982 The Putnam-Metz Correspondence on Mound Explorations in Ohio. *Ohio Archaeologist* 32(4):24-28.

Dimmick, Frederica R.
1987 *Trade Goods Used by the Upper Creeks: Seeing Culture Change and Continuity through Documents, Art and Archaeology.* A.L.M. thesis, Harvard University, Cambridge, Massachusetts.

Dincauze, Dina F., and Robert J. Hasenstab
1989 Explaining the Iroquois: Tribalization on a Prehistoric Periphery. In *Centre and Periphery,* edited by Timothy C. Champion, pp. 67-87. Unwin Hyman, London.

Di Peso, Charles C.
1974 *Casas Grandes: A Fallen Trading Center of the Gran Chichimeca.* The Amerind Foundation and Northland Press, Dragoon and Flagstaff, Arizona.

Dobyns, Henry F.
1983 *Their Number Became Thinned.* University of Tennessee Press, Knoxville.

Dodd, Christine F., Dana R. Poulton, Paul A. Lennox, David G. Smith, and Gary A. Warrick
1990 The Middle Ontario Iroquoian Stage. In *The Archaeology of Southern Ontario to A.D. 1650,* edited by Chris J. Ellis and Neal Ferris, pp. 321-59. Ontario Archaeological Society, London, Ontario.

Dole, Gertrude
1968 Tribe as the Autonomous Unit. In *Essays on the Problem of Tribe: Proceedings of the 1967 Annual Spring Meeting of the American Ethnological Society,* edited by June Helm, pp. 83-100. American Ethnological Society, Seattle.

Dorwin, John T.
1971 The Bowen Site: An Archaeological Study of Culture Process in the Late Prehistory of Central Indiana. *Indiana Historical Society Prehistory Research Series* 44:192-411.

Douglas, Mary
1972 Symbolic Orders in the Use of Domestic Space. In *Man, Settlement, and Urbanism,* edited by Peter J. Ucko, Ruth Trigham, and G. W. Dimbleby, pp. 513-21. Duckworth, London.

Dragoo, Don W.
1963 *Mounds for the Dead: An Analysis of the Adena Culture.* Annals, Vol. 37, Carnegie Museum, Pittsburgh.

Drooker, Penelope B.
1991a Mississippian Lace: A Complex Textile Impressed on Pottery from the Stone Site, Tennessee. *Southeastern Archaeology* 10(2):79-97.
1991b The Shawnee Female Deity in Political Perspective. Manuscript.
1992a Fort Ancient Westerly Exchange: The Catlinite Connection. Manuscript.
1992b Madisonville Bell, Cincinnati Musuem of Natural History. Manuscript on file, Cincinnati Museum of Natural History, Cincinnati.
1992c Metal and Glass Artifacts. Manuscript on file, Cincinnati Museum of Natural History, Cincinnati.
1992d Metal from the Madisonville Site in the Collection of the Cincinnati Museum of Natural History. Manuscript on file, Cincinnati Museum of Natural History, Cincinnati.
1992e *Mississippian Village Textiles at Wickliffe*. The University of Alabama Press, Tuscaloosa.
1992f Theory of Mortuary Analysis: Review of Literature and Assessment of Current Practice. Special Field Examination for Doctoral Candidacy, Department of Anthropology, The University at Albany, State University of New York.
1993a Chemical Analysis of Blue Glass Beads from the Madisonville Site: Report to Harvard University Peabody Museum of Archaeology and Ethnology. Manuscript on file at the Peabody Museum, Cambridge, Massachusetts.
1993b Chemical Analysis of Metal Samples from the Madisonville Site: Report to the Cincinnati Museum of Natural History. Manuscript on file at the Cincinnati Museum of Natural History, Cincinnati.
1993c External Relations: Exotic Materials and Artifacts at Madisonville. Paper presented at the annual meeting of the Society for American Archaeology, St. Louis, April 1993.
1993d Madisonville and Its Neighbors: Fort Ancient Late Prehistoric and Protohistoric Patterns of Interaction and Exchange. Address presented at the West Virginia Archaeological Society Annual Meeting, Huntington.
1993e Methodological Models for the Analysis of Prehistoric and Protohistoric Trade Systems. Special Field Examination for Doctoral Candidacy, Department of Anthropology, The University at Albany, State University of New York.
1993f Radiocarbon Dating of Corn from the Madisonville and Hahn's Field, Ohio, Sites: Report to Harvard University Peabody Museum of Archaeology and Ethnology. Manuscript on file at the Peabody Museum, Cambridge, Massachusetts.
1994a Background Information for "Protohistoric Madisonville: Interaction and Change in the Central Ohio River Valley ca. 1450-1650." Manuscript on file, Peabody Museum Collections Department, Harvard University, Cambridge, Massachusetts.
1994b Chemical Analysis of Blue Glass Bead Fragments from the Rolf Lee Site (46Ms51). Manuscript.
1994c Fort Ancient and the Southeast: Late Prehistoric and Protohistoric Interaction. Paper presented at the Southeastern Archaeological Conference, Lexington, Kentucky.
1994d Representations of Gender in Fort Ancient versus Mississippian Culture Areas. Paper presented at the Third Archaeology and Gender Conference, Boone, North Carolina.
1995 Fort Ancient Social Organization and Interregional Interaction. *Museum Anthropology* 19(3):1-16.
1996a Madisonville Focus Revisited: Reexcavating Fort Ancient from Museum Collections. In *Cultures Before Contact: The Late Prehistory of the Ohio Region*, edited by Robert Genheimer. Ohio Archaeological Council, Cincinnati (in press).
1996b Madisonville Metal and Glass Artifacts: Implications for Western Fort Ancient Chronology and Interaction Networks. *Midcontinental Journal of Archaeology* 21(2):1-46.
1996c *The View from Madisonville: Continuity and Change in Late Prehistoric: Protohistoric Western Fort Ancient Interaction Patterns*. Unpublished Ph.D. dissertation, The University at Albany, State University of New York.
in press *The View from Madisonville: The Data on CD-ROM.* University of Michigan Museum of Anthropology. Ann Arbor.

Dunavan, Sandra L.
1991 Fort Ancient Paleoethnobotany: New Data and Perspectives. Paper presented at the Society of Ethnobiology Annual Conference, St. Louis.
1993 Madisonville Paleoethnobotany: Crops aqnd Other Plants. Paper presented at the Society for American Archaeology Annual Meeting, St. Louis.
n.d. Madisonville Paleoethnobotany. Report submitted to the Cincinnati Museum of Natural History, Cincinnati.

Dye, David H.
1990 Warfare in the Sixteenth-Century Southeast: The de Soto Expedition in the Interior. In *Columbian Consequences, Vol. 2: Archaeological and Historical Perspectives on the Spanish Borderlands East,* edited by David H. Thomas, pp. 211-22. Smithsonian Institution Press, Washington, D.C.
1995 Feasting with the Enemy: Mississippian Warfare and Prestige-Goods Circulation. In *Native American Interactions: Multiscalar Analyses and Interpretations in the Eastern Woodlands,* edited by Michael S. Nassaney and Kenneth E. Sassaman, pp. 289-316. The University of Tennessee Press, Knoxville.

Dye, David H., and Ronald C. Brister (editors)
1986 *The Protohistoric Period in the Mid-South: 1500-1700: Proceedings of the 1983 Mid-South Archaeological Conference.* Mississippi Department of Archives and History, Jackson.

Dye, David H., and Camille Wharey
1989 Exhibition Catalog. In *The Southeastern Ceremonial Complex: Artifacts and Analysis, The Cottonlandia Conference,* edited by Patricia Galloway, pp. 321-82. University of Nebraska Press, Lincoln.

Earle, Timothy K.
1977 A Reappraisal of Redistribution: Complex Hawaiian Chiefdoms. In *Exchange Systems in Prehistory,* edited by Timothy K. Earle and Jonathon E. Ericson, pp. 213-29. Academic Press, New York.
1994 Positioning Exchange in the Evolution of Human Society. In *Prehistoric Exchange Systems in North America,* edited by Timothy G. Baugh and Jonathon E. Ericson, pp. 419-37. Plenum Press, New York.

Earle, Timothy K., and Jonathon E. Ericson (editors)
1977 *Exchange Systems in Prehistory.* Academic Press, New York.

Edmunds, R. David
1984 *Tecumseh and the Quest for Indian Leadership.* Little, Brown, and Company, Boston.

Ehrenreich, Robert M., Carole L. Crumley, and Janet E. Levy (editors)
1995 *Heterarchy and the Analysis of Complex Societies.* Archaeological Papers No. 6. American Anthropological Association, Washington, D.C.

Ellis, Chris J., and Neal Ferris (editors)
1990 *The Archaeology of Southern Ontario to A.D. 1650.* London Chapter, Ontario Archaeological Society, London, Ontario.

Ellis, Owen W.
1948 *Copper and Copper Alloys.* American Society for Metals, Cleveland.

Emerson, Thomas A.
1983 The Bostrom Figure Pipe and the Cahokian Effigy Style in the American Bottom. *Midcontinental Journal of Archaeology* 8:257-67.
1982 *Mississippian Stone Images in Illinois.* Circular 6. Illinois Archaeological Survey, Urbana.
1989 Water, Serpents, and the Underworld: An Exploration into Cahokian Symbolism. In *The Southeastern Ceremonial Complex: Artifacts and Analysis (The Cottonlandia Conference),* edited by Patricia Galloway, pp. 45-92. University of Nebraska Press, Lincoln.

Emerson, Thomas J., and James A. Brown
1992 The Late Prehistory and Protohistory of Illinois. In *Calumet & Fleur-de-Lys: Archaeology of Indian and French Contact in the Midcontinent,* edited by John A. Walthall and Thomas E. Emerson, pp. 77-128. Smithsonian Institution Press, Washington, D.C.

Emerson, Thomas E., and R. Barry Lewis (editors)
1991 *Cahokia and the Hinterlands: Middle Mississippian Cultures of the Midwest.* University of Illinois Press, Urbana.

Engelbrecht, William
1991 Erie. *The Bulletin: Journal of the New York State Archaeological Association* (102):2-12.
1995 The Case of the Disappearing Iroquoians: Early Contact Period Superpower Politics. *Northeast Anthropology* 50:35-59.

Ericson, Jonathon E.
1977 Egalitarian Exchange Systems in California: A Preliminary View. In *Exchange Systems in Prehistory,* edited by Timothy K. Earle and Jonathon E. Ericson, pp. 109-26. Academic Press, New York.
1981 Exchange and Production Systems in California Prehistory. *British Archaeological Reports, International Series* 110:1-240.

Ericson, Jonathon E., and Timothy G. Baugh (editors)
1993 *The American Southwest and Mesoamerica: Systems of Prehistoric Exchange.* Plenum Press, New York.
1994 Systematics of the Study of Prehistoric Regional Exchange in North America. In *Prehistoric Exchange Systems in North America,* edited by Timothy G. Baugh and Jonathon E. Ericson, pp. 3-15. Plenum, New York.

Esarey, Duane
1990 Style Geography and Symbolism of Mississippian Spiders. Paper presented at the Southeastern Archaeological Conference, Mobile.

Esarey, Duane, and Sharron K. Santure
1990 The Morton Site Oneota Component and the Bold Counselor Phase. In *Archaeological Investigations at the Morton Village and Norris Farms 36 Cemetery,* edited by Sharron K. Santure, Alan D. Harn, and Duane Esarey, pp. 162-66. Illinois State Museum Reports of Investigations, No. 45, Springfield.

Essenpreis, Patricia S.
1978 Fort Ancient Settlement: Differential Response at a Mississippian-Late Woodland Interface. In *Mississippian Settlement Patterns,* edited by Bruce D. Smith, pp. 141-67. Academic Press, New York.
1982 *The Anderson Village Site: Redefining the Anderson Phase of the Fort Ancient Tradition of the Middle Ohio Valley.* Ph.D. Dissertation, Harvard University.
1988 An Introduction to the Fort Ancient Cultural Complexes of the Middle Ohio Valley. In *A History of 17 Years of Excavation and Reconstruction: A Chronicle of 12th Century Human Values and the Built Environment,* edited by James M. Heilman, Malinda C. Lileas, and Christopher A. Turnbow, pp. 1-22. The Dayton Museum of Natural History, Dayton, Ohio.

Evans, Sarah J.
1994 Mortuary Data as Indicators of Social Organization at the Incinerator Site (33MY57). Paper presented in the symposium, Refocusing on Fort Ancient: New Directions at the Incinerator Site, Midwest Archaeological Conference, Lexington, Kentucky.

Ewers, John C.
1954 The Indian Trade of the Upper Missouri before Lewis and Clark: An Interpretation. *Missouri Historical Society Bulletin* 10:429-46.

Farnsworth, Paul
1989 Native American Acculturation in the Spanish Colonial Empire: the Franciscan Missions of Alta California. In *Centre and Periphery,* edited by Timothy C. Champion, pp. 186-206. Unwin Hyman, London.

Farnsworth, Kenneth B., and Thomas A. Emerson
1989 The Macoupin Creek Figure Pipe and Its Archaeological Context: Evidence for Late Woodland-Mississippian Interaction Beyond the Northern Border of Cahokian Settlement. *Midcontinental Journal of Archaeology* 14(1):18-37.

Faulkner, Charles H.
1972 *The Late Prehistoric Occupation of Northwestern Indiana: A Study of the Upper Mississippian Cultures of the Kankakee Valley.* Prehistory Research Series 5 (1). Indiana Historical Society, Indianapolis.

Fausz, Frederick J.
1985 Patterns of Anglo-Indian Aggression and Accommodation along the Mid-Atlantic Coast, 1584-1634. In *Cultures in Contact: The European Impact on Native Cultural Institutions in Eastern North America, A.D. 1000-1800,* edited by William W. Fitzhugh, pp. 225-68. Smithsonian Institution, Washington, D.C.

Featherstone, Bryan J.
1977 A Report on the Floral Remains from Two Archeological Sites in Southwestern Ohio. Paper presented at the Central States Anthropological Society Annual Meeting, Cincinnati.

Feinman, Gary, and Jill E. Neitzel
1984 Too Many Types: An Overview of Sedentary Prestate Societies in the Americas. In *Advances in Archaeological Method and Theory, vol. 7,* edited by Michael B. Schiffer, pp. 39-102. Academic Press, New York.

Fenton, William N.
1953 The Iroquois Eagle Dance: An Offshoot of the Calumet Dance. *Bureau of American Ethnology Bulletin* 156.
1978 Northern Iroquoian Culture Patterns. In *Handbook of North American Indians: Northeast,* edited by Bruce G. Trigger, pp. 296-321. Smithsonian Institution, Washington, D.C.

Findlow, Frank J., and Marisa Bolognese
1982 Regional Modeling of Obsidian Procurement in the American Southwest. In *Contexts for Prehistoric Exchange,* edited by Jonathon E. Ericson and Timothy K. Earle, pp. 103-27. Academic Press, New York.

Fitzgerald, William R.
1982 A Refinement of Historic Neutral Chronologies: Evidence from Shaver Hill, Christianson, and Dwyer. *Ontario Archaeology* 38:31-47.
1990 *Chronology to Cultural Process: Lower Great Lakes Archaeology, 1500 to 1650.* Ph.D. dissertation, McGill University, Montreal.
1991 An Analysis of Brass and Copper from the Ripley Site: The 1906 Sample. Manuscript on file, New York State Museum, Albany.
1992 Contact, Contraction, and the Little Ice Age: Neutral Iroquoian Transformation, A.D. 1450-1650. Paper presented at the 57th annual meeting of the Society for American Archaeology, Pittsburgh.

Fitzgerald, William R., and Peter G. Ramsden
1988 Copper Based Metal Testing as an Aid to Understanding Early European-Amerindian Interaction: Scratching the Surface. *Canadian Journal of Archaeology* 12:151-61.

Fitzgerald, William R., Laurier Turgeon, Ruth Holmes Whitehead, and James W. Bradley
1993 Late Sixteenth-Century Basque Banded Copper Kettles. *Historical Archaeology* 27(1):44-57.

Fletcher, Alice C., and Francis La Flesche
1992 *The Omaha Tribe.* University of Nebraska Press, Lincoln.
[1911]

Fletcher, Alice C., and James Murie
1904 The Hako: A Pawnee Ceremony. *Bureau of American Ethnology Annual Report* 22(pt. 2).

Foley, Phillip M., and Thomas F. Lipscombe
1961 A Kentucky Fort Ancient Burial Site. *Ohio Archaeologist* 11(4):126-28.

Ford, J. A., and C. H. Webb
1956 *Poverty Point, a Late Archaic Site in Louisiana.* Anthroplogy Papers, vol. 46, pt. 1. American Museum of Natural History, New York.

Ford, Richard I.
1972 Barter, Gift, or Violence: An Analysis of Tewa Intertribal Trade. In *Social Exchange and Interaction,* edited by Edwin N. Wilmsen, pp. 21-45. University of Michigan Museum of Anthropology Papers No. 46, Ann Arbor.
1983 Inter-Indian Exchange in the Southwest. In *Handbook of North American Indians, vol. 10: Southwest,* edited by Alfonso Ortiz, pp. 711-22. Smithsonian Institution, Washington, D.C.

Foster, George M.
1960 *Culture and Conquest.* Quadrangle Books, Chicago.

Foster, Morris W.
1994 Introduction to the Bison Book Edition. In *The Cheyenne in Plains Indian Trade Relations, 1795-1840,* edited by Joseph Jablow, pp. University of Nebraska Press, Lincoln.

Fox, William A.
1980 Miskwo Sinnee Munidominug. *Archaeology of Eastern North America* 8:88-98.
1990 The Odawa. In *The Archaeology of Southern Ontario to A.D. 1650,* edited by Chris J. Ellis and Neal Ferris, pp. 457-73. Ontario Archaeological Society, London, Ontario.
1991 The Serpent's Copper Scales. *Wanikan: Newsletter of the Thunder Bay Chapter, Ontario Archaeological Society* 91(3):2-15.

Fox, William A. , R. G. V. Hancock, and L. A. Pavlish
1995 Where East Met West: The New Copper Culture. *The Wisconsin Archeologist* 76(3-4):269-93.

Freeman, Joan E.
1986 Aztalan: A Middle Mississippi Village. *The Wisconsin Archaeologist* 67(3-4):339-64.

Freidin, Nicholas
1987 Report on the Investigations at Clover (46-Cb-40), West Virginia, by the Marshall University Archaeological Field School. Manuscript on file at the State Historic Preservation Office, Charleston.
1996 Physical Examination of Some Artifacts from the Clover Site (46CB40). Paper presented at the Eastern States Archeological Federation annual meeting, Huntington, West Virginia.

Fried, Morton H.
1967 *The Evolution of Political Society: An Essay in Political Anthropology.* Random House, New York.
1968 On the Concepts of "Tribe" and "Tribal Society." In *Essays on the Problem of Tribe: Proceedings of the 1967 Annual Spring Meeting of the American Ethnological Society,* edited by June Helm, pp. 3-20. American Ethnological Society, Seattle.

Fundabark, Emma Lila (editor)
1992 [1958] *Southeastern Indians, Life Portraits: A Catalogue of Pictures, 1564-1860.* American Bicentennial Museum, Fairhope, Alabama.

Fundabark, Emma L., and Mary D. F. Foreman
1957 *Sun Circles and Human Hands: The Southeastern Indians, Art, and Industries.* Emma Lila Fundabark, Luverne, Alabama.

Funk, Robert
1993 *Archaeological Investigations in the Upper Susquehanna Valley, New York State.* Persimmon Press,

Funkhauser, W. D., and Wiliam S. Webb
1928 *Ancient Life in Kentucky.* Kentucky Geological Survey Series 6, v. 34. Kentucky Geological Survey, Frankfort.

Galloway, Patricia (editor)
1989 *The Southeastern Ceremonial Complex: Artifacts and Analysis (The Cottonlandia Conference).* University of Nebraska Press, Lincoln.

Galloway, Patricia
1994 Confederacy as a Solution to Chiefdom Dissolution: Historical Evidence in the Choctaw Case. In *The Forgotten Centuries: Indians and Europeans in the American South, 1521-1704,* edited by Charles Hudson and Carmen C. Tesser, pp. 393-420. The University of Georgia Press, Athens.
1995 *Choctaw Genesis 1500-1700.* University of Nebraska Press, Lincoln.

Ganier, Albert F.
1948 The "Baton" or "Mace" Design among Aboriginal Artifacts. *Tennessee Archaeologist* 4(1 and 2):1-13.

Garraty, John A., and Peter Gay (editors)
1986 *The Columbia History of the World.* Harper & Row, New York.

Garrett, John
1988 Status, the Warrior Class, and Artificial Cranial Deformatiuon. In *The King Site: Continuity and Contact in Sixteenth-Century Georgia,* edited by Robert L. Blakely, pp. 35-46. The University of Georgia Press, Athens.

Gehring, Charles T., and William A. Starna (editors)
1988 *A Journey into Mohawk and Oneida Country, 1634-1635: The Journal of Harmen Meyndertsz van den Bogaert.* Syracuse University Press, Syracuse, New York.

Genheimer, Robert A.
1994 Bus Tour Fact Sheet. Prepared for field trip associated with Cultures Before Contact: A Conference on the Late Prehistory of the Ohio Region. Ohio Archaeological Council, Cincinnati.

Gersch, H. Kae-Brangwyn, David Pollack, Cheryl A. Munson, A. Gwynn Henderson, and J. D. Robertson
1996 Caborn-Welborn Textiles. Poster presented at the Society for American Archaeology annual meeting, New Orleans.

Gibbon, Guy E. (editor)
1982 *Oneota Studies.* Publications in Anthropology, No. 1. University of Minnesota, Minneapolis.

Gibbon, Guy E.
1972 Cultural Dynamics and the Development of the Oneota Lifeway in Wisconson. *American Antiquity* 37(2):166-85.
1986 The Mississippian Tradition: Oneota Culture. *The Wisconsin Archaeologist* 67(3-4):315-37.
1994 Northwestern Oneota. Paper presented at the conference, "Oneota Archaeology: Past, Present, and Future," Iowa City, Iowa.
1995 Oneota at the Periphery: Trade, Political Power, and Ethnicity in Northern Minnesota and on the Northeastern Plains in the Late Prehistoric Period. In *Oneota Archaeology: Past, Present, and Future,* edited by William Green, pp. 175-99. Office of the State Archaeologist Report 20. The University of Iowa, Iowa City.

Giesen, Myra J.
1992 Late Prehistoric Populations in the Ohio Area: Biological Affinities and Stress Indicators. Ph.D. dissertation, The Ohio State University, Columbus.

Glass, Sherman A.
n.d. *Return to Fox Fields—The Mason County, Kentucky, Ft. Ancient Site.*

Glotzhober, Robert C., and Bradley T. Lepper
1994 *Serpent Mound: Ohio's Enigmatic Effigy Mound.* Ohio Historical Society, Columbus.

Glowacki, Donna, Chris Turnbow, and Ronald Fields
1993 New Perspectives on the Fort Ancient Ceramics of the Madisonville Site, Southwestern Ohio. Paper presented at the 58th Annual Meeting of the Society for American Archaeology, St. Louis.

Goad, Sharon I.
1978 *Exchange Networks in the Prehistoric Southeastern United States.* Ph.D. dissertation, University of Georgia. U.M.I. Dissertation Information Service, Ann Arbor.
1980 Patterns of Late Archaic Exchange. *Tennessee Anthropologist* 5:1-16.

Goad, Sharon I., and J. Noakes
1978 Prehistoric Copper Artifacts in the Eastern United States. In *Archaeological Chemistry II,* edited by G. F. Carter, pp. 335-46. American Chemical Society, Washington, D.C.

Goldstein, Lynne G.
1976 *Spatial Structure and Social Organization: Regional Manifestations of Mississippian Society.* Ph. D. dissertation, Northwestern, Evanston, Illinois.
1980 *Mississippian Mortuary Practices: A Case Study of Two Cemeteries in the Lower Illinois Valley.* Northwestern University Archeological Program, Evanston, Illinois.
1981 One-dimensional Archaeology and Multi-dimensional People: Spatial Organisation and Mortuary Analysis. In *The Archaeology of Death,* edited by Robert Chapman, Ian Kinnes, and Klavs Randsborg, pp. 53-70. Cambridge University Press, Cambridge.

1995 Landscapes and Mortuary Practices: A Case for Regional Perspectives. In *Regional Approaches to Mortuary Analysis,* edited by Lane A. Beck, pp. 101-21. Plenum, New York.

Good, Mary E.
1972 *Guebert Site: An Eighteenth Century, Historic Kaskaskia Indian Village in Randolph County, Illinois.* Central States Archaeological Societies.

Goodenough, Ward H.
1969 Rethinking "Status" and "Role": Toward a General Model of the Cultural Organization of Social Relationships in Cognitive Anthropology. In *The Relevance of Models for Social Anthropology,* edited by M. Banton, pp. 1-24. Holt, Reinhart and Winston, New York.

Goodman, Alan H., Debra L. Martin, and George J. Armelagos
1984 Indications of Stress from Bone and Teeth. In *Paleopathology at the Origins of Agriculture,* edited by M. N. Cohen and G. J. Armelagos, pp. 13-49. Academic Press, New York.

Goss, Arthur F.
1988 Astronomical Alignments at the Incinerator Site. In *A History of 17 Years of Excavation and Research: A Chronicle of 12th Century Human Values and the Built Environment,* edited by James M. Heilman, Malinda C. Lilias, and Christopher A. Turnbow, pp. 314-34. Dayton Museum of Natural History, Dayton, Ohio.

Gramly, R. Michael
1977 Deerskins and Hunting Territories: Competition for a Scarce Resource of the Northeastern Woodlands. 42:601-5.
1988 Conflict and Defense in the Eastern Woodlands. In *Interpretations of Culture Change in the Eastern Woodlands During the Late Woodland Period,* edited by R. W. Yerkes, pp. 86-97. Occasional Papers in Anthropology No. 3. Department of Anthropology, Ohio State University, Columbus.

Grantham, Larry
1993 The Illini Village of the Marquette and Jolliet Voyage of 1673. *Missouri Archaeologist* 54:1-20.

Graybill, Jeffrey R.
1980 Marietta Works, Ohio, and the Eastern Periphery of Fort Ancient. *Pennsylvania Archaeologist* 50(1-2):51-60.
1981 *The Eastern Periphery of Fort Ancient (A.D. 1050-1650): A Diachronic Approach to Settlement Variability.* Ph.D. Dissertation, University of Washington.
1986 Fort Ancient-East: Origins, Change, and External Correlations. Paper presented at the Midwestern Archaeological Conference, Columbus, Ohio.
1987 Fort Ancient-Madisonville Horizon: Protohistoric Archeology in the Middle Ohio Valley. Paper presented at the Third Annual Uplands Archaeology in the East Symposium, Harrisonburg, West Virginia.

Green, Thomas J., and Cheryl A. Munson
1978 Mississippian Settlement Pattern in Southwestern Indiana. In *Mississippian Settlement Patterns,* edited by Bruce D. Smith, pp. 293-330. Academic Press, New York.

Green, William
1993 Examining Protohistoric Depopulation in the Upper Midwest. *The Wisconsin Archeologist* 74(1-4):290-323.

Greenman, Emerson F.
1935 Excavation of the Reeve Village Site, Lake County, Ohio. *Ohio Archaeological and Historical Quarterly* 44(1):2-64.
1937 Two Prehistoric Villages near Cleveland, Ohio. *Ohio Archaeological and Historical Quarterly* 46(4):305-66.

Griffin, James B.
1937 The Chronological Position and Ethnological Relationships of the Fort Ancient Aspect. *American Antiquity* 2(4):273-76.
1942 On the Historic Location of the Tutelo and the Mohetan in the Ohio Valley. *American Anthropologist* 44(2):275-80.
1943 *The Fort Ancient Aspect: Its Cultural and Chronological Position in Mississippi Valley Archaeology.* University of Michigan Press, Ann Arbor.
1952 *Archaeology of Eastern United States.* University of Chicago Press, Chicago.
1972 Foreword. In *The Prehistoric People of the Fort Ancient Culture of the Central Ohio Valley,* edited by Louise M. Robbins and Georg K. Neumann, pp. vii-ix. Anthropological Papers 47. University of Michigan Museum of Anthropology, Ann Arbor.
1978 Late Prehistory of the Ohio Valley. In *Handbook of North American Indians: Northeast,* edited by Bruce G. Trigger, pp. 547-59. Smithsonian Institution, Washington, D.C.
1992 Fort Ancient Has No Class: The Absence of an Elite Group in Mississippian Societies in the Central Ohio Valley. In *Lords of the Southeast: Social Inequality and the Native Elites of Southeastern North America,* edited by Alex W. Barker and Timothy R. Pauketat, pp. 53-59. Archaeological Papers No. 3. American Anthropological Association, Washington, D.C.
1993 Cahokia Interaction with Contemporary Southeastern and Eastern Societies. *Midcontinental Journal of Archaeology* 18(1):3-17.

Griffin, John W.
1945 The Pedestal Vessels of the Madisonville Site. *American Antiquity* 10:386-87.

Gruber, Jacob W.
1971 Patterning Death in a Late Prehistoric Village in Pennsylvania. *American Antiquity* 36:64-76.

Guilday, John E.
1971 *Biological and Archaeological Analysis of Bones from a Seventeenth Century Indian Village (46 Pu 31).* Report of Archaeological Investigations No. 4. West Virginia Geological and Economic Survey, Morgantown.

Gundersen, James N.
1982a Comments on the Distribution of Pipestone and Pipestone-bearing Clastics in Kansan Drift, Southeastern Nebraska. *Proceedings of the Nebraska Academy of Science* 92:2.
1982b The Mineralogy of Pipestone Artifacts of the Linwood Site (Historic Pawnee) of East Central Nebraska. *Proceedings of the Nebraska Academy of Science* 92:3.
1993 "Catlinite" and the Spread of the Calumet Ceremony. *American Antiquity* 58(3):560-62.

Hagadorn, Nancy
1991 "Faithful, Knowing, and Prudent:" Andrew Montour as Interpreter and Cultural Broker, 1740-1772. Paper presented at the Conference on Iroquois Research, Rensselaerville, New York.

Hail, Barbara A.
1983 *Hau, Kola! The Plains Indian Collection of the Haffenreffer Museum of Anthropology.* Studies in Anthropology and Material Culture 3. Haffenreffer Museum of Anthropology, Brown University, Bristol.

Hale, John R.
1981 *A Fort Ancient Village at Augusta, Kentucky: Report on Salvage Excavations at Site 15Bk200, May-August 1981.* Granger Associates Inc., Louisville, Kentucky.

Hall, Robert L.
1962 *The Archaeology of Carcajou Point: With an Interpretation of the Development of Oneota Culture in Wisconsin.* University of Wisconsin Press, Madison.
1986 Upper Mississippi and Middle Mississippi Relationships. *The Wisconsin Archaeologist* 67(3-4):365-69.
1987 Calumet Ceremonialism, Mourning Ritual, and Mechanisms of Inter-Tribal Trade. In *Mirror and Metaphor: Material and Social Construction of Reality,* edited by D. W. Ingersoll, Jr., and G. Bronitsky, pp. 29-43. University Press of America, Lanham, Maryland.
1991 Cahokia Identity and Interaction Models of Cahokia Mississippian. In *Cahokia and the Hinterlands: Middle Mississippian Cultures of the Midwest,* edited by Thomas E. Emerson and R. Barry Lewis, pp. 3-34. University of Illinois Press, Urbana.
1993 Red Banks, Oneota, and the Winnebago: Views from a Distant Rock. *The Wisconsin Archeologist* 74(1-4):10-79.
1995 Relating the Big Fish and the Big Stone: Reconsidering the Archaeological Identity and Habitat of the Winnebago in 1634. In *Oneota Archaeology: Past, Present, and Future,* edited by William Green, pp. 19-30. Office of the State Archaeologist Report 20. The University of Iowa, Iowa City.

Hally, David J.
1983 The Interpretive Potential of Pottery from Domestic Contexts. *Midcontinental Journal of Archaeology* 8:163-96.
1988 Archaeology and Settlement Plan of the King Site. In *The King Site: Continuity and Contact in Sixteenth-Century Georgia,* edited by Robert L. Blakely, pp. 3-16. The University of Georgia Press, Athens.
1994a The Chiefdom of Coosa. In *The Forgotten Centuries: Indians and Europeans in the American South, 1521-1704,* edited by Charles Hudson and Carmen Chaves Tesser, pp. 227-53. University of Georgia Press, Athens.
1994b The Spatial Dimension of Mortuary Practices at the King Site. Paper presented at the Southeastern Archaeological Conference, Lexington, Kentucky.
1996 Platform-Mound Construction and the Instability of Mississippian Chiefdoms. In *Political Structure and Change in the Prehistoric Southeastern United States,* edited by John F. Scarry, pp. 92-127. University Press of Florida, Gainesville.

Hally, David J., Marvin T. Smith, and James B. Langford Jr.
1990 The Archaeological Reality of De Soto's Coosa. In *Columbian Consequences, Vol. 2: Archaeological and Historical Perspectives on the Spanish Borderlands East,* edited by David H. Thomas, pp. 121-38. Smithsonian Institution Press, Washington, D.C.

Hamell, George R.
1983 Trading in Metaphors: The Magic of Beads, Another Perspective upon Indian-European Contact in Northeastern North America. In *Proceedings of the 1982 Glass Trade Bead Conference,* edited by Charles F. Hayes III, pp. 5-28. Rochester Museum and Science Center, Rochester.
1986-87 Strawberries, Floating Islands, and Rabbit Captains: Mythical Realities and European Contact in the Northeast during the Sixteenth and Seventeenth Centuries. *Journal of Canadian Studies* 21(4):72-94.
1988 Life's Immortal Shell: Wampum Among the Iroquois (abs.). In *Proceedings of the 1986 Shell Bead Conference,* edited by Charles F. Hayes III and Lynn Ceci, p. 205. Rochester Museum and Science Center, Research Records No. 20, Rochester, New York.
1995 Wampum: White, Bright and Light Things Are Good To Think. In *One Man's Trash Is Another Man's Treasure,* edited by Alexandra van Dongen, pp. 41-51. Museum Boymans-van Beuningen, Rotterdam.

Hamilton, Henry W.
1967 *Tobacco Pipes of the Missouri Indians.* Memoir No. 5. Missouri Archaeological Society, Columbia.

Hancock, R.G.V., L.A. Pavlish, R.M. Farquhar, R. Salloum, W.A. Fox, and G.C. Wilson
1991 Distinguishing European Trade Copper and North-Eastern North American Native Copper. *Archaeometry* 33(1):69-86.

Hanna, Charles A.
1911 *The Wilderness Trail; or, the Ventures and Adventures of the Pennsylvania Traders on the Allegheny Path, with Some New Annals of the Old West, and the Records of Some Strong Men and Some Bad Ones.* G. P. Putnam's Sons, New York.

Hanson, Lee H., Jr.
1963 *The Hardin Village Site, Gp 22, a Late Prehistoric Village in Northeastern Kentucky.* Unpublished Master's thesis, University of Kentucky, Lexington.
1966 *The Hardin Village Site.* Studies in Anthropology 4. University of Kentucky Press, Lexington.
1968 Pottery Types from the Hardin Village Site. *Southeastern Archaeological Conference Bulletin* 10:1-16.
1975 *The Buffalo Site, a Late Seventeenth Century Indian Village Site (46 Pu 31) in Putnam County, West Virginia.* Report of Archaeological Investigations 5. West Virginia Geological Survey, Morgantown.

Hantman, Jeffrey L., and Stephen Plog
1982 The Relationship of Stylistic Similarity to Patterns of Material Exchange. In *Contexts for Prehistoric Exchange,* edited by Jonathon E. Ericson and Timothy K. Earle, pp. 237-63. Academic Press, New York.

Harbottle, Garman
1976 Activation Analysis in Archaeology. In *Radiochemistry 3*, edited by G.W.A. Newton, pp. 33-72. The Chemical Society, London.
1982 Chemical Characterization in Archaeology. In *Contexts for Prehistoric Exchange*, edited by Jonathon E. Ericson and Timothy K. Earle, pp. 13-51. Academic Press, New York.

Harn, Alan D., and Nicholas W. Klobuchar
1991 Inside Morton House 7: An Oneota House from the Central Illinois River Valley. Paper presented at the Midwest Archaeological conference, La Crosse, Wisconsin.

Harper, Brett
1994 Changing Settlement Patterns in the Anderson Phase of Fort Ancient: New Evidence from South Fort Village. Paper presented at Cultures Before Contact: A Conference on the Late Prehistory of the Ohio Region. Ohio Archaeological Council, Cincinnati.

Harper, J. Russell
1956 *Portland Point: Crossroads of New Brunswick History*. History Studies No. 9. New Brunswick Museum, St. John.

Harrison, Julia
1989 "He Heard Something Laugh": Otter Imagery in the Midewiwin. In *Great Lakes Indian Art*, edited by David W. Penney, pp. 82-92. Wayne State University Press and the Detroit Institute of Arts, Detroit.

Harvey, Amy E.
1979 *Oneota Culture in Northwestern Iowa*. Report No. 12. Office of the State Archaeologist, Iowa City.

Harvey, Henry
1855 *History of the Shawnee Indians, from the Year 1681 to 1854, Inclusive*. Ephraim Morgan and Sons, Cincinnati.

Hatch, James W.
1976 *Status in Death: Principles of Ranking in Dallas Culture Mortuary Remains*. Ph. D. dissertation, Pennsylvania State University, College Park.

Hatch, James W., and Patrick S. Willey
1974 Stature and Status in Dallas Society. *Tennessee Archaeologist* 30:107-31.

Hathcock, Roy
1976 *Ancient Indian Pottery of the Mississippi River Valley*. Hurley Press, Camden, Arkansas.

Haviland, William A.
1967 Stature at Tikal, Guatemala: Implications for Ancient Demography and Social Organization. *American Antiquity* 32:316-25.

Hawkins, Rebecca A.
1994 Coming Full Circle: An Overview of the Fort Ancient Circular Village. Paper presented at Cultures Before Contact: A Conference on the Late Prehistory of the Ohio Region. Ohio Archaeological Council, Cincinnati.

Hayes, Charles F., III (editor)
1983 *Proceedings of the 1982 Glass Trade Bead Conference*. Research Records No. 16. Rochester Museum and Science Center, Rochester, New York.

Hayes, Charles F., III
1989 An Introduction to the Shell and Shell Artifact Collection at the Rochester Museum and Science Center. In *Proceedings of the 1986 Shell Bead Conference: Selected Papers*, edited by Charles F. Hayes III, Lynn Ceci, and Connie Cox Bodner, pp. 37-43. Rochester Museum and Science Center, Rochester, New York.

Hayes, Charles F., III (editor)
1991 75th Anniversary Issue: Papers of the Symposium on the Iroquoian Speaking Peoples of the Northeast. *The Bulletin: Journal of the New York State Archaeological Association* 102.

Heidenreich, Conrad E.
1990 History of the St. Lawrence-Great Lakes Area to A.D. 1650. In *The Archaeology of Southern Ontario to A.D. 1650*, edited by Chris J. Ellis and Neal Ferris, pp. 475-92. Ontario Archaeological Society, London, Ontario.
1978 Huron. In *Handbook of North American Indians: Northeast*, edited by Bruce Trigger, pp. 368-88. Smithsonian Institution, Washington, D.C.

Heilman, James M.
1988 Ceramics as Indicators of Social Organization. In *A History of 17 Years of Excavation and Research: A Chronicle of 12th Century Human Values and the Built Environment*, edited by James M. Heilman, Malinda C. Lilias, and Christopher A. Turnbow, pp. 242-60. Dayton Museum of Natural History, Dayton, Ohio.

Heilman, James M., Malinda C. Lilias, and Christopher A. Turnbow (editors)
1988 *A History of 17 Years of Excavation and Research: A Chronicle of 12th Century Human Values and the Built Environment*. Dayton Museum of Natural History, Dayton, Ohio.

Helm, June (editor)
1968 *Essays on the Problem of Tribe: Proceedings of the 1967 Annual Spring Meeting of the American Ethnological Society*. American Ethnological Society, Seattle.

Helms, Mary W.
1988 *Ulysses' Sail: An Ethnographic Odyssey of Power, Knowledge, and Geographical Distance*. Princeton University Press, Princeton, New Jersey.

Hemmings, E. Thomas
1976 Fort Ancient Pipes from the Blennerhassett Island Area. *West Virginia Archaeologist* 25:56-66.
1977 Neale's Landing: An Archaeological Study of a Fort Ancient Settlement on Blennerhassett Island, West Virginia. Draft manuscript on file at the West Virginia Geological and Economic Survey, Morgantown, West Virginia.

Henderson, A. Gwynn (editor)
1992 *Fort Ancient Cultural Dynamics in the Middle Ohio Valley.* Monographs in World Archaeology No. 8. Prehistory Press, Madison, Wisconsin.
1993 *Prehistoric Research at Petersburg, Boone County, Kentucky.* Program for Cultural Resource Assessment Archaeological Report 289. University of Kentucky, Lexington.

Henderson, A. Gwynn, Cynthia E. Jobe, and Christopher A. Turnbow
1986 *Indian Occupation and Use in Northern and Eastern Kentucky during the Contact Period (1540-1795): An Initial Investigation.* Manuscript on file, Kentucky Heritage Council, Frankfort.

Henderson, A. Gwynn, David Pollack, and Christopher A. Turnbow
1992 Chronology and Cultural Patterns. In *Fort Ancient Cultural Dynamics in the Middle Ohio Valley,* edited by A. Gwynn Henderson, pp. 253-79. Monographs in World Archaeology No. 8. Prehistory Press, Madison, Wisconsin.

Henderson, A. Gwynn, and Christopher Turnbow
1987 Fort Ancient Developments in Northeastern Kentucky. In *Current Archaeological Research in Kentucky: Volume I,* edited by David Pollack, pp. 205-23. Kentucky Heritage Council, Frankfort.

Henning, Dale R.
1970 Development and Interrelationships of Oneota Culture in the Lower Missouri River Valley. *Missouri Archaeologist* 32.
1994 Oneota Evolution and Interpretation: A Perspective from Southeast Iowa. Paper presented at the conference Oneota Archaeology: Past, Present, and Future, Iowa City, Iowa.
1995 Oneota Evolution and Interpretation: A Perspective from the Wever Terrace, Southeast Iowa. In *Oneota Archaeology: Past, Present, and Future,* edited by William Green, pp. 65-88. Office of the State Archaeologist Report 20. The University of Iowa, Iowa City.

Herbstritt, James T.
1996 Protohistoric Trade Connections: A Summary of Probable Routes, Known Sites and Hallmark Artifacts. Paper presented at the Eastern States Archaeological Federation annual meeting, Huntington, West Virginia.

Herold, Elaine Bluhm, Patricia J. O'Brien, and David J. Wenner Jr.
1990 Hoxie Farm and Huber: Two Upper Mississippian Archaeological Sites in Cook County, Illinois. In *At the Edge of Prehistory: Huber Phase Archaeology in the Chicago Area,* edited by James A. Brown and Patricia J. O'Brien, pp. 1-119. Center for American Archaeology, Kampsville, Illinois.

Hickerson, Harold
1962 Notes on the Post-Contact Origin of the Midewiwin. *Ethnohistory* 9(4):404-23.
1963 The Sociocultural Significance of Two Chippewa Ceremonials. *American Anthropologist* 65(1):67-85.
1965 The Virginia Deer and Intertribal Buffer Zones in the Upper Mississippi Valley. In *Man, Culture and Animals,* edited by Anthony Leeds and A. P. Vayda, pp. 43-65. American Association for the Advancement of Science, Washington, D.C.
1970 *The Chippewa and Their Neighbors: A Study in Ethnohistory.* Holt, Rinehart and Winston, New York.

Hill, James N.
1977 Systems Theory and the Explanation of Change. In *Explanation of Prehistoric Change,* edited by James N. Hill, pp. 59-103. University of New Mexico Press, Albuquerque.

Hill, James N., and R. K. Evans
1972 A Model for Classification and Typology. In *Models and Archaeology,* edited by D. L. Clarke, pp. 231-73. Methuen, London.

Hirth, Kenneth G.
1978 Interregional Trade and the Formation of Prehistoric Gateway Communities. *American Antiquity* 42:35-45.

Hodder, Ian
1974 Regression Analysis of Some Trade and Marketing Patterns. *World Archaeology* 6:172-89.
1978 Some Effects of Distance on Patterns of Human Interaction. In *The Spatial Organisation of Culture,* edited by Ian Hodder, pp. 155-78. University of Pittsburgh Press, Pittsburgh.
1979 Economic and Social Stress and Material Culture Patterning. *American Antiquity* 44(3):446-54.
1980 Trade and Exchange: Definitions, Identification, and Function. In *Models and Methods in Regional Exchange,* edited by Robert E. Fry, pp. 151-56. Society for American Archaeology, Washington, D.C.
1982 Toward a Contextual Approach to Prehistoric Exchange. In *Contexts for Prehistoric Exchange,* edited by Jonathon E. Ericson and Timothy K. Earle, pp. 199-209. Academic Press, New York.

Hodder, Ian, and Clive Orton
1976 *Spatial Analysis in Archaeology.* Cambridge University Press, Cambridge.

Hodson, Frank R.
1977 Quantifying Hallstatt: Some Initial Results. *American Antiquity* 42(3):394-412.

Hoffman, Michael P.
1993 The Depopulation and Abandonment of Northeastern Arkansas in the Protohistoric Period. In *Archaeology of Eastern North America: Papers in Honor of Stephen Williams,* edited by James B. Stoltman, pp. 261-75. Archaeological Report No. 25. Mississippi Department of Archives and History, Jackson.

Hoffman, Paul
1995 Did Coosa Decline between 1540 and 1560? Paper presented at the Southeastern Archaeological Conference, Knoxville, Tennessee.

Hollinger, R. Eric
1993 *Investigating Oneota Residence through Domestic Architecture.* Master's thesis, University of Missouri-Columbia, Columbia, Missouri.
1995 Residence Patterns and Oneota Cultural Dynamics. In *Oneota Archaeology: Past, Present, and Future,* edited by William Green, pp. 141-74. Office of the State Archaeologist Report 20. The University of Iowa, Iowa City.

Holmes, William F. S.
1994 *Hardin Village: A Northern Kentucky Late Fort Ancient Site's Mortuary Patterns and Social Organization.* Master's thesis. University of Kentucky, Lexington.

Holzapfel, Elaine
1995 Ohio Pipestone. *Ohio Archaeologist* 45(3):4-6.

Holzapfel, Elaine, and Robert N. Converse
1995 War Clubs and War Club Heads From Ohio. *Ohio Archaeologist* 45(4):40-42.

Hooton, Earnest A., and Charles C. Willoughby
1920 *Indian Village Site and Cemetery near Madisonville Ohio.* Papers of the Peabody Museum of American Archaeology and Ethnology, Harvard University, Vol. 8, No. 1. Peabody Museum, Cambridge, Massachusetts.

Howard, James H.
1981 *Shawnee! The Ceremonialism of a Native Indian Tribe and Its Cultural Background.* University of Ohio Press, Athens.

Howell, Nancy
1982 Village Composition Implied by a Paleodemographic Life Table: The Libben Site. *American Journal of Physical Anthropology* 59:263-69.

Howell, Todd L., and Keith W. Kintigh
1996 Archaeological Identification of Kin Groups Using Mortuary and Biological Data: An Example from the American Southwest. *American Antiquity* 61(3):537-54.

Hudson, Charles
1976 *The Southeastern Indians.* University of Tennessee Press, Knoxville.
1990 *The Juan Pardo Expeditions: Exploration of the Carolinas and Tennessee, 1566-1568.* Smithsonian Institution Press, Washington, D.C.

Hudson, Charles , Marvin T. Smith, Chester B. De Pratter, and Emilia Kelley
1989 The Tristan de Luna Expedition, 1559-1561. In *First Encounters: Spanish Explorations in the Caribbean and the United States, 1492-1570,* edited by Jerald T. Milanich and Susan Milbrath, pp. 119-34. University of Florida Press, Gainesville.

Hudson, Charles, and Carmen Chaves Tesser (editors)
1994 *The Forgotten Centuries: Indians and Europeans in the American South, 1521-1704.* University of Georgia Press, Athens.

Humpf, Dorothy A., and James W. Hatch
1994 Susquehannock Demography: A New Perspective on the Contact Period in Pennsylvania. In *Proceedings of the 1992 People to People Conference,* edited by Charles F. Hayes III, Connie C. Bodner, and Lorraine P. Saunders, pp. 65-76. Research Records No. 23. Rochester Museum and Science Center, Rochester, New York.

Hunt, George T.
1960 *The Wars of the Iroquois: A Study in Intertribal Trade Relations.* University of Wisconsin Press, Madison.

Hunter, William A.
1952 Traders on the Ohio, 1730. *Western Pennsylvania Historical Magazine* 35:85-92.
1978 History of the Ohio Valley. In *Handbook of North American Indians: Northeast,* edited by Bruce G. Trigger, pp. 588-93. Smithsonian Institution, Washington, D.C.

Irwin-Williams, Cynthia
1977 A Network Model for the Analysis of Prehistoric Trade. In *Exchange Systems in Prehistory,* edited by Timothy K. Earle and Jonathon E. Ericson, pp. 141-51. Academic Press, New York.

Jablow, Joseph
1994 [1951] *The Cheyenne in Plains Indian Trade Relations, 1795-1840.* University of Nebraska Press, Lincoln.

Jackes, Mary
1992 Paleodemography: Problems and Techniques. In *Skeletal Biology of Past Peoples: Research Methods,* edited by Shelley R. Saunders and M. Anne Katzenberg, pp. 189-224. Wiley-Liss, New York.

Jamieson, J. Bruce
1990 The Archaeology of the St. Lawrence Iroquoians. In *The Archaeology of Southern Ontario to A.D. 1650,* edited by Chris J. Ellis and Neal Ferris, pp. 385-404. Ontario Archaeological Society, London, Ontario.

Jamieson, Susan M.
1992 Regional Interaction and Ontario Iroquois Evolution. *Canadian Journal of Archaeology* 16:70-88.

Jennings, Francis
1975 *The Invasion of America: Indians, Colonialism, and the Cant of Conquest.* University of North Carolina Press, Chapel Hill.
1984 *The Ambiguous Iroquois Empire: The Covenant Chain Confederation of Indian Tribes with English Colonies from Its Beginnings to the Lancaster Treaty of 1744.* W.W. Norton, New York.

Jeske, John A.
1927 The Grand River Mound Group and Camp Site. *Milwaukee Public Museum Bulletin* 3(2):139-214.

Johnson, Allen W., and Timothy K. Earle
1987 *The Evolution of Human Societies: From Foraging Group to Agrarian State.* Stanford University Press, Stanford, California.

Johnson, William C.
1992 The Protohistoric Monongahela and the Case for an Iroquois Connection. Paper presented at the Society for American Archaeology annual meeting, Pittsburgh, Pennsylvania.
1994 The Protohistoric Monongahela and the Case for an Iroquois Connection. In *Societies in Eclipse,* edited by C. Wesley Cowan. Smithsonian Institution, Washington, D.C. In press.

Jolly, Fletcher, III
1969 Evidence of Aboriginal Trade in Late Prehistoric Times. *Journal of Alabama Archaeology* 15(2):41-47.
1973 A Catlinite Disk Pipe and Associated Vessels from Lowland Eastern Arkansas. *The Arkansas Archaeologist* 14(1):1-12.

Jones, B. Calvin
1982 Southern Cult Manifestations at the Lake Jackson Site, Leon County, Florida: Salvage Excavation of Mound 3. *Midcontinental Journal of Archaeology* 7(1):3-44.

Kapp, Kenneth M.
1961-68 Field notes, Rolf Lee site (46Ms51), West Virginia. In possession of Ronald W. Moxley, Sharples, WV.

Karklins, Karlis
1985 Early Amsterdam Trade Beads. *Ornament* 9(2):36-41.

Keesing, Felix M.
1953 *Culture Change*. Stanford Anthropological Series, No. 1. Stanford University, Palo Alto.

Keigwin, Lloyd D.
1996 The Little Ice Age and Medieval Warm Period in the Sargasso Sea. *Science* 274:1504-8.

Keller, Gordon N.
1950 Fort Ancient Manifestations in the Starved Rock Area. *Journal of the Illinois State Archaeological Society* 7(3):18-19.

Kelly, John E.
1991 Cahokia and Its Role as a Gateway Center in Interregional Exchange. In *Cahokia and the Hinterlands: Middle Mississippian Cultures of the Midwest,* edited by Thomas E. Emerson and R. Barry Lewis, pp. 61-80. University of Illinois Press, Urbana.

Kent, Barry C.
1983 The Susquehanna Bead Sequence. In *Proceedings of the 1982 Glass Trade Bead Conference,* edited by Charles F. Hayes III, Nancy Bolger, Karlis Karklins, and Charles F. Wray, pp. 75-81. Research Records No. 16. Rochester Museum and Science Center, Rochester, New York.
1984 *Susquehanna's Indians*. Anthropological Series, No. 6. Pennsylvania Historical and Museum Commission, Harrisburg.

Kent, Barry C., Janet Rice, and Kakuko Ota
1981 A Map of Eighteenth Century Indian Towns in Pennsylvania. *Pennsylvania Archaeologist* 51(4):1-18.

Kenyon, Ian T., and William Fitzgerald
1986 Dutch Glass Beads in the Northeast: An Ontario Perspective. *Man in the Northeast* 32:1-34.

Kenyon, Ian T., and Thomas Kenyon
1983 Comments on Seventeenth Century Glass Trade Beads from Ontario. In *Proceedings of the 1982 Glass Trade Bead Conference,* edited by Charles F. Hayes III, Nancy Bolger, Karlis Karklins, and Charles F. Wray, pp. 59-74. Research Records No. 16. Rochester Museum and Science Center, Rochester, New York.

Kenyon, W. A.
1982 *The Grimsby Site: A Historic Neutral Cemetery.* Royal Ontario Museum, Toronto.

Kidd, Kenneth E.
1949 *The Excavation of Sainte-Marie I.* University of Toronto Press, Toronto.
1953 The Excavation and Historical Identification of a Huron Ossuary. *American Antiquity* 18(4):359-79.
1954 Trade Goods Research Techniques. *American Antiquity* 20(1):1-8.
1983 Problems in Glass Trade Bead Research. In *Proceedings of the 1982 Glass Trade Bead Conference,* edited by Charles F. Hayes III, Nancy Bolger, Karlis Karklins, and Charles F. Wray, pp. 1-4. Research Records No. 16. Rochester Museum and Science Center, Rochester, New York.

Kidd, Kenneth E., and Martha A. Kidd
1983 A Classification System for Glass Beads for the Use of Field Archaeologists. In *Proceedings of the 1982 Glass Trade Bead Conference,* edited by Charles F. Hayes III, Nancy Bolger, Karlis Karklins, and Charles F. Wray, pp. 219-257. Research Records No. 16. Rochester Museum and Science Center, Rochester, New York.

Kidder, Alfred V.
1932 *The Artifacts of Pecos.* Yale University Press for the Phillips Academy, New Haven.

King, Adam
1995 DeSoto's Itaba: Reoccupation of an Ancient Chiefly Capital. Paper presented at the Southeastern Archaeological Conference, Knoxville, Tennessee.

Kintigh, Keith W., and Albert J. Ammerman
1982 Heuristic Approaches to Spatial Analysis in Archaeology. *American Antiquity* 47(1):31-63.

Klepinger, Linda L., Darryl Katz, Marc S. Micozzi, and Laurie Carroll
1990 Evaluation of Cast Methods for Estimating Age from the Os Pubis. *Journal of Forensic Sciences* 37:763-70.

Kneberg, Madeline
1959 Engraved Shell Gorgets and Their Associations. *Tennessee Archaeologist* 15(1):1-39.

Knight, Vernon James, Jr.
1993 Moundville as a Diagrammatic Ceremonial Center. Paper presented at the 58th Annual Meeting of the Society for American Archaeology, St. Louis.
1985 *Tukabatchee: Archaeological Investigations at an Historic Creek Town, Elmore County, Alabama, 1984.* Report of Investigations No. 45, Office of Archaeological Reseach. Alabama State Museum of Natural History, The University of Alabama, Tuscaloosa.
1986 The Institutional Organization of Mississippian Religion. *American Antiquity* 51(4):675-87.
1989 Some Speculations on Mississippian Monsters. In *The Southeastern Ceremonial Complex: Artifacts and Analysis (The Cottonlandia Conference),* edited by Patricia Galloway, pp. 205-10. University of Nebraska Press, Lincoln.
1990 Social Organization and the Evolution of Hierarchy in Southeastern Chiefdoms. *Journal of Anthropological Research* 46(1):1-23.
1993 Moundville as a Diagrammatic Ceremonial Center. Paper presented at the 58th Annual Meeting of the Society for American Archaeology, St. Louis.

Kreisa, Paul P.
1993 Oneota Burial Patterns in Eastern Wisconsin. *Midcontinental Journal of Archaeology* 18(1):33-60.

Kristiansen, Kristian
1984 Ideology and Material Culture: An Archaeological Perspective. In *Marxist Perspectives in Archaeology,* edited by Matthew Spriggs, pp. 72-100. Cambridge University Press, Cambridge.

Kuhn, Robert D.
1985 *Trade and Exchange among the Mohawk-Iroquois: A Trace Element Analysis of Ceramic Smoking Pipes*. Ph. D. dissertation, State University of New York at Albany.
1986 Interaction Patterns in Eastern New York: A Trace Element Analysis of Iroquoian and Algonkian Ceramics. *The Bulletin: Journal of the New York State Archaeological Association* (92):9-21.
1987 Trade and Exchange among the Mohawk-Iroquois: A Trace-Element Analysis. *North American Archaeologist* 8(4):305-16.

Kuhn, Robert D., and Robert E. Funk
1994 Mohawk Interaction Patterns During the Late Sixteenth Century. In *Proceedings of the 1992 People to People Conference*, edited by Charles F. Hayes III, Connie C. Bodner, and Lorraine P. Saunders, pp. 77-84. Research Records No. 23. Rochester Museum and Science Center, Rochester, New York.

Kuttruff, Jenna T.
1988 *Textile Attributes and Production Complexity as Indicators of Caddoan Status Differentiation in the Arkansas Valley and Southern Ozark Regions*. Unpublished Ph.D. dissertation. Ohio State University, Columbus.
1993 Mississippian Period Status Differentiation through Textile Analysis: A Caddoan Example. *American Antiquity* 58(1):1-27.

Laidlaw, George E.
1903 Effigy Pipes in Stone. *Annual Archaeological Report for Ontario for 1902*, pp. 37-57.
1913 Ontario Effigy Pipes in Stone. *Annual Archaeological Report for Ontario for 1913*, pp. 37-67.
1914 Ontario Effigy Pipes in Stone, Third Paper. *Annual Archaeological Report for Ontario for 1914*, pp. 44-76.
1916 Ontario Effigy Pipes in Stone, Fifth Paper. *Annual Archaeological Report for Ontario for 1916*, pp. 63-82.
1924 Effigy Pipes in Stone, Sixth Paper. *Annual Archaeological Report for Ontario for 1924*, pp. 57-80.

Laird, Allison
1989 *A Guide to Native American Artifacts in Iowa Hall*. Office of the State Archaeologist, Iowa City.

Lambert, Brooke A., and James M. Heilman
1988 Stockade Reconstruction. In *A History of 17 Years of Excavation and Research: A Chronicle of 12th Century Human Values and the Built Environment*, edited by James M. Heilman, Malinda C. Lilias, and Christopher A. Turnbow, pp. 1-7. Dayton Museum of Natural History, Dayton, Ohio.

Lane, Rebecca A., and Audrey J. Sublett
1972 Osteology of Social Organization: Residence Pattern. *American Antiquity* 37(2):186-201.

Langdon, Frank W.
1880 Notice of Some Recent Archaeological Discoveries in the Little Miami Valley. In *The North Americans of Antiquity*, edited by John Thomas Short, pp. 523-31. Harper Bros., New York.
1881 The Madisonville Pre-Historic Cemetery: Anthropological Notes. *Journal of the Cincinnati Society of Natural History* 4(3):237-57.

Lankford, George
1984 Saying Hello to the Timucua. *Mid-America Folklore* 12:7-23.
1988 Saying Hello in the Mississippi Valley. *Mid-America Folklore* 16:24-39.

Lapham, Heather A.
1995 *The Analysis of European Glass Trade Beads Recovered from Monongahela Sites in Greene County, Pennsylvania*. Report submitted to The Bead Society of Greater Washington, Washington, D.C.

Larson, Clark S.
1995 Regional Perspectives on Mortuary Analysis. In *Regional Approaches to Mortuary Analysis*, edited by Lane A. Beck, pp. 247-64. Plenum, New York.

Larson, Lewis H., Jr.
1971 Archaeological Implications of Social Stratification at the Etowah Site, Georgia. In *Approaches to the Social Dimensions of Mortuary Practices*, edited by James A. Brown, pp. 39-57. Society for American Archaeology, Washington, D.C.
1972 Functional Considerations of Warfare in the Southeast during the Mississippian Period. *American Antiquity* 37:383-92.
1993 An Examination of the Significance of a Tortoise-Shell Pin from the Etowah Site. In *Archaeology of Eastern North America: Papers in Honor of Stephen Williams*, edited by James B. Stoltman, pp. 169-85. Archaeological Report No. 25. Mississippi Department of Archives and History, Jackson.

Larson, Lewis H., Jr., and A. R. Kelly
1957 Explorations at Etowah, Georgia, 1954-1956. *Archaeology* 10(1):39-48.

Latta, Martha A.
1987 Iroquoian Stemware. *American Antiquity* 52(4):717-24.
1990 The Stem of the Matter: Reply to Ramsden and Fitzgerald. *American Antiquity* 55(1):162-65.
1991 The Captive Bride Syndrome: Iroquoian Behavior or Archaeological Myth? In *The Archaeology of Gender: Proceedings of the 22nd Annual Chacmool Conference*, edited by Dale Walde and Noreen D. Willows, pp. 375-92. Archaeological Association of the University of Calgary, Calgary.

Lawshe, Fred E.
1947 The Metro Site: Diamond Bluff, Pierce County, Wisconsin. *Minnesota Archaeologist* 13(4):74-95.

Lenig, Donald
1965 The Oak Hill Horizon and Its Relation to the Development of Five Nations Iroquois Culture. *Researches and Transactions of the New York State Archaeological Association* 15(1):1-114.

Lennox, Paul A.
1981 The Hamilton Site: A Late Historic Neutral Town. *National Museum of Man, Archaeological Survey of Canada Mercury Series Paper* 103:211-403.

Lennox, Paul A., and William R. Fitzgerald
1990 The Culture History and Archaeology of the Neutral Iroquoians. In *The Archaeology of Southern Ontario to* A.D.

1650, edited by Chris J. Ellis and Neal Ferris, pp. 405-56. Ontario Archaeological Society, London, Ontario.

Le Page du Pratz, Antoine S.
1763 *The History of Louisana.* T. Becket and T.A. de Hondt, London.

Leute, Ulrich
1987 *Archaeometry: An Introduction to Physical Methods in Archaeology and the History of Art.* VCH, Weinheim, Germany.

Levy, Janet E.
1989 Archaeological Perspectives on Death Ritual: Thoughts from Northwest Europe. *Anthropological Quarterly* 62(4):155-61.

Lewis, Thomas M. N.
1934 Kentucky's "Ancient Buried City". *Wisconsin Archaeologist* 13(2):25-31.
1947 News and Comments. *Tennessee Archaeologist* 3(4):64.

Lewis, Thomas M. N., and Madeline D. Kneberg
1946 *Hiwassee Island: An Archaeological Account of Four Tennessee Indian Peoples.* The University of Tennessee Press, Knoxville.

Lewis, Thomas M. N., and Madeline D. Kneberg Lewis
1995 *The Prehistory of the Chickamauga Basin in Tennessee.* The University of Tennessee Press, Knoxville.

Lileas, Malinda
1988 History of the Dayton Museum of Natural History's Involvement with the Incinerator Site. In *A History of 17 Years of Excavation and Research: A Chronicle of 12th Century Human Values and the Built Environment,* edited by James M. Heilman, Malinda C. Lilias, and Christopher A. Turnbow, pp. 36-54. Dayton Museum of Natural History, Dayton, Ohio.

Lindsey, Mrs. E. M.
1964 Cooper Farm Salvage Project. *Journal of Alabama Archaeology* 10(1):22-29.

Linton, Ralph
1936 *The Study of Man.* D. Appleton Century, New York.

Linton, Ralph (editor)
1940 *Acculturation in Seven American Indian Tribes.* D. Appleton-Century, New York.

Litfin, James C., Pamela C. Jackson, and Kent D. Vickery
1993 A Chronological Seriation Approach to Fort Ancient Triangular Arrowpoints in the Central Ohio Valley. Paper presented at the 58th Annual Meeting of the Society for American Archaeology, St. Louis.

Little, Elizabeth A.
1987 Inland Waterways in the Northeast. *Midcontinental Journal of Archaeology* 12(1):55-76.

Little, Keith, and Cailup B. Curran
1981 Site 1Ce308: A Protohistoric Site on the Upper Coosa River in Alabama. *Journal of Alabama Archaeology* 27(2):117-40.

Logan, Michael H., and Douglas A. Schmittou
1995 The Crow Problem: A Test of the Boyd and Richerson Hypothesis. Paper presented at the symposium Expressions of Ethnicity: Evolutionary and Historical Persectives on Plains Indian Art, Knoxville, Tennessee.

Lovejoy, C. Owen
1985 Dental Wear in the Libben Population: Its Functional Pattern and Role in the Determination of Adult Skeletal Age at Death. *American Journal of Physical Anthropology* 68:47-56.

Lovejoy, C. Owen, Richard S. Meindl, Thomas R. Pryzbeck, Thomas S. Barton, Kingsbury G. Heiple, and David Kotting
1977 Paleodemography of the Libben Site, Ottawa County, Ohio. *Science* 198:291-93.

Lovejoy, C. Owen, Richard S. Meindl, Thomas R. Pryzbeck, and Robert P. Mensforth
1985a Chronological Metamorphosis of the Auricular Surface of the Ilium: A New Method for the Determination of Adult Skeletal Age at Death. *American Journal of Physical Anthropology* 68:15-28.

Lovejoy, C. Owen, Richard S. Mendl, Robert P. Mensforth, and Thomas J. Barton
1985b Multifactorial Determination of Skeletal Age at Death: A Method and Blind Tests of Its Accuracy. *American Journal of Physical Anthropology* 68:1-14.

Low, Charles F.
1880 Archaeological Explorations near Madisonville, Ohio. *Journal of the Cincinnati Society of Natural History* 3:40-68, 128-39, 203-20.

Lurie, Nancy O.
1960 Winnebago Protohistory. In *In Culture and History: Essays in Honor of Paul Radin,* edited by Stanley Diamond, pp. 790-808. Columbia University Press, New York.

Lurie, Rochelle
1994 New Insights on the Protohistoric Period in Northeastern Illinois: The New Lenox Site. Paper presented at the joint Southeastern Archaeological Conference–Midwest Archaeological Conference, Lexington, Kentucky.

MacCord, Howard A.
1952 The Susquehannock Indians in West Virginia, 1630-1677. *West Virginia History* 13(4):239-53.

MacCurdy, George G.
1913 Shell Gorgets from Missouri. *American Anthropologist* 15:395-414.
1917a Some Mounds of Eastern Tennessee. *Proceedings of the 19th Annual International Congress of Americanists* 19:59-74.
1917b The Wesleyan University Collection of Antiquities from Tennessee. *Proceedings of the 19th Annual International Congress of Americanists* 19:75-94.

Mackay, Gene
1989 A Selection of Drawings by Gene Mackay. In *Proceedings of the 1986 Shell Bead Conference: Selected Papers,* edited by Charles F. Hayes III, Lynn Ceci, and Connie Cox Bodner, pp. 45-61. Rochester Museum and Science Center, Rochester, New York.

Mainfort, Robert C., Jr.
1979 Indian Social Dynamics in the Period of European Contact: Fletcher Site Cemetery, Bay County, Michigan. *Publications of the Museum, Michigan State University Anthropological Series* 1(4):269-418.
1985 Wealth, Space, and Status in a Historic Indian Cemetery. *American Antiquity* 50(3):555-79.
1996 Late Period Chronology in the Central Mississippi Valley: A Western Tennessee Perspective. *Southeastern Archaeology* 15(2):172-81.

Mairs, Oscar L.
1960 Preliminary Report on Site 46Pu31. *West Virginia Archaeologist* 12:15-16.

Malinowski, Bronislaw
1945 *The Dynamics of Culture Change*. Yale University Press, New Haven.

Mallam, R. C.
1976 *The Iowa Effigy Mound Manifestastion: An Interpretive Model*. Report No. 9. Office of the State Archaeologist, The University of Iowa, Iowa City.

Mandzy, Adrian O.
1992 *History of Cayuga Acculturation: An Examination of the Seventeenth Century Cayuga Iroquois Archaeological Data*. Master's thesis. Michigan State University, East Lansing.
1994 The Results of Interaction: Change in Cayuga Society during the Seventeenth Century. In *Proceedings of the 1992 People to People Conference,* edited by Charles F. Hayes III, Connie C. Bodner, and Lorraine P. Saunders, pp. 133-56. Research Records No. 23. Rochester Museum and Science Center, Rochester, New York.

Manson, Carl P., and Howard A. MacCord
1941 An Historic Iroquois Site near Romney, West Virginia. *West Virginia History* 2:290-93.
1944 Additional Notes on the Herriot Farm Site. *West Virginia History* 5:201-11.

Margry, Pierre
1876-86 *Decouvertes et Etablissements de Francais dans L'ouest et dans le Sud de l'Amerique Septentrionale (1614-1754)*. Paris.

Maslowski, Robert F.
1984 Protohistoric Villages in Southern West Virginia. In *Upland Archaeology in the East, Symposium 2,* edited by Michael B. Barber, pp. 148-65. USDA Forest Service Southern Region, Atlanta, Georgia.
1991 Clover Archaeological Site. Application to U.S. Department of the Interior, National Park Service, for appointment to the National Register of Historic Places.

Mason, Carol I.
1976 Historic Identification and Lake Winnebago Focus Oneota. In *Cultural Continuity and Change,* edited by Charles E. Cleland, pp. 335-48. Academic Press, New York.
1986 The Historic Period in Wisconsin Archaeology. *The Wisconsin Archaeologist* 67(3-4):370-92.

Mason, Ronald J.
1981 *Great Lakes Archaeology*. Academic Press, New York.
1986 *Rock Island: Historical Indian Archaeology in the Northern Lake Michigan Basin*. MCJA Special Paper No. 6. The Kent State University Press, Kent, Ohio.
1993 Oneota and Winnebago Ethnogenesis: An Overview. *The Wisconsin Archaeologist* 74(1-4):347-68.

Mathews, David S.
1988 The Massacre: The Discovery of De Soto in Georgia. In *The King Site: Continuity and Contact in Sixteenth-Century Georgia,* edited by Robert L. Blakely, pp. 101-16. The University of Georgia Press, Athens.

Mathews, Zena P.
1980 Of Man and Beast: The Chronology of Effigy Pipes among Ontario Iroquoians. *Ethnohistory* 27(4):295-307.
1981 Janus and Other Multiple-Image Iroquoian Pipes. *Ontario Archaeology* 35:3-22.

Mauss, Marcel
1957 *The Gift*. Cohen, London.

Mayer-Oakes, William J.
1954 *The Speidel Site (46OH7), Ohio County, West Virginia*. Publication Series No. 2. West Virginia Archaeological Society, Moundsville.
1955 *Prehistory of the Upper Ohio Valley; An Introductory Archeological Study*. Annals of Carnegie Museum, Vol. 34, Anthropological Series, No. 2. Carnegie Museum, Pittsburgh.

McClellan, Catharine
1975 *My Old People Say: An Ethnographic Survey of the Southern Yukon Territory*. National Museum of Canada, Ottawa.

McConnell, Michael N.
1987 Peoples "in Between": The Iroquois and the Ohio Indians, 1720-1768. In *Beyond the Covenant Chain,* edited by Daniel K. Richter and James Merrell, pp. 93-112. Syracuse University Press, Syracuse.

McGuire, Randall H., and Christian E. Downum
1982 A Preliminary Consideration of Desert-Mountain Trade Relations. In *Mogollon Archaeology: Proceedings of the 1980 Mogollon Conference,* edited by Patrick H. Beckett and Kira Silverbird, pp. 111-22. Acoma Books, Ramona, California.

McGuire, Randall H., and Dean J. Saitta
1996 Although They Have Petty Captains, They Obey Them Badly: The Dialectics of Prehispanic Western Pueblo Social Organization. *American Antiquity* 61(2):197-216.

McKenzie, Douglas H.
1973 A Shell Ornament Assemblage of Probable Florida Origin at the Late Woodland Eiden Site, Lorain County, Ohio. *Ohio Archaeologist* 23(1):4-6.

McKern, William C.
1939 The Midwestern Taxonomic Method as an Aid to Archaeological Culture Study. *American Antiquity* 4(4):301-14.
1945 Preliminary Report of the Upper Mississippian Phase in Wisconsin. *Milwaukee Public Museum Bulletin* 16(3):109-285.

McKivergan, David A., Jr.
1995 Balanced Reciprocity and Peer Polity Interaction in the Late Prehistoric Southeastern United States. In *Native American Interactions: Multiscalar Analyes and Interpretations in the Eastern Woodlands,* edited by Michael S. Nassaney and Kenneth E. Sassaman, pp. 229-46. The University of Tennessee Press, Knoxville.

McMichael, Edward V.
1962 Three Seasons Work at the Buffalo Site, Putnam County, West Virginia. *Eastern States Archaeological Federation Bulletin* 25:11-12.
1963 1963 Excavations at the Buffalo Site, 46-Pu-31. *West Virginia Archeologist* 16:13-23.

McWilliams, Richebourg G. (editor)
1953 *Fleur de Lys and Calumet: Being the Penicaut Narrative of French Adventure in Louisiana.* Baton Rouge.

Meindl, Richard S., and C. Owen Lovejoy
1985 Ectocranial Suture Closure: A Revised Method for the Determination of Skeletal Age at Death Based on the Lateral-Anterior Sutures. *American Journal of Physical Anthropology* 68:57-66.

Meindl, Richard S., C. Owen Lovejoy, Robert P. Mensforth, and Lydia Don Carlos
1985a Accuracy and Direction of Error in the Sexing of the Skeleton: Implications for Paleodemography. *American Journal of Physical Anthropology* 68:79-85.

Meindl, Richard S., C. Owen Lovejoy, Robert P. Mensforth, and Robert A. Walker
1985b A Revised Method of Age Determination Using the Os Pubis, with a Review and Tests of Accuracy of Other Current Methods of Pubic Symphyseal Aging. *American Journal of Physical Anthropology* 68:29-45.

Merrell, James H.
1989 *The Indians' New World: Catawbas and Their Neighbors from European Contact through the Era of Removal.* University of North Carolina Press, Chapel Hill.

Merwin, Bruce W.
1911 Madisonville Prehistoric Cemetery Explorations of 1911. Manuscript on file in the Harvard University Peabody Museum Collections Department, Accession File No. 11-10.

Metress, James
1971 *An Osteobiography of the Buffalo Site, Fulton (Putnam) County, West Virginia.* Ph.D. dissertation. Indiana University, Bloomington.

Metz, Charles L.
1878 The Prehistoric Monuments of the Little Miami Valley. *Journal of the Cincinnati Society of Natural History* 1:119-28.
1881 The Prehistoric Monuments of Anderson Township, Hamilton County, Ohio. *Journal of the Cincinnati Society of Natural History* 4:293-305.
1885a *Explorations in the "Hahn Field."* Field Notes on file, Harvard University Peabody Museum, Cambridge, Massachusetts.
1885b *Explorations, Phil Turpin's Farm (Various Parts) Sept.-Nov. 1885, near Newtown, Anderson Township, Ohio.* Field notes on file, Harvard University Peabody Museum, Cambridge, Massachusetts.

Meuser, Gordon F.
1954 Smoking Pipes Found on the Surface in Ohio. *Ohio Archaeologist* 4(1):ii, 1.

Michalik, Laura K, and James A. Brown
1990 Ceramic Artifacts. In *At the Edge of Prehistory: Huber Phase Archaeology in the Chicago Area,* edited by James A. Brown and Patricia J. O'Brien, pp. 199-217. Center for American Archaeology, Kampsville, Illinois.

Milanich, Jerald T.
1996 Laboring in the Fields of the Lord. *Archaeology* 49(1):60-67.

Milanich, Jerald T., and Susan Milbrath
1989 *First Encounters: Spanish Explorations in the Caribbean and the United States, 1492-1570.* University of Florida Press, Gainesville.

Miller, Christopher L., and George R. Hamell
1986 A New Perspective on Indian-White Contact: Cultural Symbols and Colonial Trade. *The Journal of American History* 73(2):311-28.

Miller, Donald A., and Ken Duerksen
1995 Excavation of a Prehistoric Feature at Big Bone Lick, Boone County, Kentucky. In *Current Archaeological Research in Kentucky: Volume Three,* edited by John F. Doershuk, Christopher A. Bergman, and David Pollack, pp. 137-59. Kentucky Heritage Council, Frankfort.

Miller, Henry M., Dennis J. Pogue, and Michael A. Smolek
1983 Beads from the Seventeenth Century Chesapeake. In *Proceedings of the 1982 Glass Trade Bead Conference,* edited by Charles F. Hayes III, Nancy Bolger, Karlis Karklins, and Charles F. Wray, pp. 127-44. Research Records No. 16. Rochester Museum and Science Center, Rochester, New York.

Mills, William C.
1904 Explorations of the Gartner Mound and Village Site. In *Certain Mounds and Village Sites in Ohio,* vol. 1, pt. 2, pp. 1-65. Fred J. Heer, Columbus.
1906 Explorations of the Baum Village Site. In *Certain Mounds and Village Sites in Ohio,* vol. 1, pt. 3, pp. 1-96. Fred J. Heer, Columbus.
1907 The Explorations of the Edwin Harness Mound. *Ohio Archaeological and Historical Quarterly* 16:113-93.
1917 Exploration of the Feurt Mounds and Village Site. *Ohio Archaeological and Historical Quarterly* 26(3):305-449.

Milner, George R.
1980 Epidemic Disease in the Postcontact Southeast: A Reappraisal. *Midcontinental Journal of Archaeology* 5:39-56.
1984 Social and Temporal Implications of Variation among American Bottom Mississippian Cemeteries. *American Antiquity* 49(3):468-88.
1995 An Osteological Perspective on Prehistoric Warfare. In *Regional Approaches to Mortuary Analysis,* edited by Lane A. Beck, pp. 221-44. Plenum, New York.

Milner, George R., David G. Anderson, and Marvin T. Smith
1992 The Distribution of Eastern Woodlands Peoples at the Prehistoric and Historic Interface. Paper presented at the Annual Meeting of the Society for American Archaeology, Pittsburgh.

Milner, George R, Eve Anderson, and Virginia Smith
1991 Warfare in Late Prehistoric West-Central Illinois. *American Antiquity* 56(4):581-603.

Milner, George R., Thomas E. Emerson, Mark W. Mehrer, Joyce A. Williams, and Duane Esarey
1984 Mississippian and Oneota Period. In *American Bottom Archaeology,* edited by James W. Porter, pp. 158-86. University of Illinois Press, Urbana.

Milner, George R., and Virginia G. Smith
1990 Oneota Human Skeletal Remains. In *Archaeological Investigations at the Morton Village and Norris Farms 36 Cemetery,* edited by Sharron K. Santure, Alan D. Harn, and Duane Esarey, pp. 111-48. Illinois State Museum Reports of Investigations, No. 45, Springfield.

Mitchem, Jeffrey M., and Bonnie G. McEwan
1988 New Data on Early Bells from Florida. *Southeastern Archaeology* 7(1):39-49.

Moore, Clarence B.
1894 Certain Sand Mounds of the St. John's River, Florida, Pt. II. *Journal of the Academy of Natural Sciences of Philadelphia* 10.
1899 Certain Aboriginal Remains of the Alabama River. *Journal of the Academy of Natural Sciences of Philadelphia* 11:289-337.
1907 Notes on the Ten Thousand Islands, Florida. *Journal of the Academy of Natural Sciences of Philadelphia* 13 (2nd series).
1920 Letter of 9/28/20 to Charles C. Willoughby. Harvard University Archives UAV677.46, Box C.
1996 *The Moundville Expeditions of Clarence Bloomfield Moore.* University of Alabama Press, Tuscaloosa.

Moorehead, Warren K.
1897 Report of Field Work Carried on in the Muskingum, Scioto and Ohio Valleys during the Season of 1896. *Ohio Archaeological and Historical Publications* 5:165-274.
1906 A Narrative of Explorations in New Mexico, Arizona, Indiana, etc.... *Phillips Academy Department of Archaeology Bulletin* 3.

Moreau, J.-F.
1993 INNA Study of "Turquoise" Glass Beads from the Saguenay-Lac Saint-Jean Region. In *Annual Report for the Period July, 1992 to June, 1993,* edited by S Aufreiter, R. G. V. Hancock, and B. Cox, p. 32. University of Toronto Slowpoke Reactor Facility, Toronto.

Morgan, Lewis H.
1959 *The Indian Journals 1859-1862.* University of Michigan Press, Ann Arbor.

Morgan, Richard G., and H. Holmes Ellis
1943 The Fairport Harbor Village Site. *Ohio Archaeological and Historical Quarterly* 52:3-64.

Morrell, L. Ross
1965 *The Woods Island Site in Southeastern Acculturation, 1625-1800.* Notes in Anthropology 11. Florida State University, Tallahassee.

Morris, Ian
1991 The Archaeology of Ancestors: The Saxe/Goldstein Hypothesis Revisited. *Cambridge Archaeological Journal* 1(2):147-69.

Morris, William (editor)
1969 *The American Heritage Dictionary of th English Language.* American Heritage Publishing Company, New York.

Morse, Dan F., and Phyllis A. Morse
1983 *Archaeology of the Central Mississippi Valley.* Academic Press, New York.

Morse, Phyllis A.
1981 Parkin. *Arkansas Archaeological Survey Research Series* 13.

Morton, James
1984 Toward a Late Woodland Taxonomy for the Central Muskingum Valley. *Ohio Archaeologist* 34(1):41-47.
1992a Late Late Prehistoric and Protohistoric Sites in the Upper Ohio Valley. Map.
1992b A Late Woodland/Late Prehistoric Culture Sequence for East Central Ohio.

Morton, James, and Brian DaRe
1996 Toward a Revised Taxonomy and Culture History Scheme for Eastern Ohio Late Prehistoric. *Ohio Archaeologist* 46(4):32-39.

Moxley, Ronald W.
1985 Recent Excavations at the Man Site (46LG5). *West Virginia Archaeologist* 37(1):44-46.
1988a The Orchard Site: A Proto-Historic Fort Ancient Village Site in Mason County, West Virginia. *West Virginia Archaeologist* 40(1):33-41.
1988b The Orchard Site: A Proto-Historic Fort Ancient Village Site in Mason County, West Virginia. *Ohio Archaeologist* 38(3):4-11.
1993 The Rolfe Lee Site. Paper presented at the West Virginia Archaeological Society annual meeting, Huntington.

Moxley, Ronald W., and J. D. Bloemker
1985 The Man Site: A Preliminary Report on a Late Prehistoric Village in Logan County, West Virginia. *West Virginia Archaeologist* 37(2):3-22.

Muller, Jon D.
1966 Archaeological Analysis of Art Style. *Tennessee Archaeologist* 22:25-39.
1989 The Southern Cult. In *The Southeastern Ceremonial Complex: Artifacts and Analysis,* edited by Patricia Galloway, pp. 11-26. University of Nebraska, Lincoln.

Munson, Cheryl A.
1994? Archaeological Survey and Testing of Caborn-Welborn Phase Occupations at the Murphy Site and Its Environs, Posey County, Indiana. Manuscript.

Munson, Cheryl A., Marjorie M. James, and Bret J. Ruby
1989 The 1988 Test Excavations at the Caborn Site, a Protohistoric Mississippian Village in Posey County, Indiana. In *Current Research in Indiana Archaeology and Prehistory, 1987 and 1988,* edited by Christopher Peebles, pp. 41-42. Glenn A. Black Laboratory of Archaeology, Indiana University, Bloomington.

Munson, Cheryl A., and Patrick J. Munson
1969a The Palos Site. *Field Museum of Natural History Bulletin* 40(3):5-6.
1969b Preliminary Report on an Early Historic Site, Cook County, Illinois. *Wisconsin Archaeologist* 50(3):184-88.

Munson, Cheryl A., and David Pollack
1990 Slack Farm: A Protohistoric Caborn-Welborn Phase Settlement in Union County, Kentucky. Manuscript on file, Kentucky Heritage Council, Frankfort.

Murphy, Carl, and Neal Ferris
1990 The Late Woodland Western Basin Tradition in Southwestern Ontario. In *The Archaeology of Southern Ontario to A.D. 1650,* edited by Chris J. Ellis and Neal Ferris, pp. 189-278. Ontario Archaeological Society, London, Ontario.

Murphy, James L.
1971 The Fairport Harbor Site, (33-La-5), Lake County, Ohio. *Pennsylvania Archaeologist* 41(3):26-43.
1974 Pedestal Vessels in the Eastern United States. *American Archaeologist* 1(1):42-45.
1996 Comments on the Composition of Catlinite and Ohio Pipestone. *Ohio Archaeologist* 46(1):10-11.

Myer, William E.
1928 Indian Trails of the Southeast. *Bureau of American Ethnology Annual Report* 42:727-857.

Nass, John P. , Jr.
1987 *Use-Wear Analysis and Household Archaeology: A Study of the Activity Structure of the Incinerator Site, an Anderson Phase Fort Ancient Community in Southwestern Ohio.* Ph.D. dissertation, Ohio State University, Columbus.
1988 Fort Ancient Agricultural Systems and Settlement: A View from Southwestern Ohio. *North American Archaeologist* 9(4):319-47.
1989 Household Archaeology and Functional Analysis as Procedures for Studying Fort Ancient Communities in the Ohio Valley. *Pennsylvania Archaeologist* 59(1):1-13.

Nass, John P., Jr., and Richard W. Yerkes
1995 Social Differentiation in Mississippian and Fort Ancient Societies. In *Mississippian Communities and Households,* edited by J. Daniel Rogers and Bruce D. Smith, pp. 58-80. The University of Alabama Press, Tuscaloosa.

Neitzel, Jill E.
1995 Elite Styles in Hierarchically Organized Societies: The Chacoan Regional System. In *Style, Society, and Person: Archaeological and Ethnological Perspectives,* edited by Christopher Carr and Jill E. Neitzel, pp. 393-417. Plenum Press, New York.

Nickerson, W. B.
1885 Log Book of Archaeological Notes of Hamilton County, 1885 (2 vols.). Manuscripts in the collection of the Cincinnati Historical Society, MSS/M596/RM, Box 4, Volume 9 and Folder 7.

Niemczycki, Mary Ann
1984 *The Origin and Development of the Seneca and Cayuga Tribes of New York State.* Research Records No. 17. Rochester Museum and Science Center, Rochester, New York.

Niquette, Charles M., and Jonathan P. Kerr
1993 Late Woodland Archaeology at the Parkline Site, Putnam County, West Virginia. *West Virginia Archaeologist* 45(1 & 2):42-59.

Noble, William C.
1992 Neutral Iroquois Smoking Pipes. In *Proceedings of the 1989 Smoking Pipe Conference,* edited by Charles F. Hayes III, Connie C. Bodner, and Martha L. Sempowski, pp. 41-49. Research Records No. 22. Rochester Museum and Science Center, Rochester, New York.

Noel-Hume, Ivor
1982 *Martin's Hundred.* Random House, New York.

Nolan, David J., and Lawrence A. Conrad
1993 Oneota Occupations along the Mississippi Valley in West Central Illinois. Paper presented at the Midwest Archaeological Conference, Milwaukee.

O'Brien, Michael J.
1994 *Cat Monsters and Head Pots: The Archaeology of Missouri's Pemiscot Bayou.* University of Missouri Press, Columbia.

Oehler, Charles M.
1950 *Turpin Indians: A Report on the Findings of the Cincinnati Museum of Natural History's Archaeological Exploration of the Turpin Site, Hamilton County, Ohio, 1946 to 1949.* Popular Publication Series, No. 1. Cincinnati Museum of Natural History, Cincinnati.
1973 Turpin Indians. *Journal of the Cincinnati Museum of Natural History* 23(2).

O'Gorman, Jodie A., and Holly Halverson
1993 Patterns of Oneota Mortuary Behavior at the La Crosse Locality, Wisconsin. Paper presented at the Midwest Archaeological Conference, Milwaukee.

Olafson, Sigfus
1960 Gabriel Arthur and the Fort Ancient People. *The West Virginia Archeologist* 12:32-42.

Orr, Kenneth G.
1949 The Historic Upper Mississippian Phase in Northern Illinois: LaSalle County Excavations, 1947. *Proceedings of the Fifth Plains Conference for Archaeology, Notebook No.* 1:100-105.

Orser, Charles E., Jr.
1980 *An Archaeological and Historical Socioeconomic Analysis of Arikara Mortuary Practices.* Ph.D. dissertation, Southern Illinois University-Carbondale.

Orton, C. R., and F. R. Hodson

1981 Rank and Class: Interpreting the Evidence from Prehistoric Cemeteries. In *Mortality and Immortality: The Anthropology and Archaeology of Death,* edited by Sarah C. Humphreys and Helen King, pp. 103-15. Academic Press, New York.

Osborne, Chris

1996 A Bird Effigy Pipe from Mercer County, Pennsylvania. *Ohio Archaeologist* 46(1):30-31.

O'Shea, John M.

1981 Social Configurations and the Archaeological Study of Mortuary Practices: A Case Study. In *The Archaeology of Death,* edited by Robert Chapman, Ian Kinnes, and Klavs Randsborg, pp. 39-52. Cambridge University Press, Cambridge.

1984 *Mortuary Variability: An Archaeological Investigation.* Academic Press, Orlando.

1985 Cluster Analysis and Mortuary Patterning: an Experimental Assessment. In *To Pattern the Past,* edited by Albertus Voorips and S. Loving, pp. 91-110. PACT 11.

1988 Social Organization and Mortuary Behavior in the Late Woodland Period in Michigan. In *Interpretations of Culture Change in the Eastern Woodlands during the Late Woodland Period,* edited by R. Yerkes, pp. 67-84. Ohio State University, Columbus.

Overstreet, David F.

1978 Oneota Settlement Patterns in Eastern Wisconsin: Some Considerations of Time and Space. In *Mississippian Settlement Patterns,* edited by Bruce D. Smith, pp. 21-52. Academic Press, New York.

1995 The Eastern Wisconsin Oneota Regional Continuity. In *Oneota Archaeology: Past, Present, and Future,* edited by William Green, pp. 33-64. Office of the State Archaeologist Report 20. The University of Iowa, Iowa City.

Pader, Ellen-Jane

1982 *Symbolism, Social Relations and the Interpretation of Mortuary Remains.* BAR International Series, No. 130. British Archaeological Reports, Oxford.

Pailes, Richard A., and Joseph W. Whitecotton

1979 The Greater Southwest and the Mesoamerican "World System": An Exploratory Model of Frontier Relationships. In *The Frontier: Comparative Studies,* vol. 2, edited by W. Savage, Jr., and S. Thompson, pp. 105-21. University of Oklahoma Press, Norman.

Paper, Jordan

1988 *Offering Smoke: The Sacred Pipe and Native American Religion.* University of Idaho Press, Moscow.

1992 The Iroquoian and Pan-Indian Sacred Pipes: Comparative Ritual and Symbolism. In *Proceedings of the 1989 Smoking Pipe Conference,* edited by Charles F. Hayes III, Connie C. Bodner, and Martha L. Sempowski, pp. 163-69. Research Records No. 22. Rochester Museum and Science Center, Rochester, New York.

Parker, Arthur C.

1918 A Prehistoric Iroquoian Site on the Reed Farm, Richmond Mills, Ontario County, N.Y. *Researches and Transactions of the New York State Archaeological Association* 1(1):5-41.

1922 The Archaeological History of New York. *New York State Museum Bulletin* 235-36

Parsons, J. R.

1972 Archaeological Settlement Patterns. *Annual Review of Anthropology* 1:127-50.

Pauketat, Timothy R.

1992 The Reign and Ruin of the Lords of Cahokia: A Dialectic of Dominance. In *Lords of the Southeast: Social Inequality and the Native Elites of Southeastern North America,* edited by Alex W. Barker and Timothy R. Pauketat, pp. 31-51. Archaeological Papers No. 3. American Anthropological Association, Washington, D.C.

1994 *The Ascent of Chiefs: Cahokia and Mississippian Politics in Native North America.* University of Alabama Press, Tuscaloosa.

Peebles, Christopher S.

1971 Moundville and Surrounding Sites: Some Structural Considerations of Mortuary Practices II. In *Approaches to the Social Dimensions of Mortuary Practices,* edited by James A. Brown, pp. 68-91. Society for American Archarology, Washington, D.C.

1972 Monothetic-Divisive Analysis of the Moundville Burials: An Initial Report. *Newsletter of Computer Archaeology* 8(2):1-13.

1974 *Moundville: The Organization of a Prehistoric Community and Culture.* Ph.D. dissertation, University of California-Santa Barbara.

1978 Determinants of Settlement Size and Location in the Moundville Phase. In *Mississippian Settlement Patterns,* edited by Bruce D. Smith, pp. 369-416. Academic Press, New York.

1987 The Rise and Fall of the Mississippian in Western Alabama: The Moundville and Summerville Phases, A.D. 1000 to 1600. *Mississippi Archaeology* 22(1):1-31.

Peebles, Christopher S., and Susan M. Kus

1977 Some Archaeological Correlates of Ranked Societies. *American Antiquity* 42(3)::421-48.

Pena, Elizabeth S.

1990 *Wampum Production in New Netherland and Colonial New York: The Historical and Archaeological Context.* Ph.D. dissertation, Boston University, Boston.

Pendergast, James F.

1985 Huron-St. Lawrence Relations in the Terminal Prehistoric Period. *Ontario Archaeology* 44:23-39.

1989 The Significance of Some Shell Excavated on Iroquoian Archaeological Sites in Ontario. In *Proceedings of the 1986 Shell Bead Conference: Selected Papers,* edited by Charles F. Hayes III, Lynn Ceci, and Connie Cox Bodner, pp. 97-111. Rochester Museum and Science Center, Rochester, New York.

1991a The Massawomeck: Raiders and Traders into the Chesapeake Bay in the Seventeenth Century. *American Philosophical Society Transactions* 81(pt. 2).

1991b The St. Lawrence Iroquoians: Their Past, Present, and Immediate Future. *The Bulletin: Journal of the New York State Archaeological Association* (102):47-74.

1992 Some Notes on Ceramic Smoking Pipes from St. Lawrence Iroquoian Archaeological Sites. In *Proceedings of the 1989*

Smoking Pipe Conference, edited by Charles F. Hayes III, Connie C. Bodner, and Martha L. Sempowski, pp. 51-70. Research Records No. 22. Rochester Museum and Science Center, Rochester, New York.

1994 The Introduction of European Goods into the Native Community in the Sixteenth Century. In *Proceedings of the 1992 People to People Conference,* edited by Charles F. Hayes III, Connie C. Bodner, and Lorraine P. Saunders, pp. 7-18. Research Records No. 23. Rochester Museum and Science Center, Rochester, New York.

Peregrine, Peter

1993 An Archaeological Correlate of War. *North American Archaeologist* 14(2):139-51.

Perttula, Timothy K.

1992 *"The Caddo Nation": Archaeological and Ethnohistoric Perspectives.* University of Texas Press, Austin.

Perzigian, Anthony J., Patricia Tench, and Donna J. Braun

1984 Prehistoric Health in the Ohio River Valley. In *Paleopathology at the Origins of Agriculture,* edited by M. N. Cohen and G. J. Armelagos, pp. 347-66. Academic Press, New York.

Phenice, T. W.

1969 A Newly Developed Visual Method of Sexing the Os Pubis. *American Journal of Physical Anthropology* 30:297-301.

Phillips, Philip

1970 *Archaeological Survey in the Lower Yazoo Basin, Mississippi, 1949-1955.* The Peabody Museum, Cambridge, Massachusetts.

Phillips, Philip, and James A. Brown

1978 *Pre-Columbian Shell Engravings from the Craig Mound at Spiro, Oklahoma,* Part 1. Peabody Museum Press, Cambridge, Massachusetts.

1984 *Pre-Columbian Shell Engravings from the Craig Mound at Spiro, Oklahoma,* Part 2. Peabody Museum Press, Cambridge, Massachusetts.

Plog, Fred

1977 Modeling Economic Exchange. In *Exchange Systems in Prehistory,* edited by Timothy K. Earle and Jonathon E. Ericson, pp. 127-40. Academic Press, New York.

Plog, Stephen

1980 Village Autonomy in the American Southwest, An Evaluation of the Evidence. In *Models and Methods in Regional Exchange,* edited by Robert E. Fry, pp. 135-46. Society for American Archaeology, Washington, D.C.

1983 Analysis of Style in Artifacts. *Annual Review of Anthropology* 12:125-42.

1986 *Spatial Organization and Exchange.* Southern Illinois Press, Carbondale.

Polanyi, Karl

1975 Traders and Trade. In *Ancient Civilizations and Trade,* edited by Jeremy A. Sabloff, pp. 133-54. University of New Mexico Press, Albuquerque.

Polhemus, Richard

1985 *The Toqua Site: A Late Mississippian Dallas Phase Town.* University of Tennessee Department of Anthropology Report of Investigations No. 41, TVA Publications in Anthropology No. 44.

Pollack, David, and A. Gwynn Henderson

1984 A Mid-Eighteenth Century Historic Indian Occupation in Greenup County, Kentucky. In *Late Prehistoric Research in Kentucky,* edited by David Pollack, Charles D. Hockensmith, and Thomas N. Sanders, pp. 1-24. Kentucky Heritage Council, Frankfort.

1992 Toward a Model of Fort Ancient Society. In *Fort Ancient Cultural Dynamics in the Middle Ohio Valley,* edited by A. Gwynn Henderson, pp. 281-94. Monographs in World Archaeology No. 8. Prehistory Press, Madison, Wisconsin.

Pollack, David, and Cheryl Ann Munson

1995 Caborn-Welborn Ceramics: Inter-Site Comparisons and Extra-Regional Interaction. Paper presented at the 1994 Southeastern Archaeological Conference, Lexington, Kentucky, and the 1995 Kentucky Heritage Council Archaeology Conference.

Pollack, David, Cheryl Ann Munson, and A. Gwynn Henderson

1996 *Slack Farm and the Caborn-Welborn People.* Education Series No. 1. Kentucky Archaeological Survey, Lexington.

Pollack, David, Mary Lucas Powell, and Audrey Adkins

1987 Preliminary Study of Mortuary Patterns at the Larkin Site, Bourbon County, Kentucky. In *Current Archaeological Research in Kentucky: Volume One,* edited by David Pollack, pp. 188-203. Kentucky Heritage Council, Frankfort.

Potter, Stephen R.

1989 Early English Effects on Virginia Algonquian Exchange and Tribute in the Tidewater Potomac. In *Powhatan's Mantle: Indians in the Colonial Southeast,* edited by Peter H. Wood, Gregory A. Waselkov, and M. Thomas Hatley, pp. 151-72. University of Nebraska Press, Lincoln.

1993 *Commoners, Tribute, and Chiefs: The Development of Algonquian Culture in the Potomac Valley.* University Press of Virginia, Charlottesville.

Powell, Mary L.

1988 *Status and Health in Prehistory: A Case Study of the Moundville Chiefdom.* Smithsonian Institution Press, Washington, D.C.

1992 In the Best of Health? Disease and Trauma Among the Mississippian Elite. In *Lords of the Southeast: Social Inequality and the Native Elites of Southeastern North America,* edited by Alex W. Barker and Timothy R. Pauketat, pp. 81-97. Archaeological Papers No. 3. American Anthropological Association, Washington, D.C.

Pratt, Marjorie K.

1991 The St. Lawrence Iroquois of Northern New York. *The Bulletin: Journal of the New York State Archaeological Association* (102):43-46.

Prentice, Guy

1987 Marine Shells as Wealth Items in Mississippian Societies. *Midcontinental Journal of Archaeology* 122:193-223.

Price, Barbara
1977 Shifts in Production and Organization: A Cluster-Interaction Model. *Current Anthropology* 18:209-13.

Prufer, Olaf
1970 *Blain Village and the Fort Ancient Tradition in Ohio*. Kent State University Press, Kent, Ohio.

Prufer, Olaf H., and Ellen Andors
1967 The Morrison Village Site (33Ro-3): A Terminal Prehistoric Site in Ross County, Ohio. In *Studies in Ohio Archaeology*, edited by Olaf H. Prufer and Douglas H. McKenzie, pp. 187-229. The Press of Western Reserve University, Cleveland.

Pustmueller, A. E.
1950 The Copper Serpent. In *Cahokia Brought to Life*, edited by R. E. Grimm, pp. 13-14. The Greater St. Louis Archaeological Society, St. Louis.

Putnam, Frederic W.
1881 Account of Explorations. *Proceedings of the Boston Society of Natural History for 1881*:216-22.
1882 Madisonville, May 2nd 1882 to May 16. Manuscript on file, Harvard University Peabody Museum Collections Department, Accession File No. 82-35B.
1886 Report of the Curator. *Peabody Museum Annual Report* 18:401-19, 477-502.
1973a Archaeological Explorations at Madisonville and Other Sites in the Little Miami River Valley, Ohio. Sixteenth Annual Report, 1883. In *The Archeological Reports of Frederic Ward Putnam, Selected from the Annual Reports of the Peabody Museum of Archaeology and Ethnology, Harvard University 1875-1903*, edited by Philip Phillips, pp. 197-208. AMS Press, New York.
1973b Archaeological Explorations at Madisonville, Ohio. Fifteenth Annual Report, 1882. In *The Archeological Reports of Frederic Ward Putnam, Selected from the Annual Reports of the Peabody Museum of Archaeology and Ethnology, Harvard University 1875-1903*, edited by Philip Phillips, pp. 185-90. AMS Press, New York.
1973c Archaeological Explorations in Tennessee. Eleventh Annual Report, 1878. In *The Archeological Reports of Frederic Ward Putnam, Selected from the Annual Reports of the Peabody Museum of Archaeology and Ethnology, Harvard University 1875-1903*, edited by Philip Phillips, pp. 37-133. AMS Press, New York.
1973d Notes on Copper Objects from North and South America, Contained in the Collections of the Peabody Museum. Fifteenth Annual Report, 1882. In *The Archeological Reports of Frederic Ward Putnam, Selected from the Annual Reports of the Peabody Museum of Archaeology and Ethnology, Harvard University 1875-1903*, edited by Philip Phillips, pp. 91-134. AMS Press, New York.
1973e Rose Mound. Fourteenth Annual Report, 1881. In *The Archeological Reports of Frederic Ward Putnam, Selected from the Annual Reports of the Peabody Museum of Archaeology and Ethnology, Harvard University 1875-1903*, edited by Philip Phillips, pp. 181-84. AMS Press, New York.

Quimby, George I.
1939 European Trade Articles as Chronological Indicators for the Archaeology of the Historic Period in Michigan. *Papers of the Michigan Academy of Science, Arts, and Letters* 27:25-31.
1960 *Indian Life in the Upper Great Lakes*. University of Chicago Press, Chicago.
1966a The Dumaw Creek Site: A Seventeenth Century Prehistoric Indian Village and Cemetery in Oceana County, Michigan. *Fieldiana: Anthropology* 56(1):1-91.
1966b *Indian Culture and European Trade Goods*. University of Wisconsin Press, Madison.

Quimby, George I, and Alexander Spoehr
1951 Acculturation and Material Culture, I. *Fieldiana: Anthropology* 36(6):107-47.

Raemsch, Carol A.
1991 *A Description and Analysis of Cutmarks Found on Human Skeletal Remains from the Riviere aux Vase Site*. Master's thesis, The University at Albany, State University of New York.
1993 Mechanical Procedures Involved in Bone Dismemberment and Defleshing in Prehistoric Michigan. *Midcontinental Journal of Archaeology* 18(2):217-44.

Rafferty, Janet E.
1974 *The Development of the Fort Ancient Tradition in Northern Kentucky*. Ph.D. dissertation, University of Washington. U.M.I. Dissertation Information Service, Ann Arbor.

Railey, Jimmy A.
1992 Chipped Stone Artifacts. In *Fort Ancient Cultural Dynamics in the Middle Ohio Valley*, edited by A. Gwynn Henderson, pp. 137-69. Monographs in World Archaeology No. 8. Prehistory Press, Madison, Wisconsin.

Ramenofsky, Ann F.
1987 *Vectors of Death: The Archaeology of European Contact*. University of New Mexico Press, Albuquerque.
1990 Loss of Innocence: Explanation of Differential Persistence in the Sixteenth-Century Southeast. In *Columbian Consequences, Volume 2: Archaeological and Historical Perspectives on the Spanish Borderlands East*, edited by David Hurst Thomas, pp. 31-48. Smithsonian Institution, Washington, D.C.

Ramsden, Peter G.
1990a The Hurons: Archaeology and Culture History. In *The Archaeology of Southern Ontario to A.D. 1650*, edited by Chris J. Ellis and Neal Ferris, pp. 385-404. Ontario Archaeological Society, London, Ontario.
1990b Saint Lawrence Iroquoians in the Upper Trent River Valley. *Man in the Northeast* 39:87-95.

Ramsden, Peter G., and William R. Fitzgerald
1990 More (or Less) on Iroquoian Stemware. *American Antiquity* 55(1):159-61.

Randsborg, Klavs
1974 Social Stratification in Early Bronze Age Denmark. *Praehistorische Zeitschrift* 49:38-61.

Rapoport, Amos
1990 Systems of Activities and Systems of Settings. In *Domestic Architecture and the Use of Space: An Interdisciplinary Cross-Cultural Study*, edited by Susan Kent, pp. 9-20. Cambridge University Press, Cambridge.

Rapp, George, Jr.
1985 The Provenance of Artifactual Raw Materials. In *Archaeological Geology*, edited by George Rapp Jr. and John A. Gifford, pp. 353-75. Yale University Press, New Haven.

Rapp, George, Jr., Eiler Henrickson, and James Allert
1990 Native Copper Sources of Artifact Copper in Pre-Columbian North America. In *Archaeological Geology of North America*, edited by N. P. Lasca and J. Donahue, pp. 479-95. Geological Society of America, Boulder, Colorado.

Rathje, William L.
1973 Models for the Mobile Maya: A Variety of Constraints. In *The Explanation of Culture Change: Models in Prehistory*, edited by Colin Renfrew, pp. 731-57. Duckworth, London.

Ray, Arthur J.
1974 *Indians in the Fur Trade: Their Role as Hunters, Trappers and Middlemen in the Lands Southwest of Hudson Bay, 1660-1870*. University of Toronto Press, Toronto.
1978 History and Archaeology of the Northern Fur Trade. *American Antiquity* 43:26-34.

Redfield, Robert , Ralph Linton, and Melville J. Herskovits
1936 A Memorandum on the Study of Acculturation. *American Anthropologist* 38:149-52.

Redmond, Brian G.
1993 The 1991 Excavations at the Clampitt Site (12 Lr 329): An Oliver Phase Village Site in Lawrence County, Indiana. In *Current Research in Indiana Archaeology and Prehistory: 1991-1992. Abstracts of Papers Presented at the Annual Meeting of the Indiana Historical Society, 1991 and 1992*, edited by Brian G. Redmond, pp. 39-42. Research Reports No. 14. Indiana University, Glenn A. Black Laboratory of Archeology, Bloomington.
1994 *The Archaeology of the Clampitt Site (12 Lr 329), an Oliver Phase Village in Lawrence County, Indiana*. Research Report No. 16. Glenn A. Black Laboratory of Archaeology, Indiana University, Bloomington.

Redmond, Brian G., and Robert G. McCullough
1996 *Excavations at the Cox's Woods Site (12 or 1), a Late Prehistoric Oliver Phase Village in the Pioneer Mothers Memorial Forest, Orange County, Indiana*. Research Report No. 17. Glenn A. Black Laboratory of Archaeology, Indiana University, Bloomington.

Reidhead, V. A., and W. F. Limp
1974 The Haag Site (12D19): A Preliminary Report. *Indiana Archaeological Bulletin* 1(1):4-19.

Renfrew, Colin
1969 Trade and Culture Process in European Prehistory. *Current Anthropology* 10:151-69.
1975 Trade as Action at a Distance: Questions of Integration and Communication. In *Ancient Civilizations and Trade*, edited by Jeremy A. Sabloff, pp. 3-59. University of New Mexico Press, Albuquerque.
1976 Megaliths, Territories and Populations. In *Acculturation and Continuity in Atlantic Europe*, edited by S. J. De Laet, pp. 198-220. De Tempel, Brugge.
1977 Models for Exchange and Spatial Distribution. In *Exchange Systems in Prehistory*, edited by Timothy K. Earle and Jonathon E. Ericson, pp. 71-90. Academic Press, New York.
1986 Introduction: Peer Polity Interaction and Socio-Political Change. In *Peer Polity Interaction and Socio-Political Change*, edited by Colin Renfrew and John F. Cherry, pp. 1-18. Cambridge University Press, Cambridge.

Renfrew, Colin, and Cherry, John F. (editors)
1986 *Peer Polity Interaction and Socio-Political Change*. Cambridge University Press, Cambridge.

Renfrew, Colin, J. E. Dixon, and J. R. Cann
1966 Obsidian and Early Culture Contact in the Near East. *Proceedings of the Prehistoric Society* 32:30-72.

Reyman, Jonathan E.
1978 Pochteca Burials at Anasazi Sites? In *Across the Chichimec Sea: Papers in Honor of J. Charles Kelley*, edited by Carroll L. Riley and Basil C. Hedrick, pp. 242-59. University of Southern Illinois Press, Carbondale.

Rice, Prudence
1987 *Pottery Analysis: A Sourcebook*. The University of Chicago Press, Chicago.

Richter, Daniel K.
1983 War and Culture: The Iroquois Experience. *William and Mary Quarterly* 40:528-59
1992 *The Ordeal of the Longhouse: The Peoples of the Iroquois League in the Era of European Colonization*. University of North Carolina Press, Chapel Hill.

Riggs, Rodney E.
1977 *The Turpin Site Fort Ancient Burial Mound and Surrounding Burial Pattern (33 Ha 19): A Biological Comparison Using Non-Metric Traits of the Cranial and Post-Cranial Skeleton*. Master's thesis, University of Cincinnati, Cincinnati.
1986 New Stratigraphic Sequences from the Lower Little Miami Valley. *The West Virginia Archaeologist* 38(2):1-21.
1994 Ceramic Change from the Middle Woodland to the Terminal Fort Ancient in the Lower Little Miami Valley. Manuscript.

Riley, Carroll L.
1978 Pecos and Trade. In *Across the Chichimec Sea: Papers in Honor of J. Charles Kelley*, edited by Carroll L. Riley and Basil C. Hedrick, pp. 53-64. University of Southern Illinois Press, Carbondale.

Riordan, Robert V.
1994 Small but Significant: Diversity at Late Prehistoric Components. Paper presented at Cultures Before Contact: A Conference on the Late Prehistory of the Ohio Region. Ohio Archaeological Council, Cincinnati.

Ritzenthaler, Robert E., and Frederick A. Peterson
1956 *The Mexican Kickapoo Indians*. Publications in Anthropology, No. 2. Milwaukee Public Museum, Milwaukee.

Robbins, Louise M.
1968 *Identification of the Prehistoric Shawnee Indians: The Description of the Population of the Fort Ancient Aspect*. Ph.D. dissertation, Indiana University,

Robbins, Louise M., and Georg K. Neumann
1972 *The Prehistoric People of the Fort Ancient Culture of the Central Ohio Valley.* Anthropological Papers 47. University of Michigan Museum of Anthropology, Ann Arbor.

Robertson, James A.
1984 Chipped Stone and Functional Interpretations: A Fort Ancient Example. *Midcontinental Journal of Archaeology* 9(2):251-67.

Robinson, Paul A., Marc A. Kelley, and Patricia E. Rubertone
1985 Preliminary Biocultural Interpretations from a Seventeenth-Century Narragansett Indian Cemetery in Rhode Island. In *Cultures in Contact: The Impact of European Contacts on Native American Cultural Institutions* A.D. *1000-1800,* edited by William W. Fitzhugh, pp. 107-30. Smithsonian Institution Press, Washington, D.C.

Rogers, J. Daniel
1990 *Objects of Change: The Archaeology and History of Arikara Contact with Europeans.* Smithsonian Institution Press, Washington, D.C.

Rogers, J. Daniel, and Bruce D. Smith (editors)
1995 *Mississippian Communities and Households.* The University of Alabama Press, Tuscaloosa.

Rogers, Rhea J.
1995 Tribes as Heterarchy: A Case Study from the Prehistoric Southeastern United States. In *Heterarchy and the Analysis of Complex Societies,* edited by Robert M. Ehrenreich, Carole L. Crumley, and Janet E. Levy, pp. 7-16. Archaeological Papers No. 6. American Anthropological Association, Washington, D.C.

Romain, William F
1992 More Astronomical Alignments at Hopewell Sites in Ohio. *Ohio Archaeologist* 42(1):38-47.

Rossen, Jack
1992 Botanical Remains. In *Fort Ancient Cultural Dynamics in the Middle Ohio Valley,* edited by A. Gwynn Henderson, pp. 189-208. Monographs in World Archaeology No. 8. Prehistory Press, Madison, Wisconsin.

Rossen, Jack, and Richard B. Edging
1987 East Meets West: Patterns in Kentucky Late Prehistoric Subsistence. In *Current Archaeological Research in Kentucky: Volume One,* edited by David Pollack, pp. 225-34. Kentucky Heritage Council, Frankfort.

Rothschild, Nan A.
1975 *Age and Sex, Status and Role, in Prehistoric Societies of Eastern North America.* Ph. D. dissertation, New York University, New York.
1979 Mortuary Behavior and Social Organization at Indian Knoll and Dickson Mounds. *American Antiquity* 44(4):658-75.

Rountree, Helen C. (editor)
1993a *Powhatan Foreign Relations, 1500-1722.* University Press of Virginia, Charlottesville.

Rountree, Helen C.
1993b The Powhatans and Other Woodland Indians as Travelers. In *Powhatan Foreign Relations, 1500-1722,* edited by Helen C. Rountree, pp. 21-52. University Press of Virginia, Charlottesville.

Rowe, John H.
1962 Worsaae's Low and the Use of Grave Lots for Archaeological Dating. *American Antiquity* 28:129-37.

Rumrill, Donald A.
1991 The Mohawk Glass Trade Bead Chronology: ca. 1560-1785. *Beads: Journal of the Society of Bead Researchers* 3:5-45.

Rutsch, Edward S.
1973 *Smoking Technology of the Aborigines of the Iroquois Area of New York State.* Associated University Presses, Cranbury, New Jersey.

Sahlins, Marshall
1972 *Stone Age Economics.* Aldine-Atherton, Chicago.

Saitta, Dean J.
1983 On the Evolution of "Tribal" Social Networks. *American Antiquity* 48(4):820-24.

Salter, Andrew H.
1977 *Catlinite Calumets: Artifactual Clues to Late Prehistoric and Historic Interactions in Eastern North America.* Honors thesis, Harvard University Department of Anthropology, Cambridge, Massachusetts.

Santure, Sharron K.
1990 Social Conflict. In *Archaeological Investigations at the Morton Village and Norris Farms 36 Cemetery,* edited by Sharron K. Santure, Alan D. Harn, and Duane Esarey, pp. 154-59. Illinois State Museum Reports of Investigations, No. 45, Springfield.

Santure, Sharron K., Alan D. Harn, and Duane Esarey
1990 *Archaeological Investigations at the Morton Village and Norris Farms 36 Cemetery.* Illinois State Museum Reports of Investigations, No. 45, Springfield.

Sasso, Robert F.
1993 La Crosse Region Oneota Adaptation: Changing Late Prehistoric Subsistence and Settlement Patterns in the Upper Mississippi Valley. *The Wisconsin Archeologist* 74(1-4):324-69.

Saunders, Lorraine P.
1994 A Consideration of Local Origins for Epidemic Disease in Certain Native American Populations. In *Proceedings of the 1992 People to People Conference,* edited by Charles F. Hayes III, Connie C. Bodner, and Lorraine P. Saunders, pp. 105-14. Research Records No. 23. Rochester Museum and Science Center, Rochester, New York.

Saunders, Lorraine P., and Martha L. Sempowski
1991 The Seneca Site Sequence and Chronology: The Baby or the Bathwater? *The Bulletin: Journal of the New York State Archaeological Association* (102):13-26.

Saxe, Arthur A.
1970 *Social Dimensions of Mortuary Practices.* Ph.D. dissertation, University of Michigan, Ann Arbor, Michigan.

Saxe, Arthur A., and Patricia Gall
1977 Ecological Determinants of Mortuary Practices: The Tenuan of Malaysia. In *Cultural-Ecological Perspectives on South East Asia,* edited by William Wood, pp. 74-82. Ohio University Center for International Studies, Athens.

Scarry, John F.
1994a The Apalachee Chiefdom: A Mississippian Society on the Fringe of the Mississippian World. In *The Forgotten Centuries: Indians and Europeans in the American South, 1521-1704,* edited by Charles Hudson and Carmen Chaves Tesser, pp. 156-78. University of Georgia Press, Athens.
1994b The Late Prehistoric Southeast. In *The Forgotten Centuries: Indians and Europeans in the American South, 1521-1704,* edited by Charles Hudson and Carmen Chaves Tesser, pp. 17-35. University of Georgia Press, Athens.

Scarry, John F. (editor)
1996 *Political Structure and Change in the Prehistoric Southeastern United States.* University Press of Florida, Gainesville.

Scarry, John F., and Bonnie G.. McEwan
1995 Domestic Architecture in Apalachee Province: Apalachee and Spanish Residential Styles in the Late Prehistoric and Early Historic Period Southeast. *American Antiquity* 60(3):482-95.

Schiffer, Michael B.
1987 *Formation Processes of the Archaeological Record.* University of New Mexico Press, Albuquerque.

Schneider, Jane
1977 Was There a Pre-Capitalist World-System? *Peasant Studies* 6:20-29.

Schnell, Gail S.
1974 *Hotel Plaza: An Early Historic Site with a Long Prehistory.* Reports of Investigations, No. 29. Illinois State Museum, Springfield.

Schoolcraft, Henry R.
1851 *Historical and Statistical Information Respecting the History, Condition, and Prospects of the Indian Tribes of the United States, Pt. 1.* Lippincott, Grambo & Co., Philadelphia.

Schortman, Edward M.
1989 Interregional Interaction in Prehistory: The Need for a New Perspective. *American Antiquity* 54(1):52-65.

Schortman, Edward M., and Patricia A. Urban
1987 Modeling Interregional Interaction in Prehistory. In *Advances in Archaeological Method and Theory, Vol. 11,* edited by Michael B. Schiffer, pp. 37-95. Academic Press, New York.
1992a Current Trends in Interaction Research. In *Resources, Power, and Interregional Interaction,* edited by Edward M. Schortman and Patricia A. Urban, pp. 235-55. Plenum, New York.
1992b The Place of Interaction Studies in Archaeological Thought. In *Resources, Power, and Interregional Interaction,* edited by Edward M. Schortman and Patricia A. Urban, pp. 3-15. Plenum, New York.

Schroedl, Gerald F. (editor)
1986 *Overhill Cherokee Archaeology at Chota-Tanasee.* University of Tennessee Department of Anthropology Report of Investigations 38 and Tennessee Valley Authority Publications in Anthropology 42, Knoxville.

Schurr, Mark R., and Margaret J. Schoeninger
1995 Associations between Agricultural Intensification and Social Complexity: An Example from the Prehistoric Ohio Valley. *Journal of Anthropological Archaeology* 14:315-39.

Sears, William H.
1973 The Sacred and the Secular in Prehistoric Ceramics. In *Variation in Anthropology: Essays in Honor of J. C. McGregor,* edited by D. W. Lathrap, pp. 31-42. Illinois Archaeological Survey, Urbana.

Sempowski, Martha L.
1986 Differential Mortuary Treatment of Seneca Women: Some Social Inferences. *Archaeology of Eastern North America (Journal of the Eastern States Archaeological Federation)* (14):50-57.
1989 Fluctuations Through Time in the Use of Marine Shell at Seneca Iroquois Sites. In *Proceedings of the 1986 Shell Bead Conference: Selected Papers,* edited by Charles F. Hayes III, Lynn Ceci, and Connie Cox Bodner, pp. 81-96. Rochester Museum and Science Center, Rochester, New York.
1991 A Possible Explanation for a Shift in Burial Orientation among the Early Historic Seneca. Paper presented at the Annual Meeting of the Society for American Archaeology, New Orleans.
1994 Early Historic Exchange Between the Seneca and the Susquehannock. In *Proceedings of the 1992 People to People Conference,* edited by Charles F. Hayes III, Connie C. Bodner, and Lorraine P. Saunders, pp. 51-64. Research Records No. 23. Rochester Museum and Science Center, Rochester, New York.

Service, Elman R.
1962 *Primitive Social Organization: An Evolutionary Perspective.* Random House, New York.

Sharer, Robert J, and Wendy Ashmore
1979 *Fundamentals of Archaeology.* Benjamin/Cummings, Menlo Park, California.

Sharp, William E.
1990 Fort Ancient Period. In *The Archaeology of Kentucky: Past Accomplishments and Future Directions,* edited by David Pollack, pp. 467-557. Kentucky Heritage Council, Frankfort.

Shennan, Susan
1975 The Social Organization at Branc. *Antiquity* 49:279-88.
1982 From Minimal to Moderate Ranking. In *Ranking, Resource, and Exchange,* edited by Colin Renfrew and G. Shennan, pp. 27-32. Cambridge University Press, Cambridge.

Shennan, Stephen
1986 Interaction and Change in Third Millennium BC Western and Central Europe. In *Peer Polity Interaction and Socio-Political Change,* edited by Colin Renfrew and John F. Cherry, pp. 137-48. Cambridge University Press, Cambridge.
1988 *Quantifying Archaeology.* Edinburgh University Press, Edinburgh.

Shetrone, Henry C.
1926 The Campbell Island Village Site and the Hine Mound and Village Site. In *Certain Mounds and Village Sites in Ohio,* vol. 4, edited by William C. Mills. F. J. Heer, Columbus.

Shotton, F. W., and G. L. Hendry
1979 The Developing Field of Petrology in Archaeology. *Journal of Archaeological Science* 6:75-84.

Shriver, Phillip
1987 The Miami and the Illinois (Peoria) at the Time of Historic Contact: The Journal of Father Marquette. *Ohio Archaeologist* 37(4):11-17.

Sigstad, John S.
1973 *The Age and Distribution of Catlinite and Red Pipestone.* Ph.D. dissertation, University of Missouri, Columbia.

Skinner, Alanson
1913 Social Life and Ceremonial Bundles of the Menomini Indians. *American Museum of Natural History Anthropological Papers* 9(1):1-179.
1920 Medicine Ceremony of the Menomini, Iowa, and Wahpeton Dakota, with Notes on the Ceremony among the Ponca, Bungi Ojibwa, and Potawatomi. *Museum of the American Indian, Heye Foundation, Indian Notes and Monographs* 4.
1926 An Unusual Canadian Disc Pipe. *Indian Notes* 3:39-41.

Sleen, W. N. R., van der
1963 Bead-Making in Seventeenth-Century Amsterdam. *Archaeology* 16(4):260-63.

Smith, Bruce D.
1978 Variation in Mississippian Settlement Patterns. In *Mississippian Settlement Patterns,* edited by Bruce D. Smith, pp. 479-503. Academic Press, New York.
1986 The Archaeology of the Southeastern United States: From Dalton to de Soto, 10,500-500 B.P. *Advances in World Archaeology* 5:1-92.
1990 Research on the Origins of Mississippian Chiefdoms in Eastern North America. In *The Mississippian Emergence,* edited by Bruce D. Smith, pp. 1-8. Smithsonian Institution Press, Washington, D.C.

Smith, Carol A.
1974 Economics of Marketing Systems: Models from Economic Geography. *Annual Review of Anthropology* 3:167-201.

Smith, D.C., and Frank M. Hodges Jr.
1968 The Rankin Site, Cocke County, Tennessee. *Tennessee Archaeologist* 26(2):36-91.

Smith, Harlan I.
1910 The Prehistoric Ethnology of a Kentucky Site. *Anthropological Papers of the American Museum of Natural History* 6 (part 2).

Smith, Kevin E.
1992 *The Middle Cumberland Region: Missippian Archaeology in North Central Tennessee.* Ph.D. dissertation. University of Tennessee, Nashville.

Smith, Marvin T.
1977 The Chevron Trade Bead in North America. *The Bead Journal* 3(2):15-17.
1983 Chronology from Glass Beads: The Spanish Period in the Southeast, c. A.D. 1513-1670. In *Proceedings of the 1982 Glass Trade Bead Conference,* edited by Charles F. Hayes III, Nancy Bolger, Karlis Karklins, and Charles F. Wray, pp. 147-58. Research Records No. 16. Rochester Museum and Science Center, Rochester, New York.
1987 *Archaeology of Aboriginal Culture Change in the Interior Southeast: Depopulation during the Early Historical Period.* University Presses of Florida, Gainesville.
1992 Glass Beads in the Spanish Trade, with Comments on Central American Assemblages of the Sixteenth Century. Paper presented at the Bead Trade in the Americas Conference, Santa Fe.
1993 Seventeenth Century Aboriginal Settlement on the Coosa River. *Alabama Museum of Natural History Bulletin* 15:63-70.
1994 Aboriginal Depopulation in the Postcontact Southeast. In *The Forgotten Centuries: Indians and Europeans in the American South, 1521-1704,* edited by Charles Hudson and Carmen Chaves Tesser, pp. 257-75. University of Georgia Press, Athens.

Smith, Marvin T., and Mary Elizabeth Good
1982 *Early Sixteenth-Century Glass Beads in the Spanish Colonial Trade.* Cottonlandia Museum, Greenwood, Mississippi.

Smith, Marvin T., and David J. Hally
1992 Chiefly Behavior: Evidence from Sixteenth Century Spanish Accounts. In *Lords of the Southeast: Social Inequality and the Native Elites of Southeastern North America,* edited by Alex W. Barker and Timothy R. Pauketat, pp. 99-109. American Anthropological Association, Washington, D.C.

Smith, Marvin T., and Julie B. Smith
1989 Engraved Shell Masks in North America. *Southeastern Archaeology* 8(1):9-18.

Smith, Michael E.
1992 Braudel's Temporal Rhythms and Chronology Theory in Archaeology. In *Annales, Archaeology, and Ethnohistory,* edited by A. Bernard Knapp, pp. 25-36. Cambridge University Press, Cambridge.

Snider, Duke
1991 Eagle Creek Site, Brown County, Ohio - A Preliminary Assessment and Observation. *Ohio Archaeologist* 41(1):16-21.

Snow, Dean R.
1987 The Effects of War and Conflict on Mohawk Settlement and Demography. Paper presented at the 20th Annual Conference of the Archaeological Association of the University of Calgary.
1994 Iroquoians and Europeans: Disunited Nations in the Early Contact Period. In *Proceedings of the 1992 People to People Conference,* edited by Charles F. Hayes III, Connie C.

Bodner, and Lorraine P. Saunders, pp. 1-5. Research Records No. 23. Rochester Museum and Science Center, Rochester, New York.
1995a Microchronology and Demographic Evidence Relating to the Size of Pre-Columbian North American Indian Populations. *Science* 268:1601-1604.
1995b Migration in Prehistory: The Northern Iroquoian Case. *American Antiquity* 60(1):59-79.
1995c *Mohawk Archaeology*. Institute for Archaeological Studies, Albany.
1996 The Lessons of Northern Iroquoian Demography. Paper presented at the Conference on Integrating Appalachian Highlands Archaeology, Albany, New York.

Snow, Dean R., and Kim M. Lamphear
1988 European Contact and Indian Depopulation in the Northeast: The Timing of the First Epidemics. *Ethnohistory* 35:15-33.

Snow, Dean R., and William A. Starna
1989 Sixteenth-Century Depopulation: A View from the Mohawk Valley. *American Anthropologist* 91:142-49.

South, Stanley
1977 *Method and Theory in Historical Archaeology*. Academic Press, New York.

South, Stanley, Russell K. Skowronek, and Richard E. Johnson
1988 *Spanish Artifacts from Santa Elena*. South Carolina Institute of Archaeology and Anthropology Anthropological Series No. 7. University of South Carolina, Columbia.

Spaulding, Albert C.
1960 The Dimensions of Archaeology. In *Essays in the Science of Culture in Honor of Leslie A. White*, edited by G.E. Dole and Robert L. Carneiro, pp. 437-56. Crowell, New York.
1977 On Growth and Form in Archaeology: Multivariate Analysis. *Journal of Anthropological Research* 33:1-15

Speck, Frank G.
1907 *Ethnology of the Yuchi Indians*. Anthropological Publications, vol. 1, no. 1. University Museum, University of Pennsylvania, Philadelphia.

Spence, Michael W.
1994 Mortuary Programmes of the Early Ontario Iroquoians. *Ontario Archaeology* 58:6-26.

Spence, Michael W., Robert H. Pihl, and Carl R. Murphy
1990 Cultural Complexes of the Early and Middle Woodland Periods. In *The Archaeology of Southern Ontario to A.D. 1650*, edited by Chris J. Ellis and Neal Ferris, pp. 125-70. Ontario Archaeological Society, London, Ontario.

Spicer, Edward H.
1961 Types of Contact and Processes of Change. In *Perspectives in American Indian Culture Change*, edited by Edward H. Spicer, pp. 517-44. University of Chicago Press, Chicago.
1972 Types of Contact and Processes of Change. In *The Emergent Native Americans: A Reader in Culture Contact*, edited by Deward E. Walker Jr., pp. 50-69. Little, Brown, Boston.

Spielmann, Katherine A.
1983 Late Prehistoric Exchange between the Southwest and the Southern Plains. *Plains Anthropologist* 28(102, part 1):257-72.

Spielmann, Katherine A.
1989 Colonists, Hunters, and Farmers: Plains-Pueblo Interaction in the Seventeenth Century. In *Columbian Consequences, vol. 1, Archaeological and Historical Perspectives on the Spanish Borderlands West*, edited by David Hurst Thomas, pp. 101-13. Smithsonian Institution Press, Washington, D.C.
1991 *Farmers, Hunters, and Colonists: Interaction between the Southwest and the Southern Plains*. The University of Arizona Press, Tucson.

Squier, E.G., and E.H. Davis
1848 *Ancient Monuments of the Mississippi Valley...* Smithsonian Contributions to Knowledge, No. 1. Smithsonian Institution, Washington, D.C.

Starna, William A., George R. Hammell, and William L. Butts
1984 Northern Iroquoian Horticulture and Insect Infestation: A Cause for Village Removal. *Ethnohistory* 31(3):197-207.

Starr, S. Frederick
1960 The Archaeology of Hamilton County, Ohio. *The Journal of the Cincinnati Museum of Natural History* 23(1):1-130.

Steckley, John
1990 The Early Map "Novvelle France": A Linguistic Analysis. In *Ontario Archaology*, edited by pp. 16-29. Ontario Archaeological Society, Willowdale, Ontario.

Steinen, Karl T.
1992 Ambushes, Raids, and Palisades: Mississippian Warfare in the Interior Southeast. *Southeastern Archaeology* 11(2):132-39.

Steponaitis, Vincas P.
1978 Location Theory and Complex Chiefdoms: A Mississippian Example. In *Mississippian Settlement Patterns*, edited by Bruce D. Smith, pp. 417-53. Academic Press, New York.
1983 *Ceramics, Chronology, and Community Patterns: An Archaeological Study at Moundville*. Academic Press, New York.
1991 Contrasting Patterns of Mississippian Settlement. In *Chiefdoms: Their Evolutionary Significance*, edited by Timothy Earle, pp. 193-228. Cambridge University Press, Cambridge.

Stewart, Marilyn C.
1973 A Proto-Historic Susquehannock Cemetery near Nichols, Tioga County, New York. *The Bulletin: Journal of the New York State Archaeological Association* (58):1-21.

Stiles, Henry R. (editor)
1906 *Joutel's Journal of LaSalle's Last Voyage, 1684-7*. Joseph McDunough, Albany.

Stoltman, James B. (editor)
1991 *New Perspectives on Cahokia: Views from the Periphery*. Monographs on World Archaeology No. 2. Prehistory Press, Madison, Wisconsin.

Stone, Lyle M., and Donald Chaput
1978 History of the Upper Great Lakes Area. In *Handbook of North American Indians: Northeast*, edited by Bruce G. Trigger, pp. 602-9. Smithsonian Institution, Washington, D.C.

Stothers, David M.
1978 The Western Basin Tradition: Algonquin or Iroquois? *Michigan Archaeologist* 24(1):11-36.
1981 Indian Hills (33WO4), A Protohistoric Assistaeronon Village in the Maumee River Valley of Northwestern Ohio. *Ontario Archaeology* 36:47-56.
1991 Lost in Time: The Forgotten Tribal Groups of Northern Ohio. *Ohio Archaeologist* 41(3):26-27.
1994 The Protohistoric Time Period in the Southwestern Lake Erie Region: European-Derived Trade Material, Population Movement and Cultural Realignment. Paper presented at Cultures Before Contact: A Conference on the Late Prehistory of the Ohio Region. Ohio Archaeological Council, Cincinnati.
1995 The "Michigan Owasco" and the Iroquois Co-Tradition: Late Woodland Conflict, Conquest, and Cultural Realignment in the Western Lower Great Lakes. *Northeast Anthropology* 49:5-41.
in press The Protohistoric Time Period in the Southwestern Lake Erie Region: European-Derived Trade Material, Population Movement and Cultural Realignment. In *Cultures Before Contact: The Late Prehistory of the Ohio Region*, edited by Robert Genheimer. Ohio Archaeological Council, Cincinnati.

Stothers, David M., and Timothy J. Abel
1991 Beads, Brass, and Beaver: Archaeological Reflections of Protohistoric "Fire Nation" Trade and Exchange. *Archaeology of Eastern North America* 19:121-34.

Stothers, David M., James R. Graves, and Susan B. Conway
1984 The Weiser Site: A Sandusky Village in Transition. *The Michigan Archaeologist* 29(4):59-89.

Stothers, David M., James R. Graves, Susan K. Bechtel, and Timothy J. Abel
1994 Current Perspectives on the Late Prehistory of the Western Lake Erie Region: An Alternative to Murphy and Ferris. *Archaeology of Eastern North America* 22:135-96.

Strong, John A.
1989 The Mississippian Bird-Man Theme in Cross-Cultural Perspective. In *The Southeastern Ceremonial Complex: Artifacts and Analysis (The Cottonlandia Conference)*, edited by Patricia Galloway, pp. 211-38. University of Nebraska Press, Lincoln.

Stuiver, Minze, and Paula J. Reimer
1986 A Computer Program for Radiocarbon Age Calibration. *Radiocarbon* 28:1022-30.
1987 *User's Guide to the Programs* CALIB *and* DISPLAY. Quaternary Isotope Laboratory, Quaternary Research Center, University of Washington, Seattle.
1993 Extended ^{14}C Data Base and Revised Calib 3.0 ^{14}C Age Calibration Program. *Radiocarbon* 35(1):215-30.

Sugiyama, Saburo
1992 Rulership, Warfare, and Human Sacrifice at the Ciudadela: An Iconographic Study of Feathered Serpent Representations. In *Art, Ideology, and the City of Teotihuacan*, edited by Janet C. Berlo, pp. 205-30. Dumbarton Oaks Research Library and Collection, Washington, D.C.

Sullivan, Lynne P.
1986 *The Late Mississippian Village: Community and Society of the Mouse Creek Phase in Southeastern Tennessee*. Ph.D. dissertation, University of Wisconsin-Milwaukee, Milwaukee.
1995 Variation in the Tennessee Portion of the Coosa Province. Paper presented at the Southeastern Archaeological Conference, Knoxville, Tennessee.

Sullivan, Lynne P., and Gwenyth A. D. Coffin
1995 Ripley Site Mortuary Customs. In *Reanalyzing the Ripley Site: Earthworks and Late Prehistory on the Lake Erie Plain*, edited by Lynne P. Sullivan, pp. 157-86. New York State Museum Bulletin. State Education Department, Albany.

Sullivan, Lynne P., Sarah W. Neusius, and Phillip D. Neusius
1995 Earthworks and Mortuary Sites on Lake Erie: Believe It or Not at the Ripley Site. *Midcontinental Journal of Archaeology* 20(2):115-42.

Sutherland, Leslie D., and Judy Myers Suchey
1991 Use of the Ventral Arc in Pubic Sex Determination. *Journal of Forensic Sciences* 36:501-11.

Sutton, Richard E.
1995 New Approaches for Identifying Prehistoric Iroquoian Migrations. In *Origins of the People of the Longhouse*, edited by Andre Bekerman and Gary Warrick, pp. 71-85. Proceedings of the 21st Annual Symposium of the Ontario Archaeological Society Inc., North York, Ontario.

Swagerty, William R.
1988 Indian Trade in the Trans-Mississippi West to 1870. In *Handbook of North American Indians, vol. 4, History of Indian-White Relations*, edited by Wilcomb E. Washburn, pp. 351-74. Smithsonian Institution, Washington.
1991 Protohistoric Trade in Western North America: Archaeological and Ethnohistorical Considerations. In *Columbian Consequences, vol. 3, The Spanish Borderlands in Pan-American Perspective*, edited by David Hurst Thomas, pp. 471-99. Smithsonian Institution Press, Washington, D.C.

Swanton, John R.
1897 Field Notebooks, 1897 Excavations, Madisonville Cemetery. Manuscript on file in the Harvard University Peabody Museum Collections Department, Accession File No. 97-38A.
1922 Early History of the Creek Indians and Their Neighbors. *Bureau of American Ethnology Bulletin* 73.
1928 Religious Beliefs and Medical Practices of the Creek Indians. *Annual Report of the Bureau of American Ethnology* 42:473-672.
1930 The Kaskinampo Indians and Their Neighbors. *American Anthropologist* 32(3):405-18.

1943 Siouan Tribes and the Ohio River. *American Anthropologist* 45:49-66.
1946 The Indians of the Southeastern United States. *Bureau of American Ethnology Bulletin* 137.

Swauger, James L.
1974 *Rock Art of the Upper Ohio Valley*. Akademische Druk und Verlagsanstalt, Graz, Austria.

Syms, Leigh
1979 The Devil's Lake-Sourisford Burial Complex on the Northeastern Plains. *Plains Anthropologist* 24(86):283-308.

Tainter, Joseph A.
1973 The Social Correlates of Mortuary Patterning at Kaloko, North Kona, Hawaii. *Archaeology and Physical Anthropology in Oceania* 8:1-11.
1975a *The Archaeological Study of Social Change: Woodland Systems in West-Central Illinois*. Ph.D. dissertation, Northwestern University, Evanston, Illinois.
1975b Social Inference and Mortuary Practices: An Experiment in Numerical Classification. *World Archaeology* 7(1):1-14.
1976 Spatial Organization and Social Patterning in the Kaloko Cemetery, North Kona, Hawaii. *Archaeology and Physical Anthropology in Oceania* 11:91-105.
1977a Modeling Change in Prehistoric Social Systems. In *For Theory Building in Archaeology*, edited by Lewis R. Binford, pp. 327-51. Academic Press, New York.
1977b Woodland Social Change in West-Central Illinois. *Midcontinental Journal of Archaeology* 2(1):67-98.
1978 Mortuary Practices and the Study of Prehistoric Social Systems. In *Advances in Archaeological Method and Theory*, edited by Michael B. Schiffer, pp. 105-41. Academic Press, New York.
1980 Behavior and Status in a Middle Woodland Mortuary Population from the Illinois Valley. *American Antiquity* 45(2):308-13.
1981 Reply to "A Critique of Some Recent North American Mortuary Studies." *American Antiquity* 48(2):416-20.

Tainter, Joseph A., and Ross H. Cordy
1977 An Archaeological Analysis of Social Ranking and Residence Groups in Prehistoric Hawaii. *World Archaeology* 9(1):95-112.

Tankersley, Kenneth B.
1981 A Bison Beamer from the Madisonville Site, Hamilton County, Ohio. *Ohio Archaeologist* 31(4):14.
1985 The Potential for Early-Man Sites at Big Bone Lick, Kentucky. *Tennessee Anthropologist*:10(1):27-49.
1986a Bison Exploitation by Late Fort Ancient Peoples in the Central Ohio River Valley. *North American Archaeologist* 7(4):289-303.
1986b The Geoarchaeology of the Madisonville Site. Paper presented at the Midwest Archaeological Conference, Columbus, Ohio.
1992 Bison and Subsistence Change: The Protohistoric Ohio River Valley and Illinois Valley Connection. In *Research in Economic Anthropology, Supplement 6*, edited by Barry Isaac, pp. 103-30. JAI Press, Greenwich, CT.

Tankersley, Kenneth B., and William R. Adams
1991 Holocene Bison Remains, (*Bison bison*), from Greene County, Indiana. *Proceedings of the Indiana Academy of Science* 99(2):229-36.

Tankersley, Kenneth B., and John Meinhart
1982 Physical and Structural Properties of Ceramic Materials Utilized by a Fort Ancient Group. *Midcontinental Journal of Archaeology* 7:225-43.

Tanner, Helen H.
1987 *Atlas of Great Lakes Indian History*. University of Oklahoma Press, Norman.
1989 The Land and Water Communication Systems of the Southeastern Indians. In *Powhatan's Mantle: Indians in the Colonial Southeast*, edited by Peter H. Wood, Gregory A. Waselkov, and M. Thomas Hatley, pp. 6-20. University of Nebraska Press, Lincoln.

Theler, James L.
1978 *The Vertebrate Faunal Remains from Sand Ridge (33 HA 17): A Stratified Habitation Site in Southwestern Ohio*. Master's thesis, University of Wisconsin, Madison.

Thomas, Cyrus
1894 Report on the Mound Explorations of the Bureau of Ethnology. *Bureau of Ethnology Annual Report for 1890-91* 12:1-742.

Thomas, David Hurst (editor)
1990 *Columbian Consequences, Volume 2: Archaeological and Historical Perspectives on the Spanish Borderlands East*. Smithsonian Institution, Washington, D.C.

Thruston, Gates P.
1890 *The Antiquities of Tennessee and the Adjacent States and the State of Aboriginal Society in the Scale of Civilization Represented by Them*. Robert Clarke, Cincinnati.
1897 *The Antiquities of Tennessee and the Adjacent States and the State of Aboriginal Society in the Scale of Civilization Represented by Them*. 2nd ed. Robert Clarke, Cincinnati.

Thwaites, Reuben G. (editor)
1896-1901 *The Jesuit Relations and Allied Documents; Travel and Explorations of the Jesuit Missionaries in New France, 1610-1791*. Burrows Brothers, Cleveland.

Tooker, Elisabeth
1978 The League of the Iroquois: Its History, Politics, and Ritual. In *Handbook of North American Indians: Northeast*, edited by Bruce G. Trigger, pp. 418-41. Smithsonian Institution, Washington, D.C.

Torrence, Robin
1986 *Production and Exchange of Stone Tools: Prehistoric Obsidian in the Aegean*. Cambridge University Press, Cambridge.

Trigger, Bruce G.
1968 The Determinants of Settlement Patterns. In *Settlement Archaeology*, edited by K. C. Chang, pp. 53-78. National Press, Palo Alto, California.
1971 The Mohawk-Mahican War (1624-1628): The Establishment of a Pattern. *Canadian Historical Review* 52(3):276-86.
1976 *The Children of Aataentsic: A History of the Huron People to 1660*. 2 vols. McGill-Queen's University Press, Montreal.
1978a Early Iroquoian Contacts with Europeans. In *Handbook of North American Indians, vol 13: Northeast*, edited by Bruce G. Trigger, pp. 344-56. Smithsonian Institution, Washington, D.C.

Trigger, Bruce G. (editor)
1978b *Handbook of North American Indians, vol 15: Northeast.* Smithsonian Institution, Washington, D.C.

Trigger, Bruce G.
1986 *Natives and Newcomers: Canada's "Heroic Age" Reconsidered.* McGill-Queen's University Press, Kingston, Ontario.

Trigger, Bruce G., L. Yaffe, M. Diksic, J.-L. Galinier, H. Marshall, and James F. Pendergast
1980 Trace-Element Analysis of Iroquoian Pottery. *Canadian Journal of Archaeology* 4:119-45.

Trowbridge, C. C.
1938 *Meerarmeer Traditions.* Occasional Contributions No. 7. University of Michigan Museum of Anthropology, Ann Arbor.
1939 *Shawnese Traditions: C. C. Trowbridge's Account.* Occasional Contributions from the Museum of Anthropology of the University of Michigan, No. 9. University of Michigan Press, Ann Arbor.

Tuck, James A.
1971 *Onondaga Iroquois Prehistory: A Study in Settlement Archaeology.* Syracuse University Press, Syracuse.
1978 Northern Iroquoian Prehistory. In *Handbook of North American Indians: Northeast,* edited by Bruce G. Trigger, pp. 322-33. Smithsonian Institution, Washington, D.C.

Tukey, John
1977 *Exploratory Data Analysis.* Addison-Wesley, Reading, Massachusetts.

Turgeon, Laurier
1990 Basque-Amerindian Trade in the Saint Lawrence during the Sixteenth Century: New Documents, New Perspectives. *Man in the Northeast* (40):81-87.

Turnbow, Christopher A.
1992 The Fox Farm Site. In *Fort Ancient Cultural Dynamics in the Middle Ohio Valley,* edited by A. Gwynn Henderson, pp. 51-68. Monographs in World Archaeology No. 8. Prehistory Press, Madison, Wisconsin.

Turnbow, Christopher A., and A. Gwynn Henderson
1992 Ceramic Analysis. In *Fort Ancient Cultural Dynamics in the Middle Ohio Valley,* edited by A. Gwynn Henderson, pp. 113-35. Monographs in World Archaeology No. 8. Prehistory Press, Madison, Wisconsin.

Turnbow, Christopher A., and Cynthia Jobe
1984 The Goolman Site: A Late Fort Ancient Winter Encampment in Clark County, Kentucky. In *Late Prehistoric Research in Kentucky,* edited by David Pollack, Charles D. Hockensmith, and Thomas N. Sanders, pp. 25-48. Kentucky Heritage Council, Frankfort.
1990 The Augusta Site (15Bk200). In *Continuity and Change: Fort Ancient Cultural Dynamics in Northeastern Kentucky,* edited by A. Gwynn Henderson, pp. 109-20. Manuscript on file, Kentucky Anthropological Research Facility, Lexington.
1992 The Augusta Site. In *Fort Ancient Cultural Dynamics in the Middle Ohio Valley,* edited by A. Gwynn Henderson, pp. 83-97. Monographs in World Archaeology No. 8. Prehistory Press, Madison, Wisconsin.

Turnbow, Christopher A., Cynthia E. Jobe, Nancy O'Malley, Dee Ann Wymer, Michelle Seme, and Irwin Rovner
1983 *Archaeological Excavations of the Goolman, Devary, and Stone Sites in Clark County, Kentucky.* Archaeological Report No. 78. Department of Anthropology, University of Kentucky, Lexington.

Turnbow, Christopher A., and William E. Sharp
1988 *Muir: An Early Fort Ancient Site in the Inner Bluegrass.* Archaeological Report No. 165. Program for Cultural Resource Assessment, University of Kentucky, Lexington.

Turner, E. Randolph
1985 Socio-Political Organization within the Powhatan Chiefdom and the Effects of European Contact, A.D. 1607-1646. In *Cultures in Contact: The European Impact on Native Cultural Institutions in Eastern North America, A.D. 1000-1800,* edited by William W. Fitzhugh, pp. 193-224. Smithsonian Institution, Washington, D.C.

Turner, Robert L., Jr.
1978 The Tuck Carpenter Site and its Relation to Other Sites within the Titus Focus. *Bulletin of the Texas Archeological Society* 49:1-110.

Ublaker, Douglas H.
1989 *Human Skeletal Remains: Excavation, Analysis, Interpretation.* Tarqaxacum, Washington, D.C.

Ubelaker, Douglas H., and Waldo R. Wedel
1975 Bird Bones, Burials, and Bundles in Plains Archaeology. *American Antiquity* 40(4):444-52.

Ucko, Peter J.
1969 Ethnography and Archaeological Interpretation of Funerary Remains. *World Archaeology* 1:262-81.

Upham, Steadman
1986 Imperialists, Isolationists, World Systems and Political Realities: Perspectives on Mesoamerican -Southwestern Interaction. In *Ripples in the Chichimec Sea: New Considerations of Southwestern-Mesoamerican Interaction,* edited by Frances J. Mathien and Randall H. McGuire, pp. 205-19. Southern Illinois University Press, Carbondale and Edwardsville.

Usner, Daniel H., Jr.
1992 *Indians, Settlers, and Slaves in a Frontier Exchange Economy: The Lower Mississippi Valley Before 1783.* University of North Carolina Press, Chapel Hill.

van der Merwe, Nikolaas J., and J. C. Vogel
1978 ^{13}C Content of Human Collagen as a Measure of Prehistoric Diet in Woodland North America. *Nature* 276:815-16.

Van de Velde, Pieter
1979 The Social Anthropology of a Neolithic Cemetery in the Netherlands. *Current Anthropology* 20(1):37-58.

Vickery, Kent D., and Robert A. Genheimer
1994 Report of Excavations at the Fort Ancient State Line Site, 33Ha58, in the Central Ohio Valley. Paper presented at Cultures Before Contact: A Conference on the Late Prehistory of the Ohio Region. Ohio Archaeological Council, Cincinnati.

Vietzen, Raymond C.
1946 *The Ancient Ohians and Their Neighbors.*
1974 *The Riker Site.* Sugar Creek Valley Chapter of the Archaeological Society of Ohio.

Voegelin, Charles F.
1936 *The Shawnee Female Deity.* Publications in Anthropology, 10. Yale University, New Haven.

Voegelin, Erminie Wheeler
1944 Mortuary Customs of the Shawnee and Other Eastern Tribes. *Indiana Historical Society, Prehistory Research Series* 2(4):225-444.

von Gernet, Alexander D.
1992 Hallucinogens and the Origins of the Iroquoian Pipe/Tobacco/Smoking Complex. In *Proceedings of the 1989 Smoking Pipe Conference,* edited by Charles F. Hayes III, Connie C. Bodner, and Martha L. Sempowski, pp. 171-85. Research Records No. 22. Rochester Museum and Science Center, Rochester, New York.

Wachtel, H. C.
1952 Saga of the Olla. *Ohio Archaeologist* 2(3):9-11.

Wagers, Charlie
1993 The Atkinson Spider. *Central States Archaeological Journal* 40(2):55.

Wagner, Gail E.
1983 Fort Ancient Subsistence: The Botanical Record. *West Virginia Archaeologist* 35(2):27-39.
1984 Fort Ancient Plant Remains from Northern Kentucky. In *Late Prehistoric Research in Kentucky,* edited by David Pollack, Charles D. Hockensmith, and Thomas N. Sanders, pp. 50-66. Kentucky Heritage Council, Frankfort.
1986 The Corn and Cultivated Beans of the Fort Ancient Indians. *Missouri Archaeologist* 47:107-35.
1987 *Uses of Plants by the Fort Ancient Indians.* Ph.D. dissertation, Washington University, U.M.I., Ann Arbor.

Waisberg, L. G.
1977 *The Ottawa: Traders of the Upper Great Lakes 1615-1700.* Master's thesis, McMaster University, Hamilton, Ontario.

Walker, Deward E., Jr. (editor)
1972 *The Emergent Native Americans: A Reader in Culture Contact.* Little, Brown, Boston.

Wallace, Antoinette B.
1993 Southeastern American Indian Body Decoration: Forms and Functions. Master's thesis. Harvard University, Cambridge, Massachusetts.

Wallerstein, Immanuel
1974 *The Modern World-System I.* Academic Press, New York.
1980 *The Modern World-System II.* Academic Press, New York.

Walthall, John A. (editor)
1991 *French Colonial Archaeology: The Illinois Country and the Western Great Lakes.* University of Illinois Press, Urbana.

Walthall, John A., and Thomas E. Emerson (editor)
1992 *Calumet and Fleur-de-Lys: Archaeology of Indian and French Contact in the Midcontinent.* Smithsonian Institution Press, Washington, D.C.

Walthall, John A., F. Terry Norris, and Barbara D. Stafford
1992 Woman Chief's Village: An Illini Winter Hunting Camp. In *Calumet & Fleur-de-Lys: Archaeology of Indian and French Contact in the Midcontinent,* edited by John A. Walthall and Thomas E. Emerson, pp. 129-53. Smithsonian Institution Press, Washington, D.C.

Warren, Robert E.
in press Freshwater Mussels from the Madisonville Site, a Fort Ancient Village in Southwestern Ohio. In *Recent Research at the Madisonville Village Site, Hamilton County, Ohio,* edited by C. Wesley Cowan. Occasional Papers in Anthropology, No. 1. Cincinnati Museum of Natural History, Cincinnati.

Warrick, Gary A.
1990 *A Population History of the Huron-Petun, A.D. 900-1500.* Ph.D. dissertation. McGill University, Montreal.

Waselkov, Gregory
1978 Evolution of Deer Hunting in the Eastern Woodlands. *Midcontinental Journal of Archaeology* 3(1):15-34.
1989 Seventeenth-Century Trade in the Colonial Southeast. *Southeastern Archaeology* 8(2):117-33.
1993 Historic Creek Indian Responses to European Trade and the Rise of Political Factions. In *Ethnohistory and Archaeology: Approaches to Postcontact Change in the Americas,* edited by J. Daniel Rogers and Samuel M. Wilson, pp. 123-31. Plenum Press, New York.
1994 The Macon Trading House and Early European-Indian Contact in the Colonial Southeast. In *Ocmulgee Archaeology 1936-1986,* edited by David J. Hally, pp. 190-96. University of Georgia Press, Athens.
1996 *The Archaeology of French Colonial North America.* Guides to the Archaeological Literature of the Immigrant Experience in America.

Waselkov, Gregory A., and R. Eli Paul
1981 Frontiers and Archaeology. *North American Archaeologist* 2(4):309-29.

Wauchope, Robert
1956 *Seminars in Archaeology: 1955.* Society for American Archaeology Memoir No. 11. Salt Lake City.

Webb, William S.
1927 A Note on Recently Discovered Evidence Throwing Light on the Possible Age of a Kentucky Site. *American Anthropologist* 29:62-68.
1939 An Archaeological Survey of Wheeler Basin on the Tennessee River in Northern Alabama. *Bureau of American Ethnology Bulletin* 122
1955 Comments on the Artifacts Taken from Graves in the Excavation of the Cellar at the Home of Louie Edwards, Augusta, Bracken County, Kentucky. Manuscript on file, Museum of Anthropology, University of Kentucky, Lexington.

Webb, William S., and Charles G. Wilde
1951 *An Archaeological Survey of Guntersville Basin on the Tennessee River in Northern Alabama.* University of Kentucky Press, Lexington.

Wedel, Mildred M.
1959 Oneota Sites on the Upper Iowa River. *Missouri Archaeologist* 21(2-4):1-180.
1981 The Ioway, Oto, and Omaha Indians in 1700. *Journal of the Iowa Archeological Society* 1-13.
1986 Peering at the Ioway Indians through the Mist of Time: 1650-circa 1700. *Journal of the Iowa Archeological Society* 1-74.

Wedel, Waldo R.
1937 The Direct-Historical Approach in Pawnee Archaeology. *Smithsonian Miscellaneous Collections* 97(7):1-21.
1959 An Introduction to Kansas Archaeology. *Bureau of American Ethnology Bulletin* 174.

Weiss, Kenneth M.
1972 *Demographic Models for Anthropology.* Memoirs of the Society for American Archaeology, No. 27,
1976 Demographic Theory and Anthropological Inference. *Annual Review of Anthropology* 5:351-81.

Welch, Paul D.
1991 *Moundville's Economy.* University of Alabama Press, Tuscaloosa.

Welch, Paul D., and C. Margaret Scarry
1995 Status-Related Variation in Foodways in the Moundville Chiefdom. *American Antiquity* 60(3):397-419.

West, George A.
1934 Tobacco, Pipes and Smoking Customs of the American Indians. *Bulletin of the Public Museum of the City of Milwaukee* 17:1-994.

Whallon, Robert, and James A. Brown (editors)
1982 *Essays in Archaeological Typology.* Center for American Archaeology Press, Evanston, Illinois.

Wheelersburg, Robert P.
1992 An Archaeobotanical Study of Fort Ancient Subsistence in Southwestern Ohio: the State Line Site. *Pennsylvania Archaeologist* 62:45-65.

Wheeler-Voegelin, Erminie
1974 Ethnohistory of Indian Use and Occupancy in Ohio and Indiana Prior to 1795. In *Indians of Ohio and Indiana Prior to 1795,* edited by Helen Hornbeck Tanner and Erminie Wheeler-Voegelin. Garland, New York.

White, Bruce M.
1994 Encounters with Spirits: Ojibwa and Dakota Theories about the French and Their Merchandise. *Ethnohistory* 41(3):369-405.

White, John R.
1975 Historic Contact Sites as Laboratories for the Study of Culture Change. *The Conference on Historic Site Archaeology Papers 1974* 9:153-63.

White, Karli, and Bonnie Styles
1993 Preliminary Analysis of Faunal Remains from the Madisonville Site (33HA36). Paper presented at the Society for American Archaeology Annual Meeting, St. Louis.

White, Marian E.
1976 Late Woodland Archaeology in the Niagara Frontier of New York and Ontario. In *The Late Prehistory of the Lake Erie Drainage Basin: A 1972 Symposium Revised,* edited by David S. Brose, pp. 110-36. Cleveland Museum of Natural History, Cleveland.
1978 Erie. In *Handbook of North American Indians, vol 13: Northeast,* edited by Bruce G. Trigger, pp. 412-17. Smithsonian Institution, Washington, D.C.

White, Richard
1991 *The Middle Ground: Indians, Empires, and Republics in the Great Lakes Region, 1650-1815.* Cambridge University Press, Cambridge.

White, Tim D.
1991 *Human Osteology.* Academic Press, San Diego.

Whitman, Janice K.
1975 *An Analysis of the Ceramics from the Riker Site, Tuscarawas County, Ohio.* Master's thesis. Kent State University, Kent, Ohio.

Whittlesey, Stephanie M.
1978 *Status and Death at Grasshopper Pueblo: Experiments toward an Archaeological Theory of Correlates.* Ph.D. dissertation, University of Arizona. U.M.I. Dissertation Services, Ann Arbor.

Widmer, Randolph J.
1994 The Structure of Southeastern Chiefdoms. In *The Forgotten Centuries: Indians and Europeans in the American South, 1521-1704,* edited by Charles Hudson and Carmen Chaves Tesser, pp. 125-55. University of Georgia Press, Athens.

Wiessner, Polly
1983 Style and Social Information in Kalahari San Projectile Points. *American Antiquity* 48(2):253-76.
1985 Style or Isochrestic Variation? A Reply to Sackett. *American Antiquity* 50:160-66.
1990 Is There a Unity to Style? In *The Uses of Style in Archaeology,* edited by Margaret W. Conkey and Christine A. Hastorf, pp. 103-12. Cambridge University Press, Cambridge.

Wilcox, David R.
1986 A Historical Analysis of the Problem of Southwestern-Mesoamerican Connections. In *Ripples in the Chichimec Sea: New Considerations of Southwestern-Mesoamerican Interactions,* edited by Frances J. Mathien and Randall H. McGuire, pp. 181-204. Southern Illinois University Press, Carbondale.

Wilford, Lloyd A., and John W. Brink
1974 Hogback: A Proto-historic Oneota Burial Site. *Minnesota Archaeologist* 33(1-2):1-79.

Wilkinson, Leland, MaryAnn Hill, and Erin Vang
1992 *SYSTAT: Statistics.* SYSTAT, Inc., Evanston, Illinois.

Wilkinson, Richard G., and Karen M. Van Wagenen
1993 Violence Against Women: Prehistoric Skeletal Evidence from Michigan. *Midcontinental Journal of Archaeology* 18(2):190-216.

Willey, Gordon R. (editor)
1956 *Prehistoric Settlement Patterns in the New World.* Viking Fund Publications in Anthropology 23.

Willey, Gordon R., and Philip Phillips
1958 *Method and Theory in American Archaeology.* University of Chicago Press, Chicago.

Williams, Paul
1989 Wampum of the Six Nations Confederacy at the Grand River Territory: 1784-1986. In *Proceedings of the 1986 Shell Bead Conference,* edited by Charles F. Hayes III and Lynn Ceci, pp. 199-204. Rochester Museum and Science Center, Research Records No. 20, Rochester, New York.

Williams, Samuel C. (editor)
1928 *Early Travels in the Tennessee Country, 1540-1800.* The Watauga Press, Johnson City, Tennessee.

Williams, Stephen
1980 Armorel: A Very Late Phase in the Lower Mississippi Valley. *Southeastern Archaeological Conference Bulletin* 22:105-10.
1990 The Vacant Quarter and Other Late Events in the Lower Valley. In *Towns and Temples Along the Mississippi,* edited by David H. Dye and Cheryl Anne Cox, pp. 170-80. The University of Alabama Press, Tuscaloosa.

Williamson, Ronald
1978 Preliminary Report on Huronian Interment Patterns of the Draper Site. *Canadian Journal of Archaeology* 2:117-21.
1990 The Early Iroquoian Period of Southern Ontario. In *The Archaeology of Southern Ontario to A.D. 1650,* edited by Chris J. Ellis and Neal Ferris, pp. 291-320. Ontario Archaeological Society, London, Ontario.

Williamson, Ronald F., and David A. Robertson
1994 Peer Polities Beyond the Periphery: Early and Middle Iroquoian Regional Interaction. *Ontario Archaeology* 58:27-48.

Willoughby, Charles C.
1923a Letter of January 13, 1923, to Charles L. Wilhelm. UAV677.46, Box E, Harvard University Archives, Cambridge, Massachusetts.
1923b Letter of January 17, 1923, to H. L. Madison. UAV677.46, Box E, Harvard University Archives, Cambridge, Massachusetts.

Wilmsen, E. N. (editor)
1972 *Social Exchange and Interaction.* Anthropological Papers No. 46. Museum of Anthropology, University of Michigan, Ann Arbor.

Wilson, Terry P.
1988 *The Osage.* Chelsea House Publishers, New York.

Winters, Howard D.
1968 Value Systems and Trade Cycles of the Late Archaic in the Midwest. In *New Perspectives in Archaeology,* edited by Sally R. Binford and Lewis R. Binford, pp. 175-221. Aldine, Chicago.

Witthoft, John
1952 Comments on the Cultural Position of the Herriot Farm Site. *West Virginia History* 13(4):249-53.
1959 Ancestry of the Susquehannocks. In *Susquehannock Miscellany,* edited by John Witthoft and W. Fred Kinsey III, pp. 19-60. Pennsylvania Historical and Museum Commission, Harrisburg.
1966 Archaeology as a Key to the Colonial Fur Trade. *Minnesota History* 40(4):203-9.

Witthoft, John, and William A. Hunter
1955 The Seventeenth-Century Origins of the Shawnee. *Ethnohistory* 2(1):42-57.

Witthoft, John, Harry Schoff, and Charles F. Wray
1953 Micmac Pipes, Vase-Shaped Pipes, and Calumets. *Pennsylvania Archaeologist* 23(3-4):89-107.

Wittry, Warren
1963 The Bell Site, Wn 9: An Early Historic Fox Village. *The Wisconsin Archeologist* 44:1-57.

Wobst, H. Martin
1974 Boundary Conditions for Paleolithic Social Systems: A Simulation Approach. *American Antiquity* 39:147-78.
1977 Stylistic Behavior and Information Exchange. In *For the Director: Research Essays in Honor of James B. Griffin,* edited by Charles E. Cleland, pp. 317-42. Anthropological Papers No. 61. Museum of Anthropology, University of Michigan, Ann Arbor.

Wolf, Eric R.
1982 *Europe and the People without History.* University of California Press, Berkeley.

Wood, Peter H., Gregory A. Waselkov, and M. Thomas Hatley (editors)
1989 *Powhatan's Mantle: Indians in the Colonial Southeast.* University of Nebraska Press, Lincoln.

Wood, W. Raymond
1972 Contrastive Features of Native North American Trade Systems. In *For the Chief: Essays in Honor of Luther S. Cressman,* edited by Fred W. Voget and Robert L. Stephenson, pp. 153-69. University of Oregon Anthropological Papers No. 4,
1980 Plains Trade in Prehistoric and Protohistoric Inter-Tribal Relations. In *Anthropology on the Great Plains,* edited by W. Raymond Wood and M. Liberty, pp. 98-109. University of Nebraska Press, Lincoln.

Woodward, Arthur
1932 The Value of Indian Trade Goods in the Study of Archaeology. *The Pennsylvania Archaeologist* 3(1):8-9, 16-19.

Worth, John E.
1994 Late Spanish Military Expeditions in the Interior Southeast, 1597-1628. In *The Forgotten Centuries: Indians and Europeans in the American South, 1521-1704,* edited by Charles Hudson and Carmen C. Tesser, pp. 104-22. The University of Georgia Press, Athens.

Wray, Charles F.
1983 Seneca Glass Trade Beads, c. A.D. 1550-1820. In *Proceedings of the 1982 Glass Trade Bead Conference,* edited by Charles F. Hayes III, Nancy Bolger, Karlis Karklins, and Charles F. Wray, pp. 41-49. Research Records No. 16. Rochester Museum and Science Center, Rochester, New York.
1985 Firearms among the Seneca: The Archaeological Evidence (abs.). In *Proceedings of the 1984 Trade Gun Conference,* edited by Charles F. Hayes III and Jan P. Puype, pp. 106-7. Research Records No. 18 (part 2). Rochester Museum and Science Center, Rochester, New York.

Wray, Charles F., and Harry L. Schoff
1953 A Preliminary Report on the Seneca Sequence in Western New York (1550-1687). *Pennsylvania Archaeologist* 23(2):53-63.

Wray, Charles F., Martha L. Sempowski, and Lorraine P. Saunders
1991 *Tram and Cameron: Two Early Contact Era Sites.* The Charles F. Wray Series in Seneca Archaeology, vol. 2, Research Records No. 21. Rochester Museum and Science Center, Rochester, New York.

Wray, Charles F., Martha L. Sempowski, Lorraine P. Saunders, and Gian C. Cervone
1987 *The Adams and Culbertson Sites.* Charles F. Wray Series in Seneca Archaeology, vol. 1, Research Records No. 19. Rochester Museum and Science Center, Rochester, New York.

Wright, Gary A.
1967 Some Aspects of Early and Mid-Seventeenth Century Exchange Networks in the Western Great Lakes. *Michigan Archaeologist* 13(4):181-97.
1968 A Further Note on Trade Friendship and Gift Giving in the Western Great Lakes. *Michigan Archaeologist* 14(3-4):165-66.

Wright, J. Leitch, Jr.
1986 *Creeks and Seminoles: The Destruction and Regeneration of the Muscogulge People.* University of Nebraska Press, Lincoln.

Wright, J. V.
1994 The Prehistoric Transportation of Goods in the St. Lawrence River Basin. In *Prehistoric Exchange Systems in North America,* edited by Timothy G. Baugh and Jonathon E. Ericson, pp. 47-71. Plenum Press, New York.

Yerkes, Richard W.
1983 Microwear, Microdrills, and Mississippian Craft Specialization. *American Antiquity* 48:499-518.
1989 Shell Bead Production and Exchange in Prehistoric Mississippian Populations. In *Proceedings of the 1986 Shell Bead Conference: Selected Papers,* edited by Charles F. Hayes III, Lynn Ceci, and Connie Cox Bodner, pp. 113-23. Rochester Museum and Science Center, Rochester, New York.
1991 Current Research: Great Lakes. *American Antiquity* 86(3):538-44.

Youse, Hillis J.
1965 Excavation at Rolf Lee Farm Site 46-Ms-51. *West Virginia Archaeologist* 18:15-24.
1976 The Man Site, 46LO5. *West Virginia Archaeologist* 25:15-19.
1988 Marmet Village: Archaeological Site 46KA9. *The West Virginia Archaeologist* 40(1):47-49.

Zentai, Tunde
1979 The Sign-Language of Hungarian Graveyards. *Folklore* 90:131-40.

Index

C

D

E

H

I

N

T